HENRIQUES AND WINTER ON LOCAL AUTHORITY PROSECUTIONS

Cavendish
Publishing
Limited

London • Sydney

HENRIQUES AND WINTER ON LOCAL AUTHORITY PROSECUTIONS

A Complete Guide to the Investigation and Presentation of Local Authority Prosecutions before the Magistrates' Court

Jack Henriques
and
Richard Winter

Cavendish
Publishing
Limited

London • Sydney

First published in Great Britain 2002 by Cavendish Publishing Limited, The Glass House, Wharton Street, London WC1X 9PX, United Kingdom

Telephone: +44 (0)20 7278 8000   Facsimile: +44 (0)20 7278 8080
Email: info@cavendishpublishing.com
Website: www.cavendishpublishing.com

© Henriques, J and Winter, R   2002

All rights reserved. No part of this publication may be reproduced, stored in a retrieval system, or transmitted, in any form or by any means, electronic, mechanical, photocopying, recording, scanning or otherwise, except under the terms of the Copyrights Designs and Patents Act 1988 or under the terms of a licence issued by the Copyright Licensing Agency, 90 Tottenham Court Road, London W1P 9HE, UK, without the prior permission in writing of the publisher.

British Library Cataloguing in Publication Data

Henriques, Jack
Henriques and Winter on Local Authority Prosecutions
1 Local government – law and legislation – England
2 Local government – law and legislation – Wales
I Title II Winter, Richard
342.4'2'09

ISBN 1 85941 697 7

Printed and bound in Great Britain

To Liz Adams
JRQH

To Sarah, Sophie and Daniel
RJW

PREFACE

This work is primarily intended for local authority investigators and their lawyers. It provides a systematic approach to the investigatory process that leaves nothing to chance, while also including a wealth of precedents and case law. As a natural consequence of providing a balanced view of the authorities and alerting readers to the pitfalls of various stages of the prosecution, this work might also be a useful tool for private practitioners to expose the weaknesses in the prosecution's case. The book is therefore a double-edged sword. It will assist local authorities to present a watertight case, while also identifying numerous authorities which enable cases to be dismissed on the most compelling evidence. The various groups who might benefit from the work are as follows:

Local authority investigators

Included in the systematic approach to the investigatory process are checklists, precedents, standard forms and breakdowns of the elements of offences in key areas. Authorities and legislation in these key areas support these materials. The book also contains answers to a number of frequently asked questions such as: 'Am I required to provide full disclosure before interview?' (see Imran and Hussain, in which refusal to supply evidence before an interview was approved); 'Am I entitled to prosecute for "no insurance" or any other offence?' (yes, see Jarret and Steward, which confirms that councils have very wide prosecution powers). For the more advanced investigator, there is advice on useful interviewing techniques and detailed case law on how to prove service of notices, etc, when personal service has failed. The chapters on key legislation will be of particular interest to the following officers.

Trading standards

In addition to legislation and case law, there is advice on how to investigate and prosecute offences which amount to future promises. See *BAB v Taylor*.

Licensing

For those officers who find that plying for hire is a particular problem, there are strategies to prevent booking clerks from recording false bookings (prosecution as aiders and abettors) and case law to assist in proving the substantive offence. (See *Ogwr BC v Baker* and many other cases).

On appeal, there are cases which neutralise common arguments such as, 'the local authority should be confined to its grounds of appeal set out in its notice'. There are further lists of authorities, which effectively turn the normal rules of evidence and procedure on their head to work in favour of the local authority.

Environmental health officers

It is believed the book has more case law legislation and materials for this area of the law than any other. It includes an in-depth analysis on the investigation of Housing Act notices, unlawful eviction, harassment and litter prosecutions whilst not omitting food safety and health and safety.

Local authority lawyers

Even the best of cases may fail on the issues of authority principal. A whole chapter is therefore devoted to this issue. It is accompanied by a detailed reference to case law which has been presented in a manner which is not designed to overcomplicate the issue. There are also numerous informations and specialist lists of authorities to enable more effective and efficient case management and presentation.

For those who believe that the rules of evidence and procedure are weighted too heavily in favour of the defendant, there are cases on the concept of 'fairness to the prosecution' (*Oliphant, Warner* and others), there is a chapter on the obligations of the defence advocate and a further chapter on dealing with defence objections at court. This includes common applications such as 'no case to answer', 'exclusion of unfair evidence', 'missing elements of the offence', and how to deal with them.

The question of costs is now a burning issue for many cash-strapped local authorities. The chapter on costs sets out the case law and practice directions which should enable the local authority to avoid having to pay costs in most cases and recover expenses, etc, in full where appropriate.

Lawyers in private practice

Not only does the work include the main cases and materials on the most litigious areas of the law, it also gives an in-depth analysis of the authority principle which is often the Achilles' heal of many local authorities. As the structure of local authorities is constantly changing, fresh gaps begin to appear in the authorisation. It is surprising how few solicitors challenge the local authority on this issue which can be fatal to both civil and criminal/regulatory proceedings.

As the book is primarily designed for local authorities, the case law which allows for challenge on technicalities is not well flagged, although it has not been left out. These include authorities on 'abuse of process'. There is also reference to the decision in *Maltedge* which can be used to challenge any prosecution for non-compliance with a notice if the period of compliance is not set out in the charge or proved in evidence. The decision in *Sandhu* enables a case to be challenged on appeal if the evidence contained material which goes beyond that which is necessary to prove a case. One often wonders how many cases proceeded in the absence of a defendant which included statements containing this category of evidence!

Magistrates' court clerks

For most magistrates' courts the cost of an encyclopaedia on local authority law is prohibitive. This area of the law is undeniably complex and there is therefore a need for more literature than is presently available without having to go to such expense. The rules of evidence and procedure are often far different for local authority proceedings and this work includes key legislation, together with the case law and materials, which should be of much assistance to the magistrates' clerks.

CPS and other public prosecutors

The notion of fairness to the prosecution seems to be an area of law which is relatively unknown, yet this concept is well recognised by the higher courts. The book examines this concept and highlights the cases, which have been alive to the issue. The cases of *Oliphant* and *Warner* are two of the cases which have been mentioned.

The obligations of the defence advocate is another field of law which has had little attention paid to it in the past. A chapter is devoted to this subject. There is also a chapter on dealing with objections and other defence applications, with detailed authorities in support.

Colleges and universities

The absence of a specialist work on this subject may explain why this is not a subject in its own right and yet there is a significant percentage of practising lawyers in this field. The work also adds a practical dimension to those teaching planners and environmental health officers.

CONTENTS

Preface	*vii*
Table of Cases	*xv*
Table of Statutes	*xxix*
Table of Statutory Instruments	*xxxix*
Table of European Legislation	*xlv*
Introduction	*xlvii*

1	CODE OF PRACTICE FOR INVESTIGATION AND PROSECUTION OF CRIMINAL OFFENCES	1
2	THE STATUTORY FRAMEWORK FOR CRIMINAL OFFENCE INVESTIGATIONS	7
3	PLANNING AN INVESTIGATION	19
4	HUMAN RIGHTS	25
5	INTERVIEWING WITNESSES AND OBTAINING WITNESS STATEMENTS	31
6	PREPARATION OF A STATEMENT – INADMISSIBLE EVIDENCE	35
7	INTERVIEWING AND REPORTING THE ALLEGED OFFENDER	41
8	PREPARING A FILE OF EVIDENCE	55
9	CHECKING AUTHORISATIONS AND REVIEWING EVIDENCE	57
10	DRAFTING SUMMONSES/INFORMATIONS AND SERVICE OF NOTICES AND SUMMONSES	63
11	TRANSFORMING A WEAK CASE INTO A SUCCESSFUL PROSECUTION	71
12	PREPARATION FOR THE HEARING	77
13	OBJECTION HANDLING AND DEALING WITH DEFENCE APPLICATIONS	87
14	OBLIGATIONS OF THE DEFENCE ADVOCATE	99
15	GIVING EVIDENCE IN COURT	103

16	**PROGRESS OF A CASE TO ITS RESOLUTION**	**111**
17	**COSTS IN CRIMINAL AND CIVIL PROCEEDINGS BEFORE THE MAGISTRATES' COURT**	**113**
18	**ENVIRONMENTAL HEALTH LEGISLATION**	**117**
19	**PLANNING AND ADVERTISEMENT LEGISLATION**	**245**
20	**TRADING STANDARDS LEGISLATION**	**253**
21	**HOUSING BENEFIT AND COUNCIL TAX BENEFIT PROSECUTIONS**	**299**
22	**LICENSING LEGISLATION**	**305**
23	**HIGHWAYS LEGISLATION**	**327**

APPENDICES

Appendix 1	Magistrates' Court Forms	359
Appendix 2	Housing Benefit and Council Tax Benefit Precedents	369
Appendix 3	Case Report Form	379
Appendix 4	Witness Statement Form	381
Appendix 5	Certificate of Service	383
Appendix 6	Record of Interview Forms	385
Appendix 7	Caution Form and Public Interest Matrix	393
Appendix 8	Authorisation of Legal Proceedings	397
Appendix 9	Precedents for Planning and Building Control, Enforcement and Prosecution	399
Appendix 10	Precedents for Highways Matters	417
Appendix 11	Precedents for Environmental Health and Housing Matters	439
Appendix 12	Precedents for Hackney Carriage and Private Hire Prosecutions	489
Appendix 13	Precedents for Investigation and Prosecution of Waste Management	509
Appendix 14	Precedents for Trading Standards Investigations and Prosecutions	519

Appendix 15	Precedents for Investigation and Prosecution of Education Matters	525
Appendix 16	Precedents for Investigation and Prosecution of Countryside and Highways Offences	533
Appendix 17	List of Authorities	557
Appendix 18	List of Statutory Time Limits for Offences	585
Appendix 19	Briefing Note; Guidance Document; Schedules of Unused Information	587
Appendix 20	Regulation of Investigatory Powers Authorisations	593

Index 599

TABLE OF CASES

Ackroyds Air Travel Ltd v DPP [1950] 1 All ER 933. . . . . 72, 580
Adamson v Waveney DC [1997] 2 All ER 898 572
Aitken v South Hams DC [1994] 3 All ER 400 561
Albon v Railtrack plc [1998] EHLR 83 59
Alex Lawrie Factors Ltd v Morgan [1999] TLR, 18 August. 31
Allan v Wiseman [1975] RTR 217 92
Allen v Ireland [1984] 1 WLR 903 93
Allerton v Brown [1945] KB 122. 64
Amec Building Ltd and Others v Camden LBC
  [1997] Env LR 330 . . . . 118, 221, 561, 582
Apothecaries Co v Bentley (1824) Ry and M 159 93
Atterton v Browne [1945] KB 122 . . . . 91, 93
Attorney General v Wilcox [1938] Ch 934; [1938] 2 All ER 367 329
Attorney General's Reference (No 1 of 1989) [1989] 1 WLR 1117. 96
Attorney General's Reference (No 1 of 1990) [1992] 1 QB 630 . . . . 25, 95, 574
Attorney General's Reference (No 2 of 2001), Lawtel 2/7/2001 25

Bannister v Clarke [1920] 3 KB 598; 85 JP 12 96
Barber v CWS Ltd (1983) 147 JP 296 567
Barnes v CC of Durham (1997) The Times, 6 May 19, 92
Barnes v Sheffield CC (1995) 27 HLR 719. . . . . 220, 581
Barnet LBC v Eastern Electricity Board
  [1973] 2 All ER 319; 137 JP 486. 577
Barras v Reeve [1980] 3 All ER 705 . . . . 377, 583
Barton v Director of Public Prosecution [2001] EWHC Admin
  233, 13 March; (2001) Archbold News, Issue 5, 27 June 66
Bastin v Davies [1950] 2 KB 579 567
Batley v Hampshire Justices, Lawtel 20/2/98. 51
Bedingfield v Jones (1959) 124 JP 11 225
Berni Inns Ltd v Reynolds (1981) unreported 65
Blakemore v Bellamy (1983) 147 JP 89; [1983] RTR 303 . . . . 255, 261, 265, 570
Blunden v Gravelle Ltd (1986) 151 JP 701 558
British Airways Board v Taylor [1976] 1 All ER 65. . . . . 66, 72, 263, 265, 267
Brown v Procurator Fiscal Dunfermline [2000] TLR, 14 February 50
Brown v Stott [2001] 2 WLR 817. 27
Browne v Dunn (1894) 6 R 67 . . . . 101, 572
Bruce Springsteen v Flute International and Others
  [2001] ILR, 24 April. 572
Bryan Roy Lewis v Barratt Homes Ltd (1999) unreported 265, 267

Buckman v Button [1943] 2 All ER 82 93
Bukate v Netherlands (1995) 19 EHRR 477 25

CD Carter v Eastbourne BC, Lawtel 4/2/2000 247
Camden LBC v Gunby [1999] 4 All ER 602;
   [1999] TLR, 12 July 118, 216
Camden LBC v Marshall [1996] 1 WLR 1345 .... 221, 586
Campbell v Wallsend Slipway and Engineering
   Company [1978] ICR 1015 59
Canterbury CC v Bern [1981] JPL 749 .... 219, 221
Carrick DC v Taunton Vale Meat Traders Ltd [1994] QBD,
   28 January; (1994) The Times, 15 February 568
Chichester DC v Silvester (1992) The Times, 6 May 73, 313
Chichester DC v Wood [1997] EWHC 266 309
Chief Constable of Derbyshire v Arthur Newton and Albert
   Thomas Goodman, Lawtel 2/4/98 114
City of Bradford MDC v E Booth High Court [2000] TLR, 31 May 114
City of Bradford MDC v Sabih Thiyab Obaid (2001) LTL, 29 June 307
City of Oxford Tramway Co v Sankey (1890) 54 JPN 564 92
Clear v Smith [1981] 1 WLR 399 .... 378, 584
Clode v Barnes [1974] 1 All ER 1166 19
Cogley v Sherwood [1959] 2 All ER 313 573
Connolly v Director of Public Prosecution [1964] AC 1254;
   [1964] 2 All ER 401; 128 JP 418 96
Cooke v Adatia and Others (1989) 153 LGR 189 561
Cooke v HM Advocate 2000 SCCR 922 26
Copeland (Stephen Anthony) v Smith and Others
   [1999] TLR, 20 October 99
Coppen v Moore (No 2) [1898] 2 QB 306 .... 19, 21
Corfield v Sevenways Garage Ltd
   (1984) 148 JP 648; [1985] RTR 109 .... 255, 261, 265
Costelloe v Camden LBC [1986] Crim LR 249 .... 227, 563
Cow and Gate Nutricia Ltd v Westminster CC
   [1995] QBD; (1995) The Independent, 14 March 568
Crook v Howells Garage (Newport) Ltd [1980] RTR 434 559
Crossdill v Ratcliff (1862) 26 JP 165 336

D v HM Advocate [2000] TLR, 14 April 26
DSS v Bavi [1996] COD 260 .... 377, 583

Table of Cases

DSS v Cooper (1994) 158 JPN 354 301–03
Da Silva and R v South Ribble Magistrates ex p Cochrane
   (1996) The Times, 24 June. 86
Darlington BC v Paul Wakefield (1989) LGR, 16 September 571
Darmalingum v State [2000] TLR, 18 July, PC. 25, 26
Daventry DC v Olins (1990) 154 JP 478 . . . . 12, 94, 574
Davies v Sumner [1984] 3 All ER 831;
   [1984] 1 WLR 1301; 149 JP 110, HL. 255, 261, 265
Davis v Morton [1913] 2 KB 479; 77 JP 223. 96
Dennis and Sons Ltd v Good (1918) 17 LGR 9 334
Devlin v Hall [1990] RTR 320; [1990] Crim LR 897. . . . . 255, 261, 265
Dilks v Tilley [1979] RTR 459 . . . . 40, 41, 75
Director of Public Prosecution v Anderson [1991] RTR 269 578
Director of Public Prosecution v Boardman [1975] AC 421 575
Director of Public Prosecution v Majewski [1976] 2 All ER 142. 561
Director of Public Prosecution v P [1991] 2 AC 447 575
Director of Public Prosecution v Wilson [2001] TLR, 21 March. 27
Dittah v Birmingham CC (1993) 157 JP 1110; [1993] RTR 356. 579
Dixon v Attfield [1975] 3 All ER 265 329
Dring v Mann (1948) 112 JP 270 92
Durham CC v Scott [1990] Crim LR 726. 329

Eccles v Jeremy (1982) 5 EHRR 1 26
Edwards v Llaethdy Meiron Ltd (1957) 107 LJ 133 567
Elder v Crowe 1996 SCCR 38 570
Empress Car Company Ltd v NRA [1998] EHLR 3 579
Enfield LBC v Devonish (1996) 28 HLR 641 67
Evans v Dell [1937] All ER 349. . . . . 377, 578, 583
Ewing v UK (1996) 10 EHRR 141. 26
Exeter Corporation v Heaman (1877) 42 JP 503 92

Ferguson v Weaving [1951] 1 KB 814, DC 65
Francisco Teixeiro de Castro v Portugal
   (1999) 28 EHRR 101; [1998] Crim LR 751 30
Frankland and Moore v R [1987] 2 WLR 1251. 228

Garfield v Maddocks [1974] 1 QB 7. 91
Garrett v Boots the Chemist (1980) unreported 263, 266, 277

Gatland v Metropolitan Police Commissioner
  [1968] 2 QB 279; [1968] 2 All ER 100; 132 JP 323 336
George v Kumar [1980] LGR 526 65
Giovianni v The Queen (1985) 156 CLR 473 578
Goodman v J Egan Ltd [1954] 1 All ER 753 59
Greenwich BC v Millcroft Construction Ltd (1987) 85 LGR 66 334
Griffiths (Richard) v Pembrokeshire CC
  (2000) CO/4941/99; [2000] TLR, 19 April 116, 121, 126

HSE v Spindle Select Ltd (1996) The Times, 9 December 66
Hamilton-Johnson v RSPCA (2000) 4 April, CO/3185/1999 113
Harley v McDonald Glasgow Harley (A Firm)
  v McDonald [2001] TLR, 25 May 116
Hayter v L [1998] 1 WLR 854 .... 39, 73, 95
Health and Safety Executive v Spindle Select Ltd
  (1996) The Times, 9 December, DC 128
Heaney and McGuinness v Ireland [2001] Crim LR 481 27
Heaton v Costello [1984] Crim LR 485 65
Hewlings v Mclean Homes East Anglia Ltd CO/4680/2000 119
Heywood v Whitehead (1897) 76 LT 781 567
HM Advocate v Little 1999 SLT 1145 26
HM Advocate v McGlinchey 2000 SLT 995 26
Hicks v Sullam Ltd (1983) 147 JP 493 .... 264, 266
Hilliers Ltd v Sefton MBC (1996) CO-2165-96, 29 November 59
Hirst and Agu, The v Chief Constable of West Yorkshire
  (1987) 151 LG Rev 130 329
Honig v Islington BC [1972] Crim LR 126 .... 217, 219, 582
Hotchin v Hindmarsh (1891) 2 QB 181; 55 JP 775 567
Howitt, R v Nottingham CC ex p Hamilton CO 4028/98 572
Hunter v Coombs [1962] 1 All ER 126 .... 64, 93
Hurley v Martinez & Co Ltd (1990) 154 JP 821 .... 264, 266

James v South Glamorgan CC
  (1992) The Independent, 6 January 89
Jeffry v Black [1978] QB 490 44
Jemmison v Priddle [1972] 1 All ER 540 65
Jevons v Cosmosair (1998) 162 JP 68 92
Jolley v Director of Public Prosecution (2000) LSG, 5 May 89

Table of Cases

Kavanagh v CC of Devon and Cornwall
 [1974] 1 QB 625; [1974] 2 All ER 697 .... 73, 571
Keating v Horwood (1926) 90 JP 141; 135 LT 29 262
Kelly v Lewes DC (1997) 7(1) Licensing Bulletin, 3 March 571
Kenneth Johnson v David Valks, Lawtel 15/3/2000 99
Kent CC v Brockman [1996] PLR 1; [1994] Crim LR 295 .... 217, 219, 582
Kent CC v Upchurch River Golf Course Ltd (1998) P & CR D37 217
Kinchin v Ashton Park Scooters Ltd (1984) 148 JP 540 266
Kirklees Metropolitan Council v Lees [1998] Env LR 337 .... 119, 561

Lambert (A) Flat Management Ltd v Lomas
 [1981] 2 All ER 280; [1981] 1 WLR 898 .... 118, 218, 221, 561, 582
Lambeth LBC v Mullings (1990) The Times, 6 January;
 (1990) The Times, 16 March; [1990] COD 281 .... 67, 119, 217, 219, 560, 580
Lau Pak Ngam v R [1966] Crim LR 443 112
Lawrence v Same [1968] 2 QB 93; [1968] 1 All ER 1191 .... 92, 93
Leathley v Drummond [1972] RTR 293 .... 573, 579
Leeds CC v Azam (1989) LGR, 11 March 306
Lewin v Fuel (1990) 155 JP 206 .... 266, 558
Lister v Quaife [1983] 2 All ER 29 83
Lomas v Peek [1947] 2 All ER 574 64
Lombard North Central Plc v Power-Hines [1995] CCLR 24 67
London LBC v Ezedinma [1981] 3 All ER 438 .... 220, 581
London Borough of Southwark v Time Computer Systems Ltd
 (1997) ILT, 14 July 263
London CC v Agricultural Food Products [1955] 2 QB 218 59
Lunn v Colston-Hayter (1991) 155 JP 384 313
Lyons v May [1948] 2 All ER 1062 579

MB Building Contractors Ltd v Nazir Ahmed, Lawtel 18/11/98 114
MFI Warehouses Ltd v Nattrass [1973] 1 All ER 762 265
MGN Ltd v Northampton CC (1997) CO-686-97 277
McCall v Abelesz and Another [1976] QB 585;
 [1976] All ER 727, CA 228, 565
McCool v Rushcliffe BC [1998] 3 All ER 889 .... 571, 572
McDonalds Hamburgers Ltd v Windle (1986) 151 JP 333 567
McGillivray v Stephenson [1950] 1 All ER 942 560
McNab v Alexanders of Greenock Ltd 1971 SLT 121 559
Maidstone BC v Mortimer [1980] 3 All ER 552 .... 247, 577

xix

Makin v Attorney General for New South Wales
 [1894] AC 57, PC 575, 576
Maltedge v Wokingham DC (1992) The Times, 21 May;
 (1992) 64 P & CR 487.. 64, 119, 218, 245, 247
Manley v Newforest DC CO/1050/99 119
Marco T/A A & J Bull Containers v Metropolitan Police
 [1984] RTR 24 92
Mathews v Morris [1981] Crim LR 495... 89
Mayes v Mayes [1971] 2 All ER 397; 135 JP 487.. 572
Meah v Roberts [1978] 1 All ER 97.. 567
Mendip v Glastonbury Festivals Ltd
 (1993) 91 LGR, 18 February 66, 312
Millard v Wastall [1898] 1 QB 342 560
Milton v Argyle and Clyde Health Board
 1997 SLT 565; 1996 SCLR 1072.. 114
Moody v Godstone RDC [1966] 1 WLR 1085 68
Morris v Lawrence [1977] Crim LR 170 92

Nagy v Weston [1965] 1 All ER 78... 329
Naish v Gore [1971] 3 All ER 737.. 558
National Coal Board v Gamble [1958] 3 All ER 203 580
Network Housing Association v Westminster CC
 (1994) The Times, 8 November 560
Neville and Westminster City Council
 v Gardner Merchants Ltd (1983) 5 Cr App R(S) 349 113
Newham LBC v Singh and Another (1988) 752 JP 223 558
Newport BC v Khan [1990] 1 WLR 1185;
 [1991] 1 EGLR 287, CA 577
Newton v West Vale Creamery Co Ltd (1956) 120 JP 318 567
Norman v Bennett [1974] 3 All ER 355... 266, 558
North Tyneside Council v Duchet (2000) unreported 115
North Yorkshire Trading Standards v Williams
 (1994) The Times, 22 November; (1995) 159 JP 383 .... 19, 92
Norton v Knowles [1967] 3 All ER 1061.. 227, 564
Nottingham CC v Amin [2000] 2 All ER 946;
 (1999) TLR, 2 December 30, 90, 324
Nottingham CC v Farooq [1998] TLR, 28 October 572
Nottingham CC v Woodings [1993] COD 350... 573
Numister v Austria (No 1) (1968) 1 EHRR 91 26

Table of Cases

O'Connell v Adams [1973] Crim LR 113 .... 85, 88
Ogwr BC v Baker [1989] COD 489 .... 73, 573
Onley v Gee (1861) 25 JP 342 65
Owens v Minoprio [1942] KB 193; [1942] 1 All ER 30; 106 JP 53 96

Pappin v Maynard (1863) 27 JP 745 336
Pearks Gunstein and Tee Ltd v Ward [1902] 2 KB 1; 66 JP 774 568
Pennycuick v Lees (1991) The Times, 13 December 41, 75
Perry v Garner [1953] 1 QB 335 560
Pitts v Lewis [1988] QBD, 16 May 579
Pollway Nominees Ltd v London Borough of Croydon
  [1985] 1 WLR 241 217
Polychronakis v Richards and Jerrom Ltd
  (1997) The Times, 19 November 93, 561
Practice Direction (Costs in Criminal Proceedings)
  (1991) 93 Cr App R 89 115
Practice Direction (Costs in Criminal Proceedings) (No 2)
  [2001] 1 Cr App R 60 115
Practice Direction (Crime Costs in Criminal Proceedings)
  (No 2 of 1999) [1999] 4 All ER 436;
  [1999] 1 WLR 1832; [1999] TLR, 6 October 115
Practice Note [1961] 1 All ER 448 89
Practice Notice (Criminal Law: Costs)
  [1991] 2 All ER 924; [1982] 3 All ER 1152 115
Prince Blucher, Re [1931] 2 Ch 70 59
Provident Mutual Life Assurance v Derby CC [1981] 1 WLR 173 .... 58, 59

R v Abrol [1972] Crim LR 318 .... 228, 565
R v Alath Construction Ltd [1990] 1 WLR 1255 .... 247, 252, 577, 578
R v Alford (JF) Transport and Others
  (1997) Archbold News, Issue 4 578
R v Alford
  See R v John James Shannon (Aka Alford)—
R v Alladice (1988) The Times, 11 May 42, 92
R v Argent (1996) The Times, 19 December 42, 50, 61
R v Associated Octel Ltd [1996] 4 All ER 846 130
R v Baldwin [1925] All ER 402 .... 45, 88, 100
R v Barron [1914] 2 KB 570; 78 JP 311 96
R v Belmarsh Magistrates' Court ex p Fiona Watts,
  Lawtel 11/2/99; [1999] 2 Cr App R 188 95

R v Birmingham City Justices ex p Guppy (1987) 152 JP 159 560
R v Blackburn Justices ex p Holmes
  (1999) The Independent, 29 November 92
R v Bow Street Metropolitan Stipendiary Magistrates
  ex p Screen Multimedia Ltd and Another
  [1998] TLR, 28 January 113
R v Bradford Stipendiary Magistrates' Court
  ex p Daniel and Wood, Lawtel 9/6/97; ILR 16/6/97 .... 95, 100
R v Brennan & Brennan [1969] Crim LR 603 563
R v Brentford Justices ex p Catlin [1975] 2 All ER 201 59
R v Brentford Justices ex p Wong [1981] QB 445;
  [1981] 1 All ER 888; [1981] 2 WLR 203 .... 53, 59, 574
R v British Steel plc [1995] 1 WLR 1356; [1995] Crim LR 654 130
R v Burke (1990) 22 HLR 433; [1990] All ER 385 .... 227, 228, 563
R v Burt ex p Presburg [1960] 1 QB 625 113
R v Canale [1990] 2 All ER 187 .... 51, 52
R v Collett [1994] 2 All ER 372 67
R v Court Marshall Administration Officer
  ex p Jordan [2000] COD 106, DC 25
R v Croydon Justices ex p Dean [1993] 3 All ER 129 95
R v Croydon Justices ex p WH Smith Ltd
  [2000] TLR, 22 November 128
R v Da Silva [1990] 1 All ER 29; (1990) Cr App R 233 .... 86, 112
R v Darlington BC ex p Association of Darlington
  Taxi Owners (No 2) (1994) The Times, 14 April 20
R v Day (1940) 27 Cr App R 168 89
R v Delaney (1989) 88 Cr App R 338 43
R v Derby Crown Court ex p Brooks (1985) Cr App R 164 .... 95, 574
R v Director of Public Prosecution
  ex p Lee [1999] 2 All ER 737 .... 16, 56
R v Doldur [1999] TLR, 7 December 50, 61
R v Doran (1972) 56 Cr App R 429 89
R v Eastbourne Justices ex p Kirsten
  (1984) The Times, 22 December 93
R v Edwards [1975] QB 27 .... 74, 93
R v Emmett [1999] TLR, 15 October 79
R v Evangelos Polycarpou (1978) 9 HLR 129 .... 564, 565
R v F Howe & Son (Engineers) Ltd [1999] 2 All ER 249 .... 97, 113, 128
R v Falmouth & Truro Port HA ex p SW Water Ltd [2000] 3 All ER 306 .... 119, 561

R v Francis (1990) 91 Cr App R 271;
  (1990) The Times, 31 January. 60, 89, 90
R v Frost [1839] 9 CLP 129. 89
R v Galbraith [1981] 2 All ER 1060. 89
R v Gateshead Justices ex p Tesco Stores [1981] 1 All ER 1027. 59
R v Gateway Foodmarkets Ltd [1997] 3 All ER 78 128
R v Ghosh [1982] 2 All ER 689 . . . . 303, 304
R v Godstone Justices ex p Secretary of State for the
  Environment [1974] Crim LR 110. 92
R v Gordon Mitchel Stewart [1999] Crim LR 746 . . . . 90, 100
R v Governor of Brixton Prison and Another ex p Osman
  (1990) The Times, 17 December. 95
R v Greater Manchester Justices
  ex p Aldi A Gaish and Co (1995) 159 JP 717 . . . . 59, 92
R v H [1987] AC 35R. 74
R v Hammertons Cars Ltd
  [1976] 3 All ER 578; (1976) 152 JP 207. . . . . 266, 558
R v Hay Halkett ex p Rush [1929] 2 KB 431. 92
R v Haydon (1975) 60 Cr App R 304 113
R v Hobstaff (1993) 14 Cr App R(S) 605 . . . . 79, 96, 589
R v Hunt [1987] AE 352 93
R v Imran & Hussain 96/5613/p 3; [1997] Crim LR 754. . . . . 16, 42, 49
R v Jarrett and Steward, Archbold News, 7 May 1997 . . . . 260, 300, 324
R v John Boyle [1995] Cr App R(S) 927; [1995] Crim LR 514, CA. 113
R v John James Shannon (Aka Alford) [2001] 1 WLR 51 30
R v Keenan [1990] 2 QB 54; [1989] 3 All ER 598 . . . . 43, 51, 52
R v Khan [1996] 3 All ER 289 44
R v Kidd (1997) The Times, 21 July, CA 78, 87, 94, 589
R v King (1897) 1 AB 214; 61 JP 329. 96
R v Lambert [1967] Crim LR 480 . . . . 22, 32, 97
R v Lambeth LBC ex p Wilson (1997) TLR, 25 March 116
R v Lester (1975) 63 Cr App R 144. 94
R v London Borough of Camden ex p Jarram
  [1999] EWHC 338; CO 4234/98. 116
R v London Quarter Sessions Appeal Committee
  ex p Rossi [1956] 1 QB 682. 68
R v Loughlin [1959] Crim LR 518 228
R v McLean (1956) 52 Cr App R 80 35
R v Maidstone Crown Court ex p Olson [1992] COD 498. 571

R v Mason [1986] Crim LR 349, CA.. 44
R v Matthews (1990) 91 Cr App R 43 .... 51, 52
R v Merthyr Tydfil CC ex p CC of Dyfed-Powes
  [1998] TLR, 17 December 114
R v Munnery (Vincent) (1992) 94 Cr App R 164 .... 60, 93
R v Murphy [1965] NI 138.. 44, 90
R v Mussell (1991) 155 JP 521 96
R v Nadir, R v Turner (1993) The Times, 2 July....................................... 86, 97
R v Nelson Group Services (Maintenance) Ltd
  [1998] 4 All ER 331; [1999] 1 WLR 1526, CA................................... 130
R v Newcastle-upon-Tyne Justices ex p John Bryce
  (Contractors) Ltd [1976] 2 All ER 611.. 59, 93
R v North Allerton Magistrates' Court
  ex p Dove [1999] TLR, 17 June... 113
R v North Hertfordshire DC ex p Cobbold [1985] 3 All ER 486......................... 312
R v Nottingham Crown Court ex p Director of Public
  Prosecution [1996] 1 Cr App R(S) 283; [1995] Crim LR 902............... 79, 87, 94, 96, 589
R v Oliphant [1992] Crim LR 41.. 100
R v Oliver [1943] 2 All ER 613.. 93
R v Oliver (1989) 11 Cr App R(S) 10 113
R v O'S (1993) 14 Cr App R(S) 63.. 79, 96, 589
R v Page [1996] Crim LR 439; (1996) 161 JP 308;
  (1995) The Times, 20 November....................................... 50, 75, 270, 291
R v Patel [1993] 1 All ER 402; (1993) 97 Cr App R 294 100
R v Patel [1996] 3 September CA No 96/4220/5;
  (1996) Archbold News, Issue 9, 14 November 87, 105
R v Phekoo [1981] Crim LR 399; [1981] 3 All ER 84 .... 227, 563
R v Pipe (1967) Cr App R 17 39
R v Price (Christopher Michael) (1996) unreported 86
R v Ram [1893] 17 Cox 609 580
R v Redbridge ex p Guppy [1997] BPIR 441 .... 217, 219, 582
R v Ribas (1976) 63 Cr App R 147 94
R v Richardson [1971] 2 All ER 773; [1971] 2 WLR 889 .... 86, 112
R v Ronald Wilson (1969) Cr App R 83... 65
R v Russen (1981) 3 Cr App R(S) 134 .... 78, 94, 589
R v Sandhu (1997) The Times, 2 January 87, 94, 96
R v Sang [1980] AC 402 .... 30, 43, 90
R v Scott (1921) 86 JP 69.. 93

R v Scunthorpe Justices ex p M and Another
  [1998] TLR, 10 March; (1998) 162 JP 635 .... 92, 93
R v Secretary of State for the Environment
  ex p Hillingdon BC [1986] 1 All ER 816.. 58
R v Secretary of State for the Environment, Transport and
  The Regions ex p Masters (1999) The Independent,
  15 November 355
R v Secretary of State for the Home Department
  ex p Macneil (1994) The Times, 26 May.. 325
R v Secretary of State for the Home Office ex p Patel
  (Dhirubhai Gordhanbhai) [1986] Imm AR 515................................... 85, 88
R v Senior [1895] All ER 511 .... 217, 219, 581
R v Shephard (1991) 93 Cr App R 139; [1993] 1 All ER 225............................... 38
R v Smith (1915) 11 Cr App R 576
R v South Central Division Magistrates' Court ex p Secretary
  of State for Social Security (2000) LTL 14 November 584
R v South Ribble Stipendiary Magistrate ex p Cochrane
  (1996) The Times, 4 June.. 112
R v South Tyneside MBC ex p Mill Garages and Another
  [1995] CO 2501/94 (unreported) 43, 95, 574
R v Southwood [1987] 3 All ER 556... 558
R v St Edmundsbury BC ex p Walton
  [1999] Env LR 879; [1999] JPL 805... 59
R v Straffen [1952] 2 QB 911 576
R v Stratford Justices ex p Imbert [1999] TLR, 25 February 80
R v Sunair Holidays Ltd [1973] 2 All ER 1233.. 267
R v Supremeplan Ltd [2001] 1 Cr App R(S) 71 97
R v Thomas (1976) 63 Cr App R 65 .... 377, 578, 583
R v Thomson Holidays Ltd [1974] All ER 823................................... 261, 558
R v Truro and South Powder Magistrates' Court
  ex p McCullagh (1990) 155 JP 411; [1991] RTR 374 96
R v Waldon-Jones ex p Coton [1963] Crim LR 839..................................... 121
R v Walsh (1990) 91 Cr App R 161 .... 43, 90
R v Warner (1993) Cr App R 324 100
R v Watton (Joseph) (1979) 68 Cr App R 293; [1979] Crim LR 246....................... 112
R v Yuthiwattana (1984) 16 HLR 49... 227, 564
R (McDonnell) v Tyrone Justices [1912] 2 IR 44.. 96
Ratnagopal v Attorney General [1969] 3 WLR 1056................................... 59
Redbridge LBC v Jacques [1971] 1 All ER 260; 135 JP 98................................ 329
Rhondda Waste Disposal Co Ltd, Re [2000] TLR, 2 March................................ 1

Rhymney Iron Co v Gelligaer DC [1917] 1 KB 589...560
Richmond LBC v Motor Sales (Hounslow) Ltd
  (1971) 135 JP 239..559
Roberts v Leonard (1995) 159 JP 711..255, 261, 265
Robertson v Banham & Co (A Firm) [1997] 1 All ER 79;
  (1996) The Times, 26 November...69, 217, 219
Rogers v Islington LBC [1999] TLR, 30 August...220
Rotherham MBC v Rayson (UK) Ltd (1988) 153 JP 37................................264, 266
Rushmore BC v Reynolds (1991) 23 HLR 495..................67, 119, 217, 219, 571, 580

Saddleworth UDC v Aggregate and Sand (1971) 69 LGR 103.............44, 217, 219, 582
Sagnata Investments v Norwich Corp [1971] 2 All ER 1441..................................571
Salford CC v McNally [1976] AC 379..560
Sandys v Jackson (1905) 69 JP 171..567
Sheldon (J) Deliveries Ltd v Willis [1972] RTR 217..............................377, 578, 583
Simmons v Potter [1975] RTR 347..558
Simmons v Ravenhill (1983) 148 JP 109...559
Simpson v Roberts (1984) The Times, 21 December..93
Slough v Stevenson (1943) 4 DLE 433..377, 583
Smith, Re [1858] 3 H & N 227...65
Southworth v Whitewell Dairies Ltd (1958) 122 JP 322......................................567
Spice v Peacock [1875] 39 JP 581...329
Squire v Squire [1949] P 51..228
St Helens MBC v Hill (1992) 156 JP 602..19, 21
Stagecoach Ltd v MacPhail 1988 SCCR 289.......................118, 217, 221, 561, 582
Stepney BC v Joffe and Others [1949] 1 All ER 256...571
Stevenage BC v Wright (1997) 161 JP Rep 13..309
Stott (Procurator Fiscal, Dunfermline) and Another
  v Brown [2000] TLR, 6 December...270, 291
Subramanium v Public Prosecutor [1956] 1 WLR 965....................................35, 74
Suffolk CC v Rexmore Wholesale Services Ltd
  (1994) 159 JP 390...115, 264, 266

Tan v Cameron [1992] 2 AC 205..95
Tapsell v Maslen [1967] Crim LR 53, DC...579
Tasci v Pekalp of London Ltd [2001] TLR, 17 January..129
Taylors Central Garage Ltd v Roper (1951) 115 JP 449.........................377, 578, 583
Teixeiro de Castro v Portugal
  See Francisco Teixeiro de Castro v Portugal—

Tesco Supermarkets Ltd v Natress
 [1972] AC 153; [1971] 2 All ER 127 .... 264, 266, 277
Thomas v Lindop [1950] 1 All ER 966 72
Thomas v University of Bradford [1987] 2 WLR 677 20
Thomson Travel Ltd v Roberts (1984) 148 JP 637 .... 263, 265
Tonkin v Victor Value Ltd [1962] 1 All ER 257 567
Torbay BC v Cross [1995] 159 JP 682 329
Torridge DC v Turner (1991) The Times, 27 November 64
Trebor Bassett Ltd v the Football Association
 [1997] FSR 211, Ch D 254, 570
Turner v Johnston (1886) 51 JP 22 93

Waltham Forest LBC v TS Wheatley (1977) 76 LGR 195 558
Wandsworth LBC v Bentley [1980] RTR 429 559
Waring v Wheatley (1951) JP 630 64
Wellingborough BC v Gordon [1993] 1 Env LR 218 561
West Bromwich BS v Townsend (1983) ICR 257 128
Westminster CC v Ali Elmasoglu (1996) unreported 309
Westminster CC v Peart (1968) 66 LGR 561 .... 228, 565
Westminster CC v Riding (1995) 94 LGR 489 237
Westminster CC v Zestfair Ltd (1989) 88 LGR 29 .... 73, 571
Whatling v Rees [1914] 84 LJ KB 1122 560
William Frank Smith v T & S Stores plc
 [1994] Trading Law Reports 337 .... 264, 266
Williams v Russel (1933) 97 JP 128 93
Williams and O'Hara v Director of Public Prosecution
 [1993] Crim LR 775 90
Woodford UDC v Henwood (1900) 64 JP 148 67

X v Austria [1967] CD 8 26

Young v Scampion (1988) 87 LGR 240 573

TABLE OF STATUTES

Accessories and Abettors Act 1861—
  s 8 . . . . 65, 72

Agricultural Produce (Grading
and Marketing) Act 1928—
  s 2 262

Agricultural Produce (Grading
and Marketing) (Amendment)
Act 1931 262

Agriculture Act 1967'
  ss 5, 6(1) 262

Agriculture Act 1970—
  Pt IV 262
  ss 25(1), 70 262

Agriculture and Horticulture
Act 1964 262

Animal Health Act 1981 214
  s 73 445–47

Animal Bonding Establishments
Act 1963 585
  ss 1–3 585

Animals (Scientific Procedures)
Act 1986 139
  Sched 3 140

Broadcasting Act 1990 280
  Sched 20 280
  Sched 21 280

Building Act 1959—
  s 59 21

Building Act 1984—
  s 95 . . . . 399, 414

Business Names Act 1985 71
  s 1 271
  s 2 271–73
  s 2(1) 274
  s 3 . . . . 272, 273
  s 4 . . . . 20, 253, 270, 272, 273
  ss 5, 6 273
  s 7 . . . . 271, 273, 274
  ss 8, 18 274

Charities Act 1992—
  Sched 6 312

Children and Young Persons Act 1933—
  s 18(1) 525, 529
  s 20(1) 530
  s 21 . . . . 529, 530
  s 20(1) 525

Children and Young Persons Act 1969—
  ss 5(8), 34(2), 70 54

Clean Air Act 1956 127

Clean Air Act 1993 . . . . 123, 125, 585
  s 1 . . . . 124, 125, 585
  s 1(5) 125
  s 2 . . . . 117, 126, 127, 439, 459
  s 2(1)–(5) 126
  s 2(4)–(7) 127
  s 3 . . . . 117, 123, 127
  Sched 4 124

Companies Act 1985 . . . . 271, 273, 274
  s 731 273
  s 732(3) 274

Consumer Credit Act 1968—
  Sched 4 269

Consumer Protection
Act 1987 . . . . 262, 292, 296
  Pt II 296
  Pt IV 296
  s 10 . . . . 281, 294
  s 12(1)–(3) 281
  s 13 295
  ss 13(4), 14(6) 281, 296
  s 18 282
  s 20 . . . . 253, 276–79
  s 20(1) 280, 281
  s 20(2) 280
  s 20(4)–(6) 277
  s 21 277–80
  s 24 . . . . 277, 280
  s 26 280
  ss 37, 38 296
  s 38(2)(a)–(c) 269, 291
  s 39 . . . . 277, 280, 281
  s 39(1) 297
  s 40 281
  s 42(3), (4) 296

xxix

Consumer Protection
  Act 1987 (contd)—
    Sched 3 .... 133, 137
    Sched 4 269
Control of Pollution Act 1974 561
  s 5. 236
  s 58 .... 118, 119, 217, 219,
                         221, 580, 582
  s 58(4) 218
  s 58(4) 118
  s 60. .... 118, 217, 221, 582
  ss 61, 65, 66. 120
  s 67. 121
  s 71. 124
  s 93 .... 75, 509, 510, 518
  s 93(3) 509

Control of Pollution (Amendment)
  Act 1989 236
  ss 1(3), 2 236

Copyright Designs and Patents
  Act 1988—
    ss 1–6. 260
    s 107 .... 253, 256–58, 260
    ss 107A, 108 260
    s 198 .... 253, 258–60
    s 198A 260
    Sched 2 259

Countryside Act 1968—
  s 30(1) 356

Crime and Disorder Act 1998—
  ss 65, 66. 54

Criminal Justice Act 1967 ...... 55, 56, 77, 80,
                              82, 359
  s 9. .... 37, 82, 83, 359, 364,
                         366, 381–83, 481
  s 10. .... 37, 83, 100

Criminal Justice Act 1969 31

Criminal Justice Act 1982—
  s 35. 233
  s 38 .... 233, 270, 554
  s 46 .... 133, 270, 554
  s 46(1) 233

Criminal Justice Act 1988—
  s 1. 39
  ss 23–26 37

Criminal Justice Act 1988 (contd)—
  s 27. .... 96, 572
  ss 33A, 34 .... 33, 39

Criminal Justice Act 1991—
  s 52(1) 33, 39

Criminal Justice and Public
  Order Act 1994 .... 7, 49, 61, 74, 406
  ss 34–38. .... 42, 49
  s 34. .... 7, 53
  s 34(1) 42
  ss 36, 37. .... 61, 74
  s 165. 260
  s 167. 573
  s 168. .... 33, 39
  Sched 9 .... 33, 39

Criminal Law Act 1977—
  s 28 .... 133, 230, 275
  s 32. 275
  Sched 1 133
  Sched 6 .... 133, 140

Criminal Procedure and
  Investigations Act 1996.......... 7–11, 15,
                       16, 56, 96, 591
  Pt II 591, 592
  s 1(1) 12
  ss 3, 5. 13
  ss 5(1), (6), 6(2). 14
  s 8(2) 13
  s 9. .... 14, 15, 22
  s 11(1), (3) 14
  s 13. 13
  s 13(1) 12
  s 23(1)(b) 11
  s 24(3) 13
  s 26(1) 8, 11
  s 49. 81

Criminal Procedure (Scotland)
  Act 1975—
    s 331. 298

Dangerous Dogs Act 1991—
  ss 1, 3. 585

Dogs (Fouling of Land)
  Act 1996 .... 230, 440, 482
  s 1. 230

Dogs (Fouling of Land)
  Act 1996 (contd)—
    s 2 .... 230, 481
    s 3 .... 117, 231, 232, 482, 484
    ss 4, 6 231

Education Act 1996—
  s 559(1) 525, 526, 531
  s 559(2) 525, 527, 528, 532
  s 559(3) 526
  s 559(3)(a) 531
  s 559(3)(b) 532

Employment Protection Act 1975—
  Sched 15 .... 129, 133

Environment Act 1995—
  Sched 17 .... 121, 124
  Sched 19 518
  Sched 22 .... 124, 127
  Sched 24 .... 124, 127

Environmental
  Protection Act 1990—
  Pt II 476, 478
  Pt III 476, 478
  Pt IV 516
  ss 6(1), 9(2), 19(2) 585
  ss 23, 33, 34, 80, 87 585
  s 33 .... 234–36, 509, 513
  s 33(1) 512
  s 33(1)(a) 117, 233
  s 33(6) 512
  s 33(8), (9) 233
  s 34 .... 117, 235–37
  s 34(1)–(3) 510
  s 34(1) 509, 513
  s 34(1)(c), (3) 510
  s 34(6) 509, 513, 514
  s 35 236
  s 47(2) 515
  s 47(6) 509, 515
  s 54 234
  s 58(3) 582
  s 60 120
  s 75(4) 233
  s 79 .... 117, 121, 124, 126
  s 79(1)–(8) 122
  s 79(1) 120, 121, 124

Environmental Protection
  Act 1990 (contd)—
    s 79(1A), (1B) 124
    s 79(2) 121
    s 79(7)(d), (8), (9) 123
    s 79(9)(d) 124
    s 79(10)–(12) 124
    s 80 .... 21, 117–19, 121, 121,
                  216, 217, 221, 439, 462,
                  463, 557, 560, 561, 582
    s 80(1), (2) 119
    s 80(2)(a)–(c) 120
    s 80(3)–(9) 120
    s 80(5), (6) 119
    s 80(9)(b), (c), (10) 121
    s 80A 121
    s 80A(1) 119
    s 81A(9) 123, 124
    s 87 .... 117, 237, 238, 336
    s 87(1) 509, 516
    s 87(3) 235
    Sched 3 .... 440, 476, 478
    Sched 16 124

European Communities Act 1972—
  s 2(2) 292, 453

Fire Precautions Act 1971—
  s 43(1) 137

Food and Drugs Act (Northern
  Ireland) 1958 262

Food Safety Act 1990 .... 57, 142, 154,
                  262, 292, 441, 585
  s 1 296
  s 2 .... 146, 153, 183, 567
  s 3 .... 146, 153, 183
  s 5 296
  s 5(1)(c) 182
  s 6(4) 142, 154
  s 7 .... 215, 239, 585
  s 7(1) 211
  s 8 .... 117, 146, 183, 211, 215,
                  239, 439, 585
  s 8(1) 448
  ss 9–13 118
  s 9 .... 212, 239, 240, 296,
                      439, 465, 466
  s 10 .... 240, 296, 439, 449

Food Safety Act 1990 (contd)—
  s 10(3)(b) 241, 468
  s 11 .... 240–42, 439, 467, 468
  s 11(2), (3) 243
  s 12 .... 242, 243
  s 12(6) 585
  s 13 244
  s 13(6) 585
  s 14 .... 117, 146, 183, 211–13, 215,
                   439, 450, 557, 567, 585
  s 15 .... 146, 183, 585
  s 16 .... 439, 453
  s 16(1) 142
  s 16(1)(e), (f) 154
  s 17(1) 142, 154
  s 19 .... 140, 141
  s 20 .... 146, 183
  s 21 .... 21, 146, 183, 557, 567, 568
  s 22 183
  s 26(1), (3) 142, 154
  ss 29, 30 296
  s 30(8) 146, 183
  s 32 .... 183, 213, 214, 296, 439,
                                 470, 472
  s 32(1)(a) 183
  s 33 .... 117, 146, 183, 214, 215,
                                 439, 441
  s 33(1) 183, 215, 585
  s 33(2) 183
  s 34 .... 140, 141, 146, 211, 212,
                              215, 585, 586
  s 35 .... 211, 212, 215, 216, 450
  s 35(1)–(3) 183
  s 35(2) 215
  s 36 .... 146, 183, 216
  s 36(1) 146
  s 44 .... 146, 183
  s 48(1) 142, 154

Food Standards Act 1999—
  Sched 6 244

Forestry Act 1967—
  s 15 252

Forgery and Counterfeiting
  Act 1981—
  s 30 133
  Sched 1 133

Health and Safety at Work
  etc Act 1974 .... 59, 61, 585
  ss 2–7 .... 132, 585
  s 2 .... 66, 96, 117, 128, 129
  s 2(1) 454, 455
  s 2(2)–(6) 129
  s 2(2) 66, 128
  s 2(2)(b) 439, 454
  s 2(2)(c) 439, 455
  s 2(7) 129
  s 3 .... 117, 130, 131
  s 3(3) 131
  s 7 .... 117, 131
  ss 8, 9, 14 132
  s 15(6)(d) 132, 133
  s 15(6)(e) 133
  s 19 134
  s 20 .... 117, 132, 134, 585
  s 20(2)(h) 585
  s 20(2)(j)–(m) 135
  s 20(3)–(8) 135
  s 20(7) 136
  s 21 .... 117, 118, 134, 136, 137
  s 22 .... 118, 134, 136, 137
  s 23 .... 118, 137
  s 24 .... 136, 137
  s 25 .... 118, 132, 138
  s 25(f) 585
  s 25A 132
  s 27(1), (4) 132
  s 28 132
  s 33 .... 128, 130, 132, 133, 439, 585
  s 33(1)(a) 454, 455
  s 33(1)(c) 458
  s 33(1)(d) 585
  s 33(1)(g) 456, 457
  s 33(1A) 454, 455
  s 33(3) 131
  s 37 439
  s 37(1) 456
  s 38 128
  s 42 132
  Sched 3 133

Highways Act 1980 .... 248, 533, 544, 547
  Pt VIIA 312
  s 112 311
  s 130 334
  s 131 .... 327, 334, 335

Highways Act 1980 (contd)—
   s 131A 327, 333, 334,
                                              533, 549
   s 132. 72
   s 137 . . . . 217, 327–30, 417,
                                          418, 533, 550
   s 137A(1). 333
   s 139 . . . . 327, 330, 331
   s 139(1) 417, 419
   s 139(2) 420
   s 139(3) 330, 417, 419
   s 139(4) 330, 417, 420
   s 143. . . . . 533, 534
   s 145. . . . . 533, 535
   s 146. . . . . 533, 536
   s 146(2) 536
   s 154 . . . . 533, 537, 538
   s 161. 336
   s 161(1) 327, 335, 533, 551
   s 161(2) 335
   ss 161A, 163 336
   s 164 . . . . 328, 356, 533, 539
   s 169(1) 417, 421
   s 169(3) 417, 421, 422
   s 169(4) 422
   s 172 . . . . 327, 331–33, 417
   s 172(1) 423
   s 172(5) 423
   ss 289, 292. . . . . 328, 356
   s 293. . . . . 328, 357
   s 297 . . . . 328, 357, 533, 544, 545
   s 297(1) 552, 553
   s 297(2) 533, 552
   s 297(3) 533, 553
   ss 303, 310, 311, 320. . . . . 328, 358
   s 321. 358
   s 322. . . . . 328, 358
   s 328(1) 328
   s 329. . . . . 311, 333, 336

Horticulture Act (Northern
   Ireland) 1966 262

Housing Act 1961—
   s 15 . . . . 217, 219, 582

Housing Act 1985 . . . . 218, 439, 586
   Pt II 475
   s 190(1)(a). 460
   s 193(2) 216, 226
   ss 196, 197. . . . . 118, 225

Housing Act 1985 (contd)—
   s 198. . . . . 117, 118, 225
   s 198A. 118, 216–18, 226, 439
   s 198A(1). 460
   s 207. 216
   s 365. . . . . 221, 222
   s 345. 220
   s 352 . . . . 117, 218, 222, 223,
                                                224, 461, 586
   s 354. 223
   s 369. . . . . 223, 224
   s 372 . . . . 117, 218, 223, 224,
                                                557, 580, 586
   s 373. 224
   s 375. . . . . 223, 224
   s 376 . . . . 117, 218–21, 224, 439, 586
   s 376(1) 461
   s 377A 219
   s 397. 475
   s 397(1)(a). 474
   s 398. 218
   s 617. . . . . 217, 219

Housing Act 1988. 460
   s 29. 230
   Sched 15 . . . . 225, 226

Housing Act 1996—
   s 71(1) 223
   s 78. 224

Housing and Planning
   Act 1986—
   s 39(2) 252

Human Rights Act 1998 . . . . 17, 25, 27, 30

Industrial and Provident
   Societies Act 1965 163

Interpretation Act 1889—
   s 33. 276

Interpretation Act 1978. 68
   s 7. . . . . 67, 68, 119, 217, 219
   s 16(1) 561

Jobseekers Act 1995 304

Law of Property Act 1925—
    s 193(1) 230
Licensing Act 1964—
    s 74(4) 320
    s 169(1) 519, 523
Local Government Act 1972............ 274
    s 101................................59
    s 222......................... 260, 577
    s 233 .... 67, 68, 119, 217,
                                   219, 580
Local Government Act 2000.............. 58
Local Government and Housing
    Act 1989.......................... 461
    Sched 9 223–25
    Sched 12 223–25
Local Government etc (Scotland)
    Act 1994—
    s 2............................... 123
Local Government
    (Miscellaneous
    Provisions) Act 1976...... 80, 323, 557, 579
    Pt II 490–95, 500
    s 16..................... 27, 71, 533, 540,
                                   541, 554
    s 45........................... 323, 324
    s 46........................... 21, 306
    s 46(1)(a)................. 305, 489, 490
    s 46(1)(b)...................... 489, 491
    s 46(1)(c)...................... 489, 492
    s 46(1)(d)...................... 489, 493
    s 46(1)(e)........................... 579
    s 46(1)(e)(i) 489, 494
    s 46(1)(e)(ii) 489, 495
    s 46(2).................. 305, 491–95, 579
    s 46(6)(a), (b) 489
    s 48.................... 305, 306, 490, 494,
                                   496, 497
    s 51 .... 306, 491, 492, 495, 498
    s 54............................ 489, 498
    s 54(1) 498
    s 55 .... 306, 493–95, 579
    s 63........................... 307, 499
    s 64........................... 305–07
    s 64(3) 489, 499
    s 73 .... 60, 305, 325
    s 73(1) 489, 500
    s 75(1) 305

Local Government
    (Miscellaneous Provisions)
    Act 1976 (contd)—
    s 76 .... 306, 307, 492, 493
    s 80............................... 306
    s 80(1) 60, 305
    s 80(2) 579
Local Government (Miscellaneous
    Provisions) Act 1982—
    s 1................................ 506
    Sched 1................. 305, 311–23, 489,
                                   506–08
    Sched 4............ 305, 309, 310, 489, 505
Local Government (Scotland)
    Act 1973 274
Local Government (Wales)
    Act 1994 143
    Sched 9 124

Magistrates' Courts Act 1980 .... 80, 359,
                                   362, 588
    s 1................................. 82
    ss 5A(3)(a), 5B 381, 382, 481
    s 12.................... 77, 82, 359, 360,
                                   362, 364, 383
    s 12(3) 77, 80
    s 12(3)(a)......................... 360
    s 12(3)(b)......................... 362
    s 13................................ 82
    ss 17A–21 .... 146, 251
    s 44............................. 65, 72
    s 64............................... 114
    s 100(2) 91
    s 101 .... 74, 93, 305
    s 102.............................. 366
    s 104.......................... 359, 365
    s 108(3)(b)........................ 113
    s 123............................ 83, 91
    s 123(1), (2)........................ 91
    s 127.............. 119, 125, 126, 153, 218,
                        221, 227–29, 231, 232, 238,
                        271, 298, 306–08, 310, 312,
                        313, 328, 330, 332–35, 337,
                        339, 341, 342, 344,
                        346, 347, 349–54
    Sched 3 .... 80, 82

Magistrates' Courts (Procedure)
Act 1998—
  s 1 80
  s 9 77

Medicines Act 1968 .... 143, 292, 296
  Pt V 263
  s 105 263
  ss 108–15, 119, 132(1) 296
  Sched 3 296

Mock Auctions Act 1961 275
  s 1 .... 253, 274, 275
  s 2 275
  s 3 276
  s 3(1), (2) 274

National Assistance Act 1948—
  s 29 231

National Parks and Access to the
Countryside Act 1949—
  ss 27(b), 53(1) 337
  s 57 .... 327, 335, 337, 338,
                                        533, 548
  s 108 338

New Roads and Street
Works Act 1991—
  Pt IV 123
  s 48 .... 339, 340, 342
  s 51 .... 327, 338–40, 343, 417
  s 51(1), (2) 424
  s 52 .... 327, 340
  s 54 .... 327, 340, 341, 345, 346
  s 54(1) 417, 425, 426
  s 54(4) 417, 426
  s 54(5) 417, 425, 426
  s 55 .... 327, 342–45
  s 55(1), (5) 417, 427
  s 56 .... 327, 343–45
  s 56(1), (3) 417, 428
  s 57 .... 327, 344, 345
  s 57(2) 417, 429
  s 57(4) 429
  s 58 .... 327, 345–47, 430
  s 58(4), (5) 417, 430
  s 67 .... 327, 347, 348, 417, 431
  s 67(1)–(3) 431
  s 68 .... 327, 348, 349

New Roads and Street
Works Act 1991 (contd)—
  s 68(1), (2) 417, 432
  s 69 .... 327, 349, 350
  s 69(1), (2) 417, 433
  s 70 .... 327, 350, 351, 417
  s 70(1) 352, 434
  s 70(2) 434
  s 70(6) 352, 434
  s 71 .... 327, 352, 417
  s 71(1), (2), (5) 353, 435
  s 73 353
  s 79 .... 327, 353, 354
  s 79(1) 417, 436
  s 79(4) 417
  s 79(4)(a) 436
  s 80 353
  s 92 327
  s 92(1) 417
  s 92(1)(a), (b) 437
  s 92(2) 417, 437
  s 97 341
  s 104 .... 340–42, 347
  s 105 .... 339, 340, 342

Noise and Statutory
Nuisance Act 1993—
  s 2 124
  s 3 121
  s 10 124

Offshore Safety Act 1992—
  s 4 133

Opencast Coal Act 1958—
  s 2(4) 252

Pedlars Act 1871 .... 309, 311

Planning and Compensation
Act 1991 .... 415, 416
  Pt I 408
  s 8 408
  s 11 .... 250, 251
  Sched 3 413

Planning (Listed Buildings and
Conservation Areas) Act 1990—
  s 38 413
  s 43 .... 399, 413

Plant Varieties Act 1997.................. 262
Plant Varieties and Seeds
  Act 1964 262
Police and Criminal Evidence
  Act 1984................... 7, 8, 21, 38, 43,
                            48, 53, 75, 79,
                            90, 391, 404, 439,
                            442, 444, 584, 590
  s 19............................. 260
  s 25........................... 8, 309, 482
  s 58............................. 43, 90
  s 66................................ 50
  s 67(9) 7, 48, 75
  s 69................................ 38
  s 76 .... 37, 43, 44, 74
  s 76(2) 37
  s 78..................... 7, 30, 37, 43, 44,
                            61, 90, 100
  s 82................................ 36
  s 82(3) 43
Police, Factories, etc
  (Miscellaneous
  Provisions) Act 1916.................. 312
Pollution Prevention and
  Control Act 1999—
  Sched 2 124
  Sched 3 124
Property Misdescriptions Act 1991....... 267
Prosecution of Offences Act 1985—
  s 10................................. 6
  s 16............................... 114
  s 19............................... 115
Protection Against Cruel Tethering
  Act 1988—
  s 1................................ 140
Protection from Eviction
  Act 1977 .... 229, 586
  s 1..................... 117, 226–30, 557,
                            562, 563, 586
  s 1(2) 464, 563
  s 1(3) 564, 565
  s 1(4) 563
  s 2................................ 439
  s 3B 228

Protection of
  Animals Act 1911 586
  s 1..................... 117, 138–40, 586
Protection of Animals
  (Amendment) Act 1912—
  s 1................................ 140
Protection of Animals
  (Amendment) Act 1921—
  s 1................................ 140
Protection of Animals
  (Penalties) Act 1987—
  s 1................................ 140
Public Health Act 1936........... 44, 67, 121,
                            217, 219, 439, 474,
                            475, 582
  s 287(1) 474
  s 287(2) 475
Public Health Act 1961—
  s 75............................... 323
Public Health (Control of
  Disease) Act 1984—
  s 2................................ 123
Public Health (Scotland) Act 1897—
  s 172.............................. 123
Refuse Disposal (Amenity)
  Act 1978 .... 117, 232, 586
  s 2 .... 232, 233, 509, 586
  s 2(1)(b).......................... 517
Registration of Business Names
  Act 1916—
  s 2................................ 274
Regulation of Investigatory
  Powers Act 2000 .... 27, 593
  Pt II 596
  s 26............................... 28
  s 26(3)–(5)........................ 29
  ss 26(9), 28, 29 28
  ss 30, 32.......................... 29
Rent Act 1965—
  s 30(2) 228, 565

Rights of Way Act 1990—
  s 1 549
Road Traffic Act 1930 579
Road Traffic Act 1988—
  Pt VII 504
  s 143 .... 489, 504, 557, 579
Road Traffic Regulation Act 1984—
  ss 7, 27 504
  s 64 307
  s 112 27
  Sched 13 307

Seeds Act (Northern Ireland) 1965 262
Slaughter of Animals (Scotland)
  Act 1980—
  s 6 215
Slaughterhouses Act 1974—
  s 1 215
Social Security Administration
  Act 1992 .... 369, 375,
                                 377, 557, 583
  s 110 .... 302, 304
  s 111A 299, 300, 302–04
  s 111A(1)(a) 369, 374
  s 111A(1)(b) 369, 373
  s 111A(1)(c) 369
  s 112 .... 299–302, 377, 583
  s 112(1)(b), (2) 369, 372
  s 116 .... 301, 302
Social Security Administration
  (Fraud) Act 1997—
  s 13 .... 302, 303, 373, 374
  s 25(5) 300, 302, 303
Statute Law (Repeals) Act 1993—
  Sched 1 274
Supreme Court Act 1981—
  s 48(2) 113
Supplementary Benefits Act 1976 .... 378, 584

Theft Act 1968 .... 299, 300
  s 15(1) 376
  s 17(1)(a) 369, 370, 376
  s 17(1)(b) 371, 376

Town and Country Planning
  Act 1971—
  s 102(1) 252
Town and Country Planning
  Act 1990 .... 67, 400, 401, 586
  Pt VII 408, 415, 416
  s 179 245–47
  s 179(2) 399, 408
  s 179(8) 249
  s 188 246
  s 196A 245, 250, 251, 415, 416
  s 196B 245, 250, 251, 399, 415, 416
  s 196C 245, 251
  ss 197–225 252
  s 198 .... 245, 252, 577
  ss 207–09 252
  s 210 .... 245, 248, 403, 557, 577
  s 210(1) 247, 252, 586
  s 210(2) 247, 586
  s 210(3) 400
  s 210(4) 247, 399, 409, 586
  s 211 .... 557, 577
  s 211(1) 409
  s 224 .... 248, 399, 411
  s 224(3) 249
  s 224(4) 19
  s 329 .... 67, 68
  s 330 .... 27, 399, 412
  s 336 19
Town Police Clauses
  Act 1847 .... 323, 325, 502
  s 34 503
  s 38 .... 308, 573
  s 45 .... 305, 308, 489, 503, 557
  s 47 .... 309, 489, 502
  s 68 .... 489, 501
Trade Descriptions Act 1968 .... 60, 63, 66, 72,
                                 253, 254, 256,
                                 258, 260, 261, 570
  s 1 .... 253, 261–65
  s 1(1)(a) 266
  s 1(1)(b) 519, 524
  ss 2–6 264
  s 2 .... 262, 263, 265
  s 3 .... 263, 265
  s 4 261
  s 6 .... 19, 261
  s 7(1)(a) 264, 266

Trade Descriptions Act 1968 (contd)—
  s 14 . . . . 253, 261, 263,
                                           265–68, 277
  s 14(1)(b) 519, 520
  s 18 . . . . 264, 267
  s 19 . . . . 261, 264, 265, 267
  s 23 . . . . 253, 261, 265, 268,
  . . . . 519, 522, 524
  s 24 . . . . 263, 264, 266, 557–59
  s 28 . . . . 253, 268–70
  s 29 . . . . 75, 253, 270
  s 130 63
Trade Marks Act 1968—
  s 23 19
Trade Marks Act 1994 . . . . 253–56, 260
  s 1 570
  s 92 . . . . 253–56, 260, 519,
                                                 557, 570
  s 92(1)(b) 521
  s 97 . . . . 260, 570
Transport Act 1985 323

Vehicles Excise and Registration
  Act 1994 123
  Sched 3 124

Visiting Forces Act 1952 122
  Pt I 161

Water Industry Act 1991 480
  Pt III 142
  s 18 143
  s 80 . . . . 143, 440
  ss 80(1), 84 480
  s 93(1) 143
  Sched 6 480
Water (Scotland) Act 1980—
  Pt VIA 142
  s 11(2) 143
  s 76E 142
  ss 76G, 76L(1) 143
Weights and Measures Act 1985 179
Wildlife and Countryside Act 1981—
  s 53(1) 355
  s 59 . . . . 328, 354, 355
  s 66 . . . . 355, 356

TABLE OF STATUTORY INSTRUMENTS

Bread and Flour Regulations
   1995 SI 1995/3202.................. 154
   reg 4.............................. 169

Bovine Animals (Records
Identification and Movement)
Order 1995 SI 1995/12.............. 585

Cheese and Cream Regulations
   1995 SI 1995/3240.................. 183

Cocoa and Chocolate Products
Regulations 1976 SI 1976/541 .... 155, 162

Coffee and Coffee Products
Regulations 1978 SI 1978/1420....... 162

Colours in Food Regulations
   1995 SI 1995/3124.................. 154

Condensed Milk and Dried Milk
Regulations 1977 SI 1977/928......... 162

Costs in Criminal Cases (General)
Regulations 1986 SI 1986/1335 115

Council Tax Benefit (General)
Regulations 1992 SI 1992/1814........ 301
   reg 2........................... 302, 303
   reg 65.............................. 303

Criminal Justice Act 1988
Commencement Order
1989 SI 1989/264..................... 96

Criminal Procedure and Investigations
Act (Defence Disclosure Time
Limits) Regulations
1997 SI 1997/6684—
   reg 2................................ 13

Dairy Products (Hygiene)
Regulations 1995 SI 1995/1086........ 144

Dairy Products (Hygiene) (Scotland)
Regulations 1995 SI 1995/1372........ 144

Deregulation (Slaughterhouses Act
1974 and Slaughter of Animals
(Scotland) Act 1980) Order
1996 SI 1996/2235................... 216

Dogs (Fouling of Land)
Order 1998 .... 230, 231

Drinking Water in Containers
Regulations 1994 SI 1994/743......... 143

Egg Products Regulations 1993
SI 1993/1520 144

Environmental Protection
(Duty of Care) Regulations
1991 SI 1991/2839................... 510
   reg 2(1), (2)........................ 514

Extraction Solvents in Food
Regulations 1993 SI 1993/1658—
   reg 4(3) 163

Flavourings in Food Regulations
1992 SI 1992/1971................... 154

Food Additives Labelling Regulations
1992 SI 1992/1978................... 154

Food Hygiene (General)
Regulations 1970 .... 65, 440, 586
   reg 4.............................. 439
   reg 6.......................... 439, 586
   reg 16(1)(a)......................... 65
   regs 25, 29......................... 65

Food Labelling (Amendment)
Regulations 1998 SI 1998/141 .... 154, 184
   regs 3, 4, 6–9...................... 184
   regs 14–16......................... 184
   Sched 1 184

Food Labelling (Amendment)
Regulations 1998 SI 1998/1398........ 154

Food Labelling (Amendment)
Regulations 1998 SI 1998/2424........ 154

Food Labelling (Amendment)
Regulations 1999 SI 1999/747......... 154

Food Labelling (Amendment) (No 2)
Regulations 1999 SI 1999/1136........ 154
   reg 3.............................. 185

Food Labelling (Amendment)
Regulations 1999 SI 1999/1483........ 154

Food Labelling (Amendment)
  Regulations 1999 SI 1999/1540. 154

Food Labelling Regulations 1984
  SI 1984/1305 183
  reg 40(f). 453

Food Labelling Regulations
  1996 SI 1996/1499 . . . . 117, 153, 154
  reg 2. 155–61
  reg 2(1) 185
  reg 3. . . . . 161, 162
  reg 4 . . . . 153, 162–64
  reg 4(3) 153, 163
  reg 5 . . . . 164, 172, 174, 175
  reg 5(a), (c), (e). 177
  reg 5(e)(i), (f) 173–75
  reg 6 . . . . 153, 164, 165
  regs 6(2), 7–11 185
  reg 11(2) 191
  regs 12–17. 169
  reg 12 . . . . 165, 166, 169
  reg 13. . . . . 165, 166
  reg 13(5) 170
  reg 14. . . . . 166, 167
  reg 14(4) 168, 183, 191
  reg 14(9) 183, 184, 193
  reg 14(11) 184
  reg 15. . . . . 167, 168
  reg 16. . . . . 166, 168
  reg 17. . . . . 153, 168
  reg 18 . . . . 153, 168, 169
  reg 19. . . . . 169, 170
  reg 20. . . . . 170, 171
  reg 21. 171
  reg 22. . . . . 171, 172
  reg 23 . . . . 172, 173, 174, 177, 178
  reg 24. 173
  reg 25. . . . . 173, 174
  reg 26. . . . . 174, 179
  reg 27 . . . . 172, 174, 175, 177
  reg 28. 175
  reg 29 . . . . 162, 175, 176, 181
  reg 30. . . . . 176, 194
  reg 30(1) 208, 209
  reg 31 . . . . 161, 176, 177
  reg 32 . . . . 173–76, 179
  reg 33 . . . . 162, 173–76, 184
  reg 34 . . . . 162, 170, 173–75, 177
  reg 35. . . . . 162, 177

Food Labelling Regulations
  1996 SI 1996/1499 (contd)—
  reg 36 . . . . 177–79, 184
  reg 36(3), (4). 175
  reg 36(4A), (4B) 181
  reg 37. 179
  reg 38 . . . . 162, 179, 184
  reg 39. 179
  reg 40 . . . . 162, 179, 180, 195
  reg 41 . . . . 162, 180, 195
  reg 41(3), (4). 202
  reg 42 . . . . 180, 181, 205
  reg 42(1) 162
  reg 43. . . . . 181, 209
  reg 44. . . . . 181, 182
  reg 44(1)(a). 161, 183, 184
  reg 44(1)(c)–(e). 161
  reg 44(1)(f) 184
  regs 45–47. 182
  regs 48, 49. 183
  reg 50. 183–85
  Sched A1. 185
  Sched 1 . . . . 165, 185–91
  Sched 2 . . . . 165, 191
  Sched 3 . . . . 166, 183, 191–93
  Sched 4 . . . . 167, 183, 193, 194
  Sched 5 . . . . 176, 194, 195
  Sched 6 . . . . 158, 159, 162, 175,
                                179, 180, 191,
                                195–203, 208
  Sched 7 . . . . 159, 175, 180, 202–05
  Sched 8 . . . . 162, 180, 181, 205–10

Food Labelling (Scotland)
  Regulations 1984 SI 1984/1519. 183

Food (Lot Marking) Regulations
  1992 SI 1992/1357. 172

Food Safety (Fishery Products and
  Live Shellfish) (Hygiene)
  Regulations 1998 SI 1998/994. 144

Food Safety (General Food Hygiene)
  (Amendment) Regulations 1995
  SI 1995/2148. 142

Food Safety (General Food Hygiene)
  (Amendment) Regulations
  1995 SI 1995/2200. 142

Food Safety (General Food Hygiene)
(Amendment) Regulations
1995 SI 1995/3205................... 142

Food Safety (General Food Hygiene)
(Amendment) Regulations
1997 SI 1997/2537................... 142

Food Safety (General Food Hygiene)
(Amendment) Regulations
1999 SI 1999/1360................... 142

Food Safety (General Food Hygiene)
(Amendment) Regulations
1999 SI 1999/1540............... 142, 161
reg 4.............................. 147

Food Safety (General Food
Hygiene) Regulations 1995
SI 1995/1763 .... 117, 140–42
reg 2(1), (2)......................... 143
reg 2(3), (4)......................... 144
reg 3.............................. 144
reg 4........................... 144, 146
reg 4(1) 451
reg 4(2) 145, 147
reg 4(2)(a).......................... 452
reg 4(3) 145
reg 5........................... 144, 146
reg 6 .... 140, 141, 146, 451, 452
reg 7 .... 140, 141, 146
reg 8.............................. 146
regs 9, 10........................... 147
Sched 1 .... 140, 144–53

Food Safety (Northern Ireland)
Order 1991 SI 1991/762.............. 293
Arts 2, 8, 9, 26, 29 296
Arts 30, 31, 33 296

Fresh Meat (Hygiene and Inspection)
Regulations 1995 SI 1995/539......... 144

General Product Safety Regulations
1994 SI 1994/2328................... 292
reg 1.......................... 292, 293
reg 3.......................... 292, 294
regs 4–6........................... 294
reg 7.......................... 293–96
reg 8.......................... 294, 295
reg 9.............................. 295

General Product Safety Regulations
1994 SI 1994/2328 (contd)—
reg 9(a) 296
reg 9(b) 297
reg 10......................... 292, 295
reg 11..................... 293, 295, 296
reg 12......................... 296, 298
reg 13 .... 253, 292, 296, 298
reg 14 .... 292, 297, 298
reg 15......................... 297, 298
regs 16, 17..................... 292, 298
regs 18, 131......................... 298

Honey Regulations 1976
SI 1976/1832 162

Housing Benefit (General) Regulations
1987 SI 1987/1971—
reg 2.......................... 302, 303
reg 75......................... 301, 303
reg 75(1) 375

Infant Formula and Follow-on-Formula
Regulations 1995 SI 1995/77.......... 157

Magistrates' Courts (Advance
Information) Rules 1985
SI 1985/601—
r 3......................... 80, 359, 368
r 4................................ 368

Magistrates' Courts (Advance Notice
of Expert Evidence) Rules
1997 SI 1997/705.................... 101

Magistrates' Courts (Northern
Ireland) Order 1981 SI 1981/1675
Art 19 298

Magistrates' Courts Rules 1981
SI 1981/552 63
r 4(3) 93
r 12................................ 66
r 14............................... 572
r 67............................... 383
r 70 .... 366, 367, 381, 382, 481
r 99............................... 383
r 100........................... 63, 93
r 100(1) 91

Management of Health and Safety at Work Regulations 1992 SI 1992/2051 586

Meat Products (Hygiene) Regulations 1994 SI 1994/3082 144

Milk Labelling (Scotland) Regulations 1983 SI 1983/938 183

Minced Meat and Meat Preparations (Hygiene) Regulations 1995 SI 1995/3205 144

Miscellaneous Food Additives Regulations 1995 SI 1995/3187 154
    reg 14(3)(a) 184

Natural Mineral Water, Spring Water and Bottled Drinking Water Regulations 1999 SI 1999/1540 .... 143, 158

Package Travel, Package Holidays and Package Tours (Amendment) Regulations 1995 SI 1995/1648 282

Package Travel, Package Holidays and Package Tours (Amendment) Regulations 1998 SI 1998/1208 282

Package Travel, Package Holidays and Package Tours Regulations 1992 SI 1992/3288 282
    reg 1 282
    reg 2 .... 282, 283
    regs 3–15 283
    reg 4 .... 253, 266, 283
    reg 5 .... 282–84, 286–88
    reg 6 284
    reg 7 .... 284, 286–88
    reg 8 284–88
    regs 9–22 285
    reg 9 288
    regs 16–22 283
    regs 16, 22 286–88
    reg 23 .... 286, 288
    reg 24 286
    reg 25 .... 286, 287
    reg 26 .... 282, 287
    regs 27, 28 287

Package Travel, Package Holidays and Package Tours Regulations 1992 SI 1992/3288 (contd)—
    Sched 1 .... 282, 283, 287, 288
    Sched 2 288
    Sched 3 286–91

Poultry Meat, Farmed Game Bird Meat and Rabbit Meat (Hygiene and Inspection) Regulations 1995 SI 1995/540 144

Regulation and Investigatory Powers (Prescription of Offences Ranks and Positions) Order 2000 SI 2000/2417 .... 29, 593

Reporting of Injuries, Diseases and Dangerous Occurrences Regulations 1985 SI 1995/3163 439
    reg 3(1), (2) 458

Sheep Scab Order 1997 SI 1997/968 .... 446, 447
    Art 5 447

Social Security Administration (Fraud) Act 1997 (Commencement No 1) Order 1997 SI 1997/1577 ..... 300, 302, 303

Specified Sugar Products Regulations 1976 SI 1976/509 162

Street Works (Qualifications Supervisors and Operatives) Regulations 1992 SI 1992/1687 347

Street Works (Registers, Notices, Directions and Designs) (Amendment) Regulations 1999 SI 1999/1049 .... 341, 342, 344

Street Works (Registers, Notices, Directions and Designs) Regulations 1992 SI 1992/2985 .... 341, 342, 344

Sweeteners in Food Regulations 1995 SI 1995/3123 .... 154, 177

Textile Products (Indications
  of Fibre Content)
  Regulations 1986 SI 1986/26—
  reg 5..............................519
  reg 7.........................519, 522
  reg 11............................522
  Sched 1 522
Town and Country Planning (Control
  of Advertisements) Regulations
  1992 SI 1992/666..................71, 72
  reg 3(2) 249
  regs 5, 27................. 245, 249, 411
  Sched 2 249

Town and Country Planning
  (Trees) Regulations 1999
  SI 1999/1892 252

Wild Game Meat (Hygiene and
  Inspection) Regulations 1995
  SI 1995/2148 144

TABLE OF EUROPEAN LEGISLATION

Decisions

94/371/EC 162

Directives

79/112/EEC 155, 159, 182, 184, 185
    Arts 2, 3, 4(2), 5(1) 161
    Art 7 155
    Art 8(4) 169
85/7/EEC 185
86/197/EEC 185
87/250/EEC 155, 161, 182
89/107/EEC 176
89/395/EEC 185
89/398/EEC 155, 161, 182
90/314/EEC 282
90/496/EEC 155, 161, 182
91/72/EEC 185
92/59/EEC 293, 294
93/43/EEC 142
    Arts 3, 5.5–5.8 147
93/102/EEC 185
94/54/EC 155, 161, 182
95/42/EC 185
96/3/EC 142, 143
96/21/EC 155
97/4/EC 184, 185
98/28/EC 143
99/10/EC 155

Regulations

822/87/EEC 157, 193
    Annex 1 .... 157, 158, 160, 181
2658/87/EEC 172
1576/89/EEC 163
    Art 1.4(r) 209
2136/89/EEC 163, 185
2391/89/EEC—
    Art 2 .... 158, 160
2392/89/EEC 162
3773/89/EEC 163
3886/89/EEC 164
1014/90/EEC 163
1759/90/EEC 164
1906/90/EEC 168
1907/90/EEC 162
3702/90/EEC 164
3750/90/EEC 164
1180/91/EEC 164
1274/91/EEC 162
1538/91/EEC 168
1601/91/EEC—
    Art 2 154
1785/91/EEC 164
3540/91/EEC 163
3895/91/EEC 163
3897/91/EEC 164
3901/91/EEC 163
1536/92/EEC 163, 185
2221/92/EEC 163
2333/92/EEC 162
3458/92/EEC 164
2551/93/EEC 172
2617/93/EEC 163
2891/93/EEC 168
3300/93/EC 163
1259/94/EC 163
2991/94/EC 162
3117/94/EC 163
3239/94/EC 163

786/95/EC 163
2401/95/EC 163
2200/96/EC 163
2597/97/EC 159
  Art 3(1) 159, 160
1139/98/EC 159, 161, 177–79,
                                181, 183, 184
  Art 1(1), (2) 178
  Art 2(2) 178
  Art 2(3) 157, 178

Treaties

Act of Accession (Austria, Finland
  and Sweden) 185
Act of Accession (Hellenic Republic) 185
Act of Accession (Kingdom of
  Spain and Portuguese Republic) 185

EC Treaty—
  Art 9(2) 161
European Convention
  on the Protection of
  Human Rights and
  Fundamental Freedoms 80, 90, 115
  Art 6 .... 15, 25, 26
  Art 6(1) 25, 26
European Economic Area
  Agreement 1992
  (EEA Agreement) 156, 161, 185, 293
European Economic Area
  Agreement Protocol 1993 .... 156, 293

INTRODUCTION

This book is intended as a guide to investigators, prosecutors and magistrates clerks who deal with local authority prosecutions. It is intended to be a reasonably comprehensive statement of the steps that should be taken during the investigation and prosecution of cases before the Magistrates Court.

The book originated from in-house courses, which were designed for environmental health officers, planners and other investigatory officers working for Local Authorities. Many of these courses have been presented externally to other bodies including the Local Government Group of the Law Society. These courses have been amalgamated and further developed into the book in its present form.

The authors

The authors of this book are John (known as Jack) Henriques – a solicitor admitted in March 1991 after gaining a law degree at the University of Central Lancashire and solicitors finals at Chester College of Law and Richard Winter, a solicitor admitted in September 1981 after gaining a law degree and solicitors finals through Liverpool Metropolitan University.

Jack has worked in Local Government for some 12 years. He commenced work as a Trainee Solicitor with Macclesfield Borough Council in 1989 and qualified as a solicitor in March 1991 taking up the post as litigation solicitor with South Tyneside Metropolitan Borough Council. In 1995, he joined Bradford City Council as Senior Solicitor in the criminal litigation team, working with Richard.

Richard has worked in Local Government for some 20 years and throughout that time has dealt with a wide range of local authority prosecutions. He worked as a trainee solicitor from 1979–1981 with Wakefield Metropolitan District Council, spent two years in private practice undertaking criminal defence, returning to Wakefield Council in 1983. Thereafter, Richard spent two further years with Wakefield and then joined Leeds City Council for 10 years in 1985 as manager of the prosecutions team. In 1995 he joined Bradford City Council as manager of the criminal litigation team.

Bradford Council is the fourth largest Metropolitan District Council in England and Wales and undertakes thousands of prosecutions annually.

CHAPTER 1

CODE OF PRACTICE FOR INVESTIGATION AND PROSECUTION OF CRIMINAL OFFENCES

The Code for Crown Prosecutors (the Code) last revised in 1999 is set out below with the authors' commentary in italics and bold.

1 INTRODUCTION

1.1 The decision to prosecute an individual is a serious step. Fair and effective prosecution is essential to the maintenance of law and order. But even in a small case, a prosecution has serious implications for all involved - the victim, a witness and a defendant. The Crown Prosecution Service (and local authority prosecutors) should apply the Code for Crown Prosecutors so that it can make fair and consistent decisions about prosecutions.

The purpose of the Code is to show that the CPS are reasonable and fair when making decisions to prosecute. As local authorities should be reasonable and fair in making similar decisions, then local authority prosecutors may consider it reasonable to adopt the Code to support their decision making procedures. We recommend such adoption.

1.2 The Code contains information that is important to Police Officers, to others who work in the criminal justice system and to the general public. It helps the Crown Prosecution Service to play its part in making sure that justice is done.

2 GENERAL PRINCIPLES

2.1 Each case is unique and must be considered on its own but there are general principles that apply in all cases.

1 The duty of the Crown Prosecution Service is to make sure that the right person is prosecuted for the right offence and that all relevant facts are given to the Court.

1 Crown Prosecutors must be fair, independent and objective. They must not let their personal views of the ethnic or national origin, sex, religious beliefs, political views or sexual preference of the offender, victim or witness influence their decisions. They must also not be affected by improper or undue pressure from any source.

2.4 An insolvent company may be prosecuted although leave of the court is normally required.[a] In such situations one might also have regards to the position of the companies' creditors who may be adversely affected by any financial penalty

3 REVIEW

3.1 Proceedings are usually started by the Police. Sometimes they may consult the Crown Prosecution Service before charging a Defendant. Each case that the Police send to the Crown Prosecution Service is reviewed by a Crown Prosecutor to make sure that it meets the tests set out in this Code. Crown Prosecutors may decide to continue with the original charges, to change the charges or sometimes to stop the proceedings.

Local Authority solicitors, upon receipt of prosecution files, are advised to do likewise.

---

[a] See *Re Rhondda Waste Disposal Co Ltd* [2000] TLR, 2 March.

3.2 Review, however, is a continuing process so that Crown Prosecutors can take into account any change in circumstances. Wherever possible, they talk to the Police first if they are thinking about changing the charges or stopping the proceedings. This gives the Police the chance to provide more information that may affect the decision. The Crown Prosecution Service and the Police work closely together to reach the right decision, but the final responsibility for the decision rests with the Crown Prosecution Service.

Similar principles of review apply to local authority prosecutions and the decision whether to start proceedings on the basis of sufficiency of evidence rests with the local authorities lawyers. The public interest primarily rests with the investigating officers, or with the appropriate committee of the council. The public interest is open to review by lawyers also and officers and councillors should take heed of their lawyers' advice in this area also. However, the final decision in relation to public interest issues rests with the elected members of the council.

4 THE CODE TESTS

4.1 There are two stages in the decision to prosecute. The first stage is the evidential test. If the case does not pass the evidential test, it must not go ahead, no matter how important or serious it may be. If the case does pass the evidential test, Crown Prosecutors must decide if a prosecution is needed in the public interest.

4.2 This second stage is the public interest test. The Crown Prosecution Service will only start or continue a prosecution where the case has passed both tests. The evidential test is explained in s 5 and the public interest test is explained in s 6.

5 THE EVIDENTIAL TEST

5.1 Crown Prosecutors must be satisfied that there is enough evidence to provide a 'realistic prospect of conviction' against each Defendant on each charge. They must consider what the defence case may be and how that is likely to affect the prosecutions case.

5.2 A realistic prospect of conviction is an objective test. It means that a jury or bench of magistrates, properly directed in accordance with the law, is more likely than not to convict the Defendant of the charge alleged.

5.3 When deciding whether there is enough evidence to prosecute, Crown Prosecutors must consider whether the evidence can be used and is reliable. There will be many cases in which the evidence does not give any cause for concern. But there will also be cases in which the evidence may not be as strong as it first appears. Crown Prosecutors must ask themselves the following questions:

Can the evidence be used in court?

(a) Is it likely that the evidence will be excluded by the court? There are certain legal rules which might mean that evidence which seems relevant cannot be given at a trial. For example, is it likely that the evidence will be excluded because of the way in which it was gathered or because of the rule against using hearsay as evidence? If so, is there enough other evidence for a realistic prospect of conviction?

Is the evidence reliable?

(b) Is it likely that a confession is unreliable, for example, because of the Defendant's age, intelligence or lack of understanding?

Chapter 1: Code of Practice for Investigation and Prosecution

(c) Is the witness's background likely to weaken the prosecution case? For example, does the witness have any dubious motive that may affect his or her attitude to the case or a relevant previous conviction?

(d) If the identity of the Defendant is likely to be questioned, is the evidence about this strong enough?

5.4 Crown Prosecutors should not ignore evidence because they are not sure that it can be used or is reliable. But they should look closely at it when deciding if there is a realistic prospect of conviction.

6 THE PUBLIC INTEREST TEST

6.1 In 1951, Lord Shawcross, who was Attorney General, made the classic statement on public interest, which has been supported by Attorneys General ever since: 'It has never been the rule in the country – I hope it never will be – that suspected criminal offences must automatically be the subject of prosecution.' (House of Commons Debates, volume 483, column 681, 29 January 1951.)

6.2 The public interest must be considered in each case where there is enough evidence to provide a realistic prospect of conviction. A prosecution will usually take place unless there are public interest factors tending against prosecution which clearly outweigh those tending in favour. Although there may be public interest factors against prosecution in a particular case, often the prosecution should go ahead and those factors should be put to the court for consideration when sentence is being passed.

6.3 Crown Prosecutors must balance factors for and against prosecution carefully and fairly. Public interest factors that can affect the decision to prosecute usually depend on the seriousness of the offence or the circumstances of the offender. Some factors may increase the need to prosecute but others may suggest that another course of action would be better.

The following lists of some common public interest factors, both for and against prosecution, are not exhaustive. The factors that apply will depend on the facts in each case.

Some common public interest factors in favour of prosecution

6.4 The more serious the offence, the more likely it is that a prosecution will be needed in the public interest. A prosecution is likely to be needed if:

(a) a conviction is likely to result in a significant sentence;

(b) a weapon was used or violence was threatened during the commission of the offence;

(c) the offence was committed against a person serving the public (for example, a police or prison officer, or a nurse);

(d) the Defendant was in a position of authority or trust;

(e) the evidence shows that the Defendant was a ringleader or an organiser of the offence;

(f) there is evidence that the offence was pre-meditated;

(g) there is evidence that the offence was carried out by a group;

(h) the victim of the offence was vulnerable, has been put in considerable fear, or suffered personal attack, damage or disturbance;

(i) the offence was motivated by any form of discrimination against the victim's ethnic or national origin, sex, religious, political views or sexual preference;

(j) there is a marked difference between the actual or mental ages of the Defendant and the victim, or if there is any element of corruption;

(k) the Defendant's previous convictions or cautions are relevant to the present offence;

(l) the Defendant is alleged to have committed the offence whilst under an order of the court;

(m) there are grounds for believing that the offence is likely to be continued or repeated, for example, by a history of recurring conduct; or

(n) the offence, although not serious in itself, is widespread in the area where it was committed.

Some common public interest factors against prosecution

6.5 A prosecution is less likely to be need if:

(a) the court is likely to impose a very small or nominal penalty;

(b) the offence was committed as a result of a genuine mistake or misunderstanding (these factors must be balanced against the seriousness of the offence);

(c) the loss or harm can be described as minor and was the result of a single incident, particularly if it was caused by a misjudgment;

(d) there has been a long delay between the offence taking place and the date of the trial, unless:
- offence is serious;
- the delay has been caused in part by the Defendant;
- the offence has only recently come to light; or
- the complexity of the offence has meant that there has been a long investigation;

(e) a prosecution is likely to have a very bad effect on the victim's physical or mental health, always bearing in mind the seriousness of the offence;

(f) the Defendant is elderly or is, or was at the time of the offence, suffering from significant mental or physical ill health unless the offence is serious or there is a real possibility that it may be repeated. The Crown Prosecution Service, where necessary, applies Home Office guidelines about how to deal with mentally disordered offenders. Crown Prosecutors must balance the desirability of diverting a Defendant who is suffering from significant mental or physical ill health with the need to safeguard the general public;

(g) the Defendant has put right the loss or harm that was caused but Defendants must not avoid prosecution simply because they can pay compensation); or

(h) details may be made public that could harm sources of information, international relations or national security.

6.6 Deciding on the public interest is not simply a matter of adding up the number of factors on each side. Crown Prosecutors must decide how important each factor is in the circumstances of each case and go on to make an overall assessment.

The relationship between the victim and the public interest

6.7 The Crown Prosecution Service acts in the public interest, not just in the interests of any one individual. But Crown Prosecutors may always think very carefully about the interests of the victim, which are an important factor, when deciding where the public interest lies.

Youth offenders

6.8 Crown Prosecutors must consider the interests of a youth when deciding whether it is in the public interest to prosecute. The stigma of a conviction can cause very serious harm to the prospects of a youth offender or a young adult. Young offenders can sometimes be dealt with without going to court. But Crown Prosecutors should not avoid prosecuting simply because of the Defendant's age. The seriousness of the offence or the offender's past behaviour may make prosecution necessary.

Police cautions

6.9 The Police make the decision to caution an offender in accordance with Home Office guidelines. If the Defendant admits the offence, cautioning is the most common alternative to a court appearance. Crown Prosecutors, where necessary, apply the same guidelines and should look at the alternatives to prosecution when they consider the public interest. Crown Prosecutors should tell the Police if they think that a caution would be more suitable than a prosecution.

Local authorities are equally entitled to offer cautions to offenders where they think it is appropriate. They may also wish to recover costs of the investigation and legal consideration of the evidence when offering the caution. This is appropriate bearing in mind that resources is a factor to be taken into account when considering whether it is in the public interest to prosecute.

7 CHARGES

7.1 Crown Prosecutors should select charges which:

 (a) reflect the seriousness of the offending;

 (b) give the court adequate sentencing powers; and

 (c) enable the case to be presented in a clear and simple way.

This means that Crown Prosecutors may not always continue with the most serious charge where there is a choice. Further, Crown Prosecutors should not continue with more charges than are necessary.

7.2 Crown Prosecutors should never go ahead with more charges than are necessary just to encourage a Defendant to plead guilty to a few. In the same way, they should never go ahead with a more serious charge just to encourage a Defendant to plead guilty to a less serious one.

7.3 Crown Prosecutors should not change the charge simply because of the decision made by the court or the Defendant about where the case will be heard.

8 MODE OF TRIAL

8.1 The Crown Prosecution Service applies the current guidelines for magistrates who have to decide whether cases should be tried in the Crown Court when the offence gives the option. (See the 'National Mode of Trial Guidelines' issued by the Lord Chief Justice.) Crown Prosecutors should recommend Crown Court trial when they are satisfied that the guidelines require them to do so.

8.2 Speed must never be the only reason for asking for a case to stay in the Magistrates' Courts. But Crown Prosecutors should consider the effect of any likely delay if they send a case to the Crown Court, and any possible stress on victims and witnesses if the case if delayed.

9 ACCEPTING GUILTY PLEAS

9.1 Defendants may want to plead guilty to some, but not all, of the charges. Or they may want to plead guilty to a different, possibly less serious, charge because they are admitting only part of the crime. Crown Prosecutors should only accept the Defendant's plea if they think the court is able to pass a sentence that matches the seriousness of the offending. Crown Prosecutors must never accept a guilty plea just because it is convenient.

10 RE-STARTING A PROSECUTION

10.1 People should be able to rely on decisions taken by the Crown Prosecution Service. Normally, if the Crown Prosecution Service tells a suspect or Defendant that there will not be a prosecution, or that the prosecution has been stopped, that is the end of the matter and the case will not start again. But occasionally there are special reasons why the Crown Prosecution Service will re-start the prosecution, particularly if the case is serious.

10.2 These reasons include:

(a) rare cases where a new look at the original decision shows that it was clearly wrong and should not be allowed to stand;

(b) cases which are stopped so that more evidence which is likely to become available in the fairly near future can be collected and prepared. In these cases, the Crown Prosecutor will tell the Defendant that the prosecution may well start again;

(c) cases which are stopped because of a lack of evidence but where more significant evidence is discovered later.

11 CONCLUSION

11.1 The Crown Prosecution Service is a public service headed by the Director of Public Prosecutions. It is answerable to Parliament through the Attorney General. The Code for Crown Prosecutors is issued under s 10 of the Prosecution of Offences Act 1985 and is a public document. This is the third edition and it replaces all earlier versions. Changes to the Code are made from time to time and these are also published.

11.2 The Code is designed to make sure that everyone knows the principles that the Crown Prosecution Service applies when carrying out its work. Police Officers should take account of the principles of the Code when they are deciding whether to charge a Defendant with an offence. By applying the same principles, everyone involved in the criminal justice system is helping the system to treat victims fairly, and to prosecute Defendants fairly but effectively.

11.3 The Code is available from:

Crown Prosecution Service

Information Branch

50 Ludgate Hill

London

EC4M 7EX

The code should be applied by local authority lawyers and enforcement officers, if not on a statutory basis, then in its spirit of fairness. The matrix at Appendix 7 lists public interest factors in favour and against prosecution. The matrix may be used to assist in deciding whether or not to prosecute.

CHAPTER 2

THE STATUTORY FRAMEWORK FOR CRIMINAL OFFENCE INVESTIGATIONS

THE POLICE AND CRIMINAL EVIDENCE ACT 1984, THE CRIMINAL JUSTICE AND PUBLIC ORDER ACT 1994 AND THE CRIMINAL PROCEDURE AND INVESTIGATIONS ACT 1996

2.1 Broadly speaking, the Police and Criminal Evidence Act 1984 (the Act will later be referred to as PACE) was brought about to standardise the procedures adopted by Police Forces and other prosecuting agencies when investigating crimes and reporting offenders. It goes without saying that the Codes of Practice specified in the Act are aimed specifically at Police Officers, as it is such Officers who primarily have to enforce the law on a day today basis. However, PACE does apply to investigations by local authority investigators (see s 67(9) of the Act).

2.2 The importance of cautioning the defendant before interviewing him cannot be overstressed. Failure to do so may result in the evidence obtained during the interview being excluded by the court as being unfairly prejudicial.[a] Consideration should also be given to the question of cautioning wherever an officer wishes to make inquiries of a potential defendant for the purpose of obtaining evidence. If questions are put to the defendant for other purposes, for example, to establish identity or ownership of a vehicle or property, there is no need for a caution. The words of the caution are as follows:

> You do not have to say anything. But it may harm your defence if you do not mention when questioned something which you later rely on in Court. Anything you do say may be given in evidence.

The caution was amended[b] in 1994 by the then Home Secretary Michael Howard to readjust the balance between the defence and prosecution in the prosecution's favour.

2.3 Minor deviations do not constitute a breach of this requirement provided that the sense of the caution is preserved. Therefore, it is not essential to remember this caution verbatim so long as the general meaning of it is conveyed to the suspect.

2.4 Chapter 7 provides a more detailed analysis of interviewing and reporting the offender. However, some of the more salient points which arise in connection with the caution are examined briefly in this chapter.

2.5 As a matter of good practice, it is recommended that a caution is recorded either in a pocket book or written down as an original contemporaneous note as soon as possible. Such documents will be important evidence in the case.

2.6 It was intended that PACE would provide fairness for all concerned. This includes the investigator as well as the suspect. PACE also makes provision for dealing with

---

(a) PACE 1984, s 78.
(b) Criminal Justice and Public Order Act 1994, s 34. The old caution states: 'You do not have to say anything unless you wish to do so, but anything you do say may be taken down and used in evidence.'

suspects who provide dubious names and addresses. PACE enables a Police Officer to arrest a person to verify his name and address.[c] If there are reasonable grounds to suspect that an offence has been or is being committed, and the suspect's name and address cannot be verified, investigators are advised to seek the assistance of the Police. This section applies to any offence which is not an arrestable offence.

2.7 The Police are well aware of their powers of arrest and should assist with the investigation of the offence.

2.8 Enforcement officers and prosecuting solicitors should be aware of the Criminal Procedure and Investigations Act 1996 which came into force for all prosecutions first investigated after 1 April 1997. The Act will be later referred to as the CPIA 1996.

2.9 The HELA[d] Circular for Local Authorities No 45/16 gives guidance to local authority enforcement officers and is reproduced below. It makes reference to the Home Office Code of Practice made under the CPIA 1996.

THE HELA CIRCULAR FOR LOCAL AUTHORITIES

Introduction

2.10 The CPIA 1996 made significant changes in the arrangements for disclosure of material in criminal cases. Following a series of Court of Appeal rulings, the common law required disclosure to the defence in Crown Court cases of *all information which is relevant to the case*, unless previously disclosed as part of the prosecution case. The Government of the time believed that the practical effect of the disclosure requirements has been to place heavy burdens on investigating and prosecuting authorities, with results that may not be in the interests of justice. The Act placed on a *statutory* footing procedures for the recording and retention of material, for disclosure by prosecution and defence, and for court decisions on public interest immunity. The procedures apply to summary proceedings as well as trials on indictment, and include proceedings against companies as well as individuals.

2.10.1 The Home Office Code of Practice lays down procedures for the recording, retention and disclosure of material gathered during an investigation. The code has been written to reflect the working arrangements of the Police, but other criminal investigators, including enforcement officers of local authorities, will need to have regard to it.[a] The code has implications for the procedures of ALL those involved in investigations which may lead to a prosecution, including those providing expert reports and opinions. There will also be some changes to court procedures as a result of the Act.

2.10.2 Paragraph 2.10.4 sets out the most important provisions of the Act for enforcement officers – these do not apply in Scotland; para 2.10.6 below outlines what the requirements mean in practice.

(c) PACE 1984, s 25.
(d) HELA is a group comprising of Health and Safety executives and Local Authority officers.
(a) Criminal Procedure and Investigation Act 1996, s 26(1).

Chapter 2: The Statutory Framework for Criminal Offence Investigations

2.10.3 Any local authority enforcement officer requiring legal advice on the Act and Code should seek this from their own local authority lawyers.

2.10.4 The following are the main matters for enforcement officers:

(1) Judges have the power to make a binding ruling at pre-trial hearings in the Crown Court on any question relating to admissibility of evidence or any other point of law.

(2) A statutory scheme for prosecution and defence disclosure in criminal proceedings.

(3) A Home Office Code of Practice containing provisions designed to secure the following:

(a) that material which is obtained in a criminal investigation and which may be relevant to it, is recorded, retained and revealed to *the prosecutor* (the prosecuting authority – in practice a designated person);

(b) that material is disclosed to the accused at the request of the prosecutor; and

(c) that the prosecutor is given a written statement certifying compliance with the requirements of the Code of Practice.

(4) A requirement on defendants to indicate their plea before the decision is taken on whether the trial should take place in the magistrates' court or the Crown Court.

(5) Removal of the requirement on witnesses to give oral evidence at committal hearings in the magistrates' court.

(6) Provision for the reading out at the trial without further proof of written statements and depositions admitted in evidence in modified committal proceedings.

2.10.5 The code of practice defines *an investigation* as one conducted 'with a view to it being ascertained whether a person should be charged with an offence, or whether a person charged with an offence is guilty of it'.

2.10.6 Implications of the Act and Code of Practice for local authority enforcement Officers and others involved in investigations.

2.10.7 Binding rulings

(1) Enforcement officers must bear in mind the judges' new power when preparing for pre-trial hearings.

2.10.8 Code of Practice

(1) The Code of Practice will affect a broad range of enforcement officers' activities including inspections, investigations of complaints and accidents, and audits. To a large degree, the code of practice should build on what local authorities and enforcement officers do already. The code requires systems, which will ensure the disclosure to the defence of

previously undisclosed material, if it meets certain tests. *Material*, for purposes of the Act, means 'material of any kind, including information and objects'. In each case, it will be necessary to identify:

(a) the officer-in-charge of the investigation;

(b) the disclosure officer; and

(c) the prosecutor.

Some or all of these roles may be undertaken by the same person.

(3) Material from an investigation will need to be separated into the following categories:

(a) intended for prosecution use at trial;

(b) not intended for prosecution use at the trial but which may need to be disclosed to the accused;

(c) sensitive material (ie, which it is not in the public interest to disclose); and

(d) irrelevant material.

(4) Under the code of practice, disclosure will be in three stages:

(a) *primary prosecution disclosure* of any previously undisclosed material which might undermine the prosecution case;

(b) *defence disclosure* of the nature of their case (required in Crown Court cases, voluntary in summary trials following a not guilty plea);

(c) *secondary prosecution disclosure* of any previously undisclosed material which might reasonably be expected to assist the defence's declared line of argument.

(5) Among the practical considerations are how to:

(a) allocate the roles mentioned in para 2 above;

(b) keep notebooks which record factual information, but not opinion, or considerations of a possible prosecution;

(c) decide what material from an investigation is 'relevant' and should be retained;

(d) produce the required schedules of relevant material which has not previously been disclosed;[b]

(e) avoid difficulties that could arise from the disclosure of draft statements (particularly by expert witnesses) prepared before the full circumstances were known and had been fully considered;

(f) decide the period for which various types of material should be kept; and

(g) cope with these requirements in the context of a major incident and/or complex investigation.

(b) See Appendix 19.

CRIMINAL PROCEDURE AND INVESTIGATIONS ACT (CPIA) 1996 AND CODE OF PRACTICE UNDER PT II

2.11 Provisions

2.11.1 Section 26(1) enacts that 'other investigators' – that is, local authorities – 'should have regard to any relevant provision'.

Definitions

2.11.2 *'The Officer in Charge of the investigation'* (OIC) has been defined as the police officer responsible for directing a criminal investigation. He is also responsible for ensuring that the proper procedures are in place for recording information and retaining records of information and other material in the investigation. The responsibilities of this position will obviously fall to the lead investigating officer (IO) for the local authority.

2.11.3 *'Disclosure Officer'* (DO) is the person responsible for examining material retained by the Police during the investigation and criminal proceedings resulting from it, and certifying that he has done this; and disclosing material to the accused at the request of the prosecutor', as this position includes disclosure of any material which might help the defence case (Code, para 8.2). A comprehensive knowledge of the case beyond the file evidence is required. For this reason, it is believed that the lead investigating officer best fits this role.

2.11.4 *'Material relevant to the investigation'* includes any material which 'has some bearing on any offence under investigation or any person being investigated, or on the surrounding circumstances of the case, unless it is capable of having any impact on the case'.

2.11.5 *'Material'* includes reports, telephone calls, final statements, draft statements which are materially different from the final version, interview records, communications between police and forensic experts, and material casting doubt on the reliability of a confession or witness (Code, para 5.4). Much of the above will naturally form part of the file of evidence. However, particular note should be taken of material, which is often generated routinely, which is not sent to the legal department as part of the case. This would include draft statements, as described above, and communications – that is, details of telephone calls, as well as letters to public analysts.

Recording of information

2.11.6 All relevant material must be recorded (s 23(1)(b) of the CPIA, and Code, para 4) in a durable, retrievable form. This information should be recorded at the time it is obtained or as soon as practicable.

Preparation of material for the prosecutor

2.11.7 The disclosure provisions are triggered by a not guilty plea in the magistrates' court (s 1(1) of the CPIA) or, alternatively, by committal or transfer to the Crown Court (again s 13(1) of the CPIA). Subject to this, the defence are not entitled to disclosure under the Act, although the old common law principles relating to unused information will apply.

Schedule of unused information

2.11.8 The DO is required to provide a schedule of information which he believes will not form part of the prosecution case, which is not sensitive (Code, para 6.2). All material in a schedule must be listed separately and numbered consecutively and a description should make clear the nature of the item. It should also contain sufficient details to enable the prosecutor to decide whether he needs to inspect the material before deciding whether or not it should be disclosed (Code, para 6.9). This schedule may be described as 'unused non-sensitive information' (this terminology has no specific authority).

Schedule of sensitive material

2.11.9 In addition to the above, there must also be a Schedule of Sensitive Material (Code, para 6.3). If there is no such material, it is advisable to draw one up, nonetheless, and insert the words 'no sensitive material', or words to that effect, to confirm that consideration has been given to this obligation. This schedule must be drawn up to comply with the same requirements as to numbering and description, etc, as the Schedule of Unused Information. In addition to this, the schedule must also contain a statement that the DO believes that the material is sensitive and the reason for that belief (Code, para 6.12). The Code gives numerous examples of sensitive material (Code, para 6.12). This includes material given in confidence and material relating to the identity or activities of informants or other persons supplying information to the police who may be in danger if their identities are revealed. Presumably, this protection would not be afforded to complainants (*Daventry DC v Olins* (1990) 154 JP 478), unless this might put them in danger.

Schedule of additional material

2.11.10 (Code, para 8.1.) This is to be drawn up by the DO and is only required 'where necessary'. It is the author's interpretation that, if the officer leading the investigation has included all information in either the File Report on Evidence or the schedules mentioned above, this will not be necessary. The information to be included as additional material is that:

'Which may be relevant to the investigation;
which does not form part of the case against the accused;
which is not already listed on the schedule; and
which he believes is not sensitive.'

Certification by the DO

2.11.11 (Code, para 9.1.) The DO must certify, to the best of his knowledge and belief, that all material which has been retained and made available to him has been made available in accordance with the Code. He must sign and date the certificate. It will be necessary to certify not only at the time when the schedule and accompanying material is submitted to the prosecutor, but also when material which has been retained is reconsidered after the accused has given a defence statement. There is no provision for automatic disclosure of this schedule to the defence. However, the court may order disclosure (ss 3(6) and 8(2) of the CPIA).

Disclosure of material to the accused

2.11.12 *Primary disclosure* (Code, para 10.1.)

The prosecution duty of disclosure arises 'as soon as reasonably practicable' after committal, notice of transfer to the Crown Court or entry of a not guilty plea in the magistrates' court to any charge against a person over 18 who is to be tried summarily (s 13 of the CPIA). The information to be disclosed is *any material 'which might undermine the case for the prosecution'*, or give a written statement that there is no such material (s 3 of the CPIA). This requirement could, presumably, be fulfilled by a letter from the prosecuting solicitor after receipt of a written memorandum from the lead investigating officer to the same effect. In addition to the above, the prosecution must also disclose to the defence any Schedule of Non-Sensitive Information which he has received from the IO (s 24(3)). Given that the prosecutor should be given all the schedules at the same time as the File Report on Evidence (Code, para 7.1) is received from the IO, he should be in a position to forward this information to the accused. At this stage, the DO must also draw the attention of the prosecutor to any material which an investigator has retained (whether or not listed on a Schedule) which may fall within the test for primary disclosure, and should explain why he has come to that view.

Compulsory disclosure by the accused (s 5 of the CPIA)

2.11.13 Within 14 days of primary disclosure by the prosecution, the accused is required to file a defence Statement.[a] The defence statement should include a written statement:

(a) CPIA (Defence Disclosure Time Limits) Regulations 1997 SI 1997/6684, reg 2.

(a) setting out in general terms the nature of the accused's defence;
(b) indicating the matters on which he takes issue with the prosecution; and
(c) setting out, in the case of each such matter, the reason why he takes issue with the prosecution (s 5(6) of the CPIA).

2.11.14 Compulsory disclosure by the accused does not apply to any offences which are tried in the magistrates' court (s 5(1) of the CPIA). However, the accused may give a defence statement voluntarily (s 6(2) of the CPIA), which might prompt further disclosure by the prosecution.

Sanctions against the accused for non-compliance with the duty of disclosure

2.11.15 Sanctions arise in the following circumstances:
(a) failure or delay in giving a defence statement;
(b) setting out an inconsistent defence in a defence statement;
(c) putting forward a defence at trial, which is inconsistent with the defence statement;
(d) contravening the rules vis-à-vis alibi notification, etc (s 11(1) of the CPIA).

Sanctions applicable are:
(a) The court or, with the leave of the court, any other party may make such comment as appears appropriate.
(b) The court or jury may draw such inferences as appears proper in deciding whether the accused is guilty of the offence concerned (s 11(3) of the CPIA).

Secondary disclosures

2.11.16 'After a defence statement has been given, the Disclosure Officer must look again at the material which has been retained and must draw the attention of the prosecutor to *any material which might reasonably be expected to assist the defence disclosed by the accused,*' (para 8.2). 'Section 9 of the Act imposes a *continuing duty on the prosecutor ... to disclose material which meets the test for disclosure.*'

2.12 Attorney General's guidelines and disclosure

2.12.1 Main principles:

The DO must inspect, view or listen to all material that has been retained by the Investigator, and must provide a personal declaration to the effect that this task has been done. An example of a declaration, which might appear at the foot of the schedules, is as follows:

I have inspected, viewed and listened to all material that has been retained by the investigator and certify to the best of my knowledge and belief that all material that has been retained and made available to me has been available in accordance with the code of practice under Part 11 pursuant to the Criminal Procedure and Investigation Act 1996

Signed ....
Officer in Charge of Investigation/Disclosure Officer

Dated ....

The Schedules of Sensitive and Non-Sensitive Material must be, 'detailed, clear and accurate'. The Guidelines advise that descriptions may require a summary of the contents of the retained material.

2.12.2 The following highlights some of the main points arising from the above Guidelines.

At the beginning of the Guidelines, it is advised that, 'every accused person has a right to a fair trial, a right long embodied in our law and guaranteed under Art 6 of the European Convention of Human Rights. Fair disclosure to an accused is an inseparable part of a fair trial'. It is, therefore, essential that all IOs as well as prosecutors are fully aware of the disclosure provisions. Any failure to disclose material information to the accused could result in the case being dismissed. It might also result in costs being awarded against the prosecutor on the grounds that the prosecution process has been carried out improperly.

2.12.3 *Obligations of IOs and DOs*

1 DOs must inspect, view or listen to all material that has been retained by the Investigator, and the DO must provide a personal declaration to the effect that this task has been done. There is, however, an exception in para 9, where investigators seize large volumes of material, which may not, because of its source, general nature or other reasons, seem likely ever to be relevant. In these circumstances, its existence should be made known to the accused in general terms at the primary stage. Furthermore, a s 9 statement should be completed by the IO or the DO, describing this material by general category and justifying it not having been examined if that is the case.

2 To enable DOs to inspect, view and listen to all the material, it is essential that all disclosure material is properly recorded. This will also include telephone calls with third parties during the course of the investigation.

3 The Schedules of Sensitive and Non-Sensitive Material must be 'detailed, clear and accurate'. The Guidelines advise that descriptions may require a summary of the contents of the retained material. It is, therefore, no longer appropriate to simply refer to a letter from X to Y. Some detail must be included to enable the prosecutor and the defence to become aware of the essential nature of the document.

4 The DO/Investigator must err on the side of caution in recording and retaining all material if there is any doubt as to whether or not it may be relevant.

5   The DO must draw to the prosecutor's attention any detail, which might undermine the prosecution case, or reasonably be expected to assist the defence disclosed by the accused.

2.12.4   *Prosecutors generally*

There may be occasions when a defence statement points the prosecution to other lines of enquiry. Further investigation, in these circumstances, is possible, and evidence obtained as a result of enquiring into a defence statement may be used as part of the prosecution case or to rebut the defence.

Prosecutors must review schedules prepared by DOs thoroughly and must be alert to the possibility that material may exist which has not been revealed to them. If no schedules have been provided, or there are apparent omissions from the schedules or documents or other items are insufficiently described or are unclear, the prosecutor must at once take action to obtain properly completed schedules.

Prosecutors must ensure that they record in writing all actions and decisions they make in discharging their disclosure responsibilities.

2.12.5   *Defence practitioners*

A defence statement should set out the nature of the defence, the matters on which issue is taken and the reasons for taking issue. It is, therefore, clear that a comprehensive defence statement is required. Paragraph 28 advises that, wherever possible, the accused should sign the defence statement to evidence his or her agreement.

2.12.6   *Secondary disclosure*

If no defence statement has been served or if the prosecutor considers that the defence statement is lacking specific information and/or clarity, a letter should be sent to the defence, indicating that secondary disclosure will not take place or will be limited (as appropriate), and inviting the defence to specify and/or clarify the accused's case. The prosecutor should consider raising the issue at a preliminary hearing if the position is not resolved satisfactorily to enable the court to give directions.

2.12.7   *Summary trial*

The prosecutor should, in addition to complying with the obligations under the CPIA, provide to the defence all evidence upon which the prosecution proposes to rely, in a summary trial.

2.12.8   *Disclosure prior to the disclosure provisions under CPIA 1996*

This issue was considered by the court in *R v Imran & Hussain* ([1997] Crim LR 754), in which the court clearly indicated that the defence were not entitled to be informed of the prosecutions case at the interview stage. The issue was again considered at the pre committal stage in *R v DPP ex p Lee* ([1999] 2 All ER 737) 18 March, where the court took the view that although some disclosure may be required prior to committal, the statutory provisions would be undermined if pre-committal discovery exceeded discovery obtainable after committal pursuant to statute. The court went on to say that a reasonable prosecutor should ask himself what, if any, immediate disclosure justice and fairness required him to make in the particular circumstances of the case. Examples of what should be disclosed were: (i) the previous convictions of the victim; (ii) material relevant to an abuse of process application; (iii) material relevant to an application that there should be no committal or committal on a lesser charge; and (iv) material for defence to prepare for trial where delay would affect the evidence, for example names of eye-witnesses who the prosecution would not call.

With the recent implementation of the Human Rights Act 1998 practitioners may take the view that disclosure is ripe for reconsideration. In the Attorney General's Guidelines on Disclosure, paras 34–35 nothing over and above the decision in Lee was added. It is clear from the introduction that this issue was not considered in the absence of the Human Rights Act. The commentary also confirms that the decision in Lee was considered before the guidelines were finalised. It is therefore submitted that the position set out in Lee is good law under the Human Rights Act.

Full details of the Attorney General's Guidelines can be found on website www.lslo.gov.uk.

PLANNING AN INVESTIGATION

3.1 THE ELEMENTS OF THE OFFENCE

An investigation usually begins with either a complaint or following a routine inspection, for example, house in multiple occupation or food premises inspection. The Investigating Officer (IO) will therefore have a good idea of the offence or offences, which he is investigating. It is therefore advisable to look closely at the statute which gives rise to the alleged offence and breakdown the alleged offence into its individual elements. This having been done the officer should then establish in his mind, if not on paper, how each element of the offence will be investigated. In breaking down the offence into individual elements, the officer should look to any case law or statutes, which may define any of the offence making provisions.[a]

3.2 WHO IS TO BE INVESTIGATED?

At the risk of stating the obvious, the officer should decide who he is to investigate[b] and the capacity of that person. For example, he might not charge the maker of a false trade description but the person whose fault it is.[c] Under the control of Advertisement Regulations, the owner of the land or the person whose business is being publicised may be prosecuted for unlawful advertising.[d] It is also worth bearing in mind that an employer may be vicariously liable for the acts of his staff.[e]

3.3 THE DEFENDANT'S LEGAL STATUS

3.3.1 A common mistake of novice investigators is to neglect the status of the defendant. For example, is the defendant a limited company or a sole trader? If it is a company, the full name of the company will be required as well as the registered office address. It might otherwise be a partnership in which case the names of the partners will be required together with an address for service of documents. If the sole trader or partnership does have a trading name, this should also be sought.

(a) Eg, Trade Descriptions Act 1968, s 6, defines the meaning of 'supply of goods' and Town and Country Planning Act 1990, s 336, defines the meaning of 'advertisement'.

(b) If there is any doubt as to the identity of the defendant, this should be verified at an early stage in the investigation. If the issue of identity arises for the first time at trial the authorities are conflicting as to whether a dock identification is permissible in the magistrates' court. *Barnes v CC of Durham* [1997] TLR, 6 May is in favour, *North Yorkshire Trading Standards v Williams* [1994] TLR, 22 November, (1995) 159 JP 383 is generally against.

(c) Trade Marks Act 1968, s 23.

(d) Town and Country Planning Act 1990, s 224(4).

(e) *St Helens MBC v Hill* (1992) 156 JP 602, *Coppen v Moore (No 2)* [1898] 2 QB 306, *Clode v Barnes* [1974] 1 All ER 1166.

3.3.2 All details relating to business names and addresses should be available on all business documentation, that is, receipts and all correspondence.(f) Furthermore, most if not all of this information should also be displayed in a prominent place on the business premises and failure to comply amounts to an offence.(g)

3.3.3 As regards clubs and associations, these have no legal status(h) and therefore cannot be prosecuted. Prosecutions should therefore be taken against named individuals in these circumstances.

3.3.4 Charities have no legal status. In the unlikely event that it is necessary to take proceedings against a charity, the trustees should be named in the summons unless there is an exceptional reason why an individual should be prosecuted for his personal involvement in the offence.

3.3.5 For proceedings against universities it is likely that most if not all of these will be corporations set up by royal charter.(i) They should therefore be served in the proper name of the university, although the documents could be marked for the attention of a person who is likely to be the most appropriate person to accept the proceedings, depending on the internal management structure. This could be the 'secretary' or the 'registrar and secretary'.

3.4 WITNESS STATEMENTS

It is usual in most investigations to start by taking a witness statement from the complainant and/or any lay witnesses. Sometimes expert evidence will be required and, exceptionally, in a food hygiene case, for example, the first step in the investigation will be to commission an analytical report from an expert as to the state and condition of the food, as close as possible to the time of sale or exposure for sale. Other steps in the investigation might include inspection of the premises. In the case of a food hygiene or health and safety investigation, it is recommended that this take place as soon as possible.

3.5 THE INTERVIEW OF THE DEFENDANT

Having taken statements from witnesses and carried out all other investigation it is usual to interview the defendant. Chapter 7 deals with this subject more comprehensively. Whereas there is no rule from preventing the officer from interviewing the defendant at the outset of the investigation, the effect of delaying this is to enable the officer to make further probing inquiries of the defendant on the strength of the evidence already

---

(f) Business Names Act 1985, s 4.
(g) *Ibid*, s 4.
(h) See *R v Darlington BC ex p Association of Darlington Taxi Owners (No 2)* [1994] TLR, 14 April which established that the association had no capacity to institute legal proceedings.
(i) See *Thomas v University of Bradford* [1987] 2 WLR 677 which confirms that the university is a corporation set up by royal charter. The presence of the universities names on numerous case reports suggests that they are legal entities although this is not conclusive.

collated. If, for example, the defendant cannot recall being on the premises when his employee sold cigarettes to a person under 16 years, it might be open to the investigating officer to put to the defendant at interview that he was seen entering the premises 10 minutes earlier. Furthermore, subsequent investigations often give rise to the need for further interviews. This could pose problems for the officer if the defendant is reluctant to be re-interviewed. If the defendant has already been told that he will be reported, a further interview would likely be a breach of the Police and Criminal Evidence Act 1984 code of conduct. The practice of interviewing the defendant at the closing stages of the investigation should not prevent the officer from cautioning the defendant at the early stages and asking him a few brief pertinent questions. Late interviews give the defendant the opportunity to consider his position carefully and enable him to give answers which he might not have given if questioned closer to the event. An example which might illustrate this point occurred when a publican was charged with allowing indecent acts on stage. There was a defence of due diligence open to him until the police officer asked whether he had laid down any ground rules as to what the performers were entitled to do. The answer was given in the negative and a guilty plea followed to a charge of breach of condition of a public entertainment licence.

3.6 POSSIBLE DEFENCES

The IO should also have regard to any express statutory defence such as 'due diligence'.[j] Regulatory offences often contain the words 'knowingly' or 'without reasonable excuse'.[k] An astute investigator will not only take up these issues with the defendant at interview, but also as far as possible close the door to any unexpected excuses, etc, that might arise at trial. To ensure that any matter which requires investigation have not been omitted, reference may be made to the checklist which can be found below.

3.7 CHECKLIST

Evidence required of the five W's:

3.7.1   *Who is the defendant?*
- (DOB) Employer (vicarious liability: *St Helens MBC v Hill* (1992) 156 JP 602 Employee + *Coppen v Moore (No 2)* [1898] 2 QB 306
- Employer, employee, person responsible, etc

3.7.2   *What is defendant's status?*
- Individual/sole trader
- Partnership

(j) Food Safety Act 1990, s 21.
(k) Environmental Protection Act 1990, s 80, Building Act 1959, s 59 (reasonable excuse), Local Government (Miscellaneous Provisions) Act 1976, s 46 (knowingly).

	– Limited company
	– plc
	NB clubs and associations have no legal status.
3.7.3	*What is the defendant's address/registered office?*
	– Individual and last known place of abode
	– Sole trader/partnership – business address as above
	– Company – registered office
3.7.4	*Where did the offence take place?*
	– locus in quo
3.7.5	*When did the offence take place?*
	– Is it within statutory time limits?
3.7.6	*Elements of offence*
	– See statute
	– See any legal definitions of words and phrases

3.8 COLLATION OF EVIDENCE

3.8.1	*Plan of action*
	– List evidence required, including breakdown of elements of offence
	– Decide how to obtain evidence and from whom or where
3.8.2	*Visit locus in quo (ASAP)*
	– Take photos[1] if appropriate and details on reverse
	– Contemporaneous notes, for example, when and where
	– Remove posters etc as evidence
3.8.3.	*Take statements from witness*
	– Must be in s 9 form
	– See notes on evidence for content
	– Seek corroborative evidence, for example, other witnesses, documents, etc

3.9 LETTER OF DEFENDANT FOR INTERVIEW

3.9.1	*Letter*
	– Outline allegation

---

[1] There is no need to call a photographer or some other person to prove photographs showed what in fact had taken place (*R v Lambert* [1967] Crim LR 480). If a digital camera is used this case may not readily apply, particularly if there is any reason to suggest that the pictures may have been altered. It is therefore suggested that investigators use conventional cameras.

- Caution at bottom, for example,. it should be borne in mind that should legal proceedings be instituted in this case any information that you give in response to this letter may be tendered in evidence
- Authority to speak on behalf of Co
- Seek evidence, that is, elements of offence and five W's
- details of defence/explanation
- diarise for reply
- follow up letter

3.9.2 *Interview*

- Proper form and formalities
- Outline allegation

   Caution: 'You do not have to say anything unless you wish to do so but it may harm your defence if you fail to mention when questioned something you later rely on. Anything you do say may be given in evidence.

   You have a right to see a solicitor, you are not under arrest and are free to go at any time.'

- Speak on behalf of Co
- Seek evidence including documents and probing questions
- Defence/explanation
- Signature by defendant

3.10 COLLATION OF REPORT

- Written authority to prosecute from person so entitled (see below)
- Case summary with page references to the evidence
- Draft informations
- Index
- Witness statements with exhibits attached to each statement
- Notice of intended proceedings (if necessary)
- Previous convictions (date, fine, cost, court offence, statement and provisions)

3.11 AUTHORISATIONS

See Appendix 8 and Chapter 9 for information regarding authorisations.

HUMAN RIGHTS

This chapter sets out some of the main human rights principles, which affect local authority investigators.

4.1 HUMAN RIGHTS AND DELAY

Main principles

The Human Rights Act (HRA) 1998 has awakened renewed interest in the question of delay. The courts may still dismiss charges for delay even though the charges are within the statutory time limit.

4.1.1 It has always been open to defendants to apply for a stay of proceedings on account of delay. Until the HRA 1998 came into force, applications for stays for reasons of delay were made under the head of 'abuse of process'.

4.1.2 The issue of delay has been raised by Art 6(1), which states that:
> Everyone is entitled to a fair and public hearing within a reasonable time by an independent and impartial tribunal established by law.

4.1.3 Past experience has shown that applications for stays on the grounds of abuse of process for delay have not been particularly successful. These applications have tended to decrease in popularity. The coming into force of the HRA 1998 in October 2000 has precipitated renewed interest in delay by virtue of Art 6, although little seems to have changed.[a]

4.1.4 The Home Office Guidelines advise that the passage of time in itself is not a violation of the Convention if it can be shown:

4.1.5 that the trial is heard within a reasonable time, *Darmalingum v State* (2000) *The Times*, 18 July, PC; that a fair trial can still take place; see, *obiter*, in *R v Court Marshall Administration Officer ex p Jordan* [2000] COD 106, DC; *Bukate v Netherlands* (1995) 19 EHRR 477.

4.1.6 The *dicta* by Lord Justice Simon Brown in the Jordan case seems to echo the position on abuse of process very closely. At p 6, Lord Justice Brown advises that 'in the first place, it is settled law that stays on grounds of delay should themselves only be granted in exceptional circumstances'. This view was also adopted in the abuse process case of *AG's Ref (No 1 of 1990)* which might have been regarded as a corner stone in the prosecution's response to an application for abuse of process. The second most compelling argument that a prosecutor might raise in response to an abuse of process argument was that such applications ought to be refused in circumstances where a fair trial was still possible. Lord Justice Simon Brown reiterated this view, as follows (p 5):

---

[a] See *AG Reference (No 2 of 2001)*, Lawtel 2/7/2001. The Court of Appeal had the following to say on the subject of delay: 'a stay was the appropriate remedy if the defendant had been prejudiced to an extent that interfered with his right to a fair trial. In the absence of that prejudice, there was no justification for granting a stay.'

> In my judgment the Strasbourg case law is not to be understood as laying down in principle that whenever delays are identified of such a character as to involve a violation of Art 6, that fact of it necessarily precludes there being a fair trial with the result that any outstanding criminal process must immediately be discontinued. That would be a surprising conclusion, and one which I would not readily accept.

4.1.7 This approach does not accord with the Scottish case of *Cooke v HM Advocate* 2000 SCCR 922 in which it was said that lack of prejudice was not fatal to a submission based on Art 6(1) of the Convention. A similar approach was also taken in other Scottish cases such as *HM Advocate v McGlinchey* 2000 SLT 995, *HM Advocate v Little* 1999 SLT 1145 and in the case of *D v HM Advocate* [2000] TLR, 14 April the issue of prejudice does not appear to have been raised.

4.1.8 Given the inconsistency of the decision making on the question of delay, IOs would be well advised to set up file review systems to ensure as far as possible that undue delay is avoided. The *Attorney General's Guidelines* also identified other factors for consideration on the question of delay as follows:

1. the complexity and number of enquiries;
2. the complexity of the legal and evidential issues;
3. the strong public interest in prosecuting cases involving serious criminal misconduct, which may take more time to prepare;
4. obtaining evidence from abroad;
5. obtaining expert evidence;
6. the conduct of the parties including any absconding or numerous requests for adjournments by the defendant.

4.1.9 It was said in the case of *D v HM Advocate* that the purpose of Art 6(1) of the Convention was to avoid a person remaining too long in a state of uncertainty about his fate. It is for this reason that the court is not likely to focus on any delays which have occurred at the outset of the investigation as it might have done and may still do if abuse of process is alleged. In *Ewing v UK* (1996) 10 EHRR 141 and *Numister v Austria (No 1)* (1968) 1 EHRR 91, it was established that time started to run for the purposes of Art 6 when a defendant is officially notified of a charge. In *X v Austria* [1967] CD 8, time started to run when the defendant was aware that he was under suspicion and, in the cases of *Eccles v Jeremy* (1982) 5 EHRR 1 and *Darmalingum v State* [2000] TLR, 18 July, PC, the starting point was when the defendant became aware that he was under investigation.

4.1.10 In most instances, delays which cannot be accounted for are not likely to occur if the files are properly managed. Common reasons for delay include lack of response to correspondence from third parties and absences for whatever reason by the person in charge of the file. Most public offices operate quality systems, which include regular reviews thereby avoiding the vast majority of successful applications for stays on the ground of delay.

4.2 PRIVILEGE AGAINST SELF-INCRIMINATION

4.2.1 *Main principles*

The law concerning use of statutory powers requiring suspects to provide information and subsequent use of any information given for the purposes of proceedings should be treated with caution. Investigators may be well advised to look for other methods of obtaining information if it is required to prove an offence.

There has been much debate as to whether or not a local authority is entitled to ask questions pursuant to its statutory powers if the answers given might incriminate a suspect. Not only have there been serious questions as to the right to ask these questions and any convictions for failing to comply with such a request, but also any subsequent conviction which is based upon evidence which has been supplied in consequence of any such request. The relevant cases, therefore, apply to statutory requests by the local authority such as s 16 of the Local Government (Miscellaneous Provisions) Act 1976 requesting details of ownership, s 330 of the Town and Country Planning Act 1990 requesting similar information and s 112 of the Road Traffic Regulation Act 1984, and other similar provisions.

The cases of *Brown v Stott* [2001] 2 WLR 817 and *DPP v Wilson* [2001] TLR, 21 March are authority for the principle that an admission by a defendant in answer to a statutory question may be used against him in a subsequent prosecution. The contrary approach was taken in *Heaney and McGuinness v Ireland* [2001] Crim LR 481 and *Quinn v Ireland* (2000) 21 December, App No 36887/97. As the law is clearly in a state of flux, investigators are advised to look for other methods of obtaining information if it is required to prove an offence. One obvious approach is to put these questions to the suspect at the interview.

Useful articles on this issue are 'Human rights round up, drivers in the frame', by Professor Andrew Ashworth, All Souls College, Oxford in Archbold News, Issue 10, 22 December, 2000 and, more recently, 'The self-incrimination saga', Archbold News, Issue 5, 27 June 2001 by the same author.

NB It is recommended no change is required in connection with prosecutions for failure to provide information when no information is received.

4.3 REGULATION OF INVESTIGATORY POWERS ACT (RIPA) 2000

4.3.1 *Main principles*

Any inspection/surveillance that is likely to result in obtaining private information about an individual is likely to require prior authorisation. For example, a visit to inspect a person's house or garden as a result of a complaint regarding a nuisance will require prior approval. Should an inspection take place without prior approval, it is likely that the evidence obtained will not be admissible.

4.3.2 As a consequence of the HRA 1998, the RIPA 2000 now regulates conduct that amounts to be surveillance of suspects. There are, in fact, three major forms of surveillance pursuant to s 26 of the RIPA 2000 which are: 'directed surveillance'; 'intrusive surveillance'; 'conduct and use of covert human intelligence sources'.

4.3.3 The only type of surveillance that is likely to effect the way local authorities investigate cases is directed surveillance. In the vast majority of instances, the two remaining forms of surveillance will be either extremely difficult to justify or not used for practical purposes.

4.3.4 Section 26 of the RIPA 2000 defined directed surveillance as being covert surveillance, that is, undertaken in relation to a specific investigation or specific operation which is likely to result in the obtaining of private information about a person (whether or not specifically identified for the purposes of the investigation or operation); and otherwise than by way of an immediate response to events or circumstances the nature of which is such that it would not be reasonably practicable for an authorisation under this part to be sought for the carrying out of surveillance. By sub-s (9), surveillance will be covert where it is carried out in a manner calculated to ensure that the person or persons subjected to the surveillance are unaware that it is or may be taking place.

4.3.5 The definition of 'covert', therefore, excludes any routine food hygiene or other inspection in the presence of the subject or addressee.

4.3.6 The words 'otherwise than by way of an immediate response to events or circumstances' confirm that, if surveillance is carried out by way of an immediate response to suspicious circumstances whilst on site, the statutory provisions would not apply. However, if for any reason, the IO returns to the office or carries out another activity and then returns to the *'locus in quo'* this would amount to directed surveillance and the appropriate authorisations will be required.

4.3.7 *Specific grounds for authorisation of directed surveillance*

In accordance with ss 28 and 29 of the RIPA 2000 authorisations for directed surveillance and authorisation of covert human intelligence sources cannot be granted unless specific criteria are satisfied, namely that:

4.3.8 The authorisation is necessary on specific grounds; and the authorised activity is proportionate to what is sought to be achieved by it.

4.3.9 The specific grounds are that the authorisation is necessary:
- in the interests of national security;
- for the purpose of preventing or detecting crime or preventing disorder;
- in the interests of the economic well being of the UK;
- in the interests of public safety;
- for the purpose of protecting public health;
- for the purpose of assessing or collecting any tax duty levy or other imposition, contribution or charge payable to a government department; or
- for other purposes which may be specified by order of the Secretary of State.

4.3.10 For all practice purposes, the most likely grounds which will apply are the interests of public safety and for the purpose of protecting public health. The detection of crime or preventing disorder might be regarded as stretching the interpretation for the purposes of local authority prosecutions. It is important to bear in mind that, in addition to the specific grounds, it is also necessary to establish that the authorised activity is proportionate to what is sought to be achieved by it.

4.3.11 In addition to the above, there are two further criteria in relation to covert human intelligence sources. In broad terms these tend to relate to undercover informants, which is highly unlikely in the context of local authority prosecutions.

4.3.12 As regards 'intrusive surveillance', in accordance with s 32 of the RIPA, authorisations cannot be granted unless specific criteria are satisfied, namely that the Secretary of State or senior authorising officer believes that:
- the authorisation is necessary on specific grounds and;
- the authorised activity is proportionate to what is sought to be achieved by it.

The specific grounds in this case are that it is necessary:
- in the interests of national security;
- for the purposes of preventing or detecting serious crime; or
- In the interests of economic well being of the United Kingdom.

4.3.13 As the specific grounds are highly unlikely to apply to local authority prosecutions, intrusive surveillance is most unlikely to receive authorisation.

4.3.14 Intrusive surveillance is defined in sub-ss 26(3)–(5). Covert surveillance carried out in relation to anything taking place on residential premises or any private vehicle. This kind of surveillance may take place by means either of a personal device located inside residential premises or a private vehicle of the person who is subject to the surveillance or by means of a device placed outside which consistently provides a produce of the equivalent quality and detail as a product which would be obtained from a device located inside.

4.3.15 In short, this amounts to carrying out surveillance from other premises or vehicles by way of telescopes or cameras with zoom lens or electronic surveillance, which is most unlikely in the context of local authority prosecutions.

4.3.16 *Authorisation of directed surveillance*

In accordance with the Regulation and Investigatory Powers (Prescription of Offences Ranks and Positions) Order 2000 SI 2000/2417 an assistant chief officer and officer responsible for the management of an investigation may authorise directed surveillance in accordance with s 30 of the RIPA.

4.3.17 As a consequence of the above, it is advisable that before any directed surveillance takes place, there is authorisation in writing from the appropriate person. Such authorisation should set out the statutory ground or grounds upon which that authorisation is given. Furthermore, an authorisation is highly unlikely to be effective if it is given retrospectively. Officers must therefore seek proper authorisation before conducting any form of directed surveillance.

4.3.18 The key case decided on this question is that of *Sultan Khan v UK* which was a case involving covert recordings based on intrusive surveillance. In this case, the applicant was held to have received a fair trial, however, the article entitled 'The future of covert policing: will it rest in peace – Pt 2', by Anthony F Jennings and

Danny Friedman, Issue 9, 29 November, Archbold News, 2000, suggests that this case may be limited in its application.

4.3.19 Officers are also advised to have regard to the Code of guidance on covert surveillance which is available in draft form on the website (www.homeoffice.gov.uk).

4.4 ENTRAPMENT

Until the enactment of the HRA 1998, it was settled law that entrapment was no defence (*R v Sang* [1980] AC 402), although use of an *agent provocateur* to incite a person to commit an offence that he would not otherwise commit may have resulted in the exclusion of evidence as being unfair under s 78 of the Police and Criminal Evidence Act 1984. The cases decided under the HRA 1998 do not seem to alter the position to any material degree. The European Court of Human Rights excluded evidence obtained as a result of incitement by undercover police officers in *Francisco Teixeiro de Castro v Portugal* (1999) 28 EHRR 101; [1998] Crim LR 751. The Court of Appeal in *R v Alford* [2001] 1 WLR 51 also seemed to recognise that incitement could amount to a breach of human rights. A decision which is likely to impinge more closely upon local authorities is the case of *Nottingham CC v Amin* [2000] 2 All ER 946 in which a plain-clothed policeman flagged down a taxi driver. In this case, the court noted that there was no evidence of pressure exerted by the police or any persuasion and the defendant was not wheedled into doing what he did. Accordingly, the court held that there had been no breach of the convention. The *dicta* in *Amin* seem to suggest that any pressure exerted on a suspect could be a breach of human rights, however, the court of appeal in *R v John James Shannon (Aka Alford)* [2001] 1 WLR 51 confirmed that entrapment is no defence and went on to decide that the case of *Teixeiro de Castro v Portugal* (1999) 28 EHHR 101 (which found that the public interest could not justify the use of evidence obtained as a result of incitement) was decided on its own facts and circumstances and was concerned with the activities of police officers. The authorities are therefore somewhat inconsistent as to the measures which can be taken to conduct entrapment exercises. IOs are therefore well advised to accept any hesitation on the part of a suspect in these circumstances as being outside their remit.

INTERVIEWING WITNESSES AND OBTAINING WITNESS STATEMENTS

5.1 THE COMPLAINT

The majority of offences come to light as a result of a complaint by a member of the public who has witnessed an illegal act or by way of routine inspection by enforcement officers. As such, the member of public will make a complaint to the enforcing authority and an officer will be assigned to investigate the complaint. It is important that all complainants are dealt with courteously. The enforcement officer must bear in mind that whilst this may be a relatively routine matter as far as he is concerned, yet to the person who has witnessed an offence it may be of great importance. The officer must therefore do everything he can to prevent undermining the enthusiasm of the witness by playing the matter down.

5.2 WITNESSES' DIRECT EVIDENCE

It is important to ascertain when interviewing witnesses that they actually saw or witnessed in some way the offence they describe and that they have not obtained the information which they pass on to the officer from elsewhere. If the witness is unable to give a first hand account, the officer will have to explore every possible avenue of evidence and interview more than one witness. When interviewing a person who is providing information, it is best to discuss the full incident with the witness so as to elicit all the relevant evidence and ensure that nothing is left out. A signed witness statement should then be drawn up. It is perfectly acceptable after hearing and making notes of a witness's evidence to write the statement on the witness's behalf and obtain a signature to it. It is best practice to use the witness's own words wherever possible. The language but not necessarily the grammar of the witness should, therefore, be included in the statement.[a]

5.3 CRIMINAL JUSTICE ACT 1969 FORMAT: CHRONOLOGY OF EVENTS

Witness statements should be taken on approved Criminal Justice Act Statement Forms which are endorsed accordingly and which have a certificate included which the person who gives the statement should sign saying that the evidence he gives is true. There is an art in taking witness statements which tends to follow from a thorough knowledge of the ground rules and experience. However, if a statement is taken in chronological sequence,

---

(a) See *Alex Lawrie Factors Ltd v Morgan* [1999] TLR, 18 August, which establishes that affidavits must be drawn up in the words of the witnesses, not lawyers.

things will not go far wrong. If the sequence of events is taken in a logical order it will make it easier for the officer presenting the case at court to read the statements and to glean the appropriate facts. Furthermore, when writing a witness statement, it is best to keep the statement as short as possible without losing any of the facts. A useful question to ask in these circumstances is: is this information relevant to the offence charged either as an element of the offence or as an aggravating feature? Steps should also be taken to prevent the inclusion of hearsay or other inadmissible evidence (refer to Chapter 6 regarding inadmissible evidence), remembering that any statement made by the defendant is not likely to be hearsay.

5.4 EXHIBITS

On taking the statement, the witness may produce certain items which are to be included as exhibits. These exhibits could form either documentary exhibits or other hard exhibits, which have been taken or collected by the witness. Documentary exhibits include any letters received or any other document and may include photographs.[b] Hard exhibits include all other items which have been obtained by the witness and which he wishes to produce. When producing an exhibit it must be referred to in the witness statement and when referring to that item the words 'which I produce' should be included after the item is mentioned for the first time only. Furthermore, after the words 'which I produce', an open bracket should be inserted containing the phrase 'Ex No', leaving a space for the exhibit number to be included, with, after the space, the word REF should be written, which is short for reference the initials of the person who provides the statement, that is: if the person is called John Smith then it should read REF JS and then the number of the exhibit (if it is the first exhibit it should read 1, second exhibit 2, etc). After the reference number, brackets should be closed and a continuance with the statement follows. An example of this should read as follows, 'on the 3rd October I received a letter from the defendant which I now produce. (Exhibit No ... REF JS1.)' The purpose of introducing the exhibit should be apparent from the statement. If there are a number of pages forming one exhibit the statement should identify the relevant part of that document. If there are a number of documents in the exhibit this raises the question as to whether these should be separated into individual exhibits.

5.5 CONFIRMATION OF COURT ATTENDANCE

Finally, when closing a lay witness statement, if at all possible, the final line on the statement should read: 'I am prepared to attend court if necessary.' It must be impressed upon the person providing the statement that he is a witness to a possible criminal action and that the end result may mean that he is required to give evidence in court.

(b) There is no need to call the photographer or some other person to prove photographs showed what in fact had taken place (*R v Lambert* [1967] Crim LR 480). If a digital camera is used this case may not readily apply, particularly if there is any reason to suggest that the pictures may have been altered. It is therefore suggested that investigators use conventional cameras.

5.6 CONTEMPORANEOUS NOTES

5.6.1 *Pocket book notes/ original notes*

Clearly, during the process of preparing witness statements, and the collection of evidence generally by the enforcement officer, there should be notes made by the officer of what he has been told, or has seen. These original notes are likely to be the 'contemporaneous' notes which, in the case of police officers, would be notes recorded in a pocket book. Although it is best practice to keep a pocket book of contemporaneous notes, the form in which notes are kept is not the important issue. What is important is to make accurate notes as soon as possible after the incident, for it is at this time that the facts are the most fresh in the mind of the officer and are likely to be more accurate.

5.6.2 *Use of contemporaneous notes in court*

In a later court hearing where evidence is being contested (which is likely to be in excess of six months after the incident), the most contemporaneous record of the incident is the one that may be seen to be the most reliable by the magistrates. Usually, only the 'contemporaneous note' can be used in the witness box when giving evidence, although a witness can refresh their memory from a statement, which may not be contemporaneous. If the memory of the enforcement officer has faded in court as a result of nerves, or the passage of time, the aide memoire of a contemporaneous note is a blessing to both the officer himself and the solicitor conducting the trial!

5.6.3 *Safeguarding the notes*

Contemporaneous notes are important and should never be thrown away in any circumstances, however untidily presented they may appear.

5.7 INTERVIEWING UNDER-AGE WITNESSES

5.7.1 Until recently the rules on admissibility of child witnesses meant that great care was needed when taking statements from children to ensure that the evidence was admissible. The position now is that 'a child's evidence shall be received unless it appears to the court that the child is incapable of giving intelligible testimony'.[a] Furthermore, all evidence from children under 14 is unsworn.[b] Such evidence no longer requires corroboration from another person and there is no need for the judge to give a warning of the dangers of convicting on uncorroborated evidence simply because the witness is a child.[c]

(a) Criminal Justice Act 1988, s 33A(2A), as inserted by Criminal Justice and Public Order Act 1994, s 168 and Sched 9, para 33.
(b) Criminal Justice Act 1988, s 33A, as inserted by Criminal Justice Act 1991, s 52(1)
(c) Criminal Justice Act 1988, s 34. For a detailed analysis, see the article by Stephen O'Doherty entitled 'Child witnesses – a decade of progress' (1988) 162 JP 76.

For the above reasons, the IO should not be too concerned over the admissibility provided that the child seems reasonably intelligent and there are no other exclusionary rules that may apply, that is, hearsay, etc.

5.7.2 The questions which might be in the forefront of the IO's mind will be the weight which the court might attach to the child's evidence and whether or not there are any procedural rules which should have been followed at an earlier stage, for example, special rules for children in making test purchases. Although the rule requiring corroboration does not now exist, it would be advisable nonetheless to look for supporting evidence if the defence is likely to be able to bring contradictory evidence.

5.7.3 As regards the actual taking of the statement, care should be taken so as not to suggest the evidence that is required. This approach should apply particularly to young children who might be tempted to say what a adult wishes to hear. The IO should also be mindful that the defence will be entitled to see the draft statements which could be provide fertile grounds for cross-examination.

CHAPTER 6

PREPARATION OF A STATEMENT – INADMISSIBLE EVIDENCE

6.1 HEARSAY EVIDENCE

6.1.1 As all officers will be aware, there is a very important rule with respect to the preparation and presentation of evidence. The rule is that hearsay evidence is inadmissible in the magistrates' court. Hearsay evidence can be fairly summarised as follows:

> Evidence of a statement made to a witness by a person who is not himself called as witness may or may not be hearsay. It is hearsay and inadmissible when the object of the evidence is to establish the truth of what is contained in the statement. It is not hearsay and is admissible when it is proposed to establish by the evidence, not the truth of the statement, but the fact that it was made.

6.1.2 An example of hearsay evidence can be found in the leading case of *Subramanium v Public Prosecutor* [1956] 1 WLR 965.

S was charged with unlawful possession of ammunition under Emergency Regulations. It was a defence to have a lawful excuse for possession and the accused sought to give evidence that he had been captured by terrorists and was acting under duress. The trial judge ruled that he could not state in evidence what the terrorists had said to him on the basis that it was hearsay. However, the Privy Council quashed the conviction on the following basis:

> Evidence of a statement made to a witness by a person who is not called himself as a witness may or may not be hearsay. It is hearsay and admissible when the object of the evidence is to establish the truth of what is contained in the statement. It is not hearsay and is admissible when it is proposed to establish by the evidence not the truth of the statement but the fact that it was made.

6.1.3 A further illustration of the rule against hearsay evidence can be found in the case of *R v McLean* (1956) 52 Cr App R 80.

G was the victim of a robbery. A few minutes later he dictated something that he could not afterwards remember to C. C wrote down on a card a car registration number. At the trial of McLean for the robbery, it was alleged that this was the registration number of the car used in the robbery and that McLean had hired a car with that registration number. G did not see what C had written down. The issue was whether C could testify as to the car registration mark. (*NB:* G could not refresh his memory from the card, as he had not read it over – see below.) The Court of Appeal found that C's testimony was inadmissible hearsay.

6.1.4 The rule against the admission of hearsay evidence is based on the following reasons. It is not the best evidence. The best evidence is that which is given in person, before a court, having taken an oath on the Bible, or otherwise, to speak the truth. A person present, giving evidence can also be judged upon their demeanour as to whether or not they are telling the truth or have a good or bad recollection of the events. They can also be cross-examined.

6.1.5 As a matter of practice, it is better not to include statements that are hearsay in the statement of the reporting officer. Of course, it is proper to include in such statements the response given to a request for an explanation as to the alleged offence by the proposed defendant in the investigation. Statements by the defendant fall within the exception to the hearsay rule, but the Investigating Officer (IO) is advised to caution him if he intends to refer to the defendant's statement in giving evidence.

6.1.6 It is good practice to include any verbal statements made to the officer, other than those made by the defendant in personal witness statements of the person making the statement, so that all evidence can be called through individual witnesses, in person, and on oath.

6.1.7 A description of the method of presentation and preparation of prosecution files is given in Chapter 8.

6.1.8 An example of common hearsay evidence arising in a local authority prosecution for the sale of a mouldy pork pie could be, for example, the statement of Mrs S Mathews:

> My husband told me he bought the mouldy pie for me from the grocers on Main Street, Lowtown, whilst I was at work.

6.1.9 The statement is hearsay because the witness is giving second hand evidence. Mr Mathews should be interviewed and, if possible, asked to produce the receipt or package identifying the grocers as the seller of the pie. On occasions, hearsay evidence may not be disputed, but correct technical presentation of evidence avoids criticism in court by the bench or defence solicitors.

6.1.10 A further example of hearsay evidence arising in a planning investigation alleging the breach of an Enforcement Notice could be, for example, the statement of Mr C Smith:

> Mrs Smith told me that the Graingers have put up a conservatory without planning permission.

6.1.11 Again, this is hearsay evidence if a statement was taken from Mr Smith. The statement should be obtained from Mrs Smith. In any event, Mrs Smith cannot give evidence of planning permission or lack of it. This evidence should be produced through the council's enforcement officer.

6.1.12 *Exceptions to hearsay*

6.1.12.1 Confessions

(a) Almost anything that the defendant says is likely to be an exception to the hearsay rule on the grounds that it is likely to be a confession. The following is the statutory definition of a confession:

(b) 'Confession includes any statement wholly or partly adverse to the person who made it whether or not made to a person in authority or not and whether or not made in words or otherwise.' (Section 82 of the Police and Criminal Evidence Act (PACE) 1984.)

(c) To be admissible as evidence, a confession must be relevant and it is important to bear in mind that a confession like any other evidence may be excluded under s 78 of PACE 1984. These two sections are therefore quoted verbatim, as follows:

(d) Section 76 of PACE 1984: 'In any proceedings a confession made by an accused person may be given in evidence against him insofar as it is relevant to any matter in issue in the proceedings and is not excluded by the court in pursuance of this section.'

(e) Sub-section (2) disallows a confession if it is obtained by oppression or in any circumstances which render it unreliable.

(f) Section 78 of PACE 1984: 'In any proceedings the court may refuse to allow evidence on which the prosecution proposes to rely to be given if it appears to the court that having regard to all the circumstances including the circumstances in which the evidence was obtained the admission of the evidence would have such an adverse effect on the fairness of the proceedings that the court ought not to admit it.'

6.1.12.2 *Section 9 of the CJA 1967*

Section 9 statements are admissible if they are in the proper form, that is. they must have the name of the witness, who should sign and date the statement, the age of the witness should be provided if over 18, the statement should be dated and the standard declaration as to the truthfulness of the statement should be included. Provided these requirements have been complied with and the s 9 Notice has been sent to the other side, the statement will be admissible in evidence if it is either agreed or the other party does not object within seven days.

6.1.12.3 *Section 10 of the CJA 1967*

Facts agreed in writing by the defence are regarded as conclusive evidence.

6.1.12.4 *First hand hearsay*

(a) Section 23 of the CJA 1988 refers to a statement made by a person in a document who is either:
   – dead, or unfit to attend court due to ill health;
   – is outside the UK and it is not reasonably practicable to secure his attendance;
   – or cannot be found after having taken reasonable steps.

(b) A statement made to an IO by a person in fear subject to ss 25 and 26 of the CJA 1988.

(c) Business, etc, documents.

Section 24 of the CJA 1988 states that business documents are admissible if created or received in the course of a business or profession and supplied by a person with personal knowledge of those matters dealt with.

NB Any number of persons may make a supply provided that those persons are acting in the course of a business or profession (this includes a local authority).

NB A statement prepared for the purposes of pending criminal proceedings are excluded, unless the person cannot be found or cannot reasonably remember having regard to the lapse of time, for example, receipt, booking records, diary.

6.1.12.5 *Real evidence*

For example, posters, t-shirts, photographs, etc.

6.1.12.6 *Computer records*[a]

Section 69 of PACE 1984 states that computer records are admissible. However, it is necessary to satisfy the court that the computer was working properly at the time, for example, by way of certificate from a person responsible for the computer.

6.1.12.7 *Public documents*

A document made by a Public Officer for the purpose of the public making use of it is receivable in evidence provided it purports to be sealed, stamped or signed as may be required by any Act applying to it without further proof. It is usually produced by way of examined or certified copy, for example, electoral rolls, or minutes of Council meetings.

6.1.12.8 *Expert reports*

These are admissible in court as evidence. It is good practice to agree expert reports with the other side. If an agreement cannot be reached then the expert will be required to give oral evidence.

NB Experts may give opinion evidence whereas any other witness may not. An expert will include an environmental health or planning officer with the relevant qualifications.

6.1.12.9 *Interview records*

These will be admissible provided that there has been full compliance with PACE 1984 regarding cautioning, etc.

Points to note

Code C16(5), PACE 1984 Code of Practice:

Questions relating to an offence may not be put to a person after he has been charged with that offence or confirm that he may be prosecuted for it, unless they are necessary for the purpose of clearing up an ambiguity in a previous answer or statement ... and before the questions are put the person should be cautioned ...

Experience has shown that a number of IOs are not aware of the above rule that prevents further questioning of defendants once they have been informed that they may be reported for an offence. It is often the case that at the conclusion of an interview the defendant has been informed that he will be reported for an offence and further questioning subsequently takes place. This can be most prejudicial to the prosecution's case, particularly when further letters of enquiry are sent to the defendant after proceedings have been instituted. Whereas it is advisable to inform the prospective defendant that the

---

[a] Eg, a till roll. See *R v Shephard* (1991) 93 Cr App R 139; [1993] 1 All ER 225.

Chapter 6: Preparation of a Statement – Inadmissible Evidence

matter may be reported, it is not good practice to give this warning until the IO is satisfied that he has concluded all his inquiries.

6.1.12.10 *Similar fact evidence and* res gestae

These are exceptions to the rule against hearsay – for further details see *Cross on Evidence* and Appendix 17.

6.2 OTHER INADMISSIBLE EVIDENCE

6.2.1 *Character evidence*

Section 1 of the CJA 1988 prevents the prosecution from referring to evidence of previous conduct or character of the accused, unless the accused attacks the character of any of the prosecution witnesses or that evidence is necessary to prove the offence charged.

6.2.2 *Co-accused*

He is not a competent witness against himself or against the co-accused except:[a]

(a) following an acquittal after a decision to offer no evidence;

(b) following a plea of guilty (and sentence);

(c) following the grant of a *nolle prosequi*, that is, an undertaking not to proceed against the co-accused;

(d) following separate trials of accused and co-accused.[b]

6.2.3 *The accused's spouse*

He is competent but only compelled to give evidence in certain cases, for example, assault.

6.2.4 *Evidence from children*

It is often assumed evidence from children is of limited admissibility. The position now is that 'a child's evidence shall be received unless it appears to the court that the child is incapable of giving intelligible testimony'.[aa] Furthermore, all evidence from children under 14 is unsworn.[ab] Such evidence no longer requires corroboration from another person and there is no need for the judge to give a warning of the dangers of convicting on uncorroborated evidence simply because the witness is a child.[c]

6.2.5 *A practical application of the above rules*

6.2.5.1 Having established that almost anything that a suspect says which is of any value to the prosecution will be an exception to the hearsay rule on the

---

(a) It seems that this rule applies even if the witness has accepted a caution. See *Hayter v L* [1998] 1 WLR 854.

(b) Note the strong criticism of this practice in *R v Pipe* (1967) Cr App R 17.

(aa) CJA 1988, s 33A(2A), as inserted by Criminal Justice and Public Order Act 1994, s 168 and Sched 9, para 33.

(ab) CJA 1988, s 33A, as inserted by CJA 1991, s 52(1).

(c) CJA 1988, s 34. For a detailed analysis see Stephen O'Doherty's article entitled 'Child witnesses – a decade of progress' (1988) 162 JP 76.

ground that it will be a confession, there are only a limited number of grounds on which that evidence may be excluded. The most likely ground is the failure to caution. Less likely are reasons relating to reliability, fairness and relevance. A caution need only be given to 'a person whom there are grounds to suspect of an offence'.[a] A caution is not therefore required solely to establish identity or ownership of a vehicle (or presumably house) 'or to obtain information in accordance with any relevant statutory requirement'.[b] If, therefore, an officer requires information pursuant to any of his statutory powers,[c] there is no need to caution. In fact, no offence would be committed if there was no response to such a request.[d]

Not every statement will be regarded as hearsay. According to the strict common law definition, a statement will not be hearsay if the purpose of adducing it is not to establish the truth of it but the fact that it was made.[e] It follows that warnings (verbal or written) to the defendant and meetings on site stipulating the necessary work for compliance will be admissible provided that it does not amount to evidence of previous offences. For the same reason, any conversations with the defendant adduced solely for continuity purposes will be admissible unless they could be regarded as prejudicial to his case or a caution is required. Evidence of a defendant's obstruction, acts or failure to act, for example, non compliance with notices will be also admissible, as a witness will be recalling details of events rather than statements.

(a) PACE, Code C 10.1. In the case of *Dilks v Tilley* [1979] RTR 459, a caution was not required at the gathering information stage. However, this case is very close to the dividing line and those who intend to rely on this case should do so with care.
(b) PACE, Code C 10.1.
(c) Eg, Local Government (Miscellaneous Provisions) Act 1976, s 16.
(d) *R v Page* [1996] Crim LR 439; [1995] TLR, 20 November.
(e) *Subramanium v Public Prosecutor* [1956] 1 WLR 965.

CHAPTER 7

INTERVIEWING AND REPORTING THE ALLEGED OFFENDER

7.1 PREPARING FOR THE INTERVIEW

7.1.1   The starting point should be a reference to the elements of the offence as discussed in Chapter 4. This should enable the investigator to work out the matters that require further investigation at interview with the suspect. The key to a successful interview is preparation. Before interviewing a suspect, an enforcement officer should have some idea of the questions he intends to ask. The interview will usually commence by the customary caution,[a] entitlement to legal representation and the fact that the suspect is not under arrest and is free to go at any time.[b] The investigating officer will then usually outline the nature of the allegations to the defendant. It will be followed by the more routine questions such as please confirm that you are in a position to speak on behalf of the Company. The full name of the Company is ... The registered office address is ... There then follows a detailed questioning of the offence and possible defence in accordance with the preparation made beforehand. Preparation may take the form of a list of questions/issues based on the plan discussed in Chapter 3. Routine questions present no difficulty. Other questions may result in evasive or incomplete answers. For many novice investigators the case does not progress beyond answers given regardless of the value of those answers. The more experienced investigator is expected to ask further probing questions until a proper or truthful answer is given.

7.1.2   Some thought should also be given to the answers that the suspect might give. Experienced interviewers might be forgiven for thinking that if there is an answer to a charge a canny suspect will find it. Interviewers would be advised to be mindful to potential answers, and should also be alert to the existence of any evidence that will enable them to detect a dishonest suspect. An example of this might be a sample of the defendant's handwriting, which on analysis, proves that he wrote incriminating material or records showing ownership of a business if it is anticipated that ownership is going to be denied.

(a) The is no rule of law which requires that a suspect be cautioned before any questions are put to him (*Pennycuick v Lees* [1991] TLR, 13 December). A caution must be given to a 'person whom there are grounds to suspect of an offence'. Further a person need only be cautioned if questions 'are put to him regarding his involvement or suspected involvement in that offence'. 'He need not be cautioned if questions are put to him for other purposes, for example, solely to establish his identity or his ownership of a vehicle' – PACE, Code C 10. There is therefore a compelling argument that questions with the objective of securing compliance with a notice or securing removal of waste in circumstances where proceedings are not contemplated at the time do not need to be prefixed by a caution. This appears to be the sentiment in the case of *Dilks v Tilley* [1979] RTR 459 in which DSS officers were not required to caution at the 'gathering information stage' of the enquiry.

(b) PACE, Code C 10.2.

7.2 PSYCHOLOGY OF THE INTERVIEW

7.2.1 There are certain dilemmas that often face a suspect when he attends for interview. Attending an interview can be a useful method of making an early assessment of the prosecutions case and perhaps deterring a prosecution. This can sometimes be achieved by setting out a good defence or mitigation. In seeking to account for incriminating circumstances the suspect may provide the essential evidence that is required to convict him. He is also depriving himself of the opportunity to ambushing[a] the prosecution with a defence or mitigation that has little merit. Some defendants seek to minimise the risk of providing evidence to the prosecution by asking for full disclosure prior to the interview. The provision of this information will not only give the defence the opportunity to reduce the risk but also to tailor his evidence. The investigator is therefore advised to refuse this information save for the provision of an outline at the beginning of the interview. The decision to refuse advance disclosure at this stage is lawful[b] and it is advisable to limit the information to that which is necessary to enable the suspect to provide meaningful answers. If having refused to disclose the prosecutions case the suspect declines to attend interview it may be advisable to issue warnings that adverse inferences may be invited from the court. Such inferences are likely to be made if the suspect relies on a fact which would have been reasonable for him (in all the circumstances) to have mentioned at the time.[c]

7.2.2 It is not only right and proper that an interviewer should be open minded and detached, it is also in his interests to ensure that the same impression is given to the suspect. If the suspect takes the impression that the interview is simply a process to gather further evidence against him his replies are likely to less open.

7.2.3 Interviewers might wish to consider how relaxed they wish the suspect to be. There is a theory that a suspect who is relaxed is more likely to speak freely, and in doing so provide the information required. However if a suspect is guilty of an offence and is determined to lie and admit nothing unnecessarily there may be no advantage in encouraging him to feel totally relaxed. If such a person is put under legitimate pressure he may be prepared to answer honestly as this is often much easier than inventing a story.

(a) In *R v Alladice* [1988] TLR, 11 May it was said that it was 'high time that proper comment was permitted on the silence of a detainee when interviewed by police but who produced at trial an explanation or defence to the charge which the police had no chance to verify.'

(b) 'In support of the application it is submitted that the tenor of ss 34–38 of the Criminal Justice and Public Order Act 1994 require the police to give as full a briefing as possible of disclosing all material to a legal representative before the interview with a suspect commences. We do not agree.' *R v Imran and Hussain* 96/5613/ye page 3; [1997] Crim LR 754. The issue is more fully discussed in Chapter 4.

(c) See Criminal Justice and Public Order Act 1994, s 34(1) and *R v Argent* [1996] TLR, 19 December which sets out the conditions precedent for inferences to be drawn including that the defendant 'failed to mention a fact which in the circumstances existing at the time he could reasonable have been expected to mention when so questioned'. It is submitted that if a suspect is asked to account for incriminating evidence, is warned that inferences may been taken against him and refuses to provide a fact which was known to him at the time, it is likely that adverse inferences will be drawn unless there is a good reason to do otherwise.

Chapter 7: Interviewing and Reporting the Alleged Offender

7.3 QUESTIONS THAT MAY BE ASKED

7.3.1 A suspect or his solicitor might reasonably object to unfair questions yet the courts would not necessarily exclude answers given to those questions or discipline the investigator for asking them.[a] Although the common law exclusionary rules still exist the courts are only likely exclude an unfair question if there was a breach of PACE and only then if its prejudicial effect outweighed its probative value.[b] There are no formal set of rules as to the type of questions that can be asked, which in any event vary from case to case. If questions are strictly limited to the case law on admissibility of answers given it is likely that a number of suspects will be advised not to answer. The interviewer will then be faced with choice of arguing the validity of the question or warning that adverse inferences may be taken. This approach is not likely to be as productive as a form of enquiry which excludes questions which a suspect might reasonably object to rather than

---

(a) It is only natural that a suspect would object to a question that is in any way unfair. However, unfairness does not automatically lead to exclusion of the evidence (see note (b)) and the discretion of the court to exclude evidence should not be used as a stick with which to beat the local authority. This is demonstrated by the case of *R v South Tyneside MBC ex p Mill Garages and another* CO 2501/94. Simon O'Hare, the learned clerk at first instance, gave the following advice to the court in an application to exclude evidence on the ground of abuse of process:

    A ...

    B ...

    C The object of this power is to ensure that there should be a fair trial according to law, that involves both fairness to the defendant and the prosecution.

    D The court would not be using its discretion judicially if it were to dismiss these proceedings as a disciplinary measure against the prosecution. Mr Justice Keen said that this was an admirable summary of the principles (p 18). See also *R v Delaney* (1989) 88 Cr App R 338 in which Lord Lane CJ said: 'it is no part of the duty of the court to rule a statement inadmissible simply in order to punish the police for failure to observe the code of practice.' (Approved in *R v Keenan* [1990] 2 QB 54.)

(b) The test applied by the House of Lords in *R v Sang* [1980] AC 402 for the exclusion of evidence was whether its prejudicial effect outweighed its probative value; but with the exception of evidence (including confession evidence) obtained from the accused after the commission of the offence, the judge had no discretion to exclude relevant admissible evidence on the ground that it was obtained by improper or unfair means (*per* Lord Diplock at p 437). The rules on exclusion of evidence are now codified in PACE, although the discretion to exclude evidence at common law is expressly preserved by s 82(3) of PACE.

Whereas the court may still exclude evidence under the common law rules they should be regarded as supplementary to rather than replacement of PACE. The exclusionary provisions are set out in ss 76 and 78 of PACE. Section 76 enables confession evidence to be excluded for a number of reasons including the ground of unreliability. Section 78 allows evidence to be excluded on the ground that the admission of the evidence would have such an adverse effect on the fairness of the proceedings that the court ought not to admit it. This clearly requires a balancing exercise to be carried out by the court which is somewhat analogous to the decision in *R v Sang* and the mere existence of a breach of PACE or unfairness is not enough on its own to invoke the provision. The court of appeal in *R v Walsh* (1990) 91 Cr App R 161 confirmed this position:

    So far as a defendant is concerned, it seems to us to follow that to admit evidence against him which has been obtained in circumstances where these standards have not been met, cannot but have an adverse effect on the fairness of the proceedings. This does not mean of course that in every case of a significant or substantial breach of s 58 or the code of practice the evidence concerned will automatically be excluded. Section 78 does not so provide. The task of the court is not merely to consider whether there would be an adverse effect on the fairness of the proceedings, but such an adverse effect that justice requires the evidence to be excluded.

It is arguable that the decision in *Walsh* is consistent with the balancing exercise advanced by the House of Lords in *R v Sang* above.

adherence to strict legal principles. The following should therefore be regarded as guidance as to good practice rather than a definitive statement.

7.4 RELEVANT QUESTIONS

7.4.1 The interviewer may only ask questions that are relevant to the offence that is being investigated. This may include aggravating features such as abusive or insulting conduct alleged against the subject during the course of the investigation. It does not include questions relating to the character or convictions of the defendant, his reputation or matters which are not under investigation. A more difficult question is whether the subject may be asked questions of his means and financial resources. The answer to this will depend entirely on the nature of the charge. If there is a defence of reasonable excuse, due diligence or the words wilfully or intentionally appear it is likely that the answer will be yes unless there is case law to suggest otherwise.[a]

7.5 FAIR QUESTIONS

7.5.1 Evidence in court may be excluded on the grounds that it is unreliable[aa] or the it would adversely effect the fairness of the proceedings.[b] On the basis of this a suspect would be entitled to object to any question which would be unfair or would lead to an unreliable answer. Long questions which are really a series of statements with a number of questions included could be excluded on the basis that the answer is unreliable. Short questions which are clear and to the point are therefore infinitely preferable. There is a difference between evidence which is likely to have an adverse effect on the fairness of the proceedings and evidence which is merely obtained by unfair means. The difference is that the former affects the defendants ability to formulate his case or challenge the evidence against him and the latter relates only the manner in which evidence is obtained. Although the courts have a discretion to exclude evidence under the common law and statute they have refused to exclude evidence obtained by unfair or improper[c] means. To adopt this approach at interview is likely to attract criticism in court. Trick questions are likely to be received in the same way although case law is conflicting on this.[d]

(a) In *Saddleworth UDC v Aggregate and Sand* (1971) 69 LGR 103 lack of finance could not amount to a reasonable excuse for a company in defence to a prosecution for non compliance with a notice under the Public Health Act 1936, but see case law on individual area of law for an answer which is relevant to the offence which is being investigated.

(aa) Police and Criminal Evidence Act 1984, s 76.

(b) Police and Criminal Evidence Act 1984, s 78. See also footnote to para 7.4.

(c) *R v Khan* [1996] 3 All ER 289.

(d) In *R v Murphy* [1965] NI 138 the court said 'a trick is a method as old as the constable in plain clothes ... and the day has not come when it would be safe to say that the law could be enforced without resort to it'. The same view was taken in *R v Mason* [1986] Crim LR 349 (CA). However Lord Chief Justice in the case of *Jeffry v Black* [1978] QB 490 said that there was a discretion to exclude evidence where there was trickery.

Chapter 7: Interviewing and Reporting the Alleged Offender

7.5.2 Questions that cannot fairly be answered should also be avoided. Loaded questions such as 'when did stop beating your wife' should be avoided unless it has been established with the defendant that he did actually beat his wife.

7.6 QUESTIONS MUST RELATE TO EVIDENCE THAT IS WITHIN THE KNOWLEDGE OF THE DEFENDANT

A suspect should not therefore be asked questions as to why another person acted in a particular way or what another person might have thought.

7.7 QUESTIONS ON EXPERT OPINION

Certain questions should only be asked of experts, for example, a question asking a suspect to compare handwriting is likely to be excluded by the court. As a rule of thumb, use of the word 'opinion' should be avoided.

7.8 ARGUMENTATIVE OR SARCASTIC QUESTIONS

This type of questioning should be avoided by advocates in court[a] and the same should apply to the investigating officer. This line of questioning does not tend to further the main purpose of the interview, that is, to establish relevant facts and admissible evidence. This does not mean that the suspect should not be asked questions which are designed to probe, test or evaluate his evidence. An example of an argumentative/sarcastic question is 'come on now, you don't really expect us to believe that do you?' On the other hand it is acceptable to say 'given that you freely admit to x how do you account for y'.

7.9 INTERVIEWING STYLES AND TECHNIQUES

7.9.1 *Style*

A technique is not to be confused with a style. A technique is a combination of skill/expertise and method or procedure whereas style relates to a manner or approach (for example, relaxed, coercive, informal, sympathetic, friendly) which is often peculiar to the interviewer. It cannot be said that one particular style of interview is more productive than another. Much will depend on the situation and the person being interviewed. It is hardly surprising that a formal, almost officious style employed on site may result in some suspects walking away. On the other hand a suspect who has attended the office for interview has already made a commitment and is less likely to leave if the questions become taxing. Some investigators are well known to ask crucial questions on site that close the

---

[a] *R v Baldwin* [1925] All ER 402.

door to a defence which could have been manufactured when a suspect had more time to think. The time period immediately after the offence is a time when the suspect may not have had the opportunity to invent a story with the benefit of legal advice. If he believes that he has committed an offence he may be prepared to co-operate if questioned about it at the time. From his point of view it he may be better off mitigating in the hope of being dealt with more leniently rather than pursue a defence that he has not thought of at the time. This way of thinking may alter after a suspect has had many weeks if not months to concoct a story. The time immediately after the offence is therefore a golden opportunity for an investigator. A relaxed open-minded approach to the investigation at this time is not likely to deter a defendant from admitting valuable evidence. If a less that open minded/sympathetic approach to questioning is taken at this stage the suspect might well think that if he admits the offence he will be prosecuted in any event and his best interests might be to take legal advice before admitting anything.

7.9.2 *Technique*

Teamwork between interviewers can complement or ruin good technique. Whilst one person is going through the list of questions or issues of enquiry the other should be evaluating the answers given and to enable further questions to be asked if the issue has not been fully explored or an inadequate answer is given. Either one should be ready to step in if the other is floundering.

7.9.3 *Probing questions*

These should be adopted when the replies given do not give an an answer which can be believed or fails to answer the question properly. Sometimes the question will be designed to require the suspect to answer to the question more fully, for example, 'you haven't explained exactly what you said to the tenant when you visited her on such and such a day'. If a suspect is simply not believed he may be asked to elaborate by asking the 'W' Type questions, ie, who, what, when, where, why.

7.9.4 *Short concise questions*

The form of question should not give rise to an ambiguous answer. The shorter the question the less thinking time with which to invent an answer. If a suspect is lying this may result in him either inventing an answer which is inconsistent with previous answers or deciding 'to play safe', that is, giving a truthful answer if there is insufficient time to invent a lie that fits the facts. If a suspect's lawyer objects[a] to a question the other interviewer should be ready with the next so that there is no break in the questioning. The use of who, what, when, where, why

---

(a) Code C, para 6D: 'The solicitor's only role in the police station is to protect and advance the legal rights of his client. On occasions this may require the solicitor to give advice which has the effect of his client avoiding giving evidence which strengthens a prosecution case. The solicitor may intervene in order to seek clarification or challenge an improper question to his client or the manner in which it is put, or to advise his client not to reply to a particular questions, or if he wishes to give his client further legal advice ...'

type questions are easier to apply at short notice. The solicitor should not prevent the proper putting of questions.[b]

7.9.5 *Robust questioning*

Questions should not only be short, they should be direct and avoid qualification unless necessary. A question to avoid is; 'we could be wrong', 'but we sort of think', you owned three houses which you 'do' let out 'don't you', and 'maybe' you did have enough money to do the repairs 'if you don't really mind us asking too much about your private affairs.' There are too many qualifications that undermine the strength of the questioning. The length of the question and number of issues raised gives the suspect plenty of time to choose which issue to speak on, and plenty of time to think of an answer or a reason not to answer. In fact the question contains a reason for not answering at all. After establishing that the suspect is claiming poverty as a reason for not repairing a HIMO[a] an alternative form of questioning might be as follows:

Q You own other rental houses do you not?

A Yes.

Q Which ones?

A Well there's 4 Red Lane and 3 Blue Grove but that's not let at the moment.

Q And?

A Well there's another house but I sold it.

Q When?

A Last month.

Q Who to?

A My wife.

Q Up to last month what was the gross income on these properties?

A I don't know.

Q How much do you think?

A About three or four thousand a month.

Q How much are the properties worth?

(b) Code C, paras 6.9–6.11 states that a solicitor can be asked to withdraw if an officer of the rank of superintendent or above considers that by his conduct he is preventing the proper putting of questions to his client. As this is such a serious decision the senior officer should consider whether a report to the Law Society is appropriate. This paragraph only applies 'if the solicitors approach or conduct prevents or unreasonably obstructs proper questions being put to the suspect or his response is being recorded. Examples of unacceptable conduct include answering questions on a suspect's behalf or providing written replies for him to quote.' – Code C, para 6D. If a decision is made to exclude a solicitor this decision must be capable of satisfying the court that it was properly made – Code C, para 6E.

(a) House in multiple occupation.

7.9.6   *A bold opening to the interview*

The technique of asking a suspect a question to commit him to a lie and immediately confronting him with it is somewhat controversial during proceedings. It does nonetheless undermine a suspects confidence. The intended effect is to unsettle the suspect thereby making it more difficult to invent a story and become wary of telling more lies.

7.9.7   *Questions out of sequence*

Questions which are asked out of sequence should be easy to answer for the honest witness but more difficult for someone who intends to fabricate a defence.

7.9.8   *Commit a suspect to detail*

A prime objective of the interview is to obtain as much relevant evidence as possible. Therefore a suspect should be encouraged to set out his case in detail. Open questions such as 'what is your version of events' are often very productive. There are additional reasons for asking a suspect to provide detail. If his account is untruthful he will be forced to invent facts that can later be examined against other evidence. The more detail that a suspect provides the more difficult it will be to change his evidence at a later date.

7.10 IS THERE A NEED FOR AN INTERVIEW?

Once an enforcement officer is satisfied that he gathered enough evidence to incriminate the offender and thus has reasonable cause to believe that an offence has been committed then consideration should be given to interviewing the defendant. The purpose of an interview will be either in to allow the accused to put his version of the events or for the investigating officer to fill gaps in the evidence or confirm existing evidence or to address possible lines of defence or all four of those issues.

The defendant should be given the opportunity to answer the allegations by way of mitigation or explanation in order that the Prosecutor has a balanced file. The prosecutor is under a duty to present mitigation and explanations to the court whether the defendant is legally represented or not. Furthermore, the interview could indicate any possible line of defence that may be put forward by the alleged offender at court.

7.11 THE POLICE AND CRIMINAL EVIDENCE ACT 1984

All interviews or persons suspected of committing criminal offences must be carried in accordance with the Police and Criminal Evidence Act of 1984[a] and must be preceded with a caution. The caution is set out in Chapter 2. In interviewing an offender under caution all the relevant facts of the case must be put to him on a question and answer basis and whenever possible a note of those questions and answers must be made at the time either in a pocket book or on an interview record form or tape recorder, whichever is

---

[a] PACE 1984, s 67(9) which confirms that the code applies to Local Authority Investigators.

available. If it is not possible to have an interview record form or pocket book or tape recorder then notes of the interview must be made as soon as practicable after the interview as those notes may be required in evidence. If a record of interview is made when the defendant is not present, he must be given the opportunity to read and sign the notes. If there is an undue delay in the preparation of interview notes (especially question and answer interviews) the court may refuse to accept that evidence at any subsequent trial. The investigator must not be afraid to put the open facts to the person and actually accuse him of the offence if this is necessary to encourage the defendant to account for himself. Frequently, it is only when the bare facts are put to the defendant that he will usually give his reasons as to why he has committed the offence or any reason as to why he is not guilty of the offence. At the end of the interview, and once the investigator is satisfied there is sufficient evidence to bring a prosecution against the defendant, then the offender should be informed that he will be reported for the offence of ... which must be clearly identified. Unless the interview is confident that the suspect has committed the offence he should warn as set out above. Once the warning is given it would be a breach of the PACE code to ask further questions unless it is to clear up some ambiguity.[b] The alternative is to say that the file will be submitted to the managers to decide whether or not to institute proceedings.

7.12 THE ACCUSED'S RIGHT TO SILENCE AND ADVERSE INFERENCES

Now that the provisions of the Criminal Justice and Public Order Act of 1994 are in force, the accused has a limited right to silence. The caution has not removed the accused's right to rely on silence, however, it can influence a court in the event of the defendant relying on something which he later adduces as evidence providing he has had the opportunity to adduce that evidence at the investigation/interview stage. The purpose of the caution is designed to warn the defendant that he cannot rely on total silence in the future, however, on balance, any questions put to the defendant should have direct relevance to the offence for which he is suspected and, it is advised, that the significance of the question ought to be made perfectly clear to the defendant. After being cautioned, the defendant should be advised that he is not under arrest and is free to go at any time. This should be recorded on the interview record. Special warnings should be put to the defendant in order to allow the court to draw adverse inferences these should also be fully recorded in the interview. The defendant is not entitled to know the full extent of the case against him before agreeing to answer questions.[a]

(b) Code C16(5) PACE code of conduct.
(a) 'In support of the application it is submitted that the tenor of ss 34 to 38 of the Criminal Justice and Public Order Act 1994 require the police to give as full a briefing as possible of disclosing all material to a legal representative before the interview with a suspect commences. We do not agree.' R v Imran and Hussain 96/5613/page 3; [1997] Crim LR 754. See Chapter 4 for a more detailed examination.

7.13 PACE, CODE C 10.5B

Inferences may be made if the suspect fails to answer questions but only where he has been warned in accordance with PACE, Code C 10.5B. If the investigating officer intends to invite the Court to make adverse inferences[a] from the defendant's failure to answer questions those special warnings should be given. However it should be noted that adverse inferences alone are insufficient to convict a person.[b]

7.14 THE RIGHT TO SILENCE IN THE CONTEXT OF PACE AND HUMAN RIGHTS

Certain statutes enable investigators to require suspects to provide information on the pain of prosecution. The high court has recently ruled that evidence tendered as a result of being required to answer such questions would be an infringement of a persons human rights and accordingly allowed an appeal against conviction.[c] This presents an investigator with something of a dilemma in that if a statutory power to require information is used the evidence obtained cannot be used against the accused. On the other hand if a caution is given at the same time as the exercise of a statutory right the court is unlikely to convict a person to for failing to comply with a requirement.[d] It is therefore suggested that investigators should still use the statutory procedure to obtain information but nonetheless obtain that evidence via a different method if it is required to prove an offence.

7.15 KEEPING A RECORD OF INTERVIEW BY TAPE RECORDER OR IN MANUSCRIPT

An interview is the questioning of a person regarding his involvement or suspected involvement in a criminal offence or offences. Questioning a person only to establish identity or ownership of a vehicle or property does not constitute an interview (Notes for Guidance, Police and Criminal Evidence Act 1984 Section 66 Code of Practice 10 and 11, Part C) and therefore there is no need to caution a suspect at this stage.

(a) See *R v Argent* [1996] TLR, 19 December – Court may draw an adverse inference from a failure to mention a fact when questioned if the accused could reasonably have been expected to mention it in the circumstances existing at the time. The case outlines six formal conditions which should be met before an adverse inference can be drawn. See also the list of questions (warnings) at Appendix 11.
(b) *R v Doldur* [1999] TLR, 7 December.
(c) *Brown v Procurator Fiscal Dunfermline* [2000] TLR, 14 February.
(d) *R v Page* [1996] Crim LR 439; [1995] TLR, 20 November.

Chapter 7: Interviewing and Reporting the Alleged Offender

7.16 INTERVIEW RECORDS

7.16.1 Normally any discussion between a suspect and an officer about an alleged offence will be an interview.(a) Officers are therefore well advised to ensure that the full effect of PACE is complied with including recording the discussion in the proper form, that is, date, time, place, persons present etc + the usual endorsements.

7.16.2 This advice arises from subtle changes in PACE which appear to had very little publicity. Non compliance with the formalities is likely to give rise to serious and substantial breaches of PACE. This could result in the case being dismissed if the evidence is crucial to the case. An examination of the changes is as follows:

7.16.3 Looking at an out of date edition of the Code, guidance is given at Code C, para 11(a) as follows:

7.16.4 An interview is defined at paragraph 11.1A as being the questioning of a person regarding his involvement or suspected involvement in a criminal offence or offences which by virtue of para 10.1 of Code C is required to be carried out under caution.

7.16.5 Looking at the up-to-date edition of the PACE Codes, the note for guidance at para 11.A is marked 'not used'. This is important in as much as the deletion of this guidance prevents the Local Authority from arguing that a questioning of a person to obtain an explanation of the facts etc is not an interview. The ramifications of this are that if questioning for that purpose is an interview, the following formalities need to be complied with:

> 11.5(a) An accurate record must be made of each interview with a person suspected of an offence whether or not the interview takes place at a Police Station.
>
> 11.5(b) The record must state the place of the interview, the time it begins and ends, the time the record of is made (if different), any breaks in the interview and the names of all those present and must be made on the forms provided for this purpose or in the Officer's pocket book or in accordance with the Code of Practice for tape recording of Police interviews with suspects (Code E).
>
> 11.5(c) The record must be made during the course of the interview, unless in the investigating officer's view this would not be practicable or would interview with the conduct of the interview, and must constitute the verbatim record of what has been said or failing this, an account of the interview which adequately and accurately summarises it.

(a) *R v Matthews* (1990) 91 Cr App R 43. The Court of Appeal in the case of *R v Matthews* (1990) 91 Cr App R 43 advises that 'normally any discussion or talk between the suspect or a prisoner and a Police Officer about an alleged crime would amount to an interview. On this occasion the Court took the view that evidence should not be excluded, however, the contrary view was taken in *R v Keenan* [1990] 2 QB 54, [1989] 3 All ER 598 and *R v Canale* [1990] 2 All ER 187 in which it was said that significant and substantial breaches of these provisions would lead to evidence being excluded. See also *Batley v Hampshire Justices* 5 March 1998 and Lawtel 20/2/98 for meaning of interview and need to obtain signature in police officers note book. In this case it was said that a caution was not required where the officers had no more than hunch that an offence was being committed however the appellant was suspected of committing an offence and this did activate the code.

1   If an interview record is not made during the course of the interview, it must be made as soon as practicable after completion.

1   Written interview records must be timed and signed by the maker.

1   If an interview record is not completed in the course of the interview, the reason must be recorded in the Officer's note book.

11.10 Unless it is impracticable the person interviewed shall be given the opportunity to read the interview record and sign it as correct or to indicate the respects in which he considers it inaccurate ... if the person concerned cannot read or refuses to read the record or to sign it the Senior Police Officer present shall read it to him and ask him whether or not he would like to sign it as correct (or make his mark) or to indicate the respects in which he considers it inaccurate. The Police Officer shall then certify on the interview record itself what has occurred.

11.12 Any refusal by a person to sign an interview record when asked to do so in accordance with the provisions of the Code must itself be recorded.

11.13 A written record shall also be made of any comments made by a suspected person, including unsolicited comments, which are outside the context of an interview but which might be relevant to the offence. Any such record must be timed and signed by the maker. Where practicable the person shall be given the opportunity to read the record and sign it as correct or to indicate the respects in which he considers it inaccurate. Any refusal to sign shall be recorded.

7.16.6 For the above reasons, it may well have been good practice in the past not to comply with the formalities set out if the Officer is simply asking the Defendant for his explanation as to the facts which have been put to him. The removal of guidance note 11A would now suggest otherwise. Furthermore, the Court of Appeal in the case of *R v Matthews* (1990) 91 Cr App R 43 advises that 'normally any discussion or talk between the suspect or a prisoner and a Police Officer about an alleged crime would amount to an interview'. On this occasion the Court took the view that evidence should not be excluded, however, the contrary view was taken in *R v Keenan* [1990] 2 QB 54, [1989] 3 All ER 598 and *R v Canale* [1990] 2 All ER 187 in which it was said that significant and substantial breaches of these provisions would lead to evidence being excluded.

7.16.7 If an interview takes place other than 'on site' or is an in-depth interview, a record of interview must be made on the prescribed form (Appendix 6).

7.16.8 Interview records should be maintained in accordance with the requirements of para 11.5 of Part C of the Codes of Practice.

7.17 DEVIATIONS FROM PACE

Evidence may be excluded by the Court if a record of interview is not made in accordance with the codes of practice. PACE Code E deals with tape recording of Police interviews and in accordance with PACE Code E:3:1 all interviews which take place at a Police Station for indictable and either way offences should be tape recorded. Local Authority investigators are advised to apply these provisions and tape-record all interviews wherever possible especially if they are either way matters. Interviews relating to summary offences do not need to be tape-recorded.

7.18 INTERVIEWS THROUGH CORRESPONDENCE

7.18.1 It is possible (and in some ways an advantage) for an interview to be conducted by letter. At Appendix 9 is an example of a letter that could be used in an investigation of a planning offence. The disadvantages of this approach are that the suspect has greater opportunity to tailor his evidence and probing questions are restricted to secondary correspondence.

7.18.2 The letter contains the caution and a list of questions similar to those which would be put at a face to face interview on site or in the office or a formal tape recorded interview.

7.18.3 Bearing in mind the new caution the use of a letter of interview is an advantage. No response can be used against the defendant, ie, the magistrates may draw adverse inferences under s 34 of the CJPOA 1994. Of course, the usual PACE warning and evidence that it was received is required for those inferences to be drawn and the warning under Code C 10.5B.

7.18.4 Further the use of an interview letter avoids face to face contact with an aggressive defendant in circumstances where investigating officers do not have police powers or support.

7.19 INVESTIGATING OFFENCES AFTER CHARGING THE DEFENDANT

A suspect should not be questioned after he has been charged with an offence or informed that he may be prosecuted for it. See PACE, Code C, para 16.5.

It is also an abuse of the process of the court to lay an information for the purpose of protecting the statutory time limit for laying proceedings when no decision had been taken to prosecute.[a] It follows from this that the courts would deprecate any practice of investigating an offence after the laying of an information (unless information became available as a consequence of making further enquiries upon receipt of a defence statement pursuant to the disclosure procedure).

7.20 INTERVIEWING CHILDREN AND YOUNG PERSONS

7.20.1 There are detailed provisions regarding this which are included in PACE, Code C 3. If the suspect is interviewed at the police station/office there is a detailed procedure to follow including the duty to inform an appropriate adult, that is, parent or guardian as soon as possible after arrest (or presumably attendance at office). It also extends to informing the appropriate adult of the grounds of

---

(a) See *R v Brentford Justices ex p Wong* [1981] 1 All ER 888.

detention and his whereabouts and the appropriate adult should be asked to attend the police station (office). Information about the suspect's right to legal advice and to inform someone else of his arrest and the right to consult the codes must be given to the juvenile in the adults presence or if not it must be given when he arrives at the police station. If the adult arrives later the advice must be repeated in the adult's presence.

7.20.2 When the appropriate adult arrives at the police station (office) the juvenile must be informed that he is there and that he has the right to consult privately with the adult at any time. The juvenile must not be interviewed or asked to sign any written statement except in the presence of that adult. Juveniles may only be interviewed at school in exceptional circumstances. For special rules see para 3.13.

7.20.3 For practical purposes it is much safer to interview the juvenile at his home in the presence of an appropriate adult.

7.21 ACTION FOLLOWING INTERVIEW OF CHILD OR YOUNG PERSON

Anyone who decides to lay a charge against a child[a] or young person[b] must notify the local authority[c] that is, social services. In the case of a child or young person aged 13 or older no proceedings may begin unless the prosecutor has given notice to a probation officer.[d] The practice of cautioning will be replaced by a scheme of reprimands and warnings.[e]

(a) Child is (*inter alia*) person under 18 – Children and Young Persons Act 1969, s 70.
(b) Young person 'means a person who has attained the age of 14 and is under the age of 18' – Children and Young Persons Act 1969, s 70.
(c) Children and Young Persons Act 1969, s 5(8).
(d) Children and Young Persons Act 1969, s 34(2).
(e) These will apply when ss 65 and 66 of the Crime and Disorder Act 1998 come into force.

PREPARING A FILE OF EVIDENCE

8.1 Investigating Officers (IOs) of all council departments are advised to use a standard report form, that is, something similar to that the report form that is enclosed at Appendix 3. The form describes the name of the defendant; the legislation under which the defendant is charged; the date of the offence; the place of the offence; the IO of the council and the designation of that officer.

8.2 Details of the report usually describes how the complaint was received by the council and then summarises the investigation. If reference is made to the page numbers in the evidence, this will facilitate the person evaluating it. At a later stage, a summary in this form may also assist in the presentation of the case should the court decide to proceed in the absence of the defendant. Not surprisingly, the court will often refuse to hear verbatim accounts of statements and interview records, etc, if this will take more than 10 or 15 minutes. The court often calls for summary of the statements and much time and expense may be saved if a draft is already on file.

8.3 Any observations made by officers of the defendant (or in the case of a company, its officers) are recorded in the report. Evidence is obtained from the defendants themselves or their representative (if the defendant is a company), then the information is transcribed into the officer's own Criminal Justice Act (CJA) 1967 statement.

8.4 The method of interviewing potential witnesses and the recording of information in a CJA statement are discussed in Chapters 5 and 6 of this book.

8.5 In situations where multiple offences are committed, care should be taken by the IO to prepare his report in a logical or usually chronological, manner.

8.6 The report should be divided into sub-paragraphs (usually with an introduction), background information and information whether notices have been served and incidents between service of notices (if any) and alleged contraventions, that is, the salient points of the investigation and aggravating circumstances.

8.7 The reports should be divided into sub-headings and include lists of witnesses and exhibits, a conclusion and a recommendation of offences.

8.8 Often, there is correspondence between the council and the complainants and/or the defendant company. These documents should be referred to as exhibits in either the CJA statement of the person who has written the letter or, alternatively, as exhibits in the statement of the person who has received the letter.

8.9 Before submitting a report to the legal department, the IO should be alert to the possibility that the case may be proved in the absence of the defendant by reading or summarising the statements. For this reason, it is worth checking the statements to ensure that they contain all the information that should be brought to the attention of the court. If, for example, the report contains useful photographs, the court may refuse to look at these if they have not been exhibited to a statement.

8.10 Contemporaneous notes should be passed to the council's solicitor for consideration as part of the evidence. These notes should be appended to the IO's report rather than to a CJA statement. This evidence will then only form part of the case if required by the legal department or by the defence if they ask to see it.

8.11 It is also important to note that at common law and, since 1 April 1997 under the Criminal Procedure and Investigations Act 1996, the defence have a right to see unused information.[a] Furthermore, the prosecution should disclose any evidence which may undermine its case whether or not it is asked for by the defence.

8.12 As all actions by officers of the council require authorisation by the council, an 'authorisation' should to be issued before the file of evidence is referred to the council's solicitors for prosecution and, in any event, before proceeding are laid.

8.13 Before submitting the file for prosecution, the officer may wish to view the checklist in Chapter 3 to ensure that all the steps have been taken in the investigation.

(a) See *R v DPP ex p Lee* [1999] 2 All ER 737. The Act does not apply prior to committal for trial in indictable proceedings or prior to a not guilty plea in summary proceedings (see Chapter 2). In these circumstances, the common law will apply. The defendant will therefore be entitled to ask for unused information as of right and a prosecutor should supply it whether asked or not, if 'justice and fairness' requires him to do so.

CHAPTER 9

CHECKING AUTHORISATIONS AND REVIEWING EVIDENCE

9.1 AUTHORISATIONS GENERALLY

A local authority is a creature of statute. It follows from this that every action taken by a local authority must have some statutory foundation without which such action will be deemed to be *ultra vires*, that is, without authority and may be declared null and void. Likewise any action or decision taken by an officer of a local authority must be authorised by that local authority. Any such action or decision taken without authority may be declared null and void. An officer may be authorised in either one of four ways.

9.2 COMMITTEE AUTHORISATION

9.2.1 A committee resolution of a local authority may authorise an officer to act. For example, it is not uncommon for a sub-committee of the council to authorise an officer prosecute a person or to take legal proceedings against an individual for providing public entertainment without a licence.

9.2.2 It is also worth bearing in mind that a sub-committee of a council may not act upon everything or authorise any action or decision unless it has the authority to do so from a parent committee. Furthermore, that parent committee will also be acting without authority in authorising the sub-committee unless its authority is granted by a resolution of the full council.

9.3 DELEGATED AUTHORITY FROM COMMITTEE

9.3.1 Many local authorities take the view that officers should institute legal proceedings on routine matters without reference to a committee. The consequence of doing otherwise would be to inundate councillors with routine matters which take second place to the mainstream political agenda. In these circumstances, authority will be given to an individual officer by reference to this position or one officer in consultation with another. For example, a chief environmental health officer may be given authority to institute proceedings under the Food Safety Act 1990 in consultation with a director of legal services. For authorisations involving criminal or quasi-criminal prosecutions, consideration should be given to the Home Office guidance before issuing proceedings. This involves consideration of the evidence which requires a thorough understanding of the rules of evidence and procedure. It is submitted that the person most qualified to make such a decision is a lawyer. Such a person is properly qualified to weigh up the evidence and is likely to be detached from the investigation. Given that this was one of the reasons for transferring the decision to prosecute mainstream criminal offences from the police, there is much to be said in favour of requiring the consent of an independent and legally qualified person before taking regulatory proceedings. If the decision to prosecute is taken by a person who has not properly considered the evidence and is considered partisan in his approach, it is not difficult to envisage a time when there are adverse implications in the courts. This could result in an award of costs being made against the officer and, bearing in mind that the door to new grounds for abuse of process have not been closed, there is potential for judicial review in extreme circumstances.

9.3.2 If an officer is acting under delegated powers, it is advisable to check the standing order giving effect to the resolution, so that it does, in fact, authorise the intended prosecution. If a standing order is not sufficiently precise, or otherwise incorrectly drafted, the charges may be dismissed without even the evidence having been considered. It is also worth checking the actual resolution giving rise to the standing order. It is not uncommon for there to be a variance between the resolution and the standing order. Furthermore, the possibility that such a resolution cannot be located due to the passage of time, or for a multitude of other reasons, cannot be discounted. In either case, questions may be raised over the authorisation and, hence, the validity of the proceedings. It is for these reasons that many local authorities have adopted the practice of approving the standing orders annually. This practice is to be commended.

9.4 AUTHORITY DELEGATED TO AN OFFICER IN CONSULTATION WITH CHAIRPERSON AND VICE-CHAIRPERSON OF THE APPROPRIATE COMMITTEE

Matters of political importance which require action to be taken at short notice are often dealt with by a standing order which enables an officer, in consultation with a chairperson and a vice-chairperson, to authorise a named officer to institute proceedings. Decision taking powers prior to the Local Government Act 2000 could not be delegated to a single councillor, even if that person is a committee chairperson.[a] As with all authorisations, it is advisable to check the wording of the standing order and the authorisation to the committee from the full council.

9.5 AUTHORISATION FROM A SUPERIOR OFFICER

It is important to distinguish the difference between a ministerial and a judicial decision. A ministerial decision may be delegated where a judicial decision may not except under limited circumstances. Ministerial decisions are routine, rubber stamp-type operations, such as sending out routine correspondence in an authorised officer's name. Judicial

---

[a] See Raymond Knowles' article, 'A councillor has no executive authority' (1998) 162 JP 92 and *R v Secretary of State for the Environment ex p Hillingdon BC* [1986] 1 All ER 816, but can delegate to a single officer. See *Provident Mutual Life Assurance v Derby CC* [1981] 1 WLR 173. This has been altered by the Local Government Act 2000.

decisions require a balancing exercise to be undertaken, having considered all relevant factors. A decision to institute criminal or quasi-criminal proceedings, for example, food safety offences will always be a judicial consideration. That being the case, the person instituting proceedings must not only be properly authorised,[a] but he must make a judicial decision. Such a decision cannot be delegated if the statute specifically names a particular person, for example, the Health and Safety at Work Act etc 1974.[b] The only circumstances which enable an officer to delegate a judicial function is if he has the requisite committee authority to delegate that function.[c] Provided that the authorised person has taken a judicial decision to prosecute,[d] a facsimile rubber stamp of his signature may be used to denote that decision. That authority may be either general or specific. The procedure of signing over the rubber stamp and including 'pp' before initialling is good practice.[e]

9.6 THE CONTENT OF THE AUTHORISATION

9.6.1 The authorisation should refer to the correct section and sub-section of the offence, together with a brief description of that offence. This should all be checked for accuracy along with the name, date of offence and date of authorisation. An authorisation post-dating the laying of an information would be defective.[aa] Furthermore, an authorisation which pre-dated a relevant fact in the investigation would also open the authorisation up to questioning.

9.6.2 The defendant's name on a summons cannot be altered.[ab] The same may well apply to a written authorisation unless it is altered before proceedings are laid.

9.6.3 It is also worth checking the *locus standi* of the person instituting the proceedings, for example, the Health and Safety at Work etc Act 1974 stipulates that an authorised environmental health officer may bring proceedings.

(a) *R v St Edmundsbury BC ex p Walton* [1999] Env LR 879; [1999] JPL 805. Power to prosecute must be formally delegated under the Local Government Act 1972, s 101, but see *Campbell v Wallsend Slipway and Engineering Company* [1978] ICR 1015 for presumption as to validity of appointment and requirement to state section of the Act not being necessary.

(b) *Delegatus non potest delegare*: see *R v Gateshead Justices ex p Tesco Stores* [1981] 1 All ER 1027 and *Re Prince Blucher* [1931] 2 Ch 70.

(c) *Hilliers Ltd v Sefton MBC* (1996) CO-2165-96, 29 November. Standing orders may give officers power to authorise subordinates. Furthermore, there is no obligation to evidence a decision to prosecute in writing and still less to serve the evidence on the proposed defendants.

(d) See *R v Brentford Justices ex p Catlin* [1975] 2 All ER 201, use of rubber stamp also approved in *Goodman v J Egan Ltd* [1954] 1 All ER 753. There is authority to suggest that there is no power to sub-delegate in the absence of express authority in the statute (see *Ratnagopal v AG* [1969] 3 WLR 1056 and *R v Gateshead Justices ex p Tesco Stores* [1981] 1 All ER 1027). However, where it is impracticable for one person to carry out all the decisions, there is likely to be an exception (*Provident Mutual Life Assurance v Derby CC* [1981] 1 WLR 173). A liberal approach was also taken in the more recent case of *Hilliers v Sefton MBC* (1996) CO-2165-96, 29 November.

(e) *London CC v Agricultural Food Products* [1955] 2 QB 218 and *Albon v Railtrack plc* [1998] EHLR 83, p 87.

(aa) *R v Brentford Justices ex p Wong* [1981] 2 WLR 203 – an information laid before final decision to prosecute to gain time was an abuse of process. See, also, *R v Newcastle-upon-Tyne Justices ex p John Bryce Ltd* [1976] 2 All ER 611.

(ab) *R v Greater Manchester Justices ex p Aldi A Gaish and Co* (1995) 159 JP 717, *R v Newcastle-upon-Tyne Justices ex p John Bryce Ltd* [1976] 2 All ER 611.

9.7 EVIDENCE

9.7.1 The Home Office Guidelines and the Code for Crown Prosecutors[a] stipulate that a person should not be charged with an offence unless the evidence supports a 'realistic prospect of conviction'. This is often taken to mean more than a 50% chance of conviction.

9.7.2 When evaluating the evidence, it is advisable for the solicitor to break down the offence into individual elements, having particular regard to any hidden element which may exist. In a prosecution for[b] obstruction or failure to provide evidence of insurance at the request of an authorised private hire/hackney carriage officer, there is a hidden element which arises from the definition of authorised officer. In accordance with this definition, it is necessary to call evidence at trial that the officer was, in fact, authorised in writing. Any failure to prove this or any other element of the prosecution case, however small, may leave the prosecution open to a submission of no case to answer. Advocates who find themselves in this position may find it helpful to ask the court to recall evidence.[c]

9.7.3 In addition to evaluating the evidence, it is necessary to carry out a number of other routine checks. These include checking that the date of the allegation is supported by the evidence and is consistent with the authorisation. The name of the defendant needs to be correctly stated. There must also be evidence that the name given is the correct name. If the defendant is known to the officer, this should not be a problem. Alternatively, if a person's name and address is previously unknown, and has not been verified, it is open to the defendant to give a false name and deny any connection with the allegation at a subsequent hearing. In this situation, it would probably be inappropriate for an officer to identify the defendant in court, although the authorities are divided on the issue (see Chapter 3 under the heading 'Who is to be investigated'). In addition to the above, the name must amount to a legal entity. Proceedings against a firm or a club are a nullity for want of legal status. Checks should be also made of the particular authorising statute[d] for any conditions precedent before or ancillary to laying the information, for example, service of notice on the Office of Fair Trading prior to proceedings or the requirement that an inspector authorised on that behalf by any enforcing authority institutes and, therefore, also authorises proceedings under some statutes.[e]

9.7.4 If the defendant has a foreign sounding name, inquiries with the investigating officer (IO) are recommended to establish his ability to understand English, particularly if the offence involves *mens rea*.

(a) See the Code of Crown Prosecutors for other considerations to be taken into account when deciding whether or not to prosecute as referred to in greater detail in Chapter 1. A copy of the Code can be obtained from the Crown Prosecution Service, London, telephone 0207 273 8049.

(b) See Local Government (Miscellaneous Provisions) Act 1976, s 73, and, for the definition of authorised officer, s 80(1).

(c) *R v Munnery* (1992) 94 Cr App R 164. See, also, *R v Francis* [1990] TLR, 31 January.

(d) The Trade Descriptions Act 1968 requires such notice.

(e) The Health and Safety at Work Act etc 1974 authorises the investigating environmental health officer to lay the information before the magistrates.

Chapter 9: Checking Authorisations and Reviewing Evidence

9.7.5   The IO should at all times comply with the rules of natural justice.[f] Any failure to do so may result in an application for evidence to be excluded.[g] A common breach of natural justice in local authority investigations is to ask further substantive questions of the defendant after informing him that he may be reported. Any subsequent questioning of the defendant should be confined to clarification of issues already raised.[h]

9.7.6   Evidence is most likely to be excluded where the defendant has not been cautioned. However, it is worth noting that preliminary questions to establish identity or ownership of vehicles, etc, need not be made the subject of a caution.[i]

9.7.7   Before making a final assessment of the evidence, the solicitor should take into account any inferences which the court might be prepared to make of the defendant's failure or refusal to answer questions.

9.7.8   For inferences to be drawn,[j] special warnings should be given.[k]

9.7.9   The use of the special warnings and the Criminal Justice and Public Order Act 1994 will sometimes have a part to play in local authority proceedings,[l] although a court cannot convict on adverse inferences alone.[m]

(f) Embodied in some detail but not exhaustively in the Police and Criminal Evidence Act (PACE) 1984, Codes of Practice.
(g) PACE 1984, s 78.
(h) See PACE 1984, Codes of Practice, Code C16.
(i) See PACE 1984, Codes of Practice, Code C10.
(j) Criminal Justice and Public Order Act 1994, ss 36 and 37.
(k) PACE 1984, Codes of Practice, Code C, para 10.5.
(l) The case of *R v Argent* [1996] TLR, 19 December sets out the six conditions which must be satisfied before a jury may make an appropriate inference.
(m) *R v Doldur* [1999] TLR, 7 December.

CHAPTER 10

DRAFTING SUMMONSES/INFORMATIONS AND SERVICE OF NOTICES AND SUMMONSES

10.1 JURISDICTION OF THE COURT AND CONSENT TO PROSECUTION

10.1.1 The alleged offence must arise within the jurisdiction of the court or be connected to an allegation that is.

10.1.2 Consent to prosecution may be required in special cases, for example, consent of local authority in respect of prosecutions against children and young persons. There may also be a requirement to give external notification in respect of Trade Descriptions Act 1968 matters to the Office of Fair Trading.[a]

10.2 GENERAL PRINCIPLES – R 100 OF THE MAGISTRATES' COURTS RULES 1981

The drafting of informations and summonses are governed by r 100 of the Magistrates' Courts Rules 1981 as summarised in 10.3 below.

10.3 DESCRIPTION OF A SPECIFIC OFFENCE

Every information, summons, warrant or other document laid, issued or made for the purposes of or in connection with any proceedings before a magistrates' court for an offence shall be sufficient if it describes the specific offence with which the accused is charged or of which he is convicted in ordinary language avoiding as far as possible the use of technical terms and without necessarily stating all the elements of the offence,[aa] but giving such particulars as may be necessary for giving reasonable information of the nature of the charge. Reference should also be made to any amending statute or regulation.

10.4 REFERENCE TO A SECTION OF A STATUTE

If the offence charged is one created by or under any Act the description of the offence shall contain a reference to a section of the Act or as the case may be the rule, order, regulation, byelaw or other instrument creating the offence. Reference should also be made to any amending statute or regulation.

---

[a] Trade Descriptions Act 1968, s 130.
[aa] Failure to include all the elements of the offence may result in a challenge on the grounds that the information is insufficient for the defendant to know the charge against him. It is, therefore, safer to include all elements of the offence in the information.

10.5 OMISSION OF A SECTION

Omission to state the section or state it correctly may be fatal.[a]

10.6 USE OF PRECEDENTS

To avoid re-inventing the wheel, it is often helpful to refer to a precedent either in the appendices, or on an earlier file, or in a standard text such as *Oke's Magisterial Formulist*. However, it can be dangerous to assume that the precedent is correct in every case. Statutes are often amended or deleted and it is advisable to check for such alterations. As a general rule, an Information will often outline the offence in the wording of the statute and then set out how, or in what manner, the offence is being alleged. See appendices for examples.

10.7 NON-FEASANCE OFFENCES

Special care should be taken for non-feasance offences, that is, offences arising from a failure to act. It is sometimes difficult to identify the date(s) for these types of offences. Once this type of offence has been recognised, it becomes easier to identify the date(s) by asking the questions when or for what period of time did the defendant fail to act and did this time period arise when failure to act constituted an offence. If the failure to act relates to non-compliance with a notice, the period for compliance must be set out in the summons and supported by evidence.[aa] In arriving at a date or time period for the offence, care should be taken to avoid future applications to exclude evidence on the basis that it refers to events which took place outside the dates for which the defendant is charged. For offences involving non-compliance with notices, it is often preferable to state that these offences have been committed between certain dates for the above reasons. The same approach would also be the norm for any other continuing offence.[b]

(a) See *Allerton v Brown* [1945] KB 122, p 109, JP 25; *Hunter v Coombs* [1962] 1 All ER 126, JP 300. In accordance with the case of *Lomas v Peek* [1947] 2 All ER 574, the words 'knowingly and wilfully' need not appear in the summons but the contrary view was taken in. *Waring v Wheatley* (1951) JP 630.

(aa) *Maltedge v Wokingham DC* [1992] TLR, 21 May; (1992) 64 P & CR 487.

(b) *Torridge DC v Turner* [1991] TLR, 27 November confirms that failure to comply with the building regulations is a continuing offence.

10.8 MISFEASANCE OFFENCES

For situations in which offences have been committed on a date that is unknown, charges may also be laid by reference to it having been committed between two dates.(a) Alternatively, it is also sufficient to use such phrases as 'on or before' or 'on or about'.

10.9 DRAFTING INFORMATIONS AGAINST ACCESSORIES

10.9.1 There is no statutory obligation to charge aiders and abettors, etc, as secondary parties.(aa) However, good practice would dictate that it is better to do so, as this would set out the nature of the charge with greater clarity. The words 'aid and abet, counsel and procure' may all be used together when drafting the information.(b) Each word has a different meaning, and inclusion of them all at the drafting stage ensures maximum flexibility at the hearing.

10.9.2 The suggested formula is to recite the substantive offence against the principle and add the words 'and you, Mr/Mrs Y, did aid and abet, counsel and procure Mr/Mrs X to commit the said offence, contrary to s 44, Magistrates' Courts Act 1980' for summary offences, or 'contrary to s 8, Accessories and Abettors Act 1861' for either way offences.

10.10 DUPLICITY

10.10.1 Unless it can be established that an offence is a continuing offence or constitutes a single activity,(ba) the information must refer to one offence only. If an information

---

(a) *Onley v Gee* (1861) 25 JP 342.

(aa) Magistrates' Courts Act 1980, s 44, which creates liability for secondary parties in summary proceedings, includes the words 'whether or not he is charged as a principal'.

(b) *Re Smith* [1858] 3 H & N 227; *Ferguson v Weaving* [1951] 1 KB 814 DC.

(ba) *Jemmison v Priddle* [1972] 1 All ER 540 – two shots in quick succession at deer passing from one person's land to another was one single activity and, therefore, it was proper to include this as a single charge. This principal was applied in *R v Ronald Wilson* (1969) Cr App R 83. Where counts in an indictment each charge theft of a number of separate items from different departments, the counts are not bad for duplicity, for it is legitimate to charge in a single count one activity even though that activity may involve more than one act. *Heaton v Costello* [1984] Crim LR 485. Theft of clothing and a bottle of cider (latter by label switching) from a department store was not bad for duplicity when included on a single count. The High Court ruled that the magistrates had applied the wrong test in asking whether or not the theft of the cider by label switching and theft of the clothing were separate acts. The test to apply was whether the various acts could properly and fairly be described as comprising one single activity having regard to all the facts of the case. See, also, the following decision under the Food Hygiene Regulations 1970, which are now replaced: *George v Kumar* [1980] LGR 526. Thirty informations were laid under the Food Hygiene (General) Regulations 1970. Regulation 16(1)(a) required that every sanitary convenience situated in or regularly used in connection with any food premises shall be kept clean and in efficient working order. This regulation created two offences. Regulation 25 also created two offences, namely: failure to keep the structure of every food room clean and failure to keep the structure of every food room in good order, repair and condition. The *Kumar* case approved the decision of: *Berni Inns Ltd v Reynolds* (1981) unreported, 27 March. Regulation 29 of the 1970 Regulations, which stipulated that a wash-hand basin should have soap, a nailbrush and a clean towel, created three separate offences in respect of each item.

alleges more than one offence, the prosecutor can anticipate an objection on the ground of duplicity. In such a case, the prosecutor shall elect on which offence he desires the court to proceed.(b) There is no known authority requiring the information to be dismissed if the prosecutor makes such an election. If there a number of charges in one information the charge may still succeed if some but not all are proved.(c)

10.11 SPECIAL CONSIDERATIONS FOR CERTAIN TYPES OF OFFENCES

10.11.1 Numerous breaches of a Public Entertainment Licence on the same day normally amount to one offence only.(a) The same offence on different dates would normally merit a further charge.

10.11.2 For health and safety at work offences pursuant to s 2 of the Health and Safety At Work etc Act 1974, the matters referred to in s 2(2) are mere examples of the breach of the general duty, these may therefore all be included in the same charge (without the issue of duplicity arising) and there is no need specifically to refer to these examples in the information.(ab)

10.11.3 For allegations pursuant to the Trade Descriptions Act 1968, there can be no offence if the charge amounts to a future promise. However, a future promise may include a 'statement of present intention', for example, to ensure that a travel company has put in place the arrangements, such as booking sufficient numbers of three-star hotels to put that promise into effect. If companies are charged in these terms, the informations should be drafted accordingly.(ac)

10.12 SERVICE OF STATUTORY NOTICES

10.12.1 *Notices*

Generally speaking, notices that are required to be served in accordance with statutory procedures can be served in a number of different ways. The first option and most easily available is by ordinary post. Alternatively, a notice may be served by recorded delivery letter, registered post, insertion by hand through the letter box, or by personal service.

10.12.2 The authors do not recommend service of notices that might ultimately be the subject of proceedings to be served other than personally, unless steps will be taken by the officer serving the notice to ascertain whether the person to whom the notice is addressed has received the notice.

(b) Magistrates' Courts Rules 1981, r 12.
(c) *Barton v DPP* [2001] EWHC Admin 223, 13 March; Archbold News (2001) issue 5, 27 June.
(a) *Mendip v Glastonbury Festivals Ltd* (1993) 91 LGR, 18 February.
(ab) *HSE v Spindle Select Ltd* [1996] TLR, 9 December.
(ac) *British Airways Board v Taylor* [1976] 1 All ER 65.

Chapter 10: Drafting Summonses/Informations and Service of Notices and Summonses

10.12.3 The most reliable form of service is, of course, by personal service, but this is a time consuming and expensive way to serve a summons or notice. However, it is the only way to be absolutely certain that the person to whom the notice is addressed has received it.

10.12.4 There are certain provisions contained in various statutes relating to local government law which set out in detail the manner in which notices issued under a particular Act in question are to be served. If the document is served in accordance with the provisions of s 233 of the Local Government Act 1972, or the Public Health Act 1936, or s 329 of the Town and Country Planning Act 1990, the recipient will be deemed to have been duly served although, in point of fact, it never reached him.[a]

10.12.5 It is also possible for a person to be convicted of failing to comply with an enforcement notice in circumstances where he has not been served with it.[aa] However, the magistrates would regard the lack of service strong mitigation and this would reflected in the penalty.

10.12.6 Practically speaking, in the event that a notice is served by ordinary post, or even by recorded delivery, and there has been a non-compliance, the first question that ought to be asked is whether or not the recipient has received the notice. If receipt is denied at the interview stage of the investigation, the officer should have with him a spare copy to serve it there and then and inform the recipient that he has an additional length of time to comply with the notice. It is also advisable to endorse the extended time limit on the notice and retain a signed copy.

10.12.7 There are certain provisions contained in various statutes relating to local government law which set out in detail the manner in which notices issued under an Act are to be served.[ab]

---

[a] *Woodford UDC v Henwood* (1900) 64 JP 148, *Lombard North Central Plc v Power-Hines* [1995] CCLR 24, *R v Collett* [1994] 2 All ER 372, see, also, *Lambeth LBC v Mullings* [1990] TLR 16 March for service of an abatement notice through a letter box applying Local Government Act 1972, s 233; *Rushmore BC v Reynolds* (1991) 23 HLR 495 which confirms that Local Government Act 1972, s 233, and Interpretation Act 1978, s 7, create an irrebuttable presumption that service has been effected (receipt of a notice denied after it was pushed through a letter box) and *Enfield LBC v Devonish* (1996) 28 HLR 641 which limits s 233 to documents required or authorised by any enactment (therefore, would not apply to a notice to quit which is not so required or authorised).

[aa] *R v Collett* [1994] 2 All ER 372 and Town and Country Planning Act 1990. It should also be noted that the ruling in *R v Collett* only applies to enforcement notices. (*Stones Justices Manual* sets out different methods for serving notices in some cases.)

[ab] Eg, the Town and Country Planning Act 1990, s 329, which relates to the service of notices states:

Any notice or other document required or authorised to be served or given under this Act may be served or given either:

1   (a) by delivering it to the person on whom it is to be served or to whom it is to be given; or

     (b) by leaving it at the usual or last known place of abode of that person, or, in a case where an address for service has been given by that person, by leaving it at the usual or last known place of at that address; or

     (c) by sending it in a pre-paid registered letter, or by the recorded delivery service at his usual or last known place of abode or, in a case where an address for service has been given by that person, at that address or ... [cont]

10.12.8 In some cases, even though it is sufficient in law to serve the notice/order on the owner/occupier of the land, consideration should be given to affixing the notice/order to a conspicuous place on the land itself. Taking such action could prevent a misunderstanding between the owner/occupier of the land who may reside elsewhere and any contractor he has assigned to carry out work on the land.

10.12.9 Section 7 of the Interpretation Act 1978 may be used in tandem with s 329 above as a method of establishing service of documents by post.

10.12.10 Under s 7 of the Interpretation Act 1978, it seems that, where the time of service of a document authorised or requested to be served by post is not vital, the presumption that it is served is irrebuttable.[aa] In these circumstances, a person is deemed to have received a document even where the contrary is proved. On the other hand, the time of service is important. Evidence may be called to establish that service did not take place at all.[b] It seems that the authorities under the Interpretation Act 1978 are more restrictive as to what constitutes service. Local government officers are therefore advised to rely more on s 233 of the Local Government Act 1972.

10.12.11 Regardless of whether or not it is intended to rely on the deeming provisions, it is preferable to satisfy the court that the notice has been served either by serving it personally or, alternatively, by taking steps to check that the notice has been duly

---

(a) [cont]

    (d) in the case of an incorporated company or body, by delivering it to the secretary or clerk of the company or body at their registered or principal office, or sending it in a pre-paid registered letter, or by the recorded delivery service, addressed to the secretary of clerk of the company or body at that office.

2   Where the notice or document is required or authorised to be served on any person as having an interest in premises and, the name of that person cannot be ascertained after reasonably enquiry, or where the Notice of document is required or authorised to be served on any person as an occupier of premises, the notice or document should be taken to be duly served if:

    (a) it is addressed to him/her either by name or by the description of 'the owner' or, as the case may be, 'the occupier' of the premises (describing them) and is delivered or sent in a manner specified in sub-section (1)(a)(b) or (c); or

    (b) it is so addressed and is marked in such manner as may be prescribed for securing that it is plainly identifiable as a communication of importance and –

        (i) It is sent to the premises in a pre-paid registered letter or by the recorded delivery services and is not returned to the authority sending it, or

        (ii) it is delivered to some person on those premises, or is affixed conspicuously to some object on those premises.

3   Where–

    (a) the notice or other document is required to be served on or given to all persons who have interest in or are occupiers of premises comprised in any land, and it appears to the authority required or authorised to serve the notice or other document that any part of that land unoccupied.

The notice or document shall be taken to be duly served on all persons having interest in, or on any occupiers of, premises comprised in that part of the land (other than a person who has given to that authority an address for the service of the notice or document on him/her, if it is addressed to 'the owners and any occupiers' of that part of the land (describing it) and is affixed conspicuously to some object on the land.

(aa) *Moody v Godstone RDC* [1966] 1 WLR 1085.

(b) *R v London Quarter Sessions Appeal Committee ex p Rossi* [1956] 1 QB 682.

Chapter 10: Drafting Summonses/Informations and Service of Notices and Summonses

received as soon as the date for compliance in the notice has expired. This will avoid the mitigation of lack of knowledge being presented to the court.

10.12.12 There are, of course, provisions in many Acts relating to the service of documents. When documents or notices are to be served under the provisions of any particular Act, the Act should always be referred to.

10.12.13 Whenever a notice or summons is served, a certificate of service should be affixed to a copy of the notice (see Appendix 5) or summons.

10.12.14 A person who is charged in his private capacity would normally be served at his private address. The position would be reversed if the defendant is a businessman or professional being proceeded against in that capacity. In the case of *Robertson v Banham & Co (A Firm)* [1996] TLR, 26 November; [1997] 1 All ER 79, the court confirmed that the phrase 'usual or last known address' was not to be confined to residential addresses and interpreted these words to mean the address where a person practised if that person was a professional.

CHAPTER 11

TRANSFORMING A WEAK CASE INTO A SUCCESSFUL PROSECUTION

11.1 REVIEW OF EVIDENCE

A prosecuting solicitor is likely to receive a number of case reports where the standard of the evidence does not satisfy the Code of Practice for Crown Prosecutors.

11.2 PUBLIC INTEREST REQUIREMENTS

In circumstances where the public interest dictates that a prosecution should be brought, it will be one of the prosecutions objectives to ensure that the case is presented at its highest. In accordance with the duty of the prosecution, as laid down by both the solicitors' and barristers' Code of Conduct, the prosecution should not go so far as to attempt to obtain a conviction by all means at his command, nor should he regard himself as appearing for a party. He should lay before the court the whole of the facts that comprise the case, fairly and impartially. His position is that of a minister of justice rather than an advocate in the cause. We have therefore set out the following steps that are intended to assist in reaching this objective.

11.3 FURTHER INVESTIGATIONS BY THE CLIENT DEPARTMENT

Sometimes, there is a lacuna in the evidence that has gone unnoticed by the investigating officer. Occasionally, this may relate to the legal status of the defendant, that is, whether the defendant is a partnership trading under a trading name or a limited company. In some cases, the name of the defendant is not supported by evidence. In either event, the Business Names Act 1985 can be used to investigate the name of the defendant. This Act requires the name of the individual(s) or company to be placed in a prominent position in the business premises and on all receipts, correspondence and business documents. It is also an offence not to comply with a written request to supply this information. For local government investigators, use may also be made of s 16 of the Local Government (Miscellaneous Provisions) Act 1976 to establish the owner of any land.

11.4 CONSIDER PROCEEDING ON LEGISLATION THAT IS MORE APPROPRIATE TO THE FACTS

This sometimes requires an overall knowledge of all the relevant legislation pertaining to the individual prosecution. For example, it may be more advantageous to prosecute a fly-posting offence under the Town and Country Planning (Control of Advertisements)

Regulations 1992 as opposed to s 132 of the Highways Act 1980. This approach may be adopted to take advantage of the deeming provisions in the regulations that extend liability to a person whose business is being advertised on the poster. This may be useful in circumstances where the evidence pointing to the defendant is weak.

11.5 CONSIDER CHARGING THE DEFENDANT AS AN AIDER AND ABETTOR

Experience of local authority prosecutions has shown that investigating officers tend to think in terms of a prosecution against the defendant as a principal only. It is possible, in many instances, to charge a person as a secondary party where the evidence does not support a prosecution as a principal – for example, prosecutions against aiders and abettors.[a] There are only two elements to this offence. The first element is that the defendant has knowledge of the offence and, secondly, that he has assisted or encouraged the commission of that offence.[b] A prosecution against a booking clerk as a secondary party to plying for hire and not having insurance is an example of proceedings that can be taken in this way in the context of local authority prosecutions.

11.6 IDENTIFYING IMPLIED STATEMENTS

The Trade Descriptions Act 1968 does not regulate future promises. This is an important restriction upon the use of the Act that is justifiable on the grounds that supervening events can alter a persons ability to keep an earlier promise. The other side of the coin is that some promises contain implied statements that are relied on. The House of Lords[aa] appear to have recognised this and concluded that a letter confirming a reservation on a certain flight contained both an implied statement of existing fact and a statement of present intention. The letter amounted to saying: 'Not only have we secured your seat for you but we have the intention to ensure that it will remain reserved and available to you on the designated flight.' To rely on this doctrine, it is necessary to lay informations on this basis and argue the point at first instance. This is not an issue that can be taken up for the first time at the appellate stage.

11.7 USE OF UNUSED INFORMATION

11.7.1 The main issues in the case are not always obvious until the later stages of the investigation or, sometimes, until the case report is submitted to a council's lawyers. This may account for the existence of relevant evidence in the unused information or in the officer's notebook without any express mention if it is in the case report. An example of this might be a reference in a notebook to an admission

---

(a) Magistrates' Courts Act 1980, s 44, for summary offences and the Accessories and Abettors Act 1861, s 8, for either way offences.
(b) See *Ackroyds Air Travel Ltd v DPP* [1950] 1 All ER 933 and *Thomas v Lindop* [1950] 1 All ER 966.
(aa) *British Airways Board v Taylor* [1976] 1 All ER 65.

by a defendant that he is in charge of a business that is inconsistent with a later interview.

11.7.2 A further source of unused information is the remainder of the interview record now that interview summaries are fast replacing the complete transcript.

11.8 RESEARCH THE AUTHORITIES

A detailed knowledge of all the relevant case law is necessary to present the case at its highest. Reference to some cases can greatly enhance the prosecution case to the extent that a successful prosecution might not otherwise be likely.[a]

11.9 GRANTING A *NOLLE PROSEQUI* TO A SECONDARY PARTY IN RETURN FOR QUEEN'S EVIDENCE

11.9.1 An example of this might be to ask the entertainers to give evidence against the organisers of unlicensed entertainment in return for a promise not to prosecute. However, if this approach is adopted, care should be taken to ensure that the door is firmly closed to the possibility of a private prosecution being launched as this would invoke the principle of self incrimination.[aa]

11.9.2 Sometimes opportunities of this nature arise, but only if the investigating officer or solicitor is sufficiently astute to raise the question. In a prosecution against a defendant who refused to desist from erecting fly-posters on lampposts, it became apparent that one of the prosecution's lay witnesses had actually erected fly-posters on the direct instructions from the defendant. This was a fact that was known to all the prosecution witnesses except the investigating officer and only surfaced during a conversation after an aborted hearing.

11.10 TAKING FULL ADVANTAGE OF THE RULES OF EVIDENCE

11.10.1 Hearsay evidence is permissible in appeals against a local authority decision in the magistrates' court.[ba]

11.10.2 It is also noteworthy that any statements made by the defendant to newspaper reporters, although hearsay, will be admissible as a confession within the meaning

---

(a) There are two cases in particular which fall in this category. In the case of *Chichester DC v Silvester* [1992] TLR, 6 May, the driver of a van was found guilty of being concerned in the organisation of a public entertainment as well as the disc jockey and the hirer of audio equipment. Another significant case is that of *Ogwr BC v Baker* [1989] COD 489. This was a plying for hire prosecution in which the driver was found guilty even though the passenger had pre-booked the journey with the firm albeit with a different driver.

(aa) *Hayter v L* [1998] 1 WLR 854.

(ba) *Westminster CC v Zestfair Ltd* (1989) 88 LGR 29, and *Kavanagh v CC of Devon and Cornwall* [1974] 2 All ER 697 goes beyond *Zestfair* to include matters not strictly proven within the ambit of admissible evidence in these type of appeals.

of s 76 of the Police and Criminal Evidence Act (PACE) 1984. The main issues are likely to relate to accuracy and reliability. Newspaper reporters tend to keep contemporaneous notes of interviews and it is therefore advisable to take all necessary steps to secure this evidence at an early stage.

11.10.3 Close attention should also be paid to the definition of hearsay that lets in statements not tendered in evidence for the purpose of establishing the truth of those statements.[b]

11.10.4 In very exceptional cases, the rules on similar fact evidence may apply to evidence not otherwise admissible. It might also be worth remembering that a court may draw proper inferences from established facts.

11.11 ELECTION TO PROSECUTE OR SUSPEND/REVOKE

Taxi drivers who commit offences may be prosecuted or disciplined by committee of the council or both. If the decision of the local authority is contested there will either be a trial, if the driver is prosecuted, or an appeal, if his licence is either suspended or revoked. In deciding which course of action to take, the committee/officer would do well to have regard to the rules of procedure and evidence that differs according to the type of hearing. If the evidence of a recent offence is insufficient to satisfy the civil standard of proof, a prosecution is highly unlikely to succeed. On the other hand if the drivers appeals against a decision to revoke or suspend this evidence will be admissible along with any other relevant matters which may have not been strictly proven. For these reasons, the decision whether to prosecute or suspend/revoke will often determine the success of any subsequent proceedings.

11.12 PROPER APPLICATION OF THE STATUTORY PROVISIONS

11.12.1 The prosecution is not always required to prove every evidential issue at trial. In accordance with s 101 of the Magistrates' Courts Act 1980 where the defendant to an information relies for his defence on any exception proviso excuse or qualification the burden of proving that exemption, etc, shall be on him.[a]

11.12.2 The Criminal Justice and Public Order Act 1994 now enables adverse inferences to be made from a defendant's failure to answer questions, provided that special warnings are given when appropriate under ss 36 and 37. See Chapter 7 for a more in-depth examination of adverse inferences.

(b) *Subramanium v DPP* [1956] 1 WLR 956 establishes this exception.
(a) This rule was applied widely in *R v Edwards* [1975] QB 27, but narrowly in *R v H* [1987] AC 35R.

11.13 KNOWING WHEN A CAUTION SHOULD BE ISSUED

11.13.1 The admissibility of statements made by a defendant will often depend on whether he should have been cautioned by the officer investigating the case. These statements can be crucial to the outcome of a trial. It is, therefore, essential to be aware of PACE 1984, Code C, para 10, which sets out when a caution must be given. This is normally when there are grounds to suspect that a person is guilty of an offence.[a] A caution is not required to establish his identity or ownership of a vehicle. No caution is required for obtaining information in accordance with any relevant statutory requirement. Therefore, requests for information pursuant to s 29 of the Trade Descriptions Act 1968, or s 93 of the Control of Pollution Act 1974, for example, do not require a caution. On the contrary, should a caution be given, this would amount to a reasonable excuse for refusing to comply.[b]

11.13.2 Police officers and investigators are required to comply with PACE 1984,[c] but not any lay person. Statements made by the defendant to a press officer or any other prosecution witness, are admissible without a caution. For defendants who will not attend an interview, but will talk freely to the press, this evidence is not only admissible, but may also be crucial. The press employees tend to retain their notes. These notes have proved to be reliable evidence. Steps should therefore be taken to ensure that this evidence is admitted by calling the press as witnesses and asking them to produce their notes of interview.

(a) *Dilks v Tilley* [1979] RTR 459; no caution was required at the scene of an accident from a police officer, as he was at the 'gathering information' stage. See, also, *Pennycuick v Lees* [1991] TLR, 13 December, which established that there is no rule of law that required a suspect to be cautioned before any question is put to him.
(b) *R v Page* [1995] TLR, 20 November.
(c) PACE 1984, s 67(9).

PREPARATION FOR THE HEARING

12.1 UNCONTESTED HEARING – GUILTY PLEAS

12.1.1 *Preparation*

Preparation is a key factor with an emphasis on a thorough knowledge of the facts to enable a prompt response to any important detail that may not have been fairly put by an opposing advocate.

12.1.2 *The law*

Assuming that research has previously been made into the particular area of law it is useful for the advocate to be armed with a summary of the law, that is, a list of authorities as set out at Appendix 17 in the event that a legal point arises.

12.1.3 *Drafting a statement/summary of facts*

At the hearing of a guilty plea, a pre-prepared 'statement of facts' will be presented to the court in the format prescribed by the Magistrates' Court Forms Rules, if the written plea procedure is used under s 12 of the Magistrates' Court Act (MCA) 1980. If the written plea procedure is not adopted the formalities on the written plea form are not required. Guidance as to the content of a statement of facts is set out below.

1.2.1.3.1 *The department's prosecution summary*

A starting point for the person drafting a statement of facts is the summary that is usually included in the prosecution report. This should provide a global view of the evidence and identify the important features as perceived by the client department.

12.1.3.2 *The prosecution are confined to statement of facts in s 12 of the MCA 1980 proceedings*

When drawing up a statement of facts, it is important to bear in mind that the prosecution will be confined to this if the written plea[a] procedure is adopted. If photographs or any other documents are to be produced to the court, these should be appended to the statement as exhibits.

12.1.3.3 *Content and objectives of the statement of facts*

The offences and public interest

If an introduction is necessary, it should be short, and ideally no more than two or three lines. This can include a summary of the offence if the charges or legislation are complex. In simpler cases, there is no need to recite the legislation as this will be apparent from the court list that will be before the magistrates. Local authority prosecutions are often unfamiliar to the

---

(a) By Magistrates' Courts (Procedure) Act 1998, s 9, Criminal Justice Act (CJA) 1967 statements may be used instead of a 'statement of facts' by amending the MCA 1980, s 12(3). *NB* not yet in force. The authors are not aware of any proposals to implement this procedure.

magistrates. It is suggested that it is appropriate to set out the public interest criteria and/or the mischief that the legislation is seeking to address if this is not apparent.

12.1.3.4 *Fairness*

The overall objective is one of fairness, that is, to present a fair and balanced version of events to include all aggravating and mitigating circumstances. The format and style of the statement should enable the court readily to identify and evaluate the important features, both for and against. If the significance of such a feature is only apparent from a fact mentioned in another context, special care is required to ensure that the point is not lost. The statement should be drafted in a dispassionate manner.

12.1.3.5 *Precision and clarity*

All material should be set out with precision and clarity. Failure in this regard will often result in prejudice to either one party or the other.

12.1.3.6 *Brevity and relevance*

Aspirations to include all material facts should not be at the expense of brevity. A short statement containing only the necessary information for sentencing purposes is more effective and enables the court to concentrate on the main issues that affect sentencing. This requires a judicious approach from the draftsperson, who should dismiss any facts which are not relevant to an issue in the case, unless it is necessary for continuity purposes. The relevance of issues should then be condensed into short sentences whilst, at the same time, complying with the criteria in this chapter.

12.1.3.7 *Sample charging*

On the principle that a person can only be sentenced for an offence[a] that has been admitted, or proved the statement should be drafted accordingly. If, for example, the informations are for counterfeit t-shirts which are representative of a larger number of items seized, the statement should only contain items which have been mentioned in the charges (this would not prevent a number of items being referred to in one charge, provided this does not amount to duplicity). This rule would not apply to items that the defendant has admitted as being counterfeit.[b]

12.1.3.8 *Previous convictions, cautions and warnings*

Warnings are sometimes the by-product of previous offences. Whereas warnings are essential to the sentencing process and should be included, no reference can be made to earlier offences unless they are made the subject of charges. Previous convictions and evidence of bad character should not be included in the statement/summary of facts, but can be mentioned at the end of the prosecutor's address to the court. Previous convictions, etc, should not

---

(a) *R v Kidd* [1997] TLR, 21 July.
(b) *R v Russen* (1981) 3 Cr App R(S) 134.

be confused with aggravating features that should be included.(c) One can be distinguished from the other by the existence of an evidential link to the proceedings that can be found in the aggravating feature.

12.1.3.9 *Effect on the victim and damage to society*

If a person sustains personal injury as a consequence of an offence, this is admissible provided an expert's report has been made available to the defence in advance of a hearing.(d) In the case of counterfeit goods, reference can be made to financial damage to the producer of the genuine product and to the quality of the goods falsely described. These are, however, questions of fact and degree and reference to damage that is too remote may raise questions of the ability of the prosecution to be dispassionate.

12.1.3.10 *Dealing with mitigation*

Not all defendants are represented and, therefore, cannot be expected to mention all the mitigating circumstances. According to the solicitors' Code of Practice, prosecuting solicitors are to be regarded as ministers of justice rather than advocates in the cause. The statement/summary of facts should, therefore, include a fair account of the mitigation. If the defendant's statement contains mitigation that differs from the prosecution's version of the events, this should be made apparent to the prosecutor. The overall effect of the statement/summary of facts should not be one of undue gravity and the overall objective should be to present a balanced version of the facts. This should include any explanations given by the defendant. In seeking to put forward a balanced version of events, care should be taken not only to protect the defendant's position, but also the interests of justice.

12.1.3.11 *Hearsay and other statements*

Any relevant statements made by the defendant will be admissible. A Police and Criminal Evidence Act 1984 caution, however, is a necessary pre-requisite for any statement made to an officer. It would not usually be appropriate to include every statement made by the defendant. Only matters that are likely to affect sentencing should be included, for example, that which tends to indicate culpability or mitigation. Care should be taken before including statements made by other persons as questions of relevance and admissibility may arise.

12.1.3.12 *Other matters for inclusion*

The statement should include any financial gain made by the defendant. Exhibits do not need to be enclosed unless they are to be presented to the court, for example, photographs. As a general rule, the statement should follow a chronological sequence and end by claiming costs and referring to any applications for compensation or forfeiture orders sought.(e)

(c) *R v Nottingham Crown Court ex p DPP* [1996] 1 Cr App R(S) 283.
(d) *R v Hobstaff* (1993) 14 Cr App R(S) 605 and *R v O'S* (1993) 14 Cr App R(S) 63.
(e) *R v Emmett* [1999] TLR, 15 October – crown required to notify defence before making application for costs. The courts tend to apply the same reasoning to forfeiture orders and compensation.

12.1.4 Checklist

1. Introduction – public interest/mischief legislation is directed at.
2. The facts including aggravating features.
3. The investigation and mitigation and reference to documents to be presented to the court, for example, photographs.
4. Previous convictions, cautions and warnings.
5. Reference to other applications, for example, costs, forfeiture, compensation.

12.1.5 MCA 1980 procedure

In the event that the matter is summary, such as an offence under the Local Government (Miscellaneous Provisions) Act 1976 and the defendant has pleaded guilty in writing under the MCA 1980 guilty plea procedure, the advocate must read only from the statement of facts[a] in order to comply with the procedure. It is not acceptable to depart from the statement unless there is no prejudice to the defendant and prejudice is a matter for the court to decide.

It may be considered good practice for the prosecution to rely on both the MCA 1980 and CJA 1967 procedure in summary matters in order that the case can be proved in the defendant's absence in the event that he does not attend the first hearing. In this manner, public money may be saved for the authority and the court in avoiding unnecessary adjournments.

12.1.6 CJA procedure, advance disclosure and election

In the event that the case is an either way matter, it is necessary for the defendant to attend court (if the defendant is a limited company the case may still proceed without representation).[aa]

12.1.7 Service of CJA statements

In accordance with the Magistrates' Courts (Advance Information) Rules 1985, r 3, the prosecution must in all either way matters serve a copy of all CJA 1967 statements to be relied upon by them or a summary thereof. In practical terms, most prosecutors prefer to serve copies of the statements, exhibits and records of interview.

12.1.8 Failure to comply with advance disclosure

Failure to include evidence in the advance disclosure is likely to result in it being objected to when it is presented to the court. In summary cases, the defence does not have a right to advance disclosure,[ba] although he would be entitled to any evidence which might reasonable assist his defence. In either way cases, either a summary or all the statements are required to be served. If the prosecution proposes to rely on important evidence that is not included in the advance disclosure, it is advisable to serve a notice of further evidence in the form of

---

[a] By Magistrates' Courts (Procedure) Act 1998, s 1, CJA 1967 statements may be used instead of a 'statement of facts' by amending MCA 1980, s 12(3). *NB* not yet in force.

[aa] MCA 1980, Sched 3, para 3.

[ba] *R v Stratford Justices ex p Imbert* [1999] TLR, 25 February; neither did this amount to an unfair trial in terms of the European Convention on Human Rights. *The Attorney General's Guidelines* now take the contrary view.

statement. In the authors' view, the best practice is to serve all statements, exhibits and records of interviews in both summary and either way prosecutions. Unless the defendant has refused to be interviewed, this approach is often taken. The advantage being that, if the defendant's position is comprehensively investigated at interview, the prosecution is less likely to be taken by surprise and a guilty plea is more likely if the evidence is sufficiently compelling.

12.1.9 *The mode of trial and statement/summary of facts*

For an either way matter, there is now no need for the advocate to address the court as to mode of trial in the event of a guilty plea. The case is automatically heard before the magistrates' court. The court will then pass sentence unless, after having heard the facts and antecedents, it is decided to commit the case to the crown court for sentencing. If the case is to be adjourned, the court will often still require representations from both parties as to venue as set out in more detail below.

12.1.10 *Plea before venue/election and the clerk's duties*[a]

The clerk of the court will invite the defendant to indicate a plea. If the plea indicated is guilty, then the court does not now move onto mode of trial and the hearing will proceed. In the event of a not guilty plea or a refusal to indicate a plea, plea before venue will be dealt with. In those circumstances, a prosecutor should be able to outline reasons for the prosecution's suggested venue. The reasons should be based upon the seriousness of the case, that is, aggravating circumstances and the powers of sentencing held by the court on summary trial in the event of a conviction.[b] If, taking the case at its highest, the court has in all probability adequate sentencing powers, in the circumstances, the prosecution should recommend summary trial.

12.1.11 *Prosecution address*

The court having determined its choice of venue and the defendant having elected trial before the magistrates, the prosecutor may then make representations. The Law Society's Guidance to prosecution solicitors is that evidence should be presented 'dispassionately and with scrupulous fairness', but ensuring that all relevant points are made which supports the prosecution including aggravating factors. See above for more details of the content of the prosecution's address.

12.1.12 *Preparation of address*

It is considered good practice for prosecution advocates to prepare a written statement/summary of facts prior to the hearing which contains all relevant points and include all aggravating factors. There may be some advantage if the statement is forwarded to clients beforehand. This enables the investigatory department to mention anything that they believe ought to be added to the address.

(a) Criminal Procedure and Investigation Act 1996, s 49.
(b) See *National Mode of Trial Guidelines* 1995.

12.1.13 *Defence mitigation*

At the conclusion of the prosecutor's address, the defence advocate is entitled to mitigate. The prosecutor should be aware that the defence advocate is under an obligation not to mislead the Court. A prosecutor may correct misleading information put to the court. The most appropriate time is usually at the close of the address made on behalf of the defendant. See Chapter 14 for details setting out the obligations of the defence advocate.

12.1.14 *Costs applications*

Finally, it is essential that realistic prosecution costs, that is, investigative and legal, are sought and these should be supported by breakdowns. See Chapters 16 and 17. An award of costs is in the absolute discretion of the court. Prior notification of the costs should be given to the defence.

12.1.15 *Proceedings in the absence of the defendant*

In the event that a defendant (an individual) does not attend in answer to a summons on an either way matter, the case cannot be dealt with in the defendant's absence, unless the defendant is a limited company.[a] A warrant for the arrest of the defendant is usually sought in these circumstances (usually with bail on the first occasion of non-attendance and without bail if this does not secure his attendance). The court is normally willing to grant the application if the offence is imprisonable. The information is substantiated on oath and service of the summons is established on oath or by way of a certificate of service within a reasonable time of the hearing.[b] If the offence is not punishable by imprisonment, a warrant for an indictable offence can still be issued provided that the written information is substantiated on oath.[c] The use of the word 'substantiated' rather than 'prove' is significant. This evidence can be given by a person who is not a witness to the proceedings. Before the Crown Prosecution Service conducted criminal proceedings this was often undertaken by the police officer having conduct of the file. This is presumably the reason why the courts have not objected to the solicitor carrying out this function, if the officer in charge of the case is not in attendance. If the defendant fails to attend on a summary matter, the case is normally dealt with in his absence.[d]

(a) See the MCA 1980, Sched 3, para 3, that allows mode of trial to be dealt with in the absence of a representative from a company. There is therefore no reason why any case, be it summary or either way, cannot proceed in the absence of any representation from a company.

(b) MCA 1980, s 13.

(c) *Ibid*, s 1.

(d) See *ibid*, s 12 for the procedure to be adopted if a guilty plea is entered by post or the procedure pursuant to the CJA 1967, s 9, for proof in absence of the accused by reading the statements. (The court will often require long statements to be summarised rather than read verbatim. The advocate should, therefore, prepare himself for this possibility.) The CJA statements must be served at least seven days prior to the hearing, or this will prevent the case being dealt with in the absence of the defendant.

12.2 A CONTESTED HEARING

12.2.1 Introduction

Preparation is without doubt a key factor in effectively presenting a trial in court. This includes having a thorough knowledge of the whole file and all the relevant law. The checklist in Chapter 3 is a useful management tool for ensuring that the all the elements of the offence are included in the evidence.

12.2.2 Research – the law

The most useful authorities are not always referred to in footnotes of legal texts and extensive research into a statutory provision each time an advocate prepares for court is not the most effective use of time. It is suggested that the advocate prepares a standard list of authorities, in the form outlined in Appendix 17, which can be used on all subsequent proceedings of the same nature. An advocate will, hopefully, find the approach useful, that is, to collate all useful case references in one document and add to it whenever the opportunity arises. A pro-active approach to this is more preferable. When time is spent researching the law, the list of authorities is updated. The information can be shared with colleagues and clients.

12.2.3 Review the informations and evidence

Check that all the elements of the offence are included in the information, although this may not be strictly necessary in every case. Ensure that the evidence supports each element of the offence as referred to in the information and that the date, time and place are correctly stated.

Typographical errors and minor defects can be amended before close of the prosecution's case. See s 123 of the MCA 1980, in Chapter 13. To avoid the cost of a potential adjournment, advocates are advised to notify all parties of any proposed amendments as soon as possible and amend sooner rather than later.

12.2.4 Agree s 10 of the CJA 1967 formalities

Bearing in mind that as a general rule the prosecution is required to prove every element of the offence, court time and sometime attendance by witnesses can be saved by agreeing formalities or non-contentious matters pursuant to s 10 of the CJA 1967. Alternatively, defence solicitors are sometimes prepared to accept s 9 statements in their entirety. This does not amount to agreement of the evidence contained in the s 9 statement and the defence are still entitled to call evidence[a] to rebut the statement, unless they have agreed not to dispute the evidence.

12.2.5 Prepare opening address to court

The format of an opening address is very much a question of style. It should, however, have a logical structure to it and the following headings might assist in formulating a structure to the speech:

(a) Introduction/background (public interest);

---

[a] *Lister v Quaife* [1983] 2 All ER 29.

(b) facts;[a]

(c) law;

(d) submissions upon the law and facts (optional).

12.2.5.1 *Introduction/background (public interest)*

This should outline a brief synopsis of what the case is all about in layman's terms. It might also make reference to the public interest criteria for taking the proceedings. See Public Interest Matrix, Appendix 7.

12.2.5.2 *Facts (elements of the offence)*

On the whole, this section should be limited to the facts necessary to prove the case, save for the salient aggravating and mitigating circumstances. It should also mention which witness will prove those facts.

12.2.5.3 *Legal submissions*

It is often tempting to make extensive references to case law during an opening address. Lay magistrates on the whole do not seem to welcome this approach and the appellate courts have deprecated the practice of reading long passages from the law reports. It is normally more effective to refer to the general principles that arise from the various cases and link them to the facts of the case. This enables the law to be more easily applied to the facts and the overall effect is a shorter and clearer address to the court. If the opposing advocate disagrees with the general principals, a more detailed exposition of the law can be provided at the close of the proceedings.

12.2.5.4 *Submissions relating to the interpretation of facts*

These can be made at any time or at the close of the address. These are often reasons put before the court explaining why certain important issues should be resolved in favour of maker. For example, an advocate may wish to submit reasons why certain evidence may corroborate or lend colour to a witness statement.

Having drafted out the opening address in the first instance, it is usually worth looking at it again to estimate the overall length of the address. Most opening addresses in local authority prosecutions can be delivered between five and 30 minutes. The address can sometimes be shortened by putting some of the less salient issues to the defence witnesses in the form of questions. In this way, the address remains short and the case should improve as it progresses. For example, a submission that a booking record in a plying for hire charge is incomplete or inconsistent with other evidence could be put to the booking clerk. Assuming, of course, that the prosecuting advocate knows that the booking clerk will be giving evidence.

As a matter of practice, it is often more effective to concentrate on a few good reasons which support your case rather than peppering the court with a multitude of submissions.

---

[a] Some lawyers prefer to put the law before the facts so that the legal significance of the facts are immediately apparent.

12.2.5.5 *Prepare examination in chief*

It is essential that all the elements of the offence are included in the witness statements. One method of ensuring this is to list the elements of the offence under the headings to the relevant witnesses and add to those lists any other important evidence. Another method is simply to highlight the relevant passages in the witness statements. Presenting the evidence in a chronological fashion is easier for the court to follow and helps a witness to recall events easily.

12.2.6 Cross-examination

12.2.6.1 *List of issues/questions*

Prepare a list of questions or issues for each defence witness and add to this as the evidence in chief raises further questions.

12.2.6.2 *Scope of questions*

The questioning should touch upon all issues which the advocate disagrees with, although failure to cross-examine on an issue does not mean that it is automatically accepted.[a]

12.2.6.3 *Use of open and closed questions*

Proper use should be made of 'open' and 'closed' questions. Closed questions, such as 'the defendant has been a friend of yours for 10 years', generally require a yes or no answer and can be used to elicit points in favour of the cross-examiner which are not in dispute. It is also a technique used when it is anticipated that open questions might give a witness the opportunity to damage your case. Open questions, such as, how was a person dressed on a particular day, give a witness much more latitude. They do not generally require a yes or no answer. They are often used to prompt a witness into giving information on a subject area that is not potentially damaging to your case. This type of questioning is frequently used to tie a witness down to a particular version of events by asking him to supply details. It then becomes difficult for him to change his version of events without damaging his credibility.

12.2.6.4 *Detailed questioning*

Asking a witness 'open questions' that require minute details of his version of events can be very damaging to two or more opposing witnesses who are purporting to give the same evidence. Whereas witnesses can collaborate to concoct a common story, they do not always consider the events in minute detail.

12.2.7 *Meeting with lay witnesses*

12.2.7.1 *Preparation of lay witnesses*

12.2.7.2 Most lay witnesses will not have been inside a magistrates' court, let alone given evidence. It is therefore essential that steps are taken to put the lay witnesses at ease and prepare them to give evidence so that they are fully

---

[a] *O'Connell v Adams* [1973] Crim LR 113 and *R v Secretary of State for the Home Office ex p Patel (Dhirubhai Gordhanbhai)* [1986] Imm AR 515.

aware of what will happen, what is expected of them and to ensure that they are not taken by surprise. It is recommended that a meeting is arranged with the witnesses before the hearing preferably at court, so that they can be taken into the court room and shown where they will give evidence. The seating positions of everyone in the courtroom should be identified and the role of the magistrates and justices' clerk in particular should be explained. The whole procedure of giving evidence should be explained to the lay witness, including the type of non-leading questions that can only be asked by the advocate who called them. These witnesses should be advised to direct all answers to the magistrates and should be given guidance on what to do if they do not fully understand a question, for example, they might ask that the question be repeated or simply say that they do not fully understand the question.[a]

12.2.7.3 *Re-interviewing witnesses*

If as a result of receiving disclosure from the defendant there is some merit in re-interviewing witnesses for the prosecution, this is acceptable,[aa] although it is also appropriate to notify the defence of any new information which comes to light as a result of further questioning.

12.2.7.4 *Avoid coaching the witnesses*

Advocates should avoid rehearsing or coaching the witnesses but it is acceptable to make provision for the witnesses to read their statements or contemporaneous notes prior to giving evidence.[ba]

12.2.8 *All witnesses – inadmissible hearsay*

If there is anything in a statement that is inadmissible hearsay, the witness attention should be drawn to it and be given a very brief explanation why it should not be repeated in court. Finally, all witnesses should be given the opportunity to ask questions of the advocate.

(a) See Chapters 15 and 16 and Appendix 19 for witness checklist.
(aa) *R v Nadir, R v Turner* [1993] TLR, 2 July.
(ba) *R v Richardson* [1971] 2 All ER 773, but see limitations in *R v Da Silva* (1990) Cr App R 233 and *R v Price (Christopher Michael)* unreported 96/1429 which followed *Da Silva* and *R v South Ribble Magistrates ex p Cochrane* [1996] TLR, 24 June which adopted a much more liberal approach in allowing a witness to refresh his memory from a statement which he had read before giving evidence but not digested.

CHAPTER 13

OBJECTION HANDLING AND DEALING WITH DEFENCE APPLICATIONS

13.1 GENERAL PRINCIPLES

Inexperienced advocates often provide too many opportunities for the opposition to object. This can undermine both their confidence and their perceived standing with the court. It is, therefore, essential for an advocate to protect themselves from valid objections as far as possible by following the basic rules of procedure.

13.2 EXAMINATION IN CHIEF AND CROSS EXAMINATION

13.2.1 *Leading questions should not be asked of one's own witness*

Leading questions are any questions that unfairly suggest the answer that is required. This is not generally considered to be an absolute rule. Advocates will often lead the witnesses on preliminary matters that are not disputed. Bearing in mind that a prosecutor will not always know all the areas of dispute, leading questions should be avoided on any issue that might be contentious.

The workings of the principle[a] can present problems even for the most experienced advocate. It is, of course, permissible to lead on a fact that has already been established, but not otherwise – for example, in a plying for hire prosecution, an advocate may ask the question: 'How long was the taxi waiting outside the public house?' This question may only be asked if the witness has already given evidence that the defendant was waiting outside a public house.

13.2.2 *Questions must be relevant*

Advocates for the prosecution are often expected by their clients to refer to a wide spectrum of events that tend to put the defendant's case in a bad light. Sometimes, these will amount to aggravating features[aa] of the offence charged, which are admissible. Examples of irrelevant material will often include conduct of a friend or witness of the defendant or evidence of matters that the defendant has not been charged with.[b]

(a) It is elaborated on by the case of *R v Patel* [1996] 3 September CA No 96/4220/5, Issue 9, 14 November 1996, Archbold News, which establishes that as a general rule, a question only requiring an answer of yes or no is likely to be a leading question.

(aa) *R v Nottingham Crown Court ex p DPP* [1996] 1 Cr App R(S) 283. See, also, *R v Sandhu* [1997] TLR, 2 January, in which it was held that evidence beyond proof of elements necessary for that offence was inadmissible at trial. Concern that the evidence would adversely sway the minds of the jury was given as a reason for the decision. Presumably, this case should not prevent such material being admissible for sentencing purposes.

(b) *R v Kidd* [1997] TLR, 21 July CA, advises that judges cannot take into account conduct not proved or admitted when sentencing. Guidance on this case should be read by prosecutors who intend to lay sample charges.

In cross-examination, the question of relevance often arises where the advocate is seeking to lead the opposing witness down a certain route whilst, at the same time, closing off all other avenues of escape. If the relevance of the question was obvious to the witness, a truthful answer might not be forthcoming. The answer to a challenge in this situation could be that the relevance of the question will become apparent very shortly if further questioning is permissible in the interim.

13.2.3 *References can only be made to evidence that is admissible*

This naturally precludes hearsay and character evidence, whether or not amounting to a previous conviction – see Chapter 6.

13.2.4 *Questions should not be argumentative*

The Court of Appeal[a] has given examples of certain types of questions that are argumentative and should not be put to the witness. These include the following:

- Can you suggest any reason why the girl should invent the story?;
- Do you regard her story as blackmail?;
- Do you agree that she is trying to shield some boy?

There are a number of other questions that seem to have common usage, but have been deprecated by the Court of Appeal. These include:

- I suggest to you that ... ; or
- Is your evidence to be taken as suggesting that ... ?;
- Do you ask the jury to believe ... ?

13.2.5 *In examining a witness, an advocate must not repeat what some other witness has said*

This rule also applies to what a witness is expected to say. Defence solicitors have an obligation to put their case to the prosecution witnesses in cross-examination and can easily fall into this trap. However, failure to challenge evidence in cross-examination does not require the court to accept that evidence.[aa]

13.2.6 *Avoid asking a witness for his opinion unless he is an expert*

Whereas the definition of an 'expert' has a broad meaning, the witness must, in fact, be giving evidence as an expert. Environmental health officers, for example, will usually be regarded as experts. Questions to these witnesses must, of course, be confined to their field of expertise. As a fail safe rule, it is advisable to avoid the use of the word 'opinion' when examining witnesses who are not experts.

13.2.7 *Emotive language*

Prosecuting advocates should be regarded as ministers of justice rather than advocates in the cause. The case should be proved on the facts without reference to emotive language. Prosecutors should not seek to improve the prospects of conviction by presenting a case in a manner that is likely to incite sympathy for the victim. However, the court should nonetheless be informed of effect that the offence has had on the victim for the purpose of sentencing. This issue is set out in

---

(a) *R v Baldwin* [1925] All ER 402.
(aa) *R v Secretary of State for the Home Office ex p Patel* [1986] Imm AR 515, *O'Connell v Adams* [1973] Crim LR 113.

Chapter 13: Objection Handling and Dealing with Defence Applications

more detail later in this chapter. A prosecutor should not be striving for a conviction at all costs.

13.3 COMMON OBJECTIONS AND DEFENCE APPLICATIONS

13.3.1 *Application of no case to answer*

The basis upon which a no case to answer submission is set out in practice note PN [1961] 1 All ER 448 as follows:

> Where there has been no evidence to prove an essential element in the alleged offence.
>
> Where the evidence adduced by the prosecution has been so discredited as a result of cross-examination or is so manifestly unreliable that no reasonable tribunal could safely convict on it ... if however a submission is made that there is no case to answer, *the decision should depend not so much on whether the adjudicating tribunal (if compelled to do so) would at that stage convict or acquit* but on whether the evidence is such that a reasonable tribunal *might* convict.
>
> To a submission that an element of the offence is not made out it might be argued that it is not necessary to prove beyond all reasonable doubt at the half-way stage of the proceedings that every element of the offence is made out to that degree and therefore the mere existence of a doubt as to any element of the offence is not necessarily sufficient for he defence to succeed in its application if the court is of the opinion that they might convict on the evidence.[a]
>
> An alternative to the submission that an element of the offence has not been made out is to make an application before the court to call further evidence if an element of the offence has been inadvertently missed out. The general rule is that evidence should be called at the proper time.[b]
>
> The exceptions to this rule are matters arising *ex improviso* with leave of the court[c] and the calling of fresh evidence that has not previously been available.[d] Evidence inadvertently missed by the prosecution.[e]

(a) See *R v Galbraith* [1981] 2 All ER 1060, in which Lord Lane CJ advised that where on one possible view of the facts, there is evidence on which the jury 'could' properly come to the conclusion that the defendant is guilty and then the judge should allow the matter to be tried by the jury.

(b) *R v Day* (1940) 27 Crim App R 168.

(c) *R v Frost* [1839] 9 CLP 129. Fresh evidence that has not previously been available.

(d) *R v Doran* (1972) 56 Cr App R 429. See, also, *James v South Glamorgan CC* (1992) *The Independent*, 6 January. Evidence inadvertently missed from the prosecution.

(e) The general principle is that it is the duty of the prosecution to call its evidence at the proper time, however, in the case of *R v Munnery* (1992) 94 Cr App R 164, CA, the court allowed an adjournment for the Crown to obtain evidence to rectify an alleged lacuna in its case. See, also, *R v Francis* [1990] TLR, 31 January, (1990) 91 Cr App R 271. *Mathews v Morris* [1981] Crim LR 495 (prosecution re-opening case after omitting to produce statement). In the more recent case of *Jolley v DPP*, LSG 5 May 2000, it was decided that it is now beyond argument that there was a general discretion to permit the calling of evidence at a later stage, which extended in the magistrates' court up to the time when the bench retired; that before exercising that discretion the court would look carefully at the interests of justice overall and, in particular, the risk of any prejudice whatsoever to the defendant; that the discretion would be sparingly exercised, but it was doubtful whether it assisted any longer to speak of 'exceptional circumstances'; that each case had to be considered on its own facts, and in the circumstances the magistrates had been entitled to admit the evidence.

Furthermore, it seems that the discretion to allow further evidence to answer an application of no case to answer is not limited to the well established principles of:

(a) evidence arising *ex improviso* and

(b) cases where what has been omitted is a mere formality as distinct from a central issue.(f)

To a submission that the evidence has been discredited as a result of cross-examination or that it is unreliable, it might be argued that the fact that it has been discredited and/or unreliable is not enough. The damage to the prosecution has to be to the extent that no reasonable tribunal could safely convict.

13.3.2 *Exclusion of unfair evidence*

The submission in these circumstances is that admission of the evidence would have such an adverse effect on the fairness of the proceedings that the court ought not to admit it. Note that Police and Criminal Evidence Act (PACE) 1984 allows evidence to be excluded on the basis of fairness of the proceedings. It seems, at least arguable, that there discretion to exclude material on the grounds that it was obtained improperly or by unfair means is to be used sparingly if at all.(a)

Nothing in s 78 of PACE 1984 suggests that the prosecution should be punished for breach of the code etc. It also envisages that the admission of the evidence may have an adverse effect on the proceedings and yet still be admitted.(b) Fairness of the proceedings in the context of s 78 of PACE 1984 must have regard not only to the interests of the accused, but also the interests of the prosecution and the interests of justice as a whole.(c)

13.3.3 *Claims of* agent provocateur/*entrapment*

Entrapment is no defence to a criminal charge although convictions based on the activities of an *agent provocateur* may qualify for mitigation.(aa) The European Convention of Human Rights may restrict this rule if persuasion was used to secure the commission of an offence, however, given that inciting a person to

---

(f) *R v Francis* [1990] TLR, 31 January; (1990) 91 Cr App R 271.

(a) PACE 1984, s 78.

(b) *R v Walsh* (1990) 91 Cr App R 161. The court of appeal advised: 'So far as a defendant is concerned, it seems to us to follow that to admit evidence against him which has been obtained in circumstances where these standards have not been met cannot but have an adverse effect on the fairness of the proceedings. This does not mean of course that in every case of a significant or substantial breach of s 58 or the code of practice the evidence concerned will automatically be excluded. Section 78 does not so provide. The task of the court is not merely to consider whether there would be an adverse effect on the fairness of the proceedings, but such an adverse effect that justice requires the evidence to be excluded.' As regards evidence obtained by trickery the courts do not appear to be consistent. In *R v Murphy* [1965] NI 138, the Northern Ireland Courts Martial Appeal court said: 'A trick is as old as a constable in plain clothes ... and the day has not come when it would be safe to say that the law could be enforced without resort to it.' Having regard to this case, the Court might be invited to consider whether or not there is a causal link between the admission of the evidence and the effect on the fairness of the proceedings and ask whether or not the prejudicial effect outweighs its probative value.

(c) *R v Gordon Mitchel Stewart* [1999] Crim LR 746.

(aa) See *Williams and O'Hara v DPP* [1993] Crim LR 775 and *R v Sang* [1980] AC 402. See, also, *Nottingham CC v Amin* [1999] TLR, 2 December, in which the court refused to exclude evidence of entrapment in a plying for hire case.

commit an offence that he would not otherwise do is wrong, it might appear that the convention has little to add.

13.3.4 Informations bad for duplicity

This is an area of law that is not entirely consistent. If the court decides that the informations are duplicitous, this should not entail that the charge(s) should being dismissed. The correct approach is for the prosecution to be required to elect the charge that it intends to proceed with. See Chapter 10 on drafting informations for more detailed analysis.

13.3.4.1 Information/summons incorrect

13.3.4.2 General principles

In accordance with s 123(1) of the Magistrates' Courts Act (MCA) 1980, there can be no objection to the substance or form of an information or complaint or for any variance between it and the prosecution evidence,[a] *Stones Justices Manual* (1999 edn, para 1-424), puts errors into three classifications:

(1) errors which are 'so fundamental' which cannot be amended and cause the prosecution to fail;

(2) errors 'substantial enough to require amendment';

(3) errors so trivial that no amendment is required.

The words of s 123 of the MCA 1980 are extremely wide, however, prosecutors would be well advised to amend the information whenever there is a legitimate challenge, however trivial.[b] This may present convictions from being quashed in circumstances where a higher court recognises that an information could and should have been amended.[c] The sooner the amendment is applied for the less likely is the need for an adjournment. In essence, a court should allow an amendment even to a substantial and fundamental error unless the court finds (in the words of *Stones*) that the error

---

(a) MCA 1980, s 123(1): 'No objection shall be allowed to any information or complaint or to any summons or warrant to procure the presence of the defendant, for any defect in it in substance or in form, or for any variance between it and the evidence adduced on behalf of the prosecutor or complainant at the hearing of the information or complaints.' See, also, Magistrates' Courts Rules 1981, r 100(1) for content of information.

(b) *Garfield v Maddocks* [1974] 1 QB 7, Lord Widgery CJ: 'Those extremely wide words which on their face seem to legalise almost an discrepancy between the evidence and the information, have in fact always been given a more restricted meaning, and in modern times the Section is construed in this way, that if the variance between the evidence and the information is slight and does no injustice to the defence, the information may be allowed to stand notwithstanding the variance which occurred. On the other hand, if the variance is so substantial that it is unjust to the defendant to allow it to be adopted without prior amendment of the information, then the practice is for the court to require the prosecution to amend in order to bring their information into line. Once they do that, of course there is provision in s 100(2) (now MCA 1980, s 123(2)) whereby an adjournment can be ordered in the interests of the defence if the amendment requires him to seek an adjournment.'

(c) *Atterton v Browne* [1945] KB 122.

is 'so fundamental that it cannot be rescued'. An amendment may allege a different offence more than six months after the laying of the information.[d]

13.3.4.3 Absence of signature on summons

This is a minor defect and does not render the summons invalid.[a]

13.3.4.4 The wrong date or name in the information

The wrong date is always capable of amendment.[aa] An obvious misspelling of a name can be amended.[b] Generally speaking, the name on a summons cannot be changed.[c] However, an amendment to the defendant's name can be made if it alleged the same person but the wrong name.[d] Alterations to other names in the information, not being the defendant, may not be regarded as 'so fundamental'. The court may, therefore, allow an amendment but an adjournment in favour of the defence would be in order if he has been misled.[e] If the issue is one of identity, the courts tend to be against dock identifications in the crown court on the whole, however, there seems to be a greater willingness to allow this in the magistrates' court.[f] It would seem a little unfair to raise issues of identity for the first time at trial. Should this be made an issue without notice the judge is entitled to comment[g] and inferences may be drawn if the defendant was properly cautioned or no reference was made to this issue in 'defence statement' under the criminal procedure rules, if the matter is tried in crown court. The court may also take judicial notice of the due process of arrest, charge and bail to establish a *prima*

(d) *R v Scunthorpe Justices ex p M* [1998] TLR, 10 March; (1998) 162 JP 635. In this case, a charge of robbery was altered to common assault and theft. It was said that the proper test to be applied was whether both offences arose from the same or substantially the same facts, and if so, whether the amendment was in the interests of justice, having particular regard to the defendant's interests and also to the purpose of the time limit, which might be jeopardised by the need for an adjournment. However, an information could be amended, even to allege a different offence more than six months after it was laid.

(a) *R v Hay Halkett ex p Rush* [1929] 2 KB 431.

(aa) *Jevons v Cosmosair* (1998) 162 JP 68, *per* Mantel J:
> The question of the date, whether it be an information or summons or an indictment is always a matter capable of amendment and the mere fact that the date is wrongly stated, will seldom, if ever, be a matter which would lead a Court to hold that the charge was void.

See, also, *R v Godstone Justices ex p Secretary of State for the Environment* [1974] Crim LR 110, for the date of offence to be inserted after having been omitted altogether; *Exeter Corp v Heaman* (1877) 42 JP 503, wrong date and *R v Blackburn Justices ex p Holmes* (1999) *The Independent*, 29 November (date amended).

(b) *Jevons v Cosmosair* (1998) 162 JP 68, 'Mohan' could be corrected to read 'Mahon'. *Allan v Wiseman* [1975] RTR 217, name of Loach changed to Allan on an information.

(c) *Lawrence v Same* [1968] 1 All ER 1191, *City of Oxford Tramway Co v Sankey* (1890) 54 JPN 564; *R v Greater Manchester Justices ex p Aldi* (1995) 159 JP 717; *Marco T/A A & J Bull Containers v Metropolitan Police* [1984] RTR 24.

(d) *Dring v Mann* (1948) 112 JP 270; *Allan v Wiseman* [1975] RTR 217.

(e) *Morris v Lawrence* [1977] Crim LR 170.

(f) *North Yorkshire Trading Standards Department v Williams* (1995) 159 JP 383 established that the prosecution was not ordinarily entitled to rely upon dock identification however the more recent case of *Barnes v CC of Durham* [1997] TLR, 6 May is authority for the contrary view.

(g) *R v Alladice* [1988] TLR, 11 May established that 'it was high time that proper comment was permitted on the silence of a detainee when interviewed by police but who produced at trial an explanation or defence to the charge which the police had no chance to verify' the case also makes reference to fairness to prosecution and defence.

facie case that the person arrested was the defendant.[h] Furthermore, the court may allow an adjournment until the next day to allow identification evidence to be introduced after the prosecutions case had closed.[i]

13.3.4.5 *Failure to mention a negative in an information*

The information or complaint need not specify an exemption, proviso, excuse or qualification.[a] This is probably the only situation which does not call for every element of the offence to be included although case law is not entirely consistent in this area. The burden of proving the negative is on the defendant.[b] However, once a defendant has laid the evidential basis to prove a negative, it will be for the prosecution to prove otherwise beyond reasonable doubt.[c]

13.3.4.6 *Failure to state the correct offence*

The general rule is that the defendant cannot be convicted for a different offence from that stated in the information.[aa] However, an information can be amended to allege a different offence provided that the new offence alleges the 'same misdoing'.[ab] The court has also been known to amend an information to allege a different offence arising under the same section as the one charged.[ac] An amendment to the section cited has always been permitted.[d]

If the offence is described in ordinary language, there is no need to state all the elements of the offence.[e] However, it is advisable to mention every element of the offence in the summons.

(h) *Allen v Ireland* [1984] 1 WLR 903.
(i) *R v Munnery (Vincent)* (1994) Cr App R 164.
(a) Magistrates' Courts Rules 1981, r 4(3).
(b) MCA 1980, s 101. See, also, *R v Edwards* [1975] QB 27; *Buckman v Button* [1943] 2 All ER 82. *R v Oliver* [1943] 2 All ER 613. *Apothecaries Co v Bentley* (1824) Ry and M 159; *Turner v Johnston* (1886) 51 JP 22; *Williams v Russel* (1933) 97 JP 128; *R v Scott* (1921) 86 JP 69; and *R v Hunt* [1987] AE 352 where the rule was applied narrowly.
(c) *Polychronakis v Richards and Jerrom Ltd* [1997] TLR, 19 November where a defendant seeks to rely on a defence of reasonable excuse.
(aa) *Lawrence v Same* [1968] 2 QB 93. See, also, *R v Scunthorpe Justices ex p M and Another* [1998] TLR, 10 March, a case in which an information was amended to charge a different offence. The court endorsed this approach where the proposed amendment arose out of the same or substantially the same facts as gave rise to the original offence and the interests of justice favoured the amendment. This case is also authority for allowing an information to be amended out of time provided that it was laid within the time period.
(ab) *R v Scunthorpe Justices ex p M* [1998] TLR, 18 March; *Simpson v Roberts* [1984] TLR, 21 December.
(ac) *R v Newcastle-upon-Tyne Justices ex p John Bryce (Contractors) Ltd* [1976] 2 All ER 611. See, also, *Stones Justices Manual* (1998 edn), para 1-6043 which says 'the omission to state the section, or state it incorrectly, may be fatal', and also 'the information in the information'. See Victor Smith (162 JP 276) which advances a powerful argument that 'it seems highly unlikely that an omission to state the section of the act under which the prosecution is brought would, without more, be fatal'. Victor Smith refers to the authorities relied on by *Stones* (*Atterton v Browne* [1945] KB 122 and *Hunter v Coombs* [1962] 1 All ER 904) and points to additional reasons why the prosecution failed in those cases.
(d) *R v Eastbourne Justices ex p Kirsten* [1984] TLR, 22 December.
(e) See Magistrates' Court Rules 1981, r 100.

13.3.5 *Objections during opening address*

In the Crown Court if the defendant's counsel intends to object to evidence as being inadmissible he should inform the prosecutor beforehand[a] who should not mention that evidence in his opening speech. It is submitted that the same courtesy should be extended to the prosecutor in the magistrates' court. Preliminary or incidental matters should be decided as separate issues and not as a trial within the trial.[b]

13.3.6 *Defendant has not been charged with this offence*

Specimen charges

As a general rule, a court cannot take into account other similar charges that have not been proved or admitted.[aa] However, if it is clear from the defendant's statement that the matter for which he is charged with is not an isolated incident the court is entitled to take this into account when sentencing.[ab]

13.3.7 *Aggravating features which are not ingredients of the offence charged*

Aggravating features are admissible,[ba] presuming of course that they are either proved or admitted. Care should be taken when introducing this evidence at the trial stage. If the aggravating feature is necessary to prove the offence charged, it will be admissible. Evidence which goes beyond that which is necessary to prove the offence charged at the trial stage may result in the case being quashed on appeal.[bb] The reason for this is that it may adversely sway the minds of the tribunal of fact. It is therefore safer to introduce this evidence at the sentencing stage in most cases.

13.3.8 *Abuse of process*

It is becoming more common for defence advocates to argue that a case should be dismissed due to the delay of the prosecution. There is authority[ca] that enables a case to be dismissed for delay in circumstances where there has been compliance with the six months' statutory time period. Guidance on this issue has provided as follows:

> This power to stop a prosecution should only be used in exceptional circumstances
> ...
> It may be an abuse of process if either:

(a) *R v Lester* (1975) 63 Cr App R 144.
(b) *Stones Justices Manual* (2001 edn), para 1-464.
(aa) *R v Kidd* [1997] TLR, 21 July.
(ab) *R v Russen* (1981) 3 Cr App R(S) 134.
(ba) *R v Nottingham Crown Court ex p DPP* [1996] 1 Cr App R(S) 283, *per* Stuart Smith LJ: 'There is ample and varied authority also recalled in the judgment for the proposition that aggravating features of an offence, although not ingredients of that offence as defined, are to be taken into account in sentencing. It is an example of what is called "trite law".' This principle was also applied in *R v Ribas* (1976) 63 Cr App R 147.
(bb) *R v Sandhu* [1997] TLR, 2 January.
(ca) *Daventry DC v Olins* (1990) 154 JP 478.

Chapter 13: Objection Handling and Dealing with Defence Applications

(a) the prosecution have manipulated or misused the process of the court so as to deprive the defendant of a protection provided by the law or to take unfair advantage of a technicality; or

(b) on the balance of probability, the defendant has been or will be prejudiced in the preparation or conduct of his defence by delay on the part of the prosecution which is unjustifiable.[b]

Stays imposed on grounds of delay of for any other reason should only be employed in *exceptional circumstances*. If they were to become a matter of routine, it would only be a short time before the public, understandably, view the process with suspicion.

In principle, therefore, even where the delay can be said to be unjustifiable, the imposition of a permanent stay should be the exception rather than the rule. Even more rare should be cases where a stay can properly be proposed in the absence of any fault on the part of the complainant or prosecution. Delay due merely to the complexity of the case or contributed to or by the actions of the defendant himself should never be the foundation for a stay.

Also, this is also continuing in answer to the second question posed by the Attorney General, no stay should be imposed unless the Defendant shows, on the balance of probabilities, that owing to the delay he will suffer serious prejudice to the extent that no fair trial can be held ...[c]

It is not an abuse of process to prosecute a defendant after he has been cautioned by the police unless the particular circumstances of a case disclosed an abuse.[d] Alternatively, it would normally be an abuse to prosecute a defendant after informing him at an earlier stage that proceedings would not be taken.[e]

Although abuse of process is normally a point taken in favour of the defence, the ambit of the rule is not so confined. If the defendant manipulates the process of the court this can also amount to an abuse.[f]

The wide category of cases over which magistrates had jurisdiction included investigation of the *bona fides* of the prosecution or whether the prosecution had been instituted oppressively or unfairly.[g]

13.3.9 Objection to references about the effect of the offence on the victim

A practical example of this is objection to a medical report setting out the injury to a victim who sustained injuries as a consequence of an employer's breach of duty

---

(b) *R v Derby Crown Court ex p Brooks* (1985) Cr App R 164, p 168.
(c) *AG's Ref (No 1 of 1990)* [1992] 1 QB 630, p 643 G: This case was approved in *Tan v Cameron* [1992] 2 AC 205 and *R v South Tyneside Metropolitan BC ex p Mill Garages Ltd and Another* [1995] CO 2501/94. See, also, *R v Bradford Stipendiary Magistrates' Court ex p Daniel and Wood*, Lawtel 9/6/97; ILR 16/6/97. Unfairness had to be seen and considered in the context of the prosecution process, which required not only fairness to the accuses but also to victims, the state and to justice generally.
(d) See *Hayter v L* [1998] 1 WLR 854, although the facts are somewhat unusual.
(e) *R v Croydon Justices ex p Dean* [1993] 3 All ER 129.
(f) *R v Governor of Brixton Prison and Another ex p Osman* [1990] TLR, 17 December.
(g) *R v Belmarsh Magistrates' Court ex p Fiona Watts* [1999] 2 Cr App R 188.

under s 2 of the Health and Safety at Work etc Act 1974. This information should be introduced[a] at the sentencing stage (See *R v Sandhu* above.)

13.3.10 Autrefois convict, autrefois acquit

'A person cannot be tried for an offence if he has previously been acquitted or convicted of the same or substantially the same offence.'[aa] This area of the law is currently subject to review and may alter.

The above rule would not apply to a second charge if the first was dismissed due to its erroneous form and content.[b] For the rule to apply, an acquittal or conviction on the first charge must involve an acquittal or conviction on the second.[c]

The withdrawal of a summons with the consent of the justices on a preliminary point or in consequence of an informality in the proceedings is not equivalent to a dismissal or acquittal and is therefore not a bar to proceedings.[d]

13.3.11 *Double jeopardy*

This is an extension of the *autrefois* convict rule: 'A second trial involving the same or similar facts may in the discretion of the Court be stayed if to proceed would be oppressive or prejudicial and therefore an abuse of the process of the Court.'[ba]

13.3.12 *Requirement for originals*

Copies of statements contained in documents that are admissible as evidence in criminal proceedings may be admissible in evidence provided that they are authenticated in such manner as the court approves[ca] whether or not the original is in existence.

(a) *R v Hobstaff* (1993) 14 Cr App R 605 and *R v O'S* (1993) 14 Cr App R 632 establish that this evidence can be presented to the court, but the evidence must be available in proper form which can mean either an expert's report or witness statement or otherwise which must be served on the defence in advance to enable the Defendant to either contradict or take issue with the contents of the report. See, also, *R v Nottingham Crown Court ex p DPP* [1995] Crim LR 902, Stuart-Smith LJ who said that it was a cardinal principal of sentencing that the court should take into account, when considering the gravity of the offence and the appropriate sentence, the consequences on the victim. However, it was not necessary in all cases to add a more serious charge to reflect such conduct provided that the court's sentencing powers were adequate to reflect the actual gravity of the offending. See, also, *AG's Ref (No 1 of 1989)* [1989] 1 WLR 1117 and *R v Mussell* (1991) 155 JP 521 where the same view was taken.
(aa) *Stones Justices Manual* (2001 edn), para 1-66.
(b) *Ibid.*
(c) *R v King* (1897) 1 AB 214, 61 JP 329; explained and distinguished in *R v Barron* [1914] 2 KB 570, 78 JP 311; *Bannister v Clarke* [1920] 3 KB 598, 85 JP 12; and see *Connolly v DPP* [1964] AC 1254, [1964] 2 All ER 401, 128 JP 418; *R v Truro and South Powder Magistrates' Court ex p McCullagh* (1990) 155 JP 411, [1991] RTR 374.
(d) *Davis v Morton* [1913] 2 KB 479, 77 JP 223; *Owens v Minoprio* [1942] KB 193, [1942] 1 All ER 30, 106 JP 53; *R (McDonnell) v Tyrone Justices* [1912] 2 IR 44.
(ba) *Stones Justices Manual* (1999 edn), para 1-67.
(ca) Criminal Justice Act 1988, s 27 (which came into force in April 1989 – see SI 1989/264) as amended by the Criminal Procedure and Investigations Act 1996.

Chapter 13: Objection Handling and Dealing with Defence Applications

13.3.13 *Photographic evidence*

It is not necessary to call the photographer or some other person to prove that the photographs showed what in fact takes place as depicted.[a]

13.3.14 *Prosecution re-interviewing witnesses*

This is permissible after receipt of the defence statement provided the any new evidence is disclosed to the defence.[aa]

13.3.15 *Reference to warnings on a guilty plea*

These are admissible.[ab]

(a) See *R v Lambert* [1967] Crim LR 480 in which it was said (on facts in which the defendant was found in possession of photographs showing him committing offences) that to suggest that the photographs might have been faked was far fetched.

(aa) *R v Nadir, R v Turner* [1993] TLR, 2 July.

(ab) *R v F Howe & Son (Engineers) Ltd* [1999] 2 All ER 249 and *R v Supremeplan Ltd* [2001] 1 Cr App R(S) 71.

CHAPTER 14

OBLIGATIONS OF THE DEFENCE ADVOCATE

14.1 INTRODUCTION

The authors have set out below the obligations which the prosecution can expect of a defence advocate. The sources of the materials are primarily the *Solicitor's Code of Conduct and the Code of Conduct for the Bar of England and Wales* (6th edn) and case law where indicated. The overall objective of both codes must be to lay down standards of professional practice. To quote from the CCBE (the Council of the Bars and Law Societies of the European Community) reported in the LSG, 28 June 1989, Code of Conduct 1.2.2: 'The particular rules of each bar and law society nevertheless are based on the same values and in most cases demonstrate a common foundation.'

One might argue that the variation in roles between solicitor and counsel and their obligations to each other is one reason for continuing to apply different codes of practice. On the other hand, it would seem inequitable that an advocate for the defence should have different obligations to the prosecution depending on whether he is a solicitor or counsel. In reality, this is not likely to be the case. Although it seems that the Code of Conduct for the bar sets out the obligations of advocates in court in greater detail, it is submitted that many of these obligations would be covered by the general obligations of the Solicitor's Code such as unbefitting conduct.

14.2 PROVISION OF RELEVANT AUTHORITIES

The defence advocate is obliged to comply with all the general principles set out in Chapter 13. In addition to this, he is also required to inform the prosecution of all the relevant authorities within a reasonable time before the hearing. Failure to do so may result in an adjournment or the hearing of the matter being stood down. Both advocates have a duty to supply all relevant authorities to the court.[a]

14.3 NOT TO MISLEAD THE COURT[b]

Both the prosecution and the defence solicitor have an obligation not to mislead the court and there is also ample authority to support the concept of fairness to the prosecution. On a guilty plea, a prosecution advocate does not normally address the court for a second time. However, if he has reasonable cause to believe that the court has been misled in any

---

(a) *Copeland (Stephen Anthony) v Smith and Others* [1999] TLR, 20 October (p 4 of the full report). Counsel for both parties had failed in there duty to the court by failing to be aware of an authority reported in an official law report. See, also, Solicitor's Code, Chapter 22.20, notes 21A and 7.1(e). See, also, *Kenneth Johnson v David Valks*, Lawtel 15/3/2000, counsel's duty was to research issues of which he had notice, but he was not expected to be a 'walking law library'.

(b) Solicitor's Code Chapter 21.01.

way, the court may be informed of this. If this results in a material difference in the version of the facts between the prosecution and the defence, the court is entitled to hold a 'Newton'-style hearing in which both parties call evidence to enable the court to adjudicate upon the matter.

14.4 FAIRNESS TO THE PROSECUTION[c]

In extending the concept of fairness to the prosecution, it seems right to expect that advocates should gain an unfair advantage by referring to material in isolation, whether that be expert reports, or passages in reported cases. Any imbalance can sometimes be restored by asking the opposing advocate to either read the whole paragraph or, alternatively, the preceding or following paragraph.

14.5 SECTION 10 OF THE CJA 1967 ADMISSIONS

The defence advocate should consider whether any admission can be made with a view to saving time and expense at the trial, with the aim of admitting as much evidence as can properly be admitted in accordance with the duty to the court.[d]

14.6 NOTIFICATION OF CONTENTIOUS MITIGATION

Notify the prosecution in advance of any submissions in mitigation which can cast aspersions on the conduct or character of a victim or witness in the case.[e]

14.7 LIMITS OF CROSS EXAMINATION

As to the limits in which a defence advocate may attack the evidence for the prosecution, either by cross-examination or in his speech, no clearer rule can be laid down than this: 'He is entitled to test the evidence given by each individual witness and to argue that the

---

(c) *R v Warner* (1993) Cr App R 324 which mentions 'fairness not only to the defence, but to the prosecution case'; and *R v Patel* (1993) 97 Cr App R 294, which refers to 'the fairness of both sides' on the question of admitting a document; and *R v Baldwin* [1925] All ER 402; *R v Warner* [1993] Cr App R 324, which mentions 'fairness not only to the defence, but to the prosecution case'; and *R v Patel* (1993) 97 Cr App R 294, [1993] 1 All ER 402, which establishes that, 'they cannot be licensed to the defence if there is to be strictness for the prosecution'; and *R v Oliphant* [1992] Crim LR 41 refers to the need to have regard to the 'overall fairness to the prosecution and defence'. See, also, *R v Bradford Stipendiary Magistrates' Court ex p Daniel and Wood* Lawtel 9/6/97; ILR 16/6/97. Unfairness had to be seen and considered in the context of the prosecution process, which required not only fairness to the accused, but also to victims, the State and to justice generally. See, also, *R v Gordon Mitchel Stewart* Lawtel 4/10/99; [1999] Crim LR 746 in which interests of the prosecution and justice as a whole were considered on a Police and Criminal Evidence Act 1984, s 78, application.
(d) Code of Conduct for the Bar of England and Wales, Annex H, para 12.2.
(e) As for (c) above.

evidence taken as a whole is insufficient to amount to proof that the defendant is guilty of the offence charged. Further than this, he ought not to go.'[f]

14.8 RULE AGAINST EXPRESSION OF PERSONAL OPINION

When conducting proceedings at court, he must not, unless invited to do so, or where it is his duty to do so, assert a personal opinion of the facts or the law.[g]

14.9 SCANDALISATION OR VILIFICATION OF WITNESSES

He must not make statements or ask questions which are merely scandalous or intended or calculated only to vilify, insult or annoy either a witness or some other person.[h]

14.10 IMPUGNATION OF A WITNESS

He must not, by assertion in a speech, impugn a witness whom he has had an opportunity to cross-examine, unless, in cross-examination, he has given the witness an opportunity to answer the allegation.[i]

14.11 CHARACTER OF A WITNESS

He must not suggest that a victim, witness or other person is guilty of a crime, fraud or misconduct or make any defamatory aspersion on the conduct of any other person or attribute to another person a crime or conduct of which his lay client is accused, unless such allegations go to a matter in issue (including the credibility of the witness) which is material to his lay client's case and which appear to him to be supported on reasonable grounds.[j]

14.12 DISCLOSURE OF EXPERTS' REPORTS

Both sides are now required to supply each other with advance disclosure of experts' reports within a reasonable time of the hearing.[k]

(f) Code of Conduct for the Bar of England and Wales, Annex H, para 13.5.
(g) Code of Conduct for the Bar of England and Wales, code 610(b).
(h) Solicitor's Code, 21.08.
(i) Code of Conduct for the Bar of England and Wales, Pt VI, 610 and *Browne v Dunn* [1894] 6 R 67, *per* Lord Halsbury.
(j) Code of Conduct for the Bar of England and Wales, Pt VI, 610.
(k) Magistrates' Courts (Advance Notice of Expert Evidence) Rules 1997.

14.13 FRANKNESS AND GOOD FAITH[l]

All solicitors are expected to maintain personal integrity at all times and observe the requirements of good manners and courtesy. This includes honouring their word whether or not in writing. In more general terms, there is a duty to act in such a way as would not be inconsistent with the position of solicitor.

14.14 MITIGATION[m]

Solicitors will not in mitigation be entitled to suggest that the facts are such that the ingredients of the offence have not been established.

(l) Solicitor's Code, Chapter 19.0.
(m) Solicitor's Code, Chapter, 21.20, note 7.

GIVING EVIDENCE IN COURT

15.1 INTRODUCTION

15.1.1 The following paragraphs are a guide to local authority enforcement officers who become involved in court proceedings. They are intended to be advisory for officers or other witnesses who may be called upon to give evidence in either magistrates' court proceedings or, more rarely, in the Crown Court. For those who have not been a witness in court before, this may be an unsettling experience. The purpose of this guide is to set out the pitfalls and the procedure so that the officer giving evidence will know what is expected of him and perform effectively.

15.2 PERSONNEL IN THE MAGISTRATES' COURT

15.2.1 *The magistrates (and stipendiary magistrate)*

Justices of the Peace (who generally comprise of two or three on the bench) are unpaid members of the public who have volunteered to carry out this work. No formal qualifications are required, although they do sit through certain interviews and are assessed. Ideally, they should represent a true cross-section of the public. The concept behind the English legal system is that 'one should be tried by one's peers'. Occasionally, if a case raises complex questions of fact or law or is more serious, it may be listed before a district judge (magistrates' court), who is a solicitor or barrister of at least seven years' experience. A district judge is a civil servant, who is paid a salary, as opposed to lay justices, who are unpaid and receive expenses only.

15.2.2 *Justices' clerk*

This person is appointed to advise the magistrates on law and procedure only. A clerk is qualified as either a solicitor or a barrister or, alternatively, has gone through extensive legal training on evidence and magistrates' court procedures under the magistrates' clerks professional examinations. The court clerk controls the order in which the cases are dealt with and plays a prominent role in the management of the courts administration and the hearings in court. Notwithstanding this, he or she must not become involved in any decision on the facts of the case other than to refer to notes of evidence when asked by the court. For these reasons, the magistrates retire alone when the facts of the case are discussed. The clerk may only be invited to join the magistrates when advice is required upon legal issues. It is also important that the clerk is seen to be neutral and impartial and best practice suggests that advice to the magistrates is given in open court.

15.2.3 *Ushers*

In each court, there is an usher who wears a black robe and has a list of all the cases which are in that court. He or she is expected to ascertain if there are any personal appearances by the defendants and, when they are represented, which solicitor is acting. This is to ensure the smooth and timely running of the court. Also, the usher in trials must ensure that the witnesses in the case do not sit through the proceedings. The reason for this is to ensure, as far as possible, that witnesses give their own evidence, which is not coloured by any other evidence he may have heard during the course of the proceedings. The exceptions are expert or professional witnesses – for example, doctors – who are generally permitted to sit through the proceedings and give advice to the advocate on matters within their expertise as and when required. This duty also falls upon the advocate who has called the witness under the duties as officer of the court as well as prosecutor or advocate in the cause.

15.3 FORMALITIES – WITNESSES

15.3.1 A witness giving evidence during the trial is expected to sit outside the court until he or she is called. Anyone who gives evidence and is then released to leave the court by the magistrates should not discuss the evidence with any other witnesses who are sitting outside the court. This is so important that it cannot be overstressed. If a witness who has not given evidence is seen to be talking to witnesses who have just given evidence, the case may have to be re-heard altogether, and the costs of the rehearing may have to be borne by the party whose witnesses have prejudiced the proceedings.

15.4 PREPARATION FOR HEARING – WITNESSES

15.4.1 Naturally, a witness should prepare their evidence before going to court. The questions that a witness will be asked will be based on the statement that has been prepared for the purpose of the prosecution. It is usual to have a brief meeting with the lawyer presenting the case to go through the procedure, etc. A witness may refer to notes in the witness box providing that the notes have been made at, or shortly after, the incident that has occurred. Leave of the court is required before a witness may refer to his notes and it may be customary for the lawyer to introduce the notes in the following way:

Witness: 'May I refer to my notes?'

Chairperson of the magistrates: 'Could I ask when these notes were made?'

Lawyer: 'When were the notes made?'

Witness: 'Yes. I made these notes almost immediately after the incident which occurred on (such and such a date).' (Or, alternatively): 'I made notes immediately upon my return to my office, which was approximately 15 minutes after the interview took place.'

Lawyer to magistrates: 'If you are satisfied that the notes were made contemporaneously, I wonder if the witness might refer to them.'

Chairperson of the magistrates: 'Yes, of course, the witness may refer to the notes.'

15.4.2 The above scenario explains the manner in which notes can be adduced in evidence in a magistrates' court, or Crown Court. It is important that the exact time of making of the notes is recorded, otherwise it may be difficult to establish that they are contemporaneous. Furthermore, a defence advocate could argue that the notes are inaccurate or, in extreme circumstances, may have been concocted in some way if there has been a significant delay.

15.4.3 The papers that a witness intends to refer to should be in good order, usually chronological so that fumbling about in the witness box can be avoided.

15.4.4 It is also worthy of note that a witness can refer to their written statement in court. The magistrates will need to be informed as to how and when the statement came into existence in order to establish in their own minds how reliable the evidence in it is. A witness is entitled to refresh their memory from contemporaneous notes or a statement before they enter the witness box, but this should be brought to the notice of the magistrates before giving evidence in the interest of fairness and justice.

15.5 MODE OF ATTIRE

The possibility that magistrates and even judges could make assessments of witnesses from their mode of attire cannot be discounted. A tidy professional appearance is therefore desirable.

15.6 EXAMINATION-IN-CHIEF, CROSS-EXAMINATION AND RE-EXAMINATION

15.6.1 *Examination-in-chief*

This is the term given to the questions which are put by an advocate to his own witness. These are the first questions that will be asked of a witness by the lawyer calling him. The questions should not be leading questions, that is, questions which tend to suggest the answer in them.[a] The purpose of examination in chief is to elicit all the relevant evidence contained in the witness' statement. The introductory questions in examination in chief may be as follows:

Q: 'Would you please give your full name and position with the local authority?'

A: 'My name is John Smith. I am an environmental health officer.'

Q: 'What are your qualifications?'

(a) *R v Patel*, Archbold News, 14 November 1996 which establishes that as a general working rule a question only requiring an answer of 'yes' or 'no' is likely to be a leading question.

A: 'I have a BSc in environmental health and I have 10 years' experience as an environmental health officer.'

Q: 'Is it the case that you have been involved in this matter since 1996, and have had overall conduct of the investigations?'

A: 'Yes.'

15.6.2 The purpose of these questions is to establish the identity of the witness and to introduce the witness to the court. The initial questions are easy and should allow the witness to relax a little before he or she is asked to speak independently. The third question is a leading question. It does not relate to an issue in the case and for this reason no objection can be anticipated. The evidence may then continue as follows:

Q: 'Would you please tell the court how you became involved in this matter?'

15.6.3 This is the cue for the witness to tell the court their involvement from the outset, thereafter the questions should be more specific and less open-ended. In this way, the witness is not encouraged to stray into evidence that is not required. An example of such a question might be put as follows:

Q: 'After you received the complaint what did you do that afternoon?'

A: 'I interviewed the complainant and took a statement from him.'

Q: 'Where did you visit a week later on 1 May 2001?'

A: 'The defendant's premises at Oak Drive.'

Q: 'Did you notice anything of concern to you on this initial visit?'

A: 'Yes, there was an advertisement displayed at the entry to the premises.'

Q: 'Did the local authority give consent to this advertisement?'

A: 'No.'

Q: 'Did you confront the defendant about this advertisement?'

A: 'Yes, I asked him if he had sought permission for the advertisement.'

Q: 'How did he respond?'

A: 'He said that he didn't think permission was necessary but promised to take it down within a week.'

15.6.4 Whilst giving evidence, the witness should not speak too quickly. It may be helpful to watch the clerk's pen to ensure that he has an adequate opportunity to take down the evidence.

15.6.5 The witness will then be asked further questions 'in chief' to substantiate the balance of his statement.

15.7 CROSS-EXAMINATION

15.7.1 Cross-examination is a more attacking line of questioning in which leading questions may be asked. The lawyer will have full notes of the relevant points that the witness has made 'in chief' and will then cross-examine on the issues. He or she is also required to put the defence case to the prosecution witnesses so that they comment upon it insofar as they are able to do so. This should give the trained witness an insight into the possible questions that might be asked. The defence lawyer will also have a copy of the original statement made by the witness who should be mindful of this in answering the questions that are put in cross-examination. These questions will not necessarily be 'trick questions', but it is important to remember that the purpose of the questions is to assist the defence and it is perfectly legitimate to ask questions which are designed to discredit the witness. The witness should, therefore, take his time and, if uncertain about the reasons for the particular question, should say so. Any judge is likely to be sympathetic to a witness if the question is put in an unclear way. The defence lawyer would then be required to reformulate the question.

15.8 RE-EXAMINATION

15.8.1 If a question put in cross-examination has raised an issue which needs clarifying then it is open to the advocate calling him to ask questions designed to clarify that question. This is not a second bite at the cherry. Questions cannot therefore be raised on new issues or any matter that has not been raised in cross-examination.

15.9 QUESTIONS PUT BY THE DISTRICT JUDGE OR LAY MAGISTRATES

15.9.1 At any stage during the proceedings, the judge or justice may ask questions themselves.

15.9.2 Questions from the bench are most frequently asked at the close of the witness' evidence. At the conclusion of any further questioning, the prosecution advocate may ask the witness to remain at the back of court or, alternatively, for him to be released. The custom of the witness remaining in court ensures that they do not confer with other witnesses and can be recalled in the event that a matter arises *ex improviso*, that is, without having been anticipated.

15.9.3 It can be extremely helpful for witnesses who has already given evidence to remain in court, if they are a witness in a professional capacity, for example, an environmental health officer. Once an environmental health officer has given evidence about his involvement in a case, it is usual for him to sit through further witnesses' evidence on the understanding that he will normally have given expert evidence. An environmental health officer may be able to identify deficiencies in the defence's case from a technical point of view and it is often helpful for him to sit behind the advocate for advisory purposes.

15.9.4 It is usual for the prosecution to write to the witnesses informing them of the result of the case. If costs have been incurred by a witness in attending court to give evidence, these will normally be reimbursed providing that they are reasonable and are supported by the appropriate documentation.

15.10 GENERAL TIPS

15.10.1 When giving evidence it may seem natural to answer the questions directly to the person who asked them. However, in court proceedings, one should always address the bench. Increased eye contact may enable a witness to build up a report with the justices and prevent any heated exchange with the questioner. Occasionally, a witness may need a little more time to take stock of the situation. There are a number of ways in which this can be achieved without causing embarrassment in the witness box. These are as follows:

(a) ask for the question to be repeated;

(b) if a witness feels that their statement, notes or file may assist, refer to them (with the consent of the court of course) – this may assist a witness in answering the question and enable the witness to retain composure;

(c) if the question requires some thought before an answer is given, a witness may ask for a moment to think about the question for a brief period of time.

15.10.2 If, after giving due consideration, a witness is unable to answer a question s/he should say: 'I am sorry I am unable to answer that question,' or words to that effect. Under no circumstances should s/he attempt to speculate when giving evidence and s/he should restrict his evidence to matters of observation and fact only. An expert witness can express opinion on those areas of their own expertise.

15.11 SWORN EVIDENCE

A witness can either take the oath on the Bible, or other suitable holy book. Alternatively, a witness may affirm, that is, promise to tell the truth using the standard wording provided by the court. If an alternative procedure to taking the oath is preferred, it may be advisable to notify the court in advance so that adequate provision can be made.

15.12 EVIDENCE IN THE CROWN COURT

15.12.1 The Crown Court is a superior court to the magistrates' court. The more serious type of magistrates' court case is 'triable either way' (indictable) which means it can be tried in the magistrates' court or the Crown Court at the election of the defence or the court in the event of a not guilty plea.

15.12.2 Not many local authority cases are referred to the Crown Court. An example of a case being sent to the Crown Court may be a trading standards matter in which a person is alleged to have altered the odometer of a car.

15.12.3 In environmental health and planning matters, it has been known for some cases to be referred to the Crown Court but this is a rarity. Crown Court referral occurred in a planning matter in which a pizza house was opened and a 'stop notice' was served effecting closure. The defendants were also involved in a criminal fraud matter and the two cases were joined together and were committed to the Crown Court.

15.12.4 A Crown Court requires a judge and jury. The Crown Court is a more formalised setting. The judge sitting in the Crown Court would be either a circuit judge or, occasionally, a high court judge depending on the seriousness and complexity of the matter. Whereas in the magistrates' court the advocates will generally be solicitors and, sometimes, barristers, the advocates in a Crown Court do tend to be barristers or solicitors with higher rights of audience. The principles that are explained above regarding the giving evidence apply in the Crown Court, and in any other court situation. The points to remember have been summarised in a checklist for briefing lay witnesses. This can be found at Appendix 19.

PROGRESS OF A CASE TO ITS RESOLUTION

16.1 ADJOURNMENTS

A case will not often proceed the first occasion it is before a court unless a guilty plea is entered. If a not guilty plea is entered, the case is usually adjourned to a date when the court has sufficient time to deal with a contested hearing. If a trial is to be fixed, the instructing officer will be asked to canvass the availability of his witnesses for the next 3–4 months and record this information in the form of a list. The advocate with conduct of the case will keep the instructing department up to date with the court adjournments and any forthcoming trial date. The investigating officer should write to inform every witness of his obligation to attend the hearing.

16.2 NOTIFICATION TO WITNESSES OF DATE FIXED FOR TRIAL

It is the role of the Investigating Officer (IO) to ensure that all of the witnesses for the prosecution are present. If any are unable to attend he should inform the council's advocate as soon as possible.

16.3 WITNESS EXPENSES AND COSTS

Civilian witnesses claim expenses for their attendance at court and an IO is under a duty to liaise with each and every witness to ascertain what expenses they have incurred, that is, loss of earnings, fares etc. There are court guidelines for amounts payable in relation to witness expenses. IOs should pass a note to the council's advocate before the end of the prosecution case advising him of the amount of witness expenses claimed. The advocate will then be in a position to amend any application for costs.

16.4 INVESTIGATIVE COSTS REASSESSMENT – AFTER TRIAL

If officers have been engaged in court hearings as witnesses, the costs claimed by the instructing client department need to be re-assessed. The council's advocate should be informed of the revised amount of costs sought, that is, to include witness costs for officers' attendance at court. Usually, evidence is given in chronological order and it is not uncommon for the IO to give his evidence last. The advantages to this are that he can prevent witnesses from talking to each other and discussing the case. He can also prevent witnesses who are leaving the court, having given their evidence, from speaking with any person waiting to enter the court.

16.5 BAIL PENDING APPEALS

Bail should only be granted pending appeal where there are exceptional circumstances in which justice can only be done by the granting of bail.[a]

16.6 NOTEBOOKS RECORD AND EXHIBITS

IOs are not only responsible for co-ordinating witness attendance at court, but also for ensuring that witnesses bring with them any exhibits or original notes in their possession.

16.7 STATEMENTS – PROOFS OF EVIDENCE

A witness may refresh his memory before the trial from statements which are not contemporaneous but, nonetheless, made near to the time of the offence.[aa] The court also has a discretion to allow a witness to refresh his memory from a statement which he had read before going into the witness box but not digested.[b]

16.8 CONCLUSIONS

16.8.1 Many local government officers and members of the public may be called to give evidence in any court. This will generally be in the magistrates court, the court in which the vast majority of cases are dealt with. However, the same advice will apply to giving evidence in any other court.

16.8.2 A witness who is prepared for the hearing, will generally deal with it in a more composed fashion. He should therefore familiarise himself with all the evidence and allow plenty of time to arrive at the court to park his car, and to find the court building.

(a) *R v Watton (Joseph)* (1979) 68 Cr App R 293; [1979] Crim LR 246. See, also, *Stones Justices Manual*, 2001, para 1-2182, which advises that 'we would expect magistrates who have imposed a custodial sentence to be reluctant to grant bail'.

(aa) *R v Richardson* [1971] 2 WLR 889, Home Office Circular No 82/1969 and *Lau Pak Ngam v R* [1966] Crim LR 443.

(b) *R v Da Silva* [1990] 1 All ER 29: a judge has a discretion to allow a witness to read his witness statement in the box if he is satisfied (1) the witness could not remember the details because of the intervening lapse of time, (2) the statement was made nearer the time of the events and represented his recollection at that time, (3) he had not read the statement through before going into the witness box and (4) he wished to have an opportunity to read the statement before he continued to give evidence. See, also, *R v South Ribble Magistrates ex p Cochrane* [1996] TLR, 24 June; *Da Silva* is not authority for saying that a witness could only read non-contemporaneous evidence if all criteria is established by that case. The court may allow a witness to refresh his memory from a statement which he has read before going into the witness box.

COSTS IN CRIMINAL AND CIVIL PROCEEDINGS BEFORE THE MAGISTRATES' COURT

17.1 THE IMPORTANCE OF COSTS APPLICATIONS

It has been recognised that the pressures placed on local authorities budgets throughout the last two decades and presently justify applications for realistic levels of legal and investigative costs.[a] The courts generally look at the total financial penalty in relation to a person's ability to pay when awarding costs. As a rule of thumb, the courts seem to look at payment over a 12 month period as a starting point, although payment over two or three years is seldom too long, if the financial penalty is within the capacity of the offenders and default is unlikely over that period.[b] Such costs are enforced by the magistrates' court bailiffs service. Costs orders should not be confused with a civil debt. Thus, if the defendant does not pay, the council cannot enforce the costs as a civil debt. The magistrates also have the right to remit the costs orders at any time given a change of circumstances of the defendant and there is no right of appeal against such a decision. The orders for cost and the remission of those costs are in the absolute discretion of the magistrates.

17.2 SECTION 18 OF THE PROSECUTION OF OFFENCES ACT 1985

This section provides that, where any person is convicted of an offence before the magistrates' court or the Crown Court, or an appeal is dismissed, the court may make such an order as to costs to be paid by the accused to the prosecution as it considers just and reasonable. It may be argued that it is just and reasonable for the whole of the costs to be paid in order to avoid the costs of the prosecution falling upon council tax payers. Should a case proceed to appeal against sentence from the magistrates' court to the Crown Court on a criminal matter, there is a right of appeal on the questions of costs.[c]

(a) *Neville and Westminster City Council v Gardner Merchant Ltd* (1983) 5 Cr App R(S) 349. See, also, Kerr LJ in *R v Burt ex p Presburg* [1960] 1 QB 625. If the investigation arose from a specific complaint and not any routine matter, it would be (*prime facie*) right to award the whole sum. There are two cases which may not be entirely consistent on the question of whether the prosecution should be entitled to all its costs. The LCJ in the divisional court case of *R v North Allerton Magistrates' Court ex p Dove* [1999] TLR, 17 June said that the costs order should not be grossly disproportionate to the level of fine. In *R v John Boyle* [1995] Cr App R(S) 927; [1995] Crim LR 514 CA, a costs order of £1,000 and a fine of £250 was not disproportionate or unreasonable. In the court of appeal decision of *R v F Howe & Son* [1999] 2 All ER 249, it was said in a health and safety case that there was no reason why a defendant in a position to pay the whole of the prosecution costs as well as the fine should not be made to do so. In *R v Haydon* (1975) 60 Cr App R 304, it was held that the costs can be increased if the defendant has put the prosecutor to increased expense, but a defendant should not be penalised for defending himself.

(b) *R v Oliver* (1989) 11 Cr App R(S) 10.

(c) *R v Bow Street Metropolitan Stipendiary Magistrates ex p Screen Multimedia Ltd and Another* [1998] TLR, 28 January. The Magistrates' Courts Act 1980, s 108(3)(b), gave no right of appeal from a costs order in the magistrates' court. However, the decision in *Hamilton-Johnson v RSPCA* 4 April 2000 CO/3185/1999 refers to the Supreme Court Act 1981, s 48(2), which does give the Crown Court jurisdiction to reverse or vary a costs order made in the magistrates' court.

17.3 SECTION 64 OF THE MAGISTRATES' COURTS ACT 1980

The court may order costs in civil proceedings inter-parties, that is, upon complaint. An unsuccessful party's impecuniosity and the fact that he appeared in person were irrelevant considerations in determining the costs order to be made.[d] Conversely, if a party is carrying out a function which they are required to perform, costs should not automatically follow the event.[e] The same now applies to local authorities in civil proceedings. In practical terms, if an order for costs is made in favour of the council, then its finance department should be asked to raise an invoice against the person who has been ordered to pay the costs. Civil orders for costs are a civil debt and can be recovered before the County Court if they are not met.

17.4 SECTION 16 OF THE PROSECUTION OF OFFENCES ACT 1985

This section provides that where an information is not proceeded with, or that the magistrates determine not to commit the accused for trial upon an indictable offence, or the magistrates dismiss the information, the court may make an order for costs in favour of the accused from central funds. Central funds is a pool of money provided for by central government which may be used for the payment of such costs. In the magistrates'

(d) *MB Building Contractors Ltd v Nazir Ahmed*, Lawtel 18/11/98.

(e) In *R v Merthyr Tydfil CC ex p CC of Dyfed-Powes* [1998] TLR, 17 December, it was decided that the police who objected to a justices licence on the grounds that the applicant was not a fit and proper person should not be ordered to pay costs unless they have acted improperly or unreasonably as they have a function which they are required to perform. The same approach was taken in *Chief Constable of Derbyshire v Arthur Newton and Albert Thomas Goodman*, Lawtel 2/4/98, in which there was a successful appeal against the Chief Constable's revocation of a firearms license. The Chief Constable was not ordered to pay costs even though his refusal was based on an erroneous application of the law. For public bodies, the position in Scotland is against awarding expenses against a public body which defends a decision with propriety when that decision is challenged (*Milton v Argyle and Clyde Health Board* 1997 SLT 565; 1996 SCLR 1072). The position as regards administrative decisions in English law is now governed by the ruling in the case of *City of Bradford MDC v E Booth* High Court [2000] TLR, 31 May. Lord Chief Justice Bingham set out the proper approach in questions of this kind as follows:

1 Section 64(1) (Magistrates' Courts Act 1980) confers a discretion upon the magistrates' court to make such order as to costs as it thinks just and reasonable. That principal applies both to the quantum of the costs (if any) to be paid, but also as to the party (if any) which should pay them.

2 What the court thinks is just and reasonable will depend on all the relevant facts and circumstances of the case before the court. The court may think it just and reasonable that costs follow the event, but need not think so in all cases covered by the subsection.

3 Where a complainant has successfully challenged before justices an administrative decision made by a police or regulatory authority acting honestly, reasonably, properly and on grounds that reasonably appeared to be sound, in exercise of its public duty, the court should consider, in addition to any other relevant facts or circumstances, both (i) the financial prejudice to the particular complainant in the particular circumstances if an order for costs is not to be made in his favour; and (ii) the need to encourage public authorities to make and stand by honest, reasonable and apparently sound administrative decisions made in the public interest without fear of exposure to undue financial prejudice if the decision is successfully challenged.

It is submitted that the second limb in the third paragraph is referring to the danger of local authorities making 'defensive decisions' in fear of having to pay costs. On the basis that any decision that is finely balanced is likely to create an incentive to make a decisions of this nature, it is at least arguable that the second limb will be active in these circumstances.

court, it is normal for defence costs to be paid out of central funds rather than make a costs order against a private prosecutor.(f)

17.5 A DEFENDANT'S COSTS ORDER

An order should normally be made, unless there are positive reasons why such an order should not be made. There is now only one basis for refusing an order which is as follows:(g)

> The defendant's own conduct has brought suspicion on himself and has misled the prosecution into thinking that the case is stronger than it is.

Thus, as an officer of the court, the prosecutor must be aware of these issues and not simply agree with an application for costs from central funds if there are reasons not to make such an order.

17.6 SECTION 19 OF THE PROSECUTION OF OFFENCES ACT 1985

The prosecution should be aware that where proceedings result in acquittals or the case being withdrawn, there may be costs awarded against the council in certain circumstances. Those circumstances are set out in s 19 of the 1985 Act which provides that, in any case where the court is satisfied that one party to criminal proceedings has incurred costs as a result of an unnecessary or improper act or omission by or on behalf of another party to the proceedings, it may make an order for the payment of those costs. An example of this may arise if the court were to return a finding of 'no case to answer' and comment that the evidence did not support a 'realistic prospect of conviction'. In such a situation, it could be said that the prosecution had begun the proceedings unnecessarily or improperly and ought to pay defence costs. Costs may also be awarded against a local authority if the evidence is weak, even though the prosecutor has not acted improperly.(h)

17.7 SECTION 19A OF THE PROSECUTION OF OFFENCES ACT 1985

This section provides for the court to make 'wasted costs' orders in accordance with the Costs in Criminal Cases (General) Regulations 1986. In the absence of fraud, costs orders

---

(f) *Practice Notice (Criminal Law: Costs)* [1991] 2 All ER 924, [1982] 3 All ER 1152, and *Suffolk CC v Rexmore Wholesale Services Ltd* (1994) 159 JP 390. See, now, *Practice Direction (Crime Costs in Criminal Proceedings) (No 2)* (1999) *The Times*, 6 October; [1999] 4 All ER 436; [1999] 1 WLR 1832.

(g) See *Practice Direction (Crime Costs in Criminal Proceedings) (No 2)* (1999) and *Practice Direction (Costs in Criminal Proceedings) (No 2)* [2001] 1 Cr App R 60, above, that amends *Practice Direction (Costs in Criminal Proceedings)* (1991) 93 Cr App R 89, so as effectively to delete para 2.2(b). (One good reason for not making a defendant's costs order in favour of an acquitted defendant being that his defence has no merit and he was acquitted on a technicality.) The reason being that this ground was regarded as being inconsistent with the European Convention for the Protection of Human Rights. There is now only one ground for refusing to make a defendant's costs order which is set out above.

(h) *North Tyneside Council v Duchet* (2000) unreported, 23 March.

should not normally be made against local authority officials.[i] As regards an award of costs against a practitioner, the power should be invoked only in cases where there has been a serious dereliction of the practitioner's duty to the court.[j]

17.7 PROSECUTION COSTS ON APPEAL AGAINST CONVICTION

These are normally payable subject to means.[a] It would also be inappropriate to apply for judicial review where the sole issue is one of costs.[b]

(i) *R v Lambeth LBC ex p Wilson* [1997] TLR, 25 March.
(j) *Harley v McDonald Glasgow Harley (A Firm) v McDonald* [2001] TLR, 25 May.
(a) *Griffiths (Richard) v Pembrokeshire CC* (and post-judgment discussion) 2000 CO/4941/1999 Lord Justice Kennedy: 'It can, in my judgment, be cogently argued that when a defendant appeals against conviction and his appeal fails, he has put the prosecutor (and thus in a case such as this, council tax payers) to avoidable expense, and, subject to his means, he should bear the whole of the prosecutor's reasonable costs of resisting the appeal.'
(b) *R v London Borough of Camden ex p Jarram* [1999] EWHC 338 CO 4234/98.

CHAPTER 18

ENVIRONMENTAL HEALTH LEGISLATION

18.1 OFFENCE CREATING SECTIONS

This chapter sets out the following legislation together with relating checklists identifying the elements and other investigatory matters:

1. ss 79 and 80 of the Environmental Protection Act 1990 (breach of an abatement notice);
2. ss 2 and 3 of the Clean Air Act 1993 (dark smoke offences);
3. ss 2, 3 and 7 of the Health and Safety at Work etc Act 1974;
4. s 1 of the Protection of Animals Act 1911 (cruelty/neglect to animals);
5. Food Safety (General Food Hygiene) Regulations 1995;
6. Food Labelling Regulations 1996;
7. s 8 of the Food Safety Act 1990 (selling food not complying with food safety requirements);
8. s 14 of the Food Safety Act 1990 (selling food not of the nature or substance or quality demanded);
9. ss 376 and 198 of the Housing Act 1985 (repairs notices);
10. s 1 of the Protection from Eviction Act 1977 (unlawful eviction/harassment);
11. s 3 of the Dogs (Fouling of Land) Act 1996;
12. Refuse Disposal (Amenity) Act 1978 (penalty for unauthorised dumping);
13. s 33(1)(a) of the Environmental Protection Act 1990 (prohibition of unauthorised or harmful/deposit or disposal, etc, of waste);
14. s 34 of the Environmental Protection Act 1990 (duty of care, etc, as respects waste);
15. s 87 of the Environmental Protection Act 1990 (offence of leaving litter).

18.2 STATUTORY POWERS

The following statutory powers are included:

1. s 33 of the Food Safety Act 1990 (obstruction, etc, of officers);
2. s 32 of the Food Safety Act 1990 (powers of entry);
3. s 352 of the Housing Act 1985 (power to require execution of works to render premises fit for number of occupants);
4. s 372 of the Housing Act 1985 (power to require execution of works to remedy neglect of management);
5. s 20 of the Health and Safety at Work etc Act 1974 (powers of inspectors);
6. s 21 of the Health and Safety at Work etc Act 1974 (improvement notices);

7   s 22 of the Health and Safety at Work etc Act 1974 (prohibition notices);
8   s 23 of the Health and Safety at Work etc Act 1974 (provisions supplementary to ss 21 and 22);
9   s 25 of the Health and Safety at Work etc Act 1974 (power to deal with cause of imminent danger);
10 s 196 of the Housing Act 1985 (power of court to authorise owner to execute works on default of another owner);
11 s 197 of the Housing Act 1985; (powers of entry);
12 s 198 of the Housing Act 1985 (penalty for obstruction);
13 s 198A of the Housing Act 1985 (penalty for failure to execute works);
14 ss 9–13 of the Food Safety Act 1990 (emergency prohibition and condemnation orders).

18.3 BREACH OF A S 80 OF THE ENVIRONMENTAL PROTECTION ACT 1990 ABATEMENT NOTICE

Elements of the offence/investigatory matters:

(i)   Person responsible or owner[a] or occupier where this person cannot be found – the full name and address of the person upon whom the notice has been served. (If company, full name and registered office, name of trading name, partnership and address for service.)

(ii) 'Failure to comply' – evidence of non compliance and reference to the items in the notice which have not been complied with by reference to the notice.

(iii) 'Without reasonable excuse'.[b]

(a) 'Owner' includes a managing agent for the premises (*Camden London BC v Gunby* [1999] 4 All ER 602).

(b) 'Reasonable excuse' does not include matters that should have been raised on an appeal (*A Lambert Flat Management Ltd v Lomas* [1981] 2 All ER 280). In the case of *Stagecoach Ltd v McPhail* 1988 SCCR 289, it was established that matters which could have be raised by way of appeal against s 58 of the Control of Pollution Act notice could not be raised in defence to proceedings for contravention of that notice. The decision in *Stagecoach* is consistent with the view taken in *Amec Building Ltd v LB Camden* [1997] Env LR 330. The same issue arose in respect of notices served under the Environmental Protection Act 1990, s 80, and the Control of Pollution Act 1974, s 60. The court adopted the reasoning in *A Lambert Flat Management Ltd* [1981] 1 WLR 898, p 907, *per* Acker LJ:

> Can the defendant urge as a reasonable excuse for failing to comply with the notice, that the same was invalid for one or more of the reasons provided by the regulations as permissible grounds of appeal? ... The answer to my mind is clearly in the negative. Not only is the right of appeal given by statute but very detailed provisions have been made by the regulations for the prosecution of such appeals. Section 58(4) was not designed to give the recipient of the notice a choice of forum in which to mount an attack on the notice. It was designed to provide a defence to a criminal charge where he had some reasonable excuse, such as a specific difficulty in compliance with the notice.

(iv) Service of the notice[c] evidence of receipt is required for the file, but see footnotes.
(v) Existence of statutory nuisance before service and on date(s) of offence.
(vi) Reference to times for compliance in information, etc.
(vii) Best practicable means defence to prevent, or to counteract the effects of, the nuisance.
(viii) Date(s)[d] and place.
(ix) Common law defence.[e]
(x) Mitigation/explanation.

Time limit: six months (s 127 of the Magistrates' Courts Act 1980).

Mode of trial: summary.

Maximum penalty (s 80(5)).

Summary: level 5 (increased to £20,000 if offence committed on industrial, trade or business premises – s 80(6)).

18.4 SECTION 80 OF THE ENVIRONMENTAL PROTECTION ACT 1990

(1) Where a local authority is satisfied that a statutory nuisance exists, or is likely to occur or recur, in the area of the authority, the local authority shall serve a notice ('an abatement notice') imposing all or any of the following requirements –

   (a) requiring the abatement of the nuisance of prohibiting or restricting its occurrence or recurrence;

   (b) requiring the execution of such works, and the taking of such other steps, as may be necessary for any of those purposes,

   and the notice shall specify the time or times within which the requirements of the notice are to be complied with.

(2) Subject to section 80A(1) below, the abatement notice shall be served–

(c) There is authority which suggests that there is an irrebuttable presumption that service is deemed to be effected by simply pushing the notice through the letter box of the recipient, see *Rushmore BC v Reynolds* (1991) 23 HLR 495, in which service was effected under the Local Government Act 1972, s 233, and the Interpretation Act 1978, s 7, even though R did not receive the notice. See, also, *Lambeth BC v Mullings* [1990] COD 281 and [1990] TLR, 6 January which confirmed that s 233 of the above Act applied to service of a notice of an abatement notice through a letter box under the Control of Pollution Act 1974, s 58. In any event, it is the authors' view that steps should be taken to confirm that the notice has been received. Service on a company can properly be effected at its registered office or its principle office (*Hewlings v Mclean Homes East Anglia Ltd* CO/4680/2000 25/7/00).

(d) In planning law, failure to include evidence of the compliance period is fatal if it is not pleaded in the informations and referred to in the evidence (*Maltedge v Wokingham DC* [1992] TLR, 21 May). It is submitted that the same approach will apply to this Act.

(e) See list of authorities at Appendix 17 for contents of the notice, etc. Previously, if the notice required work to be done this had to be specified in the notice (*Kirklees Council v Lees* [1998] Env LR 337). *R v Falmouth & Truro Port HA ex p SW Water Ltd* CA 30/3/2000 has now overruled *Kirklees Council v Lees* in holding that the notice was not invalid for failing to specify the works to be carried out. In planning law, the information must set out the compliance period. It is submitted that the same approach will apply to this act. A s 80 notice may be served on the owner of barking dogs to reduce the number (*Manley v Newforest DC* CO/1050/99 27/07/99).

(a) except in a case falling within paragraph (b) or (c) below, on the person responsible for the nuisance;

(b) where the nuisance arises from any defect of a structural character, on the owner of the premises;

(c) where the person responsible for the nuisance cannot be found or the nuisance has not yet occurred, on the owner or occupier of the premises.

(3) A person served with an abatement notice may appeal against the notice to a magistrates' court or in Scotland, the sheriff within the period of twenty-one days beginning with the date on which he was served with the notice.

(4) If a person on whom an abatement notice is served, without reasonable excuse, contravenes or fails to comply with any requirement or prohibition imposed by the notice, he shall be guilty of an offence.

(5) Except in a case falling within subsection (6) below, a person who commits an offence under subsection (4) above shall be liable on summary conviction to a fine not exceeding *level 5* on the standard scale together with a further fine of an amount equal to *one-tenth of that level* for each day on which the offence continues after the conviction.

(6) A person who commits an offence under subsection (4) above on industrial, trade or business premises shall be liable on summary conviction to a fine not exceeding £20,000.

(7) Subject to subsection (8) below, in any proceedings for an offence under subsection (4) above in respect of a statutory nuisance it shall be a defence to prove that the best practicable means were used to prevent, or to counteract the effects of, the nuisance.

(8) The defence under subsection (7) above is not available–

(a) in the case of a nuisance falling within paragraph (a), (d), (e), (f) or (g) of section 79(1) above except where the nuisance arises on industrial, trade or business premises;

(aa) in the case of a nuisance falling within paragraph (ga) of section 79(1) above except where the noise is emitted from or caused by a vehicle, machinery or equipment being used for industrial, trade or business purposes;

(b) in the case of a nuisance falling within paragraph (b) of section 79(1) above except where the smoke is emitted from a chimney; and

(c) in the case of a nuisance falling within paragraph (c) or (h) of section 79(1) above.

(9) In proceedings for an offence under subsection (4) above in respect of a statutory nuisance falling within paragraph (g) or (ga) of section 79(1) above where the offence consists in contravening requirements imposed by virtue of subsection (1)(a) above it shall be a defence to prove–

(a) that the alleged offence was covered by a notice served under section 60 or a consent given under section 61 or 65 of the Control of Pollution Act 1974 (construction sites, etc); or

(b) where the alleged offence was committed at a time when the premises were subject to a notice under section 66 of that Act (noise reduction notice), that the level of noise emitted from the premises at that time was not such as to constitute a contravention of the notice under that section; or

(c) where the alleged offence was committed at a time when the premises were not subject to a notice under section 66 of that Act, and when a level fixed under section 67 of that Act (new buildings liable to abatement order) applied to the premises, that the level of noise emitted from the premises at that time did not exceed that level.

(10) Paragraphs (b) and (c) of subsection (9) above apply whether or not the relevant notice was subject to appeal at the time when the offence was alleged to have been committed.

Environmental Protection Act 1990, s 80, as amended by the Noise and Statutory Nuisance Act 1993, s 3, and the Environment Act 1995, Sched 17.

18.5 SECTION 79: STATUTORY NUISANCES AND INSPECTION THEREFORE

(1) Subject to subsections (2) to (6A) below, the following matters constitute 'statutory nuisances' for the purposes of this Part, that is to say–
   (a) any premises in such a state as to be prejudicial to health or a nuisance;
   (b) smoke emitted from premises so as to be prejudicial to health or a nuisance;[a]
   (c) fumes or gases emitted from premises so as to be prejudicial to health or a nuisance;
   (d) any dust, steam, smell or other effluvia arising on industrial, trade or business premises and being prejudicial to health or a nuisance;
   (e) any accumulation or deposit which is prejudicial to health or a nuisance;
   (f) any animal kept in such a place or manner as to be prejudicial to health or a nuisance;[b]
   (g) noise emitted from premises so as to be prejudicial to health or a nuisance;
   (ga) noise that is prejudicial to health or a nuisance and is emitted from or caused by a vehicle, machinery or equipment in a street or in Scotland, road;
   (h) any other matter declared by any enactment to be a statutory nuisance;
   and it shall be the duty of every local authority to cause its area to be inspected from time to time to detect any statutory nuisances which ought to be dealt with under section 80 below or sections 80 and 80A below and, where a complaint of a statutory nuisance is made to it by a person living within its area, to take such steps as are reasonably practicable to investigate the complaint.*

(2) Subsection (1)(b) and (g) above do not apply in relation to premises–
   (a) occupied on behalf of the Crown for naval, military or air force purposes or for the purposes of the department of the Secretary of State having responsibility for defence; or
   (b) occupied by or for the purposes of a visiting force;

(a) The smell of smoke, without there being any visible particles was sufficient to constitute a smoke nuisance under Environmental Protection Act 1990, s 79 (*Griffiths v Pembrokeshire CC* [2000] TLR, 19 April).
(b) *R v Walden-Jones ex p Coton* [1963] Crim LR 839. If cats strayed due to defective premises and created a nuisance this could be dealt with under the Public Health Act 1936 under the head condition of premises in which animals were kept.

and 'visiting force' means any such body, contingent or detachment of the forces of any country as is a visiting force for the purposes of any of the provisions of the Visiting Forces Act 1952.

(3) Subsection (1)(b) above does not apply to–
   (i) smoke emitted from a chimney of a private dwelling within a smoke control area,
   (ii) dark smoke emitted from a chimney of a building or a chimney serving the furnace of a boiler or industrial plant attached to a building or for the time being fixed to or installed on any land,
   (iii) smoke emitted from a railway locomotive steam engine, or
   (iv) dark smoke emitted otherwise than as mentioned above from industrial or trade premises.

(4) Subsection (1)(c) above does not apply in relation to premises other than private dwellings.

(5) Subsection (1)(d) above does not apply to steam emitted from a railway locomotive engine.

(6) Subsection (1)(g) above does not apply to noise caused by aircraft other than model aircraft.

(6A) Subsection (1)(ga) above does not apply to noise made–
   (a) by traffic,
   (b) by any naval, military or air force of the Crown or by a visiting force (as defined in subsection (2) above), or
   (c) by a political demonstration or a demonstration supporting or opposing a cause or campaign.

(7) In this Part–

'chimney' includes structures and openings of any kind from or through which smoke may be emitted;

'dust' does not include dust emitted from a chimney as an ingredient of smoke;

'equipment' includes a musical instrument;

'fumes' means any airborne solid matter smaller than dust;

'gas' includes vapour and moisture precipitated from vapour;

'industrial, trade or business premises' means premises used for any industrial, trade or business purposes or premises not so used on which matter is burnt in connection with any industrial, trade or business process, and premises are used for industrial purposes where they are used for the purposes of any treatment or process as well as where they are used for the purposes of manufacturing;

'local authority' means, subject to subsection (8) below–
   (a) in Greater London, a London borough council, the Common Council of the City of London and, as respects the Temples, the Sub-Treasurer of the Inner Temple and the Under-Treasurer of the Middle Temple respectively;
   (b) in England and Wales outside Greater London, a district council in England;
   (bb) in Wales, a county council or county borough council;
   (c) the Council of the Isles of Scilly; and

(d) in Scotland, a district or islands council or a council constituted under section 2 of the Local Government etc (Scotland) Act 1994;

'noise' includes vibration;

'person responsible'–

(a) in relation to a statutory nuisance, means the person to whose act, default or sufferance the nuisance is attributable;

(b) in relation to a vehicle, includes the person in whose name the vehicle is for the time being registered under the Vehicles Excise and Registration Act 1994 and any other person who is for the time being the driver of the vehicle;

(c) in relation to machinery or equipment, includes any person who is for the time being the operator of the machinery or equipment;

'prejudicial to health' means injurious, or likely to cause injury, to health;

'premises' includes land and, in relation to England and Wales, subject to subsection (12) and section 81A(9) below, any vessel;

'private dwelling' means any building, or part of a building, used or intended to be used, as a dwelling;

'road' has the same meaning as in Part IV of the New Roads and Street Works Act 1991;

'smoke' includes soot, ash, grit and gritty particles emitted in smoke;

'street' means a highway and any other road, footway, square or court that is for the time being open to the public;

and any expression used in this section and in the Clean Air Act 1993 have the same meaning in this section as in that Act and section 3 of the Clean Air Act 1993 shall apply for the interpretation of the expression 'dark smoke' and the operation of this Part in relation to it.

(8) Where, by an order under section 2 of the Public Health (Control of Disease) Act 1984, a port health authority has been constituted for any port health district or in Scotland where by an order under section 172 of the Public Health (Scotland) Act 1897 a port local authority or a joint port local authority has been constituted for the whole or part of a port, the port health authority, port local authority or joint port local authority, as the case may be shall have by virtue of this subsection, as respects its district, the functions conferred or imposed by this Part in relation to statutory nuisance other than a nuisance falling within paragraph (g) or (ga) of subsection (1) above and no such order shall be made assigning those functions; and 'local authority' and 'area' shall be construed accordingly.

(9) In this Part 'best practicable means' is to be interpreted by reference to the following provisions–

(a) 'practicable' means reasonably practicable having regard among other things to local conditions and circumstances, to the current state of technical knowledge and to the financial implications;

(b) the means to be employed include the design, installation, maintenance and manner and periods of operation of plant and machinery, and the design, construction and maintenance of buildings and structures;

(c) the test is to apply only so far as compatible with any duty imposed by law;

(d) the test is to apply only so far as compatible with safety and safe working conditions, and with the exigencies of any emergency or unforeseeable circumstances;

and, in circumstances where a code of practice under section 71 of the Control of Pollution Act 1974 (noise minimisation) is applicable, regard shall also be had to guidance given in it.

(10) A local authority shall not without the consent of the Secretary of State institute summary proceedings under this Part in respect of a nuisance falling within paragraph (b), (d) or (e) and, in relation to Scotland, paragraph (g) or (ga), of subsection (1) above if proceedings in respect thereof might be instituted under Part I.**

(11) The area of a local authority which includes part of the seashore shall also include for the purposes of this Part the territorial sea lying seawards from that part of the shore; and subject to subsection (12) and, in relation to England and Wales section 81A(9) below, this Part shall have effect, in relation to any area included in the area of a local authority by virtue of this subsection–

(a) as if references to premises and the occupier of premises included respectively a vessel and the master of a vessel; and

(b) with such other modifications, if any, as are prescribed in regulations made by the Secretary of State.

(12) A vessel powered by steam reciprocating machinery is not a vessel to which this Part of this Act applies.

Environmental Protection Act 1990, s 79, as amended by Sched 16 to that Act, Clean Air Act 1993, Sched 4, the Noise and Statutory Nuisance Act 1993, ss 2 and 10, the Local Government (Wales) Act 1994, Sched 9, the Vehicle Excise and Registration Act 1994, Sched 3 and the Environment Act 1995, Sched 17.

* Section 79(1) is amended and new sub-s (1A) and (1B) are inserted by the Environment Act 1995, Scheds 22 and 24, post, when in force.

** Section 79(10) is amended by the Pollution Prevention and Control Act 1999, Scheds 2 and 3, when in force.

18.6 DARK SMOKE OFFENCE (S 1 OF THE CLEAN AIR ACT 1993)

Elements of the offence/investigatory matters:

1. Place of offence (within courts jurisdiction).
2. Date of offence (within six months time limit).
3. Status of defendant, that is, individual or sole trader, partnership, limited company or plc.
4. Address of defendant or registered office address if limited company.
5. Section 1(3) applies.
6. Dark smoke is emitted from chimney of a building.
7. Defendant is the occupier.
8. Section 1(4) statutory defence.
9. Mitigation/explanation.

Time limit: six months (s 127 of the Magistrates' Courts Act 1980).

Mode of trial: summary.

Maximum penalty (s 1(5)).

Summary: level 3 (increased to level 5 if offence is not committed as respects a chimney on a private dwelling).

18.7 CLEAN AIR ACT 1993

1 Prohibition of dark smoke from chimneys

(1) Dark smoke shall not be emitted from a chimney of any building, and if, on any day, dark smoke is so emitted, the occupier of the building shall be guilty of an offence.

(2) Dark smoke shall not be emitted from a chimney (not being a chimney of a building) which serves the furnace of any fixed boiler or industrial plant, and if, on any day, dark smoke is so emitted, the person having possession of the boiler or plant shall be guilty of an offence.

(3) This section does not apply to emissions of smoke from any chimney, in such classes of case and subject to such limitations as may be prescribed in regulations made by the Secretary of State, lasting for not longer than such periods as may be so prescribed.

(4) In any proceedings for an offence under this section, it shall be a defence to prove–
   (a) that the alleged emission was solely due to the lighting up of a furnace which was cold and that all practicable steps had been taken to prevent or minimise the emission of dark smoke;
   (b) that the alleged emission was solely due to some failure of a furnace, or of apparatus used in connection with a furnace, and that–
      (i) the failure could not reasonably have been foreseen, or, if foreseen, could not reasonably have been provided against; and
      (ii) the alleged emission could not reasonably have been prevented by action taken after the failure occurred; or
   (c) that the alleged emission was solely due to the use of unsuitable fuel and that–
      (i) suitable fuel was unobtainable and the least unsuitable fuel which was available was used; and
      (ii) all practicable steps had been taken to prevent or minimise the emission of dark smoke as the result of the use of that fuel;
   or that the alleged emission was due to the combination of two or more of the causes specified in paragraphs (a) to (c) and that the other conditions specified in those paragraphs are satisfied in relation to those causes respectively.

(5) A person guilty of an offence under this section shall be liable on summary conviction–
   (a) in the case of a contravention of subsection (1) as respects a chimney of a private dwelling, to a fine not exceeding *level 3* on the standard scale; and
   (b) in any other case, to a fine not exceeding *level 5* on the standard scale.

(6) ...

18.8 DARK SMOKE OFFENCE (S 2 OF THE CLEAN AIR ACT 1993)

Elements of the offence/investigatory matters:
1. Place of offence (within court's jurisdiction).
2. Date of offence (within six months time limit).
3. Status of defendant, that is, individual or sole trader, partnership, limited company or plc.
4. Address of defendant or registered office address if limited company.
5. Dark smoke emission.[a]
6. Industrial or trade premises.
7. Occupier of the premises or person who causes or permits the emission.
8. Offence not precluded by virtue of s 2(2).
9. All practical steps defence in s 2(4).
10. Mitigation/explanation.

Time limit: six months (s 127 of the Magistrates' Courts Act 1980).

Mode of trial: summary.

Maximum penalty (s 2(5)): £20,000.

Summary: £20,000.

18.9 SECTION 2 OF THE CLEAN AIR ACT 1993

2 Prohibition of dark smoke from industrial or trade premises

(1) Dark smoke shall not be emitted from any industrial or trade premises and if, on any day, dark smoke is so emitted the occupier of the premises and any person who causes or permits the emission shall be guilty of an offence.

(2) This section does not apply–
   (a) to the emission of dark smoke from any chimney to which section 1 above applies; or
   (b) to the emission of dark smoke caused by the burning of any matter prescribed in regulations made by the Secretary of State, subject to compliance with such conditions (if any) as may be so prescribed.

(3) In proceedings for an offence under this section, there shall be taken to have been an emission of dark smoke from industrial or trade premises in any case where–
   (a) material is burned on those premises; and
   (b) the circumstances are such that the burning would be likely to give rise to the emission of dark smoke,

---

(a) Under the Environmental Protection Act 1990, s 79, the smell of smoke, without there being any visible particles was sufficient to constitute a smoke nuisance (*Griffiths v Pembrokeshire CC* [2000] TLR, 19 April).

unless the occupier or any person who caused or permitted the burning shows that no dark smoke was emitted.

(4) In proceedings for an offence under this section, it shall be a defence to prove–
   (a) that the alleged emission was inadvertent; and
   (b) that all practicable steps had been taken to prevent or minimise the emission of dark smoke.

(5) A person guilty of an offence under this section shall be liable on summary conviction to a fine not exceeding £20,000.

(6) In this section 'industrial or trade premises' means–
   (a) premises used for any industrial or trade purposes; or
   (b) premises not so used on which matter is burnt in connection with any industrial or trade process.

(7) ...

Clean Air Act 1993, s 2, as amended by the Environment Act 1995, Sched 22.

18.10 SECTION 3 OF THE CLEAN AIR ACT 1993

3 Meaning of 'dark smoke'

(1) In this Act 'dark smoke' means smoke which, if compared in the appropriate manner with a chart of the type known on 5th July 1956 (the date of the passing of the Clean Air Act 1956) as the Ringelmann Chart, would appear to be as dark as or darker than shade 2 on the chart.

(2) For the avoidance of doubt it is hereby declared that in proceedings–
   (a) for an offence under section 1 or 2 (prohibition of emissions of dark smoke);
   (b) (repealed),

   the court may be satisfied that smoke is or is not dark smoke as defined in subsection (1) notwithstanding that there has been no actual comparison of the smoke with a chart of the type mentioned in that subsection.

(3) Without prejudice to the generality of subsections (1) and (2), if the Secretary of State by regulations prescribes any method of ascertaining whether smoke is dark smoke as defined in subsection (1), proof in any such proceedings as are mentioned in subsection (2)–
   (a) that the method was properly applied; and
   (b) that the smoke was thereby ascertained to be or not to be dark smoke as so defined,
   shall be accepted as sufficient.

Section 3 of the Clean Air Act 1993, as amended by Sched 24 to the Environment Act 1995.

18.11 SECTION 2 OF THE HEALTH AND SAFETY AT WORK ETC ACT 1974

Elements of the offence/investigatory matters:

1. Place of offence (within courts jurisdiction).
2. Date of offence.
3. Status of defendant, that is, individual or sole trader, partnership, limited company or plc.
4. Address of defendant or registered office address if limited company.
5. Defendant is an employer.
6. Breach of duty.[a]
7. Breach of duty arises in connection with employee.
8. Reasonably practicable defence.[b]
9. Mitigation/explanation.
10. Common law defence.[c]

Time limit: none.

Mode of trial: either way.

Maximum penalty (s 33):

Summary: £20,000.

Indictment: unlimited fine.

18.12 SECTION 2 OF THE HEALTH AND SAFETY AT WORK ETC ACT 1974

2 General duties of employers to their employees

(1) It shall be the duty of every employer to ensure, so far as is reasonably practicable, the health, safety and welfare at work of all his employees.

(a) It is not necessary to refer to the paragraphs of s 2(2). The information may include more than one breach as matters a–e are simply examples of the duty. There is therefore no requirement to specify the individual head relied on and it would not be duplicitous to include more than one type of breach for his reason (*Health and Safety Executive v Spindle Select Ltd* (1996) *The Times*, 9 December, DC). A company could not avoid liability on the basis that the acts were not those of the 'directing mind' of the company (*R v Gateway Foodmarkets Ltd* [1997] 3 All ER 78).

(b) The degree of risk has to be weighed against the measures necessary to avert that risk *West Bromwich BS v Townsend* (1983) ICR 257. The standard of care is the same regardless of the size of the company or its financial strength *R v F Howe* [1999] 2 All ER 249. The existence of a universal practice was evidence which went to the question whether any other method was reasonably practicable, but it did not necessarily discharge the onus on employer.

(c) A health and safety officer could not delegate his power to institute proceedings under s 38 (*R v Croydon Justices ex p WH Smith Ltd* [2000] TLR, 22 November.

Chapter 18: Environmental Health Legislation

(2) Without prejudice to the generality of an employer's duty under the preceding subsection, the matters to which that duty extends include in particular–
   (a) the provision and maintenance of plant and systems of work that are, so far as is reasonably practicable, safe and without risks to health;
   (b) arrangements for ensuring, so far as is reasonably practicable, safety and absence of risks to health in connection with the use, handling, storage and transport of articles and substances;
   (c) the provision of such information, instruction, training[a] and supervision as is necessary to ensure, so far as is reasonably practicable, the health and safety at work of his employees;
   (d) so far as is reasonably practicable as regards any place of work under the employer's control, the maintenance of it in a condition that is safe and without risks to health and the provision and maintenance of means of access to and egress from it that are safe and without such risks;
   (e) the provision and maintenance of a working environment for his employees that is, so far as is reasonably practicable, safe, without risks to health, and adequate as regards facilities and arrangements for their welfare at work.

(3) Except in such cases as may be prescribed, it shall be the duty of every employer to prepare and as often as may be appropriate revise a written statement of his general policy with respect to the health and safety at work of his employees and the organisation and arrangements for the time being in force for carrying out that policy, and to bring the statement and any revision of it to the notice of all of his employees.

(4) Regulations made by the Secretary of State may provide for the appointment in prescribed cases by recognised trade unions (within the meaning of the regulations) of safety representatives from amongst the employees, and those representatives shall represent the employees in consultations with the employers under subsection (6) below and shall have such other functions as may be prescribed.

(6) It shall be the duty of every employer to consult any such representatives with a view to the making and maintenance of arrangements which will enable him and his employees to co-operate effectively in promoting and developing measures to ensure the health and safety at work of the employees, and in checking the effectiveness of such measures.

(7) In such cases as may be prescribed it shall be the duty of every employer, if requested to do so by the safety representatives mentioned in subsection (4) above, to establish, in accordance with regulations made by the Secretary of State, a safety committee having the function of keeping under review the measures taken to ensure the health and safety at work of his employees and such other functions as may be prescribed.

Health and Safety at Work etc Act 1974, s 2, as amended by the Employment Protection Act 1975, Sched 15.

---

[a] The duty to train an employee in use of a woodworking machine involves giving a comprehensive explanation in ordinary language of the dangers involved and also some appraisal as to whether the employee understood the instructions and the dangers of the machine, particularly where the employee is a refugee. *Tasci v Pekalp of London Ltd* [2001] TLR, 17 January.

18.13 SECTION 3 OF THE HEALTH AND SAFETY AT WORK ETC ACT 1974

Elements of the offence/investigatory matters:
1. Place of offence (within court's jurisdiction).
2. Date of offence.
3. Status of defendant, that is, individual or sole trader, partnership, limited company or plc.
4. Address of defendant or registered office address if limited company.
5. Defendant is an employer.
6. Exposure to a risk of health or safety.
7. Exposure to a risk arises in connection with one who is not an employee.
8. Exposure to a risk arises as a result of conduct of undertaking.
9. Reasonably practicable defence.[a]
10. Mitigation/explanation.

Time limit: none.

Mode of trial: Either way.

Maximum penalty (s 33)):

Summary: £20,000.

Indictment: unlimited fine.

18.14 SECTION 3 OF THE HEALTH AND SAFETY AT WORK ETC ACT 1974

3 General duties of employers and self-employed to persons other than their employees

(1) It shall be the duty of every employer to conduct his undertaking in such a way as to ensure, so far as is reasonably practicable, that persons not in his employment who may be affected thereby are not thereby exposed to risks to their health or safety.

(2) It shall be the duty of every self-employed person to conduct his undertaking in such a way as to ensure, so far as is reasonably practicable, that he and other persons (not

---

[a] A company could not avoid liability on the basis that the acts were not those of the 'directing mind' of the company (*R v British Steel plc* [1995] 1 WLR 1356, [1995] Crim LR 654). The decisive question in determining culpability under s 3, therefore, is not whether the employer was vicariously liable or in a position to exercise control over work carried out by an independent contractor, but simply whether the activity which has caused the risk amounts to part of the conduct by the employer of his undertaking, that being a question of fact in each case (*R v Associated Octel Ltd* [1996] 4 All ER 846, HL). If an employee is negligent, the employer may still escape liability if he can make out the statutory defence. (*R v Nelson Group Services (Maintenance) Ltd* [1998] 4 All ER 331, [1999] 1 WLR 1526, CA.)

being his employees) who may be affected thereby are not thereby exposed to risks to their health or safety.

(3) In such cases as may be prescribed, it shall be the duty of every employer and every self-employed person, in the prescribed circumstances and in the prescribed manner, to give to persons (not being his employees) who may be affected by the way in which he conducts his undertaking the prescribed information about such aspects of the way in which he conducts his undertaking as might affect their health or safety.

18.15 SECTION 7 OF THE HEALTH AND SAFETY AT WORK ETC ACT 1974

Elements of the offence/investigatory matters:
1. Place of offence (within court's jurisdiction).
2. Date of offence.
3. Defendant is an employee.
4. Address of defendant.
5. Failure to take reasonable care for the health and safety of himself and/or others.
6. Breach of duty arises whilst defendant is at work.
7. Mitigation/explanation.

Time limit: none

Mode of trial: either way.

Maximum penalty (s 33(3)):

Summary: statutory maximum.

Indictment: unlimited fine and/or two years.

18.16 SECTION 7 OF THE HEALTH AND SAFETY AT WORK ETC ACT 1974

7 **General duties of employees at work**

It shall be the duty of every employee while at work–

(a) to take reasonable care for the health and safety of himself and of other persons who may be affected by his acts or omissions at work; and

(b) as regards any duty or requirements imposed on his employer or any other person by or under any of the relevant statutory provisions, to co-operate with him so far as is necessary to enable that duty or requirement to be performed or complied with.

18.17 SECTION 33 OF THE HEALTH AND SAFETY AT WORK ETC ACT 1974

33 Offences

(1) It is an offence for a person–
- (a) to fail to discharge a duty to which he is subject by virtue of sections 2 to 7;
- (b) to contravene section 8 or 9;
- (c) to contravene any health and safety regulations or any requirement or prohibition imposed under any such regulations (including any requirement or prohibition to which he is subject to by virtue of the terms of or any condition or restriction attached to any licence, approval, exemption or other authority issued, given or granted under the regulations);
- (d) to contravene any requirement imposed by or under regulations under section 14 or intentionally to obstruct any person in the exercise of his powers under that subsection;
- (e) to contravene any requirement imposed by an inspector under sections 20 or 25;
- (f) to prevent or attempt to prevent any other person from appearing before an inspector or from answering any question to which an inspector may by virtue of section 20(2) require an answer;
- (g) to contravene any requirement or prohibition imposed by an improvement notice or a prohibition notice (including any such notice as modified on appeal);
- (h) intentionally to obstruct an inspector in the exercise or performance of his powers or duties or to obstruct a customs officer in the exercise of his powers under section 25A;
- (i) to contravene any requirement imposed by a notice under section 27(1);
- (j) to use or disclose any information in contravention of sections 27(4) or 28;
- (k) to make a statement which he knows to be false or recklessly to make a statement which is false where the statement is made–
  - (i) in purported compliance with a requirement to furnish any information imposed by or under any of the relevant statutory provisions; or
  - (ii) for the purpose of obtaining the issue of a document under any of the relevant statutory provisions to himself or another person;
- (l) intentionally to make a false entry in any register, book, notice or other document required by or under any of the relevant statutory provisions to be kept, served or given or, with intent to deceive, to make use of any such entry which he knows to be false;
- (m) with intent to deceive, to use a document issued or authorised to be issued under any of the relevant statutory provisions or required for any purpose thereunder or to make or have in his possession a document so closely resembling any such document as to be calculated to deceive;
- (n) falsely to pretend to be an inspector;
- (o) to fail to comply with an order made by a court under section 42.

(1A) Subject to any provision made by virtue of section 15(6)(d), a person guilty of an offence under subsection(1)(a) above consisting of failing to discharge a duty to which he is subject by virtue of sections 2 to 6 shall be liable–

(a) on summary conviction, to a fine not exceeding £20,000;

(b) on conviction on indictment, to a fine.

(2A) A person guilty of an offence under subsection (1)(g) or (o) above shall be liable–

(a) on summary conviction, to imprisonment for a term not exceeding six months, or a fine not exceeding £20,000, or both;

(b) on conviction on indictment, to imprisonment for a term not exceeding two years, or a fine, or both.

(2) A person guilty of an offence under paragraph (d), (f), (h) or (n) of subsection (1) above, or of an offence under paragraph (e) of that subsection consisting of contravening a requirement imposed by an inspector under section 20, shall be liable on summary conviction to a fine not exceeding level 5 on the standard scale.

(3) Subject to any provision made by virtue of section 15(6)(d) or (e) or by virtue of paragraph 2(2) of Schedule 3, a person guilty of an offence under subsection (1) above not falling within subsection (1A), (2) or (2A) above or of an offence under any of the existing statutory provisions, being an offence for which no other penalty is specified, shall be liable–

(a) on summary conviction, to a fine not exceeding the *statutory maximum*;

(b) on conviction on indictment–

(i) if the offence is one to which this sub-paragraph applies, to imprisonment for a term not exceeding two years, or a fine, or both;

(ii) if the offence is not one to which the preceding sub-paragraph applies, to a fine.

(4) Subsection (3)(b)(i) above applies to the following offences–

(a) an offence consisting of contravening any of the relevant statutory provisions by doing otherwise than under the authority of a licence issued by the Executive something for the doing of which such a licence is necessary under the relevant statutory provisions;

(b) an offence consisting of contravening a term of or a condition or restriction attached to any such licence as is mentioned in the preceding paragraph;

(c) an offence consisting of acquiring or attempting to acquire, possessing or using an explosive article or substance (within the meaning of any of the relevant statutory provisions) in contravention of any of the relevant statutory provisions;

(d) (Repealed);

(e) an offence under subsection (1)(j) above.

(5) (Repealed).

(6) (Repealed).

Health and Safety at Work etc Act 1974, s 33, as amended by the Employment Protection Act 1975, Sched 15, the Criminal Law Act 1977, s 28 and Scheds 1 and 6, the Forgery and Counterfeiting Act 1981, s 30 and Sched 1, the Criminal Justice Act 1982, s 46, the Consumer Protection Act 1987, Sched 3 and the Offshore Safety Act 1992, s 4.

18.17.1 *Section 20 of the Health and Safety at Work etc Act 1974*

Powers of inspectors

(1) Subject to the provisions of section 19 and this section, an inspector may, for the purpose of carrying into effect any of the relevant statutory provisions within the field of responsibility of the enforcing authority which appointed him, exercise the powers set out in subsection (2) below.

(2) The powers of an inspector referred to in the preceding subsection are the following, namely–

   (a) at any reasonable time (or, in a situation which in his opinion is or may be dangerous, at any time) to enter any premises which he has reason to believe it is necessary for him to enter for the purposes mentioned in subsection (1) above;

   (b) to take with him a constable if he has reasonable cause to apprehend any serious obstruction in the execution of his duty;

   (c) without prejudice to the preceding paragraph, on entering any premises by virtue of paragraph (a) above to take with him–

      (i) any other person duly authorised by his (the inspector's) enforcing authority; and

      (ii) any equipment or materials required for any purpose for which the power of entry is being exercised;

   (d) to make such examination and investigation as may in any circumstances be necessary for the purposes mentioned in subsection (1) above;

   (e) as regards any premises which he has power to enter, to direct that those premises or any part of them, or anything therein, shall be left undisturbed (whether generally or in particular respects) for so long as is reasonably necessary for the purpose of any examination or investigation under paragraph (d) above;

   (f) to take such measurements and photographs and make such recordings as he considers necessary for the purpose of any examination or investigation under paragraph (d) above;

   (g) to take samples of any articles or substances found in any premises which he has power to enter, and of the atmosphere in or in the vicinity of any such premises;

   (h) in the case of any article or substance found in any premises which he has power to enter, being an article or substance which appears to him to have caused or to be likely to cause danger to health or safety, to cause it to be dismantled or subjected to any process or test (but not so as to damage or destroy it unless this is in the circumstances necessary for the purpose mentioned in subsection (1) above);

   (i) in the case of any such article or substance as is mentioned in the preceding paragraph, to take possession of it and detain it for so long as is necessary for all or any of the following purposes, namely–

      (i) to examine it and do to it anything which he has power to do under that paragraph;

      (ii) to ensure that it is not tampered with before his examination of it is completed;

      (iii) to ensure that it is available for use as evidence in any proceedings for an offence under any of the relevant statutory provisions or any proceedings relating to a notice under section 21 or 22;

(j) to require any person whom he has reasonable cause to believe to be able to give any information relevant to any examination or investigation under paragraph (d) above to answer (in the absence of persons other than a person nominated by him to be present and any persons whom the inspector may allow to be present) such questions as the inspector thinks fit to ask and to sign a declaration of the truth of his answers;

(k) to require the production of, inspect, and take copies of or of any entry in–
   (i) any books or documents which by virtue of any of the relevant statutory provisions are required to be kept; and
   (ii) any other books or documents which it is necessary for him to see for the purposes of any examination or investigation under paragraph (d) above;

(l) to require any person to afford him such facilities and assistance with respect to any matters or things within that person's control or in relation to which that person has responsibilities as are necessary to enable the inspector to exercise any of the powers conferred on him by this section;

(m) any other power which is necessary for the purpose mentioned in subsection (1) above.

(3) The Secretary of State may by regulations make provision as to the procedure to be followed in connection with the taking of samples under subsection (2)(g) above (including provision as to the way in which samples that have been so taken are to be dealt with).

(4) Where an inspector proposes to exercise the power conferred by subsection (2)(h) above in the case of an article or substance found in any premises, he shall, if so requested by a person who at the time is present in and has responsibilities in relation to those premises, cause anything which is to be done by virtue of that power to be done in the presence of that person unless the inspector considers that its being done in that person's presence would be prejudicial to the safety of the State.

(5) Before exercising the power conferred by subsection (2)(h) above in the case of any article or substance, an inspector shall consult such persons as appear to him appropriate for the purpose of ascertaining what dangers, if any, there may be in doing anything which he proposes to do under that power.

(6) Where under the power conferred by subsection (2)(i) above an inspector takes possession of any article or substance found in any premises, he shall leave there, either with a responsible person or, if that is impracticable, fixed in a conspicuous position, a notice giving particulars of that article or substance sufficient to identify it and stating that he has taken possession of it under that power; and before taking possession of any such substance under that power an inspector shall, if it is practicable for him to do so, take a sample thereof and give to a responsible person at the premises a portion of the sample marked in a manner to identify it.

(7) No answer given by a person in pursuance of a requirement imposed under subsection 2(j) above shall be admissible in evidence against that person or the husband or wife of that person in any proceedings.

(8) Nothing in this section shall be taken to compel the production by any person of a document of which he would on grounds of legal professional privilege be entitled to withhold production on an order for discovery in an action in the High Court or, as the

case may be, on an order for the production of documents in an action in the Court of Session.

NB: s 20(7) IOs should be aware that any information obtained under this section is not admissible as evidence. Officers are therefore strongly advised to seek answers by other methods such as formal interview if questioning under this provision gives rise to information which is required to prove an offence.

18.17.2 *Section 21 of the Health and Safety at Work etc Act 1974*

Improvement notices

If an inspector is of the opinion that a person–

(a) is contravening one or more of the relevant statutory provisions; or

(b) has contravened one or more of those provisions in circumstances that make it likely that the contravention will continue or be repeated,

he may serve on him a notice (in this Part referred to as 'an improvement notice') stating that he is of that opinion, specifying the provision or provisions as to which he is of that opinion, giving particulars of the reasons why he is of that opinion, and requiring that person to remedy the contravention or, as the case may be, the matters occasioning it within such period (ending not earlier than the period within which an appeal against the notice can be brought under section 24) as may be specified in the notice.

Section 22 of the Health and Safety at Work etc Act 1974

Prohibition notices

(1) This section applies to any activities which are being or are likely to be carried on by or under the control of any person, being activities to or in relation to which any of the relevant statutory provisions apply or will, if the activities are so carried on, apply.

(2) If as regards any activities to which this section applies an inspector is of the opinion that, as carried on or likely to be carried on by or under the control of the person in question, the activities involve or, as the case may be, will involve a risk of serious personal injury, the inspector may serve on that person a notice (in this Part referred to as 'a prohibition notice').

(3) A prohibition notice shall–

(a) state that the inspector is of the said opinion;

(b) specify the matters which in his opinion give or, as the case may be, will give rise to the said risk;

(c) where in his opinion, any of those matters involves or, as the case may be, will involve a contravention of any of the relevant statutory provisions, state that he is of that opinion, specify the provision or provisions as to which he is of that opinion, and give particulars of the reasons why he is of that opinion; and

(d) direct that the activities to which the notice relates shall not be carried on by or under the control of the person on whom the notice is served unless the matters specified in the notice in pursuance of paragraph (b) above and any associated contraventions of provisions so specified in pursuance of paragraph (c) above have been remedied.

(4) A direction contained in a prohibition notice in pursuance of subsection (3)(d) above shall take effect–
   (a) at the end of the period specified in the notice; or
   (b) if the notice so declares, immediately.

Health and Safety at Work etc Act 1974, s 22, as amended by the Consumer Protection Act 1987, Sched 3.

18.17.3 *Section 23 of the Health and Safety at Work etc Act 1974*

Provisions supplementary to sections 21 and 22

(1) In this section 'a notice' means an improvement notice or a prohibition notice.

(2) A notice may (but need not) include directions as to the measures to be taken to remedy any contravention or matter to which the notice relates; and any such directions–
   (a) may be framed to any extent by reference to any approved code of practice; and
   (b) may be framed so as to afford the person on whom the notice is served a choice between different ways of remedying the contravention or matter.

(3) Where any of the relevant statutory provisions applies to a building or any matter connected with a building and an inspector proposes to serve an improvement notice relating to a contravention of that provision in connection with that building or matter, the notice shall not direct any measures to be taken to remedy the contravention of that provision which are more onerous than those necessary to secure conformity with the requirements of any building regulations for the time being in force to which that building or matter would be required to conform if the relevant building were being newly erected unless the provision in question imposes specific requirements more onerous than the requirements of any such building regulations to which the building or matter would be required to conform as aforesaid.

In this subsection 'the relevant building', in the case of a building, means that building, and, in the case of a matter connected with a building, means the building with which the matter is connected.

(4) Before an inspector serves in connection with any premises used or about to be used as a place of work a notice requiring or likely to lead to the taking of measures affecting the means of escape in case of fire with which the premises are or ought to be provided, he shall consult the fire authority.

In this subsection 'fire authority' has the meaning assigned by section 43(1) of the Fire Precautions Act 1971.

18.17.4 *Section 24 of the Health and Safety at Work etc Act 1974*

Right of appeal to an industrial tribunal against an improvement notice or a prohibition notice.

18.17.5 *Section 25 of the Health and Safety at Work etc Act 1974*

Power to deal with cause of imminent danger

(1) Where, in the case of any article or substance found by him in any premises which he has power to enter, an inspector has reasonable cause to believe that, in the circumstances in which he finds it, the article or substance is a cause of imminent danger of serious personal injury, he may seize it and cause it to be rendered harmless (whether by destruction or otherwise).

(2) Before there is rendered harmless under this section–

   (a) any article that forms part of a batch of similar articles; or

   (b) any substance,

   the inspector shall, if it is practicable for him to do so, take a sample thereof and give to a responsible person at the premises where the article or substance was found by him a portion of the sample marked in a manner sufficient to identify it.

(3) As soon as may be after any article or substance has been seized and rendered harmless under this section, the inspector shall prepare and sign a written report giving particulars of the circumstances in which the article or substance was seized and so dealt with by him, and shall–

   (a) give a signed copy of the report to a responsible person at the premises where the article or substance was found by him; and

   (b) unless that person is the owner of the article or substance, also serve a signed copy of the report on the owner,

   and if, where paragraph (b) above applies, the inspector cannot after reasonable enquiry ascertain the name or address of the owner, the copy may be served on him by giving it to the person to whom a copy was given under the preceding paragraph.

18.18 SECTION 1 OF THE PROTECTION OF ANIMALS ACT 1911

Need to prove/investigate:

1. Full name of defendant (capacity, that is, sole trader, partnership, limited company, etc).
2. Address/registered office (if limited company).
3. Place of offence.
4. Date of offence.
5. Cruelly beat, etc, or cause or permit unnecessary suffering or tether horse, ass or mule so as to cause unnecessary suffering or ... being the owner permit unnecessary suffering
6. Mitigation/explanation.

Time limit: none.

Mode of trial: summary.

Maximum penalty (s 1(1)).

Summary: level 5 and/or six months.

18.19 SECTION 1 OF THE PROTECTION OF ANIMALS ACT 1911

(1) If any person–
   (a) shall cruelly beat, kick, ill-treat, over-ride, over-drive, over-load, torture, infuriate, or terrify any animal, or shall cause or procure, or, being the owner, permit any animal to be so used, or shall, by wantonly or unreasonably doing or omitting to do any act, or causing or procuring the commission or omission of any act, cause any unnecessary suffering, or, being the owner, permit any unnecessary suffering to be so caused to any animal; or
   (b) shall convey or carry, or cause or procure, or, being the owner, permit to be conveyed or carried, any animal in such manner or position as to cause that animal any unnecessary suffering; or
   (c) shall cause, procure, or assist at the fighting or baiting of any animal; or shall keep, use, manage, or act or assist in the management of, any premises or place for the purpose, or partly for the purpose, of fighting or baiting any animal, or shall permit any premises or place to be so kept, managed, or used, or shall receive, or cause or procure any person to receive, money for the admission of any person to such premises or place; or
   (d) shall wilfully, without any reasonable cause or excuse, administer, or cause or procure, or being the owner permit, such administration of, any poisonous or injurious drug or substance to any animal, or shall wilfully, without any reasonable cause or excuse, cause any such substance to be taken by any animal; or
   (e) shall subject, or cause or procure, or being the owner permit, to be subjected, any animal to any operation which is performed without due care and humanity; or
   (f) shall tether any horse, ass or mule under such conditions or in such manner as to cause that animal unnecessary suffering,
   such person shall be guilty of an offence of cruelty within the meaning of this Act and shall be liable on summary conviction to imprisonment for a term not exceeding *six months* or to a fine not exceeding *level 5* on the standard scale, or both.

(2) For the purposes of this section, an owner shall be deemed to have permitted cruelty within the meaning of this Act if he shall have failed to exercise reasonable care and supervision in respect of the protection of the animal therefrom.

   Provided that, where an owner is convicted of permitting cruelty within the meaning of this Act by reason only of his having failed to exercise such care and supervision, he shall not be liable to imprisonment without the option of a fine.

(3) Nothing in this section shall render illegal any act lawfully done under the Animals (Scientific Procedures) Act 1986, or shall apply–
   (a) to the commission or omission of any act in the course of the destruction, or the preparation for destruction, of any animal as food for mankind, unless such destruction or such preparation was accompanied by the infliction of unnecessary suffering; or
   (b) to the coursing or hunting of any captive animal, unless such animal is liberated in an injured, mutilated, or exhausted condition; but a captive animal shall not, for the purposes of this section, be deemed to be coursed or hunted before it is liberated for the purpose of being coursed or hunted, or after it has been recaptured, or if it is under control and a captive animal shall not be deemed to be coursed or hunted

within the meaning of this subsection if it is coursed or hunted in an enclosed space from which it has no reasonable chance of escape.

Protection of Animals Act 1911, s 1; amended by Protection of Animals Act (1911) Amendment Act 1912, s 1, the Protection of Animals (1911) Amendment Act 1921, s 1, the Criminal Law Act 1977, Sched 6, the Criminal Justice Act 1982, s 46, the Animals (Scientific Procedures) Act 1986, Sched 3, the Protection of Animals (Penalties) Act 1987, s 1, and the Protection against Cruel Tethering Act 1988, s 1.

18.20 SECTION 4(2)(D), SCHED 1, CHAPTER 1 OF THE FOOD SAFETY (GENERAL FOOD HYGIENE) REGULATIONS 1995

Premises not kept clean or maintained in good repair or condition.

Need to prove/investigate:
1. Place of offence (within jurisdiction of the court).
2. Date(s) of offence (with s 19 time limit).
3. Name and capacity of defendant, for example, limited company, partnership, sole trader, individual.
4. Premises are food premises.
5. Premises are used for business purposes.
6. Premises not maintained in good repair and condition.
7. Defendant is the proprietor of the premises.
8. Due diligence defence.
9. Offence due to the act or default of the defendant.
10. Mitigation/explanation from defendant.

Time limit reg 7 and s 34 of the Food Safety Act 1990: one year from commission or three years from discovery whichever is earlier.

Mode of trial: either way.

Maximum penalty (reg 6).

Summary: statutory maximum.

Indictment: fine and/or two years.

18.21 FOOD SAFETY (GENERAL FOOD HYGIENE) REGULATIONS 1995

Articles, fittings and equipment not kept clean.

Need to prove/investigate:
1. Place of offence (within jurisdiction of the court).
2. Date(s) of offence (with s 19 time limit).

3   Capacity of defendant, for example, limited company, partnership, sole trader, individual.
4   Premises are food premises.
5   Premises are used for business purposes.
6   Articles, fittings or equipment not kept clean.
7   Defendant is the proprietor of the premises.
8   Due diligence defence.
9   Offence due to the act or default of the defendant.
10 Mitigation/explanation from defendant.

Time limit reg 7 and s 34 of the Food Safety Act 1990: one year from commission or three years from discovery whichever is earlier.

Mode of trial: either way.

Maximum penalty (reg 6).

Summary: statutory maximum.

Indictment: fine and/or two years.

18.22 FOOD SAFETY (GENERAL FOOD HYGIENE) REGULATIONS 1995

Accumulation of food waste and other refuse in food rooms.

Need to prove/investigate:

1   Place of offence (within jurisdiction of the court).
2   Date(s) of offence (with s 19 time limit).
3   Capacity of defendant, for example, limited company, partnership, sole trader, individual.
4   Premises are food premises.
5   Premises are used for business purposes.
6   Accumulation of food waste and/or other refuse in food rooms.
7   Defendant is the proprietor of the premises.
8   Due diligence defence.
9   Offence due to the act or default of the defendant.
10 Mitigation/explanation from defendant.

Time limit reg 7 and s 34 of the Food Safety Act 1990: one year from commission or three years from discovery whichever is earlier.

Mode of trial: either way.

Maximum penalty (reg 6).

Summary: statutory maximum.

Indictment: fine and/or two years.

18.23 FOOD SAFETY (GENERAL FOOD HYGIENE) REGULATIONS 1995 SI 1995/1763 AMENDED BY SI 1995/2148, 2200 AND 3205, SI 1997/2537, SI 1998/994, SI 1999/1360 AND SI 1999/1540

1 Citation and Commencement

1 Made by the Minister of Agriculture, Fisheries and Food and the Secretaries of State respectively concerned with health in England and food and health in Wales, acting jointly in relation to England and Wales, in exercise of powers conferred upon them by ss 6(4), 16(1), 17(1), 26(1) and (3) and 48(1) of the Food Safety Act 1990.

Interpretation

2(1) In these Regulations, unless the context otherwise requires–

'the Act' means the Food Safety Act 1990;

'the Directive' means Council Directive 93/43/EEC of 14th June 1993 on the hygiene of foodstuffs;

'food authority' does not include–

(a) the council of a non-metropolitan county in England or Wales, unless that council is a unitary authority; or

(b) as respects the Inner Temple or the Middle Temple, the appropriate Treasurer;

'food business' means any undertaking, whether carried on for profit or not and whether public or private, carrying out any or all of the following operations, namely, preparation, processing, manufacturing, packaging, storing, transportation, distribution, handling or offering for sale or supply, of food;

'hygiene' means all measures necessary to ensure the safety and wholesomeness of food during preparation, processing, manufacturing, packaging, storing, transportation, distribution, handling and offering for sale or supply to the consumer, and 'hygienic' shall be construed accordingly;

'list of acceptable previous cargoes for liquid oils or fats' means the list set out in the Annex to Commission Directive 96/3/EC granting a derogation from certain provisions of Council Directive 93/43/EEC on the hygiene of foodstuffs as regards the transport of bulk liquid oils and fats by sea;

'potable water' means water which at the time of supply is or was not likely in a given case to affect adversely the wholesomeness of a particular foodstuff in its finished form, and which is or was either–

(a) of the quality demanded in order for it to be regarded as wholesome for the purposes of–

(i) Part VIA of the Water (Scotland) Act 1980, or

(ii) Chapter III of Part III of the Water Industry Act 1991; or

(b) not of that quality, but the water is or was derived–

(i) from a public supply in Scotland and the Secretary of State is not required, by virtue of section 76E of the Water (Scotland) Act 1980, to make an order under

Chapter 18: Environmental Health Legislation

section 11(2) of the Water (Scotland) Act 1980 in relation to the authority supplying that water,

(ii) from a public supply in England or Wales and the Secretary of State is not required to make or confirm (with or without modifications) an enforcement order under section 18 of the Water Industry Act 1991 in relation to the company supplying that water, or

(iii) from a private supply in relation to which a private supply notice has been served or the option of a private supply notice has been considered and rejected by the local authority with remedial powers in relation to that private supply,

unless since the time of supply the quality of the water has deteriorated in a way which, in a given case, has adversely affected or is likely to affect adversely the wholesomeness of a particular foodstuff in its finished form;

'primary production' includes harvesting, slaughter and milking;

'private supply' has–

(a) in Scotland, the same meaning as in section 76L(1) of the Water (Scotland) Act 1980;

(b) in England and Wales, the same meaning as in section 93(1) of the Water Industry Act 1991;

'private supply notice' means–

(a) in Scotland, a notice under section 76G of the Water (Scotland) Act 1980;

(b) in England and Wales, a notice under section 80 of the Water Industry Act 1991;

'public supply' means a supply of water which is not a private supply;

'unitary authority' means–

(a) in England, any authority which is the sole principal council for its local government area;

(b) in Wales, a county or county borough council established under the Local Government (Wales) Act 1994;

'water' includes water in any form, but does not include water which is–

(a) natural mineral water or drinking water within the meaning of the Natural Mineral Water, Spring Water and Bottled Drinking Water Regulations 1999; or

(b) a medicinal product within the meaning of the Medicines Act 1968 ('the 1968 Act') or is a product in respect of which any provision of the 1968 Act has effect in relation to it as if it were a medicinal product within the meaning of the 1968 Act; or

(c) drinking water within the meaning of the Drinking Water in Containers Regulations 1994;

and any other words and expressions used both in these Regulations and in the Directive, Commission Directive 96/3/EC or Commission Directive 98/28/EC, shall bear the same meaning in these Regulations as they have in those Directives,

and any other words and expressions used both in these Regulations and in the Directive shall bear the same meaning in these Regulations as they have in the Directive.

(2) In determining for the purposes of these Regulations whether any matter involves a risk to food safety or wholesomeness, regard shall be had to the nature of the food, the manner in which it is handled and packed, any process to which the food is subjected before supply to the consumer, and the conditions under which it is displayed or stored.

(3) In Schedule 1,'where appropriate' and 'where necessary' mean where appropriate and where necessary respectively for the purposes of ensuring the safety and wholesomeness of food.

(4) In these Regulations, unless the context otherwise requires, a reference–

(a) to a numbered regulation or Schedule is to the regulation in or Schedule to these Regulations bearing that number;

(b) in a regulation or Schedule to a numbered paragraph is to the paragraph of that regulation or Schedule bearing that number; and

(c) in a paragraph to a numbered or lettered sub-paragraph is to the sub-paragraph in that paragraph bearing that number or letter.

Application of provisions of these Regulations

3(1) Subject to paragraphs (3) and (4), regulations 4 and 5 shall apply to neither–

(a) primary production; nor

(b) a person carrying on any activity which is regulated by or under any of the Regulations listed in paragraph (2), but only with respect to the carrying on of that activity.

(2) The Regulations referred to in paragraph (1)(b) are–

(a)–(e) revoked;

(f) the Egg Products Regulations 1993;

(g) the Meat Products (Hygiene) Regulations 1994;

(h) the Fresh Meat (Hygiene and Inspection) Regulations 1995;

(i) the Poultry Meat, Farmed Game Bird Meat and Rabbit Meat (Hygiene and Inspection) Regulations 1995;

(j) the Dairy Products (Hygiene) Regulations 1995;

(k) the Dairy Products (Hygiene) (Scotland) Regulations 1995;

(l) the Wild Game Meat (Hygiene and Inspection) Regulations 1995;

(m) the Minced Meat and Meat Preparations (Hygiene) Regulations 1995;

(n) the Food Safety (Fishery Products and Live Shellfish) (Hygiene) Regulations 1998.

(3) Notwithstanding paragraph (1)(b), the provisions of paragraph 1 of Chapter VII of Schedule 1 and of regulation 4(2)(d) in so far as it relates to that paragraph of that Chapter shall apply to a proprietor of a food business, unless–

(a) he is carrying on an activity which relates to a particular stage in the production of a product and a provision in any of the Regulations listed in paragraph (2) imposes a further or alternative requirement in relation to the supply and use of potable water in connection with that stage in the production of that product; or

(b) he is carrying out commercial operations on board a fishing vessel.

(4) Notwithstanding paragraph (1)(b), the provisions of Chapter X of Schedule 1 and of regulation 4(2)(d) in so far as it relates to that Chapter shall apply to a proprietor of a food business, unless a provision in any of the Regulations listed in paragraph (2) imposes a further or alternative requirement in relation to the instruction or training of food handlers.

Obligations upon proprietors of food businesses

4(1) A proprietor of a food business shall ensure that any of the following operations, namely, the preparation, processing, manufacturing, packaging, storing, transportation, distribution, handling and offering for sale or supply, of food are carried out in a hygienic way.

(2) A proprietor of a food business shall ensure that–

(a) the requirements set out in Chapter I of Schedule 1 are complied with as respects any food premises used for the purposes of that business;

(b) the requirements set out in Chapter II of Schedule 1 are complied with as respects any room where food is prepared, treated or processed in the course of the activities of that business, other than dining areas and premises covered by Chapter III of Schedule 1;

(c) the requirements set out in Chapter III of Schedule 1 are complied with as respects any of the following used for the purposes of that business–

(i) movable or temporary premises (such as marquees, market stalls and mobile sales vehicles);

(ii) premises used primarily as a private dwelling house;

(iii) premises used occasionally for catering purposes; and

(iv) vending machines; and

(d) the requirements set out in Chapters IV to X of Schedule 1 are complied with as respects that business.

(3) A proprietor of a food business shall identify any step in the activities of the food business which is critical ensuring food safety and ensure that adequate safety procedures are identified, implemented, maintained and reviewed on the basis of the following principles–

(a) analysis of the potential food hazards in a food business operation;

(b) identification of the points in those operations where food hazards may occur;

(c) deciding which of the points identified are critical to ensuring food safety ('critical points');

(d) identification and implementation of effective control and monitoring procedures at those critical points; and

(e) review of the analysis of food hazards, the critical points and the control and monitoring procedures periodically, and whenever the food business's operations change.

Persons suffering from certain medical conditions

5(1) Subject to paragraph (2), a person working in a food handling area who–

(a) knows or suspects that he is suffering from or that he is a carrier of a disease likely to be transmitted through food; or

(b) is afflicted with an infected wound, a skin infection, sores, diarrhoea or with any analogous medical condition,

in circumstances where there is any likelihood of him directly or indirectly contaminating any food with pathogenic micro-organisms, shall report that knowledge, suspicion or affliction to the proprietor of the food business at which he is working.

(2) This regulation shall not apply to a person unless he is working in a food handling area in which a food business proprietor, seeking to comply with regulation 4(2)(d) and paragraph 2 of Chapter VIII of Schedule 1, may be required to refuse him permission to work.

Offences and penalties

6(1) If any person contravenes regulation 4 (including any provision of Schedule 1) or 5, he shall be guilty of an offence against these Regulations.

(2) Any person guilty of an offence against these Regulations shall be liable–[a]

    (a) on summary conviction, to a fine not exceeding the *statutory maximum*;

    (b) on conviction on indictment, to a fine or imprisonment for a term not exceeding *two years* or *both*.

Application of provisions of the Act

7 The following provisions of the Act shall apply for the purposes of these Regulations as they apply for the purposes of sections 8, 14 and 15 of the Act, and unless the context otherwise requires, a reference in them to the Act shall for the purposes of these Regulations be construed as a reference to these Regulations–

    (a) section 2 (extended meaning of 'sale' etc);

    (b) section 3 (presumptions that food intended for human consumption);

    (c) section 20 (offences due to fault of another person);

    (d) section 21 (defence of due diligence);

    (e) section 30(8) (which relates to documentary evidence);

    (f) section 33 (obstruction etc. of officers);

    (g) section 34 (time limit for prosecutions);

    (h) section 36 (offences by bodies corporate), subject to the following modifications–

        (i) after the words 'body corporate', at the three places where they occur in section 36(1) of the Act, there shall be inserted the words 'or Scottish partnership'; and

        (ii) for the word 'secretary' there shall be substituted the words 'secretary, partner';

    (i) section 44 (protection of officers acting in good faith).

Enforcement and execution

8(1) Each food authority shall enforce and execute these Regulations within its area.

(2) In executing and enforcing these Regulations, a food authority shall–

    (a) ensure that–

        (i) food premises are inspected with a frequency which has regard to the risk associated with those premises; and

        (ii) inspections include a general assessment of the potential food safety hazards associated with the food business being inspected;

    (b) pay particular attention to the critical control points identified by food businesses to assess whether the necessary monitoring and verification controls are being operated;

    (c) give due consideration to whether the proprietor of a food business has acted in accordance with any relevant guide to good hygiene practice which has been–

(a) For procedure in respect of an offence which is triable either way, see the Magistrates' Courts Act 1980, ss 17A–21, in Part I: Magistrates' Courts, Procedure, *ante*.

(i) forwarded by the Secretary of State to the Commission pursuant to article 5.5 of the Directive, unless the Secretary of State has announced that it no longer complies with article 3 of the Directive; or

   (ii) developed in accordance with article 5.6 and 7 of the Directive and published in accordance with article 5.8 of the Directive.

9 Amendments to other Regulations.

10 Revocations.

SCHEDULE 1

Rules of Hygiene

Regulation 4(2)

[As amended by SI 1999/1540, Reg 4]

Chapter I

General Requirements for Food Premises (other than those specified in Chapter III)

1   Food premises must be kept clean and maintained in good repair and condition.

2   The layout, design, construction and size of food premises shall–

   (a) permit adequate cleaning and/or disinfection;

   (b) be such as to protect against the accumulation of dirt, contact with toxic materials, the shedding of particles into food and the formation of condensation or undesirable mould on surfaces;

   (c) permit good food hygiene practices, including protection against cross contamination between and during operations, by foodstuffs, equipment, materials, water, air supply or personnel and external sources of contamination such as pests; and

   (d) provide, where necessary, suitable temperature conditions for the hygienic processing and storage of products.

3   An adequate number of washbasins must be available, suitably located and designated for cleaning hands. An adequate number of flush lavatories must be available and connected to an effective drainage system. Lavatories must not lead directly into rooms in which food is handled.

4   Washbasins for cleaning hands must be provided with hot and cold (or appropriately mixed) running water, materials for cleaning hands and for hygienic drying. Where necessary, the provisions for washing food must be separate from the hand-washing facility.

5   There must be suitable and sufficient means of natural or mechanical ventilation. Mechanical air flow from a contaminated area to a clean area must be avoided. Ventilation systems must be so constructed as to enable filters and other parts requiring cleaning or replacement to be readily accessible.

6   All sanitary conveniences within food premises shall be provided with adequate natural or mechanical ventilation.

7   Food premises must have adequate natural and/or artificial lighting.

8   Drainage facilities must be adequate for the purpose intended; they must be designed and constructed to avoid the risk of contamination of foodstuffs.

9   Adequate changing facilities for personnel must be provided where necessary.

Chapter II

Specific Requirements in Rooms where Foodstuffs are Prepared, Treated or Processed (excluding Dining Areas and those Premises specified in Chapter III)

1   In rooms where food is prepared, treated or processed (excluding dining areas)–

   (a) floor surfaces must be maintained in a sound condition and they must be easy to clean and, where necessary, disinfect. This will require the use of impervious, non-absorbent, washable and non-toxic materials, unless the proprietor of the food business can satisfy the food authority that other materials used are appropriate. Where appropriate, floors must allow adequate surface drainage;

   (b) wall surfaces must be maintained in a sound condition and they must be easy to clean and, where necessary, disinfect. This will require the use of impervious, non-absorbent, washable and non-toxic materials and require a smooth surface up to a height appropriate for the operations, unless the proprietor of the food business can satisfy the food authority that other materials used are appropriate;

   (c) ceilings and overhead fixtures must be designed, constructed and finished to prevent the accumulation of dirt and reduce condensation, the growth of undesirable moulds and the shedding of particles;

   (d) windows and other openings must be constructed to prevent the accumulation of dirt. Those which can be opened to the outside environment must where necessary be fitted with insect-proof screens which can be easily removed for cleaning. Where open windows would result in contamination of foodstuffs, windows must remain closed and fixed during production;

   (e) doors must be easy to clean and, where necessary, disinfect. This will require the use of smooth and non-absorbent surfaces, unless the proprietor of the food business can satisfy the food authority that other materials used are appropriate;

   (f) surfaces (including surfaces of equipment) in contact with food must be maintained in a sound condition and be easy to clean and, where necessary, disinfect. This will require the use of smooth, washable and non-toxic materials, unless the proprietor of the food business can satisfy the food authority that other materials used are appropriate.

2   Where necessary, adequate facilities must be provided for the cleaning and disinfecting of work tools and equipment. These facilities must be constructed of materials resistant to corrosion and must be easy to clean and have an adequate supply of hot and cold water.

3   Where appropriate, adequate provision must be made for any necessary washing of the food. Every sink or other such facility provided for the washing of food must have an adequate supply of hot and/or cold potable water as required, and be kept clean.

Chapter III

Requirements for Movable and/or Temporary Premises (such as Marquees, Market Stalls, Mobile Sales Vehicles) Premises used primarily as a Private Dwelling House, Premises used occasionally for Catering Purposes and Vending Machines

1 Premises and vending machines shall be so sited, designed, constructed, and kept clean and maintained in good repair and condition, as to avoid the risk of contaminating foodstuffs and harbouring pests, so far as is reasonably practicable.

2 In particular and where necessary–
   (a) appropriate facilities must be available to maintain adequate personal hygiene (including facilities for the hygienic washing and drying of hands, hygienic sanitary arrangements and changing facilities);
   (b) surfaces in contact with food must be in a sound condition and be easy to clean and, where necessary, disinfect. This will require the use of smooth, washable, non-toxic materials, unless the proprietor of the food business can satisfy the food authority that other materials used are appropriate;
   (c) adequate provision must be made for the cleaning and, where necessary, disinfecting of work utensils and equipment;
   (d) adequate provision must be made for the cleaning of foodstuffs;
   (e) an adequate supply of hot and/or cold potable water must be available;
   (f) adequate arrangements and/or facilities for the hygienic storage and disposal of hazardous and/or inedible substances and waste (whether liquid or solid) must be available;
   (g) adequate facilities and/or arrangements for maintaining and monitoring suitable food temperature conditions must be available;
   (h) foodstuffs must be so placed as to avoid, so far as is reasonably practicable, the risk of contamination.

Chapter IV

Transport

1 Conveyances and/or containers used for transporting foodstuffs must be kept clean and maintained in good repair and condition in order to protect foodstuffs from contamination, and must, where necessary, be designed and constructed to permit adequate cleaning and/or disinfection.

2 (1) Receptacles in vehicles and/or containers must not be used for transporting anything other than foodstuffs where this may result in contamination of foodstuffs.

   (2) Subject to sub-paragraphs (3),(4) and Paragraph 2B bulk foodstuffs in liquid, granulate or powder form must be transported in receptacles and/or containers/tankers reserved for the transport of foodstuffs if otherwise there is a risk of contamination. Such containers must be marked in a clearly visible and indelible fashion, in one or more Community languages, to show that they are used for the transport of foodstuffs, or must be marked 'for foodstuffs only'.

   (3) The bulk transport in sea-going vessels of liquid oils or fats which are to be processed, and which are intended for or likely to be used for human consumption, is permitted in tanks that are not exclusively reserved for the transport of foodstuffs, subject to the following conditions–

(a) where the oil or fat is transported in a stainless steel tank, or tank lined with epoxy resin or technical equivalent, the immediately previous cargo transported in the tank shall have been a foodstuff or a cargo from the list of acceptable previous cargoes for liquid oils or fats;

(b) where the oil or fat is transported in a tank of materials other than those in paragraph (a) above, the three previous cargoes transported in the tanks shall have been foodstuffs or from the list of acceptable previous cargoes for liquid oils or fats.

(4) The bulk transport in sea-going vessels of liquid oils or fats which are not to be further processed, and which are intended for or are likely to be used for human consumption, is permitted in tanks that are not exclusively reserved for the transport of foodstuffs, subject to the following conditions–

(a) the tank shall be of stainless steel or lined with epoxy resin or technical equivalent;

(b) the three previous cargoes transported in the tank shall have been foodstuffs.

2A (1) The captain of a sea-going vessel transporting, in tanks, bulk liquid oil or fats intended for or likely to be used for human consumption shall keep accurate documentary evidence relating to the three previous cargoes carried in the tanks concerned, and the effectiveness of the cleaning process applied between these cargoes.

(2) Where the cargo has been trans-shipped, in addition to the documentary evidence required in sub-paragraph (1), the captain of the receiving vessel shall keep accurate documentary evidence that the transport of the bulk liquid oil or fat complied with the provisions in paragraph 2(3) or (4) of this Chapter during previous shipment and of the effectiveness of the cleaning process used between these cargoes on the other vessel.

(3) Upon request, the captain of the vessel shall provide the food authority with the documentary evidence described in sub-paragraphs (1) and (2).

2B (1) The bulk transport of raw sugar by sea which is not intended for use as food nor as a food ingredient without a full and effective refining process is permitted in receptacles, containers or tankers that are not exclusively used for the transport of foodstuffs.

(2) The receptacles, containers or tankers referred to in sub-paragraph (1) shall be subject to the following conditions–

(a) prior to loading the raw sugar, the receptacle, container or tanker shall be effectively cleaned to remove residues of the previous cargo and other soiling and inspected to establish that such residues have been removed effectively;

(b) the immediate previous cargo prior to the raw sugar shall not have been a bulk liquid.

2C (1) A proprietor of a food business which is responsible for the transport of raw sugar by sea under paragraph 2B shall keep documentary evidence, accurately describing in detail the immediate previous cargo carried in the receptacle, container or tanker concerned, and the type and effectiveness of the cleaning process applied prior to the transport of the raw sugar.

(2) The documentary evidence shall accompany the consignment during all stages of transport to the refinery and a copy shall be retained by the refinery. The documentary evidence shall be marked in a clearly visible and indelible fashion, in

one or more Community languages, 'This product must be refined before being used for human consumption'.

(3) On request, a proprietor of a food business responsible for the transport of the raw sugar or the refining process shall provide the competent official food control authorities with the documentary evidence referred to in sub-paragraphs (1) and (2).

(4) Raw sugar which has been transported by sea in receptacles, containers or tankers which are not exclusively reserved for the transport of foodstuffs shall be subjected to a full and effective refining process before being considered suitable for use as food or as a food ingredient.

(5) Regulation 4(3) shall apply to the transport of raw sugar by sea under paragraph 2B subject to the following modifications–

(a) a proprietor of any food business which is responsible for the transport or refining of raw sugar shall consider the cleaning process undertaken prior to the loading of the sugar for transport by sea to be a critical step in ensuring the safety and wholesomeness of food within the meaning of paragraph (3) of regulation 4, and

(b) in addition to the requirements of that paragraph, he shall also take into account the nature of the previous cargo which has been transported in any receptacle, container or tanker used for the transport of the sugar.

3 Where conveyances and/or containers are used for transporting anything in addition to foodstuffs or for transporting different foodstuffs at the same time, there must be effective separation of products, where necessary, to protect against the risk of contamination.

4 Where conveyances and/or containers have been used for transporting anything other than foodstuffs or for transporting different foodstuffs, there must be effective cleaning between loads to avoid the risk of contamination.

5 Foodstuffs in conveyances and/or containers must be so placed and protected as to minimise the risk of contamination.

6 Where necessary, conveyances and/or containers used for transporting foodstuffs, must be capable of maintaining foodstuffs at appropriate temperatures and, where necessary, designed to allow those temperatures to be monitored.

Chapter V

Equipment Requirements

1 All articles, fittings and equipment with which food comes into contact shall be kept clean and–

(a) be so constructed, be of such materials, and be kept in such good order, repair and condition, as to minimise any risk of contamination of the food;

(b) with the exception of non-returnable containers and packaging, be so constructed, be of such materials, and be kept in such good order, repair and condition, as to enable them to be kept thoroughly cleaned and, where necessary, disinfected, sufficient for the purposes intended;

(c) be installed in such a manner as to allow adequate cleaning of the surrounding area.

Chapter VI

Food Waste

1. Food waste and other refuse must not be allowed to accumulate in food rooms, except so far as is unavoidable for the proper functioning of the business.

2. Food waste and other refuse must be deposited in closable containers unless the proprietor of the food business can satisfy the food authority that other types of containers used are appropriate. These containers must be of an appropriate construction, kept in sound condition, and where necessary be easy to clean and disinfect.

3. Adequate provision must be made for the removal and storage of food waste and other refuse. Refuse stores must be designed and managed in such a way as to enable them to be kept clean, and to protect against access by pests, and against contamination food, drinking water, equipment or premises.

Chapter VII

Water Supply

1. There must be an adequate supply of potable water. This potable water must be used whenever necessary to ensure foodstuffs are not contaminated.

2. Where appropriate, ice must be made from potable water. This ice must be used whenever necessary to ensure foodstuffs are not contaminated. It must be made, handled and stored under conditions which protect it from all contamination.

3. Steam used directly in contact with food must not contain any substance which presents a hazard to health, or is likely to contaminate the product.

4. Water unfit for drinking used for the generation of steam, refrigeration, fire control and other similar purposes not relating to food, must be conducted in separate systems, readily identifiable and having no connection with, nor any possibility of reflux into, the potable water systems.

Chapter VIII

Personal Hygiene

1. Every person working in a food handling area shall maintain a high degree of personal cleanliness and shall wear suitable, clean and, where appropriate, protective clothing.

2. No person, known or suspected to be suffering from, or to be a carrier of, a disease likely to be transmitted through food or while afflicted, for example with infected wounds, skin infections, sores or with diarrhoea, shall be permitted to work in any food handling area in any capacity in which there is any likelihood of directly or indirectly contaminating food with pathogenic micro-organisms.

Chapter IX

Provisions applicable to Foodstuffs

1. No raw materials or ingredients shall be accepted by a food business if they are known to be, or might reasonably be expected to be, so contaminated with parasites, pathogenic micro-organisms, or toxic, decomposed or foreign substances, that after normal sorting and/or preparatory or processing procedures hygienically applied by food businesses, they would still be unfit for human consumption.

2. Raw materials and ingredients stored in the establishment shall be kept in appropriate conditions designed to prevent harmful deterioration and to protect them from contamination.

3. All food which is handled, stored, packaged, displayed and transported, shall be protected against any contamination likely to render the food unfit for human consumption, injurious to health or contaminated in such a way that it would be unreasonable to expect it to be consumed in that state. In particular, food must be so placed and/or protected as to minimise any risk of contamination. Adequate procedures must be in place to ensure pests are controlled.

4. Hazardous and/or inedible substances, including animal feedstuffs, shall be adequately labelled and stored in separate and secure containers.

Chapter X

Training

1. The proprietor of a food business shall ensure that food handlers engaged in the food business are supervised and instructed and/or trained in food hygiene matters commensurate with their work activities.

18.24 FOOD LABELLING REGULATIONS 1996

Need to prove/investigate:

1. Place of offence (within jurisdiction of the court).
2. Date(s) of offence.
3. Capacity of defendant, for example, limited company, partnership, sole trader, individual.
4. Food is intended for human consumption (see s 3 of the Food Safety Act 1990 for presumption).
5. Sale of food (see s 2 of the Food Safety Act 1990 for extended meaning of sale).
6. The name of the food or a list of ingredients, a list of ingredients or categories of ingredients, or the appropriate durability indication.
7. Defendant is the proprietor of the premises.
8. Due diligence defence.
9. Offence due to the act or default of the defendant.
10. Due diligence defence.
11. Within the scope of reg 4 and no exception applies, for example, regs 4(3), 17 or 18.
12. Mitigation/explanation from defendant.

Time limit: six months (s 127 of the Magistrates' Courts Act 1980).

Mode of trial: summary.

Maximum penalty (reg 6).

Summary: level 5.

Food Labelling Regulations 1996 SI 1996/1499, as amended by SIs 1998/141, 1398 and 2424, 1999/747, 1136, 1483 and 1540

Part I

Preliminary

1   Title and commencement

Made by the Minister of Agriculture, Fisheries and Food, the Secretary of State for Health and the Secretary of State for Wales in exercise of the powers conferred on them by ss 6(4), 16(1)(e) and (f), 17(1), 26(1) and (3) and 48(1) of the Food Safety Act 1990.

2   Interpretation

(1) In these Regulations, unless the context otherwise requires—

'the Act' means the Food Safety Act 1990;

'additive' means any substance not normally consumed as a food in itself and not normally used as a characteristic ingredient of food, whether or not it has nutritive value, the intentional addition of which to a food for a technological purpose in the manufacture, processing, preparation, treatment, packaging, transport or storage of such food results, or may be reasonably expected to result, in it or its by-products becoming directly or indirectly a component of such foods;

'the additives regulations' means the Flavourings in Food Regulations 1992, the Food Additives Labelling Regulations 1992, the Sweeteners in Food Regulations 1995, the Colours in Food Regulations 1995 and the Miscellaneous Food Additives Regulations 1995;

'advertisement' includes any notice, circular, invoice or other document, and any public announcement made orally or by any means of producing or transmitting light or sound, but does not include any form of labelling, and 'advertise' shall be construed accordingly;

'appropriate durability indication' means—

(a)   in the case of a food other than one specified in sub-paragraph (b) of this definition, an indication of minimum durability, and

(b)   in the case of a food which, from the microbiological point of view, is highly perishable and in consequence likely after a short period to constitute an immediate danger to human health, a 'use by' date;

'aromatised wine' has the meaning assigned to it by Article 2 of Council Regulation (EEC) No 1601/91;[1]

'biscuits' includes wafers, rusks, oatcakes and matzos;

'the Bread and Flour Regulations' means the Bread and Flour Regulations [1998];

'carbohydrate' means any carbohydrate which is metabolised in man and includes polyols;

'catering establishment' means a restaurant, canteen, club, public house, school, hospital or similar establishment (including a vehicle or a fixed or mobile stall) where, in the course of a business, food is prepared for delivery to the ultimate consumer and is ready for consumption without further preparation;

'cheese' means the fresh or matured product intended for sale for human consumption, which is obtained as follows—

(a) in the case of any cheese other than whey cheese, by the combining, by coagulation or by any technique involving coagulation, of any of the following substances, namely milk, cream, skimmed milk, partly skimmed milk, concentrated skimmed milk, reconstituted dried milk, butter milk, materials obtained from milk, other ingredients necessary for the manufacture of cheese provided that those are not used for replacing, in whole or in part, any milk constituent, with or without partially draining the whey resulting from coagulation;

(b) in the case of whey cheese–
   (i) by concentrating whey with or without the addition of milk and milk fat, and moulding such concentrated whey, or
   (ii) by coagulating whey with or without the addition of milk and milk fat;

'chocolate product' has the meaning assigned to it by the Cocoa and Chocolate Products Regulations 1976;

'clotted cream' means cream which has been produced and separated by the scalding, cooling and skimming of milk or cream;

'cream' means that part of cows' milk rich in fat which has been separated by skimming or otherwise and which is intended for sale for human consumption;

'cocoa product' has the meaning assigned to it by the Cocoa and Chocolate Products Regulations 1976;

'Community controlled wine' means wine, grape must, sparkling wine, aerated sparkling wine, liqueur wine, semi-sparkling wine and aerated semi-sparkling wine;

'confectionery product' means any item of chocolate confectionery or sugar confectionery;

'Directive 79/112' means Council Directive 79/112/EEC on the approximation of the laws of the Member States relating to the labelling, presentation and advertising of foodstuffs, as read in accordance with Schedule A1 and Commission Directive 1999/10/EC providing for derogations from the provisions of Article 7 of Council Directive 79/112/EEC as regards the labelling of foodstuffs;

'Directive 87/250' means Commission Directive 87/250/EEC on the indication of alcoholic strength by volume in the labelling of alcoholic beverages for sale to the ultimate consumer;

'Directive 89/398' means Council Directive 89/398/EEC on the approximation of the laws of the Member States relating to foodstuffs intended for particular nutritional uses;

'Directive 90/496' means Council Directive 90/496/EEC on nutrition labelling for foodstuffs;

'Directive 94/54' means Commission Directive 94/54/EC concerning the compulsory indication on the labelling of certain foodstuffs of particulars other than those provided for in Directive 79/112, as amended by Council Directive 96/21/EC;

'disease' includes any injury, ailment or adverse condition, whether of body or mind;

'edible ice' includes ice-cream, water ice and fruit ice, whether alone or in combination, and any similar food;

'EEA Agreement' means the Agreement on the European Economic Area[2] signed at Oporto on 2nd May 1992 as adjusted by the Protocol[3] signed at Brussels on 17th March 1993;

'EEA State' means a state which is a Contracting Party to the EEA Agreement;

'fancy confectionery product' means any confectionery product in the form of a figure, animal, cigarette or egg or in any other fancy form;

'fat', in the context of nutrition labelling, means total lipids, and includes phospholipids;

the noun 'flavouring' means an additive consisting of material used or intended for use in or on food to impart odour, taste or both, provided that such material does not consist entirely of–

(a) any edible substance (including herbs and spices) or product, intended for human consumption as such, with or without reconstitution, or

(b) any substance which has exclusively a sweet, sour or salt taste, and the components of which include at least one of the following–

   (i) a flavouring substance,

   (ii) a flavouring preparation,

   (iii) a process flavouring,

   (iv) a smoke flavouring;

'flavouring preparation' means a product (other than a flavouring substance), whether concentrated or not, with flavouring properties, which is obtained by physical, enzymatic or microbiological processes from appropriate material of vegetable or animal origin;

'flavouring substance' means a chemical substance with flavouring properties the chemical structure of which has been established by methods normally used among scientists and which is–

(a) obtained by physical, enzymatic or microbiological processes from appropriate material of vegetable or animal origin,

(b) either obtained by chemical synthesis or isolated by chemical processes and which is chemically identical to a substance naturally present in appropriate material of vegetable or animal origin, or

(c) obtained by chemical synthesis but not included under sub-paragraph (b) of this definition,

and for the purposes of this definition and the definition of 'flavouring preparation'–

   (i) distillation and solvent extraction shall be regarded as included among types of physical process;

   (ii) material of vegetable or animal origin is appropriate material of vegetable or animal origin if it either is raw or has been subjected to a process normally used in preparing food for human consumption and to no process other than one normally so used; and

   (iii) drying, torrefaction and fermentation shall be treated as included among the types of process normally so used to which sub-paragraph (ii) above refers.

Chapter 18: Environmental Health Legislation

'flour confectionery' means any cooked food which is ready for consumption without further preparation (other than reheating), of which a characterising ingredient is ground cereal, including shortbread, sponges, crumpets, muffins, macaroons, ratafias, pastry and pastry cases, and also includes meringues, petits fours and uncooked pastry and pastry cases, but does not include bread, pizzas, biscuits, crispbread, extruded flat bread or any food containing a filling which has as an ingredient any cheese, meat, offal, fish, shellfish, vegetable protein material or microbial protein material;

'follow-on formula' has the meaning assigned to it by the Infant Formula and Follow-on Formula Regulations 1995;

'food for a particular nutritional use' means a food intended for human consumption which–

(a) owing to its special composition or process of manufacture, is clearly distinguishable from food intended for normal human consumption,

(b) is suitable for its claimed particular nutritional purpose, and

(c) is sold in such a way as to indicate that suitability;

'the GMO particulars' means the additional specific labelling particulars required by Article 2(3) of Regulation 1139/98;

'grape must' has the meaning assigned to it by Annex I to Council Regulation (EEC) No 822/87[4] on the common organisation of the market in wine;

'infants' means children under the age of twelve months;

'infant formula' has the meaning assigned to it by the Infant Formula and Follow-on Formula Regulations 1995;

'ingredient' means any substance, including any additive and any constituent of a compound ingredient, which is used in the preparation of a food and which is still present in the finished product, even if in altered form, and a 'compound ingredient' shall be composed of two or more such substances;

'intense sweetener' means an additive with a sweetness many times that of sucrose, which is virtually non-calorific and used solely for its sweetening properties;

'ionising radiation' means any gamma rays, x-rays or corpuscular radiations which are capable of producing ions either directly or indirectly other than those rays or radiations–

(a) which are emitted by measuring or inspection devices,

(b) which are emitted at an energy level no higher than the appropriate maximum level, and

(c) the dose of energy imparted by which does not exceed 0.5 Gy,

and for the purposes of this definition the appropriate maximum level is 10 MeV in the case of x-rays and 5 MeV otherwise;

'irradiated' means subjected to treatment by ionising radiation;

'labelling', in relation to a food, includes any words, particulars, trade mark, brand name, pictorial matter or symbol relating to the food and appearing on the packaging of the food or on any document, notice, label, ring or collar accompanying the food;

'liqueur wine'–
(a) in relation to a drink produced in the European Community, has the meaning assigned to it by Annex I to Council Regulation (EEC) No 822/87, and
(b) in relation to a drink originating from elsewhere, has the meaning assigned to it by Article 2 of Council Regulation (EEC) No 2391/89;[5]

'milk' means the milk intended for sale, or sold, for human consumption of–
(a) one or more cows, and includes skimmed milk, semi-skimmed milk and whole milk, or
(b) one or more ewes, goats or buffaloes;

'mono-unsaturates' means fatty acids with one cis double bond;

'natural mineral water' has the meaning assigned to it by the Natural Mineral Water, Spring Water and Bottled Drinking Water Regulations 1999;[6]

'nutrient', in the context of nutrition labelling, means any of the following: protein, carbohydrate, fat, fibre, sodium, any vitamin or mineral listed in Table A or B in Schedule 6 and present in any food in a significant amount as described in the Note to those Tables;

'nutrition claim' means any statement, suggestion or implication in any labelling, presentation or advertising of a food that that food has particular nutrition properties, but does not include a reference to any quality or quantity of any nutrient where such reference is required by law;

'nutrition labelling', in relation to a food (other than a natural mineral water or other water intended for human consumption or any food supplement) means any information appearing on labelling (other than where such appears solely as part of a list of ingredients) and relating to energy value or any nutrient or to energy value and any nutrient, including any information relating to any substance which belongs to, or is a component of, a nutrient;

'nutrition properties' means either or both of–
(a) the provision (including provision at a reduced or increased rate), or the lack of provision, of energy,
(b) the content (including content in a reduced or increased proportion), or the lack of content, of any nutrient (including any substance which belongs to, or is a component of, a nutrient);

'particular nutritional purpose' means the fulfilment of the particular nutritional requirements of–
(a) a person whose digestive processes are, or whose metabolism is, disturbed, or
(b) a person whose physiological condition renders him able to obtain a special benefit from the controlled consumption of any substance in food, or
(c) infants or young children in good health;

'polyunsaturates' means fatty acids with cis, cis-methylene interrupted double bonds;

'prepacked', in relation to a food, means put into packaging before being offered for sale in such a way that the food, whether wholly or only partly enclosed, cannot be altered without opening or changing the packaging and is ready for sale to the ultimate consumer or to a catering establishment, and includes a food which is wholly enclosed in packaging before being offered for sale and which is intended to be cooked without opening the packaging and which is ready for sale to the ultimate consumer or to a catering establishment, but does not include individually wrapped sweets or chocolates which are not enclosed in any further packaging and which are not intended for sale as individual items;

'prepacked for direct sale', means–

(a) in relation to a food other than flour confectionery, bread, edible ices and cows' milk, prepacked by a retailer for sale by him on the premises where the food is packed or from a vehicle or stall used by him,

(b) in relation to flour confectionery, bread and edible ices, prepacked by a retailer for sale as in sub-paragraph (a) of this definition, or prepacked by the producer of the food for sale by him either on the premises where the food is produced or on other premises from which he conducts business under the same name as the business conducted on the premises where the food is produced, and

(c) in relation to cows' milk, put into containers on the premises where the milk is produced by the person owning or having control of the herd from which the milk is produced for sale by him on those premises or from a vehicle or stall used by him;

'preparation', in relation to food, includes manufacture and any form of processing or treatment, and 'prepared' shall be construed accordingly;

'prescribed nutrition labelling' means nutrition labelling given in accordance with Schedule 7;

'processing aid' means any substance not consumed as a food by itself, intentionally used in the processing of raw materials, foods or their ingredients, to fulfil a certain technological purpose during treatment or processing, and which may result in the unintentional but technically unavoidable presence of residues of the substance or its derivatives in the final product, provided that these residues do not present any health risk and do not have any technological effect on the finished product;

'process flavouring' means a product which is obtained according to good manufacturing practices by heating to a temperature not exceeding 180 degrees C for a continuous period not exceeding 15 minutes a mixture of ingredients (whether or not with flavouring properties) of which at least one contains nitrogen (amino) and another is a reducing sugar;

'protein' means the protein content calculated using the formula: protein = total Kjeldahl nitrogen x 6.25;

'raw milk', in relation to cows' milk, has the meaning assigned to it by Article 3(1) of Council Regulation (EC) No 2597/97[7] laying down additional rules on the common organisation of the market in milk and milk products for drinking milk, and in relation to the milk of ewes, goats or buffaloes means milk which has neither been heat-treated beyond 40 degrees C nor undergone any treatment having the same effect;

'recommended daily allowance', in relation to a vitamin or mineral, means the recommended daily allowance specified for that vitamin or mineral in column 2 of Table A or B in Schedule 6;

'Regulation 1139/98' means Council Regulation (EC) No 1139/98 (as corrected) concerning the compulsory indication, on the labelling of certain foodstuffs produced from genetically modified organisms, of particulars other than those provided for in Directive 79/112/EEC;

'saturates' means fatty acids without double bond;

'seasonal selection pack' means a pack consisting of two or more different items of food which are wholly or partly enclosed in outer packaging decorated with seasonal designs;

'sell' includes offer or expose for sale and have in possession for sale, and 'sale' and 'sold' shall be construed accordingly;

'semi-skimmed milk', in relation to cows' milk, has the meaning assigned to it by Article 3(1) of Council Regulation (EC) No 2597/97;

'skimmed milk', in relation to cows' milk, has the meaning assigned to it by Article 3(1) of Council Regulation (EC) No 2597/97;

'smoke flavouring' means an extract from smoke of a type normally used in food smoking processes;

'sparkling wine', 'aerated sparkling wine', 'semi-sparkling wine' and 'aerated semi-sparkling wine'–

(a) in relation to drinks produced in the European Community, have the meanings respectively assigned to them by Annex I to Council Regulation (EEC) No 822/87, and

(b) in relation to drinks produced elsewhere, have the meanings respectively assigned to them by Article 2 of Council Regulation (EEC) No 2391/89;

'sterilised cream' means cream which has been subjected to a process of sterilisation by heat treatment in the container in which it is to be supplied to the consumer;

'sugars', in the context of nutrition labelling, means all monosaccharides and disaccharides present in food, but excludes polyols;

'treating', in relation to disease, includes doing or providing anything for alleviating the effects of the disease, whether it is done or provided by way of cure or not;

'ultimate consumer' means any person who buys otherwise than–

(a) for the purpose of resale,

(b) for the purposes of a catering establishment, or

(c) for the purposes of a manufacturing business;

'whole milk', in relation to cows' milk, has the meaning assigned to it by Article 3(1) of Council Regulation (EC) No 2597/97;

'wine' has the meaning assigned to it by Annex I to Council Regulation (EEC) No 822/87;

'young children' means children aged between one and three years.

(2) Unless the context otherwise requires, all proportions mentioned in these Regulations are proportions calculated by weight.

(3) Any reference in these Regulations to a numbered regulation or Schedule shall, unless the context otherwise requires, be construed as a reference to the regulation or Schedule so numbered in these Regulations.

(4) Where any Schedule to these Regulations contains any note or notes, the provisions of that Schedule shall be interpreted and applied in accordance with such note or notes.

1   OJ No L149, 14.6.91, p 1; there is an amendment to the Council Regulation which is not relevant to these Regulations.
2   OJ No L1, 3.1.94, p 1.
3   OJ No L1, 3.1.94, p 571.
4   OJ No L84, 27.3.87, p 1, to which there are amendments not relevant to these Regulations.
5   OJ No L232, 9.8.89, p 10.
6   SI 1999/1540.
7   OJ No l351, 23.12.97, p 13.

3   Exemptions

(1) Subject to paragraph (1A) of this regulation, these Regulations shall not apply in respect of–
   (a) any food to which the provisions of the EEA Agreement apply brought into Great Britain from an EEA State in which it was lawfully produced and sold;
   (b) any food lawfully produced in another member State brought into Great Britain from a member State in which it was lawfully sold; or
   (c) any food lawfully produced outside the European Community brought into Great Britain from a member State in which it was in free circulation and lawfully sold,

   if–
   (i) the requirements of Article 2 of Directive 79/112 are met in respect of that food;
   (ii) that food is marked or labelled, in a language easily understood by the consumer, with the particulars provided for in Articles 3 and 4(2) of that Directive;
   (iii) the name of the food and any other descriptive information accompanying it is in accordance with Article 5(1) of that Directive; and
   (iv) where applicable, the requirements of Directive 87/250, Directive 89/398, Directive 90/496 and Directive 94/54 and Regulation 1139/98 are met in respect of that food.

(1A) Nothing in paragraph (1) of this regulation shall prevent the enforcement of–
   (a) regulation 44(1)(a) in relation to a contravention of regulation 31; or
   (b) regulation 44(1)(c),(d) or (e).

(2) For the purposes of paragraph (1) of this regulation 'free circulation' has the same meaning as in Article 9.2 of the Treaty establishing the European Community.

(3) These Regulations, except in so far as they relate to advertising, shall not apply to any food which is–
   (a) not intended for sale for human consumption, or
   (b) supplied under Government contracts for consumption by Her Majesty's forces or supplied for consumption by a visiting force within the meaning of any of the provisions of Part I of the Visiting Forces Act 1952, and was prepared and labelled for sale before 16th November 1992.

(4) Subject to paragraph (5) of this regulation, regulation 29 and Part III of these Regulations shall not apply to natural mineral water (other than such water which has been artificially carbonated).

(5) Regulations 40 and 41 shall apply to natural mineral water in so far as they relate to item 1 in Part II of Schedule 6, and regulation 42(1) shall apply to such water in so far as it relates to the descriptions 'dietary' and 'dietetic' in Schedule 8.

Part II

Food to be Delivered as such to the Ultimate Consumer or to Caterers

Scope and general labelling requirement

4 Scope of Part II

(1) Subject to paragraphs (2) and (3) of this regulation, this Part of these Regulations applies to food which is ready for delivery to the ultimate consumer or to a catering establishment.

(2) Except for regulations 33 and 34 and, insofar as they relate to regulations 33 and 34, regulations 35 and 38, this Part of these Regulations does not apply to–

(a) any specified sugar product as defined in the Specified Sugar Products Regulations 1976;

(b) any cocoa product or chocolate product as defined in the Cocoa and Chocolate Products Regulations 1976;

(c) any honey as defined in the Honey Regulations 1976;

(d) any condensed milk product or dried milk product as defined in the Condensed Milk and Dried Milk Regulations 1977 which is ready for delivery to a catering establishment other than any such product which is specially prepared for infant feeding and in the labelling of which there appears a clear statement that such food is intended for consumption by infants and no statement to the effect that such is intended for consumption by any other class of person;

(e) any coffee, coffee mixture, coffee extract product, chicory extract product or other designated product as defined in the Coffee and Coffee Products Regulations 1978 which is ready for delivery to a catering establishment;

(f) hen eggs, in so far as their labelling is regulated by Council Regulation (EEC) No 1907/90[1] on certain marketing standards for eggs, as amended,[2] Commission Regulation (EEC) No 1274/91[3] introducing detailed rules for implementing Regulation (EEC) No 1907/90, as amended,[4] and Council Decision 94/371/EC[5] laying down specific public health conditions for the putting on the market of certain types of eggs;

(g) spreadable fats, in so far as their labelling is regulated by Council Regulation (EC) No 2991/94[6] laying down standards for spreadable fats;

(h) wines or grape musts, in so far as their labelling is regulated by Council Regulation (EEC) No 2392/89[7] laying down general rules for the description and presentation of wines and grape musts, as amended;[8]

(i) sparkling wines and aerated sparkling wines, in so far as their labelling is regulated by Council Regulation (EEC) No 2333/92[9] laying down general rules for the description and presentation of sparkling wines and aerated sparkling wines;

Chapter 18: Environmental Health Legislation

(j) liqueur wines, semi-sparkling wines and aerated semi-sparkling wines, in so far as their labelling is regulated by Council Regulation (EEC) No 3895/91[10] laying down rules for the description and presentation of special wines, and Commission Regulation (EEC) No 3901/91[11] laying down certain detailed rules on the description and presentation of special wines;

(k) any spirit drinks, in so far as their labelling is regulated by Council Regulation (EEC) No 1576/89[12] laying down general rules on the definition, description and presentation of spirit drinks, Commission Regulation (EEC) No 3773/89[13] laying down transitional measures relating to spirituous beverages, as amended,[14] and Commission Regulation (EEC) No 1014/90[15] laying down detailed implementing rules on the definition, description and presentation of spirit drinks, as amended;[16]

(l) fresh fruit and vegetables, in so far as their labelling is regulated by Council Regulation (EC) No 2200/96[17] on the common organisation of the market in fruit and vegetables;

(m) preserved sardines, in so far as their labelling is regulated by Council Regulation (EEC) No 2136/89[18] laying down common marketing standards for preserved sardines;

(n) preserved tuna and bonito, in so far as their labelling is regulated by Council Regulation (EEC) No 1536/92[19] laying down common marketing standards for preserved tuna and bonito;

(o) any additive sold as such which is required to be labelled in accordance with regulation 4(3) of the Extraction Solvents in Food Regulations 1993, or the appropriate provisions of any of the additives regulations.

(3) This Part of these Regulations does not apply to—

(a) any drink bottled before 1st January 1983 which has an alcoholic strength by volume of more than 1.2 per cent and which is labelled in accordance with the legislation in force at the time of bottling;

(b) any food prepared on domestic premises for sale for the benefit of the person preparing it by a society registered under the Industrial and Provident Societies Act 1965;

(c) any food prepared otherwise than in the course of a business carried on by the person preparing it.

1   OJ No L173, 6.7.90, p 5 as read with Corrigendum at OJ No L195, 26.7.90, p 40.

2   Council Regulation (EEC) No 2617/93 (OJ No L240, 25.9.93, p 1) and Council Regulation (EC) No 3117/94 (OJ No L330, 12.12.94, p 4).

3   OJ No L121, 16.5.91, p 11.

4   Commission Regulation (EEC) No 3540/91 (OJ No L335, 6.12.91, p 12), Commission Regulation (EEC) No 2221/92 (OJ No L218, 1.8.92, p 81, as read with Corrigendum at OJ No L292, 8.10.92, p 34), Commission Regulation (EC) No 3300/93 (OJ No L296, 1.12.93, p 52), Commission Regulation (EC) No 1259/94 (OJ No L137, 1.6.94, p 54), Commission Regulation (EC) No 3239/94 (OJ No L338, 28.12.94, p 48), Commission Regulation (EC) No 786/95 (OJ L79, 7.4.95, p 12) and Commission Regulation (EC) No 2401/95 (OJ No L246, 13.10.95, p 6).

5   OJ No L168, 2.7.94, p 34.

6 OJ No L316, 9.12.94, p 2.
7 OJ No L232, 9.8.89, p 3.
8 Council Regulation (EEC) No 3886/89 (OJ No L378, 27.12.89, p 12) and Council Regulation (EEC) No 3897/91 (OJ No L386, 3.12.91, p 5).
9 OJ No L231, 13.8.92, p 9.
10 OJ No L368, 31.12.91, p 1.
11 OJ No L368, 31.12.91, p 15.
12 OJ No L160, 12.6.89, p 1.
13 OJ No L365, 15.12.89, p 48.
14 Commission Regulation (EEC) No 1759/90 (OJ No L162, 28.6.90, p 23), Commission Regulation (EEC) No 3207/90 (OJ No L307, 7.11.90, p 11), and Commission Regulation (EEC) No 3750/90 (OJ No L360, 22.12.90, p 40).
15 OJ No L105, 25.4.90, p 9.
16 Commission Regulation (EEC) No 1180/91 (OJ No L115, 8.5.91, p 5), Commission Regulation (EEC) No 1785/91 (OJ No L160, 25.6.91, p 5), and Commission Regulation (EEC) No 3458/92 (OJ No L350, 1.12.92, p 59).
17 OJ No L297, 2.11.96, p 1.
18 OJ No L212, 22.7.89, p 79.
19 OJ No L163, 17.6.92, p 1.

5 General labelling requirement

Subject to the following provisions of this Part of these Regulations, all food to which this Part of these Regulations applies shall be marked or labelled with–

(a) the name of the food;

(b) a list of ingredients;

(ba) the quantity of certain ingredients or categories of ingredients;

(c) the appropriate durability indication;

(d) any special storage conditions or conditions of use;

(e) the name or business name and an address or registered office of either or both of–

   (i) the manufacturer or packer, or

   (ii) a seller established within the European Community;

(f) particulars of the place of origin or provenance of the food if failure to give such particulars might mislead a purchaser to a material degree as to the true origin or provenance of the food; and

(g) instructions for use if it would be difficult to make appropriate use of the food in the absence of such instructions.

Name of the food

6 Name prescribed by law

(1) If there is a name prescribed by law for a food, that is to say if a particular name is required to be used for the food, that name shall be used as the name of the food.

(2) The name used for food specified in Schedule 1 shall be the name required by that Schedule.

(3) A name that is required to be used for a food by paragraph (1) or (2) of this regulation may be qualified by other words which make it more precise, unless such qualification is prohibited.

(4) In paragraph (1) of this regulation and in regulations 7 and 8(a) and Schedule 1, 'prescribed by law' means prescribed by European Community law or, in the absence of such law, by law in Great Britain.

7 Customary name

If there is no name prescribed by law for a food, a customary name, that is to say a name which is customary in the area where the food is sold, may be used for the food.

8 Indication of true nature of food

If–

(a) there is no name prescribed by law for a food, and

(b) there is no customary name or the customary name is not used,

the name used for the food shall be sufficiently precise to inform a purchaser of the true nature of the food and to enable the food to be distinguished from products with which it could be confused and, if necessary, shall include a description of its use.

9 Form of name

The name of a food may consist of a name or description or of a name and description and it may contain more than one word.

10 Trade marks, brand names and fancy names

A trade mark, brand name or fancy name shall not be substituted for the name of a food.

11 Indication of physical condition or treatment

(1) Where a purchaser could be misled by the omission of an indication–

(a) that a food is powdered or is in any other physical condition, or

(b) that a food has been dried, freeze-dried, frozen, concentrated or smoked, or has been subjected to any other treatment,

the name of the food shall include or be accompanied by such an indication.

(2) Without prejudice to the generality of paragraph (1) of this regulation, the name used for a food specified in Schedule 2 shall include or be accompanied by such indication as is required by that Schedule.

List of ingredients

12 Heading of list of ingredients

The list of ingredients must be headed or preceded by an appropriate heading which consists of or includes the word 'ingredients'.

13 Order of list of ingredients

(1) Subject to the following paragraphs of this regulation, when a food is marked or labelled with a list of ingredients, the ingredients shall be listed in descending order of weight determined as at the time of their use in the preparation of the food.

(2) Subject to regulation 16, water and volatile products which are added as ingredients of a food shall be listed in order of their weight in the finished product, the weight being calculated in the case of water by deducting from the total weight of the finished product the total weight of the other ingredients used.

(3) In the case of an ingredient which is used in a food in concentrated or dehydrated form and which is reconstituted during preparation of the food, the weight used in determining the order of the list of ingredients may be the weight of the ingredient before concentration or dehydration.

(4) Without prejudice to regulation 12, where a food is in concentrated or dehydrated form and is intended to be reconstituted by the addition of water, its ingredients may be listed in descending order of their weight in the food when reconstituted as directed if the heading of the list of ingredients includes or is accompanied by the words 'ingredients of the reconstituted product' or 'ingredients of the ready to use product' or by some other indication to similar effect.

(5) Where a food consists of, or contains, mixed fruit, nuts, vegetables, spices or herbs and no particular fruit, nut, vegetable, spice or herb predominates significantly by weight, those ingredients may be listed otherwise than in descending order of weight if–

   (a) in the case of a food which consists entirely of such a mixture, the heading of the list of ingredients includes or is accompanied by the words 'in variable proportion' or other words indicating the nature of the order in which the ingredients are listed, and

   (b) in the case of a food which contains such a mixture, that part of the list where the names of those ingredients appear is accompanied by the words 'in variable proportion' or other words indicating the nature of the order in which those ingredients are listed.

14 Names of ingredients

(1) Subject to the following paragraphs of this regulation, the name used for any ingredient in a list of ingredients shall be a name which, if the ingredient in question were itself being sold as a food, could be used as the name of the food.

(2) The name used in any list of ingredients for any food which has been irradiated shall include or be accompanied by the word 'irradiated' or the words 'treated with ionising radiation'.

(3) Where in any case other than one to which paragraph (2) of this regulation applies a purchaser could be misled by the omission from the name used for an ingredient of any indication which, if the ingredient were itself being sold as a food, would be required to be included in or to accompany the name of the food, the name used for the ingredient in a list of ingredients shall include or be accompanied by that indication unless the provision requiring the indication provides to the contrary.

(4) A generic name which appears in column 1 of Schedule 3 may be used for an ingredient which is specified in the corresponding entry in column 2 of that Schedule in accordance with any conditions that are laid down in the corresponding entry in column 3 of that Schedule.

(5) Where an ingredient being a flavouring is added to or used in a food it shall be identified by either–

   (a) the word 'flavouring' or, where more than one such ingredient is used, 'flavourings', or

   (b) a more specific name or description of the flavouring (or flavourings).

(6) The word 'natural', or any other word having substantially the same meaning, may be used for an ingredient being a flavouring only where the flavouring component (or components) of such an ingredient consists (or consist) exclusively of–
   (a) a flavouring substance (or flavouring substances) which is (or are) obtained, by physical, enzymatic or microbiological processes, from material of vegetable or animal origin which material is either raw or has been subjected to a process normally used in preparing food for human consumption and to no process other than one normally so used,
   (b) a flavouring preparation (or flavouring preparations), or
   (c) both (a) and (b) above.
(7) If the name of an ingredient being a flavouring refers to the vegetable or animal nature or origin of the material which it incorporates, the word 'natural', or any other word having substantially the same meaning, may not be used for that ingredient unless, in addition to satisfying the requirements of paragraph (6) of this regulation, the flavouring component (or components) of that ingredient has (or have) been isolated by physical, enzymatic or microbiological processes, or by a process normally used in preparing food for human consumption, solely or almost solely from that vegetable or animal source.
(8) In paragraphs (6) and (7) of this regulation–
   (a) distillation and solvent extraction shall be regarded as included among types of physical process, and
   (b) drying, torrefaction and fermentation shall be treated as included among the types of process normally used in preparing food for human consumption.
(9) An additive which is added to or used in a food to serve the function of one of the categories of additives listed in Schedule 4 shall be identified by the name of that category followed by the additive's specific name or serial number (if any). An additive which is added to or used in a food to serve more than one such function shall be identified by the name of the category that represents the principal function served by the additive in that food followed by the additive's specific name or serial number (if any).
(10) An additive which is required to be named in the list of ingredients of a food and which is neither a flavouring nor serves the function of one of the categories of additives listed in Schedule 4 shall be identified by its specific name.
(11) In this regulation 'serial number' means the number specified for an additive in any of the additive regulations.

15 Compound ingredients

(1) Subject to paragraphs (3) and (4) of this regulation, where a compound ingredient is used in the preparation of a food, the names of the ingredients of the compound ingredient shall be given in the list of ingredients of the food either instead of or in addition to the name of the compound ingredient itself.
(2) If the name of a compound ingredient is given, it shall be immediately followed by the names of its ingredients in such a way as to make it clear that they are ingredients of that compound ingredient.
(3) The names of the ingredients of a compound ingredient need not be given in a case where the compound ingredient would not be required to be marked or labelled with a list of ingredients if it were itself being sold prepacked as a food.

(4) The names of the ingredients of a compound ingredient need not be given in a case where—
  (a) the compound ingredient is identified in the list of ingredients by a generic name in accordance with regulation 14(4), or
  (b) the compound ingredient constitutes less than 25 per cent of the finished product, except that, subject to regulation 17, any additive which is an ingredient of such a compound ingredient shall be named in the list of ingredients in accordance with paragraph (2) of this regulation.

16 Added water
  (1) Water which is added as an ingredient of a food shall be declared in the list of ingredients of the food unless—
  (a) it is used in the preparation of the food solely for the reconstitution or partial reconstitution of an ingredient used in concentrated or dehydrated form; or
  (b) it is used as, or as part of, a medium which is not normally consumed; or
  (c) it does not exceed 5 per cent of the finished product.
  (2) Water which is added to any frozen or quick-frozen chicken carcass to which Commission Regulation (EEC) No 1538/91[1] applies, as amended by Commission Regulation (EEC) No 2891/93,[2] introducing detailed rules for implementing Council Regulation (EEC) No 1906/90 on certain marketing standards for poultry, need not be declared in the list of ingredients of the food.

1 OJ No L143, 7.6.91, p 11.
2 OJ No L263, 22.10.93, p 12.

17 Ingredients which need not be named
The following ingredients of a food need not be named in its list of ingredients:
  (a) constituents of an ingredient which have become temporarily separated during the manufacturing process and are later re-introduced in their original proportions;
  (b) any additive whose presence in the food is due solely to the fact that it was contained in an ingredient of the food, if it serves no significant technological function in the finished product;
  (c) any additive which is used solely as a processing aid;
  (d) any substance other than water which is used as a solvent or carrier for an additive and is used in an amount that is no more than that which is strictly necessary for that purpose.

18 Foods which need not bear a list of ingredients
  (1) The following foods need not be marked or labelled with a list of ingredients:
  (a) fresh fruit and vegetables, including potatoes, which have not been peeled or cut into pieces;
  (b) carbonated water, to which no ingredient other than carbon dioxide has been added, and whose name indicates that it has been carbonated;
  (c) vinegar which is derived by fermentation exclusively from a single basic product and to which no other ingredient has been added;
  (d) cheese, butter, fermented milk and fermented cream, to which no ingredient has been added other than lactic products, enzymes and micro-organism

cultures essential to manufacture or, in the case of cheese other than fresh curd cheese and processed cheese, such amount of salt as is needed for its manufacture;

  (e) flour to which no substances have been added other than those which are required to be present in the flour by regulation 4 of the Bread and Flour Regulations;

  (f) any drink with an alcoholic strength by volume of more than 1.2 per cent;

  (g) any food consisting of a single ingredient, where–
    (i) the name of the food is identical with the name of the ingredient; or
    (ii) the name of the food enables the nature of the ingredient to be clearly identified.

(2) Without prejudice to regulation 12, in the case of–

  (a) any vinegar which is derived by fermentation exclusively from a single basic product and to which any other ingredient has been added, or

  (b) any cheese, butter, fermented milk or fermented cream, to which any ingredient, other than one which is mentioned in paragraph (1)(d) of this regulation, has been added,

only those other added ingredients need be named in the list of ingredients, if the heading of the list includes or is accompanied by the words 'added ingredients' or other words indicating that the list is not a complete list of ingredients.

(3) The labelling of any food that is not required to bear a list of ingredients shall not include a list of ingredients unless the food is marked or labelled with a complete list of ingredients in accordance with regulations 12 to 17 as if it were required to be so marked or labelled.

Quantities of certain ingredients or categories of ingredients

19 Indication of quantities of certain ingredients or categories of ingredients

(1) Subject to paragraph (2) and (2A) of this regulation, the quantity of an ingredient or category of ingredients used in the preparation of a food shall be indicated where–

  (a) that ingredient or category of ingredients appears in the name of the food or is usually associated with that name by the consumer;

  (b) that ingredient or category of ingredients is emphasised on the labelling in words, pictures or graphics; or

  (c) that ingredient or category of ingredients is essential to characterise a food and to distinguish it from products with which it might be confused because of its name or appearance.

(2) Paragraph (1) of this regulation shall not apply–

  (a) in respect of an ingredient or category of ingredients–
    (i) the drained net weight of which is indicated in accordance with Article 8(4) of Directive 79/112;
    (ii) the quantities of which are already required to be given on the labelling under European Community provisions;
    (iii) which is used in small quantities for the purposes of flavouring; or
    (iv) which, though it appears in the name of the food, is not such as to govern the choice of the consumer because the variation in quantity is not

essential to characterise the food or does not distinguish it from similar foods;

(b) where specific European Community provisions stipulate precisely the quantity of an ingredient or category of ingredients without providing for the indication thereof on the labelling; or

(c) in the cases referred to in regulation 13(5).

(2A) Sub-paragraphs (a) and (b) of paragraph (1) of this regulation shall not apply in the case of–

(a) any ingredient or category of ingredients covered by the indication 'with sweetener(s)' or 'with sugar(s) and sweetener(s)' if that indication accompanies the name of the food pursuant to regulation 34; or

(b) any added vitamin or mineral if that substance is the subject of nutrition labelling relating to the food in question.

(3) The indication of quantity of an ingredient or category of ingredients required by paragraph (1) of this regulation shall–

(a) subject to paragraph 4 of this regulation, be expressed as a percentage, which shall be determined as at the time of use of the ingredient or category of ingredients in the preparation of the food; and

(b) appear–

(i) in or next to the name of the food, or

(ii) in the list of ingredients in connection with the ingredient or category of ingredients in question.

(4) Notwithstanding sub-paragraph (a) of paragraph (3) of this regulation–

(a) where the food has lost moisture as a result of treatment, the indication of quantity of the ingredient or category of ingredients used shall be expressed as a percentage which shall be determined by reference to the finished product unless that quantity, or the total quantity of the ingredients or categories of ingredients indicated, would exceed 100%, in which case the indication of quantity shall be on the basis of the weight of the ingredient or category of ingredients used to prepare 100g of the finished product;

(b) the indication of quantity of a volatile ingredient or category of volatile ingredients used shall be on the basis of its proportion by weight in the finished product;

(c) the indication of quantity of an ingredient or category of ingredients which has been used in concentrated or dehydrated form and which is reconstituted during preparation of the food may be on the basis of its proportion by weight before concentration or dehydration;

(d) where the food is in concentrated or dehydrated form and is intended to be reconstituted by the addition of water as directed in the labelling of the food, the indication of quantity of the ingredient or category of ingredients may be on the basis of its proportion by weight in the food when reconstituted as so directed.

Appropriate durability indication

20 Form of indication of minimum durability

(1) Subject to the following paragraphs of this regulation, the minimum durability of a food shall be indicated by the words 'best before' followed by–

(a) the date up to and including which the food can reasonably be expected to retain its specific properties if properly stored, and

(b) any storage conditions which need to be observed if the food is to retain its specific properties until that date.

(2) The date in the indication of minimum durability shall be expressed in terms of a day, month and year (in that order), except that–

(a) in the case of a food which can reasonably be expected to retain its specific properties for three months or less, it may be expressed in terms of a day and month only;

(b) in the case of a food which can reasonably be expected to retain its specific properties for more than three months but not more than 18 months it may be expressed in terms of a month and year only, if the words 'best before' are replaced by the words 'best before end', and

(c) in the case of a food which can reasonably be expected to retain its specific properties for more than 18 months it may be expressed either in terms of a month and year only or in terms of a year only, if (in either case) the words 'best before' are replaced by the words 'best before end'.

(3) Either–

(a) the date up to and including which a food can reasonably be expected to retain its specific properties if properly stored, or

(b) that date and any storage conditions which need to be observed if the food is to retain its specific properties until that date,

may appear on the labelling of a food separately from the words 'best before' or 'best before end', as the case may be, provided that those words are followed by a reference to the place where the date (or the date and the storage conditions) appears (or appear).

21 Form of indication of 'use by' date

(1) Where a 'use by' date is required in respect of a food it shall be indicated by the words 'use by' followed by–

(a) the date up to and including which the food, if properly stored, is recommended for use, and

(b) any storage conditions which need to be observed.

(2) The 'use by' date shall be expressed in terms either of a day and month (in that order) or of a day, a month and a year (in that order).

(3) Either–

(a) the date up to and including which a food required to bear a 'use by' date is recommended for use, or

(b) that date and any storage conditions which need to be observed,

may appear separately from the words 'use by', provided that those words are followed by a reference to the place where the date (or the date and the storage conditions) appears (or appear).

22 Foods which need not bear an appropriate durability indication

The following foods need not be marked or labelled with an appropriate durability indication:

(a) fresh fruit and vegetables (including potatoes but not including sprouting seeds, legume sprouts and similar products) which have not been peeled or cut into pieces;

(b) wine, liqueur wine, sparkling wine, aromatised wine and any similar drink obtained from fruit other than grapes;

(c) any drink made from grapes or grape musts and coming within codes 22060039, 22060059 and 22060089 of the Combined Nomenclature given in Council Regulation (EEC) No 2658/87[1] on the tariff and statistical nomenclature and on the Common Customs Tariff, as amended;[2]

(d) any drink with an alcoholic strength by volume of 10 per cent or more;

(e) any soft drink, fruit juice or fruit nectar or alcoholic drink, sold in a container containing more than 5 litres and intended for supply to catering establishments;

(f) any flour, confectionery and bread which, given the nature of its content, is normally consumed within 24 hours of its preparation;

(g) vinegar;

(h) cooking and table salt;

(i) solid sugar and products consisting almost solely of flavoured or coloured sugars;

(j) chewing gums and similar products;

(k) edible ices in individual portions.

1 OJ No L256, 7.9.87, p 1

2 Relevant amendment is Commission Regulation (EEC) No 2551/93, OJ No L241, 27.9.93, p 1.

Omission of certain particulars

23 Food which is not prepacked and similar food, and fancy confectionery products

(1) This regulation applies to–

(a) food which is–

(i) not prepacked, or

(ii) prepacked for direct sale,

other than any such food to which regulation 27 applies;

(b) any flour confectionery which is packed in a crimp case only or in wholly transparent packaging which is either unmarked or marked only with an indication of the price of the food and any lot marking indication given in accordance with the Food (Lot Marking) Regulations 1992, if there is not attached to the flour confectionery or its packaging any document, notice, label, ring or collar (other than a label (or labels) on which only the price of the food and any lot marking indication are marked); and

(c) individually wrapped fancy confectionery products which are not enclosed in any further packaging and which are intended for sale as single items.

(2) Subject to paragraph (3) of this regulation, food to which this regulation applies need not be marked or labelled with any of the particulars specified in regulation 5 except–

(a) the name of the food; and

(b) in the case of milk, the particulars required by regulation 5(f)(where the appropriate circumstances described in that regulation apply) and, if such milk is raw milk, the particulars required by regulation 5(e)(i),

nor, where but for this regulation they would otherwise be required, with any of the particulars specified in regulations 32, 33 and 34.

(3) Food to which this regulation applies which has not been irradiated and which is–

(a) not exposed for sale, or

(b) white bread or flour confectionery, or

(c) carcasses and parts of carcasses which are not intended for sale in one piece,

need not be marked or labelled with any of the particulars specified in regulation 5.

24 Indication of additives

(1) Subject to the following paragraphs of this regulation, any food which–

(a) by virtue of regulation 23 alone is not marked or labelled with a list of ingredients, and

(b) contains any additive which–

(i) but for regulation 23, would be required to be named in the list of ingredients of the food, and

(ii) was added to or used in the food or an ingredient of the food to serve the function of an antioxidant, colour, flavouring, flavour enhancer, preservative, or sweetener,

shall be marked or labelled with an indication of every such category of additive that is contained in the food.

(2) Any edible ice or flour confectionery which, but for this paragraph, would be required to be marked or labelled in accordance with paragraph (1) of this regulation need not be so marked or labelled if there is displayed in a prominent position near the edible ice or flour confectionery a notice stating, subject to paragraph (3) of this regulation, that edible ices or flour confectionery, as the case may be, sold at the establishment where the notice is displayed may contain such categories of additives.

(3) Where, in the circumstances described in paragraph (1) or (2) of this regulation, an additive serves more than one of the functions specified in the said paragraph (1), it shall only be necessary to indicate that category which represents the principal function served by the additive in the food or ingredient to which it was added or in which it was used.

(4) This regulation does not apply to food which is not exposed for sale.

25 Indication of irradiated ingredients

(1) Subject to paragraph (2) of this regulation, any food which–

(a) by virtue of regulation 23 alone is exempted from the requirement to be marked or labelled with a list of ingredients, and

(b) contains any ingredient which has been irradiated (and which comprises a particular with which, had that food not been subject to that exemption, the food would have been required by these Regulations to be marked or labelled), shall be marked or labelled with an indication that it contains that ingredient, and in such a case the reference within that indication to that ingredient shall include or be accompanied by the word 'irradiated' or the words 'treated with ionising radiation'.

(2) This regulation does not apply to food which is not exposed for sale.

26 Small packages and certain indelibly marked bottles

(1) Subject to the following paragraphs of this regulation, any prepacked food, either contained in an indelibly marked glass bottle intended for re-use and having no label, ring or collar, or the largest surface of whose packaging has an area of less than ten square centimetres, need not–

(a) by virtue of these regulations be marked or labelled with–

(i) any of the particulars specified in regulation 5 except the name of the food and, unless the food is not required to be marked or labelled with such an indication, the appropriate durability indication, or

(ii) any of the particulars specified in regulations 33 and 34, where but for this regulation they would otherwise be required, or

(b) be marked or labelled with the GMO particulars, where but for this regulation they would otherwise be required;

(2) Any bottle referred to in paragraph (1) of this regulation which contains milk shall also be marked or labelled with the particulars required by regulation 5(f)(where the appropriate circumstances described in that regulation apply) and, if such milk is raw milk, with the particulars required by regulation 5(e)(i).

(3) Subject to paragraphs (4) and (5) of this regulation, any prepacked food which–

(a) is sold or supplied as an individual portion, and

(b) is intended as a minor accompaniment to either–

(i) another food, or

(ii) another service,

need not be marked or labelled with any of the particulars specified in regulation 5 except the name of the food nor, where but for this regulation they would otherwise be required, with any of the other particulars mentioned in paragraph (3A) of this regulation. Such prepacked food shall include butter and other fat spreads, milk, cream and cheeses, jams and marmalades, mustards, sauces, tea, coffee and sugar, and such other service shall include the provision of sleeping accommodation at an hotel or other establishment at which such accommodation is provided by way of trade or business.

(3A) The other particulars for the purposes of paragraph (3) of this regulation are those specified in regulation 32 and, in the case of any food to which paragraph (1) of this regulation applies, the particulars specified in regulations 33 and 34 and the GMO particulars.

(4) This regulation does not apply to any food to which regulation 23 or 27 applies.

(5) Any bottle referred to in paragraph (1) of this regulation need not–

(a) where it contains milk, or

(b) where it contains any other food, in which case until 1st January 1997,

be marked or labelled with an appropriate durability indication.

Chapter 18: Environmental Health Legislation

27 Certain food sold at catering establishments

(1) Subject to the following paragraphs of this regulation, any food which is sold at a catering establishment and is either–

   (a) not prepacked, or

   (b) prepacked for direct sale,

   need not be marked or labelled with any of the particulars specified in regulation 5 nor, where but for this regulation they would otherwise be required, with any of the particulars specified in regulations 32, 33 and 34.

(2) In the case of any such food being milk which is prepacked for direct sale it shall be marked or labelled with the particulars required by regulations 5(f)(where the appropriate circumstances described in that regulation apply) and, if such milk is raw milk, the particulars required by regulation 5(e)(i).

(3) In the case of any such food which has been irradiated that food shall be marked or labelled with an indication of such treatment, which indication shall include or be accompanied by the word 'irradiated' or the words 'treated with ionising radiation'.

(4) In the case of any such food which contains an ingredient which has been irradiated (and which comprises a particular with which, had that food been prepacked, the food would have been required by these Regulations to be marked or labelled), that food shall (subject to regulation 36(3) and (4)) be marked or labelled with an indication that it contains that ingredient and the reference within that indication to that ingredient shall include or be accompanied by the word 'irradiated' or the words 'treated with ionising radiation'.

28 Seasonal selection packs

The outer packaging of a seasonal selection pack need not be marked or labelled with any of the particulars specified by these Regulations, provided that each item contained in the pack is individually prepacked and is marked or labelled in accordance with the provisions of these Regulations or any other Regulations applying to such item.

Additional labelling requirements for certain categories of food

29 Food sold from vending machines

(1) Subject to paragraph (2) of this regulation, where any food is sold from a vending machine, without prejudice to any other labelling requirements imposed by these Regulations, there shall appear on the front of the machine a notice indicating the name of the food (unless that name appears on the labelling of the food in such a manner as to be easily visible and clearly legible to an intending purchaser through the outside of the machine), together with–

   (a) in the event that such food is not prepacked, and there is made in respect of it (whether on the machine or elsewhere) a claim of a type described in Part II of Schedule 6, a notice giving the prescribed nutrition labelling described in paragraph 2 of Part II of Schedule 7;

   (b) in the event that such food is one which should properly be reheated before it is eaten, but suitable instructions for such reheating are not given on the packaging (if any) of the food, a notice giving such instructions.

(2) A notice required under sub-paragraph (a) or (b) of paragraph (1) of this regulation shall appear either–

   (a) on the front of the vending machine, or

(b) in close proximity to the machine and in such a way as to be readily discernible by an intending purchaser.

30 Prepacked alcoholic drinks other than Community controlled wine

(1) In the case of prepacked alcoholic drinks other than Community controlled wine, every drink with an alcoholic strength by volume of more than 1.2 per cent shall be marked or labelled with an indication of its alcoholic strength by volume in the form of a figure to not more than one decimal place (which may be preceded by the word 'alcohol' or by the abbreviation 'alc') followed by the symbol '% vol'.

(2) Positive and negative tolerances shall be permitted in respect of the indication of alcoholic strength by volume and shall be those specified in Schedule 5, expressed in absolute values.

(3) For the purposes of this regulation, the alcoholic strength of any drink shall be determined at 20 degrees C.

31 Raw milk

(1) Subject to paragraph (3) of this regulation, and except in cases to which paragraph (2) of this regulation applies, the container in which any raw milk is sold shall be marked or labelled with the words 'This milk has not been heat-treated and may therefore contain organisms harmful to health'.

(2) Subject to paragraph (3) of this regulation, in the case of any raw milk which is not prepacked and is sold at a catering establishment there shall appear–
  (a) on a label attached to the container in which that milk is sold, or
  (b) on a ticket or notice that is readily discernible by an intending purchaser at the place where he chooses that milk,

the words 'Milk supplied in this establishment has not been heat-treated and may therefore contain organisms harmful to health'.

(3) The provisions of paragraphs (1) and (2) of this regulation shall not apply to raw milk from buffaloes.

32 Products consisting of skimmed milk together with non-milk fat

The container in which any product–
  (a) consisting of skimmed milk together with non-milk fat,
  (b) which is capable of being used as a substitute for milk, and
  (c) which is neither–
    (i) an infant formula or a follow-on formula, nor
    (ii) a product specially formulated for infants or young children for medical purposes,

is sold shall be prominently marked or labelled with a warning that the product is unfit, or not to be used, as food for babies.

33 Foods packaged in certain gases

A food the durability of which has been extended by means of its being packaged in any packaging gas authorised pursuant to Council Directive 89/107/EEC,[1] concerning food additives for use in foodstuffs intended for human consumption, shall be marked or labelled with the indication 'packaged in a protective atmosphere'.

1 OJ No L40, 11.2.89, p 27.

34 Foods containing sweeteners, added sugar and sweeteners, aspartame or polyols

(1) A food containing a sweetener or sweeteners authorised pursuant to the Sweeteners in Food Regulations 1995 shall be marked or labelled with the indication 'with sweetener(s)'.

(2) A food containing both an added sugar or sugars and a sweetener or sweeteners authorised pursuant to those Regulations shall be marked or labelled with the indication 'with sugar(s) and sweetener(s)'.

(3) A food containing aspartame shall be marked or labelled with the indication 'contains a source of phenylalanine'.

(4) A food containing more than 10% added polyols shall be marked or labelled with the indication 'excessive consumption may produce laxative effects'.

(5) The indications required by paragraphs (1) and (2) above shall accompany the name of the food.

Manner of marking or labelling

35 General requirement

When any food other than food to which regulation 23, 27 or 31 applies is sold, the particulars with which it is required to be marked or labelled by these Regulations or by Regulation 1139/98 shall appear–

(a) on the packaging, or

(b) on a label attached to the packaging, or

(c) on a label that is clearly visible through the packaging,

save that where the sale is otherwise than to the ultimate consumer such particulars may, alternatively, appear only on the commercial documents relating to the food where it can be guaranteed that such documents, containing all such particulars, either accompany the food to which they relate or were sent before, or at the same time as, delivery of the food, and provided always that the particulars required by regulation 5(a),(c) and (e) shall also be marked or labelled on the outermost packaging in which that food is sold.

36 Food to which regulation 23 or 27 applies

(1) When any food to which regulation 23 or 27 applies is sold to the ultimate consumer, the particulars with which it is required to be marked or labelled by these regulations or by Regulation 1139/98 shall, except in a case to which paragraph (2) or (4A) of this regulation applies, appear–

(a) on a label attached to the food, or

(b) on a menu, notice, ticket or label that is readily discernible by an intending purchaser at the place where he chooses that food.

(2) In any case where food to which paragraph (1)(b) of this regulation applies has been or contains an ingredient which has been irradiated and that food is sold and delivered to the ultimate consumer in a catering establishment, use of alternative labelling relating to irradiation shall not alone be treated as a contravention of these Regulations and for this purpose alternative labelling is used where, instead of the particulars referred to in that paragraph appearing in the manner specified therein, alternative particulars are displayed in accordance with paragraph (3), with paragraph (4) or with paragraphs (3) and (4) of this regulation.

(3) Alternative particulars are displayed in accordance with this paragraph in relation to any ingredient which has been irradiated if there appears, in the manner specified in paragraph (1)(b) of this regulation, an indication that the food of which that irradiated ingredient forms part may contain that irradiated ingredient and if the reference within that indication to that ingredient includes or is accompanied by the word 'irradiated' or the words 'treated with ionising radiation'.

(4) Alternative particulars are displayed in accordance with this paragraph if the irradiated ingredients to which they relate are dried substances normally used for seasoning, if there appears, in the manner specified in paragraph (1)(b) of this regulation, an indication to the effect that food sold in the catering establishment contains (or may contain) those irradiated ingredients and if the reference within that indication to those ingredients includes or is accompanied by the word 'irradiated' or the words 'treated with ionising radiation'.

(4A) In any case where food–
- (a) is food to which the labelling requirements of Regulation 1139/98 apply,
- (b) is–
    - (i) not prepacked, or
    - (ii) prepacked for direct sale, and
- (c) is sold to the ultimate consumer at appropriate premises,

use of alternative labelling in place of the GMO particulars shall not alone be treated as a contravention of those labelling requirements and for this purpose alternative labelling is used where, instead of the particulars referred to in Article 2(3) of that Regulation appearing in the manner specified in paragraph (1)(a) or (b) of this regulation, alternative particulars are displayed in accordance with paragraph (4B) of this regulation.

(4B) Alternative particulars are displayed in accordance with this paragraph in relation to any food referred to in paragraph (4A) of this regulation if there appears on a menu, notice, ticket or label which is readily discernible by an intending purchaser and which is located at the place at the premises where he chooses that food, indications to the effect that some of the food sold at those premises contains ingredients produced from genetically modified soya beans or maize, or both, as the case may be, and that further information is available from the staff.

(4C) In paragraph (4A)(c) of this regulation 'appropriate premises' means premises where–
- (a) the staff provide clarification at the request of an intending purchaser as to whether particular food sold at those premises, other than food falling within Article 1(2) or 2(2) of Regulation 1139/98, is produced in whole or in part from a genetically modified product referred to in Article 1(1) of that Regulation, and
- (b) there is an established procedure at those premises for keeping staff informed of that information.

(5) When any food to which regulation 23 applies is sold otherwise than to the ultimate consumer, the particulars with which it is required to be marked or labelled by these Regulations shall appear–
- (a) on a label attached to the food, or
- (b) on a ticket or notice that is readily discernible by the intending purchaser at the place where he chooses the food, or

Chapter 18: Environmental Health Legislation

(c) in commercial documents relating to the food where it can be guaranteed that such documents either accompany the food to which they relate or were sent before, or at the same time as, delivery of the food.

37 Milk

(1) Subject to paragraph (2) of this regulation, in the case of milk that is contained in a bottle, any particulars which are required to be given under these Regulations may be given on the bottle cap.

(2) In the case of raw milk contained in a bottle, the particulars specified in regulation 31(1) shall be given elsewhere than on the bottle cap.

38 Intelligibility

(1) The particulars with which a food is required to be marked or labelled by these Regulations or by Regulation 1139/98, or which appear on a menu, notice, ticket or label pursuant to these Regulations, shall be easy to understand, clearly legible and indelible and, when a food is sold to the ultimate consumer, the said particulars shall be marked in a conspicuous place in such a way as to be easily visible.

(2) Such particulars shall not in any way be hidden, obscured or interrupted by any other written or pictorial matter.

(3) Paragraph (1) of this regulation shall not be taken to preclude the giving of such particulars at a catering establishment, in respect of foods the variety and type of which are changed regularly, by means of temporary media (including the use of chalk on a blackboard).

39 Field of vision

(1) Where a food is required to be marked or labelled with more than one of the following indications, such indications shall appear in the labelling of the food in the same field of vision–

(a) the name of the food,

(b) an appropriate durability indication,

(c) an indication of alcoholic strength by volume,

(d) the cautionary words in respect of raw milk,

(e) the warning required on certain products by regulation 32, and

(f) an indication of the net quantity as required by the Weights and Measures Act 1985 or by any Order or Regulations made thereunder.

(2) Paragraph (1)(b),(c) and (f) of this regulation shall not apply to any food sold in a bottle or packaging where such bottle or packaging is the subject of regulation 26.

Part III

Claims, Nutrition Labelling and Misleading Descriptions

40 Claims

(1) A claim of the type described in Part I of Schedule 6 shall not be made, either expressly or by implication, in the labelling or advertising of a food.

(2) A claim of a type described in Part II of Schedule 6 shall not be made, either expressly or by implication, in the labelling or advertising of a food, except in accordance with the appropriate conditions set out in that Part of that Schedule.

(3) Where a claim is a claim of two or more of the types described in Part II of Schedule 6, the conditions appropriate to each of the relevant types of claim shall be observed.

41 Supplementary provisions relating to claims

(1) Nothing in regulation 40 or Schedule 6 shall be taken to prevent the dissemination of useful information or recommendations intended exclusively for persons having qualifications in dentistry, medicine, nutrition, dietetics or pharmacy.

(2) A reference to a substance in a list of ingredients or in any nutrition labelling shall not of itself constitute a claim of a type described in Schedule 6.

(3) In Schedule 6 any condition that a food in respect of which a claim is made shall be marked or labelled with the prescribed nutrition labelling shall not apply in the case of–

(a) a food (other than a food sold from a vending machine) which is not prepacked and which is sold to the ultimate consumer at a catering establishment, or

(b) a claim contained within generic advertising,

but in respect of a food described in sub-paragraph (a) there may be given such of the elements of the prescribed nutrition labelling which, but for this paragraph, would have been required or permitted to be given, as it is wished to include, and where all or any such elements are given this shall be in accordance with Part I of Schedule 7, except that in applying paragraph 4 of that Part, in place of paragraphs (a)(i) and (ii) to that paragraph there shall be read references to–

(i) an unquantified serving of the food, and

(ii) any one portion of the food.

(4) Where nutrition labelling not being prescribed nutrition labelling is given it shall be given in all respects as if it were prescribed nutrition labelling except that in applying in this context the requirements for prescribed nutrition labelling described in Schedule 7, Part II of that Schedule shall be read as if paragraph 1(d), and the proviso to paragraph 1(a), were omitted.

42 Misleading descriptions

(1) The words and descriptions specified in column 1 of Part I of Schedule 8 shall not be used in the labelling or advertising of a food, except in accordance with the appropriate conditions set out in column 2 of that Part of that Schedule.

(2) The name specified in column 1 of Part II of Schedule 8 shall not be used in the labelling or advertising of any cheese as the name of the cheese, whether or not qualified by other words, unless–

(a) the amount of water in the cheese expressed as a percentage of the total weight of the cheese does not exceed the percentage stated in column 2 of Part II of Schedule 8 opposite that name, and

(b) the amount of milk fat in the cheese expressed as a percentage of the dry matter of the cheese is not less than 48 per cent.

(3) The name specified in column 1 of Part III of Schedule 8 shall not be used in the labelling or advertising of any cream as the name of the cream, whether or not qualified by other words, unless the cream complies with the requirements specified in column 2 of that Part of that Schedule opposite that name; except that the relevant requirement as to milk fat content need not be complied with if the

name contains qualifying words which indicate that the milk fat content of the cream is greater or less than that specified in column 2, as the case may be.

(4) In calculating the percentage of milk fat in any cream for the purposes of paragraph (3) of this regulation and Part III of Schedule 8, any ingredient added to the cream shall be disregarded.

43 The word 'wine'

(1) Subject to the following provisions of this regulation, the word 'wine' may be used in a composite name in the labelling or advertising of food for a drink which is not wine as defined in Annex I to Council Regulation (EEC) No 822/87.

(2) The word 'wine' shall not be used pursuant to paragraph (1) of this regulation as part of a composite name which is likely to cause confusion with wine or table wine as defined in Annex I to Council Regulation (EEC) No 822/87.

(3) Each word that forms part of a composite name used pursuant to paragraph (1) of this regulation must appear in lettering of the same type and colour and of such a height that the composite name is clearly distinguishable from other particulars.

(4) The composite name 'non-alcoholic wine' shall not be used pursuant to paragraph (1) of this regulation, except for a drink derived from unfermented grape juice which is intended exclusively for communion or sacramental use and which is described clearly in its labelling or advertising, as the case may be, as being exclusively for such use.

(5) When the word 'wine' is used in a composite name for a drink which is derived from fruit other than grapes, that drink shall be obtained by an alcoholic fermentation of that fruit.

Part IV

Offences and Legal Proceedings

44 Offences and penalties

(1) If any person–

 (a) sells any food which is not marked or labelled in accordance with the provisions of Part II of these Regulations, or

 (b) sells or advertises for sale any food in respect of which a claim is made, nutrition labelling is given or a description or a name is used in contravention of the provisions of Part III of these Regulations, or

 (c) sells any food from a vending machine in contravention of regulation 29, or

 (d) sells any food after the date shown in a 'use by' date relating to it, or

 (e) being a person other than whichever of–

  (i) the manufacturer,

  (ii) the packer, or

  (iii) the seller established within the European Community,

 was originally responsible for so marking the food, removes or alters the appropriate durability indication relating to that food, or

 (f) sells any food to which the labelling requirements of Regulation 1139/98 apply which is not marked or labelled with the GMO particulars, except in the case of any food to which regulation 36(4A) applies and in respect of which alternative particulars are displayed in accordance with regulation 36(4B), he shall be guilty of an offence and shall be liable on *summary* conviction to a fine not exceeding *level 5* on the standard scale.

(2) Where an offence under these Regulations is committed in Scotland by a Scottish partnership and is proved to have been committed with the consent or connivance of, or to be attributable to any neglect on the part of, a partner, he as well as the partnership shall be guilty of the offence and be liable to be proceeded against and punished accordingly.

45 Enforcement

(1) Subject to paragraph (2) of this regulation, each food authority shall enforce and execute these Regulations in its area.

(2) Each port health authority shall enforce and execute these Regulations in its district in relation to imported food.

(3) In this regulation 'food authority' does not include–

   (a) the council of a district in a non-metropolitan county in England except–

   (i) where the county functions have been transferred to that council pursuant to a structural change; or

   (ii) in relation to regulations 44(1)(d) and 44(1)(e);

   (b) the appropriate Treasurer referred to in section 5(1)(c) of the Act (which deals with the Inner Temple and the Middle Temple).

46 Defence in case of alteration of appropriate durability indication

In any proceedings for an offence under regulation 44(1)(e) it shall be a defence for the person charged to prove that each removal or alteration in respect of which the offence is alleged was effected under the written authorisation of a person capable of effecting that removal or alteration without contravention of that provision.

47 Defence in relation to exports

In any proceedings for an offence under these Regulations it shall be a defence for the person charged to prove–

   (a) that the food in respect of which the offence is alleged to have been committed was intended for export to a country which has legislation analogous to these Regulations and that it complies with that legislation; and

   (b) in the case of export to an EEA State, that the legislation complies with the provisions of Directive 79/112[1] and, where applicable, the provisions of Directive 87/250,[2] Directive 89/398,[3] Directive 90/496,[4] Directive 94/54 and Regulation 1139/98.[5]

1 Council Directive 79/112/EEC (OJ No L33, 8.2.79, p 1).

2 Council Directive 87/250/EEC (OJ No L113, 30.4.87, p 57).

3 Council Directive 89/398/EEC (OJ No L186, 30.6.89, p 27).

4 Council Directive 90/496/EEC (OJ No L276, 6.10.90, p 40).

5 Council Directive 94/54/EC (OJ No L300, 23.11.94, p 14).

48 Application of various provisions of the Act

(1) The following provisions of the Act shall apply for the purposes of these Regulations and, unless the context otherwise requires, any reference in those provisions to the Act or Part thereof shall be construed for the purposes of these Regulations as a reference to these Regulations–

section 2 (extended meaning of 'sale' etc);

section 3 (presumption that food is intended for human consumption);

section 20 (offences due to fault of another person);

section 21 (defence of due diligence) as it applies for the purposes of section 8, 14 or 15;

section 22 (defence of publication in the course of a business);

section 30(8) (which relates to documentary evidence);

section 33 (obstruction etc of officers);

section 36 (offences by bodies corporate);

section 44 (protection of officers acting in good faith).

(2) In the application of section 32 of the Act (powers of entry) for the purposes of these Regulations, the reference in subsection (1)(a) to the Act shall be construed as including a reference to Regulation 1139/98.

(3) The penalty provisions in section 35(1) of the Act (punishment of offences) shall apply in relation to an offence under section 33(1) of the Act as applied by these Regulations, and the penalty provisions in section 35(2) and (3) of the Act shall apply in relation to an offence under 33(2) of the Act as applied by these Regulations.

Part V
Revocations, Amendments and Transitional Provision

49 Revocations and amendments

50 Transitional provision

(1) Subject to the following paragraphs of this regulation, in any proceedings for an offence under these Regulations it shall be a defence to prove that–

(a)
  (i) the act was committed before 1st July 1997, or
  (ii) the act was committed in relation to food prepacked before 1st July 1997; and

(b) the matters constituting the offence would not have constituted an offence under the Food Labelling Regulations 1984, the Food Labelling (Scotland) Regulations 1984, or the Milk Labelling (Scotland) Regulations 1983 or the Cheese and Cream Regulations 1995 if those Regulations had been in operation when the act was committed or the food was prepacked.

(2) In any proceedings for an offence under regulation 44(1)(a), as read with–

(a) regulation 14(4) and Schedule 3, or

(b) regulation 14(9) and Schedule 4,

paragraph (1) of this regulation shall be read as if for the date '1st July 1997' there were substituted, in both places where it occurs, the date '1st July 1996'.

(3) In any proceedings for an offence under regulation 44(1)(a) as read with regulation 33, paragraph (1) of this regulation shall be read as if for the date '1st July 1997' there were substituted the date '1st January 1997'.

(4) In any proceedings for an offence under regulation 44(1)(a), it shall be a defence to prove that–

   (a) the food concerned was prepacked before 14th February 2000, and
   (b) the matters constituting the offence would not have constituted an offence under these Regulations if the amendments made by the following provisions of the Food Labelling (Amendment) Regulations 1998, namely–
       (i) regulations 3 and 14 and the Schedule (in so far as they include in the definition of 'Directive 79/112' a reference to European Parliament and Council Directive 97/4/EC),
       (ii) regulation 4 (in so far as it substitutes a new regulation 3(1)(iii)), and
       (iii) regulations 6 to 9, 15 and 16,
       had not been made when the food was prepacked.

(5) The following provisions of these Regulations shall not apply in relation to the sale of any relevant food before 19th September 1999–

   (a) regulation 44(1)(a), as read with regulation 36 or 38, in relation to the particulars with which food is required to be marked or labelled by Regulation 1139/98, and
   (b) regulation 44(1)(f).

(6) In any proceedings for an offence in relation to any relevant food under–

   (a) regulation 44(1)(a), as read with regulation 36 or 38, in relation to the particulars with which food is required to be marked or labelled by Regulation 1139/98, or
   (b) regulation 44(1)(f),

   it shall be a defence to prove that the food was prepared using an ingredient which was on sale before 1st September 1998.

(7) For the purposes of paragraphs (5) and (6) of this regulation, 'relevant food' means food which–

   (a) is sold to the ultimate consumer, and
   (b) is–
       (i) not prepacked, or
       (ii) prepacked for direct sale.

(8) In any proceedings for an offence under regulation 44(1)(a) as read with regulation 14(9) and (11), it shall be a defence to prove that the food concerned was prepacked before 4th November 2000 and the matter constituting the offence would not have constituted an offence under these Regulations if the amendment made by regulation 14(3)(a) of the Miscellaneous Food Additives (Amendment) Regulations 1999 had not been made when the food was prepacked.

(9) In any proceedings for an offence under regulation 44(1)(a), it shall be a defence to prove that–

(a) the food concerned was prepacked before 14th February 2000, and

(b) the matters constituting the offence would not have constituted an offence under these Regulations if the amendments made by regulations 3, 5(c) and (d) and 6 of the Food Labelling (Amendment) (No 2) Regulations 1999 had not been made when the food was prepacked.

SCHEDULE A1

Amendments to Directive 79/112

Regulation 2(1)

Directive 79/112 has been amended by, and must be read subject to–

> Act of Accession (Hellenic Republic) (OJ No L291, 19.11.79, p 17);
>
> Act of Accession (Kingdom of Spain and Portuguese Republic) (OJ No L302, 15.11.85, p 218);
>
> Council Directive 85/7/EEC (OJ No L2, 3.1.85, p 22);
>
> Council Directive 86/197/EEC (OJ No L144, 29.5.86, p 38);
>
> Council Directive 89/395/EEC (OJ No L186, 30.6.89, p 17);
>
> Commission Directive 91/72/EEC (OJ No L42, 15.2.91, p 27);
>
> EEA Agreement;
>
> Commission Directive 93/102/EEC (OJ No L291, 25.11.93, p 14), as amended by Commission Directive 95/42/EC (OJ No L182, 2.8.95, p 20);

and, except in relation to an EEA State which is not a member State,–

> Act of Accession (Austria, Finland and Sweden) (OJ No Ll, 1.1.95, p 1);
>
> European Parliament and Council Directive 97/4/EC (OJ No L43, 14.2.97, p 21).

SCHEDULE 1

Names Prescribed by Law

Regulation 6(2)

Fish

(1) Subject to subparagraphs (2) and (3) of this paragraph, the name used for any species of fish specified in column 2 of the following Table shall be a name specified for that species in the corresponding entry in column 1 of the said Table.

(2) A customary name may be used for any species of fish which has been subjected to smoking or any similar process, unless the name of the species in column 2 of the following Table is followed by an asterisk. In such cases the name used for the food when the fish is smoked shall be either–

(a) a name specified for that species in column 1 of the said Table preceded by the word 'smoked', or

(b) except in the case of Salmo salar (L), 'smoked Pacific salmon'.

(3) Subparagraph (1) of this paragraph, as read with the following Table, shall not apply to fish regulated by Council Regulation (EEC) No 2136/89 laying down common marketing standards for preserved sardines, or Council Regulation (EEC) No 1536/92 laying down common marketing standards for preserved tuna and bonito.

Column 1 Name	Column 2 Species of Fish
SEA FISH	
Anchovy	All species of Engraulis
Bass	Dicentrarchus labrax (L)
Brill	Scophthalmus rhombus (L)
Brisling	Sprattus sprattus (L) when canned
Catfish or Rockfish	All species of Anarhichas
Cod or Codling	Gadus morhua (L) (including Gadus morhua callarias and Gadus morhua morhua)
Pacific cod or cod	Gadus macrocephalus
Greenland cod or cod	Gadus ogac
Coley or Saithe or Coalfish	Pollachius virens (L)
Conger	All species of Conger
Croaker or Drum	All species of the family Scianidae
Dab	Limanda limanda (L)
Dogfish or Flake or Huss or Rigg	All species of Galeorhinus All species of Mustelus All species of Scyliorhinus Galeus melastomus Rafin Squalus acanthias (L)
Dory or John Dory or St Peter's fish	Zeus faber (L)
Eel	All species of Anguilla
Emperor	All species of Lethrinus
Flounder	Platichthys flesus (L)
Grey mullet	All species of Mugil All species of Liza All species of Chelon
Grouper	All species of Mycteroperca All species of Epinephelus
Gurnard	All species of the family Triglidae Peristedion cataphractum (L)
Haddock	Melanogrammus aeglefinus (L)
Hake	All species of Meruccius
Halibut	Hippoglossus hippoglossus (L) Hippoglossus stenolepis

	Black halibut Reinhardtius hippoglossoides (Walbaum)
Herring	Clupea harengus (L)
Hilsa	Hilsa elisha
Hoki	Macruronus novaezelandiae
Jack	All species of Caranx All species of Hemmicaranx All species of Seriola All species of Trachurus All species of Decapterus
Ling	All species of Molva
Lumpfish or Lumpsucker	Cyclopterus lumpus
Mackerel	All species of Scomber
Megrim	All species of Lepidorhombus
Monkfish or Angler	Lophius piscatorius (L)
Orange roughy	Hoplosteppus atlanticus
Parrot-fish	All species of the family Scaridae
Pilchard	Sardina pilchardus (Walbaum) Pacific pilchard Sardinops sagax caerulea (Girard) Sardinops sagax sagax (Jenyns) Sardinops sagax melanosticta (Schlegel) South Atlantic pilchard Sardinops sagax ocellata (Pappe)
Plaice	Pleuronectes platessa (L)
Pacific pollak or Pacific pollock or Alaska pollack or Alaska pollock	Theragra chalcogramma (Pallas)
Pomfret	All species of Brama All species of Stromateus All species of Pampus
Redfish or Ocean perch or Rose fish	All species of Sebastes Helicolenus maculatus Helicolenus dactylopterus (De la Roche)
Red Mullet	All species of Mullus
Sardine	Small Sardina pilchardus (Walbaum)
Sardinella	All species of Sardinella
Sea bream or Porgy	All species of the family Sparidae
Sild	Small Clupea harenus (L), when canned Small Sprattus sprattus (L), when canned

Skate or Ray or Roker	All species of Raja
Smelt or Sparling	All species of Osmerus
Sole or Dover sole	Solea solea (L) Lemon sole Microstomus kitt (Walbaum)
Snapper	All species of the family Lutjanidae
Sprat	Sprattus sprattus (L), except when canned
Swordfish	Xiphias gladius
Tuna or Tunny	All species of Thunnus
Skipjack tuna (or tuna)	Euthynnus (Katsuwonus) pelamis Albacore tuna (or tuna) Thunnus alalunga Yellowfin tuna (or tuna) Thunnus (neothunnus) albacores Bluefin tuna (or tuna) Thunnus thynnus Bigeye tuna (or tuna) Thunnus (parathunnus) obesus Bonito All species of Sarda All species of Euthynnus, with the exception of the species Euthynnus (Katsuwonus) pelamis All species of Auxis
Turbot	Scophthalmus maximus (L)
Whitebait	Small Clupea harengus (L) except when canned Small Sprattus sprattus (L) except when canned
Whiting	Merlangius merlangus (L) Blue whiting Micromesistius poutassou (Risso) Southern Blue whiting Micromesistius australis
Winter flounder	Pseudopleuronectes americanus (Walbaum)
Witch	Glyptocephalus cynoglossus (L)

SALMON AND FRESHWATER FISH

Catfish	All species of the family Ictaluridae
Carp	All species of the family Cyprinidae
Char	All species of Salvelinus Salmon or Atlantic salmon Salmo salar (L)*
Cherry salmon or Pacific salmon	Oncorhynchus masou (Walbaum)*
Chum salmon or Keta salmon	Oncorhynchus keta (Walbaum)*
Medium salmon or Coho salmon or Silver salmon	Oncorhynchus kisutch (Walbaum)*
Pink salmon	Oncorhynchus gorbuscha (Walbaum)*
Red salmon or Sockeye salmon	Oncorhynchus nerka (Walbaum)*
Spring salmon or King salmon or Chinook salmon or Pacific salmon	Oncorhynchus tschwytscha (Walbaum)*
Brown trout or trout	Salmo trutta (L) which has spent all of its life in fresh water
Sea trout or Salmon trout	Salmo trutta (L) which has spent part of its life in sea water
Cut-throat trout or trout	Oncorhynchus clarkii
Rainbow trout or Steelhead trout or trout	Oncorhynchus mykiss
Tilapia	All species of Tilapia

SHELLFISH

Abalone or Ormer	All species of Haliotis
Clam or Hard shell clam	Mercenaria mercenaria (L) Venus verrucosa (L)
Clam or Razor clam	All species of Ensis and Solen
Cockle	All species of Cerastoderma
Crab	All species of the section Brachyura All species of the family Lithodidae
Crawfish or Spiny lobster or Rock lobster	All species of the family Palinuridae Jasus
Crayfish	All species of the family Astacidae All species of the family Parastacidae All species of the family Austroastacidae
Lobster	All species of Homarus
Slipper lobster	All species of Scyllaridae
Squat lobster	All species of the family Galatheidae

Mussel	All species of the family Mytulus
Oyster	All species of Crassostrea All species of Ostrea
Oyster or Portuguese oyster	Crassostrea angulata (Lmk)
Oyster or Pacific oyster	Crassostrea gigas (Thunberg)
Oyster or Native oyster	Ostrea edulis (L)
King Prawn	All species of Penaeus where the count is less than 123 per kg (head on/shell on) or less than 198 per kg (head off/shell on) or less than 242 per kg (head off/shell off)
Prawn or Shrimp	Whole fish (of a size which, when cooked, have a count of less than 397 per kg) or tails (of a size which, when peeled and cooked, have a count of less than 1,323 per kg) of– all species of Palaemonidae, all species of Penaeidae, and all species of Pandalidae
Shrimp	Whole fish (of a size which, when cooked, have a count of less than 397 per kg or more) or tails (of a size which, when peeled and cooked, have a count of less than 1,323 per kg or more) of– all species of Palaemonidae, all species of Penaeidae, and all species of Pandalidae
Shrimp or Pink shrimp	Pandalus montagui Leach
Shrimp or Brown shrimp	All species of Crangon
Scallop	All species of Pectinidae Scallop or Queen scallop or Queen Chlamys (Acquipecton) opercularis (L)
Scampi or Norway lobster or Dublin Bay prawn or Langoustine	Nephrops norvegicus (L)
Pacific scampi	Metanephrops adamanicus Metanephrops challengeri
Tiger prawn	Penaeus monodon Penaeus semisuloalus Penaeus esculentus
Whelk	All species of Buccinum
Winkle	All species of Littorina

1   OJ No L212, 22.7.89, p 79.

2   OJ No L163, 17.6.92.

Melons

2

The name used for melons sold as such shall include or be accompanied by an indication of their variety.

Potatoes

3

The name used for potatoes sold as such shall include or be accompanied by an indication of their variety.

Vitamins

4

(1) The name used for a vitamin specified in Table A in Schedule 6 shall be the name specified for that vitamin in column 1 of that Table, except that in respect of folacin the name 'folic acid' may also be used.

(2) The name for vitamin K shall be 'vitamin K'.

SCHEDULE 2

Indications of Treatment

Regulation 11(2)

Tenderised meat

1

The name used for any meat which has been treated with proteolytic enzymes shall include or be accompanied by the word 'tenderised'.

Irradiated food

2

The name used for a food which has been irradiated shall include or be accompanied by the word 'irradiated' or the words 'treated with ionising radiation'.

SCHEDULE 3

Generic Names in List of Ingredients

Regulation 14(4)

Column 1	Column 2	Column 3
Generic name	**Ingredients**	**Conditions of use of generic name**
Cheese	Any type of cheese or mixture of cheese	The labelling of the food of which the cheese is an ingredient must not refer to a specific type of cheese
Cocoa butter	Press, expeller or refined cocoa butter	Any type of crumbled, baked cereal product Crumbs or rusks, as is appropriate

Crystallised fruit	Any crystallised fruit	The proportion if crystallised fruit in the food of which it is an ingredient must not exceed 10 per cent
Dextrose	Anhydrous dextrose or dextrose monohydrate	
Fat	Any refined fat	The generic name must be accompanied by either– (a) the description 'animal' or 'vegetable', as is appropriate, or (b) an indication of the specific animal origin or the specific vegetable origin of the fat, as is appropriate In the case of an hydrogenated fat, the generic name must also be accompanied by the description 'hydrogenated'
Fish	Any species of fish	The labelling of the food of which the fish is an ingredient must not refer to a specific species of fish
Flour	Any mixture of flour derived from two or more cereal species	The generic name shall be followed by a list of the cereals from which the flour is derived in descending order of weight
Glucose syrup	Glucose syrup or anhydrous glucose syrup	
Gum base	Any type of gum preparation used in the preparation of chewing gum	
Herb, herbs or mixed herbs	Any herb or parts of a herb or combination of two or more herbs or parts of herbs	The proportion of herb or herbs in the food of which it or they are an ingredient must not exceed 2 per cent by weight of the food
Milk proteins	Any caseins, caseinates or whey proteins, or any mixture of these	
Oil	Any refined oil, other than olive oil The generic name must be accompanied by either– (a) the description 'animal' or 'vegetable', as is appropriate, or (b) an indication of the specific animal origin or the specific vegetable origin of the oil, as is appropriate	

	In the case of an hydrogenated oil, the generic name must also be accompanied by the description 'hydrogenated'
Spice, spices or mixed spices	Any spice or any combination of two or more spices
	The proportion of spice or spices in the food of which it or they are an ingredient must not exceed 2 per cent by weight of the food
Starch	Any unmodified starch or any starch which has been modified either by physical means or by enzymes
	In the case of a starch which may contain gluten, the generic name must be accompanied by an indication of the specific vegetable origin of the starch
Sugar	Any type of sucrose
Vegetables	Any mixture of vegetables
	The proportion of vegetables in the food of which they are an ingredient must not exceed 10 per cent by weight of the food
Wine	Any type of wine defined in Council Regulation (EEC) No 822/87

SCHEDULE 4

Categories of Additives which must be Identified in a List of Ingredients by their Category Name

Regulation 14(9)

Acid

Flour treatment agent

Acidity regulator

Gelling agent

Anti-caking agent

Glazing agent

Anti-foaming agent

Humectant

Antioxidant

Modified starch

Bulking agent

Preservative

Colour

Propellant gas

Emulsifier

Raising agent

Emulsifying salts

Stabiliser

Firming agent

Sweetener

Flavour enhancer

Thickener

Notes

1   In the case of an additive which is added to or used in food to serve the function of an acid and whose specific name includes the word 'acid', it shall not be necessary to use the category name.

2   Neither the specific name nor the serial number need be indicated. In the case of a modified starch which may contain gluten, the category name must be accompanied by an indication of the specific vegetable origin of the starch.

SCHEDULE 5

Positive and Negative Tolerances Permitted in the Indication of the Alcoholic Strength by Volume of Alcoholic Drinks other than Community Controlled Wine

Regulation 30

Description of alcoholic drink

Positive or negative tolerance

1   (a) Beers having an alcoholic strength not exceeding 5.5% volume;

0.5% vol

   (b) alcoholic drinks made from grapes and falling within subheading No 2206-0093 and No 2206-0099 of the combined nomenclature (1988);

0.5% vol

2   (a) Beers having an alcoholic strength exceeding 5.5% volume;

1% vol

   (b) alcoholic drinks made from grapes and falling within subheading No 2206-0091 of the combined nomenclature (1988);

1% vol

(c) ciders, perries, fruit wines and other wines obtained from fruits other than grapes whether or not semi-sparkling or sparkling;

$$1\% \text{ vol}$$

(d) alcoholic drinks based on fermented honey;

$$1\% \text{ vol}$$

3 Alcoholic drinks containing macerated fruit or part of plants;

$$1.5\% \text{ vol}$$

4 Any other alcoholic drink.

$$0.3\% \text{ vol}$$

Note

The above tolerances shall apply without prejudice to the tolerances deriving from the method of analysis used for determining the alcoholic strength.

SCHEDULE 6

Claims

Regulations 40, 41

Part I

Prohibited Claims

1

A claim that a food has tonic properties.

Note

The use of the word 'tonic' in the description 'Indian tonic water' or 'quinine tonic water' shall not of itself constitute a claim of a type described in this item.

2

A claim that a food has the property of preventing, treating or curing a human disease or any reference to such a property.

Note

A claim of a type described in item 1 of Part II of this Schedule shall not of itself be regarded as a claim of a type described in this item.

Part II

Restricted Claims

Column 1	Column 2
Types of Claim	Conditions

Claims relating to foods for particular nutritional uses

1 A claim that a food is suitable, or has been specially made, for a particular nutritional purpose.	1 The food must be capable of fulfilling the claim.
	2 The food must be marked or labelled with an indication of the particular aspects of its composition or manufacturing process that give the food its particular nutritional characteristics.
	3 The food–
	(a) must be marked or labelled with the prescribed nutrition labelling and may be marked or labelled with further information in respect of either or both of–
	(i) any nutrient or component of a nutrient (whether or not a claim is made in respect of such nutrient or component), or
	(ii) any other component or characteristic which is essential to the food's suitability for its particular nutritional use, and
	(b) when sold to the ultimate consumer, must be prepacked and completely enclosed by its packaging.

Reduced or low energy value claims

2 A claim that a food has a reduced or low energy value.

Notes

(a) The appearance, on the container of a soft drink, of the words 'low calorie' given in accordance with the conditions specified in Schedule 8 in relation to that description for such drinks shall not of itself constitute a claim of a type described in this item.

(b) Where a food is in concentrated or dehydrated form and is intended to be reconstituted by the addition of water or other substances, condition 2 shall apply to the food when reconstituted as directed.

1 If the claim is that the food has a reduced energy value, the energy value of a given weight of the food, or of a given volume in the case of a liquid food, must not be more than three quarters of that of the equivalent weight, or volume, of a similar food in relation to which no such claim is made, unless the food is–
   (a) an intense sweetener, or
   (b) a product which consists of a mixture of an intense sweetener with other substances and which, when compared on a weight for weight basis, is significantly sweeter than sucrose.

2 If the claim is that the food has a low energy value–
   (a) the energy value of the food must not be more than 167 kJ (40 kcal) per hundred grams or hundred millilitres, as is appropriate, unless the food is–
      (i) an intense sweetener, or
      (ii) a product which consists of a mixture of an intense sweetener with other substances and which, when compared on a weight for weight basis, is significantly sweeter than sucrose,
   (b) the energy value of a normal serving of the food must not be more than 167 kJ (40 kcal), and
   (c) in the case of an uncooked food which naturally has a low energy value, the claim must be in the form 'a low energy food' or 'a low calorie food' or 'a low Joule food'.

3 The food must be marked or labelled with the prescribed nutrition labelling.

Protein claims

3   A claim that a food, other than a food intended for babies or young children which satisfies the conditions of item 1 of this Part of this Schedule, is a source of protein.

1   The quantity of the food that can reasonably be expected to be consumed in one day must contribute at least 12g of protein.

2   (1) If the claim is that the food is a rich or excellent source of protein, at least 20 per cent of the energy value of the food must be provided by protein.

(2) In any other case, at least 12 per cent of the energy value of the food must be provided by protein.

3   The food must be marked or labelled with the prescribed nutrition labelling.

Vitamin claims

4   A claim that a food, other than a food intended for babies or young children which satisfies the conditions of item 1 of this Part of this Schedule, is a source of vitamins.

Note

A reference to a vitamin in the name of a food shall not of itself constitute a claim of a type to which this item applies if the food consists solely of–
(i) vitamins, or
(ii) a mixture of vitamins and minerals, or
(iii) a mixture of vitamins, or of vitamins and minerals, and a carrying agent, or
(iv) a mixture of vitamins, or of vitamins and minerals, and other substances sold in tablet, capsule or elixir form.

1   (1) If the claim is not confined to named vitamins, every vitamin named in the claim must be a vitamin specified in column 1 of Table A below, and–

(a) where the claim is that the food is a rich or excellent source of vitamins, the quantity of the food that can reasonably be expected to be consumed in one day must contain at least one half of the recommended daily allowance of two or more of the vitamins specified in column 1 of Table A below, and

(b) in any other case, the quantity of the food that can reasonably be expected to be consumed in one day must contain at least one sixth of the recommended daily allowance of two or more of the vitamins specified in column 1 of Table A below.

(2) If the claim is confined to named vitamins, every vitamin named in the claim must be a vitamin specified in column 1 of Table A below, and–

(a) where the claim is that the food is a rich or excellent source of vitamins, the quantity of the food that can reasonably be expected to be consumed in one day must contain at least one half of the recommended daily allowance of every vitamin named in the claim, and

(b) in any other case, the quantity of the food that can reasonably be expected to be consumed in one day must contain at least one sixth of the recommended daily allowance of every vitamin named in the claim.

2   The food must be marked or labelled–

(a) in the case of a food to which nutrition labelling relates–

(i) where the claim is in respect of unnamed vitamins (whether alone or together with named vitamins), then in respect of any of those unnamed vitamins which are listed in Table A, with the prescribed nutrition labelling and, in addition, with a statement of the percentages of the recommended daily allowance for such vitamins as are contained in either a quantified serving of the food or, provided that the total number of portions contained in the sales unit of the food is stated, in one such portion of the food, and

(ii) where the claim is in respect of a named vitamin or of named vitamins (whether alone or together with unnamed vitamins), then in respect of that named vitamin or those named vitamins, with the prescribed nutrition labelling and, in addition, with a statement of the percentages of the recommended daily allowance for such vitamins as are contained in either a quantified serving of the food or, provided that the total number of portions contained in the sales unit of the food is stated, in one such portion of the food; and

(b) in the case of food supplements or waters other than natural mineral waters, in respect of any vitamins, whether unnamed, named or both–

(i) with a statement of the percentage of the recommended daily allowance of those vitamins contained in either a quantified serving or (provided that the food is prepacked) a portion of the food, and

(ii) where the food is prepacked, of the number of portions contained in the package,

and the name used in such marking or labelling for any such vitamin shall be the name specified for that vitamin in column 1 of Table A below.

Mineral claims

5   A claim that a food, other than a food intended for babies or young children which satisfies the conditions of item 1 of this Part of this Schedule, is a source of minerals.

The conditions are the same as those set out in item 4 of this Part of this Schedule with the substitution of–

(a) the word 'mineral' for 'vitamin' wherever it occurs.

(b) the word 'minerals' for 'vitamins' wherever it occurs, and

(c) the expression 'Table B' for 'Table A' wherever it occurs.

Notes

(a) A claim that a food has low or reduced levels of minerals shall not be regarded as a claim of a type described in this item.

(b) The note that applies to item 4 of this Part of this Schedule applies equally to this item with the substitution of–
(i) the word 'mineral' for 'vitamin',
(ii) the word 'minerals' for 'vitamins' wherever it occurs, and
(iii) the word 'vitamins' for 'minerals' wherever it occurs.

Cholesterol claims

6	A claim relating to the presence or absence of cholesterol in a food.	1	Subject to condition 3 the food must contain no more than 0.005 per cent of cholesterol.
		2	The claim must not be accompanied by a suggestion, whether express or implied, that the food is beneficial to human health because of its level of cholesterol.
		3	If the claim relates to the removal of cholesterol from, or its reduction in, the food and condition 1 is not met, such claims shall only be made– (a) as part of an indication of the true nature of the food, (b) as part of an indication of the treatment of the food, (c) within the list of ingredients, or (d) as a footnote in respect of a prescribed nutrition labelling.
		4	The food shall be marked or labelled with the prescribed nutrition labelling.

Nutrition claims

7	Any nutrition claim not dealt with under any other item in this Part of this Schedule.	1	The food must be capable of fulfilling the claim.
		2	The food shall be marked or labelled with the prescribed nutrition labelling.

Claims which depend on another food

8	A claim that a food has a particular value or conveys a particular benefit.	The value or benefit must not be derived wholly or partly form another food that is intended to be consumed with the food in relation to which the claim is made.

TABLE A–Vitamins in respect of which claims may be made

Column 1	Column 2
Vitamin	**Recommended daily allowance**
Vitamin A	800 micro g
Vitamin D	5 micro g
Vitamin E	10 mg
Vitamin C	60 mg
Thiamin	1.4 mg
Riboflavin	0.16 mg

Niacin	18 mg
Vitamin B6	2 mg
Folacin	200 micro g
Vitamin B12	1 micro g
Biotin	0.15 mg
Pantothenic acid	6 mg

TABLE B–Minerals in respect of which claims may be made

Column 1	Column 2
Vitamin	Recommended daily allowance
Calcium	800 mg
Phosphorus	800 mg
Iron	14 mg
Magnesium	300 mg
Zinc	15 mg
Iodine	150 micro g

Note

As a rule, a significant amount means 15% of the recommended daily allowance listed in respect of each vitamin and mineral specified in Table A and B above that is supplied by 100 g or 100 ml of a food, or per package of a food if the package contains only a single portion.

SCHEDULE 7

Nutrition Labelling

Regulation 41(3),(4)

Part I

Presentation of Prescribed Nutrition Labelling

1

Prescribed nutrition labelling shall consist of such of the following items as under Part II of this Schedule are either required or permitted to be given. Subject to paragraphs 2, 3, 4, 5 and 6 below, the items and, where applicable, their order and manner of listing, are–

energy	(x)	kJ and (x) kcal
protein	(x)	g
carbohydrate	(x)	g
of which:		
– sugars	(x)	g
– polyols	(x)	g
– starch	(x)	g

fat	(x)	g
of which:		
– saturates	(x)	g
– mono-unsaturates	(x)	g
– polyunsaturates	(x)	g
– cholesterol	(x)	mg
fibre	(x)	g
sodium	(x)	g
(vitamins)	(x units)	
(minerals)	(x units)	

2

In the event that there is also required to be given the name and amount of any substance which belongs to, or is a component of, one of the items already given such substance or component shall be listed immediately after the item to which it relates, and in the following manner–

(item)	(x)	g or mg
of which		
– (substance or component)	(x)	g or mg

3

(a) For (vitamins) and (minerals) there shall be substituted, as appropriate, the names of any vitamin or mineral listed in Table A or B in Schedule 6.

(b) For (item) there shall be substituted the name of the relevant item from the list in paragraph 1 above.

(c) For (substance or component) there shall be substituted the name of the substance or component.

(d) For (x) there shall be substituted the appropriate amount in each case and, in respect of vitamins and minerals, such amounts–

   (i) shall be expressed in the units of measurement specified in relation to the respective vitamins and minerals given in Table A or B in Schedule 6, and

   (ii) shall also be expressed as a percentage of the recommended daily allowance specified for such vitamins and minerals in those Tables.

4

All amounts given–

(a) are to be per hundred grams or hundred millilitres of the food, as is appropriate, and, where it is wished to do so, those in either–

   (i) a quantified serving of the food, or

   (ii) provided that the total number of portions contained in that sales unit of the food is stated, in one such portion of the food,

(b) shall be such amounts as are contained in the food as sold to the ultimate consumer or to a catering establishment save that, where sufficiently detailed instructions are given for the preparation for consumption of the food, they may (if expressly said to be so) be such amounts as are contained in the food after the completion of such preparation in accordance with the said instructions, and

(c) shall be averages based, either alone or in any combination, on–
   (i) the manufacturer's analysis of the food,
   (ii) a calculation from the actual average values of the ingredients used in the preparation of the food,
   (iii) a calculation from generally established and accepted data,

and 'averages' for the purposes of this sub-paragraph means the figures which best represent the respective amounts of the nutrients which a given food contains, there having been taken into account seasonal variability, patterns of consumption and any other factor which may cause the actual amount to vary.

5

In the calculation of the energy value the following conversion factors shall be employed–

(a) 1 gram of carbohydrate (excluding polyols) shall be deemed to contribute 17 kJ (4 kcal);

(b) 1 gram of polyols shall be deemed to contribute 10 kJ (2.4 kcal);

(c) 1 gram of protein shall be deemed to contribute 17 kJ (4 kcal);

(d) 1 gram of fat shall be deemed to contribute 37 kJ (9 kcal);

(e) 1 gram of ethanol shall be deemed to contribute 29 kJ (7 kcal);

(f) 1 gram of organic acid shall be deemed to contribute 13 kJ (3 kcal).

6

Any prescribed nutrition labelling shall be presented together in one conspicuous place–

(a) in tabular form with any numbers aligned, or

(b) if there is insufficient space to permit tabular listing, in linear form.

Part II

Contents of Prescribed Nutrition Labelling

1

In respect of any food other than one to which paragraph 2 below applies, prescribed nutrition labelling shall be given as follows–

(a) it shall include either–
   (i) energy and the amounts of protein, carbohydrate and fat, or
   (ii) energy and the amounts of protein, carbohydrate, sugars, fat, saturates, fibre and sodium, provided that, where sugars, saturates, fibre or sodium is, or are, the subject of a nutrition claim, it shall be given in accordance with paragraph (ii);

(b) where such is the subject of a nutrition claim, it shall also include the amounts of any polyols, starch, mono-unsaturates, polyunsaturates, cholesterol, vitamins or minerals, and in the absence of such a claim it may include any of these, provided that in either case only those vitamins or minerals present in a significant amount as described in the Note to Tables A and B in Schedule 6 above shall, or may, be so included;

(c) where labelling is given in accordance with sub-paragraph (a)(i) above and, further to sub-paragraph (b) above the amount of any of mono-unsaturates, polyunsaturates or cholesterol has been included, it shall also include the amount of saturates, and

(d) where such is the subject of a nutrition claim, it shall also include the name and amount of any substance which belongs to, or is a component of, one of the nutrients already required or permitted to be included.

2

(1) In respect of any food which is not prepacked and which is sold–
   (a) to the ultimate consumer other than at a catering establishment,
   (b) to the ultimate consumer from a vending machine, whether or not such machine is located at a catering establishment, or
   (c) to a catering establishment,

the prescribed nutrition labelling shall include such of energy and the amounts of any nutrient and the name and amount of any substance which belongs to, or is a component of, any nutrient, in respect of which a nutrition claim is made, and it may include any of the items listed in paragraph 1 of Part I of this Schedule in respect of which there is no such claim.

SCHEDULE 8

Misleading Descriptions

Regulation 42

Part I

General

Column 1	Column 2
Words and descriptions	Conditions
The description 'dietary' or 'dietetic'	Shall not be applied to any food unless it is a food for a particular nutritional use (excluding such foods formulated for infants and young children in good health) which– (a) has been specially made for a class of persons whose digestive process or metabolism is disturbed or who, by reason of their special physiological condition, obtain special benefit from a controlled consumption of certain substances, and (b) is suitable for fulfilling the particular nutritional requirements of that class of persons. Any description incorporating the name of a food in such a way as to

imply that the food, or the part of a food, being described has the flavour of the food named in the description.

Shall not be applied to any food unless the flavour of the food being described is derived wholly or mainly from the food named in the description, except that any description incorporating the word 'chocolate' which is such as to imply that the food being described has a chocolate flavour may be applied to a food which has a chocolate flavour derived wholly or mainly from non fat cocoa solids where the purchaser would not be misled by the description.

This shall not be taken to prevent the use of the word 'flavour' preceded by the name of a food when the flavour of the food being described is not wholly or mainly from the food named in the description.

A pictorial representation of a food which is such as to imply that the food to which the representation is applied has the flavour of the food depicted in the representation.

Shall not be applied to any food unless the flavour of the food to which the representation is applied is derived wholly or mainly from the food depicted in the representation.

The description 'ice cream'

Shall not be applied to any food other than the frozen product containing not less than 5 per cent fat and not less than 2.5 per cent milk protein, not necessarily in natural proportions, and which is obtained by subjecting an emulsion of fat, milk solids and sugar (including any sweetener permitted in ice cream by the Sweeteners in Food Regulations 1995), with or without the addition of other substances, to heat treatment and either to subsequent freezing or evaporation, addition of water and subsequent freezing.

The description 'dairy ice cream'	Shall not be applied to any food other than one which fulfils the conditions relating to application of the description 'ice cream' to a food (provided that the fat in respect of which a minimum of 5 per cent is specified shall here consist exclusively of milk fat) and which contains no fat other than milk fat or any fat present by reason of the use as an ingredient of such ice cream of any egg, any flavouring, or any emulsifier or stabiliser.

The word 'milk' or any other word or description which implies that the food being described contains milk	Shall not be used as part of the name of a food, which contains the milk of an animal other than a cow, unless–
	(a)
	   (i) such milk has all the normal constituents in their natural proportions, and
	   (ii) the word or description is accompanied by the name of that animal; or
	(b)
	   (i) such milk has been subjected to a process or treatment, and
	   (ii) the word or description is accompanied by the name of that animal and an indication of that process or treatment; or
	(c) the word or description is used in accordance with any regulations made, or having effect as if made, under the Act or any order having effect as if contained in regulations so made.

The word 'milk'	Shall not be used as the name of an ingredient where the ingredient is the milk of an animal other than a cow unless– (a) the word is accompanied by the name of the animal, and (b) the use of the word as the name of the ingredient complies in all other respects with these Regulations.

The description 'starch-reduced'	Shall not be applied to any food, unless– (a) less than 50 per cent of the food consists of anhydrous carbohydrate calculated by weight on the dry matter of the food, and (b) the starch content of a given quantity of the food is substantially less than that of the same quantity of similar foods to which the description is not applied.
The word 'vitamin' or any other word or description which implies that the food to which the word or description relates is a vitamin	Shall not be used in the labelling or advertising of any food, unless the food to which the word or description relates is– (a) one of the vitamins specified in column 1 of Table A in Schedule 6; or (b) vitamin K.
The description 'alcohol-free'	Shall not be applied to any alcoholic drink from which the alcohol has been extracted, unless– (a) the drink has an alcoholic strength by volume of not more than 0.05 per cent, and (b) the drink is marked or labelled with an indication of its maximum alcoholic strength (in one of the forms specified in regulation 30(1) immediately preceded by the words 'not more than') or, in an appropriate case, with an indication that it contains no alcohol.
The description 'dealcoholised'	Shall not be applied to any drink, unless– (a) the drink, being an alcoholic drink from which the alcohol has been extracted, has an alcoholic strength by volume of not more than 0.5 per cent, and (b) the drink is marked or labelled with an indication of its maximum alcoholic strength (in one of the forms specified in regulation 30(1) immediately preceded by the words 'not more than') or, in an appropriate case, with an indication that it contains no alcohol.

The description 'low alcohol' or any other word or description which implies that the drink being described is low in alcohol	Shall not be applied to any alcoholic drink unless– (a) the drink has an alcoholic strength by volume of not more than 1.2 per cent, and (b) the drink is marked or labelled with an indication of its maximum alcoholic strength (in one of the forms specified in regulation 30(1) immediately preceded by the words 'not more than').
The description 'low calorie' or any other word or description which implies that the drink being described is low in calories	Shall not be applied to any soft drink unless the soft drink (where applicable, after subsequent preparation (which may include dilution) in accordance with any accompanying instructions) contains not more than 10 kcal per 100 ml and 42 kJ per 100 ml of the drink.
The description 'non-alcoholic'	Shall not be used in conjunction with a name commonly associated with an alcoholic drink, except in the composite name 'non-alcoholic wine' when that composite name is used in accordance with regulation 43.
The name 'liqueur'	Shall not be applied to any drink other than one so qualifying under the definition of liqueur contained in Article 1.4(r) of Council Regulation (EEC) No 1576/89.
The name 'Indian tonic water' or 'quinine tonic water'	Shall not be applied to any drink unless the drink contains not less than 57 mg of quinine (calculated as quinine sulphate BP) per litre of the drink.
The name 'tonic wine'	Shall not be applied to any drink unless there appears in immediate proximity to the words 'tonic wine' the clear statement: 'the name 'tonic wine' does not imply health giving or medicinal properties'. No recommendation as to consumption or dosage shall appear in the labelling or advertising of the drink.

Part II
Cheese

Column 1	Column 2
Variety of cheese	Maximum percentage of water
Cheddar	39
Blue Stilton	42
Derby	42
Leicester	42
Cheshire	44
Dunlop	44
Gloucester	44
Double Gloucester	44
Caerphilly	46
Wensleydale	46
White Stilton	46
Lancashire	48

Part III
Cream

Column 1	Column 2
Clotted cream	The cream is clotted and contains not less than 55 per cent milk fat.
Double cream	The cream contains not less than 48 per cent milk fat.
Whipping cream	The cream contains not less than 35 per cent milk fat.
Whipped cream	The cream contains not less than 35 per cent milk fat and has been whipped.
Sterilised cream	The cream is sterilised cream and contains not less than 23 per cent milk fat.
Cream or single cream	The cream is not sterilised cream and contains not less than 18 per cent milk fat.
Sterilised half cream	The cream is sterilised cream and contains not less than 12 per cent milk fat.
Half cream	The cream is not sterilised cream and contains not less than 12 per cent milk fat.

18.24.1 Section 8 of the Food Safety Act 1990: selling food not complying with food safety requirements

Need to prove/investigate:

1. Place of offence (within courts jurisdiction).
2. Date of offence.
3. Status of defendant, that is, individual or sole trader, partnership, limited company or plc.
4. Address of defendant or registered office address if limited company.
5. Sells food.
6. Food is for human consumption.
7. Food is unfit for human consumption, contaminated or injurious to health.
8. Due diligence defence.
9. Mitigation/explanation.

Time limit: s 34 of the Food Safety Act 1990: one year from commission or three years from discovery whichever is earlier.

Mode of trial: either way.

Maximum penalty (s 35): fine level 5 and/or three months.

Summary: £20,000 and/or six months.

Indictment: fine and/or two years.

18.25 SECTION 14 OF THE FOOD SAFETY ACT 1990: SELLING FOOD NOT COMPLYING WITH FOOD SAFETY REQUIREMENTS

(1) Any person who–
 (a) sells for human consumption, or offers, exposes or advertises for sale for such consumption, or has in his possession for the purpose of such sale or of preparation for such sale; or
 (b) deposits with, or consigns to, any other person for the purpose of such sale or of preparation for such sale,
 any food which fails to comply with food safety requirements shall be guilty of an offence.

(2) For the purposes of this Part food fails to comply with food safety requirements if–
 (a) it has been rendered injurious to health by means of any of the operations mentioned in section 7(1) above;
 (b) it is unfit for human consumption; or
 (c) it is so contaminated (whether by extraneous matter or otherwise) that it would not be reasonable to expect it to be used for human consumption in that state;

and references to such requirements or to food complying with such requirements shall be construed accordingly.

(3) Where any food which fails to comply with food safety requirements is part of a batch, lot or consignment of food of the same class or description, it shall be presumed for the purposes of this section and section 9 below, until the contrary is proved, that all of the food in that batch, lot or consignment fails to comply with those requirements.

(4) For the purposes of this Part, any part of, or product derived wholly or partly from, an animal–
   (a) which has been slaughtered in a knacker's yard, or of which the carcass has been brought into a knacker's yard; or
   (b) in Scotland, which has been slaughtered otherwise than in a slaughterhouse,
   shall be deemed to be unfit for human consumption.

(5) In subsection (4) above, in its application to Scotland, 'animal' means any description of cattle, sheep, goat, swine, horse, ass or mule; and paragraph (b) of that subsection shall not apply where accident, illness or emergency affecting the animal in question required it to be slaughtered as mentioned in that paragraph.

18.26 SECTION 14 OF THE FOOD SAFETY ACT 1990: SELLING FOOD NOT OF THE NATURE OR SUBSTANCE OR QUALITY DEMANDED

Need to prove/investigate:

1. A person (capacity of defendant, that is, limited company, partnership, individual – correct identity).
2. Place of offence (within jurisdiction of the court).
3. Dates of offence (s 34: three years from commission/one year from discovery).
4. A sale of food for human consumption.
5. A purchaser.
6. Food which is not of nature, substance, or quality.[a]
7. Due diligence defence.
8. Prejudice to the purchaser (see s 14(2) for clarification).

Time limit: s 34 of the Food Safety Act 1990: one year from commission or three years from discovery which ever is earlier

Mode of trial: either way

Maximum penalty (s 35).

Summary: £20,000 and/or six months.

Indictment: fine and/or two years.

(a) One of these only must be elected for inclusion in an information.

18.27 SECTION 14 OF THE FOOD SAFETY ACT 1990: SELLING FOOD NOT OF THE NATURE OR SUBSTANCE OR QUALITY DEMANDED

(1) Any person who sells to the purchasers prejudice any food which is not of the nature or substance or quality demanded by the purchaser shall be guilty of an offence.

(2) In sub-section (1) above the reference to sale shall be construed as a reference to sale for human consumption and in proceedings under that sub-section it shall not be a defence that the purchaser was not prejudiced because he bought for analysis or examination.

18.28 SECTION 32 OF THE FOOD SAFETY ACT 1990: POWERS OF ENTRY

(1) An authorised officer of an enforcement authority shall, on producing, if so required, some duly authenticated document showing his authority, have a right at all reasonable hours–

   (a) to enter any premises within the authority's area for the purpose of ascertaining whether there is or has been on the premises any contravention of the provisions of this Act, or of regulations or orders made under it; and

   (b) to enter any business premises, whether within or outside the authority's area, for the purpose of ascertaining whether there is on the premises any evidence of any contravention within that area of any of such provisions; and

   (c) in the case of an authorised officer of a food authority, to enter any premises for the purpose of the performance by the authority of their functions under this Act,

   but admission to any premises used only as a private dwelling-house shall not be demanded as of right unless 24 hours' notice of the intended entry has been given to the occupier.

(2) If a justice of the peace, on sworn information in writing, is satisfied that there is reasonable ground for entry into any premises for any such purpose as is mentioned in subsection (1) above and either–

   (a) that admission to the premises has been refused, or a refusal is apprehended, and that notice of the intention to apply for a warrant has been given to the occupier; or

   (b) that an application for admission, or the giving of such a notice, would defeat the object of the entry, or that the case is one of urgency, or that the premises are unoccupied or the occupier temporarily absent,

   the justice may by warrant signed by him authorise the authorised officer to enter the premises, if need be by reasonable force.

(3) Every warrant granted under this section shall continue in force for a period of one month.

(4) An authorised officer entering any premises by virtue of this section, or of a warrant issued under it, may take with him such other persons as he considers necessary, and on leaving any unoccupied premises which he has entered by virtue of such a warrant shall leave them as effectively secured against unauthorised entry as he found them.

(5) An authorised officer entering premises by virtue of this section, or of a warrant issued under it, may inspect any records (in whatever form they are held) relating to a food business and, where any such records are kept by means of a computer–
   (a) may have access to, and inspect and check the operation of, any computer and any associated apparatus or material which is or has been in use in connection with the records; and
   (b) may require any person having charge of, or otherwise concerned with the operation of, the computer, apparatus or material to afford him such assistance as he may reasonably require.
(6) Any officer exercising any power conferred by subsection (5) above may–
   (a) seize and detain any records which he has reason to believe may be required as evidence in proceedings under any of the provisions of this Act or of regulations or orders made under it; and
   (b) where the records are kept by means of a computer, may require the records to be produced in a form in which they may be taken away.
(7) If any person who enters any premises by virtue of this section, or of a warrant issued under it, discloses to any person any information obtained by him in the premises with regard to any trade secret, he shall, unless the disclosure was made in the performance of his duty, be guilty of an offence.
(8) Nothing in this section authorises any person, except with the permission of the local authority under the Animal Health Act 1981, to enter any premises–
   (a) in which an animal or bird affected with any disease to which that Act applies is kept; and
   (b) which is situated in a place declared under that Act to be infected with such a disease.
(9) In the application of this section to Scotland, any reference to a justice of the peace includes a reference to the sheriff and to a magistrate.

18.29 SECTION 33 OF THE FOOD SAFETY ACT 1990: OBSTRUCTION ETC OF OFFICERS

(1) Any person who–
   (a) intentionally obstructs any person acting in the execution of this Act; or
   (b) without reasonable cause, fails to give to any person acting in the execution of this Act any assistance or information which that person may reasonably require of him for the performance of his functions under this Act,
   shall be guilty of an offence.
(2) Any person who, in purported compliance with any such requirement as is mentioned in subsection (1)(b) above–
   (a) furnishes information which he knows to be false or misleading in a material particular; or

(b) recklessly furnishes information which is false or misleading in a material particular,

shall be guilty of an offence.

(3) Nothing in subsection (1)(b) above shall be construed as requiring any person to answer any question or give information if to do so might incriminate him.

Offences

18.30 SECTION 34 OF THE FOOD SAFETY ACT 1990: TIME LIMIT FOR PROSECUTIONS

No prosecution for an offence under this Act which is punishable under section 35(2) below shall be begun after the expiry of–

(a) three years from the commission of the offence; or

(b) one year from its discovery by the prosecutor,

whichever is the earlier.

18.31 SECTION 35 OF THE FOOD SAFETY ACT 1990: PUNISHMENT OF OFFENCES

(1) A person guilty of an offence under section 33(1) above shall be liable on summary conviction to a fine not exceeding level 5 on the standard scale or to imprisonment for a term not exceeding three months or to both.

(2) A person guilty of any other offence under this Act shall be liable–

(a) on conviction on indictment, to a fine or to imprisonment for a term not exceeding two years or to both;

(b) on summary conviction, to a fine not exceeding the relevant amount or to imprisonment for a term not exceeding six months or to both.

(3) In subsection (2) above 'the relevant amount' means–

(a) in the case of an offence under section 7, 8 or 14 above, £20,000;

(b) in any other case, the statutory maximum.

(4) If a person who is–

(a) licensed under section 1 of the Slaughterhouses Act 1974 to keep a knacker's yard;

(b) (Repealed);

(c) licensed under section 6 of the Slaughter of Animals (Scotland) Act 1980 to use any premises as a knacker's yard, is convicted of an offence under Part II of this Act, the court may, in addition to any other punishment, cancel his licence or registration.

Food Safety Act 1990, s 35 as amended by SI 1996/2235. Sub-s (a) is amended, and sub-s (b) is repealed, by SI 1996/2235.

18.32 SECTION 36 OF THE FOOD SAFETY ACT 1990: OFFENCES BY BODIES CORPORATE

(1) Where an offence under this Act which has been committed by a body corporate is proved to have been committed with the consent or connivance of, or to be attributable to any neglect on the part of–

  (a) any director, manager, secretary or other similar officer of the body corporate; or

  (b) any person who was purporting to act in any such capacity,

  he as well as the body corporate shall be deemed to be guilty of that offence and shall be liable to be proceeded against and punished accordingly.

(2) In subsection (1) above 'director', in relation to any body corporate established by or under any enactment for the purpose of carrying on under national ownership any industry or part of an industry or undertaking, being a body corporate whose affairs are managed by its members, means a member of that body corporate.

18.33 NON COMPLIANCE WITH A REPAIRS NOTICE (S 198A OF THE HOUSING ACT 1985)

Elements of the offence/matters for investigation:

1 Capacity of defendant ie individual, sole trader, partnership, ltd, Co, plc.

2 Address of defendant (registered office if company).

3 Date(s) of the offence.[a]

4 Place of the offence (within the courts jurisdiction).

5 A person having control of the premises.[b]

6 Non compliance with the notice.

(a) The date of the information will normally be the period in which the offence takes place so that the case can be presented to the court by reference to the full period of non compliance and any aggravating features that arise in that time period. This date will usually be the first date after which the notice becomes effective and that latest date for non compliance as can be proved by the evidence (usually the last site visit). If an appeal is entered the date of any offence will be effected by s 193(2) which is either a date set by the court or within 21 days of any appeal having been withdrawn.

(b) A person having control of the premises is defined in s 207. Essentially, it means the owner or person entitled to the rack rent. The rack rent is usually the full rent as opposed to a nominal or peppercorn rent or ground rent. In reality those entitled to these rents are not really owners in the practical sense. It was established in the case of *Camden LBC v Gunby* [1999] TLR, 12 July that an agent is the owner for the purposes of s 80 of the Environmental Protection Act 1990. On the basis that the owner is also defined by reference to receipt of the rack rent it is the authors' view that this case would apply to s 198A.

Chapter 18: Environmental Health Legislation

7   Failure to comply is intentional.(c)

8   Service of the notice.(d)

9   Defence (if any).(e)

10 Mitigation/explanation.

(c) The courts seem to define the words intentionally and wilfully as being the same or at least as being very similar. This is demonstrated by reference to the case of *R v Senior* [1895] All ER 511, p 514I, in which Lord Russell defined wilfully to mean 'done deliberately and not by inadvertence' and the words 'wilfully neglect' were defined as 'intentional failure to take those steps which the experience of mankind shows to be generally necessary': see, also, *Kent CC v Upchurch River Golf Course Ltd* (1998) P & CR D37 it was said that wilfully under s 137 of the Highways Act 1980 meant intentionally as opposed to accidentally. The following cases on the meaning of the word wilful have been cited. A question that is frequently asked is whether or not the financial circumstances of the defendant can be taken into account when determining if there has been wilful non compliance. The case of *Kent CC v Brockman* [1996] PLR 1; [1994] Crim LR 295 has established that personal circumstances may be taken into account for failure to comply with an enforcement notice. The case of *R v Senior* [1895] All ER 511 considered the meaning of 'wilfully neglected'. The *dicta* of Lord Russell CJ, p 514H, allowed for the means of the defendant to be considered. However it was more recently decided in the case of *Saddleworth UDC v Aggregate and Sand* (1971) 69 LGR 103 that lack of finance could not amount to a reasonable excuse for a company in defence to a prosecution for non compliance with a notice under the Public Health Act 1936. In the case of *R v Redbridge ex p Guppy* [1997] BPIR 441, the defendant's failure to pay a compensation order amounted to wilful refusal after he had declared himself bankrupt as funds were available prior to the declaration. It seems therefore, that the courts tend to interpret the word wilful by looking very closely at the conduct of the offender. The approach of the appellate courts appears to be more consistent with the question of whether the non compliance was an impossibility as opposed to a more relaxed question of whether compliance is reasonably possible. An equally strict approach was taken in the case of *Honig v Islington* [1972] Crim LR 126, in which it was held that failure to comply with a s 15 of the Housing Act 1961 notice was the result of a course of conduct which the defendant has chosen to pursue and was not caused by *force majeure* (supervening event) accident or impossibility. In this case the defendant intended to purchase water heaters to enable him to conform to the notice. These were not available, the defendant made no attempt to obtain others and was convicted of wilfully failing to comply with the notice.

(d) It is essential that the correct person is served with the notice. If the wrong person is served there is no need to appeal to the county court (*Pollway Nominees Ltd v London Borough of Croydon* [1985] 1 WLR 241). This is therefore a matter which can be raised at a prosecution hearing. Section 617 sets out the procedure for service in circumstances where the 'person having control of' the premises cannot be ascertained after having made reasonable enquiry. The section is however silent as to the manner of service in any other situation. There is authority which suggests that there is an irrebuttable presumption that service is deemed to be effected by simply pushing the notice through the letter box of the recipient, see *Rushmore BC v Reynolds* (1991) 23 HLR 495, in which service was effected under s 233 of the Local Government Act 1972 and s 7 of the Interpretation Act 1978, even though R did not receive the notice. See, also, *Lambeth BC v Mullings* [1990] COD 281 and [1990] TLR, 6 January which confirmed that s 233 of the above Act applied to service of a notice of an abatement notice through a letter box under s 58 of the Control of Pollution Act 1974. In any event, it is the authors' view that steps should be taken to confirm that the notice has been received. It is also recommended that the notice is endorsed as to service on the reverse of the notice. This endorsement should be affixed at the time of service or at the first available opportunity thereafter.

Business or personal address?
A person proceeded against in his private capacity would normally be served at his private address. The position would be reversed if the defendant is a businessman or professional being proceeded against in that capacity. By virtue of s 233 of the Local Government Act 1972 a person may be served at his 'proper address' which is defined as his 'last known address' in s 233(4). In the case of *Robertson v Banham & Co (A Firm)* [1996] TLR, 26 November, the court confirmed that the phrase 'usual or last known address' was not to be confined to residential addresses and interpreted these words to mean the address where a person practised if that person was a professional.

(e) In the case of *Stagecoach Ltd v MacPhail* 1988 SCCR 289, it was established that matters which could have be raised by way of appeal against a s 58 of the Control of Pollution Act notice could not be raised in defence to proceedings for contravention of that notice. The same issue arose in respect of notices served under s 80 of the Environmental Protection Act 1990 and s 60 of the Control of Pollution ... [cont]

Time limit: six months (s 127 of the Magistrates' Courts Act 1980).

Mode of trial: summary.

Maximum penalty (s 198A).

Summary: level 4.

18.34 OTHER HOUSING ACT 1985 NOTICES

For a draft information/allegation relating to s 376 of the Housing Act 1985, see Appendix 11.

The legislation covering offences for non-compliance with notices is set out below in more detail:

18.35 SECTION 376 OF THE HOUSING ACT 1985

Penalty for failure to execute works (see below).

18.36 SECTION 376 OF THE HOUSING ACT 1985

The investigatory matters and elements of the offence are:

(i) 'A person' – The full name and address of the person upon whom the notice has been served, that is, person managing the house (for ss 352 and 372 offences as defined in s 398) or person having control of the house (for a s 352 offence as defined in s 398) supported by admissible evidence.

(ii) 'failure to comply' – evidence of inspection scheduling the items in the notice which have not been complied with by reference to the notice.

(e) [cont] Act 1974. The court adopted the reasoning in *A Lambert Flat Management Ltd* [1981] 1 WLR 898, per Acker LJ, p 907:

> Can the defendant urge as a reasonable excuse for failing to comply with the notice, that the same was invalid for one or more of the reasons provided by the regulations as permissible grounds of appeal? ... The answer to my mind is clearly in the negative. Not only is the right of appeal given by statute but very detailed provisions have been made by the regulations for the prosecution of such appeals. Section 58(4) was not designed to give the recipient of the notice a choice of forum in which to mount an attack on the notice. It was designed to provide a defence to a criminal charge where he had some reasonable excuse, such as a specific difficulty in compliance with the notice.

The authors suggest that the above cases relate to legislation that is similar to s 198A and are applicable.

Failure to include evidence of the compliance period is fatal if it is not pleaded in the informations and referred to in the evidence (*Maltedge v Wokingham DC* [1992] TLR, 21 May).

Chapter 18: Environmental Health Legislation

(iii) 'wilfully'[a] – the owner or manager should be interviewed by the Investigating Officer to determine why there has been a failure to comply as wilfully means 'a requirement by the accused of basic *mens rea* (guilty mind) in the sense of intention.

(iv) Service of the notice[b] – evidence of receipt is required for the file, but see footnotes.

(v) Service of preliminary notice[c] (s 377A) unless urgent.

(a) A question which is frequently asked is whether or not the financial circumstances of the defendant can be taken into account when determining if there has been wilful non compliance. The case of *Kent CC v Brockman* [1996] PLR 1; [1994] Crim LR 295 has established that personal circumstances may be taken into account for failure to comply with an enforcement notice. The case of *R v Senior* [1895] All ER 511 considered the meaning of 'wilfully neglected'. The *dicta* of Lord Russell CJ, p 514H, allowed for the means of the defendant to be considered. However, it was more recently decided in the case of *Saddleworth UDC v Aggregate and Sand* (1971) 69 LGR 103 that lack of finance could not amount to a reasonable excuse for a company in defence to a prosecution for non compliance with a notice under the Public Health Act 1936. In the case of *R v Redbridge ex p Guppy* [1997] BPIR 441, the defendant's failure to pay a compensation order amounted to wilful refusal after he had declared himself bankrupt as funds were available prior to the declaration. It seems, therefore, that the courts tend to interpret the word wilful by looking very closely at the conduct of the offender. The approach of the appellate courts appears to be more consistent with the question of whether the non compliance was an impossibility as opposed to a more relaxed question of whether compliance is reasonably possible. An equally strict approach was taken in the case of *Honig v Islington* [1972] Crim LR 126 in which it was held that failure to comply with a s 15 of the Housing Act 1961 notice was the result of a course of conduct which the defendant has chosen to pursue and was not caused by *force majeure* (supervening event) accident or impossibility. In this case, the defendant intended to purchase water heaters to enable him to conform to the notice. These were not available, the defendant made no attempt to obtain others and was convicted.

(b) Section 617 sets out the procedure for service in circumstances where the 'person having control of' the premises cannot be ascertained after having made reasonable enquiry. The section is, however, silent as to the manner of service in any other situation. There is authority which suggests that there is an irrebuttable presumption that service is deemed to be effected by simply pushing the notice through the letter box of the recipient, see *Rushmore BC v Reynolds* (1991) 23 HLR 495, in which service was effected under s 233 of the Local Government Act 1972 and s 7 of the Interpretation Act 1978, even though R did not receive the notice. See, also, *Lambeth BC v Mullings* [1990] COD 281 and [1990] TLR, 6 January, which confirmed that s 233 of the above Act applied to service of a notice of an abatement notice through a letter box under s 58 of the Control of Pollution Act 1974. In any event, it is the authors' view that steps should be taken to confirm that the notice has been received. It is also recommended that the notice is endorsed as to service on the reverse of the notice. This endorsement should be affixed at the time of service or at the first available opportunity thereafter.

Business or personal address?

A person proceeded against in his private capacity would normally be served at his private address. The position would be reversed if the defendant is a businessman or professional being proceeded against in that capacity. By virtue of s 233 of the Local Government Act 1972, a person may be served at his 'proper address' which is defined as his 'last known address' in s 233(4). In the case of *Robertson v Banham & Co (A Firm)* [1996] TLR, 26 November, the court confirmed that the phrase 'usual or last known address' was not to be confined to residential addresses and interpreted these words to mean the address where a person practised if that person was a professional.

(c) Another preliminary consideration may arise from the decision in *Canterbury CC v Bern* [1981] JPL 749, in which is was established that the notice must specify the works required, not merely the effect that unspecified works are required to achieve.

(vi) House is a house in multiple occupation (HIMO).(d)

(d) See s 345 which defines a HIMO to mean 'a house which is occupied by persons who do not form a single household'. The case of *Barnes v Sheffield CC* (1995) 27 HLR 719 decided that it would be wrong to suggest that there was a litmus test that could be applied to the question the court of appeal nonetheless regarded the following factors to be 'helpful' in determining whether the occupiers formed a single household:

A   whether the persons living in the house came to it as a single group or whether they were independently recruited;
B   what facilities were shared;
C   whether the occupiers were responsible for the whole house or just their particular rooms;
D   whether individual tenants were able to, or did lock other occupiers out of his room;
E   whose responsibility it was to recruit new occupiers when individuals left;
F   who allocated rooms;
G   the size of the rooms;
H   how stable the group composition was;
I   whether the mode of living was communal.

Sir Thomas Bingham MR, pp 723–24, made it clear that the order of these factors should not be regarded as significant and the weight given to any particular factor will vary widely from case to case depending on the overall picture. A similar list is to be found at DOE Circular 12/93 which sets out the following criteria:

A   whether cooking facilities are shared;
B   whether washing facilities are separate or shared;
C   whether occupants eat together;
D   whether cleaning is shared between occupants;
E   whether occupants have separate contracts;
F   whether vacancies are filled by occupants or landlord;
G   whether occupants come and go frequently.

In the more recent decision of *Rogers v Islington LBC* [1999] TLR, 30 August, the Court of Appeal recognised that the reasoning in the *Barnes* case was difficult to apply and further clarification was desirable. In the interests of safety and welfare of the occupants, the court emphasised that houses which ought to be treated as HIMOs did not escape statutory control. The house consisting of nine young adults who had all completed their further education, described by the owner as a private residential club, was a HIMO. The *Barnes* case was distinguished on two grounds: firstly, in that case the occupants were only four or five in number and, secondly, they came together as a pre-formed group for a predetermined period. Lord Justice Nourse deduced a good working test from the *Barnes* case as follows:

Where a small group of students at the same university joined together to occupy a house or flat for an academic year they would normally form a single household, notwithstanding that they might not have known each other beforehand and might pay rent individually.

The above test seems to be confined to students and people who form households in that way. Whilst recognising the dangers of seeking to 'define the indefinable' the court was reluctant to provide a universal test. Since the purpose of the legislation is to protect those who are not in a single household, it may be possible to design a test with this in mind, provided that the dynamics of the situation can be appreciated. The existence of more than one household not only exposes each household to the dangers caused by the other, it also creates an environment in which there is a fracture in the social responsibility between households. That is to say, in case of an emergency the degree of responsibility to warn and assist others will depend on whether or not the other occupant is a member of the same household. In the case of a fire, it is likely be 'each man for himself' unless there is a sufficient nexus between the occupants which is so compelling as to warrant one person warning the other and coming to his assistance if this is reasonable possible. This must be the reasoning behind the requirements for alarms and other devices such as half-hour fire-resistant doors, etc, which are designed to give anyone still remaining in the building a improved chance to escape the danger. For genuine family units and other single households where there is some form of obligation to assist, the need for such devices is not so essential. With this in mind, it might be helpful to have regard to the questions raised in *Barnes* and the circular above and ask whether there is a nexus between the household which is sufficiently compelling to ensure that everyone will be assisted by the other occupants to the extent that he has an equal chance of escaping in case of fire. The case of *London LBC v Ezedinma* [1981] 3 All ER 438 held that three groups of people, each sharing a separate kitchen from the other group are capable of being three separate households.

Chapter 18: Environmental Health Legislation

(vii) Date(s)[e] and place.

(viii) Common law defence.[f]

Time limit: six months (s 127 of the Magistrates' Courts Act 1980).

Mode of trial: summary.

Maximum penalty (s 376(1)).

Summary: level 4.

Subject to s 365 the local housing authority may serve a notice under this section where in the opinion of the authority, a house in multiple occupation fails to meet one or more of the requirements in paragraphs (a) to (e) of subsection (1A) and, having regard to the number of individuals or households or both for the time being accommodated on the premises, by reason of that failure the premises are not reasonably suitable for occupation by those individuals or households.

(e) For the purpose of drafting the information and authorisation of legal proceedings it is important to know when an offence has taken place. It is also necessary to give consideration to the date or more likely the period of the offence to enable to prosecution to refer to the full period of non compliance in the event of a guilty plea. If, for example, a single date is chosen for the offence it is open to the defence to argue that no reference can be made to any period of non compliance outside that date. There is some logic to this as further charges may follow, if there is further non compliance after the first offence and this would give rise to a duplication of punishment. Section 376(2) and the authority of *Camden LBC v Marshall* [1996] 1 WLR 1345 confirms that s 376 is a continuing offence. The case helpfully sets out that there are three obligations set out in the notice. The first and substantial obligation was to do the works; the second was to begin them within time; and the third to complete them within the time specified. Breach of any one of those requirements constituted non compliance. As s 376 is a continuing offence, it is advisable to lay proceedings for the full period of non compliance. It also follows that proceedings may be charged in respect of a notice served more than six months before the date of the offence provided that the alleged period of non compliance is within six months of laying the information. The date also needs to be considered in terms of the notice which must specify a treasonable date, at least 21 days after service, by which works must be begun and a reasonable period within which they must be completed. Notification must also be given to any owner lessee or mortgagee that the notice has been served.

(f) In the case of *Stagecoach Ltd v MacPhail* 1988 SCCR 289, it was established that matters which could have been raised by way of appeal against a s 58 of the Control of Pollution Act notice could not be raised in defence to proceedings for contravention of that notice. This is consistent with the view taken in *Amec Building Ltd v LB Camden* [1997] Env LR 330. The same issue arose in respect of notices served under s 80 of the Environmental Protection Act 1990 and s 60 of the Control of Pollution Act 1974. The court adopted the reasoning in *A Lambert Flat Management Ltd* [1981] 1 WLR 898, *per* Acker LJ, p 907:

> Can the defendant urge as a reasonable excuse for failing to comply with the notice, that the same was invalid for one or more of the reasons provided by the regulations as permissible grounds of appeal? ... The answer to my mind is clearly in the negative. Not only is the right of appeal given by statute but very detailed provisions have been made by the regulations for the prosecution of such appeals. Section 58(4) was not designed to give the recipient of the notice a choice of forum in which to mount an attack on the notice. It was designed to provide a defence to a criminal charge where he had some reasonable excuse, such as a specific difficulty in compliance with the notice.

The authors suggest that the above cases relate to legislation that is similar to s 376 and are applicable. Another preliminary consideration may arise from the decision in *Canterbury City Council v Bern* [1981] JPL 749 in which is was established that the notice must specify the works required, not merely the effect that unspecified works are required to achieve

For a draft information/allegation relating to HA 1985, s 376, see Appendix 11.

The legislation covering offences for non compliance with notices is set out below in more detail.

18.37 SECTION 352 OF THE HOUSING ACT 1985: POWER TO REQUIRE EXECUTION OF WORKS TO RENDER PREMISES FIT FOR NUMBER OF OCCUPANTS

(1A) The requirements in respect of a house in multiple occupation referred to in subsection (1) are the following, that is to say,–

    (a) there are satisfactory facilities for the storage, preparation and cooking of food including an adequate number of sinks with a satisfactory supply of hot and cold water;

    (b) it has an adequate number of suitably located water-closets for the exclusive use of the occupants;

    (c) it has, for the exclusive use of the occupants, an adequate number of suitably located fixed baths or showers and wash-hand basins each of which is provided with a satisfactory supply of hot and cold water;

    (d) subject to section 365, there are adequate means of escape from fire; and

    (e) there are adequate other fire precautions.

(2) Subject to subsection (2A) the notice shall specify the works which in the opinion of the authority are required for rendering the house reasonably suitable–

    (a) for occupation by the individuals and households for the time being accommodated there, or

    (b) for a smaller number of individuals or households and the number of individuals or households, or both, which, in the opinion of the authority, the house could reasonably accommodate if the works were carried out,

but the notice shall not specify any works to any premises outside the house.

(2A) Where the authority have exercised or propose to exercise their powers under section 368 to secure that part of the house is not used for human habitation, they may specify in the notice such work only as in their opinion is required to meet such of the requirements in subsection (1A) as may be applicable if that part is not so used.

(3) The notice may be served–

    (a) on the person having control of the house, or

    (b) on the person managing the house;

and the authority shall inform any other person who is to their knowledge an owner, lessee, occupier or mortgagee of the house of the fact that the notice has been served.

(4) The notice shall require the person on whom it is served to execute the works specified in the notice as follows, namely,–

    (a) to begin those works not later than such reasonable date, being not earlier than the twenty-first day after the date of service of the notice, as is specified in the notice; and

    (b) to complete those works within such reasonable period as is so specified.

(5) If the authority are satisfied that–

    (a) after the service of a notice under this section the number of individuals living on the premises has been reduced to a level which will make the works specified in the notice unnecessary, and

(b) that number will be maintained at or below that level, whether in consequence of the exercise of the authority's powers under section 354 (power to limit number of occupants of house) or otherwise,

they may withdraw the notice by notifying that fact in writing to the person on whom the notice was served, but without prejudice to the issue of a further notice.

(5A) A notice served under this section is a local land charge.

(5B) Each local housing authority shall–
   (a) maintain a register of notices served by the authority under subsection (1) after the coming into force of this subsection;
   (b) ensure the register is open to inspection by the public free of charge at all reasonable hours; and
   (c) on request, and on payment of any such reasonable fee as the authority may require, supply copies of entries in the register to any person.

(7) Where a local housing authority serve a notice under this section in respect of any of the requirements specified in subsection (1A), and the works specified in the notice are carried out, whether by the person on whom the notice was served or by the local housing authority under section 375, the authority shall not, within the period of five years from the service of the notice, serve another notice under this section in respect of the same requirement unless they consider that there has been a change of circumstances in relation to the premises.

(8) Such a change may, in particular, relate to the condition of the premises or the availability or use of the facilities mentioned in subsection (1A).

Housing Act 1985, s 352, as amended by the Local Government and Housing Act 1989, Scheds 9 and 12 and the Housing Act 1996, s 71(1).

18.38 SECTION 372 OF THE HOUSING ACT 1985: POWER TO REQUIRE EXECUTION OF WORKS TO REMEDY NEGLECT OF MANAGEMENT

(1) If in the opinion of the local housing authority the condition of a house is defective in consequence of–
   (a) neglect to comply with the requirements imposed by regulations under section 369 (regulations prescribing management code), or
   (b) repealed,

the authority may serve on the person managing the house a notice specifying the works which, in the opinion of the authority, are required to make good the neglect.

(2) If it is not practicable after reasonable inquiry to ascertain the name or address of the person managing the house, the notice may be served by addressing it to him by the description of 'manager of the house' (naming the house to which it relates) and delivering it to some person on the premises.

(3) The notice shall require the person on whom it is served to execute the works specified in the notice as follows, namely–

(a) to begin those works not later than such reasonable date, being not earlier than the twenty-first day after the date of service of the notice, as is specified in the notice; and

(b) to complete those works within such reasonable period as is so specified.

(4) Where the authority serve a notice under this section on the person managing a house, they shall inform any other person who is to their knowledge an owner, lessee or mortgagee of the house of the fact that the notice has been served.

(5) References in this section to the person managing a house have the same meaning as in section 369 (and accordingly are subject to amendment by regulations under that section).

Housing Act 1985, s 372 as amended by the Local Government and Housing Act 1989, Sched 9.1.

18.39 SECTION 373 OF THE HOUSING ACT 1985: APPEAL AGAINST NOTICE UNDER S 372

The next paragraph is para 18.40.1.

18.40.1 Section 376 of the Housing Act 1985: Penalty for failure to execute works

(1) A person on whom a notice has been served under section 352 or 372 (notices requiring the execution of works) who wilfully fails to comply with the notice commits a summary offence, and is liable on conviction to a fine not exceeding level 5 on the standard scale.

(2) The obligation to execute the works specified in the notice continues notwithstanding the expiry of the period which under section 375(2) is appropriate for completion of the works in question; and a person who wilfully fails to comply with that obligation, after being convicted of an offence in relation to the notice under subsection (1) or this subsection, commits a further offence and is is liable on conviction to a fine not exceeding level 5 on the standard scale.

(3) References in this section to compliance with a notice shall be construed in accordance section 375(2).

(4) Repealed.

(5) The provisions of this section are without prejudice to the exercise by the local housing authority of their power under section 375 to carry out the works themselves.

Housing Act 1985, s 376 amended by the Local Government and Housing Act 1989, Scheds 9 and 12 and the Housing Act 1996, s 78.

Chapter 18: Environmental Health Legislation

18.40.2 Section 196 of the Housing Act 1985: Power of court to authorise owner to execute works on default of another owner[a]

(1) If it appears to a magistrates' court, on the application of an owner of premises in respect of which a repair notice has been served, that owing to the default of another owner of the premises in executing works required to be executed, the interests of the applicant will be prejudiced, the court may make an order empowering the applicant forthwith to enter on the premises and execute the works within a period fixed by the order.

(2) Where the court makes such an order, the court may, where it seems to the court just to do so, make a like order in favour of any other owner.

(3) Before an order is made under this section, notice of the application shall be given to the local housing authority.

18.40.3 Section 197 of the Housing Act 1985: Powers of entry

(1) A person authorised by the local housing authority or the Secretary of State may at any reasonable time, on giving seven days' notice of his intention to the occupier, and to the owner if the owner is known, enter premises for the purpose of survey and examination–

   (a) where it appears to the authority that survey or examination is necessary in order to determine whether any powers under this Part should be exercised in respect of the premises, or

   (b) where a repair notice has been served in respect of the premises, or

(2) An authorisation for the purposes of this section shall be in writing stating the particular purpose or purposes for which the entry is authorised and shall, if so required, be produced for inspection by the occupier or anyone acting on his behalf.

Housing Act 1985, s 197 as amended by the Local Government and Housing Act 1989, Scheds 9 and 12.

18.40.4 Section 198 of the Housing Act 1985: Penalty for obstruction

(1) It is a summary offence intentionally to obstruct an officer of the local housing authority or of the Secretary of State, or a person authorised in pursuance of this Part to enter premises, in the performance of anything which that officer, authority or person is required or authorised by this Part to do.

(2) A person who commits such an offence is liable on conviction to a fine not exceeding level 3 on the standard scale.

Housing Act 1985, s 198 as amended by the Housing Act 1988, Sched 15 and the Local Government and Housing Act 1989, Sched 9.

(a) This is a general power, not depending upon reasonable ground to suspect the existence of any state of things (*Bedingfield v Jones* (1959) 124 JP 11).

18.40.5 Section 198A of the Housing Act 1985

Penalty for failure to execute works

(1) A person having control of premises to which a repair notice relates who intentionally fails to comply with the notice commits a summary offence and is liable on conviction to a fine not exceeding level 4 on the standard scale.

(2) The obligation to execute the works specified in the notice continues notwithstanding that the period for completion of the works has expired.

(3) Section 193(2) shall have effect to determine whether a person has failed to comply with a notice and what is the period for completion of any works.

(4) The provisions of this section are without prejudice to the exercise by the local housing authority of the powers conferred by the preceding provisions of this Part.

Housing Act 1985, s 198A, as inserted by the Housing Act 1988, Sched 15.

18.41 UNLAWFUL HARASSMENT AND EVICTION

For evidential reasons these cases can be very difficult to prove. An offence may arise from a dispute between landlord and tenant where both parties are to blame to a greater or lesser degree. Even if the tenant has not discredited his evidence by his own conduct, the essential evidence often boils down to the word of the tenant against that of the landlord, with little or no supporting evidence. For these reasons, the investigating officer is advised to take steps to alert himself to potential offences at the earliest possible stage so that steps can be taken to collate supporting evidence. The practice of issuing leaflets for display in council offices and citizens advice bureaux, informing tenants of advice and assistance given by local authorities to distressed tenants, is to be commended, as is the practice of asking homeless advice officers to liaise with the investigator of any potential offence. This enables the investigating officer to warn the defendant of his conduct and arrange with the tenant for another witness to be present at any expected visit from the landlord if harassment is anticipated. Advice can also be given to the tenant to retain any notices that amount to harassment. On past experience, notices left by landlords after changing locks, etc, have proved to be decisive in a prosecution after the notice has been sent to a graphologist to analyse and compare against known handwriting belonging to the defendant.

18.42 SECTION 1 OF THE PROTECTION FROM EVICTION ACT 1977

The elements of the offence/investigatory matters for unlawful eviction are as follows:

1. Status of the defendant, that is, individual, sole trader partner, limited company or plc.
2. Address of the defendant or registered office if limited company.
3. Date or dates of the offence.
4. Place of offence (within court's jurisdiction).

5 Deprivation[a] of premises[b] or part of it or attempts to do so.
6 The persons was an residential occupier[c] in occupation at the time.
7 The deprivation was unlawful.
8 Defence (common law if any).
9 Mitigation/explanation.

Time limit: six months (s 127 of the Magistrates' Courts Act 1980).

Mode of trial: either way

Maximum penalty (s 1(4)).

Summary: statutory maximum and/or six months.

Indictment: fine and/or two years.

18.43 SECTION 1 OF THE PROTECTION FROM EVICTION ACT 1977

The elements of the offence/investigatory matters for unlawful harassment by any person are (whether or not the landlord):

1 Status of the defendant, that is, individual, sole trader, partner, limited company or plc.
2 Address of defendant or registered office if limited company.
3 Date or dates of the offence.
4 Place of offence (within courts jurisdiction).
5 The person was a residential occupier[aa] in occupation of premises[ab] at the time.

(a) *R v Yuthiwattana* (1984) 16 HLR 49: not every locking-out amounted to an eviction. To constitute the offence of deprivation of occupation, there must be something having the character of an eviction; that does not mean permanent eviction. On this occasion, locking the tenant out for one night was harassment but not sufficient to amount to a deprivation of the tenant's right to occupation of the room. Furthermore, it was not necessary for an act by the defendant to be actionable as a civil wrong in order to constitute an offence under the Protection of Eviction Act 1977, s 1(3). This was approved by the House of Lords in *R v Burke* (1990) 22 HLR 433 which also confirmed that refusal to replace a lost key was harassment. The *Yuthiwattana* case was also applied in the decision of *Costelloe v Camden LBC* [1986] Crim LR 249. In this case, entry was refused but re-entry was offered an hour later after police intervention. The tenant collected her property and left. The court held that in the absence of a finding as to whether the tenant was intended to be evicted only for a short time the conviction could not stand. The corollary of this decision is that an eviction even for a period of one hour is an unlawful eviction if a more permanent eviction was intended at the time. This approach is not inconsistent with the *Yuthiwattana* case that can be distinguished having regard to the degree of permanence envisaged by the landlord.
(b) Premises may include a caravan (*Norton v Knowles* [1967] 3 All ER 1061).
(c) The definition in s 1(1) is wide enough to include tenant, lodger or licensee.
(aa) The case of *R v Phekoo* [1981] Crim LR 399 establishes that this is not a strict liability offence. If the defendant claims that he honestly believed the person harassed was not a residential occupier, the prosecution had to negative that belief.
(ab) Premises may include a caravan (*Norton v Knowles* [1967] 3 All ER 1061).

6 Acts likely to interfere with the peace and comfort of the residential occupier or members of his household or persistently[c] withdraws or withholds services reasonable required for the occupation of the premises as a residence.
7 Acts are intended[d] to cause the residential occupier to give up part or whole of the premises or to refrain from exercising any right or pursuing any remedy in respect of the premises or any part of it.
8 Absence of reasonable grounds for acts set out in (v) above (s 3B).
9 Defence (common law if any).
10 Mitigation/explanation.

Time limit: six months (s 127 of the Magistrates' Courts Act 1980).

Mode of trial: either way

Maximum penalty (s 1(4)).

Summary: statutory maximum and/or six months.

Indictment: fine and/or two years.

18.44 SECTION 1 OF THE PROTECTION FROM EVICTION ACT 1977

The elements of the offence/investigatory matters for unlawful harassment by the landlord are:

[1–6 as above.]
7 Defendant is a landlord or agent of a landlord.
8 Defendant knows or has reasonable cause to believe that his conduct is likely to cause the residential occupier to leave or not exercise any right or remedy as set out in 7 above.
9 Whether there are reasonable grounds for doing acts or withholding services as set out in 6 above (s 3B defence).
10 Defence (common law if any).
11 Mitigation/explanation.

(c) In *R v Abrol* [1972] Crim LR 318, it was established that the information/indictment should not omit the word 'persistently' which must also be proved as part of the prosecutions case. A similar approach was taken in the case of *Westminster CC v Peart* (1968) 66 LGR 561, in which it was held that the informations were invalid inasmuch as they did not allege (a) that the withholding of the services was persistent and (b) that the boarding up of the lavatory was calculated to interfere with the peace and comfort of the residential occupier.

(d) Ormerod J in *McCall v Abelesz* [1976] QB 585, p 598, confirmed that a positive intent to cause the residential occupier to give up premises had to be shown, not merely a hopeful inactivity over services. Lord Griffiths in *R v Burke* (1990) 22 HLR 433, p 438, defined intention in s 30(2) of the Rent Act 1965 (the predecessor to s 1(3) of the Protection from Eviction Act 1977) as meaning 'with the purpose or motive of causing the occupier to give up occupation of the premises'. The common law definition of intention refers to a rebuttable presumption of fact that a man intended the natural and probable consequences of his acts (*Frankland and Moore v R* [1987] 2 WLR 1251; *R v Loughlin* [1959] Crim LR 518; and *Squire v Squire* [1949] P 51).

Time limit: six months (s 127 of the Magistrates' Courts Act 1980).

Mode of trial: either way

Maximum penalty (s 1(4)).

Summary: statutory maximum and/or six months.

Indictment: fine and/or two years.

18.45 PROTECTION FROM EVICTION ACT 1977

PART I
UNLAWFUL EVICTION AND HARASSMENT

1   Unlawful eviction and harassment of occupier

(1) In this section 'residential occupier', in relation to any premises, means a person occupying the premises as a residence, whether under a contract or by virtue of any enactment or rule of law giving him the right to remain in occupation or restricting the right of any other person to recover possession of the premises.

(2) If any person unlawfully deprives the residential occupier of any premises of his occupation of the premises or any part thereof, or attempts to do so, he shall be guilty of an offence unless he proves that he believed, and had reasonable cause to believe, that the residential occupier had ceased to reside in the premises.

(3) If any person with intent to cause the residential occupier of any premises–

   (a) to give up the occupation of the premises or any part thereof; or
   (b) to refrain from exercising any right or pursuing any remedy in respect of the premises or part thereof;

   does acts likely to interfere with the peace or comfort of the residential occupier or members of his household, or persistently withdraws or withholds services reasonably required for the occupation of the premises as a residence, he shall be guilty of an offence.

(3A) Subject to subsection (3B) below, the landlord of a residential occupier or an agent of the landlord shall be guilty of an offence if–

   (a) he does acts likely to interfere with the peace of comfort of the residential occupier or members of his household, or
   (b) he persistently withdraws or withholds services reasonably required for the occupation of the premises in question as a residence,

   and (in either case) he knows, or has reasonable cause to believe, that that conduct is likely to cause the residential occupier to give up the occupation of the whole or part of the premises or to refrain from exercising any right or pursuing any remedy in respect of the whole or part of the premises.

(3B) A person shall not be guilty of an offence under subsection (3A) above if he proves that he had reasonable grounds for doing the acts or withdrawing or withholding the services in question.

(3C) In subsection (3A) above 'landlord' in relation to a residential occupier of any premises, means the person who, but for–
  (a) the residential occupier's right to remain in occupation of the premises, or
  (b) a restriction on the person's right to recover possession of the premises,
would be entitled to occupation of the premises and any superior landlord under whom that person derives title.

(4) A person guilty of an offence under this section shall be liable–
  (a) on summary conviction, to a fine not exceeding the statutory maximum or to imprisonment for a term not exceeding 6 months or to both;
  (b) on conviction on indictment, to a fine or to imprisonment for a term not exceeding 2 years or to both.

(5) Nothing in this section shall be taken to prejudice any liability or remedy to which a person guilty of an offence thereunder may be subject in civil proceedings.

(6) Where an offence under this section committed by a body corporate is proved to have been committed with the consent or connivance of, or to be attributable to any neglect on the part of, any director, manager or secretary or other similar officer of the body corporate or any person who was purporting to act in any capacity, he as well as the body corporate shall be guilty of that offence and shall be liable to be proceeded against and punished accordingly.

Protection from Eviction Act 1977, s 1, as amended by the Criminal Law Act 1977, s 28 and the Housing Act 1988, s 29.

18.46 DOG FOULING PROSECUTIONS

Some councils have adopted bylaws designating land for the purpose of the Dog Fouling of Land Act 1996. Once land has been designated in thus way prosecutions under the 1996 Act may be taken for dog fouling in respect of any land in the district that has been designated. The following is an extract from a bylaw which has been adopted by the council by the City of Bradford Metropolitan District Council pursuant to the 1996 Act. It is the Dogs (Fouling of Land) Order 1998 made under s 2 of the Act. This bylaw designated all land in the district as designated except:

(i) land comprised in or running alongside a highway which comprises a carriageway unless the driving of motor vehicles on the carriageway is subject, otherwise than temporarily, to a speed limit of 40 miles per hour or less;

(ii) land used for agriculture or for woodlands;

(iii) land which is predominantly marshland, moor or heath and;

(iv) common land to which the public are entitled or permitted to have access otherwise than by virtue of s 193(1) of the Law of Property Act 1925 (right of access to urban common land, that is, rural common land).[a]

(a) These types of land are excluded by s 1 of the Act.

18.47 SECTION 3 OF THE DOGS (FOULING OF LAND) ACT 1996

The elements of the offence/investigatory matters are as follows:

Need to prove/investigate:

1. Place of offence (within jurisdiction of the Court) and on designated land.
2. Date or dates of offence(s) within six months time limit.
3. Full name and address of defendant.
4. Evidence the defendant was in charge of the dog.
5. The defecation (photographs) and failure to remove faeces.
6. Mitigation/explanation from the defendant.
7. No reasonable excuse.

Time limit: six months (s 127 of the Magistrates' Courts Act 1980).

Mode of trial: summary

Maximum penalty (s 3(2)).

Summary: level 3.

Section 4 of the Act allows for the service of fixed penalty notices.

Section 6 of the Act has the effect of nullifying all existing bylaws that relate to land designated by the council's 1998 Order, that is, all bylaws other than those relating to land referred to in para 1.5 above, for example, woodland, marshland, moor, heath or common land in parks.

18.48 SECTION 3 OF THE DOGS (FOULING OF LAND) 1996 ACT

(1) If a dog defecates at any time on designated land and a person who is in charge of the dog at that time fails to remove the faeces from the land forthwith, that person shall be guilty of an offence unless–

    (a) he has a reasonable excuse for failing to do so; or

    (b) the owner, occupier or other person or authority having control of the land has consented (generally or specifically) to his failing to do so.

(2) A person who is guilty of an offence under this section shall be liable on summary conviction to a fine not exceeding level 3 on the standard scale.

(3) Nothing in this section applies to a person registered as a blind person in a register compiled under section 29 of the National Assistance Act 1948.

(4) For the purposes of this section –

    (a) a person who habitually has a dog in his possession shall be taken to be in charge of the dog at any time unless at that time some other person is in charge of the dog;

    (b) placing the faeces in a receptacle on the land which is provided for the purpose, or for the disposal of waste, shall be a sufficient removal from the land; and

(c) being unaware of the defecation (whether by reason of not being in the vicinity or otherwise), or not having a device for or other suitable means of removing the faeces, shall not be a reasonable excuse for failing to remove the faeces.

18.49 SECTION 2 OF THE REFUSE DISPOSAL (AMENITY) ACT 1978

Elements of the offence/investigation:
1 Place of offence (within courts jurisdiction) being part of highway or land in the open air.
2 Date of offence (within six months time limit).
3 Full name and status of defendant, that is, individual or sole trader, partnership, limited company or plc.
4 Address of defendant or registered office address if limited company.
5 Date of birth (particularly if young person).
6 Absence of lawful authority.
7 Abandoned rubbish or other matter within the meaning of sub-s (2).
8 Mitigation/explanation.

Time limit: six months (s 127 of the Magistrates' Courts Act 1980).

Mode of trial: summary

Maximum penalty (s 2(1)).

Summary: level 4 and/or three months.

18.50 REFUSE DISPOSAL (AMENITY) ACT 1978

2 Penalty for unauthorised dumping

(1) Any person who, without lawful authority–
   (a) abandons on any land in the open air, or on any other land forming part of a highway, a motor vehicle or anything which formed part of a motor vehicle and was removed from it in the course of dismantling the vehicle on the land; or
   (b) abandons on any such land anything other than a motor vehicle, being a thing which he has brought to the land for the purpose of abandoning it there,
   shall be guilty of an offence and liable on summary conviction to a fine of an amount not exceeding level 4 on the standard scale or imprisonment for a term not exceeding three months or both.

(2) For the purposes of subsection (1) above, a person who leaves any thing on any land in such circumstances or for such a period that he may reasonably be assumed to have abandoned it or to have brought it to the land for the purpose of abandoning it there shall be deemed to have abandoned it there or, as the case may be, to have brought it to the land for the purpose unless the contrary is shown.

(3) Scotland.

Refuse Disposal (Amenity) Act 1978, s 2, as amended by the Criminal Justice Act 1982, ss 35, 38 and 46.1.

18.51 SECTION 33(1)(A) OF THE ENVIRONMENTAL PROTECTION ACT 1990: PROHIBITION OF UNAUTHORISED OR HARMFUL/DEPOSIT OR DISPOSAL, ETC, OF WASTE

Elements of the offence/investigation:

1. Full name and capacity of defendant ie individual, sole trader, partnership, limited company or plc.
2. Place of offence (within court's jurisdiction) not being within the curtilage of a dwelling if household waste.
3. Date of offence.
4. Status of defendant, that is, individual or sole trader, partnership, limited company or plc.
5. Address or registered office address if limited company.
6. Date of birth (not essential).
7. The waste was 'deposited' in the alleged place.
8. The defendant deposited that waste.
9. The waste deposited was controlled waste as defined in s 75(4) as being 'household, industrial and commercial waste or any such waste' (see waste management: Duty of Care Code of Practice, March 1996 for guidance on what is not controlled waste).
10. If not deposit controlled waste alternatively knowingly cause or knowingly permit controlled waste to be deposited.
11. There is no waste management licence in force to authorise the deposit.
12. Defence of doing all that can reasonable be expected.
13. Mitigation/explanation.

Time limit: none.

Mode of trial: either way.

Maximum penalty (s 33(8)).

Summary: £20,000 and/or six months.

Indictment: fine and/or two years. *NB* increase in penalty for special waste – s 33(9).

18.52 SECTION 33 OF THE ENVIRONMENTAL PROTECTION ACT 1990: PROHIBITION ON UNAUTHORISED OR HARMFUL DEPOSIT, TREATMENT OR DISPOSAL, ETC, OF WASTE

33 (1) Subject to subsection (2) and (3) below and, in relation to Scotland, to section 54 below, a person shall not–

   (a) deposit controlled waste, or knowingly cause or knowingly permit controlled waste to be deposited in or on any land unless a waste management licence authorising the deposit is in force and the deposit is in accordance with the licence;

   (b) treat, keep or dispose of controlled waste, or knowingly cause or knowingly permit controlled waste to be treated, kept or disposed of–

      (i) in or on any land, or

      (ii) by means of any mobile plant,

   except under and in accordance with a waste management licence;

   (c) treat, keep or dispose of controlled waste in a manner likely to cause pollution of the environment or harm to human health.

(2) Subsection (1) above does not apply in relation to household waste from a domestic property which is treated, kept or disposed of within the curtilage of the dwelling by or with the permission of the occupier of the dwelling.

(3) Subsection (1)(a), (b) or (c) above do not apply in cases prescribed in regulations made by the Secretary of State and the regulations may make different exceptions for different areas.

(4) The Secretary of State, in exercising his power under subsection (3) above, shall have regard in particular to the expediency of excluding from the controls imposed by waste management licences–

   (a) any deposits which are small enough or of such a temporary nature that they may be so excluded;

   (b) any means of treatment or disposal which are innocuous enough to be so excluded;

   (c) cases for which adequate controls are provided by another enactment than this section.

(5) Where controlled waste is carried in and deposited from a motor vehicle, the person who controls or is in a position to control the use of the vehicle shall, for the purposes of subsection (1)(a) above, be treated as knowingly causing the waste to be deposited whether or not he gave any instructions for this to be done.

(6) A person who contravenes subsection (1) above or any condition of a waste management licence commits an offence.

(7) It shall be a defence for a person charged with an offence under this section to prove–

   (a) that he took all reasonable precautions and exercised all due diligence to avoid the commission of the offence; or

   (b) that he acted under instructions from his employer and neither knew nor had reason to suppose that the acts done by him constituted a contravention of subsection (1) above; or

(c) that the acts alleged to constitute the contravention were done in an emergency in order to avoid danger to the public and that, as soon as reasonably practicable after they were done, particulars of them were furnished to the waste regulation authority in whose area the treatment or disposal of the waste took place.

(8) Except in a case falling within subsection (9) below, a person who commits an offence under this section shall be liable–

   (a) on summary conviction, to imprisonment for a term not exceeding six months or a fine not exceeding £20,000 or both; and

   (b) on conviction on indictment, to imprisonment for a term not exceeding two years or a fine or both.

(9) A person who commits an offence under this section in relation to special waste shall be liable–

   (a) on summary conviction, to imprisonment for a term not exceeding six months or a fine not exceeding £20,000 or both;

   (b) on conviction on indictment, to imprisonment for a term not exceeding five years or a fine or both.

18.53 SECTION 34 OF THE ENVIRONMENTAL PROTECTION ACT 1990: DUTY OF CARE, ETC, AS RESPECTS WASTE

Elements of the offence/investigation

1. Full name of defendant.
2. Place of offence, that is, public open space or highway, etc, as defined in s 87(3).
3. Date of offence.
4. Status of defendant, that is, individual or sole trader, partnership, limited company or plc.
5. Address or registered office address if limited company.
6. Defendant imports, produces, carries, keeps, treats or disposes of controlled waste.
7. Escape of waste.
8. Defendant fails to take reasonable measures to prevent escape.
9. Defence.
10. Mitigation/explanation.

Time limit: none.

Mode of trial: either way.

Maximum penalty (s 34(6)).

Summary: statutory maximum.

Indictment: fine.

18.54 SECTION 34 OF THE ENVIRONMENTAL PROTECTION ACT 1990: DUTY OF CARE, ETC, AS RESPECTS WASTE

34 (1) Subject to subsection (2) below, it shall be the duty of any person who imports, produces, carries, keeps, treats or disposes of controlled waste or, as a broker, has control of such waste, to take all such measures applicable to him in that capacity as are reasonable in the circumstances–

   (a) to prevent any contravention by any other person of section 33 above;

   (b) to prevent the escape of the waste from his control or that of any other person; and

   (c) on the transfer of the waste, to secure–

      (i) that the transfer is only to an authorised person or to a person for authorised transport purposes; and

      (ii) that there is transferred such a written description of the waste as will enable other persons to avoid a contravention of that section and to comply with the duty under this subsection as respects the escape of waste.

(2) The duty imposed by subsection (1) above does not apply to an occupier of domestic property as respects the household waste produced on the property.

(3) The following are authorised persons for the purpose of subsection (1)(c) above–

   (a) any authority which is a waste collection authority for the purposes of this Part;

   (b) any person who is the holder of a waste management licence under section 35 below or of a disposal licence under section 5 of the Control of Pollution Act 1974 [1974 c 40];

   (c) any person to whom section 33(1) above does not apply by virtue of regulations under subsection (3) of that section;

   (d) any person registered as a carrier of controlled waste under section 2 of the Control of Pollution (Amendment) Act 1989;

   (e) any person who is not required to be so registered by virtue of regulations under section 1(3) of that Act; and

   (f) a waste disposal authority in Scotland.

(4) The following are authorised transport purposes for the purposes of subsection (1)(c) above–

   (a) the transport of controlled waste within the same premises between different places in those premises;

   (b) the transport to a place in Great Britain of controlled waste which has been brought from a country or territory outside Great Britain not having been landed in Great Britain until it arrives at that place; and

   (c) the transport by air or sea of controlled waste from a place in Great Britain to a place outside Great Britain;

   and 'transport' has the same meaning in this subsection as in the Control of Pollution (Amendment) Act 1989.

(5) The Secretary of State may, by regulations, make provision imposing requirements on any person who is subject to the duty imposed by subsection (1) above as

respects the making and retention of documents and the furnishing of documents or copies of documents.

(6) Any person who fails to comply with the duty imposed by subsection (1) above or with any requirement imposed under subsection (5) above shall be liable–

(a) on summary conviction, to a fine not exceeding the statutory maximum; and

(b) on conviction on indictment, to a fine.

(7) The Secretary of State shall, after consultation with such persons or bodies as appear to him representative of the interests concerned, prepare and issue a code of practice for the purpose of providing to persons practical guidance on how to discharge the duty imposed on them by subsection (1) above.

(8) The Secretary of State may from time to time revise a code of practice issued under subsection (7) above by revoking, amending or adding to the provisions of the code.

(9) The code of practice prepared in pursuance of subsection (7) above shall be laid before both Houses of Parliament.

(10) A code of practice issued under subsection (7) above shall be admissible in evidence and if any provision of such a code appears to the court to be relevant to any question arising in the proceedings it shall be taken into account in determining that question.

(11) Different codes of practice may be prepared and issued under subsection (7) above for different areas.

18.55 SECTION 87 OF THE ENVIRONMENTAL PROTECTION ACT 1990: OFFENCE OF LEAVING LITTER

Elements of the offence/investigation:

1 Full name of defendant.
2 Place of offence, that is, public open space or highway, etc, as defined in s 87(3).
3 Date of offence.
4 Status of defendant, that is, individual or sole trader, partnership, limited company or plc.
5 Address or registered office address if limited company.
6 Without consent of owner/occupier, etc.
7 The litter[a] was thrown down, dropped or otherwise deposited in the alleged place.
8 Evidence of litter being left.[b]
9 Evidence of defacement by litter.
10 Defence.
11 Mitigation/explanation.

(a) Litter includes commercial waste. (*Westminster CC v Riding* (1995) 94 LGR 489.)
(b) Evidence of when the waste was left will normally be required to prove that it was 'left' (*Westminster CC v Riding* (1995) 94 LGR 489). If this is not known, evidence of a sufficient length of time that the litter was allowed to remain may be sufficient.

Time limit: six months (s 127 of the Magistrates' Courts Act 1980).

Mode of trial: summary.

Maximum penalty (s 87(5)).

Summary: level 4.

18.56 SECTION 87 OF THE ENVIRONMENTAL PROTECTION ACT 1990: OFFENCE OF LEAVING LITTER

87 (1) If any person throws down, drops or otherwise deposits in, into or from any place to which this section applies, and leaves, any thing whatsoever in such circumstances as to cause, or contribute to, or tend to lead to, the defacement by litter of any place to which this section applies, he shall, subject to subsection (2) below, be guilty of an offence.

  (2) No offence is committed under this section where the depositing and leaving of the thing was–
    (a) authorised by law, or
    (b) done with the consent of the owner, occupier or other person or authority having control of the place in or into which that thing was deposited.

  (3) This section applies to any public open place and, in so far as the place is not a public open place, also to the following places–
    (a) any relevant highway or relevant road and any trunk road which is a special road;
    (b) any place on relevant land of a principal litter authority;
    (c) any place on relevant Crown land;
    (d) any place on relevant land of any designated statutory undertaker;
    (e) any place on relevant land of any designated educational institution;
    (f) any place on relevant land within a litter control area of a local authority.

  (4) In this section 'public open place' means a place in the open air to which the public are entitled or permitted to have access without payment; and any covered place open to the air on at least one side and available for public use shall be treated as a public open place.

  (5) A person who is guilty of an offence under this section shall be liable on summary conviction to a fine not exceeding level 4 on the standard scale.

  (6) A local authority, with a view to promoting the abatement of litter, may take such steps as the authority think appropriate for making the effect of subsection (5) above known to the public in their area.

  (7) In any proceedings in Scotland for an offence under this section it shall be lawful to convict the accused on the evidence of one witness.

Fixed penalty notices for leaving litter.

18.57 SECTION 9 OF THE FOOD SAFETY ACT 1990: INSPECTION AND SEIZURE OF SUSPECTED FOOD

(1) An authorised officer of a food authority may at all reasonable times inspect any food intended for human consumption which–
   (a) has been sold or is offered or exposed for sale; or
   (b) is in the possession of, or has been deposited with or consigned to, any person for the purpose of sale or of preparation for sale;
   and subsections (3) to (9) below shall apply where, on such an inspection, it appears to the authorised officer that any food fails to comply with food safety requirements.

(2) The following provisions shall also apply where, otherwise than on such an inspection, it appears to an authorised officer of a food authority that any food is likely to cause food poisoning or any disease communicable to human beings.

(3) The authorised officer may either–
   (a) give notice to the person in charge of the food that, until the notice is withdrawn, the food or any specified portion of it–
      (i) is not to be used for human consumption; and
      (ii) either is not to be removed or is not to be removed except to some place specified in the notice; or
   (b) seize the food and remove it in order to have it dealt with by a justice of the peace;
   and any person who knowingly contravenes the requirements of a notice under paragraph (a) above shall be guilty of an offence.

(4) Where the authorised officer exercises the powers conferred by subsection (3)(a) above, he shall, as soon as is reasonably practicable and in any event within 21 days, determine whether or not he is satisfied that the food complies with food safety requirements and–
   (a) if he is so satisfied, shall forthwith withdraw the notice;
   (b) if he is not so satisfied, shall seize the food and remove it in order to have it dealt with by a justice of the peace.

(5) Where an authorised officer exercises the powers conferred by subsection (3)(b) or (4)(b) above, he shall inform the person in charge of the food of his intention to have it dealt with by a justice of the peace and–
   (a) any person who under section 7 or 8 above might be liable to a prosecution in respect of the food shall, if he attends before the justice of the peace by whom the food falls to be dealt with, be entitled to be heard and to call witnesses; and
   (b) that justice of the peace may, but need not, be a member of the court before which any person is charged with an offence under that section in relation to that food.

(6) If it appears to a justice of the peace, on the basis of such evidence as he considers appropriate in the circumstances, that any food falling to be dealt with by him under this section fails to comply with food safety requirements, he shall condemn the food and order–
   (a) the food to be destroyed or to be disposed of as to prevent it from being used for human consumption; and

(b) any expenses reasonably incurred in connection with the destruction or disposal to be defrayed by the owner of the food.

(7) If a notice under subsection (3)(a) above is withdrawn, or the justice of the peace by whom any food falls to be dealt with under this section refuses to condemn it, the food authority shall compensate the owner of the food for any depreciation in its value resulting from the action taken by the authorised officer.

(8) Any disputed question as to the right to or the amount of any compensation payable under subsection (7) above shall be determined by arbitration.

(9) In the application of this section to Scotland–
   (a) any reference to a justice of the peace includes a reference to the sheriff and to a magistrate;
   (b) paragraph (b) of subsection (5) above shall not apply;
   (c) any order made under subsection (6) above shall be sufficient evidence in any proceedings under this Act of the failure of the food in question to comply with food safety requirements; and
   (d) the reference in subsection (8) above to determination by arbitration shall be construed as a reference to determination by a single arbiter appointed, failing agreement between the parties, by the sheriff.

18.58 SECTION 10 OF THE FOOD SAFETY ACT 1990: IMPROVEMENT NOTICES

(1) If an authorised officer of an enforcement authority has reasonable grounds for believing that the proprietor of a food business is failing to comply with any regulations to which this section applies, he may, by a notice[1] served on that proprietor (in this Act referred to as an 'improvement notice')–
   (a) state the officer's grounds for believing that the proprietor is failing to comply with the regulations;
   (b) specify the matters which constitute the proprietor's failure so to comply;
   (c) specify the measures which, in the officer's opinion, the proprietor must take in order to secure compliance; and
   (d) require the proprietor to take those measures, or measures which are at least equivalent to them, within such period (not being less than 14 days) as may be specified in the notice.

(2) Any person who fails to comply with an improvement notice shall be guilty of an offence.

(3) This section and section 11 below apply to any regulations under this Part which make provision–
   (a) for requiring, prohibiting or regulating the use of any process or treatment in the preparation of food; or
   (b) for securing the observance of hygienic conditions and practices in connection with the carrying out of commercial operations with respect to food or food sources.

18.59 SECTION 11 OF THE FOOD SAFETY ACT 1990: PROHIBITION ORDERS

(1) If–
   (a) the proprietor of a food business is convicted of an offence under any regulations to which this section applies; and
   (b) the court by or before which he is so convicted is satisfied that the health risk condition is fulfilled with respect to that business,
   the court shall by an order impose the appropriate prohibition.

(2) The health risk condition is fulfilled with respect to any food business if any of the following involves risk of injury to health, namely–
   (a) the use for the purposes of the business of any process or treatment;
   (b) the construction of any premises used for the purposes of the business, or the use for those purposes of any equipment; and
   (c) the state or condition of any premises or equipment used for the purposes of the business.

(3) The appropriate prohibition is–
   (a) in a case falling within paragraph (a) of subsection (2) above, a prohibition on the use of the process or treatment for the purposes of the business;
   (b) in a case falling within paragraph (b) of that subsection, a prohibition on the use of the premises or equipment for the purposes of the business or any other food business of the same class or description;
   (c) in a case falling within paragraph (c) of that subsection, a prohibition on the use of the premises or equipment for the purposes of any food business.

(4) If–
   (a) the proprietor of a food business is convicted of an offence under any regulations to which this section applies by virtue of section 10(3)(b) above; and
   (b) the court by or before which he is so convicted thinks it proper to do so in all the circumstances of the case,
   the court may, by an order, impose a prohibition on the proprietor participating in the management of any food business, or any food business of a class or description specified in the order.

(5) As soon as practicable after the making of an order under subsection (1) or (4) above (in this Act referred to as a 'prohibition order'), the enforcement authority shall–
   (a) serve a copy of the order on the proprietor of the business; and
   (b) in the case of an order under subsection (1) above, affix a copy of the order in a conspicuous position on such premises used for the purposes of the business as they consider appropriate;
   and any person who knowingly contravenes such an order shall be guilty of an offence.

(6) A prohibition order shall cease to have effect–
   (a) in the case of an order under subsection (1) above, on the issue by the enforcement authority of a certificate to the effect that they are satisfied that the proprietor has taken sufficient measures to secure that the health risk condition is no longer fulfilled with respect to the business;

(b) in the case of an order under subsection (4) above, on the giving by the court of a direction to that effect.

(7) The enforcement authority shall issue a certificate under paragraph (a) of subsection (6) above within three days of their being satisfied as mentioned in that paragraph; and on an application by the proprietor for such a certificate, the authority shall–

(a) determine, as soon as is reasonably practicable and in any event within 14 days, whether or not they are so satisfied; and

(b) if they determine that they are not so satisfied, give notice to the proprietor of the reasons for that determination.

(8) The court shall give a direction under subsection (6)(b) above if, on an application by the proprietor, the court thinks it proper to do so having regard to all the circumstances of the case, including in particular the conduct of the proprietor since the making of the order; but no such application shall be entertained if it is made–

(a) within six months after the making of the prohibition order; or

(b) within three months after the making by the proprietor of a previous application for such a direction.

(9) Where a magistrates' court or, in Scotland, the sheriff makes an order under section 12(2) below with respect to any food business, subsection (1) above shall apply as if the proprietor of the business had been convicted by the court or sheriff of an offence under regulations to which this section applies.

(10) Subsection (4) above shall apply in relation to a manager of a food business as it applies in relation to the proprietor of such a business; and any reference in subsection (5) or (8) above to the proprietor of the business, or to the proprietor, shall be construed accordingly.

(11) In subsection (10) above 'manager', in relation to a food business, means any person who is entrusted by the proprietor with the day to day running of the business, or any part of the business.

18.60 SECTION 12 OF THE FOOD SAFETY ACT 1990: EMERGENCY PROHIBITION NOTICES AND ORDERS

(1) If an authorised officer of an enforcement authority is satisfied that the health risk condition is fulfilled with respect to any food business, he may, by a notice served on the proprietor of the business (in this Act referred to as an 'emergency prohibition notice'), impose the appropriate prohibition.

(2) If a magistrates' court or, in Scotland, the sheriff is satisfied, on the application of such an officer, that the health risk condition is fulfilled with respect to any food business, the court or sheriff shall, by an order (in this Act referred to as an 'emergency prohibition order'), impose the appropriate prohibition.

(3) Such an officer shall not apply for an emergency prohibition order unless, at least one day before the date of the application, he has served notice on the proprietor of the business of his intention to apply for the order.

(4) Subsections (2) and (3) of section 11 above shall apply for the purposes of this section as they apply for the purposes of that section, but as if the reference in subsection (2) to risk of injury to health were a reference to imminent risk of such injury.

(5) As soon as practicable after the service of an emergency prohibition notice, the enforcement authority shall affix a copy of the notice in a conspicuous position on such premises used for the purposes of the business as they consider appropriate; and any person who knowingly contravenes such a notice shall be guilty of an offence.

(6) As soon as practicable after the making of an emergency prohibition order, the enforcement authority shall–
   (a) serve a copy of the order on the proprietor of the business; and
   (b) affix a copy of the order in a conspicuous position on such premises used for the purposes of that business as they consider appropriate;

   and any person who knowingly contravenes such an order shall be guilty of an offence.

(7) An emergency prohibition notice shall cease to have effect–
   (a) if no application for an emergency prohibition order is made within the period of three days beginning with the service of the notice, at the end of that period;
   (b) if such an application is so made, on the determination or abandonment of the application.

(8) An emergency prohibition notice or emergency prohibition order shall cease to have effect on the issue by the enforcement authority of a certificate to the effect that they are satisfied that the proprietor has taken sufficient measures to secure that the health risk condition is no longer fulfilled with respect to the business.

(9) The enforcement authority shall issue a certificate under subsection (8) above within three days of their being satisfied as mentioned in that subsection; and on an application by the proprietor for such a certificate, the authority shall–
   (a) determine, as soon as is reasonably practicable and in any event within 14 days, whether or not they are so satisfied; and
   (b) if they determine that they are not so satisfied, give notice to the proprietor of the reasons for that determination.

(10) Where an emergency prohibition notice is served on the proprietor of a business, the enforcement authority shall compensate him in respect of any loss suffered by reason of his complying with the notice unless–
   (a) an application for an emergency prohibition order is made within the period of three days beginning with the service of the notice; and
   (b) the court declares itself satisfied, on the hearing of the application, that the health risk condition was fulfilled with respect to the business at the time when the notice was served;

   and any disputed question as to the right to or the amount of any compensation payable under this subsection shall be determined by arbitration or, in Scotland, by a single arbiter appointed, failing agreement between the parties, by the sheriff.

18.61 SECTION 13 OF THE FOOD SAFETY ACT 1990: EMERGENCY CONTROL ORDERS

(1) If it appears to the Secretary of State that the carrying out of commercial operations with respect to food, food sources or contact materials of any class or description involves or may involve imminent risk of injury to health, he may, by an order (in this Act referred to as an 'emergency control order'), prohibit the carrying out of such operations with respect to food, food sources or contact materials of that class or description.

(2) Any person who knowingly contravenes an emergency control order shall be guilty of an offence.

(3) The Secretary of State or the Food Standards Agency may consent, either unconditionally or subject to any condition that the authority giving the consent considers appropriate, to the doing in a particular case of anything prohibited by an emergency control order.

(4) It shall be a defence for a person charged with an offence under subsection (2) above to show–
   (a) that consent had been given under subsection (3) above to the contravention of the emergency control order; and
   (b) that any condition subject to which that consent was given was complied with.

(5) The Secretary of State or the Food Standards Agency–
   (a) may give such directions as appear to the authority giving the directions to be necessary or expedient for the purpose of preventing the carrying out of commercial operations with respect to any food, food sources or contact materials which the authority giving the directions believes, on reasonable grounds, to be food, food sources or contact materials to which an emergency control order applies; and
   (b) may do anything which appears to the authority giving the directions to be necessary or expedient for that purpose.

(6) Any person who fails to comply with a direction under this section shall be guilty of an offence.

(7) If the Minister does anything by virtue of this section in consequence of any person failing to comply with an emergency control order or a direction under this section, the Minister may recover from that person any expenses reasonably incurred by him under this section.

Food Safety Act 1990, s 13 as amended by the Food Standards Act 1999, Sched 6.

CHAPTER 19

PLANNING AND ADVERTISEMENT LEGISLATION

19.1 INTRODUCTION

This chapter sets out the following legislation together with relating checklists identifying the elements and other investigatory matters:

1. Section 179 of the Town and Country Planning Act 1990 (Breach of an Enforcement Notice);
2. Section 210 of the Town and Country Planning Act 1990 (Breach of a Tree Preservation Order);
3. Regulations 5 and 27 of the Town and Country Planning (Control of Advertisement Regulations) 1992 (Breach of Advertisement Regulations).

The following statutory powers are included:

1. Section 196A of the Town and Country Planning Act 1990 (rights to enter without warrant);
2. Section 196B of the Town and Country Planning Act 1990 (right to enter under warrant);
3. Section 196C of the Town and Country Planning Act 1990 (rights of entry: supplementary provisions);
4. Section 198 of the Town and Country Planning Act 1990 (power to make tree preservation orders).

19.2 STATUTORY PROVISIONS

At Appendix 9 there are draft informations for offences, arising under the above legislation, draft information for warrants to enter premises and other useful precedents.

19.3 SECTION 179 OF THE TOWN AND COUNTRY PLANNING ACT 1990: INVESTIGATORY MATTERS AND ELEMENTS OF AN OFFENCE

1. The name and address of the owner of the land (registered office address if limited company) status of defendant, that is, individual or sole trader, partnership, limited company or plc.
2. The date of the offence.[a]

---

[a] Failure to include evidence of the compliance period is fatal if it is not pleaded in the informations and referred to in the evidence (*Maltedge v Wokingham DC* [1992] TLR, 21 May).

3   Details of the steps required by the notice to be taken which has not been taken or activity which has not ceased.
4   Evidence of ownership or person who has control of or an interest in the land.
5   Proof of service or s 188 registration.
6   The existence of a valid enforcement notice (see s 179(7)).
7   The place of the offence.
8   Defence to show that the defendant did everything that could be expected of him to secure compliance with the notice.
9   Mitigation/explanation.

Time limit: no time limit.

Mode of trial: either way.

Maximum penalty (s 179(8)).

Summary: £20,000.

Either way: fine.

19.4 SECTION 179 OF THE TOWN AND COUNTRY PLANNING ACT 1990

(1) Where at any time after the end of the period for compliance with an Enforcement Notice, any step required by the Notice to be taken has not been taken or any activity required by the Notice to cease is being carried out, the person who is then the owner of the land is in breach of the Notice;

(2) where the owner of the land is in breach of an Enforcement Notice then he shall be guilty of an offence;

(3) in proceedings against any person for an offence under sub-section (2), it shall be a defence for him to show that he did everything he could be expected to do to secure compliance with the Notice;

(4) a person who has control of an interest in the land to which an Enforcement Notice relates (other than the owner) must not carry on any activity which is required by the Notice to cease or cause or permit such an activity to be carried on;

(5) a person who, at any time after the end of the period of compliance with the Notice, contravenes sub-section 4 shall be guilty of an offence;

(6) an offence under sub-section (2) or (5) may be charged by reference to any day or longer period of time the person may be convicted of a second or subsequent offence under the sub-section in question by reference to any period of time following the proceeding conviction for such an offence;

(7) where – (a) a person charged with an offence under this Section has not been served with a copy of the Enforcement Notice and (b) the Notice is not contained in the appropriate Register kept under Section 188, it shall be a defence for him to show that he was not aware of the existence of the Notice;

(8) a person guilty of an offence under this Section shall be liable - (a) on summary conviction, to a fine not exceeding £20,000 and (b) on conviction on indictment, to a fine;

(9) in determining the amount of any fine to be imposed on a person convicted of an offence under this Section, the Court shall in particular have regard to any financial benefit which has accrued or likely to accrue to him in consequence of the offence.

19.5 SECTION 210(1) OF THE TOWN AND COUNTRY PLANNING ACT 1990: CUTTING DOWN TREE, ETC, CONTRARY TO TREE PRESERVATION ORDER (TPO)

The investigatory matters and elements of the offence are as follows:

1. The name and address of the person responsible (registered office address if limited company), status of defendant, that is, individual or sole trader, partnership, limited company or plc.
2. The date of the offence.[a]
3. Evidence of the existence of a valid TPO.
4. Breach of a TPO or the cutting down, uprooting or wilful destruction of a tree or the wilful damage, topping or lopping of a tree in such a manner as to be likely to destroy it (this evidence requires an expert arboriculturist).
5. The date of the cutting, etc.
6. The place of the offence, that is, location of the tree.
7. Evidence that the tree existed at the time that the order was made.[b]
8. Defence,[c] for example, the tree was dead, dying or dangerous.
9. The mitigation/explanation.

Time limit: No time limit (NB six months for summary offence under s 210(4)).

Mode of trial: either way.

Maximum penalty (s 210(2)).

Summary: £20,000.

Either way: fine.

---

[a] Failure to include evidence of the compliance period is fatal if it is not pleaded in the informations and referred to in the evidence (*Maltedge v Wokingham DC* [1992] TLR, 21 May).

[b] Failure to prove this is fatal to the case (*CD Carter v Eastbourne BC*, Lawtel 4/2/2000).

[c] See list of authorities in Appendix 17. It is not necessary to prove that the accused knew of the existence of the preservation order (*Maidstone BC v Mortimer* [1980] 3 All ER 552). The burden of proving that the tree was dying, or dead or had become dangerous, so as to justify its felling without the local authority's consent, is on the defendant (*R v Alath Construction Ltd* [1990] 1 WLR 1255).

19.6 SECTION 210 OF THE TOWN AND COUNTRY PLANNING ACT 1990

(1) If any person, in contravention of a Tree Preservation Order –
   (a) Cuts down, uproots or wilfully destroys a tree, or
   (b) Wilfully damages, tops or lops a tree in such a manner as to be likely to destroy it, he shall be guilty of an offence.

(2) A person guilty of an offence under sub-section (1) shall be liable on the Standard Scale.
   (a) On summary conviction to a fine not exceeding £20,000.
   (b) On conviction on indictment to a fine.

(3) In determining the amount of any fine to be imposed on a person convicted of an offence under sub-section (1), the Court shall in particular have regard to any financial benefit which has accrued or appears likely to accrue to him in consequence of the offence.

(4) If any person contravenes the provisions of a Tree Preservation Order, otherwise than as mentioned in sub-section (1), he shall be guilty of an offence and liable on summary conviction to a fine not exceeding Level 4.

19.7 ADVERTISEMENT PROSECUTIONS

Prosecutions for posters and advertisements, etc, can be taken under the Highways Act 1980 for offences on the highway or under the advertisement regulations which are set out in part below. Use of the Highways Act has its limitations in that it only relates to offences in or on the highway and there are no provisions that enable the prosecutor to dispense with the need to prove display by the defendant. Conversely, the advertisement regulations have wider application and the owner or persons whose trade or business is being advertised is deemed to display the advertisement unless he proves that the advertisement was displayed without his knowledge or consent.[a] A knowledge of this provision can be very useful if the prime objective of the prosecution is to secure removal of the offending advertisement. If therefore the existence of an offending advertisement is drawn to the attention of an owner or person whose business is being publicised in such a manner that knowledge of it can not be denied, the owner, etc, would be well advised to secure its removal. Failure to do so could result in a prosecution being brought on evidence that is likely to be very compelling.

(a) Town and Country Planning Act 1990, s 224.

19.8 REGULATIONS 5 AND 27 OF THE TOWN AND COUNTRY PLANNING (CONTROL OF ADVERTISEMENT REGULATIONS) 1992

The investigatory matters and elements of the offence are as follows:
1. Name and address (registered office address if limited company), status of defendant, that is, individual or sole trader, partnership, limited company or plc.
2. The date of the offence.
3. Lack of consent.
4. Affixing of poster or being a person whose business is being advertised or on whose land the poster is attached and knowledge of advertisement in both cases.
5. Defence.
6. Mitigation/explanation.

Time limit: six months.

Mode of trial (reg 27): summary.

Maximum penalty (s 179(8)).

Summary: level 3.

19.9 REGULATIONS 5 AND 27 OF THE TOWN AND COUNTRY PLANNING (CONTROL OF ADVERTISEMENT REGULATIONS) 1992

Requirement for consent

5 (1) No advertisement may be displayed without consent granted by the local planning authority or by the Secretary of State on an application in that behalf (referred to in these Regulations as 'express consent'), or granted by regulation 6 (referred to in these Regulations as 'deemed consent'), except an advertisement displayed in accordance with paragraph (2) below.

   (2) The display-
   (a) outside any area of special control, of such an advertisement as is mentioned in regulation 3(2); or
   (b) within an area of special control, of such an advertisement as is so mentioned, other than one falling within Class A in Schedule 2,
   is in accordance with this paragraph.

Contravention of Regulations

27 A person displaying an advertisement in contravention of these Regulations shall be liable on summary conviction of an offence under section 224(3) of the Act to a fine of an amount not exceeding level 3 on the standard scale and, in the case of a continuing offence, one-tenth of level 3 on the standard scale for each day during which the offence continues after conviction.

19.10 SECTION 196A OF THE TOWN AND COUNTRY PLANNING ACT 1990: RIGHTS TO ENTER WITHOUT WARRANT

(1) Any person duly authorised in writing by a local planning authority may at any reasonable hour enter any land—
   (a) to ascertain whether there is or has been any breach of planning control on the land or any other land;
   (b) to determine whether any of the powers conferred on a local planning authority by this Part should be exercised in relation to the land or any other land;
   (c) to determine how any such power should be exercised in relation to the land or any other land;
   (d) to ascertain whether there has been compliance with any requirement imposed as a result of any such power having been exercised in relation to the land or any other land,
   if there are reasonable grounds for entering for the purpose in question.

(2) Any person duly authorised in writing by the Secretary of State may at any reasonable hour enter any land to determine whether an enforcement notice should be issued in relation to the land or any other land, if there are reasonable grounds for entering for that purpose.

(3) The Secretary of State shall not so authorise any person without consulting the local planning authority.

(4) Admission to any building used as a dwelling house shall not be demanded as of right by virtue of subsection (1) or (2) unless twenty-four hours' notice of the intended entry has been given to the occupier of the building.

19.11 SECTION 196B OF THE TOWN AND COUNTRY PLANNING ACT 1990, ADDED BY S 11 OF THE PLANNING AND COMPENSATION ACT 1991

Section 196B of the Town and Country Planning Act 1990 provides right to enter under warrant:

(1) If it is shown to the satisfaction of a justice of the peace on sworn information in writing—
   (a) that there are reasonable grounds for entering any land for any of the purposes mentioned in section 196A(1) or (2); and
   (b) that—
      (i) admission to the land has been refused, or a refusal is reasonably apprehended; or
      (ii) the case is one of urgency,
   the justice may issue a warrant authorising any person duly authorised in writing by a local planning authority or, as the case may be, the Secretary of State to enter the land.

(2) For the purposes of subsection (1)(b)(i) admission to land shall be regarded as having been refused if no reply is received to a request for admission within a reasonable period.

(3) A warrant authorises entry on one occasion only and that entry must be—
   (a) within one month from the date of the issue of the warrant; and
   (b) at a reasonable hour, unless the case is one of urgency.

19.12 SECTION 196C OF THE TOWN AND COUNTRY PLANNING ACT 1990, ADDED BY S 11 OF THE PLANNING AND COMPENSATION ACT 1991

Section 196C of the Town and Country Planning Act 1990 provides rights of entry:

(1) A person authorised to enter any land in pursuance of a right of entry conferred under or by virtue of section 196A or 196B (referred to in this section as 'a right of entry')—
   (a) shall, if so required, produce evidence of his authority and state the purpose of his entry before so entering;
   (b) may take with him such other persons as may be necessary; and
   (c) on leaving the land shall, if the owner or occupier is not then present, leave it as effectively secured against trespassers as he found it.

(2) Any person who wilfully obstructs a person acting in the exercise of a right of entry shall be guilty of an offence and liable on summary conviction to a fine not exceeding level 3 on the standard scale.

(3) If any damage is caused to land or chattels in the exercise of a right of entry, compensation may be recovered by any person suffering the damage from the authority who gave the written authority for the entry or, as the case may be, the Secretary of State.

(4) The provisions of section 118 shall apply in relation to compensation under subsection (3) as they apply in relation to compensation under Part IV.

(5) If any person who enters any land, in exercise of a right of entry, discloses to any person any information obtained by him while on the land as to any manufacturing process or trade secret, he shall be guilty of an offence.

(6) Subsection (5) does not apply if the disclosure is made by a person in the course of performing his duty in connection with the purpose for which he was authorised to enter the land.

(7) A person who is guilty of an offence[a] under subsection (5) shall be liable on summary conviction to a fine not exceeding the statutory maximum or on conviction on indictment to imprisonment for a term not exceeding two years or a fine or both.

(8) In sections 196A and 196B and this section references to a local planning authority include, in relation to a building situated in Greater London, a reference to the Historic Buildings and Monuments Commission for England.

---

[a] For procedure in respect of an offence triable either way, see the Magistrates' Courts Act 1980, ss 17A–21 in Part I: Magistrates' Courts, Procedure, *ante*.

Part VIII[a]
Special Controls

Chapter I
Trees

Tree preservation orders

Section 198 Town and Country Planning Act 1990

Power to make tree preservation orders

If it appears to a local planning authority that it is expedient in the interests of amenity they may make an order prohibiting cutting down, topping, lopping, uprooting, wilful damage or wilful destruction of trees except with consent, and to secure replanting after forestry operations. Such order not to apply to cutting down, uprooting, topping or lopping of trees which are dying or dead or have become dangerous or such work done in compliance with an Act of Parliament or to prevent or abate a nuisance.[b]

Sections 207–09 of the Town and Country Planning Act 1990

Replacement of trees

Section 209(6) states that any person wilfully obstructing the exercise of a power under s 209(1)(a) is punishable on summary conviction to a fine not exceeding level 3 on the standard scale.

(a) Part VIII contains ss 197–225.
(b) Additionally, this section has effect subject to the Housing and Planning Act 1986, s 39(2) (saving s 2(4) of the repealed Opencast Coal Act 1958) and the Forestry Act 1967, s 15 (licence to fell), Town and Country Planning Act 1990, s 198(7). Footnote taken from *Stones Justices Manual 2001*.

For procedure in respect of the making of tree preservation orders see the Town and Country Planning (Trees) Regulations 1999 SI 1999/1892. In proceedings alleging commission of an offence under s 210(1), *post*, it will be for the defendant to prove on the balance of probabilities that the conditions creating an exemption under this section existed at the time; see *R v Alath Construction Ltd* [1990] 1 WLR 1255, CA (decided under s 102(1) of the repealed 1971 Act). The burden of proof on the issue of whether the tree was dying, or dead or had become dangerous, so as to justify its felling without the local authority's consent, falls on the defendant who asserts such exemption from the preservation order (*R v Alath Construction Ltd*, above). Footnote taken from *Stones Justices Manual 2001*.

CHAPTER 20

TRADING STANDARDS LEGISLATION

20.1 OFFENCE CREATING SECTIONS

This chapter sets out the following legislation together with relating checklists identifying the elements and other investigatory matters:

1. Section 92 of the Trade Marks Act (TMA) 1994;
2. Section 107 of the Copyright Designs and Patents Act 1988 (criminal liability for making or dealing with infringing articles, etc);
3. Section 198 of the Copyright Designs and Patents Act 1988 (criminal liability for making, dealing with or using illicit recordings);
4. Section 1 of the Trade Descriptions Act 1968 (prohibition of false trade descriptions);
5. Sections 14 and 23 of the Trade Descriptions Act 1968 (s 14 false statement as to services, etc);
6. Section 4 of the Business Names Act 1985 (failure to display name and address in a prominent place in the business premises);
7. Section 1 of the Mock Auctions Act 1961 (conducting a mock auction);
8. Section 20 of the Consumer Protection Act 1987 (misleading price indications);
9. Regulation 4 of the Package Travel, Package Holidays and Package Tours Regulations 1992 (misleading descriptive matter in packages);
10. Regulation 13 of the General Product Safety Regulations 1994 (offering or agreeing to supply a dangerous product).

20.2 STATUTORY POWERS

The following statutory powers, etc, are included:

Section 28 of the Trade Descriptions Act 1968 (power to enter premises and inspect and seize goods and documents);

Section 29 of the Trade Descriptions Act 1968 (obstruction of authorised officers).

20.3 TRADE MARKS ACT 1994

20.3.1

Prior to this Act coming into force in October 1994, the Trade Descriptions Act 1968 was the main anti-counterfeiting legislation in the armoury of the local authorities. Sections 107 and 198 of the Copyright Designs and Patents Act 1988 had not come into force until later.

20.3.2

The TMA 1994 was a long over due alternative for the Trade Descriptions Act 1968. The 1968 Act can still be used against counterfeiting, although its effect has been blunted by the disclaimer doctrine that has evolved under the common law. A disclaimer may effectively neutralise a false trade description and enabled traders avoid liability under the (quasi-) criminal law by making it clear to consumers that the goods on offer were copies or fakes. The use of the word criminal law in this context is to differentiate between what has been described as regulatory offences from the civil law that enables such proceedings to be taken against counterfeiters. These proceedings are expensive and are generally not worth 'powder and shot' against a man of straw. The precise wording of s 92 of the TMA 1994 effectively writes out any common law defence of disclaimer. Furthermore, defendants may no longer rely on the due diligence defence in the 1968 Act. Section 92 of the 1994 Act does has its own statutory defence built in. It is, however, limited to those who genuinely believe on reasonable grounds that there would be no infringement, for example, use of collectible cards featuring football players wearing registered trade marks.[a]

20.3.3

A breakdown of the elements of offence etc for a charge under s 92 of the 1994 Act is as follows:

Section 92(1)(c) of the TMA 1994

Need to prove/investigate:

1. Date of offence.
2. Place of offence (within courts jurisdiction).
3. Name and status of defendant, that is, individual or sole trader, partnership, limited company or plc.
4. Address of defendant or registered office if limited company.
5. (a) With a view to gain for himself or another; or
   (b) with the intent to cause loss to another.
6. Without the consent of the proprietor.
7. (a) Has in his possession, custody or control.
   (b) With a view to doing anything by himself or another which would be an offence under paragraph.

---

[a] This was a defence to a civil claim in *Trebor Bassett Ltd v the FA* [1997] FSR 211 Ch D and may also be a defence to a TMA 1994, s 92, prosecution.

Chapter 20: Trading Standards Legislation

8   In the course of a business.(a)
9   Trade mark is registered or has a reputation in the UK and use would be detrimental, etc, to the trade mark as set out in s 92(4).
10 Section 92(5) defence, that is, belief on reasonable grounds that the use of the sign in the manner in which it was used was not an infringement of the registered trade mark.
11 Mitigation/explanation.

Time limit: no time limit.

Mode of trial: either way.

Maximum penalty (s 92(6)).

Summary: statutory maximum and/or six months.

Either way: fine and/or 10 years.

Section 92 Unauthorised use of trade mark, etc in relation to goods

(1) A person commits an offence who with a view to gain for himself or another, or with intent to cause loss to another, and without the consent of the proprietor—

   (a) applies to goods or their packaging a sign identical to, or likely to be mistaken for, a registered trade mark, or

   (b) sells or lets for hire, offers or exposes for sale or hire or distributes goods which bear, or the packaging of which bears, such a sign, or

   (c) has in his possession, custody or control in the course of a business any such goods with a view to the doing of anything, by himself or another, which would be an offence under paragraph (b).

(2) A person commits an offence who with a view to gain for himself or another, or with intent to cause loss to another, and without the consent of the proprietor—

   (a) applies a sign identical to, or likely to be mistaken for, a registered trade mark to material intended to be used—

      (i) for labelling or packaging goods,

      (ii) as a business paper in relation to goods, or

      (iii) for advertising goods, or

   (b) uses in the course of a business material bearing such a sign for labelling or packaging goods, as a business paper in relation to goods, or for advertising goods, or

---

(a) The carrying out of repairs and improvements to motor vehicles as a hobby did not amount to a trade or business in the case of *Blakemore v Bellamy* (1983) 147 JP 89, [1983] RTR 303. For activities that are incidental to the main line of business, the position is not straightforward. It was held in *Devlin v Hall* [1990] RTR 320, [1990] Crim LR 879 that transactions need to have some degree of regularity so as to form part of the normal practice of a business, although in the cases of *Davies v Sumner* [1984] 3 All ER 831, [1984] 1 WLR 1301, 149 JP 110, HL and *Corfield v Sevenways Garage Ltd* (1984) 148 JP 648, [1985] RTR 109. A one-off venture in the nature of trade, carried through with a view to profit would not necessarily fall outside the section. Contrast with *Devlin v Hall* [1990] RTR 320, [1990] Crim LR 879, in which the sale of one of four vehicles was not carried on with sufficient degree of regularity for him to be acting in the course of a trade or business. The term 'trade or business' would normally include professionals (*Roberts v Leonard* (1995) 159 JP 711).

(c) has in his possession, custody or control in the course of a business any such material with a view to the doing of anything, by himself or another, which would be an offence under paragraph (b).

(3) A person commits an offence who with a view to gain for himself or another, or with intent to cause loss to another, and without the consent of the proprietor—

(a) makes an article specifically designed or adapted for making copies of a sign identical to, or likely to be mistaken for, a registered trade mark, or

(b) has such an article in his possession, custody or control in the course of a business,

knowing or having reason to believe that it has been, or is to be, used to produce goods, or material for labelling or packaging goods, as a business paper in relation to goods, or for advertising goods.

(4) A person does not commit an offence under this section unless—

(a) the goods are goods in respect of which the trade mark is registered, or

(b) the trade mark has a reputation in the United Kingdom and the use of the sign takes or would take unfair advantage of, or is or would be detrimental to, the distinctive character or the repute of the trade mark.

(5) It is a defence for a person charged with an offence under this section to show that he believed on reasonable grounds that the use of the sign in the manner in which it was used, or was to be used, was not an infringement of the registered trade mark.

(6) A person guilty of an offence under this section is liable—

(a) on summary conviction to imprisonment for a term not exceeding six months or a fine not exceeding the statutory maximum, or both;

(b) on conviction on indictment to a fine or imprisonment for a term not exceeding ten years, or both.

20.4 SECTION 107 OF THE COPYRIGHT DESIGNS AND PATENTS ACT 1988: MAKING OR DEALING WITH INFRINGING ARTICLES, ETC

1 Date of offence.
2 Place of offence (within court's jurisdiction).
3 Name and status of defendant, that is, individual or sole trader, partnership, limited company or plc.
4 Address of defendant or registered office if limited company.
5 Defendant sells or lets for hire, or offers or exposes for sale or hire, or exhibits in public, or distributes (see 6 below).
6 In the course of a business[a] or distribution which is prejudicial to the copyright owner if not in the course of a business.
7 An article which is, and which the defendant knows or has reason to believe is, an infringing copy of a copyright work.
8 Without the licence of the copyright owner.
9 Mitigation/explanation.

---

[a] See footnotes to Trade Descriptions Act 1968 for meaning of in the course of a trade or business which will have a similar if not the same meaning.

Time limit: no time limit.

Mode of trial: either way.

Maximum penalty (s 107(4)).

Summary: statutory maximum and/or six months.

Either way: fine and/or two years.

20.5 SECTION 107 OF THE COPYRIGHT DESIGNS AND PATENTS ACT 1988: CRIMINAL LIABILITY FOR MAKING OR DEALING WITH INFRINGING ARTICLES, ETC

(1) A person commits an offence who, without the licence of the copyright owner—

    (a) makes for sale or hire, or

    (b) imports into the United Kingdom otherwise than for his private and domestic use, or

    (c) possesses in the course of a business with a view to committing any act infringing the copyright, or

    (d) in the course of a business —

        (i) sells or lets for hire, or

        (ii) offers or exposes for sale or hire, or

        (iii) exhibits in public, or

        (iv) distributes, or

    (e) distributes otherwise than in the course of a business to such an extent as to affect prejudicially the owner of the copyright,

an article which is, and which he knows or has reason to believe is, an infringing copy of a copyright work.

(2) A person commits an offence who—

    (a) makes an article specifically designed or adapted for making copies of a particular copyright work, or

    (b) has such an article in his possession,

knowing or having reason to believe that it is to be used to make infringing copies for sale or hire or for use in the course of a business.

(3) Where copyright is infringed (otherwise than by reception of a broadcast or cable programme)—

    (a) by the public performance of a literary, dramatic or musical work, or

    (b) by the playing or showing in public of a sound recording or film,

any person who caused the work to be so performed, played or shown is guilty of an offence if he knew or had reason to believe that copyright would be infringed.

(4) A person guilty of an offence under subsection (1)(a), (b), (d)(iv) or (e) is liable—

    (a) on summary conviction to imprisonment for a term not exceeding six months or a fine not exceeding the statutory maximum, or both;

    (b) on conviction on indictment to a fine or imprisonment for a term not exceeding two years, or both.

(5) A person guilty of any other offence under this section is liable on summary conviction to imprisonment for a term not exceeding six months or a fine not exceeding level 5 on the standard scale, or both.

(6) Sections 104 to 106 (presumptions as to various matters connected with copyright) do not apply to proceedings for an offence under this section; but without prejudice to their application in proceedings for an order under section 108 below.

20.6 SECTION 198 OF THE COPYRIGHT DESIGNS AND PATENTS ACT 1988: DEALING WITH OR USING ILLICIT RECORDINGS

Elements of the offence:

1. Date of offence.
2. Place of offence (within courts jurisdiction).
3. Name and status of defendant, that is, individual or sole trader, partnership, limited company or plc.
4. Address of defendant or registered office if limited company.
5. Defendant sells or lets for hire, or offers or exposes for sale or hire, or exhibits in public.*
6. In the course of a business.[a]
7. A recording which is, and which he knows or has reason to believe is, an illicit recording.
8. Without sufficient[b] consent.
9. Mitigation/explanation.

Time limit: six months.

Mode of trial: summary.

Maximum penalty (s 198(6)).

Summary: level 5.

* Penalty for person who makes, imports or distributes, etc, the following penalty, etc, is applicable.

Time limit: No time limit/six months.

Mode of trial: either way/summary.

Maximum penalty (s 198(5)).

Summary: statutory maximum and/or six months.

Either way: fine and/or two years.

(a) See footnotes to Trade Descriptions Act 1968 for meaning of in the course of a trade or business which will have a similar if not the same meaning.
(b) See s 198(3) above for meaning of sufficient.

20.7 SECTION 198 OF THE COPYRIGHT DESIGNS AND PATENTS ACT 1988: CRIMINAL LIABILITY FOR MAKING, DEALING WITH OR USING ILLICIT RECORDINGS

(1) A person commits an offence who without sufficient consent—
   (a) makes for sale or hire, or
   (b) imports into the United Kingdom otherwise than for his private and domestic use, or
   (c) possesses in the course of a business with a view to committing any act infringing the rights conferred by this Part, or
   (d) in the course of a business—
      (i) sells or lets for hire, or
      (ii) offers or exposes for sale or hire, or
      (iii) distributes,
      a recording which is, and which he knows or has reason to believe is, an illicit recording.

(2) A person commits an offence who causes a recording of a performance made without sufficient consent to be—
   (a) shown or played in public, or
   (b) broadcast or included in a cable programme service,
   thereby infringing any of the rights conferred by this Part, if he knows or has reason to believe that those rights are thereby infringed.

(3) In subsections (1) and (2) 'sufficient consent' means—
   (a) in the case of a qualifying performance, the consent of the performer, and
   (b) in the case of a non-qualifying performance subject to an exclusive recording contract—
      (i) for the purposes of subsection (1)(a) (making of recording), the consent of the performer or the person having recording rights, and
      (ii) for the purposes of subsection (1)(b), (c) and (d) and subsection (2) (dealing with or using recording), the consent of the person having recording rights.
   The references in this subsection to the person having recording rights are to the person having those rights at the time the consent is given or, if there is more than one such person, to all of them.

(4) No offence is committed under subsection (1) or (2) by the commission of an act which by virtue of any provision of Schedule 2 may be done without infringing the rights conferred by this Part.

(5) A person guilty of an offence under subsection (1)(a), (b) or (d)(iii) is liable—
   (a) on summary conviction to imprisonment for a term not exceeding six months or a fine not exceeding the statutory maximum, or both;
   (b) on conviction on indictment to a fine or imprisonment for a term not exceeding two years, or both.

(6) A person guilty of any other offence under this section is liable on summary conviction to a fine not exceeding level 5 on the standard scale or imprisonment for a term not exceeding six months, or both.

20.8 SECTIONS 107 AND 198 OF THE COPYRIGHT DESIGNS AND PATENTS ACT (CD & PA)1988

20.8.1

It might be said that ss 107 and 198 are the main enforcement provisions of the Act. Sections 107A and 198A inserted by s 165 of the Criminal Justice and Public Order Act 1994 clearly impose a duty on local authority's to enforce the provisions in these areas. Whilst is accepted that there is no duty to enforce these provisions there is a powerful argument to support the view that local authority could nonetheless use these provisions. The powers of test purchase and seizure, etc, under s 107A could not be used by trading standards officers. Instead, trading standards officers would rely on the police to exercise powers of seizure under s 19 of the Police and Criminal Evidence Act 1984. It is understood that some trading standards officers do enforce the Act in this way. The authority for so doing would be s 222 of the Local Government Act 1972.[a]

20.8.2

A comparison of the two Acts is set out below in outline.

Sections 107 and 198 of the CD & PA 1988 and s 92 of the TMA 1994

(a) Sections 107 and 198 of the CD & PA 1988–

Use: covers literary, musical or artistic works as defined in ss 1–6 of the CD & PA 1988.

Limitations: Does not automatically apply to registered trade marks.

NB: Section 198A requires local authority to enforce s 198 and power to make test purchases, inspect and seize goods, etc, inserted by s 165 of the Criminal Justice and Public Order Act 1994 – this provision is not yet in force.

Section 107A requires local authorities to enforce s 107 inserted by s 165 of the Criminal Justice and Public Order Act 1994 – see above.

(b) Section 92 of the TMA 1994:

Use: covers use of trade mark on false goods materials or articles.

Limitations: Copying where no trade mark is used. See s 107 and/or s 108 of the CD & PA 1988 which are enforceable by the police unless likely to be mistaken for a registered trade mark.

The Trade Marks Act 1994 does not apply to services – apply Trade Descriptions Act 1968.

NB: Disclaimer and brand copy defences do not apply to s 92. There is also a wide power of forfeiture of goods under s 97 of the TMA 1994.

(a) It was confirmed in the case of *R v Jarrett and Steward*, Archbold News, 7 May 1997, that a local authority has a very wide power to prosecute under this section.

Chapter 20: Trading Standards Legislation

20.9 TRADE DESCRIPTIONS ACT 1968

The offence making provisions that are examined below are:

s 1 prohibition of false trade descriptions;

s 14 false statement as to services, etc;

s 23 offences due to the fault of another person.

20.10 SECTION 1 PROHIBITION OF FALSE TRADE DESCRIPTIONS

Elements of the offence/investigatory matters:

1. Place of offence (within jurisdiction of the court).
2. Date(s)[a] of offence (with s 19 time limit).
3. Capacity of defendant (individual, sole trader, company, partnership).
4. Address or registered office (if limited company).
5. In the course of a trade or business.[b]
6. Applies[c] or supplies or offers to supply.[d]

(a) A statement in a brochure is made each time it is read (*R v Thomson Holidays Ltd* [1974] All ER 823). Any offence is therefore committed at that time.

(b) The carrying out of repairs and improvements to motor vehicles as a hobby did not amount to a trade or business the case of (*Blakemore v Bellamy* (1983) 147 JP 89, [1983] RTR 303). For activities which are incidental to the main line of business the position is not straightforward. It was held in *Devlin v Hall* [1990] RTR 320, [1990] Crim LR 879 that transactions need to have some degree of regularity so as to form part of the normal practice of a business, although in the cases of *Davies v Sumner* [1984] 3 All ER 831, [1984] 1 WLR 1301, 149 JP 110, HL and *Corfield v Sevenways Garage Ltd* (1984) 148 JP 648, [1985] RTR 109, a one-off venture in the nature of trade, carried through with a view to profit would not necessarily fall outside the section. Contrast with *Devlin v Hall* [1990] RTR 320, [1990] Crim LR 879) in which the sale of one of four vehicles was not carried on with sufficient degree of regularity for him to be acting in the course of a trade or business. The term 'trade or business' would normally include professionals (*Roberts v Leonard* (1995) 159 JP 711).

(c) Section 4 defines the word 'applies' as follows:
   Section 4
   (1) A person applies a trade description to goods if he—
      (a) affixes or annexes it to or in any manner marks it on or incorporates it with—
         (i) the goods themselves, or
         (ii) anything in, on or with which the goods are supplied;
      or:
      (b) places the goods in, on or with anything which the trade description has been affixed or annexed to, marked on or incorporated with, or places any such thing with the goods; or
      (c) uses the trade description in any manner likely to be taken as referring to the goods.
   (2) An oral statement may amount to the use of a trade description.
   (3) Where goods are supplied in pursuance of a request in which a trade description is used and the circumstances are such as to make it reasonable to infer that the goods are supplied as goods corresponding to that trade description, the person supplying the goods shall be deemed to have applied that trade description to the goods.

(d) Supply/offer to supply is defined by s 6 as follows:
   Section 6 [cont]

7 Goods.
8 Trade description[e] applied, etc, which is false.[f]

(d) [cont]
Offer to supply:
A person exposing goods for supply or having goods in his possession for supply shall be deemed to offer to supply them.
Goods held for the purpose of delivery or collection do not amount to possession for supply (*Keating v Horwood* (1926) 90 JP 141, 135 LT 29).

(e) Trade description is defined by s 2 as follows:

Section 2

Trade description

(1) A trade description is an indication direct or indirect, and by whatever means given, of any of the following matters with respect to any goods or parts of goods, that is to say–
   (a) quantity, size or gauge;
   (b) method of manufacture, production, processing or reconditioning;
   (c) composition;
   (d) fitness for purpose, strength, performance, behaviour or accuracy;
   (e) any physical characteristics not included in the preceding paragraphs;
   (f) testing by any person and results thereof;
   (g) approval by any person or conformity with a type approved by any person;
   (h) place, or date of manufacture, productions, processing or reconditioning;
   (i) person by whom manufactured, produced, processed or reconditioned;
   (j) other history, including previous ownership or use.

(2) The matters specified in subsection (1) of this section shall be taken–
   (a) in relation to any animal, to include sex, breed or cross, fertility and soundness;
   (b) in relation to any semen, to include the identity and characteristics of the animal from which it was taken and measure of dilution.

(3) In this section 'quantity' includes length, width, height, area, volume, capacity, weight, and number.

(4) Notwithstanding anything in the preceding provisions of this section, the following shall be deemed not to be trade descriptions, that is to say, any description or mark applied in pursuance of –
   (a) (Repealed);
   (b) section 2 of the Agricultural Produce (Grading and Marking) Act 1928 (as amended by the Agricultural Produce (Grading and Marking) Amendment Act 1931) or any corresponding enactment of the Parliament of Northern Ireland;
   (c) the Plant Varieties and Seeds Act 1964;
   (d) the Agriculture and Horticulture Act 1964 or any Community grading rules within the meaning of Part III of that Act;
   (e) the Seeds Act (Northern Ireland) 1965;
   (f) the Horticulture Act (Northern Ireland) 1966;
   (g) the Consumer Protection Act 1987;
   (h) the Plant Varieties Act 1997;

any statement made in respect of, or mark applied to, any material in pursuance of Part IV of the Agriculture Act 1970, any name or expression to which a meaning has been assigned under section 70 of that Act when applied to any material in the circumstances specified in that section, any mark prescribed by a system of classification compiled under section 5 of the Agriculture Act 1967 and any designation, mark or description applied in pursuance of a scheme brought into force under section 6(1) or an order made under section 25(1) of the Agriculture Act 1970.

(5) Notwithstanding anything in the preceding provisions of this section–
   (a) where provision is made under the Food Safety Act 1990, the Food and Drugs Act (Northern Ireland) 1958 or the Consumer Protection Act 1987 prohibiting the application of a description except to goods in the case of which the requirements specified in that provision are complied with, that description, when applied to goods, shall be deemed not to be a trade description;... [cont]

9 Defence of mistake, accident, etc (due diligence).(g)

(e) [cont]

    (b) where by virtue of any provision made under Part V of the Medicines Act 1968 (or made under any provisions of the said Part V as applied by an order made under section 104 or section 105 of that Act) anything which, in accordance with this Act, constitutes the application of a trade description to goods is subject to any requirements or restrictions imposed by that provision, any particular description specified in that provision, when applied to goods in circumstances to which those requirements or restrictions are applicable, shall be deemed not to be a trade description.

(f) Essentially a false trade description must be false to a material degree, as defined by s 3 below:

Section 3

False trade description

(1) A false trade description is a trade description which is false to a material degree.

(2) A trade description which, though not false, is misleading, that is to say, likely to be taken for such an indication of any of the matters specified in section 2 of this Act as would be false to material degree, shall be deemed to be a false trade description.

(3) Anything which, though not a trade description, is likely to be taken for an indication of any of those matters and, as such an indication, would be false to a material degree, shall be deemed to be a false trade description.

(4) A false indication, or anything likely to be taken as an indication which would be false, that any goods comply with a standard specified or recognised by any person or implied by the approval of any person shall be deemed to be a false trade description, if there is no such person or no standard so specified, recognised or implied.

As the meaning of a false trade description it was said in the case of *Thomson Travel Ltd v Roberts* (1984) 148 JP 637 concerning s 14 that: 'Essentially, this was a question of fact and the correct test was to decide what effect such a statement would have on the mind of the person to whom it was addressed, namely ordinary readers of the brochure.' The same view was taken in *British Airways Board v Taylor* [1976] 1 All ER 65, pp 69a and 72e. The same approach was adopted in *London Borough of Southwark v Time Computer Systems Ltd* ILR 14/7/97, in which it was asked whether a reasonable consumer would have been misled.

(g) The defence of mistake, accident, etc is set out in s 24 as follows:

Section 24

Defence of mistake, accident, etc

(1) In any proceedings for an offence under this Act it shall, subject to subsection (2) of this section, be a defence for the person charged to prove–

    (a) that the commission of the offence was due to a mistake or to reliance on information supplied to him or to the act or default of another person, an accident or some other cause beyond his control; and

    (b) that he took all reasonable precautions and exercised all due diligence to avoid the commission of such an offence by himself or any person under his control.

(2) If in any case the defence provided by the last foregoing subsection involves the allegation that the commission of the offence was due to the act or default of another person or to reliance on information supplied by another person, the person charged shall not, without leave of the court, be entitled to rely on that defence unless, within a period ending seven clear days before the hearing, he has served on the prosecutor a notice in writing giving such information identifying or assisting in the identification of that other person as was then in his possession.

(3) In any proceedings for an offence under this Act of supplying or offering to supply goods to which a false trade description is applied it shall be a defence for the person charged to prove that he did not know, and could not with reasonable diligence have ascertained, that the goods did not conform to the description or that the description had been applied to the goods.

The due diligence defence is to be found in a number of regulatory statutes. 'Reasonable precautions' involves setting up a system to ensure that things will not go wrong while 'due diligence' means seeing that the system works properly – as defined by WH Thomas, solicitor, in the article 'Food safety' (1990) 31 LSG, 5 September. The wording of the statute is such that it is for the defendant to establish both limbs for the defence to be made out. The extent of the measures required to satisfy the defence will normally depend on the size and resources of the defendant. (*Garrett v Boots the Chemist*, 16 July 1980, unreported, *per* Lane LCJ, 'of course I scarcely need to say that every case will vary in its facts, what might be reasonable for a large retailer might not be reasonable for a village shop'.) Large organisations with high turnovers can therefore be expected to carry out random sampling ... [cont]

10 Disclaimer/common law defence.(h)

11 Mitigation/explanation.

Time limit (s 19): one year commission or three years from discovery whichever is earlier.

Mode of trial: either way

Maximum penalty (s 18).

Summary: statutory maximum.

Either way: fine and/or two years.

20.11 SECTION 1 OF THE TRADE DESCRIPTIONS ACT 1968: PROHIBITION OF FALSE TRADE DESCRIPTIONS

(1) Any person who, in the course of a trade or business–

    (a) applies a false trade description to any goods; or

    (b) supplies or offers to supply any goods to which a false trade description is applied;

    shall, subject to the provisions of this Act, be guilty of an offence.

(2) Sections 2 to 6 of this Act shall have effect for the purposes of this section and for the interpretation of expressions used in this section, wherever they occur in this Act.

(g) [cont] *Hicks v Sullam Ltd* (1983) 147 JP 493 and in the case of *Rotherham Metropolitan BC v Rayson (UK) Ltd* (1988) 153 JP 37 to sample only one packet of crayons out of 7,000–10,000, was not enough. In both *Hicks* and *Rayson* verbal assurances on their own were held to be insufficient, However, in the case of *Hurley v Martinez & Co Ltd* (1990) 154 JP 821, reliance was placed solely on the tests carried out by the German wine companies and no independent tests were carried out. The rationale for this decision rests on the fact that the defendant was a small concern (two retail shops and some wholesale business), the expense of the testing procedure and the reputation of the suppliers in the context of the rigorous German statutory requirements and testing procedures. An employer may point to the default of a senior manager as his defence if all reasonable precautions have been taken as to the selection and training of that person, there is a proper system of due diligence in place and there is adequate supervision to ensure the system is carried out. (*Tesco Supermarkets Ltd v Nattrass* [1972] AC 153, [1971] 2 All ER 127.) Although the wording of the defence might suggest that it should fail if more could have been done this was not the approach taken in *William Frank Smith v T & S Stores plc* [1994] Trading Law Reports 337 in which Buxton J (as he then was) said: 'The fact that there is some other precaution that might, in one sense, be reasonable for the party to take, does not in my judgment conclude the question of whether for the purposes of s 7(1)(a) a magistrate is precluded from finding that all reasonable precautions and all due diligence in the circumstances of the case have nonetheless been taken or observed.' This seems to suggest that the defence may stand if in one sense there are other precautions which may reasonably be expected if they are not reasonable in another. An example of such a scenario might be if the precaution was reasonable but not obvious. See *Rotherham Metropolitan BC v Rayson (UK) Ltd* (1988) 153 JP 37 in which it was said that a due diligence defence cannot avail a defendant if obvious precautions are not taken.

Should this defence succeed it would not appropriate to order the prosecution to pay costs where serious and important questions relating to diligence are properly brought before the court (*Suffolk CC v Rexmore Wholesale Services Ltd* (1994) 159 JP 390). Costs would not normally be payable by the prosecutor in any event. See Chapter 17 on costs. See list of authorities relating to the due diligence defence in Appendix 17.

(h) See the list of authorities relating to s 24 in Appendix 17 for cases on the disclaimer doctrine.

20.12 SECTION 14 OF THE TRADE DESCRIPTIONS ACT 1968: FALSE STATEMENT AS TO SERVICES, ETC

The elements of a s 14 offence have been broken down into its investigatory parts. Section 23 has been added by virtue of its application to all offence making provisions. The breakdown is as follows:

Sections 23 and 14(1)(b)(i) of the Trade Descriptions Act 1968

(false statement as to services due to the fault of another person)

Need to prove/investigate:

1. Place of offence (within jurisdiction of the court).
2. Date(s) of offence (with s 19 time limit).
3. Capacity of defendant, for example, limited company, partnership, sole trader, individual.
4. In the course of a trade or business.(a)
5. Made a statement which is false.
6. False statement(b) made recklessly.(c)

(a) The carrying out of repairs and improvements to motor vehicles as a hobby did not amount to a trade or business the case of (*Blakemore v Bellamy* (1983) 147 JP 89, [1983] RTR 303). For activities that are incidental to the main line of business, the position is not straightforward. It was held, in *Devlin v Hall* [1990] RTR 320, [1990] Crim LR 879, that transactions need to have some degree of regularity so as to form part of the normal practice of a business, although in the cases of *Davies v Sumner* [1984] 3 All ER 831, [1984] 1 WLR 1301, 149 JP 110, HL and *Corfield v Sevenways Garage Ltd* (1984) 148 JP 648, [1985] RTR 109, a one-off venture in the nature of trade, carried through with a view to profit would not necessarily fall outside the section. Contrast with *Devlin v Hall* [1990] RTR 320, [1990] Crim LR 879, in which the sale of one of four vehicles was not carried on with sufficient degree of regularity for him to be acting in the course of a trade or business. The term 'trade or business' would normally include professionals (*Roberts v Leonard* (1995) 159 JP 711).

(b) Essentially, a false trade description must be false to a material degree as defined by s 3 below:

Section 3
False trade description
 (1) A false trade description is a trade description which is false to a material degree.
 (2) A trade description which, though not false, is misleading, that is to say, likely to be taken for such an indication of any of the matters specified in section 2 of this Act as would be false to material degree, shall be deemed to be a false trade description.
 (3) Anything which, though not a trade description, is likely to be taken for an indication of any of those matters and, as such an indication, would be false to a material degree, shall be deemed to be a false trade description.
 (4) A false indication, or anything likely to be taken as an indication which would be false, that any goods comply with a standard specified or recognised by any person or implied by the approval of any person shall be deemed to be a false trade description, if there is no such person or no standard so specified, recognised or implied.

As the meaning of a false trade description it was said in the case of *Thomson Travel Ltd v Roberts* (1984) 148 JP 637 concerning s 14 that: 'Essentially, this was a question of fact and the correct test was to decide what effect such a statement would have on the mind of the person to whom it was addressed, namely ordinary readers of the brochure.' A similar view was taken in *British Airways Board v Taylor* [1976] 1 All ER 65, pp 69 and 72e. This case is also relevant to the accepted principle that the Act does not apply to future promises. The case establishes that a future promise may be accompanied by an implied statement of existing fact or present intention which is actionable under the Act, for example, it is our intention to keep to the booking. To bring proceedings on this authority it is necessary to lay charges that are consistent with this argument. A similar approach was taken in the more recent case of *Bryan Roy Lewis v Barratt Homes Ltd* (1999) unreported, 19 November.

(c) 'Recklessly' is defined in s 14(2)(b) below. It is not necessary to prove dishonesty or that the defendant was deliberately closing his eyes to the truth (*MFI Warehouses Ltd v Nattrass* [1973] 1 All ER 762).

7 False statement made as to the provision of services, accommodation or facilities.(d)
8 Offence committed by some other person.
9 Offence due to the act or default of the defendant.
10 Due diligence/mistake defence s 24.(e)
11 Common law defence/disclaimer.(f)

(d) The words 'accommodation' and 'service' are terms of common usage and are not likely to be applied incorrectly if they are used in accordance with their natural meaning. However, failure to elect the appropriate element is likely to be fatal to the prosecution. The word 'facility' may not be so straightforward. One example of a 'facility' is an advertisement which offered one year's insurance free with every moped purchased (*Kinchin v Ashton Park Scooters Ltd* (1984) 148 JP 540).

(e) The due diligence defence is to be found in a number of regulatory statutes. 'Reasonable precautions' involve setting up a system to ensure that things will not go wrong while 'due diligence' means seeing that the system works properly – as defined by WH Thomas, solicitor, in the article entitled 'Food safety' (1990) 31 LSG, 5 September. The wording of the statute is such that it is for the defendant to establish both limbs for the defence to be made out. The extent of the measures required to satisfy the defence will normally depend on the size and resources of the defendant. *Garrett v Boots the Chemist* (1980) unreported, 16 July, *per* Lane LCJ, 'of course I scarcely need to say that every case will vary in its facts, what might be reasonable for a large retailer might not be reasonable for a village shop'. Large organisations with high turnovers can therefore be expected to carry out random sampling *Hicks v Sullam Ltd* (1983) 147 JP 493 and in the case of *Rotherham Metropolitan BC v Rayson (UK) Ltd* (1988) 153 JP 37 to sample only one packet of crayons out of 7,000–10,000, was not enough. In both *Hicks* and *Rayson*, verbal assurances on their own were held to be insufficient. However, in the case of *Hurley v Martinez & Co Ltd* (1990) 154 JP 821, reliance was placed solely on the tests carried out by the German wine companies and no independent tests were carried out. The rationale for this decision rests on the fact that the defendant was a small concern (two retail shops and some wholesale business), the expense of the testing procedure and the reputation of the suppliers in the context of the rigorous German statutory requirements and testing procedures. An employer may point to the default of a senior manager as his defence if all reasonable precautions have been taken as to the selection and training of that person, there is a proper system of due diligence in place and there is adequate supervision to ensure the system is carried out. (*Tesco Supermarkets Ltd v Nattrass* [1972] AC 153, [1971] 2 All ER 127.) Although the wording of the defence might suggest that it should fail if more could have been done, this was not the approach taken in *William Frank Smith v T & S Stores plc* [1994] Trading Law Reports 337, in which Buxton J (as he then was) said: 'The fact that there is some other precaution that might, in one sense, be reasonable for the party to take, does not in my judgment conclude the question of whether, for the purposes of s 7(1)(a), a magistrate is precluded from finding that all reasonable precautions and all due diligence in the circumstances of the case have nonetheless been taken or observed.' This seems to suggest that the defence may stand if in one sense there are other precautions which may reasonably be expected if they are not reasonable in another. An example of such a scenario might be if the precaution was reasonable but not obvious. See *Rotherham Metropolitan BC v Rayson (UK) Ltd* (1988) 153 JP 37 in which it was said that a due diligence defence cannot avail a defendant if obvious precautions are not taken.

Should this defence succeed it would not appropriate to order the prosecution to pay costs where serious and important questions relating to diligence are properly brought before the court (*Suffolk CC v Rexmore Wholesale Services Ltd* (1994) 159 JP 390). Costs would not normally be payable by the prosecutor in any event. See Chapter 17 on costs. See list of authorities relating to the due diligence defence in Appendix 17.

For misleading statements in connection with package holidays, consideration may also be given to reg 4 of the Package Travel, Package Holidays and Package Tour Regulations 1992 which do not attract a due diligence defence. This offence is examined below.

(f) The effect of a disclaimer is to neutralise the effect of the offending statement. To be effective the disclaimer must be as 'bold precise and compelling' as the original statement (*Norman v Bennett* [1974] 3 All ER 355) and be alongside the original statement (*Lewin v Fuel* (1990) 155 JP 206). The disclaimer doctrine does not apply to applying a false trade description under s 1(1)(a). (*R v Hammertons Cars* (1976) 152 JP 207.) For more detailed cases on the disclaimer, see the list of authorities relating to s 24 defences in Appendix 17.

Chapter 20: Trading Standards Legislation

12 Statement does not amount to a future promise.[g]
13 Mitigation/explanation from defendant.

Time limit (s 19): one year commission or three years from discovery whichever is earlier.

Mode of trial: either way.

Maximum penalty (s 18).

Summary: statutory maximum.

Either way: fine and/or two years.

20.13 SECTION 14: FALSE OR MISLEADING STATEMENTS AS TO SERVICES, ETC

(1) It shall be an offence for any person in the course of any trade or business–

    (a) to make a statement which he knows to be false; or

    (b) recklessly to make a statement which is false;

  as to any of the following matters, that is to say,

    (i) the provision in the course of any trade or business of any services, accommodation or facilities;

    (ii) the nature of any services, accommodation or facilities provided in the course of any trade or business;

    (iii) the time at which manner in which or persons by whom any services, accommodation or facilities are so provided;

    (iv) the examination, approval or evaluation by any person of any services, accommodation or facilities so provided; or

    (v) the location or amenities of any accommodation so provided.

(2) For the purposes of this section–

    (a) anything (whether or not a statement as to any of the matters specified in the preceding subsection) likely to be taken for such a statement as to any of those matters as would be false shall be deemed to be a false statement as to that matter; and

---

(g) In *R v Sunair Holidays Ltd* [1973] 2 All ER 1233, it was held that s 14 of the Trade Descriptions Act 1994 did not apply to future promises. The reason given was that it could not be said that they were true or false at the time they were made. Consequently, care should be taken to identify complaints concerning holiday brochures which may amount to future promises. Guidance was provided in the case of *British Airways Board v Taylor* [1976] 1 All ER 65 that such statements may be subject to prosecution on the basis they amount to a an implied statement of existing fact or a statement of present intention. In the context of a holiday brochure an implied statement as to existing fact may arise from a statement that a particular hotel or class of hotel is reserved. A statement of present intention may mean an intention to honour that booking against all comers. In these circumstances any over booking policy would indicate that there was no such intention. To proceed along these lines it is advisable to draft the informations accordingly. Recognition that statements under the Property Misdescriptions Act 1991 were statements of existing fact is also to be found in the case of *Bryan Roy Lewis v Barratt Homes Ltd* (1999) unreported, 19 November.

(b) a statement made regardless of whether it is true or false shall be deemed to be made recklessly, whether or not the person making it had reasons for believing that it might be false.

(3) In relation to any services consisting of or including the application of any treatment or process or the carrying out of any repair, the matters specified in subsection (1) of this section shall be taken to include the effect of the treatment, process or repair.

(4) In this section 'false' means false to a material degree and 'services' does not include anything done under a contract of service.

20.14 SECTION 23: OFFENCES DUE TO FAULT OF OTHER PERSON

Where the commission by any person of an offence under this Act is due to the act or default of some other person that other person shall be guilty of the offence, and a person may be charged with and convicted of the offence by virtue of this section.

20.15 SECTION 28: POWER TO ENTER PREMISES AND INSPECT AND SEIZE GOODS AND DOCUMENTS

(1) A duly authorised officer of a local weights and measures authority or of a Government department may, at all reasonable hours and on production, if required, of his credentials, exercise the following powers, that is to say,

(a) he may, for the purpose of ascertaining whether any offence under this Act has been committed, inspect any goods and enter any premises other than premises used only as a dwelling;

(b) if he has reasonable cause to suspect that an offence under this Act has been committed, he may, for the purpose of ascertaining whether it has been committed, require any person carrying on a trade or business or employed in connection with a trade or business to produce any books or documents relating to the trade or business and may take copies of, or of any entry in, any such book or document;

(c) if he has reasonable cause to believe that an offence under this Act has been committed, he may seize and detain any goods for the purpose of ascertaining, by testing or otherwise, whether the offence has been committed;

(d) he may seize and detain any goods or documents which he has reason to believe may be required as evidence in proceedings for an offence under this Act;

(e) he may, for the purpose of exercising his powers under this subsection to seize goods, but only if and to the extent that it is reasonably necessary in order to secure that the provisions of this Act and of any order made thereunder are duly observed, require any person having authority to do so to break open any container or open any vending machine and, if that person does not comply with the requirement, he may do so himself.

(2) An officer seizing any goods or documents in the exercise of his powers under this section shall inform the person from whom they are seized and, in the case of goods seized from a vending machine, the person whose name and address are stated on the machine as being the proprietor's or, if no name and address are so stated, the occupier of the premises on which the machine stands or to which it is affixed.

(3) If a justice of the peace, on sworn information in writing–
   (a) is satisfied that there is reasonable ground to believe either–
      (i) that any goods, books or documents which a duly authorised officer has power under this section to inspect are on any premises and that their inspection is likely to disclose evidence of the commission of an offence under this Act; or
      (ii) that any offence under this Act has been, is being or is about to be committed on any premises; and
   (b) is also satisfied either–
      (i) that admission to the premises has been or is likely to be refused and that notice of intention to apply for a warrant under this subsection has been given to the occupier; or
      (ii) that an application for admission, or the giving of such a notice, would defeat the object of the entry or that the premises are unoccupied or that the occupier is temporarily absent and it might defeat the object of the entry to await his return,

the justice may by warrant under his hand, which shall continue in force for a period of one month, authorise an officer of a local weights and measures authority or of a Government department to enter the premises, if need be by force.

In the application of this subsection to Scotland, 'justice of the peace' shall be construed as including a sheriff and a magistrate.

(4) An officer entering any premises by virtue of this section may take with him such other persons and such equipment as may appear to him necessary; and on leaving any premises which he has entered by virtue of a warrant under the preceding subsection he shall, if the premises are unoccupied or the occupier is temporarily absent, leave them as effectively secured against trespassers as he found them.

(5) If any person discloses to any person–
   (a) any information with respect to any manufacturing process or trade secret obtained by him in premises which he has entered by virtue of this section; or
   (b) any information obtained by him in pursuance of this Act;

he shall be guilty of an offence unless the disclosure was made in or for the purpose of the performance by him or any other person of function under this Act.

(5A) Sub-section (5) of this section does not apply to disclosure for a purpose specified in section 38(2)(a), (b) or (c) of the Consumer Protection Act 1987.

(6) If any person who is not a duly authorised officer of a local weights and measures authority or of a Government department purports, to act as such under this section he shall be guilty of an offence.

(7) Nothing in this section shall be taken to compel the production by a solicitor of a document containing a privileged communication made by or to him in that capacity or to authorise the taking of possession of any such document which is in his possession.

Trade Descriptions Act 1968, s 28, as amended by the Consumer Credit Act 1968, Sched 4 and the Consumer Protection Act 1987, Sched 4.

20.16 SECTION 29: OBSTRUCTION OF AUTHORISED OFFICERS

(1) Any person who–
   (a) wilfully obstructs an officer of a local weights and measures authority or of a Government department acting in pursuance of this Act; or
   (b) wilfully fails to comply with any requirement properly made to him by such an officer under section 28 of this Act; or
   (c) without reasonable cause[a] fails to give such an officer so acting any other assistance or information which he may reasonably require of him for the purpose of the performance of his functions under this Act,

   shall be guilty of an offence and liable, on summary conviction, to a fine not exceeding level 3 on the standard scale.

(2) If any person, in giving any such information as is mentioned in the preceding subsection, makes any statement which he knows to be false, he shall be guilty of an offence.

(3) Nothing in this section shall be construed as requiring a person to answer any question or give any information if to do so might incriminate him.

Trade Descriptions Act 1968, s 29 as amended by the Criminal Justice Act 1982, ss 38 and 46.

20.17 FAILURE TO DISPLAY NAME AND ADDRESS IN A PROMINENT PLACE IN THE BUSINESS PREMISES

Section 4 of the Business Names Act 1985

Need to prove/investigate:

1 Place of offence (within jurisdiction of the court).
2 Date(s) of offence (within six month time limit).
3 Capacity of defendant, for example, limited company, partnership, sole trader, individual.
4 Failure to display correct name and address in prominent place in the business.
5 Premises are defendant's business premises.
6 Suppliers or customers of the business have access to premises.
7 Non compliance is without reasonable excuse.
8 Mitigation/explanation.

---

[a] The cautioning of a suspect at the same time as requiring information to be supplied would amount to a reasonable excuse for non-compliance (*R v Page* (1996) 161 JP 308, [1996] Crim LR 439, CA). The requirement to supply information and the use of that information in criminal; proceedings is not a breach of Human Rights. (*Stott (Procurator Fiscal, Dunfermline) and Another v Brown* [2000] TLR, 6 December.)

Time limit (s 127 of the Magistrates' Court Act 1980): six months.

Mode of trial (s 7): summary.

Maximum penalty (s 18).

Summary: a fine not exceeding one-fifth of the statutory maximum.

20.18 SECTION 1 OF THE BUSINESS NAMES ACT 1985

1 Persons subject to this Act
   (1) This Act applies to any person who has a place of business in Great Britain and who carries on business in Great Britain under a name which–
      (a) in the case of a partnership, does not consist of the surnames of all partners who are individuals and the corporate names of all partners who are bodies corporate without any addition other than an addition permitted by this Act;
      (b) in the case of an individual, does not consist of his surname without any addition other than one so permitted;
      (c) in the case of a company, being a company which is capable of being wound up under the Companies Act 1985, does not consist of its corporate name without any addition other than one so permitted.
   (2) The following are permitted additions for the purposes of subsection (1)–
      (a) in the case of a partnership, the forenames of individual partners or the initials of those forenames or, where two or more individual partners have the same surname, the addition of 's' at the end of that surname; or
      (b) in the case of an individual, his forename or its initial;
      (c) in any case, any addition merely indicating that the business is carried on in succession to a former owner of the business.

2 Prohibition of use of certain business names
   (1) Subject to the following subsections, a person to whom this Act applies shall not, without the written approval of the Secretary of State, carry on business in Great Britain under a name which–
      (a) would be likely to give the impression that the business is connected with Her Majesty's Government with any part of the Scottish Administration, or with any local authority; or
      (b) includes any word or expression for the time being specified in regulations made under this Act.
   (2) Subsection (1) does not apply to the carrying on of a business by a person–
      (a) to whom the business has been transferred on or after 26th February 1982; and
      (b) who carries on the business under the name which was its lawful business name immediately before that transfer,
      during the period of 12 months beginning with the date of that transfer.

(3) Subsection (1) does not apply to the carrying on of a business by a person who–
  (a) carried on that business immediately before 26th February 1982; and
  (b) continues to carry it on under the name which immediately before that date was its lawful business name.
(4) A person who contravenes subsection (1) is guilty of an offence.

3 Words and expressions requiring Secretary of State's approval

(1) The Secretary of State may by regulations –
  (a) specify words or expressions for the use of which as or as part of a business name his approval is required by section 2(1)(b); and
  (b) in relation to any such word or expression, specify a Government department or other body as the relevant body for purposes of the following subsection.
(2) Where a person to whom this Act applies proposes to carry on a business under a name which is or includes any such word or expression, and a Government department or other body is specified under subsection (1)(b) in relation to that word or expression, that person shall–
  (a) request (in writing) the relevant body to indicate whether (and if so why) it has any objections to the proposal; and
  (b) submit to the Secretary of State a statement that such a request has been made and a copy of any response received from the relevant body.

4 Disclosure required of persons using business names

(1) A person to whom this Act applies shall–
  (a) subject to subsection (3), state in legible characters on all business letters, written orders for goods or services to be supplied to the business, invoices and receipts issued in the course of the business and written demands for payment of debts arising in the course of the business–
    (i) in the case of a partnership, the name of each partner;
    (ii) in the case of an individual, his name;
    (iii) in the case of a company, its corporate name; and
    (iv) in relation to each person so named, an address in Great Britain at which service of any document relating in any way to the business will be effective; and
  (b) in any premises where the business is carried on and to which the customers of the business or suppliers of any goods or services to the business have access, display in a prominent position so that it may easily be read by such customers or suppliers a notice containing such names and addresses.
(2) A person to whom this Act applies shall secure that the names and addresses required by subsection (1)(a) to be stated on his business letters, or which would have been so required but for the subsection next following, are immediately given, by written notice to any person with whom anything is done or discussed in the course of the business and who asks for such names and addresses.

(3) Subsection (1)(a) does not apply in relation to any document issued by a partnership of more than 20 persons which maintains at its principal place of business a list of the names of all the partners if–

   (a) none of the names of the partners appears in the document otherwise than in the text or as a signatory; and

   (b) the document states in legible characters the address of the partnership's principal place of business and that the list of the partners' names is open to inspection at that place.

(4) Where a partnership maintains a list of the partners' names for purposes of subsection (3), any person may inspect the list during office hours.

(5) The Secretary of State may by regulations require notices under subsection (1)(b) or (2) to be displayed or given in a specified form.

(6) A person who without reasonable excuse contravenes subsection (1) or (2), or any regulations made under subsection (5), is guilty of an offence.

(7) Where an inspection required by a person in accordance with subsection (4) is refused, any partner of the partnership concerned who without reasonable excuse refused that inspection, or permitted it to be refused, is guilty of an offence.

1 For penalty, see s 7, *post*.

5   Civil remedies for breach of s 4

6   Regulations

Power of Secretary of State to make regulations under ss 3 and 4.

7   Offences

(1) Offences under this Act are punishable on summary conviction.

(2) A person guilty of an offence under this Act is liable to a fine not exceeding one-fifth of the statutory maximum.

(3) If after a person has been convicted summarily of an offence under section 2 or 4(6) the original contravention is continued, he is liable on a second or subsequent summary conviction of the offence to a fine not exceeding one-fiftieth of the statutory maximum for each day on which the contravention is continued (instead of to the penalty which may be imposed on the first conviction of the offence).

(4) Where an offence under section 2 or 4(6) or (7) committed by a body corporate is proved to have been committed with the consent or connivance of, or to be attributable to any neglect on the part of, any director, manager, secretary or other similar officer of the body corporate, or any person who was purporting to act in any such capacity, he as well as the body corporate is guilty of the offence and liable to be proceeded against and punished accordingly.

(5) Where the affairs of a body corporate are managed by its members, subsection (4) applies in relation to the acts and defaults of a member in connection with his functions of management as if he were a director of the body corporate.

(6) For purposes of the following provisions of the Companies Act 1985–

   (a) section 731 (summary proceedings under the Companies Acts), and

(b) section 732(3)(legal professional privilege),

this Act is to be treated as included in those Acts.

8 Interpretation

(1) The following definitions apply for purposes of this Act–

'business' includes a profession;

'initial' includes any recognised abbreviation of a name;

'lawful business name', in relation to a business, means a name under which the business was carried on without contravening section 2(1) of this Act or section 2 of the Registration of Business Names Act 1916;

'local authority' means any local authority within the meaning of the Local Government Act 1972 or the Local Government (Scotland) Act 1973, the Common Council of the City of London or the Council of the Isles of Scilly;

'partnership' includes a foreign partnership;

and 'surname', in relation to a peer or person usually known by a British title different from his surname, means the title by which he is known.

(2) Any expression used in this Act and also in the Companies Act 1985 has the same meaning in this Act as in that.

Business Names Act 1985, s 8 as amended by the Statute Law (Repeals) Act 1993, Sched 1.

20.19 CONDUCTING A MOCK AUCTION

Section 1 of the Mock Auctions Act 1961

Need to prove/investigate:

1 Place of offence (within jurisdiction of the court).
2 Date(s) of offence.
3 Capacity of defendant, for example, limited company, partnership, sole trader, individual.
4 Correct name and identity of defendant.
5 Promoting, conducting or assisting a mock auction.
6 Sale by competitive bidding as defined in s 1(3) and s 3(1).
7 Sale relates to goods.
8 Goods are 'one or more lots to which this Act applies' as defined in s 3(2).
9 Section 1(4) exception does not apply.
10 Mitigation/explanation.

Time limit: none

Mode of trial: either way.

Maximum penalty (s 1).

Summary: statutory maximum and/or three months.

Either way: fine and/or two years.

20.20 MOCK AUCTIONS ACT 1961

1 Penalties for promoting or conducting mock auctions

(1) It shall be an offence to promote or conduct, or to assist in the conduct of, a mock auction at which one or more lots to which this Act applies are offered for sale.

(2) Any person guilty of an offence under this Act shall be liable–

  (a) on summary conviction to a fine not exceeding the statutory maximum, or to imprisonment for a term not exceeding three months, or to both such a fine and such imprisonment;

  (b) on conviction on indictment, to a fine or to imprisonment for a term not exceeding two years, or to both such a fine and such imprisonment.

(3) Subject to the following provisions of this section, for the purposes of this Act a sale of goods by way of competitive bidding shall be taken to be a mock auction if, but only if, during the course of the sale–

  (a) any lot to which this Act applies is sold to a person bidding for it, and either it is sold to him at a price lower than the amount of his highest bid for that lot, or part of the price at which it is sold to him is repaid or credited to him or is stated to be so repaid or credited; or

  (b) the right to bid for any lot to which this Act applies is restricted, or is stated4 to be restricted, to persons who have bought or agreed to buy one or more articles; or

  (c) any articles are given away or offered as gifts.

(4) A sale of goods shall not be taken to be a mock auction by virtue of paragraph (a) of the last preceding subsection, if it is proved that the reduction in price, or the repayment or credit, as the case may be–

  (a) was on account of a defect discovered after the highest bid in question had been made, being a defect of which the person conducting the sale was unaware when that bid was made; or

  (b) was on account of damage sustained after that bid was made.

Mock Auctions Act 1961, s 1, as amended by the Criminal Law Act 1977, ss 28 and 32.

2 Offences by bodies corporate

Where an offence punishable under this Act which has been committed by a body corporate is proved to have been committed with the consent or connivance or to be attributable to any neglect on the part of any director, manager, secretary or other similar officer of the body corporate or any person purporting to act in such capacity, he, as well as the body corporate, shall be deemed to be guilty of that offence and shall be liable to be proceeded against and punished accordingly.

3 Interpretation

(1) In this Act 'sale of goods by way of competitive bidding' means any sale of goods at which the persons present, or some of them, are invited to buy articles by way of competitive bidding, and 'competitive bidding' includes any mode of sale whereby prospective purchasers may be enabled to compete for the purchase of articles whether by way of increasing bids or by the offer of articles to be bid for at successively decreasing prices or otherwise.

(2) In this Act 'lot to which this Act applies' means a lot consisting of or including one or more prescribed articles; and 'prescribed articles' means any plate, plated articles, linen, china, glass, books, pictures, prints, furniture, jewellery, articles of household or personal use or ornament or any musical or scientific instrument or apparatus.

(3) In this Act 'stated', in relation to a sale of goods by way of competitive bidding, means stated by or on behalf of the person conducting the sale, by an announcement made to the persons for the time being present at the sale.

(4) For the purposes of this Act any bid stated to have been made at a sale of goods by way of competitive bidding shall be conclusively presumed to have been made, and to have been a bid of the amount stated; and any reference in this Act to the sale of a lot to a person who has made a bid for it includes a reference to a purported sale thereof to a person stated to have bid for it, whether that person exists or not.

(5) For the purposes of this Act anything done in or about the place where a sale of goods by way of competitive bidding is held, if done in connection with the sale, shall be taken to be done during the course of the sale, whether it is done at the time when any articles are being sold or offered for sale by way of competitive bidding or before or after any such time.

(6) Subject to the provisions of s 33 of the Interpretation Act 1889 (which relates to offences under two or more laws), nothing in this Act shall derogate from any right of action or other remedy (whether civil or criminal) in proceedings instituted otherwise than under this Act.

20.21 MISLEADING PRICE INDICATIONS

Section 20 of the Consumer Protection Act 1987

Need to prove/investigate:

1 Place of offence (within jurisdiction of the court).
2 Date(s) of offence (within s 20(5) time limit).
3 Capacity of defendant, for example, limited company, partnership, sole trader, individual.

4 In the course of a trade or business.(a)
5 In the course of the defendant's trade or business.
6 Indication is misleading(b) (see s 21 definition).
7 Indication relates to the price at which any goods, services, accommodation or facilities are available.
8 Indication is given by the defendant.
9 Indication is given to consumers (see s 20(6) definition).
10 Section 24 defence.
11 Section 39 defence of due diligence.(c)
12 Mitigation/explanation.

Time limit (s 20(5)): one year commission or three years from discovery whichever is earlier.

Mode of trial: either way.

Maximum penalty (s 20(4)).

Summary: statutory maximum.

Either way: fine.

20.22 CONSUMER PROTECTION ACT 1987

Section 20   Offence of giving misleading indication

(1) Subject to the following provisions of this Part, a person shall be guilty of an offence if, in the course of any business of his, he gives (by any means whatever) to any consumers an indication which is misleading as to the price at which any goods,

---

(a) See footnotes to s 14 of the Trade Descriptions Act 1968 post to the meaning of 'trade or business' in a comparative context.

(b) *MGN Ltd v Northampton CC* CO-686-97, *per* Simon Brown LJ, p 4, seems to recognise that the term misleading is subjective to the consumer and that a price is misleading if only some consumers were justifiably misled: 'It is, I should note sufficient for the prosecutor's purpose to establish that some readers might reasonably interpret the advertisement as an indication that watches are being sold elsewhere at a price approximating to their stated value, even though many more readers might, in fact take a contrary view.'

(c) The due diligence defence is to be found in a number of regulatory statutes. 'Reasonable precautions' involves setting up a system to ensure that things will not go wrong while 'due diligence' means seeing that the system works properly – as defined by WH Thomas, solicitor, in the article entitled 'Food safety' (1990) 31 LSG, 5 September. The wording of the statute is such that it is for the defendant to establish both limbs for the defence to be made out. The extent of the measures required to satisfy the defence will normally depend on the size and resources of the defendant. *Garrett v Boots the Chemist* (1980) 16 July, unreported, *per* Lane LCJ, 'of course I scarcely need to say that every case will vary in its facts, what might be reasonable for a large retailer might not be reasonable for a village shop'. An employer may point to the default of a senior manager as his defence if all reasonable precautions have been taken as to the selection and training of that person, there is a proper system of due diligence in place and there is adequate supervision to ensure the system is carried out (*Tesco Supermarkets Ltd v Nattrass* [1972] AC 153, [1971] 2 All ER 127).

services, accommodation or facilities are available (whether generally or from particular persons).

(2) Subject as aforesaid, a person shall be guilty of an offence if–
   (a) in the course of any business of his, he has given an indication to any consumers which, after it was given, has become misleading as mentioned in subsection (1) above; and
   (b) some or all of those consumers might reasonably be expected to rely on the indication at a time after it has become misleading; and
   (c) he fails to take all such steps as are reasonable to prevent those consumers from relying on the indication.

(3) For the purposes of this section it shall be immaterial–
   (a) whether the person who gives or gave the indication is or was acting on his own behalf or on behalf of another;
   (b) whether or not that person is the person, or included among the persons, from whom the goods, services, accommodation or facilities are available; and
   (c) whether the indication is or has become misleading in relation to all the consumers to whom it is or was given or only in relation to some of them.

(4) A person guilty of an offence under subsection (1) or (2) above shall be liable–
   (a) on conviction on indictment, to a fine;
   (b) on summary conviction, to a fine not exceeding the statutory maximum.

(5) No prosecution for an offence under subsection (1) or (2) above shall be brought after whichever is the earlier of the following, that is to say–
   (a) the end of the period of three years beginning with the day on which the offence was committed; and
   (b) the end of the period of one year beginning with the day on which the person bringing the prosecution discovered that the offence had been committed.

(6) In this Part–
   'consumer'–
   (a) in relation to any goods, means any person who might wish to be supplied with the goods for his own private use or consumption;
   (b) in relation to any services or facilities, means any person who might wish to be provided with the services or facilities otherwise than for the purposes of any business of his; and
   (c) in relation to any accommodation, means any person who might wish to occupy the accommodation otherwise than for the purposes of any business of his;
   'price', in relation to any goods, services, accommodation or facilities, means–
   (a) the aggregate of the sums required to be paid by a consumer for or otherwise in respect of the supply of the goods or the provision of the services, accommodation or facilities; or
   (b) except in section 21 below, any method which will be or has been applied for the purpose of determining that aggregate.

Section 21: Meaning of 'misleading'

(1) For the purposes of section 20 above an indication given to any consumers is misleading as to a price if what is conveyed by the indication, or what those consumers might reasonably be expected to infer from the indication or any omission from it, includes any of the following, that is to say–

   (a) that the price is less than in fact it is;

   (b) that the applicability of the price does not depend on facts or circumstances on which its applicability does in fact depend;

   (c) that the price covers matters in respect of which an additional charge is in fact made;

   (d) that a person who in fact has no such expectation–

   (i) expects the price to be increased or reduced (whether or not at a particular time or by a particular amount); or

   (ii) expects the price, or the price as increased or reduced, to be maintained (whether or not for a particular period); or

   (e) that the facts or circumstances by reference to which the consumers might reasonably be expected to judge the validity of any relevant comparison made or implied by the indiction are not what in fact they are.

(2) For the purposes of section 20 above, an indication given to any consumers is misleading as to a method of determining a price if what is conveyed by the indication, or what those consumers might reasonably be expected to infer from the indication or any omission from it, includes any of the following, that is to say–

   (a) that the method is not what in fact it is;

   (b) that the applicability of the method does not depend on facts or circumstances on which its applicability does in fact depend;

   (c) that the method takes into account matters in respect of which an additional charge will in fact be made;

   (d) that a person who in fact has no such expectation–

   (i) expects the method to be altered (whether or not at a particular time or in a particular respect); or

   (ii) expects the method, or that method as altered, to remain unaltered (whether or not for a particular period); or

   (e) that the facts or circumstances by reference to which the consumers might reasonably be expected to judge the validity of any relevant comparison made or implied by the indication are not what in fact they are.

(3) For the purposes of subsections (1)(e) and (2)(e) above a comparison is a relevant comparison in relation to a price or method of determining a price if it is made between that price or that method, or any price which has been or may be determined by that method, and–

   (a) any price or value which is stated or implied to be, to have been or to be likely to be attributed or attributable to the goods, services, accommodation or facilities in question or to any other goods, services, accommodation or facilities; or

   (b) any method, or other method, which is stated or implied to be, to have been or to be likely to be applied or applicable for the determination of the price or value of the goods, services, accommodation or facilities in question or of the price or value of any other goods, services, accommodation or facilities.

Section 24: defences

(1) In any proceedings against a person for an offence under subsection (1) or (2) of section 20 above in respect of any indication it shall be a defence for that person to show that his acts or omissions were authorised for the purposes of this subsection by regulations made under section 26 below.

(2) In proceedings against a person for an offence under subsection (1) or (2) of section 20 above in respect of an indication published in a book, newspaper, magazine or film or in a programme included in a programme service (within the meaning of the Broadcasting Act 1990), it shall be a defence for that person to show that the indication was not contained in an advertisement.

(3) In proceedings against a person for an offence under subsection (1) or (2) of section 20 above in respect of an indication published in an advertisement it shall be a defence for that person to show that–
   (a) he is a person who carries on a business of publishing or arranging for the publication of advertisements;
   (b) he received the advertisement for publication in the ordinary course of that business; and
   (c) at the time of publication he did not know and had no grounds for suspecting that the publication would involve the commission of the offence.

(4) In any proceedings against a person for an offence under subsection (1) of section 20 above in respect of any indication, it shall be a defence for that person to show that–
   (a) the indication did not relate to the availability from him of any goods, services, accommodation or facilities;
   (b) a price had been recommended to every person from whom the goods, services, accommodation or facilities were indicated as being available;
   (c) the indication related to that price and was misleading as to that price only by reason of a failure by any person to follow the recommendation; and
   (d) it was reasonable for the person who gave the indication to assume that the recommendation was for the most part being followed.

(5) The provisions of this section are without prejudice to the provisions of section 39 below.

(6) In this section–

'advertisement' includes a catalogue, a circular and a price list.

Consumer Protection Act 1987, s 24 as amended by the Broadcasting Act 1990, Scheds 20 and 21.

Section 39: defence of due diligence

(1) Subject to the following provisions of this section, in proceedings against any person for an offence to which this section applies it shall be a defence for that person to show that he took all reasonable steps and exercised all due diligence to avoid committing the offence.

(2) Where in any proceedings against any person for such an offence the defence provided by subsection (1) above involves an allegation that the commission of the offence was due–

   (a) to the act or default of another; or

   (b) to reliance on information given by another,

   that person shall not, without the leave of the court, be entitled to rely on the defence unless, not less than seven clear days before the hearing of the proceedings, he has served a notice under subsection (3) below on the person bringing the proceedings.

(3) A notice under this subsection shall give such information identifying or assisting in the identification of the person who committed the act or default or gave the information as is in the possession of the person serving the notice at the time he serves it.

(4) It is hereby declared that a person shall not be entitled to rely on the defence provided by subsection (1) above by reason of his reliance on information supplied by another, unless he shows that it was reasonable in all the circumstances for him to have relied on the information, having regard in particular–

   (a) to the steps which he took, and those which might reasonably have been taken, for the purpose of verifying the information; and

   (b) to whether he had any reason to disbelieve the information.

(5) This section shall apply to an offence under section 10, 12(1),(2) or (3), 13(4), 14(6) or 20(1) above.

Section 40: liability of persons other than principal offender

(1) Where the commission by any person of an offence to which section 39 above applies is due to an act or default committed by some other person in the course of any business of his, the other person shall be guilty of the offence and may be proceeded against and punished by virtue of this subsection whether or not proceedings are taken against the first-mentioned person.

(2) Where a body corporate is guilty of an offence under this Act (including where it is so guilty by virtue of subsection (1) above) in respect of any act or default which is shown to have been committed with the consent or connivance of, or to be attributable to any neglect on the part of, any director, manager, secretary or other similar officer of the body corporate or any person who was purporting to act in any such capacity he, as well as the body corporate, shall be guilty of that offence and shall be liable to be proceeded against and punished accordingly.

(3) Where the affairs of a body corporate are managed by its members, subsection (2) above shall apply in relation to the acts and defaults of a member in connection with his functions of management as if he were a director of the body corporate.

20.23 REQUIREMENTS AS TO BROCHURES

Regulation 5 Package Travel, Package Holidays and Package Tours Regulations 1992

Need to prove/investigate:

1. Place of offence (within jurisdiction of the court).
2. Date(s) of offence.
3. Capacity of defendant, for example, limited company, partnership, sole trader, individual.
4. Defendant is an organiser (see reg 2 definition).
5. Lack of price and adequate information about the matters specified in Sched 1 or said information not legible, comprehensible and accurate
6. Information etc is relevant to the package offered.
7. Brochure is made available to a possible consumer (see reg 2 definition).
8. Due diligence defence.
9. Mitigation/explanation.

Time limit (reg 26): one year commission or three years from discovery whichever is earlier.

Mode of trial: either way.

Maximum penalty (s 18).

Summary: statutory maximum.

Either way: fine and/or two years

20.24 PACKAGE TRAVEL, PACKAGE HOLIDAYS AND PACKAGE TOURS REGULATIONS 1992 SI 1992/3288, AMENDED BY SI 1995/1648 AND SI 1998/1208

1. **Citation and commencement**
2. **Interpretation**

    (1) In these Regulations–

    'brochure' means any brochure in which packages are offered for sale;

    'contract' means the agreement linking the consumer to the organiser or to the retailer, or to both, as the case may be;

    'the Directive' means Council Directive 90/314/EEC on package travel, package holidays and package tours;

    'member state' means a member state of the European Community or another state in the European Economic Area;

    'offer' includes an invitation to treat whether by means of advertising or otherwise, and cognate expressions shall be construed accordingly;

'organiser' means the person who, otherwise than occasionally, organises packages and sells or offers them for sale, whether directly or through a retailer;

'the other party to the contract' means the party, other than the consumer, to the contract, that is, the organiser or the retailer, or both, as the case may be;

'package' means the pre-arranged combination of at least two of the following components when sold or offered for sale at an inclusive price and when the service covers a period of more than twenty-four hours or includes overnight accommodation:–

- (a) transport;
- (b) accommodation;
- (c) other tourist services not ancillary to transport or accommodation and accounting for a significant proportion of the package,

and

- (i) the submission of separate accounts for different components shall not cause the arrangements to be other than a package;
- (ii) the fact that a combination is arranged at the request of the consumer and in accordance with his specific instructions (whether modified or not) shall not of itself cause it to be treated as other than pre-arranged; and

'retailer' means the person who sells or offers for sale the package put together by the organiser.

(2) In the definition of 'contract' in paragraph (1) above, 'consumer' means the person who takes or agrees to take the package ('the principal contractor') and elsewhere in these Regulations 'consumer' means, as the context requires, the principal contractor, any person on whose behalf the principal contractor agrees to purchase the package ('the other beneficiaries') or any person to whom the principal contractor or any of the other beneficiaries transfers the package ('the transferee').

3 Application of Regulations

(1) These Regulations apply to packages sold or offered for sale in the territory of the United Kingdom.

(2) Regulations 4 to 15 apply to packages so sold or offered for sale on or after 31st December 1992.

(3) Regulations 16 to 22 apply to contracts which, in whole or part, remain to be performed on 31st December 1992.

4 Descriptive matter relating to packages must not be misleading

(1) No organiser or retailer shall supply to a consumer any descriptive matter concerning a package, the price of a package or any other conditions applying to the contract which contains any misleading information.

(2) If an organiser or retailer is in breach of paragraph (1) he shall be liable to compensate the consumer for any loss which the consumer suffers in consequence.

5 Requirements as to brochures

(1) Subject to paragraph (4) below, no organiser shall make available a brochure to a possible consumer unless it indicates in a legible, comprehensible and accurate manner the price and adequate information about the matters specified in Schedule 1 to these Regulations in respect of the packages offered for sale in the brochure to the extent that those matters are relevant to the packages so offered.

(2) Subject to paragraph (4) below, no retailer shall make available to a possible consumer a brochure which he knows or has reasonable cause to believe does not comply with the requirements of paragraph (1).

(3) An organiser who contravenes paragraph (1) of this regulation and a retailer who contravenes paragraph (2) thereof shall be guilty of an offence and liable:-

    (a) on summary conviction, to a fine not exceeding level 5 on the standard scale; and

    (b) on conviction on indictment, to a fine.

(4) Where a brochure was first made available to consumers generally before 31st December 1992 no liability shall arise under this regulation in respect of an identical brochure being made available to a consumer at any time.

6 Circumstances in which particulars in brochure are to be binding

7 Information to be provided before contract is concluded

(1) Before a contract is concluded, the other party to the contract shall provide the intending consumer with the information specified in paragraph (2) below in writing or in some other appropriate form.

(2) The information referred to in paragraph (1) is:-

    (a) general information about passport and visa requirements which apply to nationals of the Member State or States concerned who purchase the package in question, including information about the length of time it is likely to take to obtain the appropriate passports and visas;

    (b) information about health formalities required for the journey and the stay; and

    (c) the arrangements for security for the money paid over and (where applicable) for the repatriation of the consumer in the event of insolvency.

(3) If the intending consumer is not provided with the information required by paragraph (1) in accordance with that paragraph the other party to the contract shall be guilty of an offence and liable:-

    (a) on summary conviction, to a fine not exceeding level 5 on the standard scale; and

    (b) on conviction on indictment, to a fine.

8 Information to be provided in good time

(1) The other party to the contract shall in good time before the start of the journey provide the consumer with the information specified in paragraph (2) below in writing or in some other appropriate form.

(2) The information referred to in paragraph (1) is the following:-

    (a) the times and places of intermediate stops and transport connections and particulars of the place to be occupied by the traveller (for example, cabin or berth on ship, sleeper compartment on train);

    (b) the name, address and telephone number-

        (i) of the representative of the other party to the contract in the locality where the consumer is to stay,

    or, if there is no such representative;

        (ii) of an agency in that locality on whose assistance a consumer in difficulty would be able to call;

or, if there is no such representative or agency, a telephone number or other information which will enable the consumer to contact the other party to the contract during the stay; and

(c) in the case of a journey or stay abroad by a child under the age of 16 on the day when the journey or stay is due to start, information enabling direct contact to be made with the child or the person responsible at the place where he is to stay; and

(d) except where the consumer is required as a term of the contract to take out an insurance policy in order to cover the cost of cancellation by the consumer or the cost of assistance, including repatriation, in the event of accident or illness, information about an insurance policy which the consumer may, if he wishes, take out in respect of the risk of those costs being incurred.

(3) If the consumer is not provided with the information required by paragraph (1) in accordance with that paragraph the other party to the contract shall be guilty of an offence and liable:-

(a) on summary conviction, to a fine not exceeding level 5 on the standard scale; and

(b) on conviction on indictment, to a fine.

9   Contents and form of contract
10 Transfer of bookings
11 Price revision
12 Significant alterations to essential terms
13 Withdrawal by consumer pursuant to regulation 12 and cancellation by organiser
14 Significant proportion of services not provided
15 Liability of other party to the contract for proper performance of obligations under contract
16 Security in event of insolvency-requirements and offences
17 Bonding
18 Bonding where approved body has reserve fund or insurance
19 Insurance
20 Monies in trust
21 Monies in trust where other party to contract is acting otherwise than in the course of business
22 Offences arising from breach of regulations 20 and 21

(1) If the other party to the contract makes a false statement under paragraph (4) of regulation 20 or paragraph (3) of regulation 21 he shall be guilty of an offence.

(2) If the other party to the contract applies monies released to him on the basis of a statement made by him under regulation 21(3)(a) or (c) for a purpose other than that mentioned in the statement he shall be guilty of an offence.

(3) If the other party to the contract is guilty of an offence under paragraph (1) or (2) of this regulation shall be liable-

(a) on summary conviction to a fine not exceeding level 5 on the standard scale; and

(b) on conviction on indictment, to a fine.

23 Enforcement

Schedule 3 to these Regulations (which makes provision about the enforcement of regulations 5, 7, 8, 16 and 22 of these Regulations) shall have effect.

24 Due diligence defence

(1) Subject to the following provisions of this regulation, in proceedings against any person for an offence under regulations 5, 7, 8, 16 or 22 of these Regulations, it shall be a defence for that person to show that he took all reasonable steps and exercised all due diligence to avoid committing the offence.

(2) Where in any proceedings against any person for such an offence the defence provided by paragraph (1) above involves an allegation that the commission of the offence was due–

(a) to the act or default of another; or

(b) to reliance on information given by another,

that person shall not, without the leave of the court, be entitled to rely on the defence unless, not less than seven clear days before the hearing of the proceedings, or, in Scotland, the trial diet, he has served a notice under paragraph (3) below on the person bringing the proceedings.

(3) A notice under this paragraph shall give such information identifying or assisting in the identification of the person who committed the act or default or gave the information as is in the possession of the person serving the notice at the time he serves it.

(4) It is hereby declared that a person shall not be entitled to rely on the defence provided by paragraph (1) above by reason of his reliance on information supplied by another, unless he shows that it was reasonable in all the circumstances for him to have relied on the information, having regard in particular–

(a) to the steps which he took, and those which might reasonably have been taken, for the purpose of verifying the information; and

(b) to whether he had any reason to disbelieve the information.

25 Liability of persons other than principal offender

(1) Where the commission by any person of an offence under regulation 5, 7, 8, 16 or 22 of these Regulations is due to an act or default committed by some other person in the course of any business of his, the other person shall be guilty of the offence and may be proceeded against and punished by virtue of this paragraph whether or not proceedings are taken against the first-mentioned person.

(2) Where a body corporate is guilty of an offence under any of the provisions mentioned in paragraph (1) above (including where it is so guilty by virtue of the said paragraph (1)) in respect of any act or default which is shown to have been committed with the consent or connivance of, or to be attributable to any neglect on the part of, any director, manager, secretary or other similar officer of the body corporate or any person who was purporting to act in any such capacity he, as well as the body corporate, shall be guilty of that offence and shall be liable to be proceeded against and punished accordingly.

(3) Where the affairs of a body corporate are managed by its members, paragraph (2) above shall apply in relation to the acts and defaults of a member in connection with his functions of management as if he were a director of the body corporate.

(4) Where an offence under any of the provisions mentioned in paragraph (1) above committed in Scotland by a Scottish partnership is proved to have been committed with the consent or connivance of, or to be attributable to neglect on the part of, a partner, he (as well as the partnership) is guilty of the offence and liable to be proceeded against and punished accordingly.

(5) On proceedings for an offence under regulation 5 by virtue of paragraph (1) above committed by the making available of a brochure it shall be a defence for the person charged to prove that he is a person whose business it is to publish or arrange for the publication of brochures and that he received the brochure for publication in the ordinary course of business and did not know and had no reason to suspect that its publication would amount to an offence under these Regulations.

26 Prosecution time limit

(1) No proceedings for an offence under regulations 5, 7, 8, 16 or 22 of these Regulations or under paragraphs 5(3), 6 or 7 of Schedule 3 thereto shall be commenced after–

(a) the end of the period of three years beginning within the date of the commission of the offence; or

(b) the end of the period of one year beginning with the date of the discovery of the offence by the prosecutor,

whichever is the earlier.

(2) For the purposes of this regulation a certificate signed by or on behalf of the prosecutor and stating the date on which the offence was discovered by him shall be conclusive evidence of that fact; and a certificate stating that matter and purporting to be so signed shall be treated as so signed unless the contrary is proved.

(3) (Scotland.)

27 Saving for civil consequences

No contract shall be void or unenforceable, and no right of action in civil proceedings in respect of any loss shall arise, by reason only of the commission of an offence under regulations 5, 7, 8, 16 or 22 of these Regulations.

28 Terms implied in contract

SCHEDULE 1

Regulation 5

Information to be included (in addition to the price) in brochures where relevant to packages offered

1   The destination and the means, characteristics and categories of transport used.

2   The type of accommodation, its location, category or degree of comfort and its main features and, where the accommodation is to be provided in a member State, its approval or tourist classification under the rules of that member State.

3   The meals which are included in the package.

4   The itinerary.

5   General information about passport and visa requirements which apply for nationals of the Member State or States in which the brochure is made available and health formalities required for the journey and the stay.

6   Either the monetary amount or the percentage of the price which is to be paid on account and the timetable for payment of the balance.

7   Whether a minimum number of persons is required for the package to take place and, if so, the deadline for informing the consumer in the event of cancellation.

8   The arrangements (if any) which apply if consumers are delayed at the outward or homeward points of departure.

9   The arrangements for security for money paid over and for the repatriation of the consumer in the event of insolvency.

SCHEDULE 2

Regulation 9

Elements to be included in the contract if relevant to the particular package

SCHEDULE 3

Enforcement

Regulation 23

Enforcement authority

1

(1) Every local weights and measures authority in Great Britain shall be an enforcement authority for the purposes of regulations 5, 7, 8, 16 and 22 of these Regulations ('the relevant regulations'), and it shall be the duty of each such authority to enforce those provisions within their area.

(2) The Department of Economic Development in Northern Ireland shall be an enforcement authority for the purposes of the relevant regulations, and it shall be the duty of the Department to enforce those provisions within Northern Ireland.

Prosecutions

2

(1) Where an enforcement authority in England or Wales proposes to institute proceedings for an offence under any of the relevant regulations, it shall as between the enforcement authority and the Director General of Fair Trading be the duty of the enforcement authority to give to the Director General of Fair Trading notice of the intended proceedings, together with a summary of the facts on which the charges are to be founded, and to postpone institution of the proceedings until either–

  (a) twenty-eight days have elapsed since the giving of that notice; or

  (b) the Director General of Fair Trading has notified the enforcement authority that he has received the notice and the summary of the facts.

(2) Nothing in paragraph 1 above shall authorise a local weights and measures authority to bring proceedings in Scotland for an offence.

Powers of officers of enforcement authority

3

(1) If a duly authorised officer of an enforcement authority has reasonable grounds for suspecting that an offence has been committed under any of the relevant regulations, he may–
   (a) require a person whom he believes on reasonable grounds to be engaged in the organisation or retailing of packages to produce any book or document relating to the activity and take copies of it or any entry in it, or
   (b) require such a person to produce in a visible and legible documentary form any information so relating which is contained in a computer, and take copies of it,
   for the purpose of ascertaining whether such an offence has been committed.

(2) Such an officer may inspect any goods for the purpose of ascertaining whether such an offence has been committed.

(3) If such an officer has reasonable grounds for believing that any documents or goods may be required as evidence in proceedings for such an offence, he may seize and detain them.

(4) An officer seizing any documents or goods in the exercise of his power under sub-paragraph (3) above shall inform the person from whom they are seized.

(5) The powers of an officer under this paragraph may be exercised by him only at a reasonable hour and on production (if required) of his credentials.

(6) Nothing in this paragraph–
   (a) requires a person to produce a document if he would be entitled to refuse to produce it in proceedings in a court on the ground that it is the subject of legal professional privilege or, in Scotland, that it contains a confidential communication made by or to an advocate or a solicitor in that capacity; or
   (b) authorises the taking possession of a document which is in the possession of a person who would be so entitled.

4

(1) A duly authorised officer of an enforcement authority may, at a reasonable hour and on production (if required) of his credentials, enter any premises for the purpose of ascertaining whether an offence under any of the relevant regulations has been committed.

(2) If a justice of the peace, or in Scotland a justice of the peace or a sheriff, is satisfied–
   (a) that any relevant books, documents or goods are on, or that any relevant information contained in a computer is available from, any premises, and that production or inspection is likely to disclose the commission of an offence under the relevant regulations; or
   (b) that any such an offence has been, is being or is about to be committed on any premises.
   and that any of the conditions specified in sub-paragraph (3) below is met, he may by warrant under his hand authorise an officer of an enforcement authority to enter the premises, if need be by force.

(3) The conditions referred to in sub-paragraph (2) above are–
   (a) that admission to the premises has been or is likely to be refused and that notice of intention to apply for a warrant under that sub-paragraph has been given to the occupier;
   (b) that an application for admission, or the giving of such a notice, would defeat the object of the entry;
   (c) that the premises are unoccupied; and
   (d) that the occupier is temporarily absent and it might defeat the object of the entry to await his return.

(4) In sub-paragraph (2) above 'relevant', in relation to books, documents, goods or information, means books, documents, goods or information which, under paragraph 3 above, a duly authorised officer may require to be produced or may inspect.

(5) A warrant under sub-paragraph (2) above may be issued only if–
   (a) in England and Wales, the justice of the peace is satisfied as required by that sub-paragraph by written information on oath;
   (b) in Scotland, the justice of the peace or sheriff is so satisfied by evidence on oath; or
   (c) in Northern Ireland, the justice of the peace is so satisfied by complaint on oath.

(6) A warrant under sub-paragraph (2) above shall continue in force for a period of one month.

(7) An officer entering any premises by virtue of this paragraph may take with him such other persons as may appear to him necessary.

(8) On leaving premises which he has entered by virtue of a warrant under sub-paragraph (2) above, an officer shall, if the premises are unoccupied or the occupier is temporarily absent, leave the premises as effectively secured against trespassers as he found them.

(9) In this paragraph 'premises' includes any place (including any vehicle, ship or aircraft) except premises used only as a dwelling.

Obstruction of officers

5

(1) A person who–
   (a) intentionally obstructs an officer of an enforcement authority acting in pursuance of this Schedule;
   (b) without reasonable excuse fails to comply with a requirement made of him by such an officer under paragraph 3(1) above; or
   (c) without reasonable excuse fails to give an officer of an enforcement authority acting in pursuance of this Schedule any other assistance or information which the officer may reasonably require of him for the purpose of the performance of the officer's functions under this Schedule,

shall be guilty of an offence.

(2) A person guilty of an offence under sub-paragraph (1) above shall be liable on summary conviction to a fine not exceeding level 5 on the standard scale.

(3) If a person, in giving any such information as is mentioned in sub-paragraph (1)(c) above–

(a) makes a statement which he knows is false in a material particular; or
(b) recklessly makes a statement which is false in a material particular,
he shall be guilty of an offence.

(4) A person guilty of an offence under sub-paragraph (3) above shall be liable–
   (a) on summary conviction, to a fine not exceeding level 5 on the standard scale; and
   (b) on conviction on indictment, to a fine.

Impersonation of officers

6

(1) If a person who is not a duly authorised officer of an enforcement authority purports to act as such under this Schedule he shall be guilty of an offence.

(2) A person guilty of an offence under sub-paragraph (1) above shall be liable–
   (a) on summary conviction, to a fine not exceeding level 5 on the standard scale; and
   (b) on conviction on indictment, to a fine.

Disclosure of information

7

(1) If a person discloses to another any information obtained by him by virtue of this Schedule he shall be guilty of an offence unless the disclosure was made–
   (a) in or for the purpose of the performance by him or any other person of any function under the relevant regulations; or
   (b) for a purpose specified in section 38(2)(a), (b) or (c) of the Consumer Protection Act 1987.

(2) A person guilty of an offence under sub-paragraph (1) above shall be liable–
   (a) on summary conviction, to a fine not exceeding level 5 on the standard scale; and
   (b) on conviction on indictment, to a fine.

Privilege against self-incrimination

8

Nothing in this Schedule requires a person to answer any question or give any information if to do so might incriminate him.

(See *R v Page* (1996) 161 JP 308, [1996] Crim LR 439, CA.) The cautioning of a suspect at the same time as requiring information to be supplied would amount to a reasonable excuse for non compliance. The requirement to supply information and the use of that information in criminal; proceedings is not a breach of human rights. (*Stott (Procurator Fiscal, Dunfermline) and Another v Brown* (2000) TLR, 6 December.)

20.25 OFFERING OR AGREEING TO SUPPLY A DANGEROUS PRODUCT

Regulation 13 of the General Product Safety Regulations 1994

Need to prove/investigate:
1 Place of offence (within jurisdiction of the court).
2 Date(s) of offence (within reg 16 time limit).
3 Capacity of defendant, for example, limited company, partnership, sole trader, individual.
4 Offer or agree to supply or expose or possess for supply.
5 Defendant is a producer or distributor.
6 Dangerous product.
7 Regulation 14, due diligence defence.
8 Product is not second hand or other item described in reg 3.
9 Compliance with reg 10 standard.
10 Mitigation/explanation.

Time limit (reg 16): 12 months.

Mode of trial: summary.

Maximum penalty (reg 17).

Summary: three months and/or level 5.

20.26 GENERAL PRODUCT SAFETY REGULATIONS 1994

Citation and commencement

1 Made by the Secretary of State, in exercise of the powers conferred on him by s 2(2) of the European Communities Act 1972.

Interpretation

(1) In these Regulations–

'the 1968 Act' means the Medicines Act 1968;

'the 1987 Act' means the Consumer Protection Act 1987;

'the 1990 Act' means the Food Safety Act 1990;

'commercial activity' includes a business and a trade;

'consumer' means a consumer acting otherwise than in the course of a commercial activity;

'dangerous product' means any product other than a safe product;

'distributor' means any professional in the supply chain whose activity does not affect the safety properties of a product;

'enforcement authority' means the Secretary of State, any other Minister of the Crown in charge of a Government Department, any such department and any authority, council and other person on whom functions under these Regulations are imposed by or under regulation 11;

'general safety requirement' means the requirement in regulation 7;

'the GPS Directive' means Council Directive 92/59/EEC on general product safety;

'the 1991 Order' means the Food Safety (Northern Ireland) Order 1991;

'producer' means–

(a) the manufacturer of the product, when he is established in the Community, and includes any person presenting himself as the manufacturer by affixing to the product his name, trade mark or other distinctive mark, or the person who reconditions the product;

(b) when the manufacturer is not established in the Community–

   (i) if the manufacturer does not have a representative established in the Community, the importer of the product;

   (ii) in all other cases, the manufacturer's representative; and

(c) other professionals in the supply chain, in so far as their activities may affect the safety properties of a product placed on the market;

'product' means any product intended for consumers or likely to be used by consumers, supplied whether for consideration or not in the course of a commercial activity and whether new, used or reconditioned; provided, however, a product which is used exclusively in the context of a commercial activity even if it is used for or by a consumer shall not be regarded as a product for the purposes of these Regulations provided always and for the avoidance of doubt this exception shall not extend to the supply of such a product to a consumer;

'safe product' means any product which, under normal or reasonably foreseeable conditions of use, including duration, does not present any risk or only the minimum risks compatible with the product's use, considered as acceptable and consistent with a high level of protection for the safety and health of persons, taking into account in particular–

(a) the characteristics of the product, including its composition, packaging, instructions for assembly and maintenance;

(b) the effect on other products, where it is reasonably foreseeable that it will be used with other products;

(c) the presentation of the product, the labelling, any instructions for its use and disposal and any other indication or information provided by the producer; and

(d) the categories of consumers at serious risk when using the product, in particular children,

and the fact that higher levels of safety may be obtained or other products presenting a lesser degree of risk may be available shall not of itself cause the product to be considered other than a safe product.

(2) References in these Regulations to the 'Community' are references to the European Economic Area established under the Agreement signed at Oporto on 2nd May 1992 as adjusted by the Protocol signed at Brussels on 17th March 1993.

Application and revocation

3

These Regulations do not apply to–

(a) second-hand products which are antiques;

(b) products supplied for repair or reconditioning before use, provided the supplier clearly informs the person to whom he supplies the product to that effect; or

(c) any product where there are specific provisions in rules of Community law governing all aspects of the safety of the product.

4

The requirements of these Regulations apply to a product where the product is the subject of provisions of Community law other than the GPS Directive in so far as those provisions do not make specific provision governing an aspect of the safety of the product.

5

For the purposes of these Regulations the provisions of section 10 of the 1987 Act to the extent that they impose general safety requirements which must be complied with if products are to be–

(i) placed on the market, offered or agreed to be placed on the market or exposed or possessed to be placed on the market by producers; or

(ii) supplied, offered or agreed to be supplied or exposed or possessed to be supplied by distributors,

are hereby disapplied.

6

Repeals and revocations

7

General safety requirement

No producer shall place a product on the market unless the product is a safe product.

Requirement as to information

8

(1) within the limits of his activity, a producer shall–
   (a) provide consumers with the relevant information to enable them to assess the risks inherent in a product throughout the normal or reasonably foreseeable period of its use, where such risks are not immediately obvious without adequate warnings, and to take precautions against those risks; and
   (b) adopt measures commensurate with the characteristics of the products which he supplies, to enable him to be informed of the risks which these products might present and to take appropriate action, including, if necessary, withdrawing the product in question from the market to avoid those risks.

(2) The measures referred to in sub-paragraph (b) of paragraph (1) above may include, whenever appropriate–

(i) marking of the products or product batches in such a way that they can be identified;
(ii) sample testing of marketed products;
(iii) investigating complaints; and
(iv) keeping distributors informed of such monitoring.

Requirements of distributors

9

A distributor shall act with due care in order to help ensure compliance with the requirements of regulation 7 above and, in particular, without limiting the generality of the foregoing–

(a) a distributor shall not supply products to any person which he knows, or should have presumed, on the basis of the information in his possession and as a professional, are dangerous products; and

(b) within the limits of his activities, a distributor shall participate in monitoring the safety of products placed on the market, in particular by passing on information on the product risks and cooperating in the action taken to avoid those risks.

Presumption of conformity and product assessment

10

(1) Where in relation to any product such product conforms to the specific rules of the law of the United Kingdom laying down the health and safety requirements which the product must satisfy in order to be marketed there shall be a presumption that, until the contrary is proved, the product is a safe product.

(2) Where no specific rules as are mentioned or referred to in paragraph (1) exist, the conformity of a product to the general safety requirement shall be assessed taking into account–

(i) voluntary national standards of the United Kingdom giving effect to a European standard; or
(ii) Community technical specifications; or
(iii) if there are no such voluntary national standards of the United Kingdom or Community technical specifications–

(aa) standards drawn up in the United Kingdom; or
(bb) the codes of good practice in respect of health and safety in the product sector concerned; or
(cc) the state of the art and technology,

and the safety which consumers may reasonably expect.

Enforcement

11

For the purposes of providing for the enforcement of these Regulations–

(a) section 13 of the 1987 Act (prohibition notices and notices to warn) shall (to the extent that it does not already do so) apply to products as it applies to relevant goods under that section;

(b) the requirements of these Regulations shall constitute safety provisions for the purposes of sections 14 (suspension notices), 15 (appeals against suspension notices), 16 (forfeiture: England, Wales and Northern Ireland), 17 (forfeiture: Scotland) and 18 (power to obtain information) of the 1987 Act;

(c)(i) subject to paragraph (ii) below a weights and measures authority in Great Britain and a district council in Northern Ireland shall have the same duty to enforce these Regulations as they have in relation to Part II of the 1987 Act, and Part IV, sections 37 and 38 and subsections (3) and (4) of section 42 of that Act shall apply accordingly;

    (ii) without prejudice to the provisions of paragraphs (a) and (b) above and sub-paragraph (i) above, in so far as these Regulations apply:–

        (aa) to products licensed in accordance with the provisions of the 1968 Act, it shall be the duty of the enforcement authority as defined in section 132(1) of the 1968 Act to enforce or to secure the enforcement of these Regulations and sections 108 to 115 and section 119 of and Schedule 3 to that Act shall apply accordingly as if these Regulations were regulations made under the said Act;

        (bb) in relation to food within the meaning of section 1 of the 1990 Act, it shall be the duty of each food authority as defined in section 5 of the 1990 Act to enforce or to secure the enforcement of these Regulations, within its area, in Great Britain and sections 9, 29, 30 and 32 of that Act shall apply accordingly as if these Regulations were food safety requirements made under the said Act and section 10 of that Act shall apply as if these Regulations were regulations made under Part II of that Act; and

        (cc) in relation to food within the meaning of article 2 of the 1991 Order, it shall be the duty of the relevant enforcement authority as provided for in article 26 of that Order to enforce or to secure enforcement of these Regulations in Northern Ireland and articles 8, 29, 30, 31 and 33 of that Order shall apply accordingly as if these Regulations were food safety requirements made under that Order and article 9 of that Order shall apply as if these Regulations were regulations made under Part II of that Order;

(d) in section 13(4) and 14(6) of the 1987 Act for the words 'six months' there shall be substituted 'three months'; and

(e) nothing in this regulation shall authorise any enforcement authority to bring proceedings in Scotland for an offence.

Offences and preparatory acts

12

Any person who contravenes regulation 7 or 9(a) shall be guilty of an offence.

13

No producer or distributor shall–

(a) offer or agree to place on the market any dangerous product or expose or possess any such product for placing on the market; or

(b) offer or agree to supply any dangerous product or expose or possess any such product for supply,

and any person who contravenes the requirements of this regulation shall be guilty of an offence.

Defence of due diligence

14

(1) Subject to the following paragraphs of this regulation, in proceedings against any person for an offence under these Regulations it shall be a defence for that person to show that he took all reasonable steps and exercised all due diligence to avoid committing the offence.

(2) Where in any proceedings against any person for such an offence the defence provided by paragraph (1) above involves an allegation that the commission of the offence was due–

 (a) to the act or default of another, or

 (b) to reliance on information given by another,

that person shall not, without leave of the court, be entitled to rely on the defence unless, not less than seven days before, in England, Wales and Northern Ireland, the hearing of the proceedings or, in Scotland, the trial diet, he has served a notice under paragraph (3) below on the person bringing the proceedings.

(3) A notice under this paragraph shall give such information identifying or assisting in the identification of the person who committed the act or default or gave the information as is in the possession of the person serving the notice at the time he serves it.

(4) It is hereby declared that a person shall not be entitled to rely on the defence provided in paragraph (1) above by reason of his reliance on information supplied by another, unless he shows that it was reasonable in all the circumstances for him to have relied on the information, having regard in particular–

 (a) to the steps which he took, and those which might reasonably have been taken, for the purpose of verifying the information; and

 (b) to whether he had any reason to disbelieve the information.

(5) It is hereby declared that a person shall not be entitled to rely on the defence provided by paragraph (1) above or by section 39(1) of the 1987 Act (defence of due diligence) if he has contravened regulation 9(b).

Liability of persons other than principal offender

15

(1) Where the commission by any person of an offence to which regulation 14 above applies is due to the act or default committed by some other person in the course of a commercial activity of his, the other person shall be guilty of an offence and may be proceeded against and punished by virtue of this paragraph whether or not proceedings are taken against the first-mentioned person.

(2) Where a body corporate is guilty of an offence under these Regulations (including where it is so guilty by virtue of paragraph (1) above) in respect of any act or default which is shown to have been committed with the consent or connivance of, or to be attributable to any neglect on the part of any director, manager, secretary or other similar officer of the body corporate or any person who was purporting to act in any such capacity he, as well as the body corporate, shall be guilty of that offence and shall be liable to be proceeded against and punished accordingly.

(3) Where the affairs of a body corporate are managed by its members, paragraph (2) above shall apply in relation to the acts and defaults of a member in connection with his functions of management as if he were a director of the body corporate.

(4) Where a Scottish partnership is guilty of an offence under regulation 14 above (including where it is so guilty by virtue of paragraph (1) above) in respect of any act or default which is shown to have been committed with the consent or connivance of, or to be attributable to any neglect on the part of, a partner in the partnership, he, as well as the partnership, shall be guilty of that offence and shall be liable to be proceeded against and punished accordingly.

Extension of the time for bringing summary proceedings

16

(1) Notwithstanding section 127 of the Magistrates' Courts Act 1980 and article 19 of the Magistrates' Courts (Northern Ireland) Order 1981, in England, Wales and Northern Ireland a magistrates' court may try an information (in the case of England and Wales) or a complaint (in the case of Northern Ireland) in respect of proceedings for an offence under regulation 12 or 131 above if (in the case of England and Wales) the information is laid or (in the case of Northern Ireland) the complaint is made within twelve months from the date of the offence.

(2) Notwithstanding section 331 of the Criminal Procedure (Scotland) Act 1975, in Scotland summary proceedings for an offence under regulation 12 or 13 above may be commenced at any time within twelve months from the date of the offence.

(3) For the purposes of paragraph (2) above, section 331(3) of the Criminal Procedure (Scotland) Act 1975 shall apply as it applies for the purposes of that section.

Penalties

17

A person guilty of an offence under regulation 12 or 13 above shall be liable on summary conviction to–

(a) imprisonment for a term not exceeding three months; or

(b) a fine not exceeding level 5 on the standard scale;

or to both.

Duties of enforcement authorities

18

(1) Every enforcement authority shall give immediate notice to the Secretary of State of any action taken by it to prohibit or restrict the supply of any product or forfeit or do any other thing in respect of any product for the purposes of these Regulations.

(2) The requirements of paragraph (1) above shall not apply in the case of any action taken in respect of any second-hand product.

HOUSING BENEFIT AND COUNCIL TAX BENEFIT PROSECUTIONS

21.1 INTRODUCTION

This chapter sets out the following legislation together with relating checklists identifying the elements and other investigatory matters:

1. Section 112 of the Social Security Administration Act (SSAA) 1992 (furnishing a false document).
2. Section 112 of the SSAA 1992 (failing to notify a change in circumstances).
3. Section 111A of the SSAA Act 1992 (dishonestly failing to notify a change in circumstances).
4. Section 111A of the SSAA 1992 (dishonestly furnishing a false document).

21.2 HOUSING BENEFIT AND COUNCIL TAX BENEFIT PROSECUTIONS

Most offences in connection with welfare legislation are likely to be a failure to notify a change in circumstances or a false statement or omission for the purposes of the claim. The breakdowns of the elements of both these offences are set out below. There is an information relating to these proceedings, together with a sample charge under the Theft Act 1968 included at Appendix 2.

21.3 CHOICE OF OFFENCE

The facts of the case tend to dictate the offence that ought to be charged. For welfare legislation, there are other factors that might be worth considering, as follows.

1 Gravity of the offence

The choice of informations should enable the court to have sufficient sentencing powers and reflect the seriousness of the offence. More serious charges may be reserved for allegations involving large sums of money over a long period of time. For such situations, use of s 111A of the SSAA 1992 may be more appropriate, if dishonesty can be proved.

2 Likely cost of the proceedings

Whereas it might not be regarded as fair to deprive a person of trial by jury purely on the question of costs, it should be born in mind that the seriousness of the charge, the availability of legal aid and other factors increase the possibility that crown court trial will be elected by the defendant if this option remains open. Proceedings under s 111A of the

SSAA 1992 are either way offences and, therefore, to avoid unnecessary costs to the public purse, care should be taken to select this option only where it is right and proper to do so.

3 Timing of the offence

The date of the offence or period of offence will often have a bearing on the offence charged. For s 112 of the SSAA 1992 offences, the time period is usually 12 months between commission and laying of the information. Proceedings under s 111A of the Act cannot be charged for offences before 1 July 1997.[a] The local authority may also lay charges under the Theft Act 1968 for very serious offences that predate 1997.[b] There is no time limit for offences under the Theft Act 1968.

4 Technical arguments

Informations alleging failure to notify a change in circumstances may present difficulties in seeking to prove a negative, unless this is admitted at interview. Arguments arising from the definition of a designated office, as discussed in footnote (d) to the s 112 breakdown at para 21.5, remain open to persons charged under this section.

5 Wording of the charge

The legislation gives rise to a number of ways in which a person can be charged. Subject to the particular facts it may be easier to prove 'furnish' rather than 'produced' a document for the reasons referred to in footnote (a) in s 112 immediately below. It might also be easier to prove a false statement in a document which is a permanent record as opposed to a verbal statement.

21.4 SOCIAL SECURITY ADMINISTRATION ACT 1992: FURNISHING A FALSE DOCUMENT (S 112)

Elements of the offence/investigatory matters:
1   A person furnishes[aa] or knowingly[bb] causes or allows to be produced.

(a) *R v Jarret and Steward* (1997) Archbold News, 7 May enables local authorities to take any proceedings that are in the interests of the inhabitants of the borough. For complete security on the issue, authorisation may be sought from the CPS to act as their agent although this should not be necessary.
(b) Section 25(5) of the Social Security Administration (Fraud) Act 1997 and SI 1997/1577 which brought this section into force on 1 July 1997.
(aa) The word 'produce' may be chosen in place of 'furnish' depending on the facts. The word 'produce' suggests that the offender played a substantial part in the making of the document and supplied it to the local authority. However, use of the word 'produce' leaves the door open to potential arguments as to manufacture and supply. Use of the word 'furnish' has a slightly wider, more embracing meaning than the word 'produce', although there is no case law to assist on its precise meaning.
(bb) For detailed authorities on the word 'knowingly', see the standard list of authorities in Appendix 17. Claim forms which require applicants to write 'yes' or 'no' in every box as opposed to ticks and/or blank spaces are more likely to demonstrate that some thought has been given to answering the questions. Claimants who are required to complete applications in this format are less likely to be in a position to claim lack of knowledge.

2   Date and place of alleged offence.[c]
3   A document.[d]
4   For the purpose of obtaining benefit or other payment, etc.
5   Document is false in a material particular.
6   Knowledge.[e]
7   Defence.
8   Mitigation/explanation.

Time limit (s 116): one year commission or three years from receipt of 'sufficient' evidence whichever is later.

Mode of trial: summary.

Maximum penalty (s 112(2)).

Summary: level 5 and/or three months.

21.5 FAILING TO NOTIFY A CHANGE IN CIRCUMSTANCES (S 112 OF THE SSAA 1992)

Elements of the offence/investigatory matters:
1   Change in circumstances.
2   Date and place of alleged offence.[a]
3   A person fails to notify change in circumstances.
4   Reasonable excuse.
5   Regulations which this act requires notification.[b]
6   Knowledge[c] of requirement to notify change of circumstances.

(c) So long as it can be proved that the defendant made the statement it is not necessary to prove the place and date of the information (*DSS v Cooper* (1994) 158 JPN 354).
(d) A claimant could be charged with making a false statement, which is written or oral. By confining the charge to the written word the scope for argument over the actual statement is reduced.
(e) For detailed authorities on the word 'knowingly', see the standard list of authorities in Appendix 17.
(a) So long as it can be proved that the defendant made the statement it is not necessary to prove the place and date of the information (*DSS v Cooper* (1994) 158 JPN 354).
(b) See reg 75 of the Housing Benefit (General) Regulations 1987 SI 1987/1971 and reg 65 of the Council Tax Benefit (General) Regulations 1992 SI 1992/1814.
(c) For detailed authorities on the word 'knowingly', see the standard list of authorities in Appendix 17.

7   Designated office.(d)
8   Defence.
9   Mitigation/explanation.

Time limit (s 116): one year commission or three years from receipt of 'sufficient' evidence whichever is later.

Mode of trial: summary.

Maximum penalty (s 112(2)).

Summary: level 5 and/or three months.

Section 112

(1) If a person for the purpose of obtaining any benefit or other payment under the legislation to which section 110 above applies whether for himself or some other person, or for any other purpose connected with that legislation—

   (a) makes a statement or representation which he knows to be false; or
   (b) produces or furnishes, or knowingly causes or knowingly allows to be produced or furnished, any document or information which he knows to be false in a material particular,

   he shall be guilty of an offence.

(2) A person guilty of an offence under subsection (1) above shall be liable on summary conviction to a fine not exceeding level 5 on the standard scale, or to imprisonment for a term not exceeding 3 months, or to both.

21.6 DISHONESTLY FAILING TO NOTIFY A CHANGE IN CIRCUMSTANCES (S 111A)

1   Change in circumstances.
2   Date and place of alleged offence.(a)
3   A person fails to notify change in circumstances.

(d) This word is defined as 'the office designated by the appropriate authority, by way of notice upon a form approved by them for the purpose of claiming housing benefit, for the receipt of claims to housing benefit' in reg 2 of the Housing Benefit Regulations. Regulation 2 of the Council Tax Regulations has a like definition. On the basis of the above definition it is incumbent on the local authority to specify the designated office on the standard claim form. Ideally, it should use the words 'designated office' although it is doubted that failure to do so would be fatal to the prosecution. This definition is unfortunate in that it gives rise to potential arguments that committee approval of the form is required. Provided that the form has been approved by a person whose authority is sufficiently broad to encompass this function there should be no difficulty. If no such person can be identified the question remains as to whether custom and usage can amount to tacit authority which would suffice or whether this is an element of the offence which requires proof.

(a) So long as it can be proved that the defendant made the statement it is not necessary to prove the place and date of the information. (*DSS v Cooper* (1994) 158 JPN 354.) NB: The offence cannot predate the coming into force of this section on 1 July 1997 (s 25(5) of the Social Security Administration (Fraud) Act 1997 and Commencement Order (SI 1997/1577) for s 13 of the Social Security Admin (Fraud) Act 1997).

Chapter 21: Housing Benefit and Council Tax Benefit Prosecutions

4 Dishonesty.(b)
5 Regulations which this act requires notification.(c)
6 Knowledge(d) of requirement to notify change of circumstances.
7 Designated office.(e)
8 Defence.
9 Mitigation/explanation.

Time limit: none.

Mode of trial: either way.

Maximum penalty (s 111A(3)).

Summary: statutory maximum and/or six months.

Either way: fine and/or seven years.

Dishonestly furnishing a false document (s 111A)

Elements of the offence/investigatory matters:
1 A person furnishes(a) or knowingly(ab) causes or allows to be produced.
2 Date and place of alleged offence.(ac)

(b) For dishonesty it must be proved that the act was dishonest according to the ordinary standards of reasonable and honest people and whether the claimant must have realised that what he was doing was by those standards dishonest (*R v Ghosh* [1982] 2 All ER 689).

(c) See reg 75 of the Housing Benefit (General) Regulations 1987 SI 1987/1971 and reg 65 of the Council Tax Benefit (General) Regulations 1992 SI 1992/1814.

(d) For detailed authorities on the word 'knowingly' see the standard list of authorities at Appendix 17.

(e) This word is defined as 'the office designated by the appropriate authority, by way of notice upon a form approved by them for the purpose of claiming housing benefit, for the receipt of claims to housing benefit' in reg 2 of the Housing Benefit Regulations. Regulation 2 of the Council Tax Regulations has a like definition. On the basis of the above definition it is incumbent on the local authority to specify the designated office on the standard claim form. Ideally, it should use the words 'designated office' although it is doubted that failure to do so would be fatal to the prosecution. This definition is unfortunate in that it gives rise to potential arguments that committee approval of the form is required. Provided that the form has been approved by a person whose authority is sufficiently broad to encompass this function there should be no difficulty. If no such person can be identified the question remains as to whether custom and usage can amount to tacit authority which would suffice or whether this is an element of the offence which requires proof.

(a) The word 'produce' may be chosen in place of 'furnish' depending on the facts. The word 'produce' suggests that the offender played a substantial part in the making of the document and supplied it to the local authority. However, use of the word 'produce' leaves the door open to potential arguments as to manufacture and supply. Use of the word 'furnish' has a slightly wider, more embracing meaning than the word 'produce' although there is no case law to assist on its precise meaning.

(ab) For detailed authorities on the word 'knowingly', see the standard list of authorities in Appendix 17.

(ac) So long as it can be proved that the defendant made the statement it is not necessary to prove the place and date of the information (*DSS v Cooper* (1994) 158 JPN 354). NB: The offence cannot predate the coming into force of this section on 1 July 1997 (s 25(5) of the Social Security Administration (Fraud) Act 1997 and commencement order (SI 1997/1577) for s 13 of the Social Security Administration (Fraud) Act 1997).

3   A document.(d)
4   For the purpose of obtaining benefit or other payment, etc.
5   Document is false in a material particular.
6   Dishonesty.(e)
7   Defence.
8   Mitigation/explanation.

Time limit: none.

Mode of trial: either way.

Maximum penalty (s 111A(3)).

Summary: statutory maximum and/or six months.

Either way: fine and/or seven years.

Section 111A

(1) If a person dishonestly–
   (a) makes a false statement or representation;
   (b) produces or furnishes, or causes or allows to be produced or furnished, any document or information which is false in a material particular;
   (c) fails to notify a change of circumstances which regulations under this Act require him to notify; or
   (d) causes or allows another person to fail to notify a change of circumstances which such regulations require the other person to notify,

   with a view to obtaining any benefit or other payment or advantage under the social security legislation (whether for himself or for some other person), he shall be guilty of an offence.

(2) In this section 'the social security legislation' means the Acts to which section 110 above applies and the Jobseekers Act 1995.

(3) A person guilty of an offence under this section shall be liable–
   (a) on summary conviction, to imprisonment for a term not exceeding six months, or to a fine not exceeding the statutory maximum, or to both; or
   (b) on conviction on indictment, to imprisonment for a term not exceeding seven years, or to a fine, or to both.

(4) In the application of this section to Scotland, in subsection (1) for 'dishonestly' substitute 'knowingly'.

(d) A claimant could be charged with making a false statement, which is written or oral. For detailed authorities on the word knowingly see the standard list of authorities in Appendix 17 confining the charge to the written word the scope for argument over the actual statement is reduced.

(e) For dishonesty it must be proved that the act was dishonest according to the ordinary standards of reasonable and honest people and whether the claimant must have realised that what he was doing was by those standards dishonest (*R v Ghosh* [1982] 2 All ER 689).

LICENSING LEGISLATION

22.1 INTRODUCTION

This chapter sets out the following legislation together with relating checklists identifying the elements and other investigatory matters:

1. Sections 46(1)(a) and 46(2) of the Local Government (Miscellaneous Provisions) Act 1976 (driving a vehicle without a private hire vehicle licence).
2. Section 64 of the Local Government (Miscellaneous Provisions) Act 1976 (parking on a hackney carriage stand).
3. Section 45 of the Town Police Clauses Act 1847 (plying for hire offence without a licence).
4. Schedule 4, para 10, of the Local Government (Miscellaneous Provisions) Act 1982 (street trading).
5. Schedule 1, para 12 of the Local Government (Miscellaneous Provisions) Act 1982 (breach of public entertainment licence condition).
6. Schedule 1, para 12 of the Local Government (Miscellaneous Provisions) Act 1982 (being concerned in the organisation or management of a Public Entertainment Licence (PEL)).
7. Section 73 of the Local Government (Miscellaneous Provisions) Act 1976 (obstruction of an authorised officer).

22.2 SECTIONS 46(1)(A) AND 46(2) OF THE LOCAL GOVERNMENT (MISCELLANEOUS PROVISIONS) ACT 1976 (DRIVING A VEHICLE WITHOUT A PRIVATE HIRE VEHICLE LICENCE)

Elements of the offence/investigatory matters:

1. Place of offence (within jurisdiction of the court).
2. Date(s) of offence (within six months time limit).
3. Defendant is the proprietor of the vehicle.
4. Vehicle is not a hackney carriage or licensed as such.
5. Use or permitted use as a private hire vehicle.
6. Absence of a vehicle licence under s 48 on the date of the allegation.
7. Controlled district.
8. Knowingly contravene the provision.
9. Possibility of statutory exception, for example, adapted for nine passengers or more (s 80(1)) or seven day contract (s 75(1)) (but see s 101 of the Magistrates' Courts Act 1980).
10. Mitigation/explanation from the defendant.

Time limit: six months (s 127 of the Magistrates' Courts Act 1980).

Mode of trial: summary.

Maximum penalty (s 76).

Summary: level 3.

22.3 SECTION 46 OF THE LOCAL GOVERNMENT (MISCELLANEOUS PROVISIONS) ACT 1976 (VEHICLES, DRIVERS AND OPERATORS LICENCES)

Section 46

(1) Except as authorised by this part of the act–
   (a) no person being the proprietor of any vehicle, not being a hackney carriage (or London cab) in respect of which a vehicle licence is in force, shall use or permit the same to be used in a controlled district as a private hire vehicle without having for such a vehicle a current licence under s 48 of this act;
   (b) no person shall in a controlled district act as a driver of any private hire vehicle[a] without having a current licence under s 51 of this act;
   (c) no person being the proprietor of any private hire vehicle licensed under this part of this act shall employ as the driver thereof for the purpose of any hiring any person who does not have a current licence under the said s 51 of this act;
   (d) no person shall in a controlled district operate any vehicle as a private hire vehicle without having a current licence under s 55 of this act;
   (e) no person licensed under the said s 55 shall in a controlled district operate any vehicle as a private hire vehicle–
      (i) if for the vehicle a current licence under the said s 48 is not in force; or
      (ii) if the driver does not have a current licence under the said s 51.

(2) If a person knowingly[b] contravenes the provisions of this section he shall be guilty of an offence.

22.3.1 Section 64 of the Local Government (Miscellaneous Provisions) Act 1976 (parking on a hackney carriage stand)

Elements of the offence/investigatory matters:
1 Full name and address of defendant.
2 Place of offence.
3 Date of offence.

(a) Private hire vehicle is defined in s 80 of the Act and was considered in the case of *Leeds CC v Azam* (1989) LGR, 11 March.
(b) 'Knowingly' is often difficult to prove. For authorities on the subject see the lists of authorities at Appendix 17.

4   Vehicle waited[a] on a hackney carriage stand.[b]
5   Vehicle waited for period of appointment.
6   Defendant was the person who caused the vehicle to wait.
7   Absence of reasonable excuse.
8   Defence.
9   Mitigation/explanation.

Time limit: six months (s 127 of the Magistrates' Courts Act 1980).

Mode of trial: summary.

Maximum penalty (s 76).

Summary: level 3.

Section 64 of the Local Government (Miscellaneous Provisions) Act 1976 (prohibition of other vehicles on hackney carriage stands)

(1) No person shall cause or permit any vehicle other than a hackney carriage to wait on any stand for hackney carriages during any period for which that stand has been appointed, or is deemed to have been appointed, by a district council under the provisions of section 63 of this Act.

(2) Notice of the prohibition in this section shall be indicated by such traffic signs as may be prescribed or authorised for the purpose by the Secretary of State in pursuance of his powers under section 64 of the Road Traffic Regulation Act 1984.

(3) If any person without reasonable excuse contravenes the provisions of this section, he shall be guilty of an offence.[aa]

(4) In any proceedings under this section against the driver of a public service vehicle it shall be a defence to show that, by reason of obstruction to traffic or for other compelling reason, he caused his vehicle to wait on a stand or part thereof and that he caused or permitted his vehicle so to wait only for so long as was reasonably necessary for the taking up or setting down of passengers.

Local Government (Miscellaneous Provisions) Act 1976, s 64, as amended by the Road Traffic Regulation Act 1984, Sched 13.

---

[a] See *City of Bradford Metropolitan DC v Sabih Thiyab Obaid* (2001) LTL, 29 June. The word 'wait' should be given its natural and ordinary meaning in the appropriate context. The word denoted stopping which was more than purely nominal. The period of time taken to drop passengers off could not be said to be purely nominal.

[b] Evidence from the hackney carriage officer is probably sufficient. The possibility that defendants will ask to see that the stand has been properly authorised is probably not unreasonable provided sufficient notice is given. Officers are therefore advised to retain all such records for inspection.

[aa] For penalty, see s 76.

22.4 SECTION 45 OF THE TOWN POLICE CLAUSES ACT 1847: PLYING FOR HIRE OFFENCE WITHOUT A LICENCE

Elements of the offence/investigatory matters.
1 Full name and address of defendant.
2 Place of offence.
3 Date of offence.
4 Within the prescribed distance.[a]
5 Plying for hire.[b]
6 Offence takes place in a street.[c]
7 Absence of hackney carriage vehicle licence.
8 Absence of pre-booked journey.
9 Defence.
10 Mitigation/explanation.

Time limit: six months (s 127 of the Magistrates' Courts Act 1980).

Mode of trial: summary.

Maximum penalty (s 45).

Summary: level 4.

22.5 SECTION 38 OF THE TOWN POLICE CLAUSES ACT 1847

Every wheeled carriage what ever may be its form or construction, used in standing or plying for hire in any street within the prescribed distance and every carriage standing on any street within the prescribed distance, having thereon any number plate required by this or the special act to be fixed upon a hackney carriage or having thereon any plate resembling or intended to resemble any such plate as aforesaid shall be deemed to be a hackney carriage within the meaning of this act and all proceedings at law or otherwise the term 'hackney carriage' shall be sufficient to describe any such carriage.

22.6 SECTION 45 OF THE TOWN POLICE CLAUSES ACT 1847: PENALTY FOR PLYING FOR HIRE WITHOUT A LICENCE

Permitting use, or driving, standing or plying for hire or not displaying licence number; maximum fine level 4 on the standard scale.

(a) Once local authorities have designated their area as being controlled districts evidence of this should suffice.
(b) See list of authorities at Appendix 17.
(c) If a driver is parked off a street seeking to attract passengers passing in a street this will amount to evidence of plying for hire in a street.

22.7 SECTION 47 OF THE TOWN POLICE CLAUSES ACT 1847

Penalty on drivers for acting without licence, or proprietors employing unlicensed drivers; maximum fine level 3 on the standard scale.

22.8 SCHEDULE 4, PARA 10 OF THE LOCAL GOVERNMENT (MISCELLANEOUS PROVISIONS) ACT 1982: STREET TRADING

Elements of the offence/investigatory matters:
1. Full name of defendant[a] (capacity, that is, sole trader, partnership, limited company, etc).
2. Address/registered office (if limited company).
3. Date of offence.
4. Place of offence.
5. Street trading.
6. Trading in a prohibited/consent street.
7. Lack of consent (if applicable).
8. Statutory exception.[b]

(a) A common problem with this type of offence is being able to approve the identity of the suspect. Local authority officers are not in a position to set up an identity parade and street traders, it seems, rarely carry proof of identity. Police officers are often willing to assist by using their powers of arrest under s 25 of the Police and Criminal Evidence Act 1984 for this purpose.

(b) The two main exceptions are sale of newspapers and periodicals and pedlars. A pedlar requires a licence and must pedal as opposed to street trade. Case law, below, suggests that pedlars do not set up a pitch; they tend to go to their customers rather than wait for them to come to him. A pedlar is defined under the Pedlars Act 1871 as:

> Any hawker, pedlar, petty chapman, tinker caster of metals, mender of chairs, or other person who, without any horse or other beast bearing or drawing burden, travels and trades on foot and goes from town to town or to other men's houses carrying, to sell or exposing for sale any goods, wares or merchandise, or procuring orders for goods, wares or merchandising immediately to be delivered, or selling or offering for sale his skill in handicraft.

The meaning of 'pedlar' has been discussed in the following cases. *Stevenage BC v Wright* (1997) 161 JP Rep 13, cited with approval in *Chichester DC v Wood* [1997] EWHC 266, 14 March. Leggatt LJ in giving the judgment said, p 10:

> Essentially a pedlar, acting as such, is travelling when he is not trading. So the length is important of those periods during which he is stationary and not selling but is prepared to do so. The use of a stall or stand may indicate an intention to remain in one place or in a succession of different places for longer than is necessary to effect a particular sale or sales ... The fact was that he was not trading from a stall did not of itself mean that he was acting as a pedlar.

In *Westminster CC v Ali Elmasoglu* (1996) unreported, 14 February, cited with approval in *Chichester DC v Wood* the learned stipendiary magistrate's opinion was cited by Forbes J in his judgment, p 6. The relevant part reads:

> I [stipendiary magistrate] was of the opinion that (a) although the appellant moved his barrow every few minutes this did not of itself bring this within the definition of a pedlar acting under the authority of a pedlar's certificate; (b) the appellant did not stop his barrow to serve customers who asked for his wares; he stopped and then waited for customers to come to him whilst he was stationary in this place.

In *Chichester DC v Wood* [1997] EWHC 266, 14 March, Mr Justice Blofeld gave the following guidance: ... [cont]

9   Due diligence defence.

10 Mitigation/explanation.

Time limit: six months (s 127 of the Magistrates' Courts Act 1980).

Mode of trial: summary.

Maximum penalty (Sched 4, para 10(4)).

Summary: level 3.

22.9 SCHEDULE 4, PARA 10 OF THE LOCAL GOVERNMENT (MISCELLANEOUS PROVISIONS) ACT 1982

(1) A person who–
  (a) engages in street trading in a prohibited street; or
  (b) engages in street trading in a licence street or a consent street without being authorised to do so under this Schedule; or
  (c) contravenes any of the principal terms of a street trading licence; or
  (d) being authorised by a street trading consent to trade in a consent street, trades in that street–
    (i) from a stationary van, cart, barrow or other vehicle; or
    (ii) from a portable stall,
    without first having been granted permission to do so under paragraph 7(8) above; or
  (e) contravenes a condition imposed under paragraph 7(9) above,
  shall be guilty of an offence.

(2) It shall be a defence for a person charged with an offence under sub-paragraph (1) above to prove that he took all reasonable precautions and exercised all due diligence to avoid commission of the offence.

(b) [cont] From these authorities, a number of matters appear to be reasonably clear:
1   Each case depends on its own facts.
2   A pedlar goes to his customers rather than allowing them to come to him.
3   A pedlar trades as he travels rather than travels to trade.
4   A pedlar is a pedestrian.
5   If a pedlar is a seller, rather than a mender, he sells reasonably small goods.
6   He is entitled to have some small means of assisting his transport of goods, such as a trolley.
7   It is necessary to consider his whole apparatus of trading and decide if it is of such a scale to take the person concerned out of the definition of 'pedlar'.
8   The use of a stall, or stand, or barrow, may indicate an intention to remain in one place or in a succession of different places for longer than is necessary to effect the particular sale or sales indicating that he is a street trader and not a pedlar.
9   If he sets up a stall or barrow and waits for people to approach him, rather than approaching them, that is an indication that he is a street trader and not a pedlar.

(3) Any person who, in connection with an application for a street trading licence or for a street trading consent, makes a false statement which he knows to be false in any material respect, or which he does not believe to be true, shall be guilty of an offence.

(4) A person guilty of an offence under this paragraph shall be liable on summary conviction to a fine not exceeding level 3 on the standard scale.

22.10 SCHEDULE 1, PARA 10 OF THE LOCAL GOVERNMENT (MISCELLANEOUS PROVISIONS) ACT 1982

(1) In this Schedule–

'consent street' means a street in which street trading is prohibited without the consent of the district council;

'licence street' means a street in which street trading is prohibited without a licence granted by the district council;

'principal terms', in relation to a street trading licence, has the meaning assigned to it by paragraph 4(3) below;

'prohibited street' means a street in which street trading is prohibited;

'street' includes–

(a) any road, footway, beach or other area to which the public have access without payment; and

(b) a service area as defined in section 329 of the Highways Act 1980,

and also includes any part of a street;

'street trading' means, subject to sub-paragraph (2) below, the selling or exposing or offering for sale of any article (including a living thing) in a street; and

'subsidiary terms', in relation to a street trading licence, has the meaning assigned to it by paragraph 4(4) below.

(2) The following are not street trading for the purposes of this Schedule–

(a) trading by a person acting as a pedlar under the authority of a pedlar's certificate granted under the Pedlars Act 1871;

(b) anything done in a market or fair the right to hold which was acquired by virtue of a grant (including a presumed grant) or acquired or established by virtue of an enactment or order.

(c) trading in a trunk road picnic area provided by the Secretary of State under section 112 of the Highways Act 1980;

(d) trading as a news vendor;

(e) trading which–

(i) is carried on at premises used as a petrol filling station; or

(ii) is carried on at premises used as a shop or in a street adjoining premises so used and as part of the business of the shop;

(f) selling things, or offering or exposing them for sale, as a roundsman;

(g) the use for trading under Part VIIA of the Highways Act 1980 of an object or structure placed on, in or over a highway;

(h) the operation of facilities for recreation or refreshment under Part VIIA of the Highways Act 1980;

(j) the doing of anything authorised by regulations made under section 5 of the Police, Factories, etc (Miscellaneous Provisions) Act 1916.*

(3) The reference to trading as a news vendor in sub-paragraph (2)(d) is a reference to trading where–

(a) the only articles sold or exposed or offered for sale are newspapers or periodicals; and

(b) they are sold or exposed or offered for sale without a stall or receptacle for them or with a stall or receptacle for them which does not–

(i) exceed one metre in length or width or two metres in height;

(ii) occupy a ground area exceeding 0.25 square metres; or

(iii) stand on the carriageway of a street.

*Amended by the Charities Act 1992, Sched 6, when in force.

22.10.1 Public entertainment licence offences: breach of licence condition

Elements of the offence/investigatory matters:

1 Full name of defendant (capacity, that is, sole trader, partnership, limited company, etc).
2 Address/registered office (if limited company).
3 Date of offence.
4 Public entertainment licence in force.
5 Defendant is licensee.
6 Breach of condition.(a)
7 Valid licence.(b)
8 Condition applies to that particular licence.
9 Due diligence defence.
10 Mitigation/explanation.

Time limit: six months (s 127 of the Magistrates' Courts Act 1980).

Mode of trial: summary.

Maximum penalty (Sched 1, para 12(2A)).

Summary: level 5.

(a) Breach of more than one condition is one offence only (*Mendip DC v Glastonbury Festivals Ltd* – (1993) 91 LGR, 18 February). Different dates may give rise to more than one offence.

(b) See *R v North Hertfordshire DC ex p Cobbold* [1985] 3 All ER 486, which stipulates that if a condition is invalid the whole licence may be invalidated unless the offensive condition can be severed from the whole licence without altering the essential character or substance of the licence that remains. If the licence is invalid it is likely that no offence is committed.

NB If condition breached relates to number of persons on the premises the fine is increased to £20,000 and/or six months (para 12(2A)).

12.10.2 Public Entertainment licence offences: Being concerned in the organisation or management of an unlicensed PEL

Elements of the offence/investigatory matters:

1. Full name of defendant (capacity, that is, sole trader, partnership, limited company, etc).
2. Address/registered office (if limited company).
3. Date of offence.
4. Public entertainment licence not in force.
5. Provision of public entertainment.[a]
6(a) Defendant is a person concerned in the organisation[b] or management of public entertainment; or
6(b) Defendant is a person who knew[c] or had reasonable cause to suspect that a public entertainment would be provided; or
6(c) Let or made it available to any person who committed an offence referred to in 6(a) or (b).
7. Due diligence defence.
8. Mitigation/explanation.

Time limit: six months (s 127 of the Magistrates' Courts Act 1980).

Mode of trial: summary.

Maximum penalty (Sched 1, para 12(2A)).

Summary: level 5.

(a) Public entertainment is defined in para 1 as public dancing or music or another public entertainment of a like kind. Note exceptions in para 1(3) and exception for bands with two members or less. Public is generally regarded as being open to the public whether or not on payment of a fee. Membership of a club cannot be used as a transparent device to argue that the entertainment is not public. See *Lunn v Colston-Hayter* (1991) 155 JP 384.
(b) See *Chichester DC v Silvester* [1992] TLR, 6 May which takes a very broad view of being concerned in provision of a public entertainment. In this case the driver of the van as well as the disc jockey and the hirer of the audio equipment were all found guilty under this section.
(c) See list of authorities in Appendix 17 for cases on the meaning of 'knowingly'.

22.11 SCHEDULE 1, PARA 1 OF THE LOCAL GOVERNMENT (MISCELLANEOUS PROVISIONS) ACT 1982: GRANT, RENEWAL AND TRANSFER OF ENTERTAINMENTS LICENCES

1

(1) An entertainment to which this paragraph applies shall not be provided in any place except under and in accordance with the terms of a licence granted under this paragraph by the appropriate authority.

(2) Subject to sub-paragraph (3) below, this paragraph applies to public dancing or music or any other public entertainment a like kind.

(3) This paragraph does not apply—
   (a) to any music—
      (i) in a place of public religious worship; or
      (ii) performed as an incident of a religious meeting or service;
   (b) to an entertainment held in a pleasure fair; or
   (c) to an entertainment which takes place wholly or mainly in the open air.

(4) The appropriate authority may grant to any applicant, and from time to time renew, a licence for the use of any place specified in it for all or any of the entertainments to which this paragraph applies on such terms and conditions and subject to such restrictions as may be so specified.

(5) The appropriate authority may grant a licence under this paragraph in respect of such one or more particular occasions only as may be specified in the licence.

2

(1) Subject to sub-paragraphs (2) and (3) below, no premises shall be used for any entertainment which consists of any sporting event to which the public are invited as spectators (a 'sports entertainment') except under and in accordance with the terms of a licence granted under this paragraph by the appropriate authority.

(2) Sub-paragraph (1) above does not require a licence in respect of any occasion when the sporting event which constitutes the entertainment is not the principal purpose for which the premises are used on that occasion; but this provision does not apply in relation to a sports complex.

(3) Sub-paragraph (1) above does not apply to a sports entertainment held in a pleasure fair.

(4) The appropriate authority may grant to any applicant, and from time to time renew, a licence for the use of any premises specified in it for any sports entertainment on such terms and conditions and subject to such restrictions as may be so specified.

(5) The appropriate authority may grant a licence under this paragraph in respect of such one or more particular occasions only as may be specified in the licence.

(6) In this paragraph—

'premises' means any permanent or temporary building and any tent or inflatable structure and includes a part of a building where the building is a sports complex but does not include a part of any other building;

Chapter 22: Licensing Legislation

'sporting event' means any contest, exhibition or display of any sport;

'sports complex' means a building—

(a) which provides accommodation and facilities for both those engaging in sport and spectators; and

(b) the parts of which are so arranged that one or more sports can be engaged in simultaneously in different parts of the building, and

'sport' includes any game in which physical skill is the predominant factor and any form of physical recreation which is also engaged in for purposes of competition or display, except dancing (in any form).

3

(1) This paragraph applies to any public musical entertainment which is held—

(a) in an area in which this paragraph and paragraph 4 below have effect; and

(b) wholly or mainly in the open air; and

(c) at a place on private land.

(2) For the purposes of this paragraph and paragraph 4 below—

(a) an entertainment is musical if music is a substantial ingredient; and

(b) land is private if the public has access to it (whether on payment or otherwise) only by permission of the owner, occupier or lessee.

(3) This paragraph does not apply—

(a) to a garden fete, bazaar, sale of work, sporting or athletic event, exhibition, display or other function or event of a similar character, whether limited to one day or extending over two or more days; or

(b) to a religious meeting or service,

merely because music is incidental to it.

(4) This paragraph does not apply to an entertainment held in a pleasure fair.

4

(1) An entertainment to which paragraph 3 above applies shall not be provided except under and in accordance with the terms of a licence granted under this paragraph by the appropriate authority.

(2) The appropriate authority may grant to any applicant, and from time to time renew, a licence for the use of any place specified in it for any entertainment to which paragraph 3 above applies.

(3) The appropriate authority may grant a licence under this paragraph in respect of such one or more particular occasions only as may be specified in the licence.

(4) A licence under this paragraph may be granted—

(a) on terms and conditions; and

(b) subject to restrictions,

imposed for all or any of the following purposes, but no others—

(i) for securing the safety of performers at the entertainment for which the licence is granted and other persons present at the entertainment;

(ii) without prejudice to the generality of paragraph (i) above, for securing adequate access for fire engines, ambulances, police cars or other vehicles that may be required in an emergency;

(iii) for securing the provision of adequate sanitary appliances and things used in connection with such appliances;

(iv) for preventing persons in the neighbourhood being unreasonably disturbed by noise.

5

(1) Subject to paragraphs 8 and 17 below, any entertainments licence other than a licence in respect of one or more particular occasions only shall, unless previously cancelled under paragraph 10 or revoked under paragraph 11A or 12(4) or (5) below, remain in force for one year or for such shorter period specified in the licence as the appropriate authority may think fit.

(2) Where an entertainments licence has been granted to any person, the appropriate authority may, if they think fit, transfer that licence to any other person on the application of that other person or the holder of the licence.

6

(1) An applicant for the grant, renewal or transfer of an entertainments licence in respect of any place shall give not less than 28 days' notice of his intention to make the application to—

(a) the appropriate authority;

(b) the chief officer of police; and

(c) the fire authority.

(2) The appropriate authority may in such cases as they think fit, after consulting with the chief officer of police and the fire authority, grant an application for the grant, renewal or transfer of an entertainments licence notwithstanding the fact that the applicant has failed to give notice in accordance with sub-paragraph (1) above.

(3) An applicant for the grant, renewal or transfer of an entertainments licence shall furnish such particulars and give such other notices as the appropriate authority may by regulation prescribe.

(4) In considering any application for the grant, renewal or transfer of an entertainments licence, the appropriate authority shall have regard to any observations submitted to them by the chief officer of police and by the fire authority.

6A

(1) This paragraph applies where the authority by whom an entertainments licence was granted under paragraph 1 above in respect of a place receive a report from the chief officer of police—

(a) stating that there is a serious problem relating to the supply or use of controlled drugs at the place or at any place nearby which is controlled by the holder of the licence; and

(b) giving reasons for his view that there is such a problem.

(2) An application for the renewal or transfer of the licence may be refused by the authority on the ground that they are satisfied that not renewing or transferring it will significantly assist in dealing with the problem.

(3) The authority shall give the reasons for their refusal of the application to—
   (a) the holder of the licence; and
   (b) in the case of an application for the transfer of the licence, the person to whom the licence would have been transferred if the application had been granted.

(4) A person to whom reasons are given may make representations to the authority; and the authority shall consider any representations within the period of 21 days beginning with the day on which they receive them.

(5) After considering any representations, the authority shall (unless the date of expiry of the licence has passed) either—
   (a) confirm the refusal of the application; or
   (b) grant the application.

(6) The authority shall have regard in exercising their functions under this paragraph to such guidance as may be issued by the Secretary of State.

7

(1) Subject to sub-paragraphs (2) and (3) below, an applicant for the grant, renewal or transfer of an entertainments licence shall pay a reasonable fee determined by the appropriate authority.

(2) No fee shall be payable if the application is for a licence for an entertainment—
   (a) at a church hall, chapel hall or other similar building occupied in connection with a place of public religious worship; or
   (b) at a village hall, parish or community hall or other similar building.

(3) The appropriate authority may remit the whole or any part of the fee that would otherwise be payable for the grant, renewal or transfer of an entertainments licence, where in the opinion of the authority the entertainment in question—
   (a) is of an educational or other like character; or
   (b) is given for a charitable or other like purpose.

8

(1) Where, before the date of expiry of an entertainments licence, an application has been made for its renewal, it shall be deemed to remain in force notwithstanding that the date has passed until the withdrawal of the application or its determination by the appropriate authority.

(2) Where, before the date of expiry of an entertainments licence, an application has been made for its transfer, it shall be deemed to remain in force with any necessary modifications until the withdrawal of the application or its determination notwithstanding that the date has passed or that the person to whom the licence is to be transferred if the application is granted is carrying on at the place in respect of which the licence was granted the functions to which it relates.

Transmission and cancellation of entertainments licences

9

In the event of the death of the holder of an entertainments licence, the person carrying on at the place in respect of which the licence was granted the functions to which the licence relates shall be deemed to be the holder of the licence unless and until—

(a) a legal personal representative of the deceased has been duly constituted; or

(b) the licence is transferred to some other person.

10

The appropriate authority may, at the written request of the holder of an entertainments licence, cancel the licence.

Power to prescribe standard terms, conditions and restrictions

11

(1) The appropriate authority may make regulations prescribing standard conditions applicable to all, or any class of, entertainments licences, that is to say terms, conditions and restrictions on or subject to which such licences, or licences of that class, are in general to be granted, renewed or transferred by them.

(2) Regulations relating to entertainments to which paragraph 3 above applies may only prescribe standard conditions for the purposes specified in paragraph 4(4) above.

(3) Where the appropriate authority have made regulations under sub-paragraph (1) above, every such licence granted, renewed or transferred by them shall be presumed to have been so granted, renewed or transferred subject to any standard conditions applicable to it unless they have been expressly excluded or varied.

(4) Where the appropriate authority have made regulations under sub-paragraph (1) above, they shall, if so requested by any person, supply him with a copy of the regulations on payment of such reasonable fee as the authority may determine.

(5) In any legal proceedings the production of a copy of any regulations made by the appropriate authority under sub-paragraph (1) above purporting to be certified as a true copy by an officer of the authority authorised to give a certificate for the purposes of this paragraph shall be prima facie evidence of such regulations, and no proof shall be required of the handwriting or official position or authority of any person giving such a certificate.

Enforcement

11A

(1) This paragraph applies where the authority by whom an entertainments licence was granted under paragraph 1 above in respect of a place receive a report from the chief officer of police—

(a) stating that there is a serious problem relating to the supply or use of controlled drugs at the place or at any place nearby which is controlled by the holder of the licence; and

(b) giving reasons for his view that there is such a problem.

(2) The authority may—
   (a) revoke the licence; or
   (b) impose terms, conditions or restrictions on or subject to which it is to be held,

   on the ground that they are satisfied that to do so will significantly assist in dealing with the problem.

(3) The authority shall give the reasons for their revocation of the licence, or the imposition of the terms, conditions or restrictions, to the holder of the licence who may make representations to the authority; and the authority shall consider any representations within the period of 21 days beginning with the day on which they receive them.

(4) After considering any representations, the authority shall (unless the date of expiry of the licence has passed) either—
   (a) confirm that the licence remains revoked or continues to have effect on or subject to the terms, conditions or restrictions which have been imposed; or
   (b) reinstate the licence or determine that it has effect free of those terms, conditions or restrictions.

(5) The authority shall have regard in exercising their functions under this paragraph to such guidance as may be issued by the Secretary of State.

12

(1) If any entertainment to which paragraph 1, 2 or 3 above applies is provided at any place in respect of which a licence under the relevant paragraph is not in force, then, subject to sub-paragraph (3) below—
   (a) any person concerned in the organisation or management of that entertainment; and
   (b) any other person who, knowing or having reasonable cause to suspect that such an entertainment would be so provided at the place—
      (i) allowed the place to be used for the provision of that entertainment; or
      (ii) let the place, or otherwise made it available, to any person by whom an offence in connection with that use of the place has been committed,

   shall be guilty of an offence.

(2) If any place in respect of which a licence under paragraph 1, 2 or 4 above is in force is used for any entertainment otherwise than in accordance with the terms, conditions or restrictions on or subject to which the licence is held, then, subject to sub-paragraph (3) and to paragraph 13 below—
   (a) the holder of the licence; and
   (b) any other person who, knowing or having reasonable cause to suspect that the place would be so used—
      (i) allowed the place to be so used; or
      (ii) let the place, or otherwise made it available, to any person by whom an offence in connection with that use of the place has been committed,

   shall be guilty of an offence.

(2A) Any person guilty of an offence under sub-paragraph (1) or (2) above shall be liable on summary conviction—

(a) in the case of an offence to which sub-paragraph (2B) below applies to a fine not exceeding £20,000 or to imprisonment for a term not exceeding six months or to both;

(b) in any other case, to a fine not exceeding level 5 on the standard scale.

(2B) This sub-paragraph applies to—

(a) any offence under sub-paragraph (1) above where the entertainment provided is entertainment to which paragraph 1 or 3 above applies; and

(b) any offence under sub-paragraph (2) above where the licence in force is a licence under paragraph 1 or 4 above and the terms, conditions or restrictions which are contravened or not complied with include one which imposes a limit on the number of persons who may be present at the entertainment.

(3) It shall be a defence for a person charged with an offence under this paragraph to prove that he took all reasonable precautions and exercised all due diligence to avoid commission of the offence.

(4) Subject to paragraph 17 below, the authority by whom an entertainments licence was granted may revoke it if its holder is convicted of an offence under sub-paragraph (2)(a) above.

(5) Where a person is convicted by a court of an offence under sub-paragraph (2) above in relation to a licence under paragraph 1 above in respect of a place, the court may revoke the licence if satisfied that—

(a) there is a serious problem relating to the supply or use of controlled drugs at the place or at any place nearby which is controlled by the holder of the licence; and

(b) it will significantly assist in dealing with the problem to revoke the licence;

and the standard of proof for the purposes of this sub-paragraph is that applicable in civil proceedings.

13

Where—

(a) a special order of exemption has been granted in respect of premises under section 74(4) of the Licensing Act 1964; and

(b) the premises form all or part of a place in respect of which a licence under paragraph 1 above is for the time being in force,

no person shall be guilty of an offence under paragraph 12(2) above by reason only of those premises being kept open on that special occasion for any of the purposes authorised by the licence after the latest hour so authorised but not later than the hour specified in that special order of exemption as the hour for closing.

14

(1) Where—

(a) a constable; or

(b) an authorised officer of the appropriate authority; or

(c) an authorised officer of the fire authority,

has reason to believe that an entertainment to which paragraph 1, 2 or 3 above applies is being, or is about to be, given in any place in respect of which an entertainments licence is for the time being in force, he may enter the place with a view to seeing whether the terms, conditions or restrictions on or subject to which the licence is held are complied with.

(2) An authorised officer of the fire authority may, on giving not less than 24 hours' notice to the occupier of any place in respect of which an entertainments licence is for the time being in force, enter the place for the purpose of—
   (a) inspecting the place to ensure that there are adequate fire precautions; and
   (b) seeing whether the terms, conditions or restrictions relating to fire precautions on or subject to which the licence is held are being complied with.

(3) A constable or authorised officer of the appropriate authority may enter any place in respect of which he has reason to suspect that an offence under paragraph 12 above is being committed if authorised to do so by a warrant granted by a justice of the peace.

(4) Where an authorised officer of the appropriate authority or of the fire authority enters any place in exercise of any power under this paragraph he shall, if required to do so by the occupier, produce to him his authority.

(5) Any person who without reasonable excuse refuses to permit a constable or officer to enter or inspect any place in accordance with the provisions of this paragraph shall be guilty of an offence and shall for every such refusal be liable on summary conviction to a fine not exceeding level 3 on the standard scale.

Provisional grant of licences

15

(1) Where application is made to the appropriate authority for the grant of an entertainments licence in respect of premises which are to be, or are in the course of being, constructed, extended or altered and the authority are satisfied that the premises would, if completed in accordance with plans deposited in accordance with the requirements of the authority, be such that they would grant the licence, the authority may grant the licence subject to a condition that it shall be of no effect until confirmed by them.

(2) The authority shall confirm any licence granted by virtue of the foregoing sub-paragraph if and when they are satisfied that the premises have been completed in accordance with the plans referred to in sub-paragraph (1) above or in accordance with those plans as modified with the approval of the authority, and that the licence is held by a fit and proper person.

Variation of licences

16

(1) The holder of an entertainments licence may at any time apply to the appropriate authority for such variations of the terms, conditions or restrictions on or subject to which the licence is held as may be specified in the application.

(2) An authority to whom an application under sub-paragraph (1) above is made may—
   (a) make the variations specified in the application;
   (b) make such variations as they think fit, including, subject to paragraph 4(4), above, the imposition of terms, conditions or restrictions other than those so specified; or
   (c) refuse the application.

16A

An applicant for the variation of the terms, conditions or restrictions on or subject to which an entertainments licence is held shall pay a reasonable fee determined by the appropriate authority.

Appeals

17

(1) Any of the following persons, that is to say—
   (a) an applicant for the grant, renewal or transfer of an entertainments licence in respect of any place whose application is refused;
   (b) an applicant for the variation of the terms, conditions or restrictions on or subject to which any such licence is held whose application is refused;
   (c) a holder of any such licence who is aggrieved by any term, condition or restriction on or subject to which the licence is held; or
   (d) a holder of any such licence whose licence is revoked under paragraph 11A or12(4) above,

may at any time before the expiration of the period of 21 days beginning with the relevant date appeal to the magistrates' court acting for the petty sessions area in which the place is situated.

(2) In this paragraph 'the relevant date' means the date on which the person in question is notified of the refusal of his application, the imposition of the term, condition or restriction by which he is aggrieved or the revocation of his licence, as the case may be; but in a case where a decision is made under paragraph 6A(5) or 11A(4) above means the date on which the person in question is notified of the decision.

(3) An appeal against the decision of a magistrates' court under this paragraph or under paragraph 12(5) above may be brought to the Crown Court.

(4) On an appeal to the magistrates' court or the Crown Court under this paragraph the court may make such order as it thinks fit.

(5) Subject to sub-paragraphs (6) to (9) below, it shall be the duty of the appropriate authority to give effect to an order of the magistrates' court or the Crown Court.

(6) The appropriate authority need not give effect to the order of the magistrates' court until the time for bringing an appeal under sub-paragraph (3) above has expired and, if such an appeal is duly brought, until the determination or abandonment of the appeal.

(7) Where any entertainments licence is revoked under paragraph 12(4) above or an application for the renewal of such a licence is refused otherwise than on the ground specified in paragraph 6A(2) above, the licence shall be deemed to remain in force—
   (a) until the time for bringing an appeal under this paragraph has expired and, if such an appeal is duly brought, until the determination or abandonment of the appeal; and
   (b) where an appeal relating to the refusal of an application for such a renewal is successful and no further appeal is available, until the licence is renewed by the appropriate authority.

(7A) A court which revokes an entertainments licence under paragraph 12(5) above may, if in the particular circumstances it would be unfair not to do so, order that the licence shall remain in force

(a) until the time for bringing an appeal against the revocation has expired; and

(b) if such an appeal is duly brought, until the determination or abandonment of the appeal.

(8) Where—

(a) the holder of an entertainments licence makes an application under paragraph 16 above; and

(b) the appropriate authority impose any term, condition or restriction other than one specified in the application,

the licence shall be deemed to be free of it until the time for bringing an appeal under this paragraph has expired.

(9) Where an appeal is brought under this paragraph against the imposition of any such term, condition or restriction, the licence shall be deemed to be free of the term, condition or restriction until the determination or abandonment of the appeal.

Miscellaneous

18

Where a place in respect of which an entertainments licence has been granted constitutes a roller skating rink within the meaning of section 75(2)(b) of the Public Health Act 1961, it shall not be subject to any byelaws made under section 75 for so long as the licence is in force.

22.12 PRIVATE HIRE AND HACKNEY CARRIAGE MATTERS

22.12.1 Introduction

The licensing regime for the operation of private hire vehicles is contained in the Local Government (Miscellaneous Provisions) Act 1976. The regime for the licensing of hackney carriages and their drivers is contained in the Town Police Clauses Act 1947, the Transport Act 1985 and the Local Government (Miscellaneous Provisions) Act 1976. There are many offences created by the provisions of the Local Government (Miscellaneous Provisions) Act 1976 relating to operators of private hire vehicles, drivers and proprietors. The main offence created by the Town Police Clauses Act 1847 is that under s 45 of the Act, that is, plying for hire. Effectively, both private hire vehicles and hackney carriage vehicles can commit an offence of plying for hire. If the driver of a private hire vehicle picks up a passenger in the street without a prior booking he is plying for hire which is contrary to s 45 of the Act. If the driver of a hackney carriage, is found waiting in a street without a prior booking this also would be plying for hire.(a)

22.12.2   Strategy for investigating plying for hire offences

The existence of radio equipment and the willingness of many booking clerks to collaborate makes the investigation of this offence very difficult. Furthermore, the financial benefits to be gained from this carrying out this illegal activity over a period of time far outweigh the risk of the occasional fine. For these reasons, it is essential to operate a strategy that deters booking clerks from taking part in the offence whilst at the same time increasing the detection rate.

Booking clerks who take part in the offence of plying for hire by encouraging errant drivers in recording bookings that are not 'genuine' may be prosecuted as aiders and abettors. To prove complicity in this offence all that is required is knowledge that an offence is taking place and either assistance or encouragement of the offence. Of course, proof of the substantive offence is normally implicit for guilt by a secondary party. For a more detailed examination of the law relating to secondary offenders, see Chapter 11. Local authorities who adopt the practice of prosecuting booking clerks will often discover that such persons will be very reluctant to record bookings that are not directly from the customer. It naturally follows from this that anyone who commits this offence is much more likely to be convicted. Furthermore, there is not the same incentive to commit the offence particularly if proceedings are also taken for not having insurance.(aa) A useful method of detecting this offence is by way of an entrapment exercise.(b)

22.13 CONCLUSION

At the conclusion of the investigation for an offence of plying for hire a compelling file of evidence can be collated using the suggested methods. Thereafter, difficulties may still be encountered in proving that the facts fit into the legal meaning of plying for hire. To assist with this regard, there is a list of authorities at Appendix 17. If the evidence is not so compelling and the investigating officer believes that an offence has taken place the local

---

(a) See Appendix 17 for list of authorities on plying for hire.
(aa) Local authorities may take proceedings for any offence. (*R v Jarret and Steward* (1997) Archbold News, 7 May.)
(b) Entrapment exercises are a legitimate and common practice in detecting plying for hire offences. However, care should be taken to ensure that the suspect is not persuaded or wheedled into doing something that he would not otherwise have done as this would amount to a breach of human rights. Use of radio wave scanners to pick up and record conversations between booking clerks and drivers can be an effective tool in obtaining very useful evidence in these type of offences. Prior consent of the home office is required before the equipment is used for investigative purposes although failure to obtain permission is not likely to result in the evidence being excluded. See, also, *Nottingham CC v Amin* (1999) TLR, 2 December, in which the court refused to exclude evidence of entrapment in a plying for hire case. Further advice on entrapment can be found in Chapter 4.

authority may still suspend the licence.[a] If there is a challenge by way of an appeal, the evidential rules will be much more relaxed.[b] The court may take into account previous convictions and other matters that would not be permissible in straightforward criminal proceedings.

Section 73 of the Local Government (Miscellaneous Provisions) Act 1976: obstruction of authorised officer

(1) Any person who—
   (a) wilfully obstructs an authorised officer or constable acting in pursuance of this Part of this Act or the Act of 1847; or
   (b) without reasonable excuse fails to comply with any requirement properly made to him by such officer or constable under this Part of this Act; or
   (c) without reasonable cause fails to give such an officer or constable so acting any other assistance or information which he may reasonably require of such person for the purpose of the performance of his functions under this Part of this Act or the Act of 1847;
   shall be guilty of an offence.

(2) If any person, in giving any such information as is mentioned in the preceding subsection, makes any statement which he knows to be false, he shall be guilty of an offence.

(a) See *R v Secretary of State for the Home Department ex p Macneil* (1994) TLR, 26 May, in which a prisoner's release on licence was revoked for alleged subsequent offences which had not been tried. The court held that this was not a breach of the European Convention of Human Rights. In this case, the correct approach was to balance the prisoner's interest in having continued liberty with the need to protect the public.
(b) See the standard list of authorities for appeal at Appendix 17.

HIGHWAYS LEGISLATION

23.1 INTRODUCTION

This chapter sets out the following legislation:
1. Section 137 of the Highways Act 1980 (penalty for wilful obstruction).
2. Section 139 of the Highways Act 1980 (control of builder's skips).
3. Section 172 of the Highways Act 1980 (hoardings to be set up during building, etc).
4. Section 131A of the Highways Act 1980 (disturbance of surface of certain highways).
5. Section 131 of the Highways Act 1980 (penalty for damaging highway).
6. Section 161(1) of the Highways Act 1980 (danger or annoyance caused by fires lit otherwise than on highways).
7. Section 57 of the National Parks and Access to the Countryside Act 1949.
8. Section 51 of the New Roads and Street Works Act 1991 (prohibition of an unauthorised street works).
9. Section 52 of the New Roads and Street Works Act 1991 (emergency works).
10. Section 54 of the New Roads and Street Works Act 1991 (advanced notice of certain works).
11. Section 55 of the New Roads and Street Works Act 1991 (notice of starting date of works).
12. Section 56 of the New Roads and Street Works Act 1991 (power to give directions as to timing of street works).
13. Section 57 of the New Roads and Street Works Act 1991 (notice of emergency works).
14. Section 58 of the New Roads and Street Works Act 1991.
15. Section 67 of the New Roads and Street Works Act 1991 (qualification of supervisors and operatives).
16. Section 68 of the New Roads and Street Works Act 1991 (facilities to be afforded to street authority).
17. Section 69 of the New Roads and Street Works Act 1991 (works likely to affect other apparatus in the street).
18. Section 70 of the New Roads and Street Works Act 1991 (duty of undertaker to reinstate).
19. Section 71 of the New Roads and Street Works Act 1991 (materials, workmanship and standards of reinstatement)
20. Section 79 of the New Roads and Street Works Act 1991 (records of location of apparatus).
21. Section 92 of the New Roads and Street Works Act 1991 (special precautions as to displaying of lights).

22 Section 59 of the Wildlife and Countryside Act 1981 (prohibition on keeping bulls on land crossed by public rights of way).

23.2 MISCELLANEOUS POWERS, ETC

1 Section 164 of the Highways Act 1980: Power to Require Removal of Barbed Wire.
2 Section 289 of the Highways Act 1980: Powers of Entry of Highway Authority for the Purpose of Service.
3 Section 292 of the Highways Act 1980: Obstruction.
4 Section 293 of the Highways Act 1980: Powers of Entry for Purposes Connected with Certain Orders Relating to Footpaths and Bridle Ways.
5 Section 297 of the Highways Act 1980: Power of Highway Authority or Council to Require Information as to Ownership of Land.
6 Section 303 of the Highways Act 1980: Penalty for Obstructing Execution of Act.
7 Section 310 of the Highways Act 1980: Summary Proceedings for Offences.
8 Section 311 of the Highways Act 1980.
9 Section 320 of the Highways Act 1980: Form of Notice, etc.
10 Section 322 of the Highways Act 1980: Service of Notices, etc.

23.3 SECTION 137 OF THE HIGHWAYS ACT 1980: PENALTY FOR WILFUL OBSTRUCTION

Need to prove/investigate:
1 Place of offence (within jurisdiction of the court).
2 Date(s) of offence (within six months time limit).
3 Full name and address and capacity of defendant, that is, whether company (ltd or plc) or partnership or sole trader. If company, full name and registered office required. If partnership, full names of partners and trading addresses. If sole trader, his full name and address and any trading name (if any).
4 Defendant obstructs the highway[a] (description of the obstruction).
5 Obstruction is done wilfully (see definition below).
6 The obstruction restricted free passage at that part (description or photographs).
7 Without lawful authority or excuse (see definition).
8 The obstruction is not *de minimis* (for example, newspaper rack attached to wall).
9 Mitigation/explanation.

Time limit: six months (s 127 of the Magistrates' Courts Act 1980).

Mode of trial: summary.

---

[a] Road/footpath is in fact a highway as defined by s 328(1) (produce extract from definitive map or highways register).

Maximum penalty (s 137(1)).

Summary: level 3.

23.4 SECTION 137 – PENALTY FOR WILFUL OBSTRUCTION

(1) If a person, without lawful authority or excuse, in any way wilfully obstructs the free passage along a highway, he is guilty of an offence and liable to a fine not exceeding level 3 on the standard scale.

NB: The onus is on the prosecution to prove that the defendant was obstructing the highway without lawful authority or excuse.

'Lawful authority' includes permits and licenses granted to market and street traders and those collecting for charitable causes.

'Lawful excuse' embraces activities, otherwise lawful in themselves, which may or may not be reasonable in all the circumstance.[a]

It is not a lawful authority or excuse:

for a livestock smallholder to erect across a bridle way three metal gates tied to hedges with twine to prevent livestock wandering on to a near-by road.[b]

To expose goods for sale on land dedicated as a footway is an obstruction unless the practice prevailed before the dedication.[c]

To erect posts on a footpath to prevent undesirable vehicle traffic may be an obstruction.[d]

It was stated that the broad interpretation of 'reasonable excuse' applied in the case of a temporary obstruction, but did not apply to a permanent obstruction.[e] The fact that neither the police nor local authority prosecute in respect of an alleged obstruction over a period of years does not give the defendant a license to perform an unlawful act of obstruction.[f]

Wilfully in law means that the act is done deliberately and intentionally not by accident or inadvertence but so the mind of the person who does the act goes with it.[g]

The test of whether a particular use of a highway – eg, by a vehicle – amounts to an obstruction is whether such use is unreasonable with regard to all circumstances, including its duration, position and purpose, and whether it causes an actual, as opposed to a potential, obstruction.[h]

(a) The *de minimis* principle applies to obstruction cases. *The Hirst and Agu v Chief Constable of West Yorkshire* (1987) 151 LG Rev 130 principle is reserved for cases of fractional obstructions.
(b) *Durham CC v Scott* [1990] Crim LR 726.
(c) *Spice v Peacock* [1875] 39 JP 581.
(d) *AG v Wilcox* [1938] Ch 934, [1938] 2 All ER 367.
(e) *Dixon v Attfield* [1975] 3 All ER 265.
(f) *Redbridge London Borough v Jacques* [1971] 1 All ER 260, 135 JP 98.
(g) *Words and Phrases Legally Defined*, Vol 2, 3rd edn, London: Butterworths, p 435. *Nagy v Weston* [1965] 1 All ER 78.
(h) *Torbay BC v Cross* [1995] 159 JP 682.

23.5 SECTION 137 OF THE HIGHWAYS ACT 1980: DRAFT INFORMATION

For a draft information, see Appendix 10.

23.6 SECTION 139(3) OF THE HIGHWAYS ACT 1980: DRAFT INFORMATION

For the draft allegation relating to s 139(3) of the Highways Act 1980, see Appendix 10.

23.7 SECTION 139 OF THE HIGHWAYS ACT 1980: CONTROL OF BUILDER'S SKIPS

The investigatory matters and elements of the offence are:
1. Full name and address and capacity of defendant, that is, whether company (limited or plc) or partnership or sole trader. If company, full name and registered office required. If partnership, full names of partners and trading addresses. If sole trader, his full name and address and trading name (if any).
2. The owner of the skip.
3. Deposit of the skip on the highway.
4. Date.
5. No permission had been obtained from the council as highway authority.
6. The place.
7. Due diligence defence.
8. Mitigation explanation.

Time limit: six months (s 127 of the Magistrates' Courts Act 1980).

Mode of trial: summary.

Maximum penalty (s 139(3)).

Summary: level 3.

23.8 SECTION 139(4) OF THE HIGHWAYS ACT 1980: DRAFT INFORMATION

For a draft information relating to s 139(4) of the Highways Act, see Appendix 10.

23.9 SECTION 139 OF THE HIGHWAYS ACT 1980: CONTROL OF BUILDER'S SKIPS

(1) A builder's skip shall not be deposited on a highway without the permission of the highways authority.

(2) A permission under this section shall be a permission for a person to whom it is granted to deposit, or cause to be deposited, a skip on the highway specified in the permission and the highway authority may grant such permission either conditionally or subject to such conditions as may be specified in the permission, including, in particular, conditions relating to the siting of the skip, its dimensions, the manner in which it is to be coated with paint and other material for the purpose of making it immediately visible to incoming traffic, the care and disposal of its contents, the manner in which it is to be lighted or guarded, its removal, at the end of the period of permission.

(3) If a builder's skip is deposited on the highway without a permission granted under this section, the owner of the skip is, subject to sub-section (6) below, guilty of an offence and liable to a fine not exceeding level 3 on the standard scale.

(4) Where a builder's skip has been deposited on the highway in accordance with a permission granted under this section, the owner of the skip shall ensure:
   (a) That the skip is properly lighted during the hours of darkness and, where regulations made by the Secretary of State under this section required to be marked in accordance with the regulations (with reflecting or fluorescent material or otherwise), that it is so marked;
   (b) That the skip is clearly and indelibly marked with the owner's name and with his telephone number or address;
   (c) That the skip is removed as soon as practicable after it has been filled;
   (d) That each of the conditions subject to which that permission was granted is complied with;
   and, if he fails to do so, he is, subject to sub-section (6) below, guilty of an offence and liable to a fine not exceeding level 3 on the standard scale.

(5) Where the commission by any person or an offence under this section is due to the act or default of some other person, that other person is guilty of the offence, and that person may be charged with and convicted of the offence by virtue of this sub-section, whether or not proceedings are taken against the first-mentioned person.

(6) If any proceedings for an offence under this section, it is a defence, subject to sub-section (7) below, for the person charged to prove that the commission of the offence was due to the act or default of another person and that he took all reasonable precautions and exercised all due diligence to avoid the commission of such an offence by himself or any other person under his control.

23.10 SECTION 172 OF THE HIGHWAYS ACT 1980: HOARDINGS TO BE SET UP DURING BUILDING, ETC

The investigatory matters and elements of the offence are:

1. Full name and address and capacity of defendant, that is, whether company (limited or plc) or partnership or sole trader. If company, full name and registered office required. If partnership, full names of partners and trading addresses. If sole trader, his full name and address and trading name (if any).
2. Date.
3. The place, that is, street or court.
4. Failure to erect a close-boarded hoarding or fence or failure to erect etc to the council's satisfaction.
5. Evidence of proposal to erect or take down a building in the street or court, or to alter or repair the outside of a building in a street or court.
6. Consent issue.
7. Due diligence defence.
8. Mitigation explanation.

Time limit: six months (s 127 of the Magistrates' Courts Act 1980).

Mode of trial: summary.

Maximum penalty (s 172(5)).

Summary: level 3.

23.11 SECTION 172 OF THE HIGHWAYS ACT 1980: HOARDINGS TO BE SET UP DURING BUILDING, ETC

(1) Subject to sub-section (2) below, a person proposing to erect or take down a building in the street or court, or to alter or repair the outside of a building in a street or court, shall, before beginning the work, erect a close-boarded hoarding or fence to the satisfaction of the appropriate highway authority, so as to separate the building from the street or court.

For the purpose of this section, the appropriate authority in relation to any street or court is the Council of the Metropolitan District.

(2) The obligation to erect a hoarding or fence imposed by sub-section (1) above may be dispensed with if the appropriate authority so consents.

(3) Where a person has erected a hoarding or fence in compliance with sub-section (1) above, he shall:
   (a) If the appropriate authority so require, makes convenient covered platform and handrail to serve as a footway for pedestrians outside the hoarding or fence;
   (b) maintain the hoarding or fence and any such platform and handrail in good condition to the satisfaction of the authority during such time as the authority may require;
   (c) if the authority so require, sufficiently light the hoarding or fence and any such platform and handrail during the hours of darkness;
   (d) remove the hoarding or fence and any such platform and handrail when required by the authority.

(4) A person aggrieved by the refusal of a consent under sub-section (2) above, or by a requirement under sub-section (3) above, may appeal to a Magistrates' Court.

(5) Subject to any order made on appeal, if a person contravenes this section he is guilty of an offence and liable to a fine not exceeding level 3 on the standard scale, and if the offence is continued after conviction he is guilty of a further offence and liable to a fine not exceeding £2 for each day on which the offence is so continued.

23.12 SECTION 172(1) OF THE HIGHWAYS ACT 1980: DRAFT INFORMATION

For a draft information/allegation under s 172(1) and (5), see Appendix 10.

23.13 SECTION 131A OF THE HIGHWAYS ACT 1980: DISTURBANCE OF SURFACE OF CERTAIN HIGHWAYS

Need to prove/investigate:
1. Place of offence (within jurisdiction of the court).
2. Date or dates of offence(s) with six months time limit.
3. Capacity of defendant, that is, whether company (limited or plc) or partnership or sole trader. If company, full name and registered office required. If partnership, full names of partners and trading addresses. If sole trader, his full name and address and trading name (if any).
4. (i) Defendant disturbs a surface of a road/footpath.
   (ii) That road/footpath being a footpath or bridleway or any other highway which consists or comprises of a carriageway other than a made up carriageway. (See s 329 for definition of footpath, bridleway and carriageway.) (Produce extract from definitive map/highways register which shows the 'highway'.)
5. Disturbance renders the road/footpath inconvenient for use as a public right of way (description of why it is inconvenient) (photographs).
6. Without lawful authority or excuse.
7. Mitigation/explanation from the defendant.

Time limit: six months (s 127 of the Magistrates' Courts Act 1980).

Mode of trial: summary.

Maximum penalty (s 137A(1)).

Summary: level 3.

23.14 SECTION 131A: DISTURBANCE OF SURFACE OF CERTAIN HIGHWAYS

(1) A person who, without lawful authority or excuse, so disturbs the surface of–
   (a) A footpath; or

(b) a bridle way; or

(c) any other highway which consists of or comprises a carriageway other than a made-up carriageway,

as to render it inconvenient for the exercise of the public right of way is guilty of an offence and liable to a fine not exceeding level 3 on the standard scale.

(2) Proceedings for an offence under this section shall be brought only by the Highway Authority or the Council of the non-metropolitan district, parish or community in which the offence is committed, and, without prejudice to section 130 (Protection of Public Rights) above, it is the duty of the Highway Authority to ensure that where desirable in the public interest, such proceedings are brought.

23.15 SECTION 131 OF THE HIGHWAYS ACT 1980: PENALTY FOR DAMAGING HIGHWAY

Need to prove/investigate:

1 Place of offence (within jurisdiction of the court).
2 Date or dates of offence(s) with six months time limit.
3 Capacity of defendant, that is, whether company (limited or plc) or partnership or sole trader. If company, full name and registered office required. If partnership, full names of partners and trading addresses. If sole trader, his full name and address and trading name (if any).
4 Deposits anything whatsoever on a highway so as to damage the highway. (Produce extract from definitive map/highways register which shows the 'highway.')
5 Damage to the highway. (Produce extract from definitive map/highways register which shows the 'highway'.)
6 Without lawful authority or excuse.
7 Mitigation/explanation from the defendant.

Time limit: six months (s 127 of the Magistrates' Courts Act 1980).

Mode of trial: summary.

Maximum penalty (s 131).

Summary: level 3.

23.16 SECTION 131: PENALTY FOR DAMAGING HIGHWAY[a]

(1) If a person, without lawful authority or excuse –[b]

(a) makes a ditch or excavation in a highway which consists of or comprises a carriageway; or

---

(a) *Dennis and Sons Ltd v Good* (1918) 17 LGR 9 held that a footway across a field is a highway within the meaning of this provision.
(b) In *Greenwich BC v Millcroft Construction Ltd* (1987) 85 LGR 66, it was held that lack of knowledge of the requirement to obtain consent of the highway was not a 'lawful excuse'.

(b) removes any soil or turf from any part of a highway, except for the purpose of improving the highway and with the consent of the Highway Authority for the highway; or

(c) deposits anything whatsoever on a highway so as to damage the highway; or

(d) lights any fire or discharges any firearm or firework within 50 feet from the centre of a highway which consists of or comprises a carriageway, and in consequence thereof, the highway is damaged,

he is guilty of an offence.

(2) If a person, without lawful authority or excuse, pulls down or obliterates a traffic sign placed on or over a highway, or a milestone or direction post (not being a traffic sign) so placed, he is guilty of an offence; but it is a defence for any proceedings under this subsection to show that the traffic sign, milestone or post was not lawfully so placed.

(3) A person guilty of an offence under this section is liable to a fine not exceeding level 3 on the standard scale.

Notes

(1) This section creates an absolute offence and proof of *mens rea* (knowledge) is unnecessary subject only to the defence of 'lawful authority or excuse'.

(2) The lawful authority will generally be a statutory power to interfere with the highway. Exceptionally it may be found in the terms or conditions subject to which the highway was originally dedicated.

23.17 SECTION 161(1) OF THE HIGHWAYS ACT 1980: DANGER OR ANNOYANCE CAUSED BY FIRES LIT OTHERWISE THAN ON HIGHWAYS

Need to prove/investigate:

1 Place of offence (within court's jurisdiction).
2 Date(s) of offence (within six months time limit).
3 Capacity of defendant (as for s 57 of the National Parks and Access to the Countryside Act (NPACA) 1949).
4 The deposit on the highway causes a person to be injured or endangered.
5 The person who was endangered, injured was using the highway at the time.
6 Mitigation/excuse.

Time limit: six months (s 127 of the Magistrates' Courts Act 1980).

Mode of trial: summary.

Maximum penalty (s 161(2).

Summary: level 3.

23.18 SECTION 161: PENALTIES FOR CAUSING CERTAIN KINDS OF DANGER OR ANNOYANCE

(1) If a person, without lawful authority or excuse, deposits anything whatsoever on a highway in consequence of which a user of the highway is injured or endangered[a] that person is guilty of an offence and liable to a fine not exceeding level 3 on the standard scale.

(2) If a person without lawful authority or excuse –
   (a) lights any fire on or over a highway which consists of or comprises a carriageway; or
   (b) discharges any firearm or firework within 50 feet of the centre of such a carriageway,

   and in consequence a user of the highway is injured, interrupted or endangered, that person is guilty of an offence and liable to a fine not exceeding level 3 on the standard scale.

(3) If a person plays at football or any other game[b] on a highway to the annoyance of a user of the highway he is guilty of an offence and liable to a fine not exceeding level 1 on the standard scale.

(4) If a person, without lawful authority or excuse, allows any filth, dirt, lime or other offensive matter or thing[c] to run or flow onto a highway from any adjoining premises, he is guilty of an offence and liable to a fine not exceeding level 1 on the standard scale.

NB (i) For offences relating to the throwing down etc of litter, see Environmental Protection Act 1990, s 87 in Part VII: title Public Health *ante*.

(ii) For meaning of 'carriageway' see s 329 *post*.

23.19 SECTION 161A: ENDANGER OR ANNOYANCE CAUSED BY FIRES LIT OTHERWISE THAN ON HIGHWAYS

(1) If a person –
   (a) lights a fire on any land not forming part of the highway which consists of or comprises a carriageway; or
   (b) directs or permits a fire to be lit on any such land and in consequence a user of any highway which consists of or comprises a carriageway, injured, interrupted or endangered by, or by smoke from that fire or any other fire caused by that fire, that person is guilty of an offence and liable to a fine not exceeding level 5 on the standard scale.

(a) It is up to the prosecution to prove that the injury or danger is caused by the thing deposited (*Gatland v Metropolitan Police Comr* [1968] 2 QB 279, [1968] 2 All ER 100, 132 JP 323).
(b) A mock hunt, with fancy dresses and trumpets, after a man dressed like a stag, is a game (*Pappin v Maynard* (1863) 27 JP 745).
(c) The flow of rainwater from the eaves of a house is not an offensive thing within the meaning of this section (*Crossdill v Ratcliff* (1862) 26 JP 165), but see s 163 *post*.

23.20 SECTION 57 OF THE NATIONAL PARKS AND ACCESS TO THE COUNTRYSIDE ACT 1949

Need to prove/investigate:

1. Place of offence (within jurisdiction of the court).
2. Date or dates of offence(s) within six months time limit.
3. Capacity of defendant, that is, whether company (ltd or plc) or partnership or sole trader. If company, full name and registered office required. If partnership, full names of partners and trading addresses. If sole trader, his full name and address and trading name (if any).
4. Defendant places or maintains a notice on a path or road.
5. Path or road is a public path or road used as a public path (see s 27(b) for definition of 'public path' or 'road used as a public path'). (Produce extract from definitive map or highways register showing highway.)
6. Notice must be on a way shown on a definitive map or on a revised map prepared in definitive form (definitive map being a map produced by a local authority under above Act which has passed the draft and provisional stage. A revised map is a revised definitive map (see s 53(1)). (Produce extract from definitive map or highways register showing highway.)
7. Notice must contain a false or misleading statement (description of why it is false or misleading, photographs).
8. The false or misleading statement must be likely to deter the public from using the way (a description of why it deters the public).
9. Mitigation/explanation from the defendant.

Time limit: six months (s 127 of the Magistrates' Courts Act 1980).

Mode of trial: summary.

Maximum penalty (s 57(1)).

Summary: level 1.

23.21 SECTION 57: PENALTY FOR DISPLAYING ON FOOTPATHS NOTICES DETERRING PUBLIC USE

(1) If any person places or maintains, on or near any way shown on a definitive map, or on a revised map prepared in definitive form, as a public path or road used as a public path, a notice containing any false or misleading statement likely to deter the public from using the way, he shall be liable on summary conviction to a fine not exceeding level 1 on the standard scale.

(2) The Court before whom a person is convicted of an offence under the last foregoing subsection may, in addition to or in substitution for the imposition of a fine, order him to remove the notice in respect of which he is convicted within such period, not being

less than four days, as may be specified in the Order; and if he fails to comply with the Order, he shall be liable on summary conviction to a fine not exceeding £2 for each day on which the failure continues.

(3) It shall be the duty of a Highway Authority to enforce the provisions of this section as respects any public path, or road used as a public path, for which they are the Highway Authority; and no proceedings in respect of any offence under those provisions shall be brought, except by the Authority required by this section to enforce those provisions as respects the path or road in question or by the Council of the district or, where they are not the Highway Authority, the Council of the Welsh county or county borough in which the notice is placed or maintained.

23.22 SECTION 108: POWERS OF ENTRY

(1) For the purpose of surveying land in connection with –
   (a) The acquisition thereof, or of any interest therein, whether by agreement or compulsorily; or
   (c) the making of an Access Order with respect thereto,
   in the exercise of any power conferred by this Act, any person duly authorised in writing by the Minister or other Authority having power so to acquire the land or to make the Order, as the case may be, may enter upon the land.

(2) For the purpose of surveying land, or of estimating its value, in connection with any claim for compensation payable under this Act by a Minister or other Authority in respect of that or any other land, any person being an Officer of the Valuation Office or a person duly authorised in writing by the Authority from whom the compensation is claimed may enter upon the land.

(3) A person authorised under this section to enter upon any land shall, if so required, produce evidence of his authority before entering; and a person shall not, under this section, demand admission as of right to any land which is occupied unless at least 14 days' notice in writing of the intended entry has been given to the occupier.

(4) Any person who wilfully obstructs a person in the exercise of his powers under this section shall be liable on summary conviction to a fine not exceeding level 1 on the standard scale.

23.23 SECTION 51 OF THE NEW ROADS AND STREET WORKS ACT 1991: UNAUTHORISED STREET WORKS

Need to prove/investigate:
1 Place of offence (within jurisdiction of the court).
2 Date or dates of offence(s) within six months time limit.
3 Capacity of defendant, that is, whether company (limited or plc) or partnership or sole trader. If company, full name and registered office required. If partnership, full names of partners and trading addresses. If sole trader, his full name and address and trading name (if any).

4	Defendant broke open a street[a] or a sewer, drain or tunnel under it, tunnelled or bore under a street.
5	The purpose of 4 above was the placing, inspecting, maintaining, adjusting, repairing, altering or renewing apparatus, or of changing the position of apparatus or removing it, otherwise than in pursuance of the statutory right or a street works licence.
6	4, above, was otherwise than in pursuance of the statutory right or street works licence.
7	Defence.
8	Mitigation/explanation from the defendant.

Time limit: six months (s 127 of the Magistrates' Courts Act 1980).

Mode of trial: summary.

Maximum penalty (s 51(2)).

Summary: level 1.

23.24 SECTION 51 OF THE NEW ROADS AND STREET WORKS ACT 1991: PROHIBITION OF AN UNAUTHORISED STREET WORKS

(1) It is an offence for a person, other than the street authority:
   (a) To place apparatus in the street;
   (b) To break up or open a street, or a sewer, drain or tunnel under it, or to tunnel or bore under a street, for the purpose of placing, inspecting, maintaining, adjusting, repairing, altering or renewing apparatus, or of changing the position of apparatus or removing it, otherwise than in pursuance of the statutory right or a street works licence.

(2) A person committing an offence under this section is liable under summary conviction to a fine not exceeding level 3 on the standard scale.

(3) This section does not apply to works for road purpose, or to emergency works of any description.

(4) If a person commits an offence under this section, the street authority may:
   (a) In the case of an offence under sub-section (1)(a), direct him to remove the apparatus in respect of which the offence was committed;
   (b) in any case, direct him to take such steps as appear to be necessary to reinstate the street or any sewer, drain or tunnel under it.

   If he fails to comply with the direction, the authority may remove the apparatus or, as the case may be, carry out the necessary work and recover from him the costs reasonably incurred by them in doing so.

(a) 'Street' is defined by ss 48 and 105.

23.25 SECTION 51 OF THE NEW ROADS AND STREET WORKS ACT 1991: DRAFT INFORMATION

For a draft information/allegation under s 51(1) and (2) of the New Roads and Street Works Act 1991, see Appendix 10.

23.26 ELEMENTS OF OFFENCE

Evidence is required of the name and address of the person whom committed the offence, the day on which it happened, the name of the street and district, and that the council had not granted a street works licence. The mitigation or an explanation for the offence is required from the defendant.

23.27 SECTION 52 OF THE NEW ROADS AND STREET WORKS ACT 1991: EMERGENCY WORKS

(1) In this part, 'emergency works' means works who excuse at the time when they are executed is required in order to put an end to, or to prevent the occurrence of, the circumstances then existing or imminent (or which the person responsible for the works believes on reasonable grounds to be existing or imminent, which are likely to cause danger to persons or property).

(2) Where works comprise items some of which fall within the preceding definition, the expression 'emergency works' shall be taken to include such of the items as do not fall within that definition as cannot reasonable be severed from those that do.

(3) Where in any civil or criminal proceedings brought by virtue of any provision of this part the question arises whether works were emergency works, it is for the person alleging that they were to prove it.

23.28 SECTION 54 OF THE NEW ROAD AND STREET WORKS ACT 1991 – FAILURE TO GIVE ADVANCED NOTICE OF CERTAIN WORKS

Need to prove/investigate:
1 Place of offence (within jurisdiction of the court).
2 Date or dates of offence(s) within six months time limit.
3 Capacity of defendant, that is, whether company (limited or plc) or partnership or sole trader. If company, full name and registered office required. If partnership, full names of partners and trading addresses. If sole trader, his full name and address and trading name (if any).
4 Circumstances must be prescribed in accordance with regulations.[a]
5 Defendant is undertaker proposing to execute street works.[b]

---

[a] See s 104.
[b] Street works are defined by ss 48 and 105.

6 Defendant fails to give prescribed[c] notice[d] or fails to give such information as may be prescribed.
7 Defence.
8 Mitigation/explanation from the defendant.

Time limit: six months (s 127 of the Magistrates' Courts Act 1980).

Mode of trial: summary.

Maximum penalty (s 54(5)).

Summary: level 1.

23.29 SECTION 54 OF THE NEW ROAD AND STREET WORKS ACT 1991: ADVANCED NOTICE OF CERTAIN WORKS

(1) In such cases as may be prescribed, an undertaker proposing to execute street works shall give the prescribed advance notice of the works to the street authority.

(2) Different periods of notice may be prescribed for different descriptions of work.

(3) The notice shall contain such information as may be prescribed.

(4) After giving advance notice under this section, an undertaker shall comply with such requirements as may be prescribed, or imposed by the street authority, as to the providing of information and other procedural steps to be taken for the purpose of co-ordinating the proposed works with any other works of any description proposed to be executed in the street.

(5) An undertaker who fails to comply with his duties under this section commits an offence and is liable on summary conviction to a fine not exceeding level 3 on the standard scale.

23.30 SECTION 54(1) OF THE NEW ROAD AND STREET WORKS ACT 1991: DRAFT INFORMATION

For a draft information/allegation under s 54(1), (4) and (5) of the New Roads and Street Works Act 1991, see Appendix 10.

23.31 ELEMENTS OF OFFENCE

Evidence is therefore required of the name and address of the undertaker who allegedly has committed the offence, which duty that undertaker has failed to comply with, on

---

(c) See s 104 for prescribed notice and the Street Works (Registers, Notices, Directions and Designs) Regulations 1992 SI 1992/2985 as amended by SI 1999/1049.
(d) See s 97 for notice.

what date and in what street and district. An explanation for the offence is required from the defendant.

23.32 SECTION 55 OF THE NEW ROADS AND STREET WORKS ACT 1991: NOTICE OF STARTING DATE OF WORKS

Need to prove/investigate:
1. Place of offence (within jurisdiction of the court).
2. Date or dates of offence(s) within six months time limit.
3. Capacity of defendant, that is, whether company (limited or plc) or partnership or sole trader. If company, full name and registered office required. If partnership, full names of partners and trading addresses. If sole trader, his full name and address and trading name (if any).
4. Defendant is undertaker proposing to execute street works.[a]
5. Street works involve breaking up or opening the street, or any sewer, drain or tunnel under it or tunnelling or boring under the street.
6. Street works have commenced.
7. Failure to give seven days' notice or such notice as may be prescribed[b] to persons set out in s 55(1).
8. Defence.[c]
9. Mitigation/explanation from the defendant.

Time limit: six months (s 127 of the Magistrates' Courts Act 1980).

Mode of trial: summary.

Maximum penalty (s 55(5)).

Summary: level 3.

23.33 SECTION 55 OF THE NEW ROADS AND STREET WORKS ACT 1991 – NOTICE OF STARTING DATE OF WORKS

(1) An undertaker proposes to begin to execute street works[d] involving:
   (a) Breaking up or opening the street, or any sewer, drain or tunnel under it;

(a) Street works are defined by ss 48 and 105.
(b) See s 104 for prescribed notice and the Street Works (Registers, Notices, Directions and Designs) Regulations 1992 SI 1992/2985 as amended by SI 1999/1049.
(c) See defence under s 55 in (6).
(d) Street works are defined by ss 48 and 105.
NB: Essential to see regulations for correct notice. Street Works (Registers, Notices, Directions and Designations) Regulations 1992 SI 1992/2985 as amended.)

(b) tunnelling or boring under the street, shall give not less than 7 working days notice (or such other notice as may be prescribed to the street authority), to the relevant authority and to any other person having apparatus in the street which is likely to be affected by the works).

(2) Different periods of notice may be prescribed for different descriptions of works and cases may be prescribed in which no notice is required.

(3) The notice shall state the date in which it is proposed to begin the works and shall contain such other information as may be prescribed.

(4) Where notice is required to be given under this section, the works shall not be begun without notice or before the end of the notice period, except with the consent of those to whom notice is required to be given.

(5) An undertaker who begins to execute any works in contravention of this section commits an offence, and is liable under summary conviction to a fine not exceeding level 3 on the standard scale.

(6) In proceedings against a person for such an offence, it is a defence for him to show that the conviction was attributable:
 (a) To his not knowing the position, or not knowing of the existence, or of another person's apparatus;
 (b) to his not knowing the identity or address of:
  (i) A relevant authority;
  (ii) the person to whom any apparatus belongs;
 and that his ignorance was not due to any negligence on his part, or to any failure to make enquiries which he ought reasonably to have made.

(7) A notice under this section shall cease to have effect if the works to which it relates are not substantially begun before the end of the period of 7 working days (or such other period as may be prescribed), beginning with the starting date specified in the notice, or such further period as may be allowed by those to whom notice is required to be given.

23.34 SECTION 51 OF THE NEW ROADS AND STREET WORKS ACT 1991: DRAFT INFORMATION

For a draft information/allegation under s 55(1) and (5) of the New Roads and Street Works Act 1991, see Appendix 10.

23.35 SECTION 56 OF THE NEW ROADS AND STREET WORKS ACT 1991: POWER TO GIVE DIRECTIONS AS TO TIMING OF STREET WORKS

(1) If it appears to the street authority:
 (a) That proposed street works are likely to cause serious disruption to traffic;
 (b) that the disruption will be avoided or reduced if the works were carried out only at certain times;

the authority may give the undertaker such directions as may be appropriate as to the times when the works may or may not be carried out.

(2) The procedure for giving a direction is prescribed by the Secretary of State.

(3) An undertaker who executes works in contravention of a direction under this section commits an offence, and is liable on conviction to a fine not exceeding level 3 on the standard scale.

(4) The Secretary of State may issue or approve for the purpose of this section a code of practice giving him practical guidance over the exercise by street authorities of the power conferred by this section; and in exercising the power a street authority shall have regard to the code of practice.

23.36 SECTION 57 OF THE NEW ROADS AND STREET WORKS ACT 1991: NOTICE OF EMERGENCY WORKS

Need to prove/investigate:

1   Place of offence (within jurisdiction of the court).
2   Date or dates of offence(s) within six month's time limit.
3   Capacity of defendant, that is, whether company (limited or plc) or partnership or sole trader. If company, full name and registered office required. If partnership, full names of partners and trading addresses. If sole trader, his full name and address and trading name (if any).
4   Defendant is undertaker proposing to execute emergency works.[a]
5   Works are of a kind in respect of which notice is required by s 55.
6   Failure to give notice within two hours or other prescribed period[b] of when the works began.
7   Notice not given to person prescribed under s 55.
8   Defence.[c]
9   Mitigation/explanation from the defendant.

Time limit: six months (s 127 of the Magistrates' Courts Act 1980).

Mode of trial: summary.

Maximum penalty (s 57(4)).

Summary: level 3.

(a) Careful consideration of the meaning of emergency works by reference to the regulations is required. See the Street Works (Registers, Notices, Directions and Designations) Regulations 1992 SI 1992/2985 as amended.
(b) Reference to the regulations as to the prescribed period is important.
(c) See defence under s 55 in (6), p 343.

23.37 SECTION 57 OF THE NEW ROADS AND STREET WORKS ACT 1991: NOTICE OF EMERGENCY WORKS

(1) Nothing in section 54 (advanced notice), section 55 (notice of starting date (or section 56 (direction as to timing of works) affects the rights of an undertaker to execute emergency works.

(2) An undertaker executing emergency works shall, if the works are of a kind in respect of which notice is required by section 55, give notice as soon as reasonably practicable, and in any event within 2 hours (or such other period as may be prescribed) of the works being begun, to the person to whom notice will be required to be given under this section.

 (3) The notice shall state his intention or, as the case may be, the fact that he has begun to execute the works, and shall contain such other information as may be prescribed.
 (4) An undertaker who fails to give notice in accordance with this section commits an offence, and is liable on summary conviction to a fine not exceeding level 3 on the standard scale.
 (5) See defence under section 55 in (6).

23.38 SECTION 57(2) OF THE NEW ROADS AND STREET WORKS ACT 1991: DRAFT INFORMATION

For a draft information/allegation under s 57(2) and (4) of the New Roads and Street Works Act 1991, see Appendix 10.

23.39 SECTION 58 OF THE NEW ROADS AND STREET WORKS ACT 1991: CONTRAVENTION OF A RESTRICTION OF WORKS FOLLOWING SUBSTANTIAL ROADWORKS

Need to prove/investigate:

1 Place of offence (within jurisdiction of the court).
2 Date or dates of offence(s) within six months time limit.
3 Capacity of defendant, that is, whether company (limited or plc) or partnership or sole trader. If company, full name and registered office required. If partnership, full names of partners and trading addresses. If sole trader, his full name and address and trading name (if any).
4 Defendant is undertaker who broke up etc a highway in contravention of a restriction.
5 An exception in s 58(5) does not apply.
7 Notice given and publication is made as prescribed in s 58(2) and (3)[(a)] defence.
8 Mitigation/explanation from the defendant.

(a) Section 58(3) this is not essential. It is however likely to affect penalty if the defendant is unaware of the notice.

Time limit: six months (s 127 of the Magistrates' Courts Act 1980).

Mode of trial: summary.

Maximum penalty (s 58).

Summary: level 3.

23.40 SECTION 58 OF THE NEW ROADS AND STREET WORKS ACT 1991: RESTRICTION OF WORKS FOLLOWING SUBSTANTIAL ROADWORKS

(1) Where it is proposed to carry out substantial roadworks in a highway, the street authority may, by notice in accordance with this section, restrict the execution of street works during the 12 months following the completion of those works.

For this purpose, substantial road works means works for road purposes, or such works together with other works of such description as may be prescribed.

(2) The notice shall be published in the prescribed manner and shall specify the nature and location of the proposed work, the date (not being less than 3 months after the notice is published or first published) on which it is proposed to begin the works, and the extent of the restriction.

(3) A copy of the notice shall be given to each of the following:
   (a) where there is a public sewer in the part of the highway to which the restriction relates, to the sewer authority;
   (b) where the part of the highway to which the restriction relates is carried or crossed by a bridge vested in a transport authority, or is crossed by another property held or used for the purpose of the street authority, to that authority;
   (c) where in any other case the part of the highway to which the restriction relates is carried or crossed by a bridge, to the bridge authority.
   (d) any person who has given notice under Section 54 (advanced notice of certain works) of his intention to execute street works in the part of the highway to which the restriction relates;
   (e) any other person having apparatus in the part of the highway to which the restrictions relate;

   but a failure to do do does not affect the validity of the restriction imposed by the notice.

(4) An undertaker shall not, in contravention of a restriction, imposed by a notice under this section, break up or open the part of the highway to which the restriction relates, except:
   (a) to execute emergency works;
   (b) with the consent of the street authority;
   (c) in such other cases as may be prescribed.

(5) If he does:
   (a) he commits an offence, and is liable on summary conviction to a fine not exceeding level 3 on the standard scale;
   (b) he is liable to reimburse the street authority any costs reasonably incurred by them in reinstating the highway.
(6) The consent of the street authority under sub-section (5)(b) shall not be unreasonably withheld, and any question whether the withholding of consent is unreasonable shall be settled by arbitration.
(7) ...
(8) ...

23.41 SECTION 58(4) OF THE NEW ROADS AND STREET WORKS ACT 1991: DRAFT INFORMATION

For a draft information/allegation under s 58(4) and (5) of the New Roads and Street Works Act 1991, see Appendix 10.

23.42 SECTION 67 OF THE NEW ROADS AND STREET WORKS ACT 1991: EMPLOYMENT OF UNQUALIFIED SUPERVISORS AND OPERATIVES

Need to prove/investigate:
1. Place of offence (within jurisdiction of the court).
2. Date or dates of offence(s) within six months time limit.
3. Capacity of defendant, that is, whether company (limited or plc) or partnership or sole trader. If company, full name and registered office required. If partnership, full names of partners and trading addresses. If sole trader, his full name and address and trading name (if any).
4. Defendant is an undertaker executing street works.
5. Work involves breaking up the street, or any sewer, drain or tunnel under it or tunnelling or boring under the street.
6. A person having a prescribed qualification as supervisor is not on site.
7. A prescribed exception does not apply.[a]
8. Defence.
9. Mitigation/explanation from the defendant.

Time limit: six months (s 127 of the Magistrates' Courts Act 1980).

Mode of trial: summary

(a) See regulations made by the Secretary of State. See s 104 and Street Works (Qualifications Supervisors and Operatives) Regulations 1992 SI 1992/1687.

Maximum penalty (s 67(3)).

Summary: level 3.

23.43 SECTION 67 OF THE NEW ROADS AND STREET WORKS ACT 1991 – QUALIFICATION OF SUPERVISORS AND OPERATIVES

(1) It is the duty of an undertaker executing street works involving;
   (a) breaking up the street, or any sewer, drain or tunnel under it;
   (b) tunnelling or boring under the street;
   to secure that, except in such cases as may be prescribed, the execution of the works is supervised by a person having a prescribed qualification as supervisor.

(2) It is the duty of an undertaker executing street works involving;
   (a) breaking up or opening the street, or any sewer, drain or tunnel under it;
   (b) tunnelling or boring under the street;
   to secure that, except in such cases as may be prescribed, there is on site at all times any such works are in progress at least one person having a prescribed qualification as a trained operative.

(3) An undertaker who fails to comply with his duty under sub-section (1) or (2) commits an offence, and is liable on summary conviction to a fine not exceeding level 3 on the standard scale.

(4) ...

23.44 SECTION 67(1) OF THE NEW ROADS AND STREET WORKS ACT 1991: DRAFT INFORMATION

For a draft information under s 67(1), (2) and (3) of the New Roads and Street Works Act 1991, see Appendix 10.

23 45 SECTION 68 OF THE NEW ROADS AND STREET WORKS ACT 1991: FAILURE TO PROVIDE FACILITIES TO THE STREET AUTHORITY

Need to prove/investigate:

1. Place of offence (within jurisdiction of the court).
2. Date or dates of offence(s) within six months time limit.
3. Capacity of defendant, that is, whether company (limited or plc) or partnership or sole trader. If company, full name and registered office required. If partnership, full names of partners and trading addresses. If sole trader, his full name and address and trading name (if any).
4. Defendant is an undertaker executing street works.

5 Defendant fails to provide facilities to the street authority for purpose of ascertaining whether he is complying with his duties under this part of the Act.
6 Facilities requested are reasonable.(a)
7 Defence.
8 Mitigation/explanation from the defendant.

Time limit: six months (s 127 of the Magistrates' Courts Act 1980).

Mode of trial: summary.

Maximum penalty (s 68(2)).

Summary: level 3.

23.46 SECTION 68 OF THE NEW ROADS AND STREET WORKS ACT 1991: FACILITIES TO BE AFFORDED TO STREET AUTHORITY

(1) An undertaker executing street works shall afford the street authority reasonable facilities for ascertaining whether he is complying with his duties under this part.

(2) An undertaker who fails to afford the street authority such facilities commits an offence in respect of each failure, and is liable on summary conviction to a fine not exceeding level 3 on the standard scale.

23.47 SECTION 68(1) OF THE NEW ROADS AND STREET WORKS ACT 1991: DRAFT INFORMATION

For a draft information under s 68(1) and (2) of the New Roads and Street Works Act 1991, see Appendix 10.

23.48 SECTION 69 OF THE NEW ROADS AND STREET WORKS ACT 1991: FAILURE TO NOTIFY OWNERS OF OTHER APPARATUS

Need to prove/investigate:
1 Place of offence (within jurisdiction of the court).
2 Date or dates of offence(s) within six months time limit.
3 Capacity of defendant, that is, whether company (limited or plc) or partnership or sole trader. If company, full name and registered office required. If partnership, full names of partners and trading addresses. If sole trader, his full name and address and trading name (if any).
4 Defendant is an undertaker executing street works.
5 Street works are likely to affect other person's apparatus.

(a) Court will no doubt take into account cost and level inconvenience when assessing reasonableness.

6   Defendant has failed to take all practical steps to that other person reasonable facilities to monitor the execution of the works or failed to comply with any reasonable requirement for the protection of the apparatus or for securing access to it.
7   Defendant fails to provide facilities to the street authority for purpose of ascertaining whether he is complying with his duties under this part of the Act.
8   Defence.[a]
9   Mitigation/explanation from the defendant.

Time limit: six months (s 127 of the Magistrates' Courts Act 1980).

Mode of trial: summary.

Maximum penalty (s 69(2)).

Summary: level 3.

23.49 SECTION 69 OF THE NEW ROADS AND STREET WORKS ACT 1991: WORKS LIKELY TO AFFECT OTHER APPARATUS IN THE STREET

(1) Where street works are likely to affect another person's apparatus in the street, the undertaker executing the works shall take all reasonably practicable steps:
   (a) To give the person to whom the apparatus belongs reasonable facilities for monitoring the execution of the works;
   (b) to comply with any requirements made by him which is reasonably necessary for the protection of the apparatus or for securing access to it.
(2) An undertaker who fails to comply with sub-section (1) commits an offence in respect of each failure, and is liable under summary conviction to a fine not exceeding level 3 on the standard scale.
(3) See defence in section 55(6) before.

23.50 SECTION 69(1) OF THE NEW ROADS AND STREET WORKS ACT 1991: DRAFT INFORMATION

For a draft information/allegation under s 69(1) and (2) of the Act, see Appendix 10.

23.51 SECTION 70 OF THE NEW ROADS AND STREET WORKS ACT 1991 – FAILURE TO REINSTATE

Need to prove/investigate:
1   Place of offence (within jurisdiction of the court).
2   Date or dates of offence(s) within six months time limit.

(a) See s 69(3) for statutory defence.

3   Capacity of defendant, that is, whether company (limited or plc) or partnership or sole trader. If company, full name and registered office required. If partnership, full names of partners and trading addresses. If sole trader, his full name and address and trading name (if any).
4   Defendant is an undertaker executing street works.
5   Defendant failed to begin reinstatement as soon as reasonably practicable after completion of part of the street works or failed to complete with such dispatch as is reasonably practicable.
6   Defence.
7   Mitigation/explanation from the defendant.

Time limit: six months (s 127 of the Magistrates' Courts Act 1980).

Mode of trial: summary.

Maximum penalty (s 70(6)).

Summary: level 3.

23.52 SECTION 70 OF THE NEW ROADS AND STREET WORKS ACT 1991: DUTY OF UNDERTAKER TO REINSTATE

(1) It is the duty of the undertaker by whom street works are executed to reinstate the street.

(2) He shall begin the reinstatement as soon after the completion of any part of the street works as is reasonably practicable and shall carry on and complete the reinstatement with all such dispatch, as is reasonably practicable.

(3) He shall, before the end of the next working day after the day on which the reinstatement is completed, inform the street authority that he has completed the reinstatement of the street, stating whether the reinstatement is permanent or interim.

(4) If it is interim, he shall complete the permanent reinstatement of the street as soon as reasonably practicable, and in any event within six months (or such other period as may be prescribed) from the date on which the interim reinstatement was completed; and he shall notify the street authority when he has done so.

(5) The permanent reinstatement of the street shall include, in particular, the reinstatement of features designed to assist people with a disability.

(6) An undertaker who fails to comply with any provisions of this section commits an offence, and is liable on summary conviction to a fine not exceeding level 3 on the standard scale.

(7) In proceedings against a person for an offence of failing to comply with sub-section (2), it is a defence for him to show that any delay in reinstating the street was in order to avoid hindering the execution of any works, or other parts of the same works, to be undertaken immediately or shortly thereafter.

23.53 SECTION 70(1) OF THE NEW ROADS AND STREET WORKS ACT 1991: DRAFT INFORMATION

For a draft information/allegation under s 70(1) and (6) of the Act, see Appendix 16.

23.54 SECTION 71 OF THE NEW ROADS AND STREET WORKS ACT 1991: STANDARDS OF REINSTATEMENT

Need to prove/investigate:
1. Place of offence (within jurisdiction of the court).
2. Date or dates of offence(s) within six months time limit.
3. Capacity of defendant, that is, whether company (limited or plc) or partnership or sole trader. If company, full name and registered office required. If partnership, full names of partners and trading addresses. If sole trader, his full name and address and trading name (if any).
4. Defendant is an undertaker executing street works.
5. Defendant failed to reinstate in accordance with prescribed standards.[a]
6. Defence.
7. Mitigation/explanation from the defendant.

Time limit: six months (s 127 of the Magistrates' Courts Act 1980).

Mode of trial: summary.

Maximum penalty (s 71(5)).

Summary: level 3.

23.55 SECTION 71 OF THE NEW ROADS AND STREET WORKS ACT 1991: MATERIALS, WORKMANSHIP AND STANDARDS OF REINSTATEMENT

(1) An undertaker executing street works shall in reinstating the street comply with such requirements as may be prescribed as to the specification of materials to be used and the standards of workmanship to be observed.

(2) He shall also ensure that the reinstatement confirms to such performance standards as may be prescribed:

(a) in the case of interim reinstatement, until permanent reinstatement is effected;

(b) in the case of permanent reinstatement, for the prescribed period after the completion of the reinstatement.

(a) See the Specification for Reinstatement of Openings in Highways, July 1992 and Code of Practice for Inspections, July 1992.

This obligation is extended in certain cases and restricted in others, by the provisions of section 73 as to cases where a reinstatement is affected by subsequent works.

(3) See Act.

(4) See Act.

(5) An undertaker who fails to comply with his duties under this section commits an offence and is liable on summary conviction to a fine not exceeding level 3 on the standard scale.

23.56 SECTION 71(1) OF THE NEW ROADS AND STREET WORKS ACT 1991: DRAFT INFORMATION

For a draft information/allegation under s 71(1), (2) and (5) of the Act, see Appendix 10.

23.57 SECTION 79 OF THE NEW ROADS AND STREET WORKS ACT 1991: FAILURE TO KEEP RECORDS OF LOCATION OF APPARATUS

Need to prove/investigate:

1. Place of offence (within jurisdiction of the court).
2. Date or dates of offence(s) within six months time limit.
3. Capacity of defendant, that is, whether company (limited or plc) or partnership or sole trader. If company, full name and registered office required. If partnership, full names of partners and trading addresses. If sole trader, his full name and address and trading name (if any).
4. Defendant is an undertaker executing street works.
5. Defendant failed to keep records of every item of apparatus after placing it in a street or being informed of its location under s 80 as soon as reasonably practicable.
6. A prescribed exception does not apply.
7. Defence.
8. Mitigation/explanation from the defendant.

Time limit: six months (s 127 of the Magistrates' Courts Act 1980).

Mode of trial: summary.

Maximum penalty (s 79(4)).

Summary: level 3.

23.58 SECTION 79 OF THE NEW ROADS AND STREET WORKS ACT 1991: RECORDS OF LOCATION OF APPARATUS

(1) An undertaker shall, except in such cases as may be prescribed, record the location of every item of apparatus belonging to him as soon as is reasonably practicable after:

(a) placing in the street or altering its position;
(b) locating it in the street in the course of executing any other works;
(c) being informed of its location under section 80 below.

(2) The records shall be kept up to date and shall be kept in such form and manner as may be prescribed.

(3) An undertaker shall make his records available for inspection, at all reasonable hours and free of charge, by any person having authority to execute works of any description in the street or otherwise appearing to the undertaker to have a sufficient interest.

(4) If an undertaker fails to comply with his duties under this section:
   (a) he commits an offence and is liable on summary conviction to a fine not exceeding level 3 on the standard scale;
   (b) he is liable to compensate any person in respect of damage or loss incurred by him as a consequence of the failure.

(5) In criminal or civil proceedings arising out of any such failure, it is a defence for the undertaker to show that all reasonable care was taken by him, and by his/her contractors and by persons in his employ or that of his contractors, to secure that no such failure occurs.

(6) ...

23.59 SECTION 59 OF THE WILDLIFE AND COUNTRYSIDE ACT 1981: KEEPING BULLS ON LAND CROSSED BY PUBLIC RIGHTS OF WAY

Need to prove/investigate:

1. Place of offence (within jurisdiction of the court).
2. Date or dates of offence(s) within six months time limit.
3. Capacity of defendant, that is, whether company (limited or plc) or partnership or sole trader. If company, full name and registered office required. If partnership, full names of partners and trading addresses. If sole trader, his full name and address and trading name (if any).
4. Defendant is the occupier of a field or enclosure.
5. The field or enclosure is a right if way which is applicable under this part of the Act.
6. Defendant permits a bull to be at large in the field or enclosure.
7. Defence.
8. Mitigation/explanation from the defendant.

Time limit: six months (s 127 of the Magistrates' Courts Act 1980).

Mode of trial: summary.

Maximum penalty (s 59(1)).

Summary: level 3.

23.60 SECTION 5: PROHIBITION ON KEEPING BULLS ON LAND CROSSED BY PUBLIC RIGHTS OF WAY

(1) If in a case not falling within sub-section (2) the occupier of a field or enclosure crossed by right of way to which this part applies permits a bull to be at large in the field or enclosure, shall be liable on summary conviction to a fine not exceeding level 3 on the standard scale.

(2) Sub-section (1) shall not apply to any bull which does not exceed the age of 10 months; or is not a recognised dairy breed and is at large in any field or enclosure in which cows or heifers are also at large.

(3) Nothing in any byelaws, whenever made, shall make unlawful any act which is, or but for sub-section (2) would be, made unlawful by sub-section (1).

(4) In this section 'recognised dairy breed' means one of the following breeds, namely Ayrshire, British Friesian, British Holstein, Dairy Shorthorn, Guernsey, Jersey and Kerry.

(5) The Secretary of State may by order add any breed to, or remove any breed from, sub-section (4); and an order under this sub-section shall be made by statutory instrument which shall be subject to annulment in pursuance of a resolution of either House of Parliament.

23.61 SECTION 66: INTERPRETATION OF PART III

(1) In this part –

'bridleway' means a highway over which the public have the following, but no other, rights of way, that is to say, a right of way on foot and a right of way on horseback or leading a horse, with or without a right to drive animals of any description along the highway;

'byway[a] open to all traffic' means a highway over which the public have a right of way for vehicular and all other kinds of traffic, but which is used by the public mainly for the purpose for which footpaths and bridleways are so used;

'definitive map and statement' has the meaning given by section 53(1);

'footpath' means a highway over which the public have a right of way on foot only, other than such a highway at the side of a public road;

'horse' includes a pony, ass and mule and 'horseback' shall be construed accordingly;

'public path' means a highway being either a footpath or a bridleway;

'right of way to which this Part applies' means a right of way such that the land over which the right subsists is a public path or a byway open to all traffic;

'surveying authority' in relation to any area, means the County Council, County Borough Council, Metropolitan District Council or London Borough Council whose area includes that area.

---

[a] See *R v Secretary of State for the Environment Transport and the Regions ex p Masters* (1999) *The Independent*, 15 November, in which the word 'byways' was given a purposive interpretation and not restricted to those routes presently being used as footpaths and bridleways.

(2) A highway at the side of a river, canal or other inland navigation shall not be excluded from any definition contained in sub-section (1) by reason only that the public have a right to use the highway for purposes of navigation, if the highway would fall within that definition if the public had no such right thereover.

(3) The provisions of section 30(1) of the 1968 Act (riding of pedal cycles on bridleways) shall not affect the definition of bridleway in sub-section (1) and any rights exercisable by virtue of those provisions shall be disregarded for the purposes of this Part.

23.62 SECTION 164 OF THE HIGHWAYS ACT 1980: POWER TO REQUIRE REMOVAL OF BARBED WIRE

(1) Where, on land adjoining a highway, there is a fence made with barbed wire or having barbed wire in or on it, and the wire is a nuisance to the highway, a competent Authority may, by Notice served on the occupier of the land, require him to abate the nuisance within such time, not being less than one month nor more than six months from the date of service of the Notice, as may be specified in it.

(2) If, at the expiration of the time specified in the Notice, the occupier has failed to comply with the Notice, a Magistrates' Court, if satisfied, on complaint made by the Authority, that the wire is a nuisance ('nuisance', at common law, being a material interference with the use and enjoyment of a person's property and, therefore, in this case, the use of the public highway), may order the occupier to abate the nuisance, and if he fails to comply with the Order within a reasonable time, the Authority may do whatever may be necessary in execution of the Order to recover from him the expenses reasonably incurred by them in doing so.

NB: See Appendix 16 for copy of a draft notice.

23.63 SECTION 289 – POWERS OF ENTRY OF HIGHWAY AUTHORITY FOR THE PURPOSE OF SERVICE

(1) A person duly authorised in writing by a Highway Authority may, at any reasonable time, enter on any land for the purpose of surveying that or any other land in connection with the exercise by that Authority, in their capacity as a Highway Authority, of any of their functions.

23.64 SECTION 292 – OBSTRUCTION

(1) A person who wilfully obstructs a person acting in the exercise of a power confirmed by section 289, or who removes or otherwise interferes with any apparatus placed or left on or in any land in the exercise of a power confirmed by section 289 above, is guilty of an offence and liable to a fine not exceeding level 3 on the standard scale.

23.65 SECTION 293: POWERS OF ENTRY FOR PURPOSES CONNECTED WITH CERTAIN ORDERS RELATING TO FOOTPATHS AND BRIDLE WAYS

(1) A person duly authorised in writing by the Secretary of State or other Authority having power under this Act to make a Public Path Creation Order, a Public Path Extinguishment Order, a Rail Crossing Extinguishment Order, a Public Path Diversion Order or a Rail Crossing Diversion Order may enter upon any land for the purpose of surveying it in connection with the making of the Order.

(3) A person authorised under this section to enter upon any land shall, if so required, produce evidence of his authority before entering, and a person shall not, under this section, demand admission as of right to any land which is occupied unless, seven days' notice in writing of the intended entry has been given to the occupier.

(4) A person who wilfully obstructs a person acting in the exercise of his powers under this section is guilty of an offence and liable to a fine not exceeding level 3 on the standard scale.

NB: Compensation is also payable under sub-s (2) if necessary.

23.66 SECTION 297: POWER OF HIGHWAY AUTHORITY OR COUNCIL TO REQUIRE INFORMATION AS TO OWNERSHIP OF LAND

(1) A Highway Authority or a Council may, for the purpose of enabling them to discharge or exercise any of their functions under this Act, require the occupier of any premises and any person who, either directly or indirectly, receives rent in respect of any premises to state in writing the nature of his interest therein and the name and address of any other person known to him as having an interest therein, whether as freeholder, mortgagee, lessee or otherwise.

(2) Any person who, having been required, in pursuance of this section, to give any information, fails to give this information is guilty of an offence and liable to a fine not exceeding level 3 on the standard scale.

(3) Any person who, having been so required to give any information, knowingly makes any misstatement in respect thereof, is guilty of an offence and is liable:

(a) On summary conviction to a fine not exceeding the prescribed sum currently £5,000.

(b) On conviction on indictment to imprisonment for a term not exceeding two years or to a fine or both.

NB: See Appendix 16 for copy of a draft notice.

23.67 SECTION 303: PENALTY FOR OBSTRUCTING EXECUTION OF ACT

A person who wilfully obstructs any person acting in execution of this Act or any byelaw or order made under it is in any case for which no other person made is guilty of an offence and liable to a fine not exceeding level 1 on the standard scale and if the offence is continued after conviction, he is guilty of a further offence and liable to a fine not exceeding £5 for each day on which the offences so continued.

23.68 SECTION 310: SUMMARY PROCEEDINGS FOR OFFENCES

All offences under this Act or under Byelaws made under it are, except as provided by sections 292(4) and 297(3) above, punishable on summary conviction.

23.69 SECTION 311: CONTINUING OFFENCES

(1) Where, by virtue of any provision of this Act or of Byelaws made under it, a person convicted of an offence is, if the offence in respect of which he was convicted is continued after conviction, guilty of a further offence and liable to a fine for each day on which the offence is so continued. The Court before whom the person is convicted of the original offence may fix a reasonable period from the date of conviction for compliance by the defendant with any directions given by the Court.

(2) Where a Court fixes such a period, the defendant is not liable to a fine in respect of the further offence for any day after the expiration of that period.

23.70 SECTION 320: FORM OF NOTICE, ETC

All Notices, Consents, Approvals, Orders, Demands, Licences or Certificates given by a Highway Authority shall be in writing and, under section 321, duly authenticated by a duly authorised Officer of the Council by his personal signature or facsimile.

23.71 SECTION 322: SERVICE OF NOTICES, ETC

(1) Any Notice, Consent, Approval, Order, Demand, Licence, Certificate or other document required or authorised by or under this Act to be given or served on a corporation is duly given or served if it is given to or served on the Secretary or Clerk of the corporation.

(2) Subject to the provisions of this section, any Notice, Consent, etc, to be given to or served on any person may be given or served either:
   (a) By delivering it to that person; or
   (b) by leaving it at his proper address; or
   (c) by post.

MAGISTRATES' COURT FORMS: MAGISTRATES' COURT ACT (MCA) 1980 AND CRIMINAL JUSTICE ACT (CJA) 1967

(a) Notice to defendant, s 12 of the MCA 1980.
(b) Statement of facts, s 12 of the MCA 1980.
(c) Notice of plea of guilty, s 12 of the MCA 1980.
(d) Reply form, s 12 of the MCA 1980.
(e) Notice of intention to cite previous convictions, s 104 of the MCA 1980.
(f) Notice to defendant proof by written procedure, s 9 of the CJA 1967.
(g) Reply form, CJA 1967.
(h) Rule 3 notice, Magistrates' Court (advance information) Rules 1985.

NOTICE TO DEFENDANT (MC ACT 1980 S12(3)(A))
PLEA OF GUILTY IN ABSENCE
IN THE]><[COUNTY OF]><[
PETTY SESSIONAL DIVISION OF]>VAR 1<[

To: The Defendant

]>var 2<[

PLEASE READ THIS NOTICE CAREFULLY

If you admit the offence(s) referred to in the Summons(es) served herewith and do not wish to appear before the Court, it is open to you, under Section 12 of the Magistrates' Courts Act 1980, to inform the Clerk of the Court in writing that you wish to plead guilty to the charge(s) without appearing. If you decide to do this, you should write to the Clerk at least three days before the date fixed for the hearing in order to avoid the unnecessary costs and possible attendance of witnesses. In writing to the Clerk you should mention any mitigating circumstances which you wish to have put before the Court. (If you write as mentioned you are required to include a statement of your date of birth and sex.) *A form which you can use for writing to the Clerk is enclosed.*

Please complete the enclosed means form. This is to enable the Court to take your income and outgoings into account should it decide to impose a fine for the offence or order you to pay the costs of the prosecution.

If you send in a written plea of guilty the enclosed Statement(s) of Facts and notices describing information about you and your Statement in mitigation will be read out in open Court before the Court decides whether to accept your plea and hear and dispose of the case in your absence. Unless the Court adjourns the case after accepting your plea and before sentencing you (in which case you will be informed of the time and place of the adjourned hearing so that you may appear) the prosecution will not be permitted to make any statement with respect to any facts relating to the offence(s) other than the Statement(s) of Facts and notices describing information about you included with your Summons.

If you send in a written plea of guilty but the Court decides not to accept the plea, the hearing will be adjourned and you will be informed of the time and place of the adjourned hearing. The case will then be heard as if you had not sent in a written plea of guilty.

If you send in a written plea of guilty you may, if you wish, withdraw it by informing the Clerk of the withdrawal at any time before the hearing. However, if the Court adjourns the hearing to enable it to dispose of the case in your absence on a later date, it is not obliged to notify you of that date unless the adjourned hearing is to be held more than four weeks after the adjournment.

You may appear before the Court at the time fixed for the hearing and plead guilty or not guilty. If you have pleaded guilty by post and changed your mind, you must tell the

Clerk before the hearing that you wish to withdraw your plea; the case will then be dealt with as if you had not sent a written plea of guilty.

If it is your intention to plead not guilty it is vital that, in order to avoid delay and expense, you inform the Clerk immediately of that fact, so that prosecution witnesses can be notified that they must attend. If the prosecution witnesses have to be called, it is likely that there will have to be an adjournment to enable the witnesses to come to Court. However, if the prosecutor has served on you notice that written statements of witnesses have been put before the Court, the hearing may proceed on the basis of written evidence unless you have informed the prosecutor that you want one or more of the witnesses to give oral evidence. IF YOU ENTER A NOT GUILTY PLEA, EITHER YOU OR YOUR LEGAL REPRESENTATIVE MUST APPEAR IN COURT.

If you pleaded guilty by post and you appear at the Court hearing and maintain that plea, OR if you have not pleaded guilty by post and you appear in Court to plead guilty, the Court may deal with the case if you were absent, provided you consent. In these circumstances, before the Court accepts your plea of guilty and before it convicts you, either you, or your legal representative (if you have one) will be entitled to make oral representations in mitigation at that hearing.

NOTES:
1. If you want any more information you may get in touch with the Clerk to the Court.
2. If you intend to consult a Solicitor you would be well advised to do so before taking any action in response to this notice.
3. Address any letter to the Clerk to the Magistrates,]>var 3<[.

To:]>var 1<[
Of:]>var 2<[

If you inform the Clerk of the Court that you wish to plead guilty to the charge set out in the Summons served herewith, without appearing before the Court and the Court proceeds to hear and dispose of the case in your absence under Section 12 of the Magistrates' Courts Act 1980, the following Statements of Facts will be read out in open Court before the Court decides whether to accept your plea.

STATEMENT OF FACTS
(Section 12(3)(b) of the MCA 1980)

The prosecution will be seeking investigative costs of £]>var 5<[and Legal costs presently standing at £]>var 6<[and to be added to at the hearing.

Name of Defendant:]>var 1<[

Date of hearing:]>var 2<[

Ref No: LEG/LIT/]>var 3<[

MAGISTRATES' COURT ACT 1980
NOTICE OF PLEA OF GUILTY

To: The Clerk of the]>var 4<[Magistrates' Court

Plea of Guilty

I have read the statement of facts relating to the charge.

I plead guilty and I desire that the Court should dispose of the case in my absence. I wish to bring to the Court's attention the mitigating circumstances set out below.

Signed ....

MITIGATING CIRCUMSTANCE

NOTES:
1 If you intend to consult a solicitor about the case you would be well advised to do so before returning this form.
2 If you propose to attend Court, please fill in the form overleaf.

If you propose to attend Court, and are willing to answer any of the questions below and to return this form the Clerk of the Court at the address overleaf within seven days, time and inconvenience may be saved.

1 Do you intend to deny the charge/any of the charges?
   If so, you should appear with any witnesses you may wish to bring.
2 Do you intend to admit the charge/any of the charges?

You are at liberty at any time to change your mind as to whether or not you will appear. If you do change your mind, please let the Clerk know before the hearing that you have done so.

If you intend to appear by solicitor or Counsel, you would be well advised not to complete this form without consulting your solicitor.

To: Solicitor to the Council
   (Name and Address of Council)
Your Ref: LEG/LIT/]>ref<[

REPLY FORM

]>WHICH<[MAGISTRATES' COURT

HEARING DATE AND TIME]>date and time<[

The Council v]>who<[

Contravention of]><[

1   I have received the following documents:
   (a)]>number<[Summons(es) dated]>date<[.
   (b) A 'Means Form'.
   (c) Notice of Previous Convictions.
   *(d) Notice under Rule 3 Magistrates' Courts (Advance Information) Rules 1985.
   (e) Copies of the statements of the witnesses –]>names<[.
   (f) Notice to Defendant – Proof by Written Statement (CJ Act 1967 s 9).
   (g) Notice to Defendant – Plea of Guilty in Absence (MC Act 1980 s 12).
   (h) Statement of Facts (MC Act 1980 s 12).
   (i) Notice of Plea of Guilty (MCA 1980).

*2 I request advance information as set out in the above Rules.

*Either

3   I do not require any of the witnesses whose statements I have received to be called.

*Or

4   I require the following witnesses to attend Court:

5   I intend to plead guilty*/not guilty to the offence(s).
   I realise I must attend Court in any event.
   NB A not guilty plea will not proceed at the first hearing.
   NNB Failure to indicate your plea five working days prior to the hearing may result in *additional costs to you*.

*6 I intend to instruct the following Solicitors: ....

Signed ....
Address ....
....
Date ....

*Delete whichever does not apply.

(Name and Address of Council)

NOTICE OF INTENTION TO CITE PREVIOUS CONVICTIONS
Section 104 of the Magistrates' Courts Act 1980

RECORDED DELIVERY

TO:]>var 1<[

You are hereby given notice that if, but only if, you are convicted of (any of) the offence(s) of

]>var 2<[

in respect of which you are summoned to appear before the]>var 3<[Magistrates' Court on the]>var 4<[day of]>var 5<[20..., the undermentioned convictions which are recorded against you will be brought to the notice of the Court; and if you are not present in person before the Court, the Court may take account of any such previous convictions as if you have appeared and admitted them.

DATE OF CONVICTION	COURT	OFFENCE	SENTENCE

Date ....

Signed ....

Solicitor to the Council

If you do not intend to appear in person at the hearing and you dispute any of the above convictions, or any of the details in connection with them, you should immediately notify the Solicitor of the Council at the address above (Ref:) so that further enquiries can be made.

Nothing in this Notice limits in any way your right to appear in person on the date fixed for the hearing and to dispute any conviction alleged against you.

NOTICE TO DEFENDANT: PROOF BY WRITTEN STATEMENT
(Section 9 of the Criminal Justice Act 1967; s 102 of the MCA 1980; r 70 of the MCA Rules 1981)

In the]>var 1<[Magistrates' Court

To:]>var 2<[

of:]>var 3<[

On the]>var 4<[day of]>var 5<[the Magistrates' Court sitting at the]>var 6<[, will hear evidence relating to the following charge(s) against you:

]>var 7<[

This offence (or these offences):
1 May be tried before a jury or by the Magistrates' Court, or
2 May be tried by the Magistrates' Court.

Written statements have been made by the witnesses named below and copies of their statements are enclosed. Each of these statements will be tendered in evidence before the Magistrates unless you want the witnesses to give oral evidence. If you want any of these witnesses to give oral evidence you should inform me as soon as possible.

If you do not do so within seven days of receiving this notice and the offence(s) is/are tried by the Magistrates' Court, you will lose your right to prevent the statement being tendered in evidence and will be able to require the attendance of the witness only with the leave of the Court. If the offence(s) is/are not tried by the Magistrates' Court this time limit will not apply, but if you have not informed me that you want the witness to attend he will not be present when you appear before the Magistrates and delay and expense will be caused if he has then to be called.

A reply form is enclosed and it will help save time and expense if you reply whether or not you wish any of these witnesses to give oral evidence.

If you intend to consult a solicitor about your case, you should do so at once and hand this notice and the statements to him so that he may deal with them.

Names of witnesses whose statements are enclosed:

]>var 8<[

Address any reply to the Solicitor to the Council, (address and name of Council)

Ref:

Appendix 1: Magistrates' Court Forms

To: Solicitor to the Council
   (enter name and address)

Your Ref:

REPLY FORM

]>WHICH<[MAGISTRATES' COURT

HEARING DATE AND TIME   ]>date and time<[

The Council v]>who<[

Contravention of]><[

1 I have received the following documents:-
   (a)]>number<[Summons(es) dated]>date<[
   (b) A 'Means Form'
   (c) Notice of Previous Convictions.
   (d) Notice under Rule 3 Magistrates' Courts (Advance Information) Rules 1985.
   (e) Copies of the statements of the witnesses]>names<[.
   (f) Record(s) of Interview.

*2 I request advance information as set out in the above Rules.

*Either

3 I do not require any of the witnesses whose statements I have received to be called.

*Or

4 I require the following witnesses to attend Court:
   ....
   ....
   ....

5 I intend to plead guilty*/not guilty to the offence(s).
   I realise I must attend Court in any event.

*6 I intend to instruct the following Solicitors:
   ....
   ....

                                        Signed ....
                                        Address ....
                                        ....
                                        Date ....

*Delete whichever does not apply.

(Name and address of Council)

RULE 3 OF THE MAGISTRATES' COURTS (ADVANCE INFORMATION) RULES 1985

To:

Of:

Offence charged:

You should read this notice carefully and, if you are represented by a Solicitor or intend to consult one, you should show it to him at once.

The offence with which you are charged is of a sort which may be tried by a Magistrates' Court or the Crown Court. Accordingly, under Rule 4 of the above Rules, you are, or a person representing you is, entitled to ask to be furnished with advance information about the evidence upon which the prosecutor proposes to rely in the proceedings. If you wish to obtain advance information you or your representative must make the request *before* the Magistrates' Court begins to consider whether you are to be tried by that Court or by the Crown Court or, if you are a juvenile, before you are asked to plead. You or your representative should make your request before the Court hearing takes place.

Rule 4 requires the prosecutor to respond to a properly made request for advance information by furnishing the accused or his representative, as soon as practicable, with *either* a copy of those parts of every witness statement which deal with facts and matters of which he proposes to adduce evidence in the proceedings *or* a summary of those facts and matters. The prosecutor has also to supply a copy of any document on which he is to rely which is referred to in the statements or summary or to give information which would enable the accused or his representative to inspect the document or a copy of it. The prosecutor may withhold disclosure of any particular fact or matter, if he is of the opinion that its disclosure might lead to the course of justice being interfered with.

If you wish to ask for advance information your request may be made on the attached reply form.

In any event please acknowledge receipt. HEREWITH ALL STATEMENTS

Dated the .... day of .... 20.....

Solicitor

Council's Name and Address

Ref:

HOUSING BENEFIT AND COUNCIL TAX BENEFIT PRECEDENTS

1. Summons, s 17(1)(a) of the Theft Act 1968.
2. Summons, s 17(1)(a) of the Theft Act 1968.
3. Section 112(1)(b) and (2) of the Social Security Administration Act 1992.
4. Section 111A(1)(b) of the Social Security Administration Act 1992.
5. Section 111A(1)(a) of the Social Security Administration Act 1992.
6. Section 111A(1)(c) of the Social Security Administration Act 1992.
7. Authorisation of legal proceedings (specimen).
8. List of Authorities (meaning of knowing under the Social Security Administration Act 1992).

SUMMONS]>VAR1<[

IN THE]>var2<[MAGISTRATES' COURT

To:]>var3<[

of:]>var4<[

INFORMATION has this day been laid before the undersigned by]　　　[on behalf of]　　[Council, that you

on]>var5<[

at]>var6<[

Did dishonestly and with a view to gain for himself/another with intent to cause loss to another falsified for accounting purposes a document namely a .... form by making therein an entry which was misleading, false or deceptive in a material particular in that .... contrary to s 17(1)(a) of the Theft Act 1968.

YOU ARE THEREFORE SUMMONED to appear before the Magistrates' Court

sitting at]>var7<[

on]>var8<[

at]>var9<[to answer to the said Information.

DATED the ....day of ....20.....

....

Clerk to the Justices/Clerk to the Court/

Justice of the Peace

If you do not respond to this Summons, the case may be dealt with in your absence.

Please note that upon conviction the prosecution will be seeking costs against you.

Appendix 2: Housing Benefit and Council Tax Benefit Precedents

SUMMONS/INFORMATION]>VAR1<[

IN THE]>VAR2<[MAGISTRATES' COURT

To:]>var3<[

of:]>var4<[

INFORMATION has this day been laid before the undersigned by   on behalf Council, that you

on or before]>var5<[

at]>var6<[

did dishonestly and with a view to gain for yourself, produced an income support review/application form, a document required for an accounting purpose, which to your knowledge was misleading, false or deceptive in a material particular, namely that were false contrary to Section 17(1)(b) of the Theft Act 1968.

YOU ARE THEREFORE SUMMONED to appear before the Magistrates' Court

sitting at]>var8<[

on]>var9<[

at]>var10<[to answer to the said Information.

DATED the .... day of .... 20.....

....

Clerk to the Justices/Clerk to the Court/

Justice of the Peace

Please note that upon conviction the prosecution will be seeking costs against you.

SUMMONS]>VAR1<[

IN THE]>var2<[MAGISTRATES' COURT

To:]>var3<[

of:]>var4<[

INFORMATION has this day been laid before the undersigned by [insert name and address of Council Solicitor] on behalf of [insert name of Council], that you

on]>var 5<[

at]>var 6<[

did for the purpose of obtaining benefit or other payments for yourself under the social security legislation]>var 7<[-delete as appropriate the following produced or furnished or]>var 8<[knowingly caused or knowingly allowed to be produced or furnished any document/information which you knew to be false in a material particular for the purpose of obtaining benefit, in that you furnished an application form dated]>var 9<[, stating that the information provided was true and complete, whereas you failed to declare that]>var 10<[(insert evidence of failure)

CONTRARY to section 112(1)(b) and (2) of the Social Security Administration Act 1992.

YOU ARE THEREFORE SUMMONED to appear before the Magistrates' Court

sitting at]>var 11<[

on]>var 12<[

at]>var 13<[to answer to the said Information.

DATED the ....day of .... 20.....

....
Clerk to the Justices/Clerk to the Court/
Justice of the Peace

If you do not respond to this Summons, the case may be dealt with in your absence.

Please note that upon conviction the prosecution will be seeking costs against you.

Appendix 2: Housing Benefit and Council Tax Benefit Precedents

SUMMONS]>VAR1<[

IN THE]>var2<[MAGISTRATES' COURT

To:]>var3<[

of:]>var4<[

INFORMATION has this day been laid before the undersigned by [insert name and address of Council Solicitor] on behalf of [insert name of Council], that you

on]>var 5<[

at]>var 6<[

did dishonestly produce/furnish/cause/allow to be produced or furnished any document or information which was false in a material particular; with a view to obtaining benefit or other payment or advantage under the social security legislation whether by himself or some other person in that]>var 7<[(set out false statement) by reason that]>var 8<[(say why document false)

CONTRARY to s 111A(1)(b) of the Social Security Administration Act 1992 as inserted by s 13 of the Social Security Administration (Fraud) Act 1997.

YOU ARE THEREFORE SUMMONED to appear before the Magistrates' Court

sitting at]>var 9<[

on]>var 10<[

at]>var 11<[to answer to the said Information.

DATED the .... day of .... 20.....

....

Clerk to the Justices/Clerk to the Court/

Justice of the Peace

If you do not respond to this Summons, the case may be dealt with in your absence.

Please note that upon conviction the prosecution will be seeking costs against you.

SUMMONS]>VAR1<[

IN THE]>var2<[MAGISTRATES' COURT

To:]>var3<[

of:]>var4<[

INFORMATION has this day been laid before the undersigned by [insert name and address of Council Solicitor] on behalf of [insert name of Council], that you

on]>var 5<[

at]>var 6<[

did dishonestly make a statement or representation during the period in which income support benefit was paid]>var 7<[- two dates with a view to obtaining benefit in that]>var 8<[(set out false statement) which was false by reason that]>var 9<[(say why statement was false)

CONTRARY to s 111A(1)(a) of the Social Security Administration Act 1992 as inserted by s 13 of the Social Security Administration (Fraud) Act 1997.

YOU ARE THEREFORE SUMMONED to appear before the Magistrates' Court

sitting at]>var 10<[

on]>var 11<[

at]>var 12<[to answer to the said Information.

DATED the .... day of .... 20.....

....
Clerk to the Justices/Clerk to the Court/
Justice of the Peace

If you do not respond to this Summons, the case may be dealt with in your absence.

Please note that upon conviction the prosecution will be seeking costs against you.

SUMMONS/INFORMATION]>VAR1<[

IN THE]>var2<[MAGISTRATES' COURT

To:]>var3<[

of:]>var4<[

INFORMATION has this day been laid before the undersigned by, on behalf of Council, that you

on]>var5<[

at]>var6<[

Did dishonestly fail to notify a change of circumstances in writing to the designated office of the Local Authority during the benefit period in that]>var7<[

as required by Regulation 75(1) of the Housing Benefit (General) Regulations 1987 (as amended) under the Social Security Administration Act 1992 as amended with a view to obtaining housing benefit.

CONTRARY TO s 111A(1)(c) of the Social Security Administration Act 1992 as inserted by s 13 of the Social Security Administration (Fraud) Act 1997.

YOU ARE THEREFORE SUMMONED to appear before the Magistrates' Court

sitting at]>var8<[

on 2001

at .... to answer to the said Information.

DATED the .... day of .... 20.....

....

Clerk to the Justices/Clerk to the Court/

Justice of the Peace

Please note that upon conviction the prosecution will be seeking costs against you.

AUTHORISATION OF LEGAL PROCEEDINGS

Authority is given to institute, and continue to a final conclusion legal proceedings against the following person(s) in respect of an alleged offence(s) against the legislation noted subject to the Director of Legal Services being satisfied on points of evidence.

Date of alleged offence	Place of alleged offence	Name and address of person against whom proceedings are to be taken	Enactment under which proceedings are to be taken*

....

on or about or between .... and .... 20 .....

Did dishonestly and with a view to gain for himself/another with intent to cause loss to another falsified for accounting purposes a .... namely a form .... by making therein an entry which was misleading, false or deceptive in a material particular in that .... contrary to s 17(1)(a)

or**

Recommended .... Authorised Signatory ....

DATED ....

*make reference to Act, section, subsection and sufficient detail to ensure that the chosen allegation is clearly set out.

**In furnishing information for obtaining housing benefit/council tax and with a view to gain for himself or another or with intent to cause loss to another produced a document required for accounting purposes namely a .... which to his/her knowledge was or might be misleading, false or deceptive in a material particular in that it purported to show that .... contrary to s 17(1)(b) of the Theft Act 1968 or;

Did dishonestly obtain from The City of Bradford Metropolitan District Council the sum of £.... on a Giro cheque number .... With the intention of permanently depriving the said Council of the same by deception, namely by falsely representing that he/she was entitled to the aforesaid sum whereas .... contrary to s 15(1) of the Theft Act 1968.

PROSECUTIONS UNDER SOCIAL SECURITY ADMINISTRATION ACT 1992

MEANING OF KNOWINGLY
LIST OF AUTHORITIES (SUBMITTED BY LEA)

AUTHORITY	PURPOSE
J Sheldon Deliveries Ltd v Willis [1972] RTR 217 @ 220c	Knowledge can be imputed to a person who shuts his mind to the obvious or allowed something to go on not caring whether an offence was committed or not.
Evans v Dell [1937] All ER 349 @ 353B	One who is put on enquiry and fails to make proper enquiries has knowledge.
Barras v Reeve [1980] 3 All ER 705	It is not necessary to show that the false representation was made with the intention of obtaining benefit. It is sufficient to establish that the person claiming the benefit made a representation he knew to be false ie acted dishonestly.
Slough v Stevenson (1943) 4 DLE 433 *per* Kellock JA	I think 'knowingly' in the statute is used in the sense that the applicant (insurance claim) is in possession of information that what is in fact stated in the application is untrue or does not disclose the truth.
DSS v Bavi [1996] COD 260	In a prosecution under s 112 of the SSAA 1992 the defendant claimed that the representation had occurred due to a misunderstanding. Held: it was not necessary to prove intention to deceive or to defraud. The defendant knew that the statement he had made was false and this was sufficient.
Taylors Central Garage Ltd v Roper (1951) 115 JP 445 @ 449/450 (see also *R v Thomas* (1976) 63 Cr App R 65)	Knowledge in law means 'actual knowledge and that the justices may infer from the nature of the act that was done and may find it (actual knowledge) of course even if the defendant gives evidence to the contrary'. AND 'knowledge of the second degree' where the justices 'consider whether what the defendant was doing was, as it has been called, shutting his eyes to an obvious means of knowledge'.

Clear v Smith [1981] 1 WLR 399   It is not necessary for the prosecution to prove an intention to defraud (Supplementary Benefits Act 1976).

CASE REPORT FORM

CASE REPORT

1 **NAME OF DEFENDANT(S)**
   DOB

2 **ADDRESS(ES)**

3 **DATE(S) OF ALLEGED OFFENCE**

4 **LOCATION OF ALLEGED OFFENCE(S)**

5 **ALLEGED OFFENCES**
   (Specify Section of Act or Regulation under which each alleged offence is to be brought)

6 **LATEST DATE FOR INFORMATIONS**

7 **REPORTING OFFICER**   (Tel No)

8 **DEPARTMENT/OFFICE ADDRESS**

9 LIST OF WITNESSES

(Statement, address and telephone number of witness) (use separate sheet if necessary)

10 LIST OF DOCUMENTARY AND OTHER EXHIBITS

(Use separate sheet if necessary)

11 PREVIOUS CONVICTIONS

(Use separate sheet if necessary)

12 SUGGESTED OFFENCE(S)

(Use separate sheet if necessary)

13 OFFENCE SUMMARY

(Include brief description of the events)
(Use separate sheet if necessary)

14 SPECIAL OBSERVATIONS (include separate sheet if necessary)

(a) Local Councillor involved (name/ward/reason for involvement)
(b) Matters to be taken into consideration (name)
(c) Caution (Yes/No)
(d) Process as charged (Yes/No)
(e) Likely plea (Guilty/Not Guilty/Don't Know)
(f) Schedule attached as to Investigative costs
(g) Interpreter required (Yes/No)

SIGNED .... (REPORTING OFFICER) .... DATE

SIGNED .... (MANAGER) ....DATE

APPENDIX 4

WITNESS STATEMENT FORM

STATEMENT OF WITNESS

(Section 9 of the CJA 1967; ss 5A(3)(a) and 5B of the MCA 1980; r 70 of the MC Rules 1981)

Statement of

Age of witness (if over 18 enter 'over 18')

Occupation of witness

(Witness to sign at the end of the statement and at the completion of the following declaration)

This statement [consisting of   pages each signed by me], is true to the best of my knowledge and belief and I make it knowing that, if it is tendered in evidence, I shall be liable to prosecution if I have wilfully stated in it anything which I know to be false or do not believe to be true.

.... being unable to read the above statement

I, ... of ....

read it to him before he signed it.

Dated the   day of   20

Dated the   day of   20

(Signed)

STATEMENT OF WITNESS

(SECTION 9 OF THE CJA 1967; SS 5A(3)(A) AND 5B OF THE MCA 1980; R 70 OF THE MC RULES 1981)

Statement of: .... **Page No:**

(Continuation Sheet)

Date of Birth of Witness ....
Address of Witness ....
....
Post Code..................................

Statement taken by ....

APPENDIX 5

CERTIFICATE OF SERVICE

RULES 67 AND 69 OF THE MAGISTRATES' COURTS RULES 1981

I, of]>(name Council)<[,]>(insert address)<[, hereby certify that I served the Defendant, with the Summons, s 12 of the MCA 1980 notice, plea form, statement of facts, statements of, s 9 of the CJA 1967 notice and s 9 form, of which these are true copies, by sending the said documents by recorded delivery service/ordinary post to the Defendant in a pre-paid letter posted by me at the]>insert<[Post Office situate at]>(insert address)<[at

on of and addressed to the Defendant at being the Defendant's last known (or usual) place of abode. (A copy of the certificate of posting is attached hereto.)

DATED the

Signature	]>(insert)<[
Name in full	]>(insert)<[
Occupation	]>(insert)<[
Address	]>(insert)<[

RECORD OF INTERVIEW FORMS

NOTICE TO PERSON WHOSE INTERVIEW HAS BEEN TAPE RECORDED

This notice explains the use which will be made of the tape recording and the provisions for access to it by the defence in the event of you being prosecuted.

GENERAL

The interview has been recorded on two tapes. One of these tapes has been sealed in your presence and will be kept securely and treated as an exhibit for the purpose of any criminal proceedings.

The other tape will be a working copy to which the Enforcement Officer(s) and defence may have access. Both tapes contain devices against tampering.

If you do not have a solicitor now you may wish to consider whether you should seek legal representation. If, however, you wish to remain unrepresented, you will be given access to a copy of the tape.

COPY TAPES

Your interview was recorded on .... tapes.

If you or your solicitor wish to obtain copy(ies) of the tape(s) send your written application, which should be addressed to:

TAPE LIBRARIAN ....

Please quote the following reference number in any correspondence:

Ref No .... Names of Person(s) interviewed..

Copy tape(s) will be despatched to you by means of Recorded Delivery.

NOTICE: AT THE CONCLUSION OF THE CASE PLEASE ENSURE PROMPT RETURN OF ALL TAPES TO THE TAPE LIBRARIAN AT THE ABOVE ADDRESS

RECORD OF TAPE RECORDED INTERVIEW

Person Interviewed   Defendant

Place and Date of Interview

Other Person(s) Present

DECLARATION: This record consisting of .... pages is the exhibit referred to in the Statement made and signed by me.

Signed

Officer's Name .... Rank........................

Signature of Officer preparing record
(if different to above)

Officer's Name.. Rank........................

Tape Times	Direct Speech	
Initials of the Investigating Officer and of Accused		Record

SENSITIVE MATERIAL ON TAPE RECORDING
FROM: Name... Rank..

TO: SECTION HEAD............................ Date.....................................

Suspects Name:

Tape Ref Number

On: .... (date) the suspect named above was interviewed at .... The interview was tape recorded on................................(quantity) Master Tapes.

Appendix 6: Record of Interview Forms

Parts of the recording include sensitive material or matters to which I would draw your attention (eg, Non-conformity with Codes of Practice, previous convictions, offences TIC or not likely to be proceeded with informant's details).

Tape Ref No .... From Min .... Sec .... To Min .... Sec .... Subject Matter ....

NOTICE TO SOLICITOR

TAPE RECORDING OF INTERVIEWS
BY ENFORCEMENT OFFICERS

Name of Defendant

Tape Reference

Court and Date

1   The enclosed copies of working tapes relate to the interview with your above-named client. These tapes have/have not* been edited to exclude sensitive material in accordance with the Home Office Directive.

2   In the event that you wish to take issue with any part of the evidence contained on this recording, or require additional material from the recorded interview to be included in the officer's record of interview, you should communicate that fact to the .... at the earliest convenient time. One of the intentions of tape recording is that any dispute arising out of the conduct of the interview, or of the evidence obtained thereby may be resolved by the defence and prosecution well before the case comes to trail so that unnecessary adjournments be eliminated.

*Delete where applicable

RECORD OF INTERVIEW

Ref No......................

Sheet No....................

Held at:

Name:

Address:

Postcode: .... Telephone No: ....

Occupation: .... Date of Birth: ....

| Date Taken: | Time From: | Time To: | Time of Caution: | By Whom: | Persons Present: | Breaks (if any): |

RECORD OF INTERVIEW

Ref No......................

Sheet No....................

Location of Interview:

Name of Person Interviewed:

Address:

Postcode:

Occupation:

Date of Birth:

Date Taken:	Time From:	Time To:	Time of Caution:	By Whom:	Persons Present:	Breaks (if any):

SPECIMEN

[INSERT QUESTIONS AND ANSWERS TO AND FROM DEFENDANT]

Initial of Officer/ Defendant Time Interview Taken

Summary of Interview

HEO   9.04 am

My name is ... I am a Highways Enforcement Officer employed by .... Council based at the Town Hall, today's date and the time is 9.04 am and we are at the Town Hall, Could you identify yourself please?

JS   John Smith

HEO   Your full address?

JS   ....

HEO   Your date of birth please?

JS   ....

HEO   You are not under arrest and you are not obliged to remain in this interview. You may wish to obtain legal advice. Do you understand?

JS   Yes thank you. I do not want legal advice.

Appendix 6: Record of Interview Forms

HEO	9.05 am. I must inform you before we commence the formal interview that you do not have to say anything unless you wish to do so but it may harm your defence if you do not mention, when questioned, something which you later rely on in Court. Anything you do say may be given in evidence. Do you understand?
JS	Yes thank you [but I'm not prepared to answer any questions].
HEO	[If refusal to answer questions then state:] Bearing in mind your refusal to answer questions then in accordance with the Police and Criminal Evidence Act 1984, I must give you the following special warnings:
HEO	[If no refusal to answer then follow with those questions marked thus] I am investigating the alleged offence that on you caused, without lawful authority or excuse, the wilful obstruction of a public footpath at Eastham thereby obstructing the free passage along the footpath by dropping cut tree branches completely across the route.
HEO	I will in a moment ask you to account for such allegations.
HEO	It is believed you have committed the alleged offence as stated.
HEO	Should this matter be made the subject of prosecution the Court may be invited to draw proper inference if you fail to or refuse to account for facts upon which you are to be questioned in relation to the alleged offence as stated or that your account or failure to account suggests a future or present explanation has been fabricated.
HEO	A copy of this interview will be placed before the Court.
HEO	Do you understand?
JS	Yes thank you.
HEO	(The questions which now follow arise from the ingredients of the offence and general requests for mitigation or explanation from the defendant.)

CAUTION FORM AND PUBLIC INTEREST MATRIX

CAUTION FORM

OFFENDER'S NAME:

ADDRESS:

DATE OF OFFENCE:

PLACE OF OFFENCE:

BRIEF CIRCUMSTANCES OF OFFENCE:

DECLARATION:

I hereby declare that I/on behalf of the above-mentioned Company, admit the offence described above and agree to accept a caution in this case. I understand that a record will be kept of this caution and that it may influence a decision to institute proceedings should I/the Company be found to be infringing the law in the future. I further understand that this caution may be cited should I/the Company subsequently be found guilty of an offence by a Court of Law.

Name: (Block Capitals)

Position with

Signed: Date:

SIGNED: On behalf of the Instructing Department

DATE:

SIGNED: Solicitor to the Council

SHOULD YOU WISH TO MAKE COMMENT PLEASE ENDORSE ON THE REVERSE OF THIS FORM

PUBLIC INTEREST MATRIX FORM

Deciding whether to prosecute or offer a formal caution

The decision to prosecute or offer a formal caution should be made using the following table as a guide:

CRITERION
OFFER CAUTION

PROSECUTE

Criterion		
Was the offence a genuine mistake/misunderstanding?	YES	NO
Is the offence serious and will likely result in significant sentence?	YES	NO
A nominal penalty will follow.	YES	NO
Is the offence stale?	YES	NO
Is the offender old or infirm?	YES	NO
Is the offender ill or suffering from stress?	YES	NO
Was there violence in the offence or investigation?	YES	NO
Has the offender a previous history of offending?	YES	NO
Was the offender a ringleader?	YES	NO
Was the offence premeditated?	YES	NO
Is the offender willing to prevent a recurrence of the problem?	YES	NO
Was the victim vulnerable?	YES	NO
Was the offence motivated by discrimination eg racial, sex, religion, political?	YES	NO
The offence is widespread in the area.	YES	NO
Is the case likely to establish a legal precedent?	YES	NO
Has the offender offered a reasonable explanation?	YES	NO
The offender has put right loss.	YES	NO
Was the offence committed whilst Defendant under order of Court?	YES	NO
The Defendant's previous are relevant to offence.	YES	NO
The offender was in a position of authority or trust.	YES	NO

Appendix 7: Caution Form and Public Interest Matrix

The offence was committed against a public servant.	YES	NO
The offence of little harm was a misjudgment.	YES	NO
TOTALS		

Weight the appropriate response to each criterion on a scale of 1–3 and total the number in each column. The decision will be influenced by the totals in each column.

Recommendation of Investigating Officer

- Formal Caution/Prosecution

Signed...................................... Date:

- Agree/Disagree (Manager)

Signed...................................... Date:

Decision of Principal Manager

Signed...................................... Date:

Delete as applicable

APPENDIX 8

AUTHORISATION OF LEGAL PROCEEDINGS

STANDARD FORM

AUTHORISATION OF LEGAL PROCEEDINGS

Authority is given to institute and continue until final conclusion legal proceedings against the following person(s) in respect of an alleged offence(s) against the legislation noted subject to the Director of Legal Services being satisfied on points of evidence.

Date of Alleged Offence
Name and address
of person against
whom proceedings
to be taken

_____
_____

Place of Alleged Offence
Enactment under
which proceedings
are to be taken

_____
_____

Recommended _____
DATE _____

Authorised Signatory _____

ALTERNATIVE FORM

AUTHORISATION OF LEGAL PROCEEDINGS

Enactment under which proceedings to be taken:

Date of alleged offence:

Details of alleged offence:

Place of alleged offence:

Name and address of person(s)
against whom proceedings to be taken:

In accordance with the powers delegated by me under the Council's Standing Orders, I, being the (state position with Council), resolve that the Council institute prosecution and continue until final conclusion proceedings in order to give effect to the resolution made on   by the Council's (name Committee) in respect of the alleged offence outlined above, subject to the Director of Legal Services being satisfied on the points of evidence.

DATED this   day of   20

Signed..

Signed..
                  Senior Officer

PRECEDENTS FOR PLANNING AND BUILDING CONTROL, ENFORCEMENT AND PROSECUTION

(a) Standard letter requesting defendant to attend interview (specimen).

(b) Example of typical reply to (a) above.

(c) Standard investigatory letters in connection with TPO investigation.

Information/summons:

(d) Section 179(2) of the TCPA 1990 (Enforcement notice).

(e) Section 210(4) of the TCPA 1990 (TPO).

(f) Section 224 of the TCPA 1990 (Advertisement regs).

(g) Section 330 of the TCPA 1990 (Information notice).

(h) Section 43 of the Planning (Listed Buildings and Conservation Areas) Act 1990.

(i) Section 95 of the Building Act 1984 (information re warrant to enter premises).

(j) Section 196B of the TCPA 1990 (information for warrant to enter premises).

(k) Warrant for (j) above.

9 February 2001

Dear Sir

TOWN AND COUNTRY PLANNING ACT 1990
UNAUTHORISED REMOVAL OF THE CROWN OF A SYCAMORE TREE

I refer to your recent correspondence with the Council's Planning and Highways Officers.

I have been informed that you are the owner of the above property and are responsible for the removal of the crown of a Sycamore Tree which stands within the curtilage of this property.

This tree is protected by a Tree Preservation Order, therefore any lopping, topping or pruning work that you might want to carry out would require written consent of the Council. Having checked the Council's records, I cannot find any such consent having been granted. Therefore, you have committed an offence under Section 210(3) of the above Act.

Given that the Local Authority considers this a serious breach of the above Act, we would wish to formally interview you. The interview would give both the Council and yourself the opportunity to state the facts. I must advise you that such an interview would be conducted under caution and, if you wanted, in the presence of your solicitor or legal adviser.

In order that this matter can be quickly concluded, such an interview should take place as soon as possible. Therefore, I would suggest that you contact me on receipt of this letter with a view to arranging a mutually convenient time and place for the interview to take place.

Yours faithfully

Area Enforcement Officer

Appendix 9: Precedents for Planning and Building Control, Enforcement and Prosecution

24 February 2001

Dear Sir

TOWN AND COUNTRY PLANNING ACT 1990
UNAUTHORISED REMOVAL OF THE CROWN OF A SYCAMORE TREE AT 26 SMITH ROAD, BRADFORD

I refer to our telephone conversation on Thursday 23 February 2001, when we discussed my letter of 9 February 1996 regarding the above.

Although you were prepared to attend a formal interview, your personal circumstances made it very difficult therefore you preferred that I write asking any questions which the interview would have included.

1. Are you the owner of   Road?
2. Were you aware of the Tree Preservation Order which protects the Sycamore Tree in the garden of this property?
3. Who carried out the pruning work?
4. If you were not responsible for carrying out the work, was the work carried out with your consent?
5. Do you know the exact date in November when the work was carried out?
6. Are you aware that this type of work on a tree covered by a Tree Preservation Order required consent by the Council?

To ensure that this matter is brought to a speedy conclusion, I must ask that you provide a written response to these questions within five days. I must remind you that 'you do not have to say anything but it may harm your defence if you do not mention when questioned something which you later rely on in Court, anything you do say may be given in evidence.

Should you require any further information, please do not hesitate to contact me at the above office.

Yours faithfully

Area Enforcement Officer
Area Planning Office

27 February 2001

Dear Sirs

26 SMITH ROAD, ALLERTON

In response to your letter of 24 February 2001, our reply to your questions is as follows:

1   Yes, we are the owner of the above property.

2   No, we were not aware of the Tree Preservation Order which protects the Sycamore Tree on the property.

3   A gardener recommended to us by someone whom he had done some work for.

4   Yes, the work was carried out with our consent. This was following two letters from Highways, Jacobs Well, advising us that if we did not cut back the overhanging branches and limbs we would be fined. Some of the work we did ourselves, but as the tree was in full foliage at the time, the tree was not cut back until it had shed its leaves.

5   No, we do not remember the exact date in November when the work was carried out. It was undertaken between mid to late November 2000.

6   No, we were not aware of a Tree Preservation Order, or in fact that we required consent to undertake this type of work until it was brought to our attention by yourselves after the tree had been pruned.

Finally, we would like to say were we aware of a Tree Preservation Order on the tree, in no way would we have pruned the tree, which was done in response to letters from your colleagues in Jacobs Well which threatened prosecution if this work was not done.

Yours sincerely

Defendant

Appendix 9: Precedents for Planning and Building Control, Enforcement and Prosecution

Dear Sir

RE: Unauthorised removal of trees protected by TPO 309
Land off ....

Further to my letters dated   2001 in which I asked that you contact me with a view to agreeing to attend a formal interview on a date which you had suggested.

You telephoned my office on   2001 and left a message for me to contact you. I telephoned you back later the same morning when you advised me that you were unwilling to attend a formal interview on the previously agreed date, in fact you refused to agree to attend any such formal interview. Instead you now suggested that we meet on site. I said I would need to check with the Council's Arboriculturist before suggesting a date.

I telephoned   who said he could meet on site on 20 December. I telephoned you again to confirm the date but stressed that I would still need to caution you and I would be taking contemporaneous notes of what was said. It was at this point that you again refused to attend the meeting/interview.

Therefore I write to advise as follows:

I have evidence before me which I believe points to the fact that certain offences have been committed under section 210 of The Town and Country Planning Act 1990. In that you have contravened tree preservation order No 309. The allegation against you is that you removed or permitted to be removed six Sycamore trees covered by a TPO without the consent of the Local Planning Authority.

From my inspections of the site and my discussions with   environmental officer, it is clear that these trees were removed to allow access from the 'tank area' to the fields, to allow the spread of the waste material on the fields to the rear of the woodland.

As you have refused to attend a formal interview to discuss this matter I now enclose a set of questions for you to complete and return to the office. These questions give you the opportunity to state your version of events with regard to the matter and which would have been carried out in accordance with the Police and Criminal Evidence Act.

Bearing in mind the allegations set out above, the Council will consider whether or not to take legal proceedings. I must caution you and advise you that:

> You do not have to say anything but it may harm your defence if you do not mention, when questioned, something which you later rely on in court. Anything you do say may be given in evidence.

I should advise you that this caution does relate to any reply and in particular any written information you may provide, therefore you may wish to discuss this with your solicitor.

1 Q Are you the owner of the land outlined red on the attached plan?

   A

2 Q Are you aware that a Tree Preservation Order is in force which protects the trees on this site?

   A

3 Q Do you remember receiving Tree Preservation Order 309 which was served upon you in October 2001?

   A

4 Q You have recently agreed a contract with England Environmental to spread their waste material on fields to the rear of this site do you recall meeting Mr Tomlinson to discuss the siting of this material and if so on which date did the meeting take place?

   A

5 Q During your meeting, on site, do you recall advising Mr Tomlinson the route which the vehicles should take when departing to spread the materials on the land and if so would you please indicate the route on the attached plan.

   A

Appendix 9: Precedents for Planning and Building Control, Enforcement and Prosecution

6 Q It is clear from my inspection of the site that a large number of trees have been removed without the prior consent of the Local Planning Authority. Do you know the date on which these trees were removed and with whose authority were they removed?

   A

7 Q Why were they removed?

   A

8 Q Who undertook this work to remove the trees?

   A

9 Q What has happened to the tree trunks?

   A

10 Q Where were you when the trees were removed?

   A

11 Q Were the trees removed for safety reasons and if so what evidence can you provide to corroborate such reasons?

   A

12 Q Were the trees removed for any other reason?

   A

13 Q Were the trees removed to create a path for vehicles in connection with the spreading of materials by an outside contractor?

   A

Warning pursuant to the Criminal Justice and Public Order Act 1994

You are asked to account for an alleged breach of a TPO as set out in this letter

You are officially informed that you may be prosecuted for the offence of causing or permitting the cutting downs of trees contrary to a tree preservation order on your land off Heights Lane.

If you now fail to mention a fact which amounts to satisfactory answer to all of the above questions or fail mention any other fact which you might reasonably be expected to provide in response to this letter. The court may be asked to draw inferences if you subsequently mention in court something that you could have mentioned at this stage. These inferences cannot be defined at this stage but may none the less include the following:

1   *You knew well in advance that the trees subject to the TPO were to be removed.*
YOUR COMMENT REQUESTED:

2   *You ordered or at alternatively permitted the removal of the trees as set out in 1 above.*
YOUR COMMENT REQUESTED:

3   *The purpose of removing the said trees was to enable a passageway for vehicles to deposit materials on your land.*
YOUR COMMENT REQUESTED:

4   *The said trees were not dead dying or dangerous and there was no legitimate reason for there removal.*
YOUR COMMENT REQUESTED:

If I do not receive a response before 8 February 2001 the Council will have to consider the most appropriate action to be taken. If you do not receive written confirmation within seven days that we have received your response you should assume that it has not been received.

Appendix 9: Precedents for Planning and Building Control, Enforcement and Prosecution

Would you please note that this letter has been served recorded delivery in order to stress the importance of your opportunity to respond to the allegations.

Yours faithfully

Area Enforcement Officer

SUMMONS]>var1<[

IN THE]>var2<[MAGISTRATES' COURT

To:]>var3<[
of:]>var4<[

INFORMATION has this day been laid before the undersigned by]><[Solicitor to the Council, on behalf of]><[Council, that you

on the]>var5<[

at]>var6<[

did fail to comply with an enforcement notice served on]>var7<[by   Council pursuant to Part VII of the Town and Country Planning Act 1990 as amended by Part I of the Planning and Compensation Act 1991 in that as owner of the land at]>var8<[you did fail before]>var9<[to]>var10<[contrary to Section 179(2) of the Town and Country Planning Act 1990 as substituted by Section 8 of the Planning and Compensation Act 1991.

YOU ARE THEREFORE SUMMONED to appear before the Magistrates' Court

sitting at]>var11<[

on]>var12<[

at]>var13<[to answer to the said Information.

DATED the   day of   20

....
Clerk to the Justices/Clerk to the Court/
Justice of the Peace

If you do not respond to this Summons, the case may be dealt with in your absence.

Please note that upon conviction the prosecution will be seeking costs against you.

SUMMONS]>var1<[

IN THE]>var2<[MAGISTRATES' COURT

To:]>var3<[
of:]>var4<[

INFORMATION has this day been laid before the undersigned by]><[, Solicitor to the Council, on behalf of]><[Council, that you

on the]>var5<[

at]>var6<[in the City first aforesaid

did permit the topping or lopping of the]>var 7<[in a conservation area designated by Bradford Council on]>var 8<[, contrary to Sections 211(1) and 210(4) of the Town and Country Planning Act 1990 as amended.

YOU ARE THEREFORE SUMMONED to appear before the Magistrates' Court sitting at]>var 9<[

on]>var 10<[

at]>var 11<[to answer to the said Information.

DATED the   day of   20

....
Clerk to the Justices/Clerk to the Court/
Justice of the Peace

If you do not respond to this Summons, the case may be dealt with in your absence. Please note that upon conviction the prosecution will be seeking costs against you.

Appendix 9: Precedents for Planning and Building Control, Enforcement and Prosecution

SUMMONS]>var1<[

IN THE]>var2<[MAGISTRATES' COURT

To:]>var3<[
of:]>var4<[

INFORMATION has this day been laid before the undersigned by]><[, Solicitor to the Council, on behalf of]><[Council, that you

on the]>var5<[

at]>var6<[in the City first aforesaid

did display an advertisement without the consent of the City of Bradford Metropolitan Council, contrary to Regulations 5 and 27 of the Town and Country (Control of Advertisements) Regulations 1992 and Section 224 of the Town and Country Planning Act 1990.

YOU ARE THEREFORE SUMMONED to appear before the Magistrates' Court

sitting at]>var7<[

on]>var8<[

at]>var9<[to answer to the said Information.

DATED the   day of   20

....
Clerk to the Justices/Clerk to the Court/
Justice of the Peace

If you do not respond to this Summons, the case may be dealt with in your absence.

Please note that upon conviction the prosecution will be seeking costs against you.

SUMMONS]>var1<[

IN THE]>var2<[MAGISTRATES' COURT

To:]>var3<[
of:]>var4<[

INFORMATION has this day been laid before the undersigned by]><[, Solicitor to the Council, on behalf of]><[Council, that you

on the]>var5<[

did without reasonable excuse fail to comply with a Notice dated]>var6<[under Section 330 of the Town and Country Planning Act 1990 requiring that you give information as to interests in land and buildings at]>var7<[, contrary to Section 330(4) of the said Act.

YOU ARE THEREFORE SUMMONED to appear before the Magistrates' Court sitting at]>var8<[

on]>var9<[

at]>var10<[to answer to the said Information.

DATED the   day of   20

....
Clerk to the Justices / Clerk to the Court /
Justice of the Peace

If you do not respond to this Summons, the case may be dealt with in your absence. Please note that upon conviction the prosecution will be seeking costs against you.

Appendix 9: Precedents for Planning and Building Control, Enforcement and Prosecution

SUMMONS]>var1<[

IN THE]>var2<[MAGISTRATES' COURT

To:]>var3<[
of:]>var4<[

INFORMATION has this day been laid before the undersigned by]><[, Solicitor to the Council, on behalf of]><[Council, that you

on the]>var5<[

at]>var6<[in the City first aforesaid

being the owner of land at]>var 7<[did fail to comply with a Notice served on]>var 8<[by the Council under Section 38 of the Planning (Listed Buildings and Conservation Areas) Act 1990 requiring that within]>var 9<[steps, namely]>var 10<[, be taken to]>var 11<[contrary to Section 43 of the Planning (Listed Buildings and Conservation Areas) Act 1990 as substituted by Paragraph 6 of Schedule 3 to the Planning and Compensation Act 1991.

YOU ARE THEREFORE SUMMONED to appear before the Magistrates' Court
sitting at]>var12<[
on]>var13<[

at]>var14<[to answer to the said Information.

DATED the   day of   20

....
Clerk to the Justices/Clerk to the Court/
Justice of the Peace

If you do not respond to this Summons, the case may be dealt with in your absence.
Please note that upon conviction the prosecution will be seeking costs against you.

Information

INFORMATION FOR WARRANT TO ENTER PREMISES

SECTION 95 OF THE BUILDING ACT 1984

]>var1<[MAGISTRATES COURT

Date:]>var2<[

The Information of]>var3<[of the]>var4<[, a duly authorised officer of the]><[Council who upon oath (or affirmation) states that for the purposes of subsection (1) of Section 95 of the Building Act 1984, he has a right at all reasonable hours to enter the premises at]>var5<[, in the occupation of]>var6<[.

And for the purposes of exercising that right having given notice to the said]>var7<[, of his intention so to do, he applies for a warrant to be issued for the reason that]>var8<[, and there are reasonable grounds for entry into the said premises for the purpose of taking any action, or executing any work, authorised or required by this Act, or by building regulations, or by an order made under this Act, to be taken, or executed, by the Local Authority.

WHEREFORE the said]>var9<[applies for a warrant authorising him to enter the said premises pursuant to Section 95(1) of the Building Act 1984.

....
Informant

SWORN before me the   day of   20

....
Clerk to the Court/Clerk to the Justices/Officer of the Court

INFORMATION FOR WARRANT TO ENTER PREMISES

Section 196B of the Town and Country Planning Act 1990

DATE:]>var 1<[

INFORMANT:]>var 2<[

INFORMATION: The above-named Informant on oath (affirmation) states that he is an Officer of the]><[Council authorised by the said Council.

And that there are reasonable grounds for entering land at]>var 3<[for the purposes of Section 196A of the Town and Country Planning Act 1990 as amended by the Planning and Compensation Act 1991:

(a) to ascertain whether there is or has been any breach of planning control on the land or any other land;

(b) to determine whether any of the powers conferred on the Local Planning Authority under Part VII of the Town and Country Planning Act 1990 as amended by the Planning and Compensation Act 1991 should be exercised in relation to the land or any other land;

(c) to determine how any such power should be exercised in relation to the land or any other land;

(d) to ascertain whether there has been compliance with any requirement imposed as a result of any power having been exercised in relation to the land or any other land.

And that admission to the land has been refused or on refusal is reasonably apprehended.

....
Informant

TAKEN before me

....
Justice of the Peace

WARRANT TO ENTER PREMISES
SECTION 196B OF THE TOWN AND COUNTRY PLANNING ACT 1990

DATE:]>var 1<[

INFORMANT:]>var 2<[

INFORMATION: The above-named Informant on oath (affirmation) states that he is an Officer of the]><[Council authorised by the said Council.

And that there are reasonable grounds for entering land at]>var 3<[for the purposes of Section 196A of the Town and Country Planning Act 1990 as amended by the Planning and Compensation Act 1991:

(a) to ascertain whether there is or has been any breach of planning control on the land or any other land;

(b) to determine whether any of the powers conferred on the Local Planning Authority under Part VII of the Town and Country Planning Act 1990 as amended by the Planning and Compensation Act 1991 should be exercised in relation to the land or any other land;

(c) to determine how any such power should be exercised in relation to the land or any other land;

(d) to ascertain whether there has been compliance with any requirement imposed as a result of any power having been exercised in relation to the land or any other land.

And that admission to the land has been refused or on refusal is reasonably apprehended.

And the undersigned Justice of the Peace being satisfied that there are such reasonable grounds.

DIRECTIONS: To the Officers of the said Council, authorised by the said Council for the purposes of Section 196B of the Town and Country Planning Act 1990 as amended by the Planning and Compensation Act 1991.

You are hereby authorised, on one occasion within a month of the date hereof, to enter the said land (at a reasonable hour).

JUSTICE OF THE PEACE ....

PRECEDENTS FOR HIGHWAYS MATTERS

INFORMATIONS/SUMMONS

(a) Section 137 of the Highways Act (HA) 1980 (obstruction).
(b) Section 139(1) and (3) of the HA 1980 (builders' skips).
(c) Section 139(4) of the HA 1980 (builders; skips).
(d) Section 169(1) of the HA 1980 (obstruction).
(e) Section 169(3) of the HA 1980 (lighting, traffic signs, etc).
(f) Section 172 of the HA 1980 (hoardings).
(g) Section 51 of the New Roads and Street Works Act (NRSWA) 1991 (breaking open a street, etc).
(h) Section 54(1) and (5) of the NRSWA 1991 (advance notice of works).
(i) Section 54(4) and (5) of the NRSWA 1991 (non compliance with requirements of street works authority).
(j) Section 55(1) and (5) of the NRSWA 1991 (seven day notice of works).
(k) Section 56(1) and (3) of the NRSWA 1991 (contravention of street authority directions).
(l) Section 57(2) of the NRSWA (emergency works notice).
(m) Section 58(4) and (5) of the NRSWA 1991 (notice contravention).
(n) Section 67 of the NRSWA 1991 (supervision of works).
(o) Section 68(1) and (2) of the NRSWA 1991 (provision of facilities).
(p) Section 69(1) and (2) of the NRSWA 1991 (facilities for monitoring execution of work).
(q) Section 70 of the NRSWA 1991 (duty to reinstate street).
(r) Section 71 of the NRSWA 1991 (specification for materials, etc).
(s) Section 79(1) and (4) of the NRSWA 1991 (failing to keep records of works).
(t) Section 92(1) and (2) of the NRSWA 1991 (failing to display lights).

INFORMATION]>var1<[

IN THE]>var2<[MAGISTRATES' COURT

To:]>var3<[
of:]>var4<[

INFORMATION has this day been laid before the undersigned by]><[on behalf of]><[Council, that you

on]>var 5<[

at]>var 6<[

without lawful authority or excuse, wilfully obstructed the free passage along a highway namely]>var 7<[by]>var 8<[contrary to Section 137 of the Highways Act 1980.

YOU ARE THEREFORE SUMMONED to appear before the Magistrates' Court sitting at]>var 9<[

on]>var 10<[

at]>var 11<[to answer to the said Information.

DATED the   day of   20

....
Clerk to the Justices/Clerk to the Court/
Justice of the Peace

If you do not respond to this Summons, the case may be dealt with in your absence. Please note that upon conviction the prosecution will be seeking costs against you.

Appendix 10: Precedents for Highways Matters

INFORMATION]>var1<[

IN THE]>var2<[MAGISTRATES' COURT

To:]>var3<[
of:]>var4<[

INFORMATION has this day been laid before the undersigned by]><[, on behalf of]><[Council, that you

on]>var 5<[

at]>var 6<[

as owner of a builder's skip did deposit on a highway]>var 7<[without the permission of the]>var 8<[as highway authority contrary to Section 139(1) and (3) of the Highways Act 1980.

YOU ARE THEREFORE SUMMONED to appear before the Magistrates' Court sitting at]>var 9<[

on]>var 10<[

at]>var 11<[to answer to the said Information.

DATED the   day of   20

....
Clerk to the Justices/Clerk to the Court/
Justice of the Peace

If you do not respond to this Summons, the case may be dealt with in your absence.

Please note that upon conviction the prosecution will be seeking costs against you.

INFORMATION]>var1<[

IN THE]>var2<[MAGISTRATES' COURT

To:]>var3<[
of:]>var4<[

INFORMATION has this day been laid before the undersigned by]><[, on behalf of]><[Council, that you

on]>var 5<[

at]>var 6<[

being the owner of a builder's skip which had been deposited on the highway at]>var 7<[in accordance with the permission granted by the]>var 8<[as highway authority under Section 139(2) of the Highways Act 1980 did fail to ensure in accordance with the permission:

(a) that the skip was properly lighted during the hours of darkness and, where Regulations made by the Secretary of State under this Section required it to be marked in accordance with the Regulations (with reflecting or fluorescent material or otherwise) that it was so marked; or
(b) that the skip was clearly and indelibly marked with the owner's name and with his telephone number or address; or
(c) that the skip was removed as soon as practicable after it had been filled; or
(d) that each of the conditions subject to which this permission was granted was complied with contrary to Section 139(4) of the said Act.

YOU ARE THEREFORE SUMMONED to appear before the Magistrates' Court

sitting at]>var 9<[

on]>var 10<[

at]>var 11<[to answer to the said Information.

DATED the   day of   20

....
Clerk to the Justices/Clerk to the Court/
Justice of the Peace

If you do not respond to this Summons, the case may be dealt with in your absence.

Please note that upon conviction the prosecution will be seeking costs against you.

INFORMATION]>var1<[

IN THE]>var2<[MAGISTRATES' COURT

To:]>var3<[
of:]>var4<[

INFORMATION has this day been laid before the undersigned by]><[, on behalf of]><[Council, that you

on]>var 5<[

at]>var 6<[

being a person in connection with building or demolition work or the alterations, repair, maintenance or cleaning of any building, erected or retained on or over the highway at]>var 7<[which obstructed the highway without authorisation or licence in writing from the]>var 8<[Council. Contrary to Section 169(1) and (3) of the Highways Act 1980.

YOU ARE THEREFORE SUMMONED to appear before the Magistrates' Court

sitting at]>var 9<[

on]>var 10<[

at]>var 11<[to answer to the said Information.

DATED the   day of   20

....
Clerk to the Justices/Clerk to the Court/
Justice of the Peace

If you do not respond to this Summons, the case may be dealt with in your absence.

Please note that upon conviction the prosecution will be seeking costs against you.

INFORMATION]>var1<[

IN THE]>var2<[MAGISTRATES' COURT

To:]>var3<[
of:]>var4<[

INFORMATION has this day been laid before the undersigned by]><[, on behalf of]><[Council, that you

on]>var 5<[

at]>var 6<[

being a person in connection with building or demolition work or the alterations, repair, maintenance or cleaning of any building, having erected or retained on or over the highway known as]>var 7<[, scaffolding or other structure with an authorisation from the]>var 8<[Council, as highway authority, failed to comply with the duties as follows:

(a) to ensure that the structure was adequately lit at all times between half an hour after sunset and half an hour before sunrise; or
(b) to comply with any directions given in writing by the authority with respect to the erection and maintenance of traffic signs in connection with the structure; or
(c) to do such things in connection with the structure as any statutory undertakers reasonably request him to do for the purpose of protecting or giving access to any apparatus belonging to or used or maintained by the undertakers.

Contrary to Section 169(3) and (4) of the Highways Act 1980.

YOU ARE THEREFORE SUMMONED to appear before the Magistrates' Court

sitting at]>var 9<[

on]>var 10<[

at]>var 11<[to answer to the said Information.

DATED the   day of   20

....
Clerk to the Justices/Clerk to the Court/
Justice of the Peace

If you do not respond to this Summons, the case may be dealt with in your absence.

Please note that upon conviction the prosecution will be seeking costs against you.

Appendix 10: Precedents for Highways Matters

INFORMATION]>var1<[

IN THE]>var2<[MAGISTRATES' COURT

To:]>var3<[
of:]>var4<[

INFORMATION has this day been laid before the undersigned by]><[, on behalf of]><[Council, that you

on]>var 5<[

at]>var 6<[

being a person proposing to erect or take down a building in the street or court known as]>var 7<[, or to alter or repair the outside of a building in a street or court known as]>var 8<[, failed before the beginning of the work to erect a close board hoarding or fence to the satisfaction of the]>var 9<[Council as highway authority, so as to separate the building from the street or court. Contrary to Section 172(1) and (5) of the Highways Act 1980.

YOU ARE THEREFORE SUMMONED to appear before the Magistrates' Court

sitting at]>var 10<[

on]>var 11<[

at]>var 12<[to answer to the said Information.

DATED the   day of   20

....
Clerk to the Justices/Clerk to the Court/
Justice of the Peace

If you do not respond to this Summons, the case may be dealt with in your absence.

Please note that upon conviction the prosecution will be seeking costs against you.

INFORMATION]>var1<[

IN THE]>var2<[MAGISTRATES' COURT

To:]>var3<[
of:]>var4<[

INFORMATION has this day been laid before the undersigned by]><[, on behalf of]><[Council, that you

on]>var 5<[

at]>var 6<[

being a person other than a street authority placed apparatus in the street or broke open a street or a sewer, drain or tunnel under it or tunnelled or bored under a street for the purpose of placing, inspecting, maintaining, adjusting, repairing, altering or renewing apparatus, or of changing the position of apparatus or removing it otherwise in pursuance of the statutory right or a street works licence. Contrary to Section 51(1) and (2) of the New Roads and Street Works Act 1991.

YOU ARE THEREFORE SUMMONED to appear before the Magistrates' Court

sitting at]>var 7<[

on]>var 8<[

at]>var 9<[to answer to the said Information.

DATED the   day of   20

....
Clerk to the Justices/Clerk to the Court/
Justice of the Peace

If you do not respond to this Summons, the case may be dealt with in your absence. Please note that upon conviction the prosecution will be seeking costs against you.

INFORMATION]>var1<[

IN THE]>var2<[MAGISTRATES' COURT

To:]>var3<[
of:]>var4<[

INFORMATION has this day been laid before the undersigned by]><[, on behalf of]><[Council, that you

on]>var 5<[

at]>var 6<[

being an undertaker did fail to comply with the duty under Section 54(1) of the New Roads and Street Works Act 1991 ie in proposing to execute street works at]>var 9<[did fail to give the prescribed advance notice of the works to the Council as street authority.

Contrary to Section 54(1) and (5) of the said Act.

YOU ARE THEREFORE SUMMONED to appear before the Magistrates' Court

sitting at]>var 9<[

on]>var 10<[

at]>var 11<[to answer to the said Information.

DATED the   day of   20

....
Clerk to the Justices/Clerk to the Court/
Justice of the Peace

If you do not respond to this Summons, the case may be dealt with in your absence.
Please note that upon conviction the prosecution will be seeking costs against you.

INFORMATION]>var1<[

IN THE]>var2<[MAGISTRATES' COURT

To:]>var3<[
of:]>var4<[

INFORMATION has this day been laid before the undersigned by]><[, on behalf of]><[Council, that you

on]>var 5<[

at]>var 6<[

being an undertaker did fail;

after giving advance notice under Section 54(1) of the New Roads and Street Works Act 1991 as undertaker to comply with the requirements as prescribed or imposed by the street works authority as to the providing of information and other procedural steps to be taken for the purpose of co-ordinating the proposed works with any other works of any description proposed to be executed in the street at]>var 8<[, contrary to Section 54(4) and (5) of the said Act.

YOU ARE THEREFORE SUMMONED to appear before the Magistrates' Court

sitting at]>var 9<[

on]>var 10<[

at]>var 11<[to answer to the said Information.

DATED the   day of   20

....
Clerk to the Justices/Clerk to the Court/
Justice of the Peace

If you do not respond to this Summons, the case may be dealt with in your absence. Please note that upon conviction the prosecution will be seeking costs against you.

INFORMATION]>var1<[

IN THE]>var2<[MAGISTRATES' COURT

To:]>var3<[
of:]>var4<[

INFORMATION has this day been laid before the undersigned by]><[, on behalf of]><[Council, that you

on]>var 5<[

at]>var 6<[

being an undertaker proposing to execute street works at]>var 7<[involving:

(a) breaking up or opening the street, or any sewer, drain or tunnel under it; or
(b) tunnelling or boarding under the street; or
(c) failing to give not less than seven working days notice to the Council or to any other person having apparatus in the street which is likely to be affected by the works.

Contrary to Section 55(1) and (5) of the New Roads and Street Works Act 1991.

YOU ARE THEREFORE SUMMONED to appear before the Magistrates' Court

sitting at]>var 8<[

on]>var 9<[

at]>var 10<[to answer to the said Information.

DATED the   day of   20

....
Clerk to the Justices/Clerk to the Court/
Justice of the Peace

If you do not respond to this Summons, the case may be dealt with in your absence.
Please note that upon conviction the prosecution will be seeking costs against you.

INFORMATION]>var1<[

IN THE]>var2<[MAGISTRATES' COURT

To:]>var3<[
of:]>var4<[

INFORMATION has this day been laid before the undersigned by]><[, on behalf of]><[Council, that you

on]>var 5<[

at]>var 6<[

being an undertaker executing street works at]>var 7<[did contravene the directions given by the]>var 8<[Council as street authority, namely]>var 9<[under Section 56(1) of the New Roads and Street Works Act 1991, contrary to Section 56(1) and (3) of the said Act

YOU ARE THEREFORE SUMMONED to appear before the Magistrates' Court

sitting at]>var 10<[

on]>var 11<[

at]>var 12<[to answer to the said Information.

DATED the   day of   20

....
Clerk to the Justices/Clerk to the Court/
Justice of the Peace

If you do not respond to this Summons, the case may be dealt with in your absence. Please note that upon conviction the prosecution will be seeking costs against you.

Appendix 10: Precedents for Highways Matters

INFORMATION]>var1<[

IN THE]>var2<[MAGISTRATES' COURT

To:]>var3<[
of:]>var4<[

INFORMATION has this day been laid before the undersigned by]><[, on behalf of]><[Council, that you

on]>var 5<[

at]>var 6<[

being an undertaker of street works failed to give notice to]>var 7<[of the said execution of emergency works at]>var 8<[as soon as was reasonably practicable and in any event within two hours of the works being begun. Contrary to Section 57(2) and (4) of the New Road and Street Works Act 1991.

YOU ARE THEREFORE SUMMONED to appear before the Magistrates' Court

sitting at]>var 9<[

on]>var 10<[

at]>var 11<[to answer to the said Information.

DATED the   day of   20

....
Clerk to the Justices/Clerk to the Court/
Justice of the Peace

If you do not respond to this Summons, the case may be dealt with in your absence.

Please note that upon conviction the prosecution will be seeking costs against you.

INFORMATION]>var1<[

IN THE]>var2<[MAGISTRATES' COURT

To:]>var3<[
of:]>var4<[

INFORMATION has this day been laid before the undersigned by]><[, on behalf of]><[Council, that you

on]>var 5<[

at]>var 6<[

being a street works undertaker did contravene a restriction imposed by a notice under Section 58 of the New Roads and Street Works Act 1991 issued by]>var 7<[in respect of works at]>var 8<[, contrary to Section 58(4) and (5) of the said Act.

YOU ARE THEREFORE SUMMONED to appear before the Magistrates' Court

sitting at]>var 9<[

on]>var 10<[

at]>var 11<[to answer to the said Information.

DATED the   day of   20

....
Clerk to the Justices/Clerk to the Court/
Justice of the Peace

If you do not respond to this Summons, the case may be dealt with in your absence. Please note that upon conviction the prosecution will be seeking costs against you.

Appendix 10: Precedents for Highways Matters

INFORMATION]>var1<[

IN THE]>var2<[MAGISTRATES' COURT

To:]>var3<[
of:]>var4<[

INFORMATION has this day been laid before the undersigned by]><[, on behalf of]><[Council, that you

on]>var 5<[

at]>var 6<[

being an undertaker executing street works as referred to in Section 67(1) and (2) of Section 67 of the New Roads and Street Works Act 1991, did fail to secure the works were supervised by a person having a prescribed qualification as supervisor or to secure there was on site at all times whilst any such works were in progress at least one person having a prescribed qualification as a trained operative respectively, contrary to Section 67(1) and (3) or 67(2) and (3) of the said Act.

YOU ARE THEREFORE SUMMONED to appear before the Magistrates' Court

sitting at]>var 7<[

on]>var 8<[

at]>var 9<[to answer to the said Information.

DATED the   day of   20

....
Clerk to the Justices/Clerk to the Court/
Justice of the Peace

If you do not respond to this Summons, the case may be dealt with in your absence.

Please note that upon conviction the prosecution will be seeking costs against you.

INFORMATION]>var1<[

IN THE]>var2<[MAGISTRATES' COURT

To:]>var3<[
of:]>var4<[

INFORMATION has this day been laid before the undersigned by]><[, on behalf of]><[Council, that you

on]>var 5<[

at]>var 6<[

being an undertaker failed to afford the street authority ie]>var 7<[Council such facilities as are reasonably required for ascertaining whether you have complied with the duties under Part]>var 8<[of the New Roads and Street Works Act 1991. Contrary to Section 68(1) and (2) of the said Act.

YOU ARE THEREFORE SUMMONED to appear before the Magistrates' Court

sitting at]>var 9<[

on]>var 10<[

at]>var 11<[to answer to the said Information.

DATED the   day of   20

....
Clerk to the Justices/Clerk to the Court/
Justice of the Peace

If you do not respond to this Summons, the case may be dealt with in your absence. Please note that upon conviction the prosecution will be seeking costs against you.

INFORMATION]>var1<[

IN THE]>var2<[MAGISTRATES' COURT

To:]>var3<[
of:]>var4<[

INFORMATION has this day been laid before the undersigned by]><[, on behalf of]><[Council, that you

on]>var 5<[

at]>var 6<[

being an undertaker executing works in a street, namely]>var 7<[did fail to take all reasonably practicable steps to give the person to whom other apparatus in the street belonged reasonable facilities for the monitoring of the execution of the works or did fail to comply with any requirements made by the apparatus owner which were reasonably necessary for the protection of the apparatus or for securing access to it, contrary to Section 69(1) and (2) of the New Roads and Street Works Act 1991.

YOU ARE THEREFORE SUMMONED to appear before the Magistrates' Court

sitting at]>var 8<[

on]>var 9<[

at]>var 10<[to answer to the said Information.

DATED the   day of   20

....
Clerk to the Justices/Clerk to the Court/
Justice of the Peace

If you do not respond to this Summons, the case may be dealt with in your absence.

Please note that upon conviction the prosecution will be seeking costs against you.

INFORMATION]>var1<[

IN THE]>var2<[MAGISTRATES' COURT

To:]>var3<[
of:]>var4<[

INFORMATION has this day been laid before the undersigned by]><[, on behalf of]><[Council, that you

on]>var 5<[

at]>var 6<[

being a street works undertaker did fail to comply with the duty to reinstate the street in accordance with Section 70(1) of the New Roads and Street Works Act 1991 OR failed to comply with those duties in reinstating the street at]>var 7<[in which you were executing the works, contrary to Section 70(1) and (6) OR 70(2) and (6) of the said Act.

YOU ARE THEREFORE SUMMONED to appear before the Magistrates' Court

sitting at]>var 8<[

on]>var 9<[

at]>var 10<[to answer to the said Information.

DATED the   day of   20

....
Clerk to the Justices/Clerk to the Court/
Justice of the Peace

If you do not respond to this Summons, the case may be dealt with in your absence.
Please note that upon conviction the prosecution will be seeking costs against you.

INFORMATION]>var1<[

IN THE]>var2<[MAGISTRATES' COURT

To:]>var3<[
of:]>var4<[

INFORMATION has this day been laid before the undersigned by]><[, on behalf of]><[Council, that you

on]>var 5<[

at]>var 6<[

being a street works undertaker did fail to comply with a duty under Section 71(1) of the New Roads and Street Works Act 1991 in relation to specification of materials to be used and the standards of workmanship to be observed or for such other reinstatements other such performance standards in relation to interim reinstatement of a prescribed period after the completion of the reinstatement in executing works in the street known as]>var 7<[, contrary to Section 71(1) and 71(5) or 71(2) and 71(5) of the said Act.

YOU ARE THEREFORE SUMMONED to appear before the Magistrates' Court

sitting at]>var 8<[

on]>var 9<[

at]>var 10<[to answer to the said Information.

DATED the   day of   20

....
Clerk to the Justices/Clerk to the Court/
Justice of the Peace

If you do not respond to this Summons, the case may be dealt with in your absence.

Please note that upon conviction the prosecution will be seeking costs against you.

INFORMATION]>var1<[

IN THE]>var2<[MAGISTRATES' COURT

To:]>var3<[
of:]>var4<[

INFORMATION has this day been laid before the undersigned by]><[, on behalf of]><[Council, that you

on]>var 5<[

at]>var 6<[

being an undertaker did fail to comply with the duties under Section 79(1) of the New Roads and Street Works Act 1991, in failing to keep records of the location of every item of apparatus belonging to you as soon as is reasonably practicable after placing in the street or altering its position, locating it in the street in the course of executing any other works or being informed of its location in accordance with Section 80 of the said Act, contrary to Section 79(1) and (4)(a) of the said Act.

YOU ARE THEREFORE SUMMONED to appear before the Magistrates' Court

sitting at]>var 7<[

on]>var 8<[

at]>var 9<[to answer to the said Information.

DATED the   day of   20

....
Clerk to the Justices/Clerk to the Court/
Justice of the Peace

If you do not respond to this Summons, the case may be dealt with in your absence.

Please note that upon conviction the prosecution will be seeking costs against you.

INFORMATION]>var1<[

IN THE]>var2<[MAGISTRATES' COURT

To:]>var3<[
of:]>var4<[

INFORMATION has this day been laid before the undersigned by]><[, on behalf of]><[Council, that you

on]>var 5<[

at]>var 6<[

being an undertaker executing street works did fail to comply with the requirement under Section 92(1)(a) or (b) of the New Roads and Street Works Act 1991, in that in executing works in a street at]>var 7<[did fail to display lights so as to avoid any risk that the light is mistaken for any signal light or other light being used for controlling direction or securing the safety of traffic or being a hindrance to the ready interpretation of any such signal or other such light, contrary to Section 92(1)(a) or (b) and (2) of the said Act.

YOU ARE THEREFORE SUMMONED to appear before the Magistrates' Court

sitting at]>var 8<[

on]>var 9<[

at]>var 10<[to answer to the said Information.

DATED the   day of   20

....
Clerk to the Justices/Clerk to the Court/
Justice of the Peace

If you do not respond to this Summons, the case may be dealt with in your absence.

Please note that upon conviction the prosecution will be seeking costs against you.

PRECEDENTS FOR ENVIRONMENTAL HEALTH AND HOUSING MATTERS

1

(a) Letter requiring information pursuant to s 33 of the Food Safety Act (FSA) 1990.
(b) Investigatory letter.
(c) List of questions with Police and Criminal Evidence Act (PACE) 1984 warnings.
(d) Notice to treat sheep scab.
(e) Order requiring isolation of sheep affected by sheep scab.
(f) Order requiring clearance of sheep on common land.
(g) Section 8 of the FSA 1990 (food not complying with safety requirements).
(h) Section 10 of the FSA 1990 (non compliance with improvement notice).
(i) Section 14 of the FSA 1990 (selling food not of the nature, substance or quality).
(j) Food Hygiene Regulations 4 and 6 (carrying out food preparation, etc, in an unhygienic way).
(k) Food Hygiene Regulation 4 (premises not permitting good food hygiene practices).
(l) Section 16 of the FSA 1990 (selling food after 'use by' date).
(m) Section 2(2)b of the Health and Safety at Work etc Act (HS@WA) 1974 (duty of care).
(n) Section 2(2)c of the HS@WA 1974 (duty to provide training, etc).
(o) Section 37 of the HS@WA 1974 (non compliance with improvement notice).
(p) Section 33 of the HS@WA 1974 (contravention of an improvement notice).
(q) Reporting of Injuries Regulations 1985 (failure to report accident).
(r) Section 2 of the Clean Air Act 1993 (dark smoke emission).
(s) Section 198A Housing Act 1985 (non compliance with repairs notice).
(t) Section 376 of the Housing Act 1985 (non compliance with repairs notice).
(u) Section 80 of the Environmental Protection Act (EPA) 1990 (non compliance with abatement notice).
(v) Section 2 of the Protection from Eviction Act 1977 (eviction of occupier).
(w) Complaint for condemnation of food order (s 9 of the FSA 1990).
(x) Order for food condemnation of food (s 9 of the FSA 1990).
(y) Prohibition order (s 11 of the FSA 1990).
(z) Application/information for warrant to enter premises (s 32 of the FSA 1990).

2

(a) Warrant to enter premises (s 32 of the FSA 1990).
(b) Information for warrant to enter premises (Housing Act 1985/Public Health Act 1936).

(c) Information for warrant to enter premises (Sched 3 of the EPA 1990).
(d) Warrant to enter premises (Sched 3 of the EPA 1990).
(e) Information for warrant to enter premises (s 80 of the Water Industry Act 1991).

3

(a) Draft witness statement for park ranger.
(b) Information Dogs (Fouling of Land) Act 1996.
(c) Information (bylaw offence).

4

(a) Standard interview plan (Food Hygiene Regulations).

(Department Name and Address)

(Insert District)

To:

Of:

Dear Sir

(insert name) DISTRICT COUNCIL
FOOD SAFETY ACT 1990
DUTY TO PROVIDE ASSISTANCE AND INFORMATION

RE ....

....

....

In accordance with Section 33 of the above Act, you are required to supply the following information with ..... days to the address.

1 ....

2 ....

3 ....

Failure to provide information in accordance with Section 33 of the above Act within the time specified or to supply false or misleading information in a material particular is an offence for which you may be liable to a fine or imprisonment if convicted.

Whereas you are obliged to supply the above information, any information you do supply in connection with this letter may be used in legal proceedings.

Yours faithfully

Insert name of
Authorised Officer of Dept

(Insert Name and Address of Department
of the Council)

Investigatory letter

Dear Sir/Madam

(SPECIFY LEGISLATION UNDER WHICH INVESTIGATION IS TO TAKE PLACE AND OTHER INFORMATION EG THE NAME OF THE ALLEGED DEFENDANT AND THE WHEREABOUTS OF THE OFFENCE)

I am writing to you as a result of failure to attend for interview as previously arranged. I have received complaints/have evidence which caused me to believe that certain offences have been committed under (specify legislation).

(Set out the short paragraph which describes the events leading up to the present position.)

The allegations against you are (specify each and every allegation which may become the subject of a charge before the Court including the date and whereabouts and nature of the offence) (this does not need to be in the form of an Information and can summarise the offences but it would be helpful to refer to the particular section of the Act or Regulations).

(The next paragraph should include the information which identifies all the relevant circumstances giving rise to concern. This outline should be in sufficient detail to enable the Defendant to answer all questions comprehensively. An appropriately drafted letter should do this without necessarily putting all our cards on the table.)

As you have failed to attend the interview scheduled to discuss the matter, I now enclose a set of questions for you to complete and return to the office. These questions give you the opportunity to state your version of events with regard to the matter and which would have been carried out in accordance with the Police and Criminal Evidence Act.

Appendix 11: Precedents for Environmental Health and Housing Matters

Bearing in mind the allegations set out above, the Council will consider whether or not to take legal proceedings. I must caution you and advise you that:

You do not have to say anything but it may harm your defence if you do not mention, when questioned, something which you later rely on in court. Anything you do say may be given in evidence.

I should advise you that this caution does relate to any written information you may provide, therefore you may wish to discuss this with your solicitor.

If I do not receive a response before (specify reasonable time in the future) the Council will have to consider the most appropriate action to be taken.

Would you please note that this letter has been served personally/recorded delivery in order to stress the importance of your opportunity to respond to the allegations.

Yours faithfully

LIST OF QUESTIONS

The questions should be a series of direct questions. In drawing up the questions, the author should give consideration to each and every element of the events including date, time, place and legal identification to the defendant ie limited company, sole trader or partnership and trading name. It should also seek details of address for service or registered office if limited company. The questions should also cover any statutory defence and the defendant should be given an opportunity to provide details of mitigation or reasons for non compliance.

The questions should include a special warning as follows:

In accordance with the Police and Criminal Evidence Act 1984, I hereby give you the following special warnings:

A   I am investigating the alleged offences as set out in my letter dated ...

B   I am asking you to account for the allegations as set out in the letter.

C   It is believed that you committed the alleged offences as set out.

D   The Court may draw up proper inference if you fail or refuse to account the facts upon which you are being questioned, namely (specific details of allegations) as alleged or that your account given has been fabricated.

E   A copy of this letter and your response may be placed before the Court. This caution applies to any written or oral response.

(INSERT NAME) DISTRICT COUNCIL

THE SHEEP SCAB ORDER 1997

NOTICE TO TREAT SHEEP SCAB

To:

Of:

Re: Sheep on land at:

Tests have been carried out on sheep kept by you on the above land. These tests confirm that the sheep thereon are infected with sheep scab. You are therefore required to take one of the following steps within   days.

1   Ensure that the sheep are slaughtered; or

2   arrange treatment of the sheep for sheep scab by a qualified Veterinary Surgeon.

AND within two weeks of compliance with this Notice send to the Veterinary Inspector:

(a) In the case of sheep treated for sheep scab, a document signed by a Veterinary Surgeon stating the date on which the treatment took place and treatment used; or

(b) in the case of sheep which were slaughtered, evidence of such slaughter.

NB Failure to comply with this Notice is an offence under s 73 of the Animal Health Act 1981 and may result in the Local Authority carrying out the treatment at your expense.

Animal Health Inspector

(Insert Name) District Council

(Insert Address)

DATED this   day of   20

(INSERT NAME) DISTRICT COUNCIL

THE SHEEP SCAB ORDER 1997

ORDER REQUIRING ISOLATION OF SHEEP VISIBLY AFFECTED WITH SHEEP SCAB

To:

Of:

Re: Sheep on land at:

It has come to my attention that sheep on the above land are visibly affected with sheep scab.

As a person in charge of the sheep you are required to take immediate steps to ensure isolation of the animals (or if they are not on a holding occupied by yourself, removal to that holding and isolation on that holding) pending the results of testing for sheep scab.

The steps that you are required to take to ensure isolation of the sheep are as follows:

NB Failure to comply with this Notice is an offence contrary to s 73 of the Animal Health Act 1981.

Animal Health Inspector

(Insert Name) District Council

(Insert Address)

DATED this   day of   20

Appendix 11: Precedents for Environmental Health and Housing Matters

(INSERT NAME) DISTRICT COUNCIL (THE LOCAL AUTHORITY)

THE SHEEP SCAB ORDER 1997 NO 968

ORDER REQUIRING THE CLEARANCE OF SHEEP ON COMMON LAND AT:

....

This Notice affects all persons keeping or intending to keep sheep on the above land.

All persons keeping sheep on the above land are required to move these sheep off the land by day of .

As from the date of this Notice, no person shall move sheep onto the above land for a period of three months without written authorisation from the Local Authority.

Take notice that in accordance with Article 5 of the above Regulations, the Local Authority may seize and detain any sheep found on the above land while this Notice is in force.

If the owner of the sheep seized by the Local Authority under Article 5 establishes his right to ownership of it within seven days of its seizure and pays to the Local Authority the expenses incurred in seizing and detaining the sheep, he may take possession of the sheep – Article 5(2).

Unless the owner of a sheep has established his right to ownership and paid the expenses of the Local Authority under paragraph (2) of Article 5 within seven days of seizure, the Local Authority may either

(a) treat and sell the sheep; or

(b) cause the sheep to be slaughtered and sell the carcass,

and deduct from the proceeds of sale expenses incurred and retain any surplus for payment to any person who can establish that the sheep belonged to him.

Any person who breaches this Order commits an offence under s 73 of the Animal Health Act 1981.

....

(Insert Name of Authorised Officer)

(Insert Address)

DATED this   day of   20

SUMMONS]>var1<[

IN THE]>var2<[MAGISTRATES' COURT

To:]>var3<[
of:]>var4<[

INFORMATION has this day been laid before the undersigned by]><[, Solicitor to the Council, on behalf of]><[Council, that you

on the]>var5<[

at]>var6<[

did offer for sale for human consumption food, namely]>var7<[, which failed to comply with food safety requirements in that they were unfit for human consumption, contrary to Section 8(1) of the Food Safety Act 1990.

YOU ARE THEREFORE SUMMONED to appear before the Magistrates' Court

sitting at]>var8<[

on]>var9<[

at]>var10<[to answer to the said Information.

DATED the   day of   20

....
Clerk to the Justices/Clerk to the Court/
Justice of the Peace

If you do not respond to this Summons, the case may be dealt with in your absence.

Please note that upon conviction the prosecution will be seeking costs against you.

Appendix 11: Precedents for Environmental Health and Housing Matters

SUMMONS]>var1<[

IN THE]>var2<[MAGISTRATES' COURT

To:]>var3<[

of:]>var4<[

INFORMATION has this day been laid before the undersigned by]><[, Solicitor to the Council, on behalf of]><[Council, that you

on the]>var5<[

being the proprietor of a food business namely]>var6<[, did fail to comply with an improvement notice, number]>var7<[, served on]>var8<[pursuant to Section 10(1) of the Food Safety Act 1990 requiring that by]>var9<[to]>var10<[contrary to Section 10 of the Food Safety Act 1990.

YOU ARE THEREFORE SUMMONED to appear before the Magistrates' Court sitting at]>var11<[

on]>var12<[

at]>var13<[to answer to the said Information.

DATED the   day of   20

....
Clerk to the Justices/Clerk to the Court/
Justice of the Peace

If you do not respond to this Summons, the case may be dealt with in your absence.

Please note that upon conviction the prosecution will be seeking costs against you.

SUMMONS]>var1<[

IN THE]>var2<[MAGISTRATES' COURT

To:]>var3<[
of:]>var4<[

INFORMATION has this day been laid before the undersigned by]><[, on behalf of]><[Council, that you

on]>var5<[

did sell to the prejudice of a purchaser food called]>var6<[which was not of the nature or not of the substance or not of the quality of the food demanded by the purchaser,

in that the said food was then adulterated with]>var7<[

CONTRARY TO Section 14 of the Food Safety Act 1990.

Penalty: fine not exceeding £20,000 – Section 35 of the Act. Triable either way.

YOU ARE THEREFORE SUMMONED to appear before the Magistrates' Court sitting at]>var8<[

on]>var9<[

at]>var10<[to answer to the said Information.

DATED the   day of   20

....
Clerk to the Justices/Clerk to the Court/
Justice of the Peace

If you do not respond to this Summons, the case may be dealt with in your absence. Please note that upon conviction the prosecution will be seeking costs against you.

Appendix 11: Precedents for Environmental Health and Housing Matters

SUMMONS]>var1<[

IN THE]>var2<[MAGISTRATES' COURT

To:]>var3<[
of:]>var4<[

INFORMATION has this day been laid before the undersigned by]><[on behalf of]><[Council, that you

on]>var5<[

being the proprietor of a food business, namely]>var6<[

at]>var7<[

did fail to ensure that the preparation or processing or manufacture or packaging or storing or transportation or distribution or handling or the offer for sale or supply of food, namely]>var8<[, was carried out in a hygienic way

CONTRARY TO Regulations 4(1) and 6 of the Food Safety (General Food Hygiene) Regulations 1995, made under the Food Safety Act 1990.

YOU ARE THEREFORE SUMMONED to appear before the Magistrates' Court

sitting at]>var8<[

on]>var9<[

at]>var10<[to answer to the said Information.

DATED the   day of   20

....
Clerk to the Justices/Clerk to the Court/
Justice of the Peace

If you do not respond to this Summons, the case may be dealt with in your absence.

Please note that upon conviction the prosecution will be seeking costs against you.

SUMMONS]>var1<[

IN THE]>var2<[MAGISTRATES' COURT

To:]>var3<[
of:]>var4<[

INFORMATION has this day been laid before the undersigned by]><[, on behalf of]><[Council, that you

on]>var5<[

being the proprietor of a food business, namely]>var6<[

at premises known as]>var7<[, used for the purposes of the business, whereat the layout, design, construction and size of the premises did not:

Permit good food hygiene practices, including protection against cross-contamination between and during operations by foodstuffs, equipment, materials, water, air supply or personal and external sources of contamination, such as pests,

in that]>var8<[

CONTRARY TO Regulation 4(2)(a) of Paragraph 2 of Chapter 1 of the Schedule and Regulation 6 of the Food Safety (General Food Hygiene) Regulations 1995, made under the Food Safety Act 1990.

YOU ARE THEREFORE SUMMONED to appear before the Magistrates' Court

sitting at]>var9<[

on]>var10<[

at]>var11<[to answer to the said Information.

DATED the   day of   20

....
Clerk to the Justices/Clerk to the Court/
Justice of the Peace

If you do not respond to this Summons, the case may be dealt with in your absence.

Please note that upon conviction the prosecution will be seeking costs against you.

Appendix 11: Precedents for Environmental Health and Housing Matters

SUMMONS]>var1<[

IN THE]>var2<[MAGISTRATES' COURT

To:]>var3<[
of:]>var4<[

INFORMATION has this day been laid before the undersigned by]><[on behalf of]><[Council, that you

on]>var5<[

at]>var6<[

did sell food, namely]>var7<[, after the date shown in the 'use by' date relating to it, contrary to regulation 40(f) of the Food Labelling Regulations 1984 as amended, made under Section 2(2) of the European Communities Act 1972 and Section 16 of the Food Safety Act 1990.

YOU ARE THEREFORE SUMMONED to appear before the Magistrates' Court

sitting at]>var8<[

on]>var9<[

at]>var10<[to answer to the said Information.

DATED the   day of   20

....
Clerk to the Justices/Clerk to the Court/
Justice of the Peace

If you do not respond to this Summons, the case may be dealt with in your absence.
Please note that upon conviction the prosecution will be seeking costs against you.

SUMMONS]>var1<[

IN THE]>var2<[MAGISTRATES' COURT

To:]>var3<[
of:]>var4<[

INFORMATION has this day been laid before the undersigned by on]><[Council, that you

on the]>var5<[

at]>var6<[

being an employer having control of premises at]>var7<[, failed to discharge a duty to which the Company was subject by Section 2(1) and 2(2)(b) of the Health and Safety at Work etc Act 1974, namely the duty to make arrangements for ensuring, so far as was reasonably practicable, safety and absence of risks to health in connection with the use, handling, storage and transport of articles and substances, in that you allowed]>var8[name]<[to]>var9<[, contrary to Section 33(1)(a) and (1A) of the Health and Safety at Work etc Act 1974.

YOU ARE THEREFORE SUMMONED to appear before the Magistrates' Court sitting at]>var10<[

on]>var11<[

at]>var12<[to answer to the said Information.

DATED the   day of   20

....
Clerk to the Justices/Clerk to the Court/
Justice of the Peace

If you do not respond to this Summons, the case may be dealt with in your absence.

Please note that upon conviction the prosecution will be seeking costs against you.

SUMMONS]>var1<[

IN THE]>var2<[MAGISTRATES' COURT

To:]>var3<[

of:]>var4<[

INFORMATION has this day been laid before the undersigned by on behalf of]><[Council, that you

on]>var5<[

at]>var6<[

being an employer having control of premises at]>var7<[, failed to discharge a duty to which the Company was subject by Section 2(1) and 2(2)(c) of the Health and Safety at Work etc Act 1974, namely the duty to provide such information, instruction, training and supervision as is necessary to ensure, so far as is reasonably practicable, the health and safety at work of his employees, in that you failed to]>var8<[, contrary to Section 33(1)(a) and (1A) of the Health and Safety at Work etc Act 1974.

YOU ARE THEREFORE SUMMONED to appear before the Magistrates' Court

sitting at]>var9<[

on]>var10<[

at]>var11<[to answer to the said Information.

DATED the   day of   20

....
Clerk to the Justices/Clerk to the Court/
Justice of the Peace

If you do not respond to this Summons, the case may be dealt with in your absence.

Please note that upon conviction the prosecution will be seeking costs against you.

SUMMONS]>var1<[

IN THE]>var2<[MAGISTRATES' COURT

To:]>var3<[

of:]>var4<[

INFORMATION has this day been laid before the undersigned by on behalf of]><[Council, that]>var5<[

on the]>var6<[

did contravene a requirement imposed by Improvement Notice]>var7<[served on]>var8<[in respect of premises at]>var9<[, in that the said Company neglected to carry out such works as were required by the Notice, namely to]>var10<[, contrary to Sections 33(1)(g) of the Health and Safety at Work etc Act 1974.

AND the said offences are attributable to the neglect of you as the manager of]>var11<[contrary to Section 33(1)(g) and 37(1) of the Health and Safety at Work etc Act 1974.

YOU ARE THEREFORE SUMMONED to appear before the Magistrates' Court sitting at]>var12<[

on]>var13<[

at]>var14<[to answer to the said Information.

DATED the   day of   20

....
Clerk to the Justices/Clerk to the Court/
Justice of the Peace

If you do not respond to this Summons, the case may be dealt with in your absence. Please note that upon conviction the prosecution will be seeking costs against you.

Appendix 11: Precedents for Environmental Health and Housing Matters

SUMMONS]>var1<[

IN THE]>var2<[MAGISTRATES' COURT

To:]>var3<[
of:]>var4<[

INFORMATION has this day been laid before the undersigned by on behalf of]><[Council, that you

on the]>var5<[

at]>var6<[

did contravene a requirement imposed by Improvement Notice]>var7<[, served on]>var8<[, namely to]>var9<[, contrary to Section 33(1)(g) of the Health and Safety at Work etc Act 1974.

YOU ARE THEREFORE SUMMONED to appear before the Magistrates' Court

sitting at]>var10<[

on]>var11<[

at]>var12<[to answer to the said Information.

DATED the   day of   20

....
Clerk to the Justices/Clerk to the Court/
Justice of the Peace

If you do not respond to this Summons, the case may be dealt with in your absence.

Please note that upon conviction the prosecution will be seeking costs against you.

SUMMONS]>var1<[

IN THE]>var2<[MAGISTRATES' COURT

To:-]>var3<[
of:-]>var4<[

INFORMATION has this day been laid before the undersigned by on behalf of]><[Council, that you

on]>var5<[

at]>var6<[

being the responsible person in respect of premises namely]>var7<[, where as a result of an accident arising out of or in connection with work on]>var8<[,]>var9[name]<[sustained an injury whilst]>var10<[, namely]>var11<[which resulted in him being admitted immediately into hospital for more than 24 hours, did fail to notify forthwith the City of Bradford Metropolitan Council, the enforcing authority thereof by the quickest possible means, contrary to Regulation 3(1) and (2) of the Reporting of Injuries, Diseases and Dangerous Occurrences Regulations 1985, as amended and Section 33(1)(c) of the Health and Safety at Work etc Act 1974, as amended.

YOU ARE THEREFORE SUMMONED to appear before the Magistrates' Court

sitting at]>var12<[

on]>var13<[

at]>var14<[to answer to the said Information.

DATED the   day of   20

....
Clerk to the Justices/Clerk to the Court/
Justice of the Peace

If you do not respond to this Summons, the case may be dealt with in your absence.

Please note that upon conviction the prosecution will be seeking costs against you.

Appendix 11: Precedents for Environmental Health and Housing Matters

SUMMONS]>var1<[

IN THE]>var2<[MAGISTRATES' COURT

To:]>var3<[
of:]>var4<[

INFORMATION has this day been laid before the undersigned by]><[to the Council, on behalf of]><[Council, that you

on the]>var5<[

at]>var6<[

you were occupier of trade premises namely]>var7<[from which dark smoke was emitted contrary to Section 2 of the Clean Air Act 1993.

YOU ARE THEREFORE SUMMONED to appear before the Magistrates' Court

sitting at]>var8<[

on]>var9<[

at]>var10<[to answer to the said Information.

DATED the   day of   20

....
Clerk to the Justices/Clerk to the Court/
Justice of the Peace

If you do not respond to this Summons, the case may be dealt with in your absence.

Please note that upon conviction the prosecution will be seeking costs against you.

SUMMONS]>var1<[

IN THE]>var2<[MAGISTRATES' COURT

To:]>var3<[
of:]>var4<[

INFORMATION has this day been laid before the undersigned by]><[to the Council, on behalf of]><[Council, that you

on the]>var5<[

at]>var6<[

you being a person having control of premises, namely]>var7<[, to which a repairs notice served under Section 190(1)(a) of the Housing Act 1985 on]>var8<[related intentionally failed to comply with the said Notice in that you did]>var9<[required by the said Notice to be completed by]>var10<[contrary to Section 198A(1) of the Housing Act 1985 as inserted by the Housing Act 1988.

YOU ARE THEREFORE SUMMONED to appear before the Magistrates' Court

sitting at]>var11<[

on]>var12<[

at]>var13<[to answer to the said Information.

DATED the   day of   20

....
Clerk to the Justices/Clerk to the Court/
Justice of the Peace

If you do not respond to this Summons, the case may be dealt with in your absence.

Please note that upon conviction the prosecution will be seeking costs against you.

Appendix 11: Precedents for Environmental Health and Housing Matters

SUMMONS]>var1<[

IN THE]>var2<[MAGISTRATES' COURT

To:]>var3<[
of:]>var4<[

INFORMATION has this day been laid before the undersigned by]><[to the Council, on behalf of]><[Council, that you

on the]>var5<[

at]>var6<[

you being a person on whom a Notice had been served under Section 352 of the Housing Act 1985 as amended by the Local Government and Housing Act 1989 on]>var7<[requiring the execution of works at a house in multiple occupation, namely]>var8<[, to be completed by]>var9<[wilfully failed to comply with the said Notice in that you]>var10<[required by the said Notice, contrary to Section 376(1) of the Housing Act 1985 as amended by the Local Government and Housing Act 1989.

YOU ARE THEREFORE SUMMONED to appear before the Magistrates' Court

sitting at]>var11<[

on]>var12<[

at]>var13<[to answer to the said Information.

DATED the   day of   20

....
Clerk to the Justices/Clerk to the Court/
Justice of the Peace

If you do not respond to this Summons, the case may be dealt with in your absence.

Please note that upon conviction the prosecution will be seeking costs against you.

SUMMONS]>var1<[

IN THE]>var2<[MAGISTRATES' COURT

To:]>var3<[
of:]>var4<[

INFORMATION has this day been laid before the undersigned by]><[to the Council, on behalf of]><[Council, that you

on the]>var5<[

did, without reasonable excuse, fail to comply with a requirement imposed by Abatement Notice]>var6<[, served on]>var7<[, under Section 80 of the Environmental Protection Act 1990, as amended, in respect of land at]>var8<[, prohibiting the recurrence of nuisance arising from]>var9<[due to]>var10<[, contrary to Section 80(4) and (5) of the Environmental Protection Act 1990 as amended.

YOU ARE THEREFORE SUMMONED to appear before the Magistrates' Court

sitting at]>var11<[

on]>var12<[

at]>var13<[to answer to the said Information.

DATED the   day of   20

....
Clerk to the Justices/Clerk to the Court/
Justice of the Peace

If you do not respond to this Summons, the case may be dealt with in your absence.
Please note that upon conviction the prosecution will be seeking costs against you.

Appendix 11: Precedents for Environmental Health and Housing Matters

SUMMONS]>var1<[

IN THE]>var2<[MAGISTRATES' COURT

To:]>var3<[
of:]>var4<[

INFORMATION has this day been laid before the undersigned by]><[to the Council, on behalf of]><[Council, that you

on]>var5<[

at]>var6<[

did without reasonable excuse fail to comply with a prohibition imposed by an Abatement Notice under Section 80 of the Environmental Protection Act 1990, as amended, in respect of]>var7<[served on]>var8<[prohibiting the recurrence of]>var9<[arising from]>var10<[, contrary to section 80(4) and (6) of the Environmental Protection Act 1990 as amended.

YOU ARE THEREFORE SUMMONED to appear before the Magistrates' Court

sitting at]>var11<[

on]>var12<[

at]>var13<[to answer to the said Information.

DATED the   day of   20

....
Clerk to the Justices/Clerk to the Court/
Justice of the Peace

If you do not respond to this Summons, the case may be dealt with in your absence.

Please note that upon conviction the prosecution will be seeking costs against you.

SUMMONS]>var1<[

IN THE]>var2<[MAGISTRATES' COURT

To:]>var3<[
of:]>var4<[

INFORMATION has this day been laid before the undersigned by]><[to the Council, on behalf of]><[Council, that you

on the]>var5<[

unlawfully deprived]>var6<[, the residential occupier of premises, namely]>var7<[, of his occupation of those premises, contrary to Section 1(2) of the Protection from Eviction Act 1977, as amended.

YOU ARE THEREFORE SUMMONED to appear before the Magistrates' Court

sitting at]>var8<[

on]>var9<[

at]>var10<[to answer to the said Information.

DATED the   day of   20

....
Clerk to the Justices/Clerk to the Court/
Justice of the Peace

If you do not respond to this Summons, the case may be dealt with in your absence.

Please note that upon conviction the prosecution will be seeking costs against you.

COMPLAINT FOR CONDEMNATION OF FOOD ORDER

SECTION 9 OF THE FOOD SAFETY ACT 1990

]>var1<[Magistrates' Court

Date:]>var2<[

the Complaint of:]>var3<[

('The Complainant')

of:]>var4<[

a duly authorised officer of the

]>var5<[

who states that on]>var6<[19]><[, at

]>var7<[

(s)he examined certain food, namely

]>var8<[

then and there [sold] [offered or exposed for sale] [in the possession of] [deposited with] [consigned to]*

]>var9<[

[for the purpose of sale or of preparation for sale]

and intended for human consumption, and that the said food then appeared to the Complainant to be unfit for human consumption, and that the Complainant then seized and removed the said food in order to have it dealt with by a Justice of the Peace.

Taken before me,

....

Justice of the Peace/Justices' Clerk/
Clerk to the Court

Delete any words within square brackets which do not apply.

*Insert name and address, where appropriate.

ORDER FOR CONDEMNATION OF FOOD

SECTION 9 OF THE FOOD SAFETY ACT 1990

]>var1<[Magistrates' Court

Date:]>var2<[

To:]>var3<[

('The Complainant')

of:]>var4<[

and to all others whom it may concern.

Whereas you, the Complainant, a duly authorised officer of the]>var5<[

have this day brought before me, the undersigned, one of Her Majesty's Justices of the Peace, certain food, namely

]>var6<[

which you, the Complainant, had on the]>var6<[20]><[at

]>var8<[

after having examined the same, lawfully seized and removed, being then and there [sold] [offered or exposed for sale] [in the possession of] [deposited with] [consigned to]*]>var9<[

[for the purpose of sale or of preparation for sale] and intended for human consumption, and then appearing to you, the Complainant, to be unfit for human consumption;

Decision: And whereas upon your application I have examined the said food and have also inquired into the circumstances of the case upon oath or otherwise, and it appears to me and I adjudge that the said food is unfit for human consumption.

Appendix 11: Precedents for Environmental Health and Housing Matters

Order: I do therefore condemn it and I hereby order it to be [destroyed] [disposed of by†

]>var10<[

so as to prevent it from being used for human consumption].

....

Justice of the Peace/Justices' Clerk/
Clerk to the Court

*Delete any words within square brackets which do not apply

†State the mode of disposal

]>VAR1<[MAGISTRATES' COURT

Date:	]>var2<[
	WHEREAS
Accused:	]>var3<[
of:	]>var4<[

being the proprietor of a food business carried on at premises at]>var5<[

has today been convicted by this court of an offence under regulations to which section 11 of the Food Safety Act 1990 applies [by virtue of section 10(3)(b) of the said Act], namely:

]>var6<[

Decision: AND WHEREAS the Court is satisfied that there exists a risk of injury to health by reason of]>var7<[

[the use for the purposes of the said food business of a certain [process] [treatment], namely

Either/or: the [construction] [state or condition] of the premises at

used for the purposes of the said food business]

the [use for the purposes of the said food business] the [state or condition] of certain equipment [used for the purposes of the said food business], namely

]>var8<[

and it is ORDERED that

Order: the use of the said [process][treatment] for the purposes of the business] [the use of the said [premises] [equipment] for the purposes of [the business] [any other food business of the same class or description, namely]>var9<[

[any food business]

and that the participation by the accused in the management of any food business [of the said class or description]

is prohibited.

[By Order of the Court]

....
Justice of the Peace/Justices' Clerk/
Clerk to the Court

APPLICATION FOR WARRANT TO ENTER PREMISES

SECTION 32 OF THE FOOD SAFETY ACT 1990

In the]>var1<[Magistrates Court

The Information and Application of]>var2<[
of]>var3<[
duly authorised on behalf of the*]>var4<[
who states that [on the]>var5<[day of]><[19]><[,
it became necessary] either/or [it is necessary] that†]>var6<[
a duly authorised Officer of the said Council should enter the premises situate at]>var7<[in the District of the said Council under the Food Safety Act 1990, [of which premises]>var8<[
is the Occupier], for the purposes of
]>var9<[

and that]>var10<[

[admission to the said premises on the   day of   20   was refused to the said †
[it is apprehended that admission to the premises will be refused]
[notice of intention to apply for a warrant has been given to the occupier]
[the premises are unoccupied]
[the occupier is temporarily absent from the premises]
[the case is one of urgency]
[an application for admission or the giving of a notice of intention to apply for a warrant would defeat the object of the entry]

and that there is reasonable ground for entry into the premises for the purpose for which entry is required.

Appendix 11: Precedents for Environmental Health and Housing Matters

Taken and [Sworn] [Affirmed] before me this
day of   20

....
Justice of the Peace/Justices' Clerk/
Clerk to the Court

Delete any words within square brackets which do not apply
*Insert name of local authority
†Insert name of officer

WARRANT TO ENTER PREMISES

FOOD SAFETY ACT 1990, S 32

In the]>var1<[Magistrates' Court

INFORMATION on [Oath] [Affirmation], on behalf of the*]>var2<[

having been laid before me, one of Her Majesty's Justices of the Peace for the said]>var3<[that [on the]>var4<[day of   20

it became necessary] [it is necessary] that†]>var5<[

a duly authorised Officer of the said Council should enter the premises situate at

]>var6<[

in the District of the said Council under the Food Safety Act 1990, [of which premises]>var7<[is the occupier], for the purpose of]>var8<[

And that [admission to the said premises on the]>var9<[day of

20 , was refused to the said†]>var10<[

[it was apprehend that admission to the said premises would be refused]

[notice of intention to apply for a warrant of entry was given to the occupier]

[the premises are unoccupied]

[the occupier is temporarily absent from the premises]

[the case is one of urgency]

[an application for admission or the giving of a notice of intention to apply for a warrant would defeat the object of the entry]

And it having been shown to my satisfaction that the allegations in the said Information are true;

And that there is reasonable ground for entry into the said premises for the purpose aforesaid;

Now I do by this Warrant authorise the said †]>var11<[

Appendix 11: Precedents for Environmental Health and Housing Matters

to enter the Premises, if need be by force.

Dated the]>var12<[day of   20 .

....
Justice of the Peace/Offices of the Court/
Clerk to the Court

Delete any words in square brackets which do not apply

*Insert name of local authority

†Insert name of officer

INFORMATION

In the]>var1<[Magistrates' Court

The Information of]>var2<[

of]>var3<[

a duly authorised Environmental Health Officer of the City of Bradford Metropolitan Council who, upon oath (or affirmation) states that for the purposes of Sub-Section (1) of Section 287 of the Public Health Act, 1936/Sub-Section (1)(a) of Section 397 of the Housing Act 1985, he has a right at all reasonable hours to enter the premises situate at]>var4<[

(in the occupation of]>var5<[ )

AND for the purpose of exercising that right (having given notice to the said

]>var6<[of his intention so to do), he applies for a warrant to be issued for the reason that:-

(1) on the   day of   20   (notwithstanding that he produced a duly authenticated document showing his authority) admission to the said premises was refused;

(2) he apprehends that he will be refused admission to the said premises;

(3) the said premises are unoccupied;

(4) the said _____ is temporarily absent;

(5) the case is one of urgency;

(6) the giving of twenty four hours' notice of the intended entry would defeat the object of the entry;

AND that there is reasonable ground for entry into the said premises for the purpose of:
(a) ascertaining whether there is, or has been, on or in connection with the said premises any contravention of the provisions of the Public Health Act 1936 or of any Byelaws made thereunder, being provisions which it is the duty of the said Council to enforce;
(b) ascertaining whether or not circumstances exist which would authorise or require the said Council to take any action or execute any work under the Public Health Act 1936 or any Byelaws made thereunder;

Appendix 11: Precedents for Environmental Health and Housing Matters

(c) taking any action or executing any work authorised or required by the Public Health Act 1936 or any Byelaws made thereunder or any Order made under the said Act to be taken or executed by the said Council;

(d) the performance generally by the said Council of their functions under the Public Health Act 1936 or any Byelaws made thereunder;

(e) survey and examination to determine whether any powers under Part II of the Housing Act 1985 should be exercised in respect of the said premises;

(f) ascertaining whether there has been a contravention of any regulations or directions made or given under Part II of the Housing Act 1985;

WHEREFORE THE said]>var7<[

applies for a warrant authorising him to enter the said premises pursuant to Section 287(2) of the Public Health Act 1936 as amended/Section 397 of the Housing Act 1985.

....
Informant

SWORN before me the   day of   20

....
Justice of the Peace/Clerk to the Justices/Officer of the Court

Case No]>var 1<[

]>var 2<[MAGISTRATES COURT

NAME:]>var 3<[

INFORMANT:]>var 4<[

ADDRESS:]>var 5<[

OCCUPATION:]>var 6<[

INFORMATION

The informant upon oath (or affirmation) states I am authorised by City of Bradford Metropolitan Council upon production of the written authority to enter any premises at any reasonable time:

(a) for the purposes of ascertaining whether or not a statutory nuisance exists;

or

(b) for the purpose of taking any action, or executing any work, authorised or required by Part III of the Environmental Protection Act 1990.

AND for the purposes of exercising that right (having given notice to]>var 7<[of my intention so to do), I apply for a Warrant to be issued for the reason that:

The case is one of emergency in that pursuant to Part II and Schedule 3 Paragraph 2 of the Environmental Protection Act 1990:

admission has been refused

or it is anticipated that admission will be refused

or the premises are unoccupied

or the occupier of the premises is temporarily absent

Appendix 11: Precedents for Environmental Health and Housing Matters

or the case is one of an emergency

or application for admission would defeat the object of entry

and that there is reasonable ground for entry into the premises for the purpose for which entry is required.

TAKEN and Affirmed/Sworn before me this   day of   20

....
Justice of the Peace

Case No]>var 1<[

WARRANT TO ENTER PREMISES

IN THE MATTER OF SCHEDULE 3 OF THE ENVIRONMENTAL PROTECTION ACT 1990

The informant]>var 2<[upon oath (or affirmation) stated that for the purpose of Part III of the Environmental Protection Act 1990, he has the right at all reasonable hours to enter the premises at]>var 3<[(in the occupation of]>var 4<[).

AND for the purposes of exercising that right (having given notice to the said]>var 5<[of his intention to do so), he applies for a warrant to be issued for the reason that:

admission has been refused

or it is anticipated that admission will be refused

or the premises are unoccupied

or the occupier of the premises is temporarily absent

or the case is one of an emergency

or application for admission would defeat the object of entry

and there is reasonable ground for entry into the premises for the purpose of ascertaining whether or not a statutory nuisance exists

or for the purpose of taking any action or executing any work authorised by Part III of the Environmental Protection Act 1990.

AND that there are reasonable grounds for entering into the said premises at]>var 7<[.

AND the undersigned Justice of the Peace is satisfied that there are such reasonable grounds.

Direction to]>var 8<[

YOU ARE HEREBY authorised together with such other persons as may be necessary to enter the said premises at]>var 9<[, if need be by force, for the purposes as aforesaid.

Pursuant to Part II and Schedule 3, Paragraph 2 of the Environmental Protection Act 1990.

Appendix 11: Precedents for Environmental Health and Housing Matters

DATED this   day of   20

....
Justice of the Peace

INFORMATION FOR WARRANT TO ENTER PREMISES

WATER INDUSTRY ACT 1991

IN THE]>var1<[MAGISTRATES' COURT

Date:]>var2<[

The information of]>var3<[of the]>var4<[a duly authorised Environmental Health Officer of the Council who, upon oath, states that the purposes of Section 84 of the Water Industry Act 1991 she has the right at all reasonable hours to enter the premises situate at]>var5<[

]>var6<[

AND that there is reasonable ground for entry to the premises for the purpose of determining whether, and if so in what manner, the power conferred on the City of Council by Section 80(1) of the Water Industry Act 1991, namely to serve a private supply Notice, should be exercised.

WHEREFORE the said]>var7<[applies for a warrant authorising her to enter the said premises pursuant to Section 84(3) and Part 1 of Schedule 6 of the Water Industry Act 1991.

....
Informant

Sworn before me

Dated

....
Justice of the Peace

(DRAFT)

STATEMENT OF WITNESS

SECTION 9 OF THE CJA 1967; SS 5A(3)(A) AND 5B OF THE MCA 1980; R 70 OF THE MC RULES 1981

Statement of:	Park Ranger
Age of witness:	Over 18
Occupation of witness:	Park Ranger
Address:	

(Witness to sign at the end of the statement and at the completion of the following declaration)

This statement [consisting of four pages each signed by me], is true to the best of my knowledge and belief and I make it knowing that, if it is tendered in evidence, I shall be liable to prosecution if I have wilfully stated in it anything which I know to be false or do not believe to be true.

I am employed by the   council in its Recreation Services Department as a Park Ranger. I have been a Park Ranger with the council for [insert number of years] years. Part of my duties are to patrol recreation grounds and public parks owned by the council in accordance with section 2 of the Dogs (Fouling of Land) Act 1996 in order to enforce the provisions of the council's byelaws relating to recreation grounds and parks and the 1996 Act. I am duly authorised to enforce the said legislation.

At [insert time on 24-hour clock] hours on [insert day, month and year], I was on duty and patrolling a recreation ground/public park/other land [insert the name and address of the ground, park or land].

The land is designated by the council in accordance with section 2 of the Dogs (Fouling of Land) Act 1996.

I now produce an Ordnance Survey plan of the area of land in question and mark it (EXHIBIT NO   PR1).

During my patrol, I noticed a dog – namely A [insert an accurate description of the dog, together with its name if known] foul an area of land [insert a description of where the area of land is situated]. A person who I now know to be [insert the full name and address of the person], who was in charge of the dog at the time, made no attempt top clean up the faeces forthwith from the land.

I watched the defendant for a few moments. S/he having made no attempt to remove the faeces and appearing to leave the area where the alleged offence was committed, I approached the defendant.

I explained to the defendant who I was – ie, a park ranger from the recreation services department of the bradford council, showed him/her my identification card and explained the nature of the offence which I believed he had committed under section 3 of the Dogs (Fouling of Land) Act 1996.

I attempted to show/showed the defendant where the actual offence took place and the faeces and explained that I was obliged to issue a fixed penalty notice under the provisions of the act unless s/he had a reasonable excuse for allowing the dog to defecate, but failing to remove the faeces forthwith.

I cautioned the defendant by explaining that if the fixed penalty ticket was issued and was not paid within 14 days, then the matter could be referred for prosecution to the magistrates' court. I further explained that I believed the defendant had committed an alleged offence under the 1996 Act. I stated 'you do not have to say anything but it may harm your defence when questioned something you later rely on in court. anything you do say may be given in evidence'. I also explained that if the defendant did not give an explanation, then that would also be referred to in the court if necessary, and the court may draw the conclusion that later explanations given by the defendant for the alleged offence were untrue.

In response, by way of explanation, the defendant stated as follows [set out the whole of the conversation/statement made by the defendant and the officer following the issue of the caution].

As the defendant was reluctant to give his/her full name and address, I advised him/her that failure to comply with my request could be enforced under section 25 of the Police and Criminal Evidence Act 1984 or, alternatively, by reference to the council's electoral roll. I also explained that any additional investigative work on the part of the council would result in an increase in costs awarded against them should the matter ultimately be placed before the magistrates' court and a finding of guilt made.

Bearing in mind that the defendant offered to clean up the faeces, I explained to the defendant that this was not a defence to the proceedings – ie, was not a reasonable excuse.

Bearing in mind that the defendant stated that it was not his/her dog, I explained also that this was not a defence, as the person responsible for the dog is the person in charge at the time the dog defecated. The defendant, in fact, confirmed that s/he was in charge of the dog.

Appendix 11: Precedents for Environmental Health and Housing Matters

I gave the white and pink copies of the fixed penalty notice to the defendant and advised him/her where payment could be made. I retained the yellow administrative and blue office's copy of the fixed penalty notice.

Finally, I confirmed with the defendant that should the fixed penalty notice be paid within 14 days, then no further action would be taken by the council. However, if payment was not received by the council, then the matter would be reported for prosecution.

I can also confirm that the council's policy is to send reminder letters to the defendant in respect of non-payment of the fixed penalty prior to the matter being reported to the council's solicitors for prosecution.

I now produce copies of those reminder letters dated [insert the dates of the reminder letters] and mark them (exhibit no   pr2).

For completeness, I now produce photographs of the faeces and the location of the incident and marked them (exhibit no   pr3) and (exhibit no   pr4) respectively.

[Please note that any additional circumstances of the case should be referred to in the statement, and also any aggravating features, such as threats or foul language.]

DATED THE   DAY OF   20

(SIGNED)

INFORMATION/SUMMONS

IN THE   MAGISTRATES' COURT

To: (Insert Defendant's full name)

of: (Insert Defendant's full address)

INFORMATION has this day been laid before the undersigned by   on behalf of Council, that you

on [insert date]

at [insert location]

did fail without reasonable excuse whilst in charge of a dog on designated land in the area of [insert location] to remove faeces forthwith from the land.

CONTRARY to Section 3 of the Dogs (Fouling of Land) Act 1996.

YOU ARE THEREFORE SUMMONED to appear before the Magistrates' Court

sitting at [insert address of court].

on [first hearing date]

at to answer to the said Information.

DATED the   day of   20 (insert date proceeding commenced)

....
Clerk to the Justices/Clerk to the Court/
Justice of the Peace

If you do not respond to this Summons, the case may be dealt with in your absence. Please note that upon conviction the prosecution will be seeking costs against you.

DRAFT INFORMATION/ SUMMONS

IN THE   MAGISTRATES' COURT

To: (Full name)

of: (Full address)

INFORMATION has this day been laid before the undersigned by, on behalf of Council, that you

on (insert date)

at (insert location)

did without reasonable excuse fail to comply with Byelaw of the Council relating to pleasure grounds, public walks and open spaces, which states 'no person shall without reasonable excuse, climb any wall or fence in or enclosing the ground, or any tree, or any barrier, railing, post or structure 'in that' [insert evidence of breach] CONTRARY to Byelaws and of the said byelaws.

YOU ARE THEREFORE SUMMONED to appear before the Magistrates' Court

sitting at

on [insert date]

at to answer to the said Information.

DATED the   day of

....
     Clerk to the Justices/Clerk to the Court/
     Justice of the Peace

If you do not respond to this Summons, the case may be dealt with in your absence.

Please note that upon conviction the prosecution will be seeking costs against you.

STANDARD INTERVIEW PLAN
FOOD HYGIENE REGULATIONS

Introductory Questions:

Formalities including caution

Owner of business

Person responsible for day to day running of business

Full name of Defendant

Status of Defendant (eg, Ltd Company, plc, Partnership etc)

Speak on behalf of Company (if Company)

Main Body of Questions:

Put all allegations/concerns individually to interviewee (refer to inspection sheet) and ask:

- whether allegation/concern accepted
- cause of alleged infringement
- when interviewee first became aware of allegation
- what remedial steps were taken or reasons for not taking any
- reasons for continuance of alleged infringement

Put any particular concerns to interviewee which arise from allegations, eg, danger of further/cross-contamination, risk to public health and awareness thereof at the time.

Due Diligence Defence:

Explanation for defects

System/steps taken to identify and prevent defects

Cleaning systems in place (daily, weekly, etc)

Maintenance contracts and provisions for inspection

Receipt for records of inspection

Pest control contracts

Receipts for and records of inspections

Appendix 11: Precedents for Environmental Health and Housing Matters

Cleaning and waste removal contracts

Receipts and contract specification and records of visits

Proposed steps to avoid future recurrence

Probing Questions:

Further questioning on answers given which are incomplete or not accepted or require clarification.

Opportunity for comment, clarify, mitigation.

Closure of interview.

PRECEDENTS FOR HACKNEY CARRIAGE AND PRIVATE HIRE PROSECUTIONS

Information/summons

(a) Section 46(1)(a) of the Local Government (Miscellaneous Provisions) Act (LGMPA) 1976 (driving without a vehicle licence).
(b) Section 46(1)(b) of the LGMPA 1976 (driving without a driver's licence).
(c) Section 46(1)(c) of the LGMPA 1976 (employing a driver without a licence).
(d) Section 46(1)(d) of the LGMPA 1976 (operating without an operator's licence).
(e) Section 46(1)(e)(i) of the LGMPA 1976 (operating a vehicle without a vehicle licence).
(f) Section 46(1)(e)(ii) of the LGMPA 1976 (operate a vehicle with an unlicensed driver).
(g) Section 48(6)(a) of the LGMPA 1976 (failure to exhibit interior plate).
(h) Section 48(6)(b) of the LGMPA 1976 (failure to exhibit exterior plate).
(i) Section 54 of the LGMPA 1976 (failure to wear Private Hire badge).
(j) Section 64(3) of the LGMPA 1976 (waiting on a hackney carriage stand).
(k) Section 73(1) of the LGMPA 1976 (failing to give information).
(l) Section 68 of the Town Police Clauses Act (TPCA) 1847 (failing to wear Hackney Carriage badge).
(m) Section 47 of the TPCA 1847 (driving without a HC licence).
(n) Section 45 of the TPCA 1847 (plying for hire without a licence).
(o) Section 143 of the Road Traffic Act 1988 (driving without insurance).
(p) Paragraph 10(1)(a), Sched 4 to the LGMPA 1982 (street trading).
(q) Section 1 and para 12(2), Sched 1 to the LGMPA 1982 (breach of PEL condition).
(r) Paragraph 12(1), Sched 1 to the LGMPA 1982 (provision of PEL without a licence).

SUMMONS]>var1<[

IN THE]>var2<[MAGISTRATES' COURT

To:]>var3<[

of:]>var4<[

INFORMATION has this day been laid before the undersigned by]><[to the Council, on behalf of]><[Council, that you

on the]>var5<[

at]>var6<[

being the proprietor of a private hire vehicle, namely an]>var7<[registration number]>var8<[, private hire plate number]>var9<[, knowingly used the said vehicle on a road called]>var10<[, in a controlled district within the meaning of Part II of the Local Government (Miscellaneous Provisions) Act 1976 without having for such vehicle a current licence under s 48 of the said Act, contrary to Section 46(1)(a) of the Local Government (Miscellaneous Provisions) Act 1976 as amended.

YOU ARE THEREFORE SUMMONED to appear before the Magistrates' Court sitting at]>var11<[

on]>var12<[

at]>var13<[to answer to the said Information.

DATED the   day of   20

....
Clerk to the Justices/Clerk to the Court/
Justice of the Peace

If you do not respond to this Summons, the case may be dealt with in your absence.

Please note that upon conviction the prosecution will be seeking costs against you.

Appendix 12: Precedents for Hackney Carriage and Private Hire Prosecutions

SUMMONS]>var1<[

IN THE]>var2<[MAGISTRATES' COURT

To:]>var3<[
of:]>var4<[

INFORMATION has this day been laid before the undersigned by]><[to the Council, on behalf of]><[Council, that you

on the]>var5<[

at]>var6<[

knowingly did act as driver of a private hire vehicle, namely a]>var7<[, registration number]>var8<[, private hire plate number]>var9<[, on a road called]>var10<[, in a controlled district within the meaning of Part II of the Local Government (Miscellaneous Provisions) Act 1976 without having a current licence under Section 51 of the said Act, contrary to Section 46(1)(b) and (2) of the Local Government (Miscellaneous Provisions) Act 1976 as amended.

YOU ARE THEREFORE SUMMONED to appear before the Magistrates' Court

sitting at]>var11<[

on]>var12<[

at]>var13<[to answer to the said Information.

DATED the   day of   20

....

Clerk to the Justices/Clerk to the Court/
Justice of the Peace

If you do not respond to this Summons, the case may be dealt with in your absence.

Please note that upon conviction the prosecution will be seeking costs against you.

SUMMONS]>var1<[

IN THE]>var2<[MAGISTRATES' COURT

To:]>var3<[

of:]>var4<[

INFORMATION has this day been laid before the undersigned by]><[to the Council, on behalf of]><[Council, that you

on the]>var5<[

at]>var6<[

being the proprietor of a private hire vehicle, namely a]>var7<[, licensed under Part II of the Local Government (Miscellaneous Provisions) Act 1976, knowingly did employ]>var8<[, to act as a driver thereof for the purposes of hiring, the said]>var9<[,

not having a current Licence under Section 51 of the said Act.

CONTRARY TO: Section 46(1)(c) and 46(2) of the Local Government (Miscellaneous Provisions) Act 1976 as amended.

PENALTY: Fine not exceeding level 3 on the standard scale: Section 76 of the said Act.

YOU ARE THEREFORE SUMMONED to appear before the Magistrates' Court

sitting at]>var10<[

on]>var11<[

at]>var12<[to answer to the said Information.

DATED the   day of   20

....
Clerk to the Justices/Clerk to the Court/
Justice of the Peace

If you do not respond to this Summons, the case may be dealt with in your absence. Please note that upon conviction the prosecution will be seeking costs against you.

Appendix 12: Precedents for Hackney Carriage and Private Hire Prosecutions

SUMMONS]>var1<[

IN THE]>var2<[MAGISTRATES' COURT

To:]>var3<[

of:]>var4<[

INFORMATION has this day been laid before the undersigned by]><[to the Council, on behalf of]><[Council, that you

on the]>var5<[

at]>var6<[

did knowingly operate a private hire vehicle, namely a]>var7<[, in a controlled district within the meaning of Part II of the Local Government (Miscellaneous Provisions) Act 1976, without having a current Operator's Licence under Section 55 of the said Act.

CONTRARY TO: Section 46(1)(d) and 46(2) of the Local Government (Miscellaneous Provisions) Act 1976 as amended.

PENALTY: Fine not exceeding level 3 on the standard scale: Section 76 of the said Act.

YOU ARE THEREFORE SUMMONED to appear before the Magistrates' Court

sitting at]>var8<[

on]>var9<[

at]>var10<[to answer to the said Information.

DATED the   day of   20

....
Clerk to the Justices/Clerk to the Court/
Justice of the Peace

If you do not respond to this Summons, the case may be dealt with in your absence.

Please note that upon conviction the prosecution will be seeking costs against you.

SUMMONS]>var1<[

IN THE]>var2<[MAGISTRATES' COURT

To:]>var3<[
of:]>var4<[

INFORMATION has this day been laid before the undersigned by]><[to the Council, on behalf of]><[Council, that you

on the]>var5<[

at]>var6<[

being a private hire vehicle operating licensed under Section 55 of the Local Government (Miscellaneous Provisions) Act 1976 knowingly did in a controlled district within the meaning of Part II of the said Act operate a vehicle namely a]>var7<[, registration number]>var8<[, private hire plate number]>var9<[as a private hire vehicle, there not being in force in relation to the said vehicle a current licence under Section 48 of the said Act, contrary to Section 46(1)(e)(i) and (2) of the Local Government (Miscellaneous Provisions) Act 1976 as amended.

YOU ARE THEREFORE SUMMONED to appear before the Magistrates' Court

sitting at]>var10<[

on]>var11<[

at]>var12<[to answer to the said Information.

DATED the   day of   20

....
Clerk to the Justices/Clerk to the Court/
Justice of the Peace

If you do not respond to this Summons, the case may be dealt with in your absence. Please note that upon conviction the prosecution will be seeking costs against you.

Appendix 12: Precedents for Hackney Carriage and Private Hire Prosecutions

SUMMONS]>var1<[

IN THE]>var2<[MAGISTRATES' COURT

To:]>var3<[

of:]>var4<[

INFORMATION has this day been laid before the undersigned by]><[to the Council, on behalf of]><[Council, that you

on the]>var5<[

at]>var6<[

being a private hire vehicle operator licensed under Section 55 of the Local Government (Miscellaneous Provisions) Act 1976 knowingly did in a controlled district within the meaning of Part II of the said Act operate a vehicle, namely a]>var7<[, registration number]>var8<[, private hire plate number]>var9<[, as a private hire vehicle, the driver of which]>var10<[, did not have a current licence under Section 51 of the said Act, contrary to Section 46(1)(e)(ii) and (2) of the Local Government (Miscellaneous Provisions) Act 1976, as amended.

YOU ARE THEREFORE SUMMONED to appear before the Magistrates' Court

sitting at]>var11<[

on]>var12<[

at]>var13<[to answer to the said Information.

DATED the   day of   20

....
Clerk to the Justices/Clerk to the Court/
Justice of the Peace

If you do not respond to this Summons, the case may be dealt with in your absence.

Please note that upon conviction the prosecution will be seeking costs against you.

SUMMONS]>var1<[

IN THE]>var2<[MAGISTRATES' COURT

To:]>var3<[

of:]>var4<[

INFORMATION has this day been laid before the undersigned by]><[to the Council, on behalf of]><[Council, that you

on the]>var5<[

at]>var6<[

used without reasonable excuse in a controlled district, a vehicle, namely a]>var7<[, registration number]>var8<[, private hire plate]>var9<[, as a private hire vehicle, a vehicle in respect of which a licence has been granted under Section 48 of the Local Government (Miscellaneous Provisions) Act 1976, without there being exhibited on the interior of the vehicle a plate issued in accordance with Section 48(5) of the said Act in such manner as prescribed by Conditions attached to the grant of the said licence, contrary to Section 48(6)(a) and (b) of the Local Government (Miscellaneous Provisions) Act 1976.

YOU ARE THEREFORE SUMMONED to appear before the Magistrates' Court sitting at]>var10<[

on]>var11<[

at]>var12<[to answer to the said Information.

DATED the   day of   20

....

Clerk to the Justices/Clerk to the Court/
Justice of the Peace

If you do not respond to this Summons, the case may be dealt with in your absence.
Please note that upon conviction the prosecution will be seeking costs against you.

Appendix 12: Precedents for Hackney Carriage and Private Hire Prosecutions

SUMMONS]>var1<[

IN THE]>var2<[MAGISTRATES' COURT

To:]>var3<[

of:]>var4<[

INFORMATION has this day been laid before the undersigned by]><[to the Council, on behalf of]><[Council, that you

on the]>var5<[

at]>var6<[

used without reasonable excuse in a controlled district a vehicle, namely a]>var7<[, registration number]>var8<[, private hire plate number]>var9<[, as a private hire vehicle in respect of which a licence had been granted under Section 48 of the Local Government (Miscellaneous Provisions) Act 1976 without there being exhibited on the vehicle an external plate issued in accordance with Section 48(5) of the said Act, in such a manner as prescribed by a Condition attached to the grant of the said Licence, contrary to Section 48(6)(b) of the Local Government (Miscellaneous Provisions) Act 1976.

YOU ARE THEREFORE SUMMONED to appear before the Magistrates' Court

sitting at]>var10<[

on]>var11<[

at]>var12<[to answer to the said Information.

DATED the   day of   20

....
Clerk to the Justices/Clerk to the Court/
Justice of the Peace

If you do not respond to this Summons, the case may be dealt with in your absence.

Please note that upon conviction the prosecution will be seeking costs against you.

SUMMONS]>var1<[

IN THE]>var2<[MAGISTRATES' COURT

To:]>var3<[

of:]>var4<[

INFORMATION has this day been laid before the undersigned by]><[to the Council, on behalf of]><[Council, that you

on the]>var5<[

at]>var6<[

when acting in accordance with a driver's licence granted to you under Section 51 of the Local Government (Miscellaneous Provisions) Act 1976 failed, without reasonable excuse, to wear the badge issued to you under Section 54(1) of the said Act in such position and manner as to be plainly and distinctly visible, contrary to Section 54 of the Local Government (Miscellaneous Provisions) Act 1976.

YOU ARE THEREFORE SUMMONED to appear before the Magistrates' Court

sitting at]>var7<[

on]>var8<[

at]>var9<[to answer to the said Information.

DATED the   day of   20

....
Clerk to the Justices/Clerk to the Court/
Justice of the Peace

If you do not respond to this Summons, the case may be dealt with in your absence.

Please note that upon conviction the prosecution will be seeking costs against you.

SUMMONS]>var1<[

Appendix 12: Precedents for Hackney Carriage and Private Hire Prosecutions

IN THE]>var2<[MAGISTRATES' COURT

To:]>var3<[

of:]>var4<[

INFORMATION has this day been laid before the undersigned by]><[to the Council, on behalf of]><[Council, that you

on the]>var5<[

at]>var6<[

did, without reasonable cause, cause a]>var7<[, motor vehicle, registration number]>var8<[not being a hackney carriage, to wait on a stand for hackney carriages at]>var9<[appointed by the City of Bradford Metropolitan Council under Section 63 of the Local Government (Miscellaneous Provisions) Act 1976, contrary to Section 64(3) of the Local Government (Miscellaneous Provisions) Act 1976.

YOU ARE THEREFORE SUMMONED to appear before the Magistrates' Court at]>var10<[

on]>var11<[

at]>var12<[to answer to the said Information.

DATED the   day of   20

....
Clerk to the Justices/Clerk to the Court/
Justice of the Peace

If you do not respond to this Summons, the case may be dealt with in your absence.

Please note that upon conviction the prosecution will be seeking costs against you.

SUMMONS]>var1<[

IN THE]>var2<[MAGISTRATES' COURT

To:]>var3<[

of:]>var4<[

INFORMATION has this day been laid before the undersigned by]>var5<[to the Council, on behalf of]>var6<[Council, that you

on the]>var7<[

at]>var8<[

did without reasonable cause fail to give to]>var9<[, Hackney Carriage Officer, information which he reasonably required for the purpose of the performance of his function as an authorised officer of the City of Bradford Metropolitan Council acting in pursuance of Part II of the Local Government (Miscellaneous Provisions) Act 1976 contrary to Section 73(1) of the Local Government (Miscellaneous Provisions) Act 1976.

YOU ARE THEREFORE SUMMONED to appear before the Magistrates' Court

sitting at]>var10<[

on]>var11<[

at]>var12<[to answer to the said Information.

DATED the   day of   20

....
Clerk to the Justices/Clerk to the Court/
Justice of the Peace

If you do not respond to this Summons, the case may be dealt with in your absence.

Please note that upon conviction the prosecution will be seeking costs against you.

Appendix 12: Precedents for Hackney Carriage and Private Hire Prosecutions

SUMMONS]>var1<[

IN THE]>var2<[MAGISTRATES' COURT

To:]>var3<[

of:]>var4<[

INFORMATION has this day been laid before the undersigned by]><[to the Council, on behalf of]><[Council, that you

on the]>var5<[

at]>var6<[

being the driver of a hackney carriage when plying for hire, did fail to wear on your left breast outside your outer garment, and in such a manner as to be at all times plainly and distinctly visible a badge provided by]><[Council, contrary to a byelaw relating to hackney carriages made by the said Council on the]><[and number]><[of the Byelaws relating to Hackney Carriages made by the]><[Council on the]><[and Section 68 of the Town Police Clauses Act 1847.

YOU ARE THEREFORE SUMMONED to appear before the Magistrates' Court

sitting at]>var7<[

on the]>var8<[

at]>var9<[to answer to the said Information.

DATED the   day of   20

....
Clerk to the Justices/Clerk to the Court/
Justice of the Peace

If you do not respond to this Summons, the case may be dealt with in your absence.

Please note that upon conviction the prosecution will be seeking costs against you.

SUMMONS]>var1<[

IN THE]>var2<[MAGISTRATES' COURT

To:]>var3<[

of:]>var4<[

INFORMATION has this day been laid before the undersigned by]><[to the Council, on behalf of]><[Council, that you

on]>var 5<[

at]>var 6<[

Did act as the driver of a hackney carriage numbered]>var 7<[, then duly licensed in pursuance of the Town Police Clauses Act 1847, to ply for hire within a prescribed distance of Bradford, as defined by the said Act:

(a) He not then having obtained a Licence to act as such driver; or

(b) during the time that his Licence to act as such driver was suspended,

contrary to Section 47 of the Town Police Clauses Act 1847.

YOU ARE THEREFORE SUMMONED to appear before the Magistrates' Court

sitting at]>var 8<[

on]>var 9<[

at]>var 10<[to answer to the said Information.

DATED the   day of   20

....
Clerk to the Justices/Clerk to the Court/
Justice of the Peace

If you do not respond to this Summons, the case may be dealt with in your absence.

Please note that upon conviction the prosecution will be seeking costs against you.

Appendix 12: Precedents for Hackney Carriage and Private Hire Prosecutions

SUMMONS]>var1<[

IN THE]>var2<[MAGISTRATES' COURT

To:]>var3<[

of:]>var4<[

INFORMATION has this day been laid before the undersigned by]><[to the Council, on behalf of]><[Council, that you

on the]>var5<[

at]>var6<[

was found plying for hire with a hackney carriage, namely a]>var7<[, registration number]>var8<[, at]>var9<[within the prescribed distance as laid down by Section 34 of the Town Police Clauses Act 1847 for which carriage a Licence plying for hire had not previously been obtained, contrary to Section 45 of the Town Police Clauses Act 1847.

YOU ARE THEREFORE SUMMONED to appear before the Magistrates' Court

sitting at]>var10<[

on]>var11<[

at]>var12<[to answer to the said Information.

DATED the   day of   20

....
Clerk to the Justices/Clerk to the Court/
Justice of the Peace

If you do not respond to this Summons, the case may be dealt with in your absence.

Please note that upon conviction the prosecution will be seeking costs against you.

SUMMONS]>var1<[

IN THE]>var2<[MAGISTRATES' COURT

To:]>var3<[

of:]>var4<[

INFORMATION has this day been laid before the undersigned by]><[to the Council, on behalf of]><[Council, that you

on the]>var5<[

at]>var6<[

did use a motor vehicle, namely a]>var7<[, registration number]>var8<[, on a road called]>var9<[, there not being in force in relation to the use of the said vehicle such policy of insurance or such security in respect of third party risk as complies with the requirements of Part VII of the Road Traffic Act 1988, contrary to Section 143 of the Road Traffic Act 1988.

YOU ARE THEREFORE SUMMONED to appear before the Magistrates' Court

sitting at]>var10<[

on]>var11<[

at]>var12<[to answer to the said Information.

DATED the   day of   20

....
Clerk to the Justices/Clerk to the Court/
Justice of the Peace

If you do not respond to this Summons, the case may be dealt with in your absence.

Please note that upon conviction the prosecution will be seeking costs against you.

Please ensure you have your current driving licence with you or, it is with the Clerk to the Court, when your case is dealt with by the Magistrates.

Additional penalties under Sections 7 and 27 of the Road Traffic Regulation Act 1984 may be imposed if the licence is not with the Court when the case has been concluded.

Appendix 12: Precedents for Hackney Carriage and Private Hire Prosecutions

SUMMONS]>var1<[

IN THE]>var2<[MAGISTRATES' COURT

To:]>var3<[

of:]>var4<[

INFORMATION has this day been laid before the undersigned by]><[on behalf of]><[Council, that you

on the]>var5<[

at]>var6<[

did engage in street trading in a prohibited street namely,]>var7<[contrary to Paragraph 10(1)(a) of Schedule 4 of the Local Government (Miscellaneous Provisions) Act 1982.

YOU ARE THEREFORE SUMMONED to appear before the Magistrates' Court

sitting at]>var8<[

on]>var9<[

at]>var10<[to answer to the said Information.

DATED the   day of   20

....
Clerk to the Justices/Clerk to the Court/
Justice of the Peace

If you do not respond to this Summons, the case may be dealt with in your absence.

Please note that upon conviction the prosecution will be seeking costs against you.

SUMMONS]>var1<[

IN THE]>var2<[MAGISTRATES' COURT

To:]>var3<[

of:]>var4<[

INFORMATION has this day been laid before the undersigned by]><[on behalf of]><[Council, that you

on the]>var5<[

at]>var6<[in the City first aforesaid

was the holder of a Licence granted under paragraph 1 of Schedule 1 to the Local Government (Miscellaneous Provisions) Act 1982 in respect of]>var7<[in relation to which a (*term/condition/restriction) namely,]>var8<[subject to which the Licence was held was (*contravened/not complied with) in that

CONTRARY to Section 1 and paragraph 12(2) of Schedule 1 to the Local Government (Miscellaneous Provisions) Act 1982, as amended.

YOU ARE THEREFORE SUMMONED to appear before the Magistrates' Court

sitting at]>var9<[

on]>var10<[

at]>var11<[to answer to the said Information.

DATED the   day of   20

....
Clerk to the Justices/Clerk to the Court/
Justice of the Peace

* Delete as appropriate

If you do not respond to this Summons, the case may be dealt with in your absence.

Please note that upon conviction the prosecution will be seeking costs against you.

Appendix 12: Precedents for Hackney Carriage and Private Hire Prosecutions

SUMMONS]>var1<[

IN THE]>var2<[MAGISTRATES' COURT

To:]>var3<[

of:]>var4<[

INFORMATION has this day been laid before the undersigned by]><[on behalf of]><[Council, that you

on the]>var5<[

at]>var6<[in the City first aforesaid

You were concerned in the (organisation or management*) of a public entertainment as set out in paragraph 1 of Schedule 1 to the Local Government (Miscellaneous Provisions) Act 1982 being a place in which no licence was in force in accordance with that paragraph.

CONTRARY to paragraph 12(1) of Schedule 1 to the Local Government (Miscellaneous Provisions) Act 1982, as amended.

YOU ARE THEREFORE SUMMONED to appear before the Magistrates' Court

sitting at]>var7<[

on]>var8<[

at]>var9<[to answer to the said Information.

DATED the   day of   20

....
Clerk to the Justices/Clerk to the Court/
Justice of the Peace

* Delete as appropriate

If you do not respond to this Summons, the case may be dealt with in your absence.

Please note that upon conviction the prosecution will be seeking costs against you.

SUMMONS]>var1<[

IN THE]>var2<[MAGISTRATES' COURT

To:]>var3<[

of:]>var4<[

INFORMATION has this day been laid before the undersigned by]><[on behalf of]><[Council, that you

on the]>var5<[

at]>var6<[in the City first aforesaid

You being a person who knew or had reasonable cause to suspect that a public entertainment to which paragraph 1 applied would be provided at the premises allowed the premises to be so used.

CONTRARY to paragraph 12(1) of Schedule 1 to the Local Government (Miscellaneous Provisions) Act 1982, as amended.

YOU ARE THEREFORE SUMMONED to appear before the Magistrates' Court

sitting at]>var7<[

on]>var8<[

at]>var8<[to answer to the said Information.

DATED the   day of   20

....
Clerk to the Justices/Clerk to the Court/
Justice of the Peace

* Delete as appropriate

If you do not respond to this Summons, the case may be dealt with in your absence.

Please note that upon conviction the prosecution will be seeking costs against you.

PRECEDENTS FOR INVESTIGATION AND PROSECUTION OF WASTE MANAGEMENT

Draft notice under:

(a) Section 93 of the Control of Pollution Act 1974.

Information/summons:

(b) Section 33 of the Environmental Protection Act (EPA) 1990 (depositing waste).
(c) Section 34(1) and (6) of the EPA 1990 (failure to keep written description of waste).
(d) Section 34(6) of the EPA 1990 (failure to complete transfer note).
(e) Section 47(6) of the EPA 1990 (failure to provide waste receptacles).
(f) Section 87(1) of the EPA 1990 (depositing waste in relevant highway).
(g) Section 2 of the Refuse Disposal Amenity Act 1978 (abandoning refuse on open land).
(h) Section 93(3) of the Control of Pollution Act 1974 (failure to comply with a request for information).

CITY OF]><[COUNCIL

SECTION 93 OF THE CONTROL OF POLLUTION ACT 1974

To:

Of:

Re: Unauthorised deposit of controlled waste at land situated on]><[(insert full location and address).

Description of Waste

Bags of builders' rubble and refuse were found containing builders' rubble and refuse. Also found was paper evidence bearing the name of]><[(insert name) of (insert address).

In accordance with s 93 of the Control of Pollution Act 1974 you are required to supply the following information to]><[of the address below within 14 days of the date of this Notice.

Failure to supply the information within 14 days of the date of this Notice is an offence for which you may be liable to a fine of £5,000. The information required is as follows:

(1) A transfer note for the waste detailed above as set out in the Environmental Protection Act 1990 (Duty of Care Regulations 1991) or confirm that no such note existed.
(2) A copy of a written description of the transfer of waste made at the time of transfer as set out in Section 34(1)(c) of the Environmental Protection Act 1990 or confirmation that no such note existed at the time of transfer.
(3) Was the waste transferred to an authorised person as set out in Section 34(3) ie a person licensed to collect waste?
(4) If the answer to (3) is yes, what is the name and address of that person.

If you fail to answer satisfactorily questions (1)–(3), the following inferences may be made at any subsequent court proceedings, namely:

(1) A transfer note was not made at the time.
(2) The transfer of the waste was not to an authorised person.
(3) A written description of the waste was not made at the time of the transfer.

Additional information required is:

(4) Your full name or the full name of your firm or limited company.
(5) Your address or registered office address if your company is a limited company.
(6) Your telephone number.
(7) Supply the name of the person(s) who collected the rubbish for disposal from your premises.
(8) The date when the rubbish was collected from your premises.
(9) Details of how the waste was generated and by whom.
(10) A brief description of the work carried out by the firm and the process used.

Appendix 13: Precedents for Investigation and Prosecution of Waste Management

(11) Confirmation that the waste was generated during the course of your business.

You are strongly advised to supply this information in writing by recorded delivery or registered post and retain proof of posting. Failure to do so may result in an inference being made by the Magistrates' Court that the information was never sent. Receipt of this information will be confirmed by Mr]><[by telephone.

NB Whereas you are required to supply the information requested. Any information you provided may be used in court proceedings.

DATED this   day of   20

....
]><[
Authorised Officer
]><[

SUMMONS]>var1<[

IN THE]>var2<[MAGISTRATES' COURT

To:]>var3<[

of:]>var4<[

INFORMATION has this day been laid before the undersigned by [insert name and address], Barrister/Solicitor, on behalf of [insert name] Council, that you

on]>var 5<[

at]>var 6<[

did deposit items of waste namely,]>var 7<[in contravention of Section 33(1) and (6) of the Environmental Protection Act 1990.

YOU ARE THEREFORE SUMMONED to appear before the Magistrates' Court

sitting at]>var 8<[

on]>var 9<[

at]>var 10<[to answer to the said Information.

DATED the   day of   20

....
Clerk to the Justices/Clerk to the Court/
Justice of the Peace

If you do not respond to this Summons, the case may be dealt with in your absence.

Please note that upon conviction the prosecution will be seeking costs against you.

Appendix 13: Precedents for Investigation and Prosecution of Waste Management

INFORMATION]>var1<[

IN THE]>var2<[MAGISTRATES' COURT

To:]>var3<[
of:]>var4<[

INFORMATION has this day been laid before the undersigned by [insert name and address], Solicitor/Barrister, on behalf of [insert name] Council, that you

on]>var 5<[

at]>var 6<[

being a product of controlled waste, namely]>var 7<[did on the transfer of that waste, fail to secure that there was transferred such a written description of the waste as to enable other persons to avoid a contravention of Section 33 of the Environmental Protection Act 1990 and to comply with the duty under Section 34(1) of the said Act as respects the escape of waste contrary to Section 34(1) and (6) of the Environmental Protection Act 1990.

YOU ARE THEREFORE SUMMONED to appear before the Magistrates' Court

sitting at]>var 8<[

on]>var 9<[

at]>var 10<[to answer to the said Information.

DATED the   day of   20

....
Clerk to the Justices/Clerk to the Court/
Justice of the Peace

If you do not respond to this Summons, the case may be dealt with in your absence.

Please note that upon conviction the prosecution will be seeking costs against you.

SUMMONS]>var1<[

IN THE]>var2<[MAGISTRATES' COURT

To:-]>var3<[

of:-]>var4<[

INFORMATION has this day been laid before the undersigned by [insert name and address], Solicitor/Barrister, on behalf of [insert name] Council, that you

on]>var 5<[

at]>var 6<[

being a transferor of controlled waste, namely]>var 7<[did fail to ensure that a transfer note as described in reg 2(2) of the Environmental Protection (Duty of Care) Regulations 1991 was completed and signed contrary to Regulation 2(1) of the said Regulations and Section 34(6) of the Environmental Protection Act 1990.

YOU ARE THEREFORE SUMMONED to appear before the Magistrates' Court

sitting at]>var 8<[

on]>var 9<[

at]>var 10<[to answer to the said Information.

DATED the   day of   20

....
Clerk to the Justices/Clerk to the Court/
Justice of the Peace

If you do not respond to this Summons, the case may be dealt with in your absence.

Please note that upon conviction the prosecution will be seeking costs against you.

Appendix 13: Precedents for Investigation and Prosecution of Waste Management

SUMMONS]>var1<[

IN THE]>var2<[MAGISTRATES' COURT

To:]>var3<[

of:]>var4<[

INFORMATION has this day been laid before the undersigned by [insert name and address], Solicitor/Barrister, on behalf of [insert name] Council, that you

on]>var5<[

at]>var6<[

did fail, without reasonable excuse, to comply with a requirement imposed under Section 47(2) of the Environmental Protection Act 1990 to provide at the premises, namely,]>var7<[, receptacles for the storage of waste as specified in a notice under the said section.

CONTRARY to Section 47(6) of the Environmental Protection Act 1990.

YOU ARE THEREFORE SUMMONED to appear before the Magistrates' Court

sitting at]>var8<[

on]>var9<[

at]>var10<[to answer to the said Information.

DATED the   day of   20

....
Clerk to the Justices/Clerk to the Court/
Justice of the Peace

If you do not respond to this Summons, the case may be dealt with in your absence.

Please note that upon conviction the prosecution will be seeking costs against you.

SUMMONS]>var1<[

IN THE]>var2<[MAGISTRATES' COURT

To:]>var3<[

of:]>var4<[

INFORMATION has this day been laid before the undersigned by [insert name and address], Solicitor/Barrister, on behalf of [insert name] Council, that you

on]>var5<[

at]>var6<[

did deposit in a relevant highway within the meaning of Part IV of the Environmental Protection Act 1990, namely]>var7<[and leave a quantity of]>var8<[refuse in such circumstances as to cause, or contribute to, or tend to lead to the defacement by litter of the said place, contrary to Section 87(1) of the Environmental Protection Act 1990.

YOU ARE THEREFORE SUMMONED to appear before the Magistrates' Court sitting at]>var9<[

on]>var10<[at]>var11<[to answer to the said Information.

DATED the   day of   20

....
Clerk to the Justices/Clerk to the Court/
Justice of the Peace

If you do not respond to this Summons, the case may be dealt with in your absence. Please note that upon conviction the prosecution will be seeking costs against you.

Appendix 13: Precedents for Investigation and Prosecution of Waste Management

SUMMONS]>var1<[

IN THE]>var2<[MAGISTRATES' COURT

To:]>var3<[
of:]>var4<[

INFORMATION has this day been laid before the undersigned by [insert name and address], Solicitor/Barrister, [insert name] Council, that you

on]>var 5<[

at]>var 6<[

did without lawful authority abandon on land in the open air known as]>var 7<[a quantity of]>var 8<[refuse, contrary to Section 2(1)(b) of the Refuse Disposal (Amenity) Act 1978.

YOU ARE THEREFORE SUMMONED to appear before the Magistrates' Court

sitting at]>var 9<[

on]>var 10<[

at]>var 11<[to answer to the said Information.

DATED the   day of   20

....
Clerk to the Justices/Clerk to the Court/
Justice of the Peace

If you do not respond to this Summons, the case may be dealt with in your absence.

Please note that upon conviction the prosecution will be seeking costs against you.

SUMMONS]>var1<[

IN THE BRADFORD MAGISTRATES' COURT

To:]>var2<[
of:]>var3<[

INFORMATION has this day been laid before the undersigned by [insert name and address], Solicitor/Barrister, on behalf of [insert name] Council, that you

on]>var4<[

at]>var5<[

did fail without reasonable excuse to comply with the requirements of a notice served in pursuance of Section 93 of the Control of Pollution Act 1974 as amended.

CONTRARY to Section 93(3) of the said Act as substituted by Schedule 19 to the Environment Act 1995.

YOU ARE THEREFORE SUMMONED to appear before the Magistrates' Court sitting at The Tyrls, Bradford, West Yorkshire.

on]>var6<[

at]>var7<[to answer to the said Information.

DATED the   day of   20

....
Clerk to the Justices/Clerk to the Court/
Justice of the Peace

If you do not respond to this Summons, the case may be dealt with in your absence.
Please note that upon conviction the prosecution will be seeking costs against you.

PRECEDENTS FOR TRADING STANDARDS INVESTIGATIONS AND PROSECUTIONS

Informations/summons:

(a) Section 14(1)(b) of the Trade Descriptions Act (TDA) 1968 (false statement in relation to services accommodation or facilities).
(b) Section 92 of the Trade Marks Act 1994 (use of trade mark without consent).
(c) Regulations 5 and 7 of the Fibre Content Regulations 1986 and s 23 of the TDA 1968 (false labelling as to fibre content).
(d) Section 169(1) of the Licensing Act 1964 (sale of alcohol to under age person).
(e) Section 1(1)(b) of the TDA 1968 (false trade description in relation to goods).

SUMMONS]>var1<[

IN THE]>var2<[MAGISTRATES' COURT
To:]>var3<[
of:]>var4<[

INFORMATION has this day been laid before the undersigned Solicitor/Barrister of the]>var5<[Council of]>var6<[that you

on]>var7<[

in the course of trade or business as a]>var8<[did recklessly make a statement which was false as to the provision/nature of any service, accommodation or facility,

namely]>var9<[

CONTRARY to Section 14(1)(b) of The Trade Descriptions Act 1968.

YOU ARE THEREFORE summoned to appear before the Magistrates' Court sitting at]>var10<[

on]>var11<[

to answer to the said Information.

Appendix 14: Precedents for Trading Standards Investigations and Prosecutions

]>VAR1<[MAGISTRATES' COURT

To:]>var2<[

of:]>var3<[

INFORMATION has this day been laid before the undersigned Solicitor/Barrister of the]>var4<[Council of]>var5<[that you

on]>var6<[

in the course of a business with a view to gain for yourself or another or with intent to cause loss to another and without the consent of the proprietor, did expose for sale]>var7<[which bore a sign likely to be mistaken for the registered trade mark]>var8<[

CONTRARY to Section 92(1)(b) of the Trade Marks Act 1994.

YOU ARE THEREFORE summoned to appear before the Magistrates' Court

sitting at]>var9<[

on]>var10<[

to answer to the said Information.

]>VAR1<[MAGISTRATES' COURT

To:]>var2<[
of:]>var3<[

INFORMATION has this day been laid before the undersigned Solicitor/Barrister of the]>var4<[Council of]>var5<[that you

on]>var6<[

committed an offence in that in the course of trade or business as]>var7<[(insert business name and type] did supply to]>var8<[a textile product namely a]>var9<[which did not comply with the requirements of Regulation 7 and Schedule 1 of the Textile Products (Indications of Fibre Content) Regulations 1986 in that it bore a label giving an indication of fibre content with was false in that it stated]>var10<[whereas the true fibre content was found to be]>var11<[

CONTRARY to Regulation 5 of the said Regulations.

AND the commission of the said offence was due to the act or default of you,]>var12<[whereby you are guilty of an offence by virtue of Regulation 11 of the said Regulations and Section 23 of the Trade Descriptions Act 1968.

YOU ARE THEREFORE summoned to appear before the Magistrates' Court

sitting at]>var13<[

on]>var14<[

to answer to the said Information.

Appendix 14: Precedents for Trading Standards Investigations and Prosecutions

]>VAR1<[MAGISTRATES' COURT

To:]>var2<[
of:]>var3<[

INFORMATION has this day been laid before the undersigned Solicitor/Barrister of the]>var4<[Council of]>var5<[that you

on]>var6<[

being the holder of the intoxicating liquor licence for]>var7<[[name premises and address] did sell to]>var8<[a person under the age of 18 years, namely]>var9<[years, intoxicating liquor, namely a]>var10<[[insert type of intoxicating liquor]

CONTRARY to Section 169(1) of the Licensing Act 1964.

YOU ARE THEREFORE summoned to appear before the Magistrates' Court

sitting at]>var11<[

on]>var12<[

to answer to the said Information.

]>VAR1<[MAGISTRATES' COURT

To:]>var2<[
of:]>var3<[

INFORMATION has this day been laid before the undersigned Solicitor/Barrister of the]>var4<[Council of]>var5<[that you

on]>var6<[

committed an offence in that]>var7<[[insert name and address and type of business] did supply to]>var8<[[name person], a]>var9<[[name product] to which a false trade description was applied, namely the statement]>var10<[appearing on the]>var11<[,

CONTRARY to Section 1(1)(b) of the Trade Descriptions Act 1968

AND the commission of the said offence was due to the act or default of you,]>var12<[whereby you are therefore guilty of an offence by virtue of Section 23 of the Trade Descriptions Act 1968.

YOU ARE THEREFORE summoned to appear before the Magistrates' Court

sitting at]>var13<[

on]>var14<[

PRECEDENTS FOR INVESTIGATION AND PROSECUTION OF EDUCATION MATTERS

Draft notices:

(a) Section 559(1) of the Education Act 1996 (notice prohibiting/restricting employment of children).
(b) Section 559(2) of the Education Act 1996 (notice requesting information as to employment of children).

Information/summons:

(c) Section 18(1) of the Children and Young Persons Act (CYPA) 1933 (employing underage people).
(d) Section 20(1) of the CYPA 1933 (employing child in street trading activities).
(e) Section 559(1) of the Education Act (EA) 1996 (contravention of s 559(1) notice).
(f) Section 559(2) of the EA 1996 (failing to comply with s 559(2) notice).

DRAFT NOTICE UNDER S 559(1) OF THE EDUCATION ACT 1996

ISSUED BY: [name Council]
[address of Council]

To: [name]
of: [address]

The [name] Council, as Local Education Authority, for [child's name], who is a registered pupil at [name school], which is a [County/Voluntary/Special School], as it appears to the Council that the child is being employed in such a manner as to be prejudicial to [his/her] health, or otherwise to render [him/her] unfit to obtain the full benefit of the education provided for [him/her].

HEREBY GIVE YOU NOTICE AS FOLLOWS:

(a) prohibiting you from employing the child; or
(b) imposing such restrictions upon his employment of the child as appears to the Council to be expedient in the interests of the child as follows:

[insert as appropriate]

....
Chief Education Officer/Authorised Officer

DATED   day of   20

NB: Insert or delete as appropriate where a square bracket appears.

NB: A person who fails to comply with this notice commits an offence under Section 559(3) of the Education Act 1996 and shall be liable on summary conviction to a fine not exceeding Level 1 on the Standard Scale or to imprisonment for a term not exceeding one month or both.

Appendix 15: Precedents for Investigation and Prosecution of Education Matters

Section 559(2) of the EA 1996

<INSERT>DISTRICT COUNCIL

NOTICE REQUESTING INFORMATION AS TO EMPLOYMENT OF CHILDREN

SECTION 559(2) OF THE EDUCATION ACT 1996

To:

of:

To enable the Local Authority to ascertain whether a child namely

of   who is a registered pupil at   school is being employed in such a manner as to render him unfit to obtain the full benefit of the education provided for him you are required to supply the following information:

1   Full name of employer.

2   Address of employer.

3   Date or approximate date when the pupil/child first became employed.

4   Number of hours per week normally worked by the pupil/child.

5   Specify times of day and days of the week that the pupil/child normally works.

6   If the pupil/child does not work a set number of hours or days estimate the number of hours worked over the last four weeks.

7   Describe what the child is employed to do according to your understanding.

In accordance with s 559(2) you are required to reply to this notice. SUCH REPLY SHOULD ARRIVE AT THE ADDRESS STATED BELOW NO LESS THAN 14 DAYS FROM THE DATE OF THIS NOTICE.

FAILURE TO COMPLY WITH S 559(2) OF THE EDUCATION ACT 1996 IS AN OFFENCE WHICH CARRIES A FINE OF UP TO LEVEL 1 ON THE STANDARD SCALE OR IMPRISONMENT FOR A TERM OF ONE MONTH OR BOTH.

NB: If you do not deliver your reply personally you are strongly advised to send it by recorded delivery or registered post and retain proof of posting. Failure to do so may result in the court being asked to infer that it was not sent.

DATED this   day of   20

....
Chief Education Officer / Authorised Officer

Address for service:

Solicitor:

Council's Name and Address:

Ref:

Appendix 15: Precedents for Investigation and Prosecution of Education Matters

SUMMONS]>var 1<[

IN THE]>var 2<[MAGISTRATES' COURT

To:]>var 3<[
of:]>var 4<[

INFORMATION has this day been laid before the undersigned by [insert name and address of Council's Chief Legal Officer] on behalf of [insert name of Council], that you

on the]>var 5<[

at]>var 6<[employed a child not over compulsory school age [insert name and date of birth]:

(a) under the age of 14 years; or
(b) before the close of school hours on any day on which he is required to attend school; or
(c) before 7.00 am or after 7.00 pm; or
(d) more than two hours on any day on which he/she is required to attend school; or
(e) for more than two hours on any Sunday.

In that]>var 7<[was employed to]>var 8<[.

Contrary to Sections 18(1)(]>a or b or c or d or e<[) and Section 21 of the Children and Young Persons Act 1933.

YOU ARE THEREFORE SUMMONED to appear before the Magistrates' Court

sitting at]>var 9<[

on]>var 10<[

at]>var 11<[to answer to the said Information.

DATED the   day of   20

....
Clerk to the Justices/Clerk to the Court/
Justice of the Peace

If you do not respond to this Summons, the case may be dealt with in your absence.

Please note that upon conviction the prosecution will be seeking costs against you.

SUMMONS]>var 1<[

IN THE]>var 2<[MAGISTRATES' COURT

To:-]>var 3<[
of:]>var 4<[

INFORMATION has this day been laid before the undersigned by [insert name and address of Council's Chief Legal Officer] on behalf of [insert name of Council], that you on the]>var 5<[

at]>var 6<[engaged or employed a child not over compulsory school age namely [insert name and date of birth of child] in street trading;

In that]>var 7<[undertook street trading activities by selling items such as]>var 8<[

Contrary to Section 20(1) and Section 21 of the Children and Young Persons Act 1933.

YOU ARE THEREFORE SUMMONED to appear before the Magistrates' Court sitting at]>var 9<[
on]>var 10<[
at]>var 11<[to answer to the said Information.

DATED the   day of   20

....
Clerk to the Justices/Clerk to the Court/
Justice of the Peace

If you do not respond to this Summons, the case may be dealt with in your absence. Please note that upon conviction the prosecution will be seeking costs against you.

Appendix 15: Precedents for Investigation and Prosecution of Education Matters

SUMMONS]>var 1<[

IN THE]>var 2<[MAGISTRATES' COURT

To:]>var 3<[
of:]>var 4<[

INFORMATION has this day been laid before the undersigned by [insert name and address of Council's Chief Legal Officer] on behalf of [insert name of Council], that you on the]>var 5<[

at]>var 6<[contravened a Notice issued under Section 559(1) of the Education Act 1996 in respect of a child, namely,]>var 7<[ ]>var 8<[[date of birth] who is a registered pupil at the]>var 9<[County/Voluntary/Special School, and being of compulsory school age such notice having been duly served in writing after it appeared to the Local Education Authority that the child was employed in such a manner as to be prejudicial to his/her health or otherwise to render him/her unfit to obtain the full benefit of the education provided for him/her in that the notice:

(a) Prohibited the employment of the child; or
(b) imposed restrictions upon the child's employment as appeared to the Local Education Authority to be expedient in the interests of the child;

by reason that the child was employed on the above date in the capacity of]>var 11<[, or the following restriction(s) were not complied with:

]>var 12<[

Contrary to Section 559(1)(a) or (b) and Section 559(3)(a) of the Education Act 1996.

YOU ARE THEREFORE SUMMONED to appear before the Magistrates' Court sitting at]>var 13<[

on]>var 14<[

at]>var 15<[to answer to the said Information.

DATED the   day of   20

....
Clerk to the Justices/Clerk to the Court/
Justice of the Peace

If you do not respond to this Summons, the case may be dealt with in your absence.

Please note that upon conviction the prosecution will be seeking costs against you.

SUMMONS]>var 1<[

IN THE]>var 2<[MAGISTRATES' COURT

To:]>var 3<[

of:]>var 4<[

INFORMATION has this day been laid before the undersigned by [insert name and address of Council's Chief Legal Officer] on behalf of [insert name of Council], that you on the]>var 5<[

at]>var 6<[, as parent/employer of a child of compulsory school age – namely,]>var 7<[[date of birth], who is a registered pupil at the]>var 8<[County/Voluntary/Special School, failed to comply with a notice requiring you to provide to the Council, within such period as specified in the Notice, information as appeared to the Council to be necessary for the purpose of enabling it to ascertain whether the child is being employed in such a manner as to render him/her unfit to obtain the full benefit of the education provided for him/her, the Notice being served on]>var 9<[, giving]>var 10<[days to comply with the Notice, you did fail to comply with the requirements of the Notice.

Contrary to Section 559(2) and Section 559(3)(b) of the Education Act 1996.

YOU ARE THEREFORE SUMMONED to appear before the Magistrates' Court

sitting at]>var 11<[

on]>var 12<[

at]>var 13<[to answer to the said Information.

DATED the   day of   20

....
Clerk to the Justices/Clerk to the Court/
Justice of the Peace

If you do not respond to this Summons, the case may be dealt with in your absence.

Please note that upon conviction the prosecution will be seeking costs against you.

PRECEDENTS FOR INVESTIGATION AND PROSECUTION OF COUNTRYSIDE AND HIGHWAYS OFFENCES

Highways Act (HA) 1980 notices:

(a) Section 143 notice to remove structure.
(b) Section 145 notice requiring enlargement or removal of gate.
(c) Section 146 notice to owner re disrepair to stile gate, etc.
(d) Section 154 notice to lop or cut overhanging vegetation.
(e) Section 154 notice to cut/fell dangerous hedge/tree.
(f) Section 164 notice to remove barbed wire.
(g) Section 16 of the Local Government (Miscellaneous Provisions) Act 1976 (Notice requesting information and reply form).
(h) Section 297 notice requesting information and reply form.
(i) Letter warning formal service of notice.

Information/Summons:

(j) Section 57 of the National Parks and Access the Countryside Act (NPACA) 1949 (notice likely to deter public from using highway).
(k) Section 131A of the HA 1980 (disturbing surface of highway).
(l) Section 137 of the HA 1980 (obstructing highway).
(m) Section 161(1) of the HA 1980 (depositing article on highway).
(n) Section 297(2) of the HA 1980 (failing to provide information).
(o) Section 297(3) of the HA 1980 (giving false information).
(p) Section 16 of the Local Government (Miscellaneous Provisions) Act 1976 (failing to give information).

NOTICE TO REMOVE STRUCTURE FROM HIGHWAYS

(NAME OF COMPETENT AUTHORITY)

SECTION 143 OF THE HIGHWAYS ACT 1980

To (name of person obstructing highway) of (address)

The Council, as competent authority for the highway known as (name) gives you notice under and in pursuance of the powers contained in Section 143 of the Highways Act 1980 that it requires you within (state period) after service of this notice upon you to remove a structure being (describe structure) erected or set up by you upon the highway (see plan attached).

If the structure is not removed within the time required by this notice the Council may itself remove the structure and recover from you the expense of so doing.

Dated:

....
(signature of proper officer)

NOTICE REQUIRING ENLARGEMENT OR REMOVAL OF GATE ACROSS HIGHWAY
(NAME OF HIGHWAY AUTHORITY)
SECTION 145 OF THE HIGHWAYS ACT 1980

To (name of owner of gate) of (address)

You are the owner of a gate at (give details) across the highway known as (name) which [consists of a carriageway or is a bridleway] and the gate is less than the minimum width of [10 or 5] feet required by the above statutory provision.

NOW the Council, as highway authority for the above highway, in pursuance of Section 145 of the Highways Act 1980, requires you as owner of the gate to enlarge the gate to the minimum width of [10 or 5] feet or remove it (see plan attached).

If you fail to comply with a requirement of this notice within 21 days from the date of the service of this notice on you will be guilty of an offence and will be liable to a fine for each day during which the failure continues.

Dated:

....
(signature of proper officer)

NOTICE TO OWNER OF LAND THAT STILE GATE, ETC, IS OUT OF REPAIR
(NAME OF APPROPRIATE AUTHORITY)
SECTION 146(2) OF THE HIGHWAYS ACT 1980

To (name of owner or occupier of land on which stile, gate etc stands) of (address)

You are the [owner or occupier] of the land over which passes a [footpath or bridleway] from (specify) to (specify) and marked with a [red] line on the map attached.

At the point marked A on the map there is across the [footpath or bridleway] a [stile or gate or (specify similar structure)] which appears to the Council to be unsafe for use and out of repair to such an extent as to interfere unreasonably with the rights of persons using the [footpath or bridleway].

NOW the Council in pursuance of Section 146 of the Highways Act 1980 gives you notice that after (number) days from the date of the service of this notice the Council intends to take all necessary steps for repairing and making good the [stile or gate or (specify similar structure)] and the Council will then be entitled to recover [from you as the owner of the land or from (name) as the owner of the land] the amount of any expenses reasonably incurred by the Council in and in connection with such repair and making good or such part of those expenses as the Council thinks fit.

[If you repair and make good the [stile or gate or (specify) similar structure] the Council will contribute not less than one quarter of any expense reasonably incurred and may make further contributions having regard to all the circumstances as it considers reasonable.

Dated:

....
(signature of proper officer)

Appendix 16: Precedents for the Investigation of Countryside and Highways Offences

NOTICE TO LOP OR CUT VEGETATION OVERHANGING HIGHWAY OR OTHER ROAD OR FOOTPATH
(NAME OF COMPETENT AUTHORITY)
SECTION 154 OF THE HIGHWAYS ACT 1980

To (name of owner of vegetation or occupier of land in which it grows) of (address)

A [hedge or tree or shrub] situated at (describe exact situation) [belonging to you or growing on land occupied by you] overhangs the [highway or road or footpath] to which the public has access known as (name) so as to [endanger or obstruct the passage of vehicles or pedestrians or obstruct or interfere with [the view of drivers of vehicles or the light from a public lamp] (see map attached).

NOW the Council in pursuance of Section 154 of the Highways Act 1980 requires you as the [owner of the [hedge or tree or shrub] or occupier of the land on which the [hedge or tree or shrub] is growing] within 14 days from the date of service of this notice so to lop or cut the [hedge or tree or shrub] as to remove the cause of danger, obstruction or interference.

If you fail to comply with this notice, the Council may carry out the work required by this notice and may recover from you the expenses reasonably incurred by it in so doing.

If you are aggrieved by the requirement of this notice you may appeal to the Magistrates' Court sitting at (address) within 21 days from the date of the service of this notice on you.

Dated:

....
(signature of proper officer)

NOTICE TO CUT OR FELL DANGEROUS HEDGE, TREE, ETC, NEAR HIGHWAY OR OTHER ROAD OR FOOTPATH
(NAME OF COMPETENT AUTHORITY)
SECTION 154 OF THE HIGHWAYS ACT 1980

To (name of owner of hedge etc or occupier of land on which it stands) of (address)

A [hedge or tree or shrub] situated at (describe exact situation) [belonging to you or growing on land occupied by you] by reason of its condition is likely to cause danger by falling on the [highway or road or footpath] to which the public has access known as (name) (see map attached).

NOW the Council in pursuance of Section 154 of the Highways Act 1980 requires you as [the owner of the [hedge or tree or shrub] or the occupier of the land on which the [hedge or tree or shrub] is growing] within 14 days from the date of service of this notice so to cut or fell the [hedge or tree or shrub] as to remove the likelihood of danger.

If you fail to comply with this notice the Council may carry out the work required by this notice and may recover from you the expenses reasonably incurred by it in so doing.

If you are aggrieved by the requirement of this notice you may appeal to the Magistrates' Court sitting at (address) within 21 days from the date of service of this notice on you.

Dated:

....
(signature of proper officer)

Appendix 16: Precedents for the Investigation of Countryside and Highways Offences

NOTICE BY COMPETENT AUTHORITY FOR REMOVAL OF BARBED WIRE WHERE NUISANCE TO HIGHWAY
(NAME OF COMPETENT AUTHORITY)
SECTION 164 OF THE HIGHWAYS ACT 1980

To (occupier) of (address)

TAKE NOTICE that in pursuance of the provisions of Section 164 of the Highways Act 1980 the Council requires you within the period of (specify) after the date of this notice to abate the nuisance caused to the highway leading from (specify) to (specify) in (authority area) by a certain fence [made with or [in or on] which there has been placed] barbed wire which is likely to be injurious to persons or animals lawfully using such highway on certain land known as or called (describe field or land where the fence is situated) of which land you are the occupier and which adjoins the highway.

AND FURTHER TAKE NOTICE that if, on the expiration of the time stated above, you have failed to comply with the above notice, the Council is authorised to apply to a Magistrates' Court for an order directing you to abate the nuisance.

Dated:

....
(signature of proper officer)

DRAFT NOTICE

IMPORTANT – THIS COMMUNICATION AFFECTS YOUR PROPERTY

SECTION 16 OF THE LOCAL GOVERNMENT (MISCELLANEOUS PROVISIONS) ACT 1976

To: [insert name]
of: [insert address]
Re premises at: [insert description]

Function: In order to ascertain details of ownership to discharge duties under the Highways Act 1980.

TAKE NOTICE that pursuant to the above provisions you are hereby required within 14 days of the date of service of this notice upon you, to furnish to the Council the particulars requested on the attached form relating to the above property.

Dated:

....
(signature of proper officer)

NOTES

If you require any help in completing the reply form, please telephone [insert number] and quote reference [insert].

By Section 16(1) of the Local Government (Miscellaneous Provisions) Act 1976, the Council is empowered to require the information requested on the attached form from you. If you fail to comply with the requirements of this notice or if you furnish any information which you know to be false, or recklessly make a statement which is false you will be guilty of an offence and liable on summary conviction to a fine not exceeding Level 5 (£5,000).

Additional copies of this notice may be purchased at a cost of £1.25 per page.

DEPARTMENT [insert name]

Appendix 16: Precedents for the Investigation of Countryside and Highways Offences

NOTICE REF NO
SECTION 16 OF THE LOCAL GOVERNMENT (MISCELLANEOUS PROVISIONS) ACT 1976 –

To: [insert name and address]

My reference [insert]

REPLY FORM

The information required in your Notice dated [insert date] relating to the premises/land at: [insert address/location].

1. Nature of my interest in the premises/land (eg owner, occupier, mortgagee, lessee, rental purchase etc):
   ....
   ....

2. Name and address of occupier(s) of the premises/land:
   ....
   ....

3. Name and address of owner(s) of the premises/land:
   ....
   ....

4. Name and address of any other person(s) having an interest in the premises/land (eg Building Society, Bank etc):
   ....
   ....

5. The nature of any person's interest mentioned at (4) above:
   ....
   ....

6. Name and address of any person authorised to manage or arrange for the letting of the said premises/land:
   ....
   ....

7. The name and address of any person who directly or indirectly receives rent for the premises/land:
   ....
   ....

I HEREBY CERTIFY that the answers to the above questions are true so far as the same are within my knowledge.

Dated this   day of   20

Signed

Full name (block capitals)

Address

DEPARTMENT [INSERT NAME]

Appendix 16: Precedents for the Investigation of Countryside and Highways Offences

A NOTICE (OF WHICH THIS IS A TRUE COPY) WAS SERVED UPON

....

[INSERT NAME AND ADDRESS] BY HANDING SAME PERSONALLY TO

....

BY .... POST AT ....

ON THE   DAY OF   20

SIGNED ....

DRAFT NOTICE
IMPORTANT – THIS COMMUNICATION AFFECTS YOUR PROPERTY
SECTION 297 OF THE HIGHWAYS ACT 1980

To: [insert name]

of: [insert address]

Re premises at: [insert description]

Function: In order to ascertain details of ownership to discharge duties under the Highways Act 1980.

TAKE NOTICE that pursuant to the above provisions you are hereby required within 14 days of the date of service of this notice upon you, to furnish to the Council the particulars requested on the attached form relating to the above property.

DATED [insert date]

....
Signature of authorised officer of the Council

NOTES

If you require any help in completing the reply form, please telephone [insert number] and quote reference [insert].

By Section 297 of the Highways Act 1980, the Council is empowered to require the information requested on the attached form from you. If you fail to comply with the requirements of this notice or if you furnish any information which you know to be false, or recklessly make a statement which is false you will be guilty of an offence and liable on summary conviction to a fine not exceeding Level 3 (£1,000), or on conviction on indictment (false statements) to imprisonment for a term not exceeding two years or to a fine or both.

Additional copies of this notice may be purchased at a cost of £1.25 per page.

DEPARTMENT [insert name]

Appendix 16: Precedents for the Investigation of Countryside and Highways Offences

NOTICE REF NO
SECTION 297 OF THE HIGHWAYS ACT 1980

To: [insert name and address]

My reference [insert]

REPLY FORM

The information required in your Notice dated [insert date] relating to the premises/land at [insert address/location]:

1. Nature of my interest in the premises/land (eg owner, occupier, mortgagee, lessee, rental purchase etc):
   ....

2. Name and address of occupier(s) of the premises/land:
   ....

3. Name and address of owner(s) of the premises/land:
   ....

4. Name and address of any other person(s) having an interest in the premises/land (eg Building Society, Bank etc):
   ....

5. The nature of any person's interest mentioned at (4) above:
   ....

6. Name and address of any person authorised to manage or arrange for the letting of the said premises/land:
   ....

7. The name and address of any person who directly or indirectly receives rent for the premises/land:
   ....

I HEREBY CERTIFY that the answers to the above questions are true so far as the same are within my knowledge.

Dated this   day of   20

Signed ....

Full name (block capitals)

....

Address

....

....

DEPARTMENT [INSERT NAME]

A NOTICE [OF WHICH THIS IS A TRUE COPY] WAS SERVED UPON

....

[INSERT NAME AND ADDRESS] BY HANDING SAME PERSONALLY TO

....

BY .... POST AT ....

ON THE   DAY OF   20

SIGNED ....

Appendix 16: Precedents for the Investigation of Countryside and Highways Offences

SPECIMEN

[insert name and address of occupier of land]

Your Ref: Our Ref:

Contact: Date:

Dear Sirs

[INSERT HIGHWAY NAME AND NATURE OF OBSTRUCTION/INTERFERENCE]

[ENTER SECTION OF HIGHWAYS ACT 1980 UNDER WHICH NOTICE MAY BE GIVEN]

I have received a complaint/am aware of a problem with regard to the above [insert nature of complaint].

I understand that the above matter causes an interference with the use of the public highway and thus restricts and prevents the highway rights of the general public. The legal situation is quite simple. The public are entitled to unhindered access to the whole of a public highway.

Any interference which restricts that right of free access constitutes a criminal offence. This Council, as Highway Authority, has a duty to assert and protect highway user rights and has no power to grant anyone permission to obstruct a highway in such a manner.

Accordingly, I request that you remove the said obstruction/interference from the highway shown in red on the plan attached hereto within the next 10 days. Should you fail to remove the obstruction/interference within this period, I will have no alternative but to serve a formal Notice on you under the provisions the Highways Act 1980 requiring its removal.

I look forward to receiving your written confirmation that the necessary action will be taken and if you have any queries, please do not hesitate to contact me.

Yours faithfully

Director of Legal Services/Countryside Officer

SUMMONS]>var1<[

IN THE]>var2<[MAGISTRATES' COURT

To:-]>var3<[
of:]>var4<[

INFORMATION has this day been laid before the undersigned by [insert name and address of the Solicitor to the Council] on behalf of [insert name and address] that you

on]>var 5<[

at]>var 6<[

placed [or maintained] on [or near] a way shown on a definitive map [or on a revised map prepared in definitive form] as a public path [or road used as a public path] namely [insert description] a notice containing the false [or misleading] statement [insert nature of statement] which was likely to deter the public from using the way

CONTRARY to Section 57 of the National Parks and Access to the Countryside Act 1949.

YOU ARE THEREFORE SUMMONED to appear before the Magistrates' Court

sitting at]>var 7<[

on]>var 8<[

at]>var 9<[to answer to the said Information.

DATED the   day of   20

....
Clerk to the Justices/Clerk to the Court/
Justice of the Peace

If you do not respond to this Summons, the case may be dealt with in your absence.

Please note that upon conviction the prosecution will be seeking costs against you.

Appendix 16: Precedents for the Investigation of Countryside and Highways Offences

SUMMONS]>var1<[

IN THE]>var2<[MAGISTRATES' COURT

To:]>var3<[

of:]>var4<[

INFORMATION has this day been laid before the undersigned by [insert name and address of the Council Solicitor] on behalf of [name of the Council], that you

on]>var 5<[

at]>var 6<[

without lawful authority or excuse so disturbed the surface of (a) a footpath or (b) a bridleway or (c) a highway consisting of or comprising of a carriageway [delete (a) or (b) or (c) leaving one option] at [specify] as to render it inconvenient for the exercise of the public right of way

CONTRARY to Section 131A of the Highways Act 1980 as inserted by Section 1 of the Rights of Way Act 1990.

YOU ARE THEREFORE SUMMONED to appear before the Magistrates' Court

sitting at]>var 7<[

on]>var 8<[

at]>var 9<[to answer to the said Information.

DATED the   day of   20

....
Clerk to the Justices/Clerk to the Court/
Justice of the Peace

If you do not respond to this Summons, the case may be dealt with in your absence.

Please note that upon conviction the prosecution will be seeking costs against you.

SUMMONS]>var1<[

IN THE]>var2<[MAGISTRATES' COURT

To:]>var3<[

of:]>var4<[

INFORMATION has this day been laid before the undersigned by [insert the name and address of the Council Solicitor] on behalf of [insert name of Council], that you

on]>var 5<[

at]>var 6<[

without lawful authority or excuse did wilfully obstruct the free passageway along [insert name of public highway] a highway by [state manner of obstruction]

CONTRARY to Section 137 of the Highways Act 1980.

YOU ARE THEREFORE SUMMONED to appear before the Magistrates' Court

sitting at]>var 7<[

on]>var 8<[

at]>var 9<[to answer to the said Information.

DATED the   day of   20

....
Clerk to the Justices/Clerk to the Court/
Justice of the Peace

If you do not respond to this Summons, the case may be dealt with in your absence.

Please note that upon conviction the prosecution will be seeking costs against you.

Appendix 16: Precedents for the Investigation of Countryside and Highways Offences

SUMMONS]>var1<[

IN THE]>var2<[MAGISTRATES' COURT

To:]>var3<[
of:]>var4<[

INFORMATION has this day been laid before the undersigned by [insert the name and address of the Council Solicitor], on behalf of [insert name of Council], that you

on]>var 5<[

at]>var 6<[

without lawful authority or excuse did deposit [specify matter or article] on [name the public highway] a highway in consequence whereof [name a person] a user of the highway was injured or endangered

CONTRARY to Section 161(1) of the Highways Act 1980.

YOU ARE THEREFORE SUMMONED to appear before the Magistrates' Court

sitting at]>var 7<[

on]>var 8<[

at]>var 9<[to answer to the said Information.

DATED the   day of   20

....
Clerk to the Justices/Clerk to the Court/
Justice of the Peace

If you do not respond to this Summons, the case may be dealt with in your absence.
Please note that upon conviction the prosecution will be seeking costs against you.

SUMMONS]>var1<[

IN THE]>var2<[MAGISTRATES' COURT

To:]>var3<[
of:]>var4<[

INFORMATION has this day been laid before the undersigned by [insert name and address of Council Solicitor] on behalf of [insert name of Council], that you

on]>var 5<[

at]>var 6<[

did as occupier of [or as person receiving rent in respect of] [specify premises] upon being so required by the [specify name] Council in accordance with Section 297(1) of the Highways Act 1980 failed to give information as to [specify]

CONTRARY to Section 297(2) of the said Act.

YOU ARE THEREFORE SUMMONED to appear before the Magistrates' Court

sitting at]>var 7<[

on]>var 8<[

at]>var 9<[to answer to the said Information.

DATED the   day of   20

....
Clerk to the Justices/Clerk to the Court/
Justice of the Peace

If you do not respond to this Summons, the case may be dealt with in your absence.

Please note that upon conviction the prosecution will be seeking costs against you.

Appendix 16: Precedents for the Investigation of Countryside and Highways Offences

SUMMONS]>var1<[

IN THE]>var2<[MAGISTRATES' COURT

To:]>var3<[

of:]>var4<[

INFORMATION has this day been laid before the undersigned by [insert name and address of Council Solicitor] on behalf of [insert name of Council], that you

on]>var 5<[

at]>var 6<[

did as occupier of [or a person receiving rent in respect of] [insert name of premises and location] in purported compliance with a requirement of the [name of Council] under Section 297(1) of the Highways Act 1980 knowingly made a misstatement that [insert details]

CONTRARY to Section 297(3) of the Highways Act 1980.

YOU ARE THEREFORE SUMMONED to appear before the Magistrates' Court

sitting at]>var 7<[

on]>var 8<[

at]>var 9<[to answer to the said Information.

DATED the   day of   20

....
Clerk to the Justices/Clerk to the Court/
Justice of the Peace

If you do not respond to this Summons, the case may be dealt with in your absence.

Please note that upon conviction the prosecution will be seeking costs against you.

INFORMATION]>var1<[

IN THE]>var2<[MAGISTRATES' COURT
To:]>var3<[
of:]>var4<[

INFORMATION has this day been laid before the undersigned by [insert name and address of Council Solicitor] on behalf of [insert name of Council], that you

on]>var 5<[

at]>var 6<[

being an *[occupier] or *[person with an interest in land] at]>var 7<[having been served with a notice pursuant to s 16 of the Local Government (Miscellaneous Provisions) Act 1976 (specifying matters set out in s 16(1) of the said Act) did fail to furnish to the authority within the period specified in the notice (not being less than 14 days beginning with the day on which the notice was served) the nature of his interest in the land and the details of any other persons who may have an interest in the land as specified in the notice.

CONTRARY to s 16(2)*[(a)] or *[(b)] of the Local Government (Miscellaneous Provisions) Act 1976 as amended by ss 38 and 46 of the Criminal Justice Act 1982.

* delete as appropriate
    if interest in the land or nature of occupation unknown you can leave both in.
    (a) for non-disclosure;
    (b) for supplying false information.

NB: Date may require careful consideration
    Information drafted on assumption of non-disclosure as opposed to false information.

YOU ARE THEREFORE SUMMONED to appear before the Magistrates' Court

sitting at]>var 8<[

on]>var 9<[

at]>var 10<[to answer to the said Information.

DATED the   day of   20

Appendix 16: Precedents for the Investigation of Countryside and Highways Offences

....
Clerk to the Justices/Clerk to the Court/
Justice of the Peace

If you do not respond to this Summons, the case may be dealt with in your absence. Please note that upon conviction the prosecution will be seeking costs against you.

APPENDIX 17

LIST OF AUTHORITIES

List of authorities pertaining to:

(a) Section 24 of the Trade Descriptions Act 1968 (statutory due diligence defence).
(b) Section 80 of the Environmental Protection Act 1990 (notice appeals and prosecutions).
(c) Section 1 of the Protection From Eviction Act 1977 (unlawful eviction/harassment).
(d) Sections 14 and 21 of the Food Safety Act (FSA) 1990 (selling food not of the substance, etc, and statutory defence).
(e) Due diligence checklist.
(f) Section 92 of the Trade Marks Act 1994 (use of trade mark without consent).
(g) Private hire and hackney carriage appeals.
(h) Section 45 of the Town Police Clauses Act 1847 (plying for hire).
(i) Abuse of process.
(j) Similar fact evidence.
(k) Sections 210 and 211 of the Town and Country Planning Act 1990 (tree preservation prosecutions)
(l) Meaning of 'knowingly'.
(m) Meaning of 'knowingly' in Local Government (MP) Act 1976.
(n) Section 143 of the Road Traffic Act 1988 (no insurance).
(o) Aiding and abetting.
(p) Section 372 of the Housing Act 1985.
(q) Meaning of 'knowing' (Social Security Administration Act 1992).

TRADE DESCRIPTIONS ACT 1968
DISCLAIMER AND S 24 DEFENCES TO CAR CLOCKING

Authority	Purpose
Disclaimer	
Simmons v Potter [1975] RTR 347	Criminal responsibility can be avoided by publishing a disclaimer of the odometers accuracy with equal prominence and force to the message given by the reading itself.
Newham LBC v Singh and Another (1988) 752 JP 223 and *R v Southwood* [1987] 3 All ER 556 and *R v Hammertons Cars Ltd* (1976) 152 JP 207	A disclaimer is only a defence to s 1(1)(b) and not s 1(1)(a).
Norman v Bennett [1974] 3 All ER 355	Disclaimer must be as bold, precise and compelling as trade description itself and must be effectively brought to the notice of the customer.
R v Hammertons Cars [1976] 3 All ER 578	If dealers do want prospective purchasers to take any notice of mileometer readings they must take positive and effective steps to ensure that the customer understands that the mileometer reading is meaningless.
Waltham Forest LBC v T S Wheatley (1977) 76 LGR 195	An effective disclaimer would have to sit along side a false trade description. A notice in the office would rarely suffice on its own.
Blunden v Gravelle Ltd (1986) 151 JP 701	Disclaimer notice displayed in a clearly visible position in showroom is not sufficient.
Lewin v Fuel (1990) 155 JP 206	Disclaimer must be alongside false trade description. Oral disclaimer insufficient. Offence is created when the goods are exposed and disclaimer must be exhibited at that time.
R v Thomson Holidays [1974] 1 All ER 823	A false statement is made when and each time it is read.
Decisions concerning enquiries of previous owner	
Naish v Gore [1971] 3 All ER 737	It is impossible to lay down as a general principle that a dealer is not required to have the log book and check with previous owners.

Appendix 17: List of Authorities

Butterworths *Trading and Consumer Law* 3 [265]	Since 1971 this decision has been considered, distinguished and not followed in a number of later cases and it should therefore be treated with caution.
Crook v Howells Garage (Newport) Ltd [1980] RTR 434	Magistrates' court allowed s 24 defence where dealer had not made enquiries of previous owners. 'It may not be a decision which we would have reached or perhaps other benches of justices would have reached but ... we should not be justified in interfering with it.' Donaldson LJ.
McNab v Alexanders of Greenock Ltd 1971 SLT 121	Section 24 defence not apply where no steps taken to ascertain if odometer was correct, for example, by asking previous owner.
Richmond LBC v Motor Sales (Hounslow) Ltd (1971) 135 SP 239	S 24 defence failed. Resp' kept no records and did not consult seller or any other persons about erroneous mileage.
Wandsworth LBC v Bentley [1980] RTR 429	S 24 defence failed, dealer failed to contact Shell UK being only previous owner named in sales document.
Simmons v Ravenhill (1983) 148 JP 109	A dealer who had taken no steps whatsoever to check a highly surprising odometer was convicted on appeal.
Butterworths *Trading and Consumer Law* 3 [260]	S 24(3) defence applies to *supplying* or offering to supply goods and not the *applying* offences.

Articles:

'Clocking and the Trade Descriptions Act 1968' (1988) 152 JP 204

'A question of disclaimer' (1988) 152 JP 223

Geoff Holgate, 'The pernicious practice of "clocking": the end of the road?' (1997) 161 JP 743

LIST OF AUTHORITIES PRODUCED BY LA
SECTION 80 OF THE ENVIRONMENTAL PROTECTION ACT 1990
(APPEALS AND PROSECUTIONS)

Authorities	Purpose
Lambeth LB v Mullings [1990] TLR, 16 Jan	Service through the letter box of the occupier of the subject premises is capable of satisfying the section.
Network Housing Association v Westminster CC [1994] TLR, 8 Nov	The notice must identify clearly and precisely the nuisance complained of even though it need not be as precise as a builder's specification.
McGillivray v Stephenson [1950] 1 All ER 942	The operative part of the request to abate the nuisance and the steps indicated whereby the abatement might be effected could be regarded as mere surplusage. The notice was not therefore bad even though it required a recipient to do something he could not be ordered to do in law.
Whatling v Rees [1914] 84 LJKB 1122	The term of the notice requiring abatement of the nuisance in a particular manner had more than one meaning. It was therefore ambiguous and could not stand.
Perry v Garner [1953] 1 QB 335	By the inclusion in the notice of the specific and, alternatively, unspecific steps to be taken, the whole notice became unspecific and, therefore, was bad.
Rhymney Iron Co v Gelligaer DC [1917] 1 KB 589	It is sufficient to satisfy the meaning of the words 'cannot be found' if, on inspection, the cause of the nuisance cannot be found.
Millard v Wastall [1898] 1 QB 342	In some situations it is sufficient to specify only that the nuisance must be stopped.
Salford CC v McNally [1976] AC 379	In other situations the works or steps required must be specified with some particularity.
R v Birmingham City Justices ex p Guppy (1987) 152 JP 159	The notice must specify a time in which the nuisance has to be abated or works concluded but does not have to state a period within which a prohibition or recurrence has to be complied with.

Appendix 17: List of Authorities

Aitken v South Hams DC [1994] 3 All ER 400	The effectiveness of a notice served under the repealed Control of Pollution Act 1974 is preserved by s 16(1) of the Interpretation Act 1978.
Stagecoach Ltd v MacPhail 1988 SCCR 289	The defendant cannot challenge the terms of a notice in a subsequent trial if the notice could have been challenged by way of appeal to the magistrates' court.
A Lambert Flat Management Ltd v Lomas [1981] 2 All ER 280	A reasonable excuse must be limited to an excuse for non compliance with the notice and cannot include a challenge to its validity, nor can it involve matters which could have been raised on appeal.
Polychronakis v Richards & Jerrom [1997] *The Times*, 19 November	The burden is on the prosecution to disprove reasonable excuse once raised by the defendant as distinct from sub-ss (1) and (9) defences where the burden is on the defendant.
Wellingborough BC v Gordon [1993] 1 Env LR 218	It is not necessary to prove that any occupiers of land were affected by the noise in question before the noise could rank as a statutory nuisance.
Amec Building Ltd and Squibb and Davies Ltd v LB of Camden [1997] Env LR 330	Decided *inter alia* 'was the magistrates' court to consider whether there was a nuisance or only whether the notices were complied with' in connection with a notice served under s 80 of the EPA 1990 and a prosecution for its contravention. Mrs Justice Ebsworth concluded 'for those reasons I would answer the ... question by saying that it was only necessary for the magistrate to consider whether the notices had been complied with'.
DPP v Majewski [1976] 2 All ER 142	'Drunkenness is not a defence in law' and thus is unlikely to be a 'reasonable excuse' under s 80(4) of the EPA 1990.
Cooke v Adatia and Others (1989) 153 LGR 189, QBD	(1) when proving that a noise amounting to a nuisance has occurred in contravention of a notice served .... the prosecution (a) need not prove that a particular occupier of the property has actually suffered interference with his reasonable enjoyment of his property; and (b) may rely solely on other evidence including expert evidence.
R v Falmouth & Truro etc ex p SW Water [2000] 3 All ER 306	The notice was not invalid for failing to specify the work to be carried out. (*Kirklees MC v Field* [1998] Env LR 337 overruled.)

PROSECUTIONS UNDER S 1 OF THE PROTECTION FROM EVICTION ACT 1977
LIST OF AUTHORITIES WHICH MAY BE PRODUCED BY LOCAL AUTHORITY

Section 1 of the Protection from Eviction Act 1977 states 'unlawful eviction and harassment of occupier':

(1) In this Section 'residential occupier', in relation to any premises, means (Note 6) a person occupying the premises as a residence, whether under a contract or by virtue of any enactment or rule of law giving him the right to remain in occupation or restricting the right of any other person to recover possession of the premises.

(2) Any person who unlawfully deprives (Note 1) the residential occupier of any premises (Note 6) of his occupation of the premises or any part thereof, or attempt to do so, he shall be guilty of an offence unless he proves that he believed, and had reasonable cause to believe (Note 3), that the residential occupier had ceased to reside in the premises.

(3) If any person within intent (Notes 8 and 11) to cause a residential occupier of any premises – (a) to give up the occupation of the premises or any part thereof or (b) refrain from exercising any right or pursuing any remedy in respect of the premises or any part thereof: does Acts (Notes 5 and 7) likely to interfere with the peace or comfort of the residential occupier or members of his household, or persistently withdraws or withholds services reasonably required for the occupation of the premises as a residence (Notes 4, 5 and 7) he shall be guilty of an offence.

   (a) Subject to sub-section 3(b) below, the landlord of a residential occupier or an agent of the landlord shall be guilty of an offence if (a) he does acts likely to interfere with the peace or comfort of the residential occupier or members of his household, or (b) he persistently withdraws or withholds services (Note 9) reasonably required for the occupation of the premises in question as a residence, and, in either case, he knows, or has reasonable cause to believe, that that conduct is likely to cause the residential occupier to give up the occupation of the whole of part of the premises or to refrain from exercising any right or pursuing any remedy in respect or whole or part of the premises.

   (b) A person shall not be guilty of an offence under sub-section 3(a) above if he proves that he had reasonable grounds for doing the acts or withdrawing or withhold the services in question.

   (c) In sub-section 3(a) above 'landlord', in relation to a residential occupier of any premises, means the person who, but for –

      (a) the residential occupiers right to remain in occupation of the premises, or

      (b) a restriction on the person's right to recover possession of the premises, would be entitled to occupation of the premises and any superior landlord under whom that person derives title.

(4) A person guilty of an offence under this section shall be liable to:

   (a) on summary conviction to a fine not exceeding the statutory maximum or to imprisonment (Note 2) for a term not exceeding six months or to both;

(b) on conviction on indictment, to a fine or to imprisonment (Note 2) for a term not exceeding two years or to both.

(5) Nothing in this section shall be taken to prejudice any liability or remedy to which a person guilty of an offence thereunder may be subject to civil proceedings.

(6) Where an offence under this section by a body corporate is proved to have been committed with the consent or connivance of, or to be attributable to any neglect on the part of, any Director, Manager or Secretary or other similar Officer of the body corporate or any person who was purporting to act in any capacity, he as well as the body corporate shall be guilty of that offence and shall be liable to be proceeded against and punished accordingly.

The authorities below are a synopsis of the main point of the cases referred to.

NOTES

1 COSTELLOE v LONDON BOROUGH OF CAMDEN [1986] CRIM LR 249, DC

Mere exclusion for one day and night is insufficient to be 'unlawful deprivation', contrary to s 1(2) and (4) of the Act.

2 R v BRENNAN & BRENNAN [1969] CRIM LR 603

Imprisonment should be the usual penalty where the landlord uses threats or force in the absence of unusual mitigation.

3 R v PHEKOO [1981] 3 ALL ER 84

Criminal law – unlawful eviction and harassment of residential occupiers – harassment – *mens rea* – Defendant believing that person harassed was not a residential occupier – whether sufficient for Crown to prove that person harassed was, in fact, a residential occupier – whether Crown required to disprove Defendant's belief whether Defendant required to have reasonable grounds for his belief – whether sufficient if defendant's belief honestly held.

HELD *INTER ALIA*:

The prosecution must show that the defendant believed the 'residential occupiers' were, in fact, so.

4 R v BURKE [1990] ALL ER 385

Criminal law – unlawful eviction and harassment of residential occupier of premises – harassment – ingredients of offence – landlord preventing tenant from using lavatory adjacent to his room – landlord disconnecting front door bell to room – tenant able to use lavatory in another part of house – whether necessary for harassment to be actionable, civil wrong – whether landlord guilty of harassment – s 1(2) and (4) of the Protection from Eviction Act 1977.

HELD:

An act likely to interfere with the peace and comfort of an occupier of residential accommodation amounted to the criminal offence of harassment under s 1(3) of the 1977 Act – if it was carried out, whether by the landlord or by another person, including another tenant, with the intention of forcing the occupier to give up occupation of the premises, notwithstanding that the act did not amount to an actionable civil wrong.

5 R v YUTHIWATTANA (1984) 16 HLR 49, CA

HELD:

(Dismissing the appeal against the harassment conviction, allowing the appeal against the unlawful eviction conviction.)

(1) There was evidence ... (before the jury) which could infer that the landlady had the intention to evict the occupier in relation to the incidents of 10 December 1980.

(2) In relation to the refusal to replace the lost key on and continuing from 11 December 1980, it was necessary for an act to amount to harassment under s 1(3) of the PEA 1977, that it should also constitute a breach of contract in relation to an express or implied term of the tenancy or licence in question.

(3) The informations were not bad for duplicity.

(4) To constitute the offence of deprivation of occupation, there must be something having the character of an eviction. This does not mean permanent eviction (only), but could include a period of weeks or months, such that the occupier has to find alternative accommodation: however, 'locking out cases' or not admitting an occupier on one or even more than one isolated occasion, so that the occupier continues to be allowed to occupy the premises, albeit that he is, on such occasion, unable to enter, constitutes a case of harassment, not unlawful eviction.

6 NORTON v KNOWLES [1967] 3 ALL ER 1061

Residential occupation – definition on facts.

HELD:

The true inference was that when the respondent first occupied the caravan, the appellant agreed he might live there on the premises on which he was allowed to reside were the land and the caravan taken together. The respondent was, therefore, a residential occupier.

7 R v EVANGELOS POLYCARPOU (1978) 9 HLR 129

FACTS:

The landlord of premises removed the tenant's sole source of heat, a gas ring. He also erected a partition, which had the effect of forcing the tenant to go out of and re-enter the house each time he wanted to go from one room to another – eg, to the bathroom.

He was prosecuted and convicted separately on each count. He appealed on a point of law that the word 'acts' in s 30(2) of the Rent Act 1965 (now s 1(3) of the Protection from Eviction Act 1977), did not include a single act.

HELD:

(Dismissing the appeal) in the context of s 30(2) of the Rent Act 1965, the word 'acts' includes a single act.

8 McCALL v ABELESZ AND ANOTHER [1976] All ER 727, CA, ORMEROD J

A positive intent to cause the residential occupier to give up the premises or to refrain to exercise any right had to be shown, not merely a hopeful inactivity (*per curiam*).

9 WESTMINSTER CC v PEART (1968) 66 LGR 561, QBD

Landlord and Tenant – protection against harassment – withholding of services – whether material to alleged that services 'persistently' withheld – landlord failing to pay for gas or electricity with the result that supply disconnected – whether 'withholding' service – acts done with intent to cause residential occupier to give up occupation of premises – whether material to allege that calculated to interfere with peace or comfort of occupier – whether one act sufficient – s 30(2) of the Rent Act 1965.

HELD:

Dismissing the appeals:

(1) That 'persistently' in s 30(2) of the Act of 1965 referred to the offence of withholding, as well as to that of withdrawing services: that an allegation of an element of persistency was a material allegation in connection with that offence; and that, accordingly, the first and second Informations were defective.

Quaere, whether by failing to pay for gas or electricity, with the result that the undertaking in question disconnects the supply, the landlord can properly be said to withhold a service.

(2) That, so far as acts done were concerned, it was a material allegation that they should be calculated to interfere with the peace or comfort of the occupier or members of his household; and that, accordingly, the third Information was also defective.

Quaere, whether a single act is capable of constituting the offence?

Yes, see *R v Evangeles* (1978) 9 HLR 129.

10 R v ABROL [1972] CRIM LR 318

Drafting of Indictments.

11 MEANING OF THE WORD 'INTENTION'

(1) The general rule of law is that a person is presumed to intend the natural reasonable and probable consequences of his/her acts, whether in fact s/he intended them or not.

(2) Where a person contemplates any result as not unlikely to follow from a deliberate act of his/her own, s/he may be said to intend that result, whether s/he desires it or not.

(Hardy-Irving, ER, in Butterworths *Law Dictionary*, 10th edn, London: Butterworths, pp 181 and 243.)

(3) Cf wilfully means that the act is done deliberately and intentionally, not by accident or inadvertence, but so that the mind of the person who does the act goes with it (*Words and Phrases Legally Defined*, Vol 2 D–J, 3rd edn, p 435).

LIST OF AUTHORITIES PRODUCED BY LOCAL AUTHORITY
SECTION 14 OF THE FOOD SAFETY ACT 1990
SECTION 21 OF THE FSA 1990 – DEFENCE OF DUE DILIGENCE

Authorities	Purpose
Hotchin v Hindmarsh [1891] 2 QB 181, 55 JP 775	A servant who sells on behalf of his master is liable to be convicted.
Meah v Roberts [1978] 1 All ER 97	A purported sale of food takes place even though something different is sold, eg, caustic soda instead of lemonade.
Section 2 Food Safety Act 1990	Extended meaning of 'sale'.
Sandys v Jackson (1905) 69 JP 171	A sale is not to the prejudice of the purchasers where it is brought clearly to his/her notice that the article offered is not of the nature, substance or quality demanded.
Heywood v Whitehead (1897) 76 LT 781	The fact that an article is offered below market price is not *prima facie* an indication to the purchaser it is below quality.
Section 2(1) and (2) Food Safety Act 1990	For the meaning of food.
Bastin v Davies [1950] 2 KB 579	An information charging not of the nature or substance or quality is bad.
Tonkin v Victor Value Ltd [1962] 1 All ER 257	An offence may be committed where in the absence of any prescribed minimum standard the standard falls below what the justices find to be reasonable.
Barber v CWS Ltd (1983) 147 JP 296	The prosecution does not need to prove that the presence of extraneous material would be deleterious to the purchaser.
Newton v West Vale Creamery Co Ltd (1956) 120 JP 318	Milk containing a dead house fly has been held to be not of the quality demanded.
Edwards v Llaethdy Meiron Ltd (1957) 107 LJ 133	The presence of a harmless article, eg, a metal milk bottle cap does not necessarily give rise to an offence under this section.
Southworth v Whitewell Dairies Ltd (1958) 122 JP 322	The presence of a source of danger, eg, a sliver of glass is adequate to create an offence.
McDonalds Hamburgers Ltd v Windle (1986) 151 JP 333	The word description may be equivalent to 'quality', ie, conviction for supplying cola instead of diet cola.

Pearks Gunstein and Tee Ltd v Ward [1902] 2 KB, 1 66 JP 774	'Purchaser' means an ordinary not a skilled purchaser and the knowledge of the purchaser cannot be taken into account except as derived from information given at time of sale.
Cow and Gate Nutricia Ltd v Westminster CC [1995] QBD *The Independent*, 14 March	*Held*: Magistrates wrong to assume *res ipsa loquitur*, ie, facts speak for themselves applied in criminal cases, ie, a fragment of bone in a jar of baby food. The defence of due diligence may still be raised.
Carrick DC v Taunton Vale Meat Traders Ltd [1994] QBD 28 January, *The Times*, 15 February	An error of judgement by a meat inspector in a report in respect of meat deemed fit for human consumption when it was not ultimately found to be fit was sufficient to raise the defence under s 21 of the FSA 1990.

DUE DILIGENCE CHECK LIST

A substantial body of case law has been built up over the last 50 years of which most important are those judgments based on the similar single-limbed defences in weights and measures and consumer safety legislation. From a study of these cases it is possible to establish certain general principles applicable to all due diligence systems:

(a) The system must be under the directing will of the company but the principal of the company may delegate responsibility for the system to superior servants under their contracts of employment with him or to agents employed by him.

(b) The precautions and checks to be taken depend on the size and resources of the company and all other relevant circumstances of the case.

(c) Reliance cannot be placed on warranties nor on general assurances from suppliers (but see sub-ss (3) and (4) person who have not prepared the food nor imported it).

(d) The due diligence system must be written down with adequate instructions and training given to staff and records kept of the training.

(e) Any reasonable precautions which can be taken must be taken and the system must be pro-active, ie, it must be capable of preventing faults and correcting them when they occur.

(f) Complaints by consumers should be recorded and analysed to detect any trends which may suggest a fault in the system.

(g) The responsibilities of directors, managers and employees should be stated in writing and acknowledged by them.

(h) Acquisition of warranties and assurances from suppliers can contribute to a due diligence system but see (c) above.

(i) The system must be modified, adjusted or amended as required.

(j) Internal and external codes of practice may contribute to the system but are not sufficient in themselves.

(k) The operation of the system must be checked and the results must be recorded.

(l) The system must cover all aspects of the business which is subject to the act or regulations made under the act including:
 - hygiene and safety of premises.
 - quality, composition and safety of premises and equipment.
 - labelling and advertising.
 - staff training.
 - registration and licensing as appropriate.
 - improvement notices, prohibition or control orders as may be applicable.

SECTION 92 OF THE TRADE MARKS ACT 1994
LIST OF AUTHORITIES

Authorities	Purpose
Blakemore v Bellamy (1983) 147 JP 89	F/T postman repairs vehicles as a hobby in spare time. Buys and sells 8 vehicles. Not a trade or business under the TDA 1968, but a hobby.
Elder v Crowe 1996 SCCR 38	300 bottles of counterfeit perfume found in house occupied by D. 'One-off' transaction claimed. *Held*: a one-off adventure in the nature of trade, with a view to profit can be a trade under TDA 1968.
Trebor Bassett Ltd v Football Assoc'n Ltd [1997] FSR 211 Ch D	TB included collectable cards featuring photographs of footballers wearing logos in its packet of candy sticks. This did not amount to 'using' the logo as a sign.

NB:See s 1 of the TMA 1994 for meaning of Trade Mark. See s 97 for forfeiture orders.

PRIVATE HIRE/HACKNEY CARRIAGE APPEALS (RULE 14 OF THE MAGISTRATES' COURT RULES 1981)
LIST OF AUTHORITIES PRODUCED BY LA

Case Report	Purpose
Rushmore BC v Richards [1996] TLR, 5 February	Evidence of fresh events admissible on appeal.
Westminster CC v Zestfair Ltd (1989) 88 LGR 29	Rule against hearsay does not apply to taxi appeals.
Kavanagh v CC of Devon and Cornwall [1974] 1 QB 625	Court obliged to consider all relevant matters whether or not strictly admissible in a court of law, p 634. Court may also consider matters not strictly proven, p 627.
Sagnata Investments v Norwich Corp [1971] 2 All ER 1441	The function of a court of appeal is to exercise its powers when it is satisfied that the judgment below is wrong, p 1457E (similar reasoning adopted in *Kavanagh*, p 643A and approved in *Zestfair*, p 293). Appeal is by way of complete rehearing. Court entitled to consider fresh evidence, p 1442.
Darlington BC v Paul Wakefield (1989) LGR, 16 September	LA not confined to its grounds of refusal on appeal but should not seek to take appellant by surprise.
Stepney BC v Joffe and Others [1949] 1 All ER 256	Magistrates may entertain the appeal on any ground that seems right to them.
R v Maidstone Crown Court ex p Olson [1992] COD 498	Approved in *McCool v Rushcliffe BC*, below, p 895e and g. It is for the applicant to establish that he is a fit and proper person. In seeking to rebut this contention the Local Authority need only satisfy the civil standard of proof where allegations amounted to a criminal offence, p 498.
Kelly v Lewes DC (1997) 7(1) Licensing Bulletin (March) 3	The council and the court should see the previous convictions even though they were all spent.
McCool v Rushcliffe BC [1998] 3 All ER 889	Objectives of licensing regime to ensure safe drivers with good driving records ... honest and not persons who would take advantage of their employment to abuse or assault passengers, p 891F. Court shall not grant licence unless they are satisfied that the applicant is fit and proper, p 896B.

Mayes v Mayes [1971] 2 All ER 397, 135 JP 487	The court may dismiss the case at the conclusion of the complainants case either on its own motion or on a submission of no case to answer.
Nottingham CC v Farooq [1998] TLR, 28 October	The court has an overriding duty to protect the public. Adopts comments made by LCJ Bingham, p 891 of *McCool* 1998 case. Confirms the guidance in Department of Transport Circular 2/92 Annex D13/97 as the overriding consideration being the protection of the public. Advocates 3–5 year ban for offences involving dishonesty
Magistrates' Courts Rules 1981, r 14	Complainant puts case first.
Adamson v Waveney DC [1997] 2 All ER 898	It is not open to the magistrates to review the question of whether or not convictions recorded in earlier criminal proceedings were incorrectly arrived at.
Browne v Dunn (1894) 6 R 67, HL	Failure to put case to opposing witnesses can be remedied by recalling that witness, this being the proper course of action.
Dept of Transport Circular 2/92 and Home Office Circular 13/92	Annex D gives guidelines relating to the relevance of convictions for the use in determining applicants for HC and PH vehicle drivers' licences.
Howitt, R v Nottingham CC ex p Hamilton CO 4028/98	Revocation of HC license after plying for hire. Local authority entitled to regard the likely insurance consequences of the offence as a reason for treating the offence as serious, para 23.
Bruce Springsteen v Flute International and Others [2001] ILR, 24 April	The best evidence rule has finally expired. See, also, s 27 of the Criminal Justice Act 1988 which enables copies to be produced whether or not the original is available.

PLYING FOR HIRE PROSECUTIONS
LIST OF AUTHORITIES PRODUCED BY LOCAL AUTHORITY

Case Report	Purpose
Cogley v Sherwood [1959] 2 All ER 313	1 Act is directing one's attention to the vehicle and asking the question whether it is plying for hire, p 317B. 2 Plying for hire can be an express or implied invitation to the public to use the vehicle By having a carriage ready for the conveyance of passengers in a place frequented by the public (even though the driver makes no sign), p 316I.
Clarke v Stanford [1871] taken from Butterworths *Words and Phrases Judicially Defined*, 3rd edn, p 386	1 There must be a soliciting or waiting to secure passengers by the driver or other person in control without any previous contract with them. 2 The owner of person in control who is engaged in or authorises the soliciting or waiting must be in possession of a carriage for which he is soliciting or waiting to obtain passengers.
Ogwr BC v Baker [1989] COD 489	1 Parking a taxi close to a Night Club between 1.20 am and 1.56 am was plying for hire even though the magistrates found no evidence that the vehicle carried any visible invitation to the public to use it or that the driver had by any means whatever invited the public to use his vehicle. 2 Prior booking with taxi firm but not the defendant's taxi did not enable defendants to escape conviction.
Nottingham CC v Woodings [1993] COD 350	Parking minicab in street, vehicle recognisable by COD 350 signs as minicab, telling passengers that he was free to carry them – plying for hire.
Leathley v Drummond [1972] RTR 293	Defendant to satisfy court that he was covered by insurance not the prosecutor.
Young v Scampion (1988) 87 LGR 240	The vehicles were not hackney carriages for the purposes of s 38 of the TPC Act 1847 as the place in which they stood plying for hire was not a 'street'. [See, now, s 167 of the Criminal Justice and Public Order Act 1994 dealing with soliciting persons to hire vehicles in a 'public place'.]

ABUSE OF PROCESS
LIST OF AUTHORITIES PRODUCED BY LA

Case Report	Purpose
R v South Tyneside MBC ex p Mill Garages Ltd (1995) unreported, 8C and 18D	Abuse of process should not be used as a measure to discipline the prosecution for delay.
R v Derby Crown Court ex p Brooks (1985) 80 Cr App R 164, p 168: Applied *R v South Tyneside MBC ex p Mill Garages Ltd and Another* (1995) unreported, CO250/94, P 12	The power to stop a prosecution should only be used in most exceptional circumstances. It may be an abuse of process if either: (a) the prosecution have manipulated or mis-used the process of the court so as to deprive the Defendant of a protection provided by the law or to take unfair advantage of a technicality; or (b) on the balance of probability the defendant has been or will be prejudiced in the preparation or conduct of his defence by delay on the part of the prosecution which is unjustifiable.
AG's Ref (No 1 of 1990) [1992] 1 QB 630, p 643G: Applied *R v South Tyneside MBC ex p Mill Garages Ltd and Another* (1995) unreported, CO250/94, P 14D	No stay should be imposed unless the defendant shows on the balance of probabilities that owing to the delay he will suffer serious prejudice to the extent that no fair trial can be held. Still more rare should be cases where a stay can properly be imposed in the absence of any fault on the part of the complainant or prosecution.
Other authorities on abuse not referred to: *Daventry DC v Olins* (1990) 154 JP 478 *R v Brentford Justices ex p Wong* [1981] QB 445	

SIMILAR FACT EVIDENCE
AUTHORITIES PRODUCED BY THE LOCAL AUTHORITY

Case Report	Purpose
DPP v Boardman [1975] AC 421	The basic principle must be that the admission of similar fact evidence (of the kind now in question) is exceptional and requires a strong degree of probative force. This probative force is derived, if at all, from the circumstances that the facts testified to by the several witnesses bear to each other such a striking similarity that they must when judged by experience and common sense, either all be true, or have arisen from a cause common to the witnesses or from pure coincidence.
DPP v P [1991] 2 AC 447	That the probative force for the admission of similar fact evidence is sufficiently great to make it just to admit the evidence notwithstanding that it is prejudicial to the accused tending to show that he is guilty of another crime. Such probative force may be derived from striking similarities in the evidence but restricting the circumstances to cases in which there is some striking similarity is not justified in principle. Similarity beyond stock in trade is sufficient.
Makin v AG for New South Wales [1894] AC 57 PC	To establish the basic principle for the admission of similar fact evidence being that the comparative evidence must have 'striking similarity'. For illustration on the facts, namely the defendants were charged with the murder of a child whose skeleton was found in the back garden and whom they had adopted from its mother in return for a sum of money, inadequate for its maintenance. The facts were consistent with the allegation that the defendant had killed the child for maintenance, but equally consistent with natural death followed by an irregular burial. It was held that the evidence of the finding of other remains of children similarly 'adopted' by the defendants which had been buried in the garden of a previous residence of the defendants was rightly admitted to show the nature of the defendants practice and so to prove the fate of the child in question.

R v Smith (1915) 11 Cr App R	For comparative illustration on the facts, namely: Where the defendant was charged with the murder of a woman whom he had gone through a ceremony of marriage, evidence of the death of two other women with whom the defendant had gone through a ceremony of marriage was held to have been rightly admitted. In each case, the deceased woman was found drowned in a bath. In each case, the door of the bathroom would not open. In each case, the defendants had informed a medical practitioner that the woman suffered from epileptic fits and in case the woman's life was insured for the benefit of the defendants.
R v Straffen [1952] 2 QB 911	For illustration as above: The defendant was charged with the murder of a girl, a murder committed during a fairly short period of time when he was an absconder from Broadmoor. Evidence was rightly admitted that the defendant had twice previously killed small girls by the same method (strangulation) and had left their bodies in a substantially similar condition, ie, unconcealed and sexually unmolested.
Archbold (1995 edn), Chapter 13, pp 13–30	'The Judge will simply have to ask himself whether explanation of the common allegations on the basis of chance or coincidence would be an affront to common sense. No particular degree of similarity is required. The reality is that independent people do not make false allegations of a like nature against the same person.'
Archbold (1995 edn), Chapter 13, pp 13–36	'A Jury properly directed would be entitled to reason that the chances of five people making the same mistake, without that mistake being revealed as a result of cross-examination, was so remote that the explanation must be that the identifications are accurate.'
Archbold (1995 edn), Chapter 13, pp 13–41	'Obviously the evidence must have clear probative value and the more remote from the date of the offence the incident sought to be proved is, the clearer the probative value must be.'

The case law has been extracted by reference to *Archbold* (1995 edn) and the facts of *Straffon*, *Smith* and *Makin* have been taken *verbatim* from *A Practical Approach to Evidence*, 2nd edn, by Peter Murphy.

SECTIONS 198, 210 AND 211 OF THE TOWN AND COUNTRY PLANNING ACT 1990
LIST OF AUTHORITIES PRODUCED BY LA

Case Authority	Purpose
R v Alath Construction Ltd [1990] 1 WLR 1255 CA [decided under 1971 Act]	It is for the defendant to prove on the balance of probabilities that the conditions creating an exemption under this section existed at the time of the alleged offence. The burden of proof on the issue of whether the tree was dying, dead or had become dangerous, so as to justify a felling without the local authority's consent, falls on the defendant who asserts such exemption from the preservation order.
Barnet LBC v Eastern Electricity Board [1973] 2 All ER 319	A tree is 'destroyed' if it ceases to have any use as an amenity, or as something worth preserving and if a competent forester, taking into account its situation, would decide it ought to be felled.
Maidstone BC v Mortimer [1980] 3 All ER 552	It is not necessary for the prosecutor to prove that the accused knew of the existence of the preservation order.
Newport BC v Khan [1990] 1 WLR 1185, [1991] 1 EGLR 287, CA	A local authority acting under s 222 of the LGA 1972 may apply for an injunction. However the discretion to grant an injunction in support of the criminal law in such a case will be exercised sparingly and with great caution.

MEANING OF 'KNOWINGLY'
LIST OF AUTHORITIES (SUBMITTED BY LEA)

Case Authority	Purpose
R v Alath Construction Ltd [1990] *R v JF Alford Transport and Others* (1997) Archbold News, Issue 4, 1 May (*Giovianni v The Queen* (1985) 156 CLR 473)	It is for the defendant to prove on the balance of: 'The failure to make such enquiries as a reasonable person would have made is not equivalent to knowledge. It is not enough to render a person liable as secondary party that he ought to have known all the facts and would have done so if he acted with reasonable care and diligence.'
J Sheldon Deliveries Ltd v Willis [1972] RTR 217, p 220c	Knowledge can be imputed to a person who shuts his mind to the obvious or allowed something to go on not caring whether an offence was committed or not.
Taylors Central Garage Ltd v Roper (1951) JP 115, p 449–50 (see, also, *R v Thomas* (1976) 63 Cr App R 65)	Knowledge means shutting one's eyes to an obvious means of knowledge or deliberately refraining from making enquiries as opposed to merely neglecting to make enquiries as a reasonable and prudent person would make.
Evans v Dell [1937] All ER 349, p 353B	One who is put on enquiry and fails to make proper enquiries has knowledge.
DPP v Anderson [1991] RTR 269	Eg, of a strict liability motoring offence (driving with excess alcohol) which can be committed recklessly by secondary party.

MEANING OF WORD 'KNOWINGLY' UNDER LOCAL GOVERNMENT (MISCELLANEOUS PROVISIONS) ACT 1976
LIST OF AUTHORITIES (SUBMITTED BY LA)

Case Authority	Purpose
Pitts v Lewis [1988] QBD 16 May	Knowledge – knowingly permit or cause a vehicle to be used in a controlled district as a private hire vehicle. Use of a vehicle in a particular manner contrary to belief does not negate knowledge (s 46(2) of the LG(MP)A 1976).
Dittah v Birmingham CC (1993) 157 JP 1110; [1993] RTR 356	S 46(1)(e) must be read subject to the provisions of s 80(2) so as to require private hire operator's licensed under s 55 to make use only of vehicles and drivers licensed by the council of the district by which the operators are licensed when operating in a controlled district.

LIST OF AUTHORITIES SUBMITTED BY LA
OFFENCES UNDER S 143 OF THE RTA 1988 – NO INSURANCE

Case Authority	Purpose
Lyons v May [1948] 2 All ER 1062	A case decided under Road Traffic Act 1930 and applicable to s 143 of the RTA 1988. A person who is ignorant of the fact that there is no policy of insurance covering a vehicle, may, nevertheless, be held to commit an offence of no insurance if he permits the use of the vehicle.
Tapsell v Maslen [1967] Crim LR 53 DC Archbold – p 2416	The offence contrary to s 143 is absolute even if the allegation is causing or permitting the uninsured use.
Leathley v Drummond [1972] RTR 293	Defendant to satisfy the court he was covered by insurance not the prosecutor.
Empress Car Company Ltd v NRA [1998] EHLR 3	A person may 'cause' an offence to be committed by creating a situation in which a third party could commit an offence – pp 12, 13 and 17.

PROSECUTIONS FOR AIDING ABETTING COUNSELLING AND PROCURING

Case Report	Purpose
Cases taken from *Stones Justices Manual*, para 1-301, *Ackroyds Air Travel v DPP* [1950] 1 All ER 933	The test is that the person knows that the acts which constitute an offence are being done and he gives assistance or encouragement to the perpetrator of the offence.
National Coal Board v Gamble [1958] 3 All ER 203	A counsellor is one who is knowingly involved before the commission of the offence in advising or assisting a principle in relation to it.
Case taken from *Archbold*, pp 18–13, *R v Ram* [1893] 17 Cox 609	A person may be an aider and abettor even if from sex or age incapable of being a principal (woman abetting rape).

SECTION 372 OF THE HOUSING ACT 1985 (APPEALS AND PROSECUTIONS) LIST OF AUTHORITIES PRODUCED BY LA

Case Authority	Purpose
Service of notices: *Lambeth LB v Mullings* [1990] TLR, 16 January	Service through the letterbox of the occupier of the subject premises is capable of satisfying s 233 of the Local Government Act 1972 and s 58 of the Control of Pollution Act 1974.
Rushmore BC v Reynolds (1991) 23 HLR 495	There was an irrebuttable presumption that service is deemed to be effected by pushing notice through letter box of the recipient under s 233 of the Local Government Act 1972.

Appendix 17: List of Authorities

Meaning of HIMO:*** *Barnes v Sheffield CC* (1995) 27 HLR 719	*Guidelines for HIMO*: A Whether the persons living in the house came to it as a single group or whether they were independently recruited; B what facilities were shared; C whether the occupiers were responsible for the whole house or just their particular rooms; D whether individual tenants were able to, or did lock other occupiers out of his room. E whose responsibility it was to recruit new occupiers when individuals left; F who allocated rooms; G the size of the rooms; H how stable the group composition was; I whether the mode of living was communal Sir Thomas Bingham MR, pp 723-24, made clear that the order of these factors should not be regarded as significant and the weight given to any particular factor will vary widely from case to case depending on the overall picture. A similar list is to be found at DOE circular 12/93 which sets out the following criteria; A whether cooking facilities are shared; B whether washing facilities are separate or shared; C whether occupants eat together; D whether cleaning is shared between occupants; E whether occupants have separate contracts; F whether vacancies are filled by occupants or landlord; G whether occupants come and go frequently.
Submission on test for HIMO***	Whether there is a nexus between the household which is sufficiently compelling to ensure that everyone will be assisted by the other occupants to the extent that he has an equal chance of escaping in case of fire.
London LBC v Ezedinma [1981] 3 All ER 438	Three groups of people, each sharing a separate kitchen from the other group are capable of being three separate households.
Meaning of 'wilfully' and related case law *R v Senior* [1895] All ER 511	The *dicta* of Lord Russell p 514H, allowed for the means of the defendant to be considered.

Saddleworth UDC v Aggregate and Sand (1971) 69 LGR 103	Lack of finance could not amount to a reasonable excuse for a company in defence to a prosecution for non-compliance with a notice under the Public Health Act 1936.
R v Redbridge ex p Guppy [1997] BPIR 441	Defendant's failure to pay a compensation order amounted to wilful refusal after he had declared himself bankrupt, as funds were available prior to the declaration.
Honig v Islington LBC [1972] Crim LR 126	Failure to comply with a s 15 of the Housing Act 1961 notice was the result of a course of conduct which the defendant has chosen to pursue and was not caused by *force majeure* (supervening event) accident or impossibility.
Kent CC v Brockman [1996] PLR 1; [1994] Crim LR 295	Personal circumstances may be taken into account for failure to comply with an enforcement notice.
Matters which can be raised in defence *Stagecoach Ltd v McPhail* 1988 SCCR 289	The defendant cannot challenge the terms of a notice in a subsequent trial if the notice could have been challenged by way of appeal to the magistrates' court (s 58 of the CPA 1974**).
A Lambert Flat Management Ltd v Lomas [1981] 2 All ER 280 (Approved in *Amec* below)	A reasonable excuse (s 58 of the CPA 1974**) must be limited to an excuse for non-compliance with the notice and cannot include a challenge to its validity, nor can it involve matters which could have been raised on appeal.
Amec Building Ltd v LB Camden [1997] Env LR 330	1 For non-compliance with s 80 of the EPA 1990* and s 60 of the CPA 1974** notice it is only necessary to consider whether the notices were complied with and not whether there was a nuisance. 2 'In my judgment an excuse cannot be "reasonable" under s 58(3) [CPA 1974**] if it involves matters which could have raised on appeal under s 58(3)'– Mrs Justice Ebsworth.

* EPA 1990 = Environmental Protection Act 1990

** CPA 1974 = Control of Pollution Act 1974

*** HIMO = House in multiple occupation

PROSECUTIONS UNDER SOCIAL SECURITY ADMINISTRATION ACT 1992
MEANING OF 'KNOWINGLY'
LIST OF AUTHORITIES (SUBMITTED BY LEA)

Authority	*Purpose*
J Sheldon Deliveries Ltd v Willis [1972] RTR 217, P 220c	Knowledge can be imputed to a person who shuts his mind to the obvious or allowed something to go on not caring whether an offence was committed or not.
Evans v Dell [1937] All ER 349, p 353B	One who is put on enquiry and fails to make proper enquiries has knowledge.
Barras v Reeve [1980] 3 All ER 705	It is not necessary to show that the false representation was made with the intention of obtaining benefit. It is sufficient to establish that the person claiming the benefit made a representation he knew to be false, ie, acted dishonestly.
Slough v Stevenson (1943) 4 DLE 433, *per* Kellock JA	I think 'knowingly' in the statute is used in the sense that the applicant (insurance claim) is in possession of information that what is in fact stated in the application is untrue or does not disclose the truth.
DSS v Bavi [1996] COD 260	In a prosecution under s 112 of the SSAA 1992, the defendant claimed that the representation had occurred due to a misunderstanding. *Held*: it was not necessary to prove intention to deceive or to defraud. The defendant knew that the statement he had made was false and this was sufficient.
Taylors Central Garage Ltd v Roper (1951) JP 115 445, pp 449–50 (see, also, *R v Thomas* (1976) 63 Cr App R 65)	Knowledge in law means 'actual knowledge and that the justices may infer from the nature of the act that was done and may find it (actual knowledge) of course even if the defendant gives evidence to the contrary' AND 'knowledge of the second degree' where the justices 'consider whether what the defendant was doing was, as it has been called, shutting his eyes to an obvious means of knowledge'.

Clear v Smith [1981] 1 WLR 399	It is not necessary for the prosecution to prove an intention to defraud (Supplementary Benefits Act 1976).
R v South Central Division Magistrates' Court ex p Secretary of State for Social Security (2000) LTL 14 November (unreported elsewhere)	The right to free legal advice under Code 3.15 of the Police and Criminal Evidence Act 1984 did not apply to interviews conducted by investigators at the Benefits Agency.

LIST OF STATUTORY TIME LIMITS FOR OFFENCES

STATUTORY TIME LIMIT FOR OFFENCES

Statute	Section	Offence Ref	Time Limit
Animal Boarding Establishments Act 1963	1	s 3	6 months
	2	s 3	
Bovine Animals (Records Identification and Movement) Order 1995			6 months
Clean Air Act 1993	1	s 1(5)	6 months
Dangerous Dogs Act	1	s 1(7)*	6 months
	3	s 3(4)*	6 months
Environmental Protection Act 1990	s 6(1), 9(2) 19(2)	s 23 "	No time limit
	33	s 33(9)	
	34	s 34(6)	
	80		6 months
	87	s 87(5)	6 months
Health and Safety at Work Act 1974	2–7	s 33	No time limit
Food Safety Act	s 33(1)	s 34 FSA 90 obstruction	6 months
Food Safety Act	s 7, 8, 12(6), 13(6) 14, 15		12 months
Health and Safety at Work Act 1974	s 33(1)(d) (e) ie s 20 and 25(f) ie s 20(2)(h) obstruction	s 33	6 months obstruction

Housing Act 1985	s 352, 372	s 376	6 months *(Camden LBC v Marshall* 1996 29 HLR Contg obligation)
Refuse Disposal Amenity Act 1978	s 2	s 2(1)	6 months
Management of HSWA Regs 1992	3	s 33(1)(c) and (3)	No time limit
Protection from Eviction Act 1977	1	s 1(4)	No time limit
Protection of Animals Act 1911	1	s 1(1)	6 months
Food Hygiene Regulations	6	7g and s 34 FSA 90	12 months
Town and Country Planning Act 1990	s 210(1)	s 210(2)	No time limit
Town and Country Planning Act 1990	s 210(4)	s 210(4)	6 months

* Please note – these offences are summary unless they are aggravated offences in which case they are triable either way and there will be no time limit.

NB: Time limits are stated in broad terms only. Cases can be dismissed for delay even if within the time limit. In some limited situations, the time limit is beyond that which is stated, eg, by reference to the close wording of the statute as it applies to the facts, extending statutory provisions or case law on continuing offences.

BRIEFING NOTE FOR LAY WITNESSES; GUIDANCE DOCUMENT FOR DRAWING UP STATEMENT OF FACTS; SCHEDULES OF UNUSED INFORMATION

BRIEFING TO LAY WITNESS BEFORE GIVING EVIDENCE

Checklist:

1. Outline the trial procedure to the witness – ie, order of speeches and evidence, etc.
2. Outline the procedure for giving evidence – ie, refer to examination-in-chief, cross-examination, re-examination and questions by the bench and clerk.
3. Explain the nature of examination-in-chief, with particular reference to leading questions.
4. Explain the nature of cross-examination – ie, the type of non-leading questions that can be asked – whilst also mentioning the basic premise that the defending Solicitor is required to put his case to the prosecution witnesses during cross-examination.
5. Explain the purpose of re-examination.
6. Explain the role of the clerk and magistrates or stipendiary magistrate, giving brief details of their qualifications and experience.
7. Explain the layout of the court, making reference to the positioning of persons taking part in the proceedings.
8. Explain the procedure before and after giving evidence so that the lay witness knows how he/she will be taken to the witness box, where the witness box will be and where he or she should be positioned after giving evidence.
9. The advocate should then give the witness the following additional advice to assist them in giving evidence:

    He or she should be advised on how to address the clerk and the magistrates and all other persons in connection with the proceedings. He/she should be advised to look directly at the magistrates, preferably the central magistrate if there are three, when giving evidence. Some advice should also be given on what to do if a question is not fully understood or more time is required to respond – eg, by asking the advocate to repeat or clarify the question or ask for a glass of water.

STATEMENT OF FACTS – GUIDANCE DOCUMENT

1 General note

A starting point for the person drafting a statement of facts is the summary that is usually included in the prosecution report. This should provide a global view of the evidence and identify the important features as perceived by the Client Department.

When drawing up a statement of facts, it is important to bear in mind that the prosecution will be confined to this if the written plea[a] procedure is used. If photographs or any other documents are to be produced to the court, these should be appended to the statement as exhibits.

2 Content and objectives of the statement of facts

2.1 Introduction – the legislation and the public interest

If an introduction is necessary, it should be short, ideally, no more than two or three lines. This can include a summary of the offence if the charges or legislation are complex. In simpler cases there is no need to recite the legislation as this will be apparent from the court list that will be before the magistrates. Local authority prosecutions are often unfamiliar to magistrates. It is suggested that it is appropriate to set out the public interest criteria and/or the mischief that the legislation is seeking to address if this is not apparent.

2.2 Fairness

The overall objective is one of fairness, that is, to present a fair and balanced version of events to include all aggravating and mitigating circumstances. The format and style of the statement should enable the court to readily identify and evaluate important features both for and against. If the significance of such a feature is only apparent from a fact mentioned in another context, special care is required to ensure that the point is not lost. The statement should be drafted in a dispassionate manner.

2.3 Precision and clarity

All material should be set out with precision and clarity. Failure in this regard will often result in prejudice to either one party or the other.

2.4 Brevity and relevance

Aspirations to include all material facts should not be at the expense of brevity. A short statement containing only the necessary information for sentencing purposes is more effective and enables the court to concentrate on the main issues that affect sentencing. This requires a judicious approach from the drafts person who should dismiss any facts

---

(a) Magistrates' Courts Act 1980.

which are not relevant to an issue in the case unless it is necessary for continuity purposes. The relevance of issues should then be condensed into short sentences whilst, at the same time, complying with the criteria in this document.

2.5 Sample charging

On the principle that a person can only be sentenced for an offence[b] which has been admitted or proved the statement should be drafted accordingly. If, for example, the informations are alleging counterfeit t-shirts that are representative of a larger number of items seized, the statement should only contain items which have been mentioned in the charges (this would not prevent a number of items being referred to in one charge provided this does not amount to duplicity). This rule would not apply to items that the defendant has admitted as being counterfeit.[c]

2.6 Character evidence and warnings

Warnings are sometimes the by-product of previous offences. Whereas warnings are essential to the sentencing process and should be included no reference can be made to earlier offences unless they are made the subject of charges. Previous convictions and evidence of bad character should not be included in the statement. This should not be confused with aggravating features that should be included.[d] One can be distinguished from the other by the existence of an evidential link to the proceedings that can be found in the aggravating feature.

2.7 Effect on the victim and damage to society

If a person sustains personal injury as a consequence of an offence, this is admissible provided an expert's report has been made available to the defence in advance of a hearing.[e] In the case of counterfeit goods reference can be made to financial damage to the producer of the genuine product and to the quality of the goods falsely described. These are, however, questions of fact and degree and reference to damage that is too remote may raise questions of the ability of the prosecution to be dispassionate.

2.8 Dealing with mitigation

Not all defendants are represented and therefore cannot be expected to mention all the mitigating circumstances. According to the Solicitor's Code of Practice, prosecuting solicitors are to be regarded as ministers of justice rather than advocates in the cause. The statement of facts should therefore include a fair account of the mitigation. Any mitigation that differs from the prosecution's version of the events should be apparent from the statement. The overall effect of the statement of facts should not be one of undue gravity and the overall objective should be to present a balanced version of the facts. This should include any explanations given by the defendant. In seeking to put forward a

---

(b) *R v Kidd* [1997] TLR, 21 July.
(c) *R v Russen* (1981) Cr App R(S) 134.
(d) *R v Nottingham Crown Court ex p DPP* [1996] 1 Cr App R(S) 283.
(e) *R v Hobstaff* (1993) 14 Cr App R(S) 605 and *R v O'S* (1993) 14 Cr App R(S) 632.

balanced version of events, care should be taken not only to protect the defendant's position but also the interests of justice.

2.9 Hearsay and other statements

Any relevant statements made by the defendant will be admissible. A PACE caution, however, is a necessary pre-requisite for any statement made to an officer. It would not usually be appropriate to include every statement made by the defendant. Only matters which are likely to affect sentencing should be included, eg, those which tend to indicate culpability or mitigation. Care should be taken before including statements made by other persons as questions of relevance and admissibility may arise.

2.10 Two or more defendants

Where there are two or more defendants there may be more than one statement of facts. If all the acts are to be included in one statement the responsibility of each defendant should be clearly identified and fairly set out.

2.11 Other matters for inclusion

The statement should include any financial gain made by the defendant. Exhibits do not need to be enclosed unless they are to be presented to the court, eg, photographs. As a general rule, the statement should follow a chronological sequence and end by claiming costs and referring to any applications for compensation or forfeiture orders sought.

Checklist

1　Introduction – public interest/mischief legislation is directed at.
2　Chronological order.
3　Aggravating features.
4　Important points from client's summary.
5　Reference to documents to be presented to the court, eg, photographs.
6　Inclusion of warnings.
7　Relevance.
8　Reference to the affect on the victim, if any.
9　Reference to other applications, eg, costs, forfeiture, compensation.
10　Reference to all relevant evidence supporting each and every charge.
11　Mitigation/explanation from the defendant.

Appendix 19: Briefing Note for Lay Witnesses

SPECIMEN

Case no: ....

R v .... (defendant)

SCHEDULE OF UNUSED (non-sensitive) PROSECUTION MATERIAL (CRIMINAL PROCEDURE AND INVESTIGATION ACT 1996)

	Date (if any)	Description of Material
1	13/01/00	Initial telephone call from Mrs Walsh (complainant) received by Adel Anwar (investigating officer)
2	14/01/00	Notes of initial interview with Mrs Walsh
3	16/01/00	Photographs taken by Adel Anwar of 2 Red Lane
4	28/02/00	Draft witness statement taken from Mrs Walsh
5	16/03/00	Draft of witness statement Adel Anwar
6	Various	Copy entries in notebook of Adel Anwar
7		
8		
9		
10		

I have inspected, viewed and listened to all material that has been retained by the investigator and certify to the best of my knowledge and belief that all material that has been retained and made available to me has been available in accordance with the code of practice under Part 11 pursuant to the Criminal Procedure and Investigation Act 1996

Signed ....
Officer in charge of Investigation/Disclosure Officer
Dated ....

SPECIMEN

Case no: ....

R v .... (defendant)

SCHEDULE OF SENSITIVE PROSECUTION MATERIAL
(CRIMINAL PROCEDURE AND INVESTIGATION ACT 1996)

Date (if any)   Description of Material

1
2
3
4
5
6
7
8
9
10

I have inspected, viewed and listened to all material that has been retained by the investigator and certify to the best of my knowledge and belief that all material that has been retained and made available to me has been available in accordance with the code of practice under Part II pursuant to the Criminal Procedure and Investigation Act 1996

Signed ....
Officer in charge of Investigation/Disclosure Officer
Dated   ....

REGULATION OF INVESTIGATORY POWERS AUTHORISATIONS

APPLICATION FOR AUTHORITY FOR DIRECTED SURVEILLANCE
APPLICATION FOR RENEWAL OF AUTHORITY FOR DIRECTED SURVEILLANCE

REGULATION OF INVESTIGATORY POWERS ACT 2000
PART II APPLICATION FOR AUTHORITY FOR DIRECTED SURVEILLANCE

Public Authority *(including full address)*	

Name of Applicant		Team	
Full Address			
Contact Details			
Operation Name *(if applicable)*		Operation Reference Number (RFS No)	

Details of application:

1 The level of authority required or recommended (where that is different): Give office, rank or position of authorising officer in accordance with the Regulation of Investigatory Powers (Prescription of Offices, Ranks and Positions) Order 2000/2417

Principal Officer	Officer in charge of the investigation

1 **Grounds on which the action is necessary:** *(Tick appropriate box)*

In the interests of national security;

for the purpose of preventing or detecting crime or of preventing disorder; ☐

in the interests of the economic well-being of the United Kingdom; ☐

in the interests of public safety; ☐

for the purpose of protecting public health; ☐

for the purpose of assessing or collecting any tax, duty, levy or other ☐
imposition, contribution or charge payable to a government department; ☐

1 **Explain why the directed surveillance is proportionate to what it seeks to achieve**

| 1 | **The identities, where known, of those to be subject of the directed surveillance:** |

Name:

Address:

DOB:

Other information as appropriate:

| 1 | The action to be authorised, including any premises or vehicles involved: |

| 1 | Give an account of the investigation or operation: |

| 1 | **Explanation of the information which it is desired to obtain as a result of the authorisation:** |

| 1 | **Collateral intrusion:** |

INDICATE ANY POTENTIAL FOR COLLATERAL INTRUSION ON OTHER PERSONS THAN THOSE TARGETED: INCLUDE A PLAN TO MINIMISE COLLATERAL INTRUSION

| 1 | **Confidential/religious material:** |

INDICATE THE LIKELIHOOD OF ACQUIRING ANY CONFIDENTIAL/RELIGIOUS MATERIAL:

| Anticipated Start: | Date: | Time: |

| 1 | **Applicant's details:** |

Name (print):   Tel No:

Grade/Rank: Date:

Signature

Appendix 20: Regulation of Investigatory Powers Authorisations

1 Authorising Officer's Comments:

1 Authorising Officer's Recommendation:		
I, [insert name], hereby authorise the directed surveillance operation as detailed above. This written authorisation will cease to have effect at the end of a period of 3 months unless renewed (see separate form for renewals).		
Name (Print)		Grade/Rank
Signature		Date

1 Confidential Material Authorisation:		
Name (Print)		Grade/ Rank
Signature		Date
From	Time:	Date:

1 Urgent Authorisation: Details of why application is urgent:		
Name (Print)		Grade/ Rank
Signature		Date/Time

1 Authorising officer's comments (this must include why the authorising officer or the person entitled to act in their absence considered the case urgent):

1 Please give the reasons why the person entitled to act in urgent cases considered that it was not reasonably practicable for the authorisation to be considered by a person otherwise entitled at act:	
Name (Print)	Grade/Rank
Signature	Date/Time

REGULATION OF INVESTIGATORY POWERS ACT 2000
PART II APPLICATION FOR RENEWAL OF DIRECTED SURVEILLANCE AUTHORITY (PLEASE ATTACH THE ORIGINAL AUTHORISATION)

Public Authority (*including full address*)	

Applicant	**Team**
Full Address	
Contact Details	
Operation Name	**Operation Number*** *RFS No
	Renewal Number

Details of renewal:

1	Renewal numbers and dates of any previous renewals	
Renewal Number	Date	

2	Detail the information as listed in the original authorisation as it applies at the time of the renewal

3	Detail any significant changes to the information in the previous authorisation

4	Detail why it is necessary to continue with the authorisation

5	Indicate the content and value to the investigation of the product so far obtained by the surveillance

Appendix 20: Regulation of Investigatory Powers Authorisations

6	Give an estimate of the length of time the authorisation will continue to be necessary

7 Applicant's Details			
Name (Print)		Tel No	
Grade/Rank		Date	
Signature			

8 Authorising Officer's Comments

9 Authorising Officer's Recommendation
I, [insert name], hereby authorise the renewal of the directed surveillance operation as detailed above. The renewal of this authorisation will last for 3 months unless renewed in writing.

Name (Print)	**Grade / Rank**
Signature	**Date**
Renewal From: Time:	Date:

INDEX

Abatement notice,
   breach 118–19
   Environmental Protection
      Act 1990 119–21
   requirements 119–21
   service 119–20

Abuse of process,
   objection handling 94–95

Accessories,
   drafting informations
      and summonses against 65

Accused
   See also Defendant
   disclosure,
      by accused 13–14
      to accused 13
   silence, right to 49–50
   spouse, evidence from 39

Additional information,
   schedule of 12–13

Additives,
   food labelling requirements 173

Adjournments 111

Admissions,
   defence 100

Advertisement prosecutions
   See also Planning investigation
   consent requirements 249
   contravention of regulations 249
   elements of offence 249
   generally 248
   investigatory matters 249
   Town and Country Planning
      (Control of Advertisement)
      Regulations 1992 249

Agent provocateur 90–91

Animal protection,
   generally 138
   Protection of Animals Act 1911 139–40

Appeal,
   bail pending 112

Attire,
   giving evidence in court 105

Auction,
   mock 274–76

Authorisations,
   checking 57–61
   committee 57
   content 59
   delegated authority,
      committee, from 57–58
   consultation with
      chairperson and
      vice-chairperson 58
   generally 57
   legal proceedings .... App 8
   superior officer 58–59

Authorities,
   list .... App 17
   researching 73
   weak cases 73

Autrefois acquit 96

Autrefois convict 96

Bail,
   appeal, pending 112

Barbed wire 356

Bodies corporate,
   food safety 216

Brochures 282, 283–84

Builder's skips, control of 330–31

Bulls on land crossed by
   public rights of way,
      keeping 354–55

Business names,
   civil remedies 273
   disclosure 272–73
   failure to display 270–71
   offences 273–74
   prohibition on use of
      certain names 271–72
   words and expressions
      requiring Secretary of
      State's approval 272

Case report form .... App 3
Cautions,
   forms .... App 7
   use 75
   weak cases 75
Certification by DO,
   Criminal Procedure and
      Investigations Act 1996 13
Character evidence 39
Charges,
   Code for Crown Prosecutors 5
Children,
   evidence from 39
   interviews 33–34, 53–54
   witnesses 33–34
Chimneys,
   dark smoke offence 125–26
Clerk,
   duties 81
   magistrates' court 103
Co-accused,
   evidence 39
Code for Crown Prosecutors 1–6
   application of code 6
   charges 5
   evidential test 2–3
   general principles 1
   guilty pleas 6
   mode of trial 5
   public interest test 3–5
   re-starting prosecution 6
   review 1
   tests, code 2
Collation of evidence,
   planning investigation 22
Computer records,
   evidence 38
Consent,
   prosecution 63
Consumer Protection Act 1987,
   misleading price indications 277–81

Contemporaneous notes,
   interviews 33
   witnesses 33
Continuing offences,
   highways legislation 358
Copyright Designs and
   Patents Act 1988,
   dealing with or using
      illicit recordings 258–60
   making or dealing with
      infringing articles 256–58, 260
Costs,
   applications 113
   defendant's costs order 115
   importance of applications 113
   investigative 111
   prosecution costs on
      appeal against conviction 116
   witnesses 111
Costs applications,
   uncontested hearing 82
Council tax benefit prosecutions
   See Housing benefit and
      council tax benefit
      prosecutions
Court,
   giving evidence in 103–09
   jurisdiction 63
   magistrates'
      See Magistrates' court
Court attendance,
   witnesses 32
Criminal offence investigations
   See Investigations
   sanctions for non-compliance
      by accused 14
   secondary disclosures 14
Criminal Procedure and
   Investigations Act 1996 11–17
   accused,
      compulsory disclosure by 13–14
   disclosure to 13

Index

sanctions for
  non-compliance with
  disclosure duty 14
additional information,
  schedule of 12–13
certification by DO 13
compulsory disclosure
  by accused 13
definitions 11
disclosure of material,
  Attorney General's
    guidelines 14–17
  by accused 13–14
  sanctions for non-compliance
    by accused 14
  secondary disclosures 14
  to accused 13
preparation of material for
  prosecutor 12
provisions 11
recording of information 11
schedules,
  additional information 12–13
  sensitive information 12
  unused information 12
sensitive information,
  schedule of 12
unused information,
  schedule of 12

Cross-examination,
  defence, by 100–01
  examination-in-chief 106–07
  limits 100–01
  preparation for hearing 85

Crown Court,
  evidence 108–09

Dangerous product, offering or
  agreeing to supply
  See Product safety

Dark smoke offence,
  chimneys 125–26
  industrial or trade premises 126–27
  meaning of dark smoke 127
  prohibition 125, 126–27

Defence,
  admissions 100
  applications
    See also Objection handling
    agent provocateur 90–91
    contentious mitigation,
      notification of 100
    entrapment 90–91
    exclusion of unfair evidence 90
    incorrect summons/
      information 91–92
    no case to answer 89–90
  contentious mitigation,
    notification of 100
  cross-examination 100–01
  expert's reports, disclosure of 101
  frankness 102
  good faith 102
  impugnation of witness 101
  misleading court 99–100
  mitigation 102
  no case to answer,
    application of 89–90
  obligations of advocate 99–102
    admissions 100
    character of witness 101
    cross-examination 100–01
    expert's reports,
      disclosure of 101
    fairness to the prosecution 100
    frankness 102
    good faith 102
    impugnation of witness 101
    misleading court 99–100
    mitigation 102
    personal opinion,
      expression of 101
    relevant authorities,
      provision of 99
    scandalisation of witnesses 101
    source 99
    vilification of witness 101
  personal opinion,
    expression of 101
  scandalisation of witnesses 101
  vilification of witness 101

Defences,
    due diligence 21
    objections from
        See Objection handling
    planning investigation 21
    possible 21

Defendant
    See also Accused
    interviewing 20–21
    interviews,
        Criminal Justice Act
            1969 format 31–32
    possible defences 21
    self-incrimination,
        privilege against 27

Delay,
    human rights 25–26

Disclosure of material,
    advance disclosure,
        uncontested proceedings 80–81
    Attorney General's guidelines 14–17
    Criminal Procedure and
        Investigations Act 1996,
        Attorney General's guidelines 14–17
        by accused 13–14
        sanctions for non-compliance
            by accused 14
        secondary disclosures 14
        to accused 13
    expert's reports 101
    preparation for hearing,
        advance disclosure 80–81
        uncontested hearing 80

Distributors,
    product safety 295

District judge, questions put by 107

Dog fouling 230–32

Double jeopardy 96

Drafting informations
    and summonses 63–69
    accessories, against 65
    consent to prosecution 63
    description of specific offence 63
    duplicity 65–66
    general principles 63

health and safety at
    work offences 66
jurisdiction of court 63
misfeasance offences 65
non-feasance offences 64
offence,
    description of specific 63
    health and safety at
        work offences 66
    misfeasance 65
    non-feasance 64
    public entertainment
        licence breaches 66
    Trade Descriptions Act
        1968 offences 66
omission of a section 64
precedents, use of 64
public entertainment
    licence breaches 66
section of statute,
    omission 64
    reference to 63
statutory notices, service of 66–69
statutory references,
    omission of a section 64
    sections of statutes 63
Trade Descriptions Act
    1968 offences 66

Drafting statement/
    summary of facts,
    uncontested hearing 77

Due diligence defence 21, 286
    product safety 297

Duplicity,
    drafting informations
        and summonses 65–66
    objection handling 91

Education precedents .... App 15

Emergency control orders 244

Emergency prohibition notices
    and orders 242–43

Emergency works 340
    notice 344–45

Index

Entrapment 90–91
   human rights 30

Entry powers,
   food safety 213–14
   highways legislation 338, 356–57
   housing 225

Environmental health 117–244
   abatement notice, breach of 118–19
   animal protection 138–40
   dark smoke offence
      See Dark smoke offence
   dog fouling 230–32
   eviction
      See Eviction, protection from
   food safety
      See Food safety
   health and safety
      See Health and safety offences
   housing
      See Housing
   litter, leaving 237
   offence creating sections 117
   precedents .... App 11
   refuse disposal 232–36
   statutory nuisance
      See Abatement notice;
      Statutory nuisance
   statutory powers 117–18
   waste .... 232–36, App 13

Environmental
   Protection Act 1990 119–21

Equipment,
   food safety 151

Eviction, protection from 226–29
   harassment 229–30
   precedents .... App 11
   unlawful eviction 229

Evidence 60–61
   See also Planning investigation
   character evidence 39
   children, evidence from 39
   co-accused 39
   collation 22
   computer records 38
   Crown Court 108–09
   evaluation 60–61
   expert reports 38

giving evidence in court 103–09
   See also Giving
      evidence in court
hearsay 35–39
inadmissible 39–40
   character evidence 39
   children, evidence from 39
   co-accused 39
   practical application of rules 39–40
   spouse of accused 39
interview records 38–39
interviews 38–39
preparing a file of 55–56
proofs 112
public documents 38
real 38
res gestae 39
similar fact evidence 39
spouse of accused 39
sworn 108
taking full advantage
   of rules 73–74
weak cases 71, 73–74

Examination-in-chief,
   argumentative questions 88
   cross-examination 106–07
   emotive language 88–89
   giving evidence in court 105–06
   leading questions 87
   opinion evidence 88
   preparation for hearing 85
   references only to
      admissible evidence 88
   relevance of questions 87
   repeating statements by
      other witnesses 88

Exemptions,
   food labelling 161–62

Exhibits 32, 112

Expenses,
   witnesses 111

Expert reports,
   disclosure by defence 101
   evidence 38

Exports,
   food labelling 182

Fairness,
  uncontested hearing 78
False document, furnishing,
  housing benefit and
  council tax benefit
  prosecutions 300–01
File,
  preparing file of evidence 55–56
Fish,
  food labelling 185–90
Food labelling,
  additives, indication of 173, 193–94
  alcoholic drinks 176, 194–95
  alteration of durability
    indication 182
  catering establishments,
    food sold at 175
  claims 179–80, 195
    minerals 202
    prohibited 195
    restricted 196–201
    vitamins 201–02
  defences,
    alternation of durability
      indication 182
    exports 182
  definitions 154–61
  delivery of food to
    ultimate consumer,
      brand names 165
      customary name 165
      durability indications 170–72
      fancy names 165
      form of name 165
      ingredient list 165–70
      labelling requirement 164
      name of food 164–65
      physical condition or
        treatment, indication of 165
      scope of regulations 162–64
      trade marks 165
      true nature of food,
        indication of 165
  durability indications 170–72
    alteration 182
    foods not requiring
      an appropriate durability
      indication 171–72

minimum durability,
  form of indication of 170–71
  use by date 171
emergency control orders 244
enforcement 182
exemptions 161–62
exports 182
fancy confectionery products 172–73
field of vision 179
fish 185–90
gases, foods
  packaged in certain 176
generally 153
generic names 191–93
indelibly marked bottles 174
indications of treatment 191
ingredient list 165–67
  added water 168
  foods not requiring list 168–69
  generic names 191–93
  heading of list 165
  ingredients which need
    not be named 168
  named of ingredients 166–68
  order of list 165–66
  quantities 169–70
  water added 168
intelligibility 179
interpretation of regulations 154–61
irradiated ingredients 173–74
manner of marking
  or labelling 177
melons 191
milk 179
  raw 176
  skimmed milk products 176
minerals 202
misleading
  descriptions 180–81, 205–10
nutrition labelling 202–05
offences 181–82
omission of certain
  particulars 172–75
penalties 181–82
potatoes 191
prepacked, food not 172–73
prescribed names,
  fish 185–90
  melons 191

Index

potatoes 191
vitamins 191
prohibited claims 195
Regulations 154–210
restricted claims 196–201
seasonal selection packs 175
small packages 174
sugar, added 177
sweeteners 177
vending machines,
   food sold from 175–76
vitamins 191, 201–02
wine 181

Food safety,
  bodies corporate 216
  emergency prohibition
    notices and orders 242–43
  enforcement 146–47
  entry powers 213–14
  equipment regulations 151
  execution 146–47
  Food Safety (General
    Food Hygiene)
    Regulations 1995 140–211
     application of provisions 144
     interpretation 143–44
     penalties 146
  food waste 152
  foodstuffs 152–53
  hygiene rules,
    equipment regulations 151
    food premises 147–48
    food waste 152
    foodstuffs 152–53
    movable premises 149
    personal hygiene 152
    preparation, treatment or
      processing of foodstuffs 148
    temporary premises 149
    training 153
    transport 149–51
    waste food 152
    water supply 152
  improvement notices 240
  interpretation of regulations 142–44
  labelling
    See Food labelling
  medical conditions,
    persons suffering from 145

movable premises 149
non-compliance with
  requirements 211
obstruction of officers 214–15
penalties 146
personal hygiene 152
powers of entry 213–14
preparation, treatment
  or processing of foodstuffs 148
prohibition orders 241–42
proprietors of food
  business, obligations of 144–45
punishment of offences 215–16
seizure of suspected food 239–40
selling food,
  not complying with
    regulations 211–12
  not of nature or
    substance or quality
    demanded 212–13
temporary premises 149
time limit for prosecution 215
training 153
transport 149–51
waste food 152
water supply 152

Forms,
  case report .... App 3
  caution .... App 7
  magistrates court .... App 1
  recording of information .... App 6
  witness statements .... App 4

Frankness,
  defence duty 102

General Product
Safety Regulations 1994,
  application 294
  conformity presumption 295
  distributor's requirements 295, 296
  due diligence defence 297
  enforcement 295
  enforcement authorities' duties 298
  extension of time for
    summary proceedings 298
  general safety requirement 294
  information requirement 294–95

interpretation 292–93
liability 297–98
offences 296
penalties 298
product assessment 295
revocation 294

Giving evidence in court 103–09
attire 105
district judge, questions put by 107
examination-in-chief 105–06
formalities 104
lay magistrates,
   questions put by 107
magistrates' court personnel 103–04
mode of attire 105
re-examination 107
sworn evidence 108
tips 108
witnesses,
   formalities 104
   preparation for hearing 104–05

Good faith,
defence duty 102

Guilty pleas,
Code for Crown Prosecutors 6
warnings on, inadmissibility of 97

Health and safety at
work offences,
drafting informations and
   summonses 66
employees' duties 131
employer's duty,
   employees, to 128–30
   persons other
      than employees, to 130–31
imminent danger, power
   to deal with cause of 138
improvement notices 136
inspectors' powers 134–36
notices,
   improvement 136
   prohibition 136–37
   supplementary provisions 137
prohibition notices 136–37

Hearing,
examination-in-chief
   See Examination-in-chief
objections at
   See Objection handling
preparation
   See Preparation for hearing
uncontested 77–82
   See also Preparation for hearing

Hearsay 35–39
contested hearing 86
inadmissibility 86
uncontested hearing 79

HELA circular 8–10

Highways Act 1980,
builder's skips, control of 330–31
disturbance of surface
   of highways 333–34
draft information .... 330, App 10
fires, danger or
   annoyance caused by 335–36
hoardings to be used
   during building 331–33
penalty for damaging
   highway 334–35
wilful obstruction 328–30

Highways legislation 327–58
advanced notice,
   failure to give 340–42
barbed wire 356
builder's skips, control of 330–31
bulls on land crossed by
   public rights of way, keeping 354–55
continuing offences 358
contravention of restriction
   of works 345–47
disturbance of surface
   of highways 333–34
draft information .... 330, App 10
emergency works 340
   notice 344–45
entry powers 338, 356–57
facilities for street
   authority, failure to provide 348–49
fires, danger or
   annoyance caused by 335–36

Index

footpaths displaying
   signs in national parks
     deterring public use 337–38
form of notice... 358
Highways Act 1980,
   builder's skips, control of 330–31
   disturbance of surface
     of highways..................................... 333–34
   draft information .... 330, App 10
   fires, danger or
     annoyance caused by 335–36
   hoardings to be used
     during building............................. 331–33
   penalty for damaging
     highway.. 334–35
   wilful obstruction 328–30
hoardings to be used
   during building................................. 331–33
miscellaneous powers............................... 328
New Roads and Street
   Works Act 1991,
   advanced notice,
     failure to give................................ 340–42
   contravention of restriction
     of works.. 345–47
   directions as to timing
     of street works 343–44
   emergency works..................................... 340
   facilities for street
     authority, failure
      to provide....................................... 348–49
   notice of emergency works 344–45
   other apparatus, failure
     to notify owners of...................... 349–50
   records of location
     of apparatus.................................. 353–54
   reinstate, failure to 350–52
   standard of reinstatement 352–53
   starting date of works
     notice of 342–43
   unauthorised street works 338–40
   unqualified supervisors
     and operative,
     employment of 347–48
notice of emergency works 344–45
notices,
   form 358
   service 358

obstruction,
   wilful... 328–30
obstruction of officers.............................. 358
other apparatus, failure to
   notify owners of................................ 349–50
overview.. 327–28
ownership of land,
   requiring information on...................... 357
penalty for damaging
   highway... 334–35
powers of entry 338, 356–57
precedents .... App 10,
                                          App 16
reinstatement,
   failure... 350–53
starting date of works,
   notice of 342–43
street works,
   contravention of restriction
     of works.. 345–47
   directions as to timing..................... 343–44
   unauthorised 338–40
summary proceedings 358
unauthorised street works 338–40
unqualified supervisors
   and operative, employment of 347–48

Hoardings to be used
   during building..................................... 331–33

Housing
   See also Eviction,
     protection from
   entry powers.. 225
   execution of works,
     authorisation of owner to
       execute works in default
       of other owner 225
     failure 218–21
   neglect of management,
     works required
       to remedy 223–24
   number of occupants,
     works required to render
       premises fit for............................. 222–23
   penalty for failure 224, 226
   power to require............................... 222–23
   failure to execute works..................... 218–21

neglect of management,
   works required to remedy............. 223–24
non-compliance with
   repairs notice 216–18
number of occupants,
   works required to render
   premises fit for................................. 222–23
obstruction of officers............................... 225
penalty for failure to
   execute works................................. 224, 226
powers of entry 225
precedents... App 11
repairs notice 216–18

Housing benefit and
council tax benefit
prosecutions... App 2,
                                                        299–304
   change in circumstances,
      failure to notify................................ 301–02
      dishonestly....................................... 302–04
   choice of offence............................... 299–300
   cost of proceedings 300
   dishonestly failing to
      notify change in
      circumstances 302–04
   false document, furnishing 300–01
   gravity of offence 299
   likely cost of proceedings................. 299–300
   offence,
      choice 299–300
      gravity.. 299
      timing... 300
   overview... 299
   Social Security
      Administration Act 1992................. 300–01
   technical arguments 300
   timing of offence 300
   wording of charge...................................... 300

Human rights 25–30
   delay... 25–26
   entrapment... 30
   Regulation of
      Investigatory Powers
      Act 2000 27–30
   self-incrimination,
      privilege against... 27
   silence, right to 50

Illicit recordings 258–60

Impersonation of officers,
   package travel, holidays
   and tours.. 291
   trading standards...................................... 291
Implied statements,
   weak cases.. 72
Improvement notices,
   food safety... 240
   health and safety at
      work offences... 136
Impugnation of witness............................... 101
Industrial or trade premises,
   dark smoke offences............................ 126–27
Informations,
   drafting
      See Drafting informations
      and summonses
   failure to mention negative in..................... 93
   negative not mentioned in 93
   wrong name/date on............................ 92–93
Interviews,
   alleged offender 41–54
      argumentative questions 45
      bold opening to interview 48
      children... 53–54
      concise questions 46–47
      correspondence,
         interviews through 53
      detail, committing suspect to................. 48
      deviations from PACE........................ 52–53
      expert opinion, questions on.................. 45
      fair questions 44–45
      need for, whether 48
      other people, questions about................ 45
      out of sequence, questions...................... 48
      Police and Criminal
         Evidence Act 1984......................... 48–49
      preparation... 41
      probing questions 46
      psychology of the interview................... 42
      questions that may be asked............ 43–44
      records... 51–52
      relating to evidence within
         knowledge of defendant,
         questions.. 45
      relevant questions 44

Index

robust questioning 47
sarcastic questions 45
short questions 46
silence, right to 49–50
style, interviewing 45–46
tape or manuscript,
    recording interview on 50
techniques 46
young persons 53–54
argumentative questions 45
children 33–34, 53–54
concise questions 46–47
contemporaneous notes 33
correspondence, through 53
defendant,
  Criminal Justice Act
    1969 format 31–32
  letter to defendant
    for interview 22–23
  planning investigation 20–21
  procedure 23
detail, committing suspect to 48
deviations from PACE 52–53
evidence 38–39
expert opinion, questions on 45
fair questions 44–45
need for, whether 48
Police and Criminal
  Evidence Act 1984 48–49
  deviations from 52–53
post-charge 53
preparation 41
probing questions 46
psychology 42
questions,
  argumentative 45
  concise 46–47
  expert opinion 45
  fair 44–45
  other people, about 45
  out of sequence 48
  possible 43–44
  probing 46
  relating to evidence within
    knowledge of defendant 45
  relevant 44
  robust 47
  sarcastic 45

short 46–47
style, interviewing 45–46
records as evidence 38–39
relevant questions 44
robust questioning 47
sarcastic questions 45
silence, right to 49–50
style, interviewing 45–46
tape or manuscript, recording
  interview on 50
techniques 46
under-age witnesses 33–34
witnesses 31–34
  complaint 31
  confirmation of court
    attendance 32
  contemporaneous notes 33
  direct evidence 31
  exhibits 32
  under-age witnesses 33–34
young persons 53–54
Investigations,
  authorisations
    See Authorisations
  Criminal Procedure and
    Investigations Act 1996 11–17
  HELA circular 8–10
  planning
    See Planning investigation
  Police and Criminal
    Evidence Act 1984 .... 7–8, 48–49
  Regulation of Investigatory
    Powers Act 2000 27–30
  statutory framework 7–17
    Criminal Justice and
      Public Order Act 1994 7–8
    Criminal Procedure and
      Investigations Act 1996 11–17
    HELA circular 8–10
    Police and Criminal
      Evidence Act 1984 7–8
    Regulation of Investigatory
      Powers Act 2000 27–30
Irradiated ingredients,
  food labelling 173–74

Labelling of food
See Food labelling

Licensing legislation 305–25
   overview 305
   private hire vehicle,
      driven without licence 305–07
      hackney stands 307
      investigation of offences 324
      overview 323–24
      plying for hire
         without licence 308–09
      precedents .... App 12
   public entertainment licences,
      being concerned in
         organisation or
         management of
         unlicensed PEL 313
      breach of licence conditions 312–13
      numerous breaches 66
   street trading 309–11
   Town Police Clauses
      Act 1847 308

List of authorities .... App 17

Litter, leaving 237

Magistrates 103

Magistrates' court,
      clerk 103
      forms .... App 1
      magistrates 103
      personnel 103–04
      stipendiary magistrates 103
      ushers 103–04

Manuscript,
   recording interview on 50

Medical conditions,
   persons suffering from,
      food safety 145

Melons,
   food labelling 191

Milk,
   food labelling 179
   raw 176
   skimmed milk products 176

Minerals,
   food labelling 202

Misfeasance offences 65

Misleading court,
   defence 99–100

Misleading descriptions,
   food labelling 180–81,
                                         205–10

Misleading price indications 275–81

Mitigation,
   contentious 100
   defence 102
   notification to prosecution
      where contentious 100
   uncontested hearing 79

Mock auction, conducting 274–76

Mode of trial,
   Code for Crown Prosecutors 5
   uncontested hearing 81

Movable premises,
   food safety 149

New Roads and Street
   Works Act 1991,
   advanced notice,
      failure to give 340–42
   contravention of
      restriction of works 345–47
   directions as to timing
      of street works 343–44
   emergency works 340
      notice 344–45
   facilities to street authority,
      failure to provide 348–49
   notice of emergency works 344–45
   other apparatus, failure to
      notify owners of 349–50
   records of location of
      apparatus 353–54
   reinstate,
      failure to 350–52
      standards of
         reinstatement 352–53
   standard of reinstatement 352–53

Index

starting date for works,
  notice of 342–43
unauthorised street works 338–40
unqualified supervisors
  and operative,
  employment of 347–48

No case to answer 89–90

Nolle prosequi,
  weak cases, use in 73

Non-feasance offences 64

Notebooks 112

Notice,
  repairs 218
  statutory
    See Statutory notices

Nuisance
  See Statutory nuisance

Nutrition labelling 202–05

Objection handling 87, 89–97
  absence of signature on
    summons 92
  abuse of process 94–95
  agent provocateur 90–91
  aggravating features not
    ingredients of offence 94
  autrefois acquit 96
  autrefois convict 96
  defendant not charged
    with offence 94
  double jeopardy 96
  duplicity 91
  entrapment 90–91
  exclusion of unfair evidence 90
  failures,
    correct offence not stated 93–94
    mention negative in
      information 93
  incorrect summons/
    information 91–92
  information,
    failure to mention
      negative in 93
    wrong name/date on 92–93

no case to answer 89–90
offence, failure to state correct 93–94
opening address,
  objections during 94
originals, requirement for 96
photographic evidence 97
re-interviewing witnesses 97
signature absent on summons 92
specimen charges 94
unfair evidence, exclusion of 90
victim, references to effect
  of offence on 95–96
warnings on a guilty plea,
  references to 97
wrong name/date on
  information 92–93

Obstruction of officers,
  food safety 214–15
  highways legislation 358
  housing 225
  package travel,
    holidays and tours 290–91
  trading standards 270, 290–91

Offences,
  See also Food safety
  dark smoke
    See Dark smoke offence
  drafting informations
    and summonses 63, 64
  failure to state correct 93
  misfeasance 65
  non-feasance 64
  statutory nuisance
    See Abatement notice;
    Statutory nuisance

Opening address to court,
  preparation 83–84

Opinion evidence,
  examination-in-chief 88

Ownership of land, requiring
  information on 357

Package travel, holidays and tours,
  application of regulations.......................... 283
  brochures.. 283–84
  disclosure of information 291
  due diligence defence............................... 286
  enforcement................................. 286, 288–90
  impersonation of officers.......................... 291
  information to be provided........ 284–85, 288
  interpretation of regulations 282
  liability.. 286–87
  misleading descriptive
    matter.. 283
  obstruction of officers.......................... 290–91
  offences.. 285–86
  self-incrimination,
    privilege against..................................... 291
  time limits for prosecutions 287

Personal hygiene,
  food safety... 152

Photographic evidence,
  objection handling 97

Planning investigation............................. 19–23
  advertisements
    See Advertisement
      prosecutions
  authorisations
    See Authorisations
  checklist... 21–22
  collation of evidence.................................... 22
  collation of report.. 23
  defences 21
  defendant's legal status 19–20
  elements of an offence.......................... 245–46
  elements of offence 19
  entry powers... 250–51
  interviewing defendant 20–21
  letter to defendant
    for interview 22–23
  powers of entry 250–51
  precedents .... App 9
  subject of investigation 19
  Town and Country
    Planning Act 1990,
      elements of offence 245–46
      investigatory matters 245–46
      tree preservation orders.......... 247–48, 252
    tree preservation orders............... 247–48, 252
    witness statements................................ 20

Planning legislation,
  investigatory matters 245–46
  overview.. 245
  statutory provisions..................... 245, App 9

Police and Criminal Evidence
  Act 1984,
    interviews... 48–49
      deviations from 52–53
    investigations 7–8, 48–49
    statutory framework for
      investigations.. 7–8

Potatoes,
  food labelling... 191

Powers of entry,
  food safety.. 213–14
  highways legislation 338, 356–57
  planning investigation........................ 250–51
  trading standards................................ 268–69

Precedents,
  use... 64

Preparation for hearing 77–86
  absence of defendant,
    proceedings in,
      uncontested hearing 82
  advance disclosure,
    uncontested hearing 80
  brevity,
    uncontested hearing 78
  checklist,
    uncontested hearing 80
  CJA procedure,
    uncontested hearing 80
  clarity,
    uncontested hearing 78
  clerk's duties,
    uncontested hearing 81
  contested hearing.................................. 83–86
    cross-examination 85
    elements of offence 84
    examination-in-chief................................ 85
    facts.. 84
    formalities, agreeing 83
    hearsay evidence 86
    informations, reviewing 83
    interpretation of facts,
      submissions relating to 84

Index

lay witnesses,
    meeting with 85–86,
        App 19
legal submissions 84
opening address to court,
    preparation of 83–84
public interest 84
researching law 83
review of evidence 83
costs applications,
    uncontested hearing 82
cross-examination 85
drafting statement/
    summary of facts,
    uncontested hearing 77
elements of offence 84
examination-in-chief 85
facts 84
failure to comply with
    advance disclosure,
    uncontested hearing 80–81
fairness,
    uncontested hearing 78
formalities, agreeing 83
hearsay evidence,
    contested hearing 86
    uncontested hearing 79
informations, reviewing 83
interpretation of facts,
    submissions relating to 84
lay witnesses, meeting with 85–86,
        App 19
legal submissions 84
MCA 1980 procedure,
    uncontested hearing 80
mitigation,
    uncontested hearing 79, 82
mode of trial 81
opening address to court,
    preparation of 83–84
plea before venue 81
precision 78
previous convictions 78–79
prosecution address 81
prosecution summary 77
public interest,
    contested hearing 84
    uncontested hearing 77–78
relevance 78

researching law 83
review of evidence 83
sample charging 78
service of CJA statements 80
statement of facts 77–80
uncontested hearing 77–82
    absence of defendant,
      proceedings in 82
    advance disclosure 80
    brevity 78
    checklist 80
    CJA procedure 80
    clarity 78
    clerk's duties 81
    costs applications 82
    drafting statement/
      summary of facts 77
    failure to comply with
      advance disclosure 80–81
    fairness 78
    hearsay statements 79
    inclusion, matters for 79
    law 77
    MCA 1980 procedure 80
    mitigation 79, 82
    mode of trial 81
    plea before venue 81
    precision 78
    preparation 77
    previous convictions 78–79
    prosecution address 81
    prosecution summary 77
    public interest 77–78
    relevance 78
    sample charging 78
    service of CJA statements 80
    statement of facts 77–80
    victim, effect on 79
victim, effect on 79
witnesses 85–86,
        104–05

Previous convictions,
    uncontested hearing 78–79

Price indications, misleading 275–81

Private hire vehicle,
    driven without licence 305–07
    licences 306–07

overview 323–24
plying for hire
  without licence 308–09
  investigating 324
precedents .... App 12
prohibition of other
  vehicles on hackney
  carriage stands 307

Product safety,
  conformity presumption 295
  distributor's requirements 295, 296
  due diligence defence 297
  enforcement authorities'
    duties 298
  General Product Safety
    Regulations 1994,
    application 294
    conformity presumption 295
    distributor's requirements 295, 296
    due diligence defence 297
    enforcement 295
    enforcement authorities'
      duties 298
    extension of time for
      summary proceedings 298
    general safety requirement 294
    information requirement 294–95
    interpretation 292–93
    liability 297–98
    offences 296
    penalties 298
    preparatory acts 296
    product assessment 295
    revocation 294
  information requirement 294–95
  offences 296
  overview 292
  preparatory acts 296
  product assessment 295

Progress of case 111–12

Prohibition orders,
  food safety 241–42

Proofs of evidence 112

Prosecution,
  consent 63
  election to prosecute 74

Prosecution summary,
  uncontested hearing 77

Protection of Animals Act 1911 139–40

Public documents,
  evidence 38

Public entertainment licences,
  being concerned in
    organisation or management
    of unlicensed PEL 313
  breach of licence conditions 312–13
  drafting informations and
    summonses 66
  numerous breaches 66
  transfer 314–23

Public interest,
  Code for Crown Prosecutors 3–5
  contested hearing 84
  matrix .... App 7
  uncontested hearing 77–78
  weak cases 71

Queen's evidence,
  nolle prosequi in return for 73

Re-examination,
  giving evidence in court 107

Re-interviewing witnesses 86
  objection handling 97

Recording of information,
  Criminal Procedure and
    Investigations Act 1996 11
  forms .... App 6
  notebooks 112

Recordings, illicit 258–60

Refuse disposal 232–36

Regulation of Investigatory
  Powers Act 2000 27–30,
                                   App 20

Repairs notice,
  non-compliance 216–18

Res gestae 39

Index

Review,
    Code for Crown Prosecutors 1
Roads
    See Highways legislation

Scandalisation of witnesses 101
Schedules,
    Criminal Procedure and
        Investigations Act 1996,
        additional material 12–13
        sensitive information 12
        unused information 12
Self-incrimination,
    privilege against,
        defendant 27
        human rights 27
        package travel, holidays
            and tours 291
Sensitive information,
    schedule of 12
Service,
    certificate .... App 5
    CJA statements 80
    statutory notices 66–69
Signature,
    absent on summons 92
Silence, right to,
    human rights 50
    interviews 49–50
Similar fact evidence 39
Skips, builder's 330–31
Social Security Administration
    Act 1992 300–01
Spouse of accused,
    evidence 39
Statement of facts,
    uncontested hearing 77–80
Statements,
    proofs of evidence 112
    witness
        See Witness statements

Statutory notices,
    service 66–69
Statutory nuisance,
    abatement notice
        See Abatement notice
        inspection where 121–24
Stipendiary magistrates 103
Street trading 309–11
Street works,
    See also Highways legislation
    contravention of
        restriction of works 345–47
    directions as to timing 343–44
    unauthorised 338–40
Summary proceedings,
    highways legislation 358
    product safety 298
Summonses,
    drafting
        See Drafting
            informations and
            summonses
    signature absent on 92
Sweeteners,
    food labelling 177
Sworn evidence 108

Tape,
    recording interview on 50
Temporary premises,
    food safety 149
Time limits for prosecutions,
    food safety 215
    list .... App 18
    package travel,
        holidays and tours 287
Town and Country Planning
    (Control of Advertisement)
    Regulations 1992 249
Town and country planning
    See Planning legislation

Town Police Clauses Act 1847 308

Trade Descriptions Act 1968,
   drafting informations and
      summonses 66
   entry powers.. 268–69
   false trade descriptions,
      prohibition of..................................... 261–64
   fault of other person,
      offences due to... 268
   obstruction of officers................................ 270
   powers of entry 268–69

Trade marks 253–56

Trading standards.................................. 253–98
   brochures... 282, 283–84
   business names
      See Business names
   Consumer Protection Act 1987 277–81
   Copyright Designs and
      Patents Act 1988,
      dealing with or using
         illicit recordings............................. 258–60
      making or dealing with
         infringing articles................. 256–58, 260
   dangerous product, offering
      or agreeing to supply
      See Product safety
   dealing with or using
      illicit recordings................................. 258–60
   entry powers.. 268–69
   false trade descriptions,
      prohibition of..................................... 261–64
   fault of other person,
      offences due to... 268
   illicit recordings................................... 258–60
   impersonation of officers......................... 291
   making or dealing with
      infringing articles...................... 256–58, 260
   misleading price indications.............. 275–81
   mock auction, conducting.................. 274–76
   obstruction of officers 270, 290–91
   offence creating sections 253
   package travel, holidays
      and tours,
      application of regulations..................... 283
      brochures.. 283–84
      disclosure of information 291
      due diligence defence........................... 286

      enforcement 286,
                                           288–90
      impersonation of officers...................... 291
      information 284–85,
                                           287–88
      interpretation of regulations 282
      liability 286–87
      misleading descriptive
         matter 283
      obstruction of officers...................... 290–91
      offences 285–86
      self-incrimination,
         privilege against.................................. 291
      time limits for
         prosecutions... 287
   power of entry 268–69
   precedents .... App 14
   price indications,
      misleading.. 277–78
   services, false
      statement as to................................... 265–68
   statutory powers 253
   Trade Descriptions Act 1968,
      entry powers...................................... 268–69
      false trade descriptions,
         prohibition of.................................. 261–64
      fault of other person,
         offences due to.................................... 268
      obstruction of officers........................... 270
      overview.. 261
      power of entry 268–69
      services, false
         statement as to............................... 265–68
   Trade Marks Act 1994......................... 253–56

Training,
   food safety 153

Transport,
   food safety 149–51

Tree preservation orders................. 247–48, 252

Trial,
   date notified to witnesses 111
   mode,
      uncontested hearing 81

Unused information,
   schedule of 12
   weak cases.. 72–73

Index

Use by date 171
Ushers 103–04

Vending machines,
   food sold from 175–76
Vilification of witness 101
Vitamins,
   food labelling 191, 201–02

Waste management .... 232–36, App 13

Water supply,
   food safety 152
Weak cases,
   aiding and abetting 72
   authorities, researching 73
   cautions, use of 75
   election to prosecute or
     suspend/revoke 74
   evidence 71, 73–74
   further investigations by
     client department 71
   implied statements 72
   proceeding on more
     appropriate legislation 71–72
   proper application of
     statutory provisions 74
   public interest 71
   Queen's evidence,
     nolle prosequi in return for 73
   researching authorities 73
   review of evidence 71
   statutory provisions,
     proper application of 74–75
   taking full advantage of
     evidential rules 73–74
   transforming into
     successful prosecution 71–75
   unused information 72–73
Wine,
   food labelling 181
Witness statements,
   chronology of events 31–32

Criminal Justice Act
   1969 format 31–32
   direct evidence of witness 31
   form .... App 4
   planning investigation 20
Witnesses,
   avoiding coaching 86
   character 101
   children 33–34
   contemporaneous notes 33
   costs 111
   court attendance 32
   direct evidence 31
   expenses 111
   formalities 104
   impugnation 101
   interviews 31–34
     complaint 31
     confirmation of court
       attendance 32
     contemporaneous notes 33
     direct evidence 31
     exhibits 32
     under-age witnesses 33–34
   lay 85–86
   notification of date
     fixed for trial 111
   preparation for hearing 85–86, 104–05
     avoiding coaching
       witness 86
     hearsay evidence 86
     re-interviewing 86
   re-interviewing 86, 97
   scandalisation 101
   statements
     See Witness statements
   vilification 101

Young persons
   See also Children 53–54
   interviews 53–54